Pornography

Pornography

The Politics of Legal Challenges

MAX WALTMAN

OXFORD
UNIVERSITY PRESS

OXFORD
UNIVERSITY PRESS

Oxford University Press is a department of the University of Oxford. It furthers the University's objective of excellence in research, scholarship, and education by publishing worldwide. Oxford is a registered trade mark of Oxford University Press in the UK and certain other countries.

Published in the United States of America by Oxford University Press
198 Madison Avenue, New York, NY 10016, United States of America.

Library of Congress Cataloging-in-Publication Data
Names: Waltman, Max, 1974– author.
Title: Pornography : the politics of legal challenges / Max Waltman.
Description: New York : Oxford University Press, 2021. | Includes index.
Identifiers: LCCN 2021008070 (print) | LCCN 2021008071 (ebook) |
ISBN 9780197598535 (hardback) | ISBN 9780197598559 (epub)
Subjects: LCSH: Pornography—Law and legislation—United States. |
Pornography—Law and legislation—Canada. | Pornography—Law and legislation—Sweden. | Pornography—Political aspects—United States. |
Pornography—Political aspects—Canada. | Pornography—Political aspects—Sweden. | Obscenity (Law)
Classification: LCC K5293 .W355 2021 (print) |
LCC K5293 (ebook) | DDC 344.05/47—dc23
LC record available at https://lccn.loc.gov/2021008070
LC ebook record available at https://lccn.loc.gov/2021008071

DOI: 10.1093/oso/9780197598535.001.0001

3 5 7 9 8 6 4 2

Printed by Sheridan Books, Inc., United States of America

Contents

Preface xiii
Credits xv

Introduction 1

PART I. HARMS AND CHALLENGES TO DEMOCRACY

1. Supply, Demand, and Production Harms 29
2. Harm Caused by Consumers 67
3. Democracy and Hierarchy 134

PART II. THE UNITED STATES

4. The Anti-pornography Civil Rights Ordinances, 1983–1991 167
5. Federal Responses, 1984–2014 216

PART III. CANADA

6. Legislative Attempts, 1983–1988 239
7. Judicial Challenges, 1982–2019 260

PART IV. SWEDEN

8. Challenging Production, 1993–2005 311
9. Substantive Equality Prostitution Law, 1999–2019 334

Conclusions 371

Notes 403
Index 521

Analytical Contents

Preface xiii
Credits xv

Introduction 1
Assessing the Harms 2
Implications for Equality 5
Gender-Based Violence as a Linchpin of Sex Inequality 5
In Context of Other Indices of Sex Inequality 8
Implications for Democracy 9
Challenging Subordination: A Problem-Driven Theory 10
Hierarchy Theory and Its Critics: A Key Summary 13
Methods and Research Design 16
Comparative Qualitative Case Studies 16
Case Selection Framework 18
Policy Output and Policy Outcome 23
Alternative Selection 24

PART I: HARMS AND CHALLENGES TO DEMOCRACY

1. Supply, Demand, and Production Harms 29
Supply and Demand 29
Men and Women's Consumption 29
Size and Economics 33
Consumer Desensitization 34
Aggression and Subordination in Popular Pornography 35
Gay Male Pornography 39
Contending Perceptions of Aggression 41
Production Harms 44
Preconditions of Abuse and Vulnerability 44
Abusive Conditions of Production 49
Mental Sequelae 51
Male Performers 54
The Myth of Alternative Production 56
Evaluating the Evidence 57
Credibility of Representation 60
Summary 63

2. Harm Caused by Consumers 67
Methods Assessing Effects from Exposure 67
Experiments and Naturalistic Studies 68
Meta-Analysis 70
Measuring Sexual Aggression, Experimental Predictors, and Attitudes 72
Experimental Research 74
Early Critical Findings on Aggression 75
Understanding Meta-Analysis on General Aggression 77
Attitudes Supporting Violence against Women (ASV) 79
Why Nonviolent Pornography Feeds Violence against Women 81
Individual Differences and Post-Treatment Bias 86
Population-Based Naturalistic Longitudinal and Cross-Sectional Surveys 96
Sexual Aggression, Attitudes Supporting Violence, and Post-Treatment Bias 96
Advantages of Longitudinal Research Designs 101
Targeted Groups, Perpetrators, Imitation 103
Impact in Battered Women's Lives 103
Evidence from Prostituted Persons 108
Evidence from Johns 110
Imitation in Population Surveys 117
Unreliable Methods 122
Aggregated Comparative Cross-Sectional Studies 124
Causal Overdetermination in Aggregated Longitudinal Studies 126
Summary 129

3. Democracy and Hierarchy 134
Substantive Inequality in Democratic Theory 135
The New Rights Approach 140
Hierarchy Theory 144
Consciousness-Raising 144
Group Representation 147
Intersectionality 152
Postmodern Theory 155
Summary 163

PART II: THE UNITED STATES

4. The Anti-pornography Civil Rights Ordinances, 1983–1991 167
Evidence, Equality, and Representation 169
Substantive Equality and Perspective 169
Representing Interests 173
Causes of Action 175
Summary Analysis 180

Public Responses and Ideological Clashes 182
Judicial Responses and Ideological Clashes 187
Representation and Ripeness 187
The Constitutional Review 190
Mill's Distinctions 192
Strict Scrutiny: Equality as a Compelling Interest 193
Intermediate Scrutiny: Viewpoint Neutrality 202
Rational Review: Alternative Balancing 207
Summary of Analysis 213

5. Federal Responses, 1984–2014 216
Civil Rights Challenges (1984–1992) 216
Attorney General Smith's Commission (1985–1986) 216
The P.R. Campaign against the Commission 220
Congressional Attempts (1984–1992) 223
Obscenity Law in the Twenty-first Century (2002–2014) 226
A New Approach to Violent, Aggressive, and Degrading Materials 226
The First Trials 227
Some Well-Known Producers in L.A. Imprisoned 230
Results, Potential, and Limitations 232

PART III: CANADA

6. Legislative Attempts, 1983–1988 239
The Fraser Committee (1983–1985) 240
Vulnerability, Legal Distinctions, Intersectionality 241
Constitutional Substantive Equality 243
Recommended Legal Definitions 245
Civil Rights versus Criminal Law 247
Concluding Analysis 249
Parliamentary Bill C-114 (1986–1987) 251
Parliamentary Bill C-54 (1987) 253
Responses to Bill C-54 (1987–1988) 256
Comparative Analysis 258

7. Judicial Challenges, 1982–2019 260
Substantive Equality in Obscenity Law (1980s) 262
Consolidation and Progression in *R. v. Butler* (1992) 269
Representation of Perspectives and Interests 269
Balancing Substantive Equality under Section 1 276
Butler's Remaining Problems 278

Post-*Butler* Law (1993–2019) 284
R. v. Hawkins (1993), Nonviolent Dehumanizing Materials Non-Obscene 284
R. v. Erotica Video (1994), Nonviolent Dehumanizing Materials Non-Obscene 288
R. v. Jorgensen (1995), "Un-knowingly" Selling Violent Obscenity 290
R. v. Price (2004), Violent Pornography Not Obscene 292
R. v. Smith (2002–2012), Violent Pornography Obscene 297
The Future of Community Standards: *R. v. Labaye* (2005), *R. v. Katigbak* (2011) 300
Gay Pornography after *Butler*: *Little Sisters v. Canada* (2000) 303
Comparative Analysis 305

PART IV: SWEDEN

8. Challenging Production, 1993–2005 311
The 1993 Prostitution Inquiry 312
The 1998 Government Demands Further Inquiry 315
The 1998–2001 Committee's Dismissal 318
The Indirect Standard 319
Child Molestation versus Child Pornography Analogy 322
Expressive Content and Underlying Crimes 324
The Seriousness of Expressive Infringement 326
Case Law Rebuts Committee's Theory 327
Law, Ideology, and Representation 332

9. Substantive Equality Prostitution Law, 1999–2019 334
Evidence from Legal Prostitution 335
The Impact of the Swedish Prostitution Law 341
Comparing Prostitution Prevalence in Scandinavia over Time 341
Corroborating Evidence of a Prostitution Decrease and Increased Safety 343
Consistent Patterns of Attitudes and Sex Purchasing 346
Unwarranted Skepticism 349
The Importance of Specialized Exit Programs 352
Symptomatic Misinformation about Sweden's Law 355
Potential of a Swedish Civil Rights Approach 360
Interpretative Problems under the Law 360
Civil Remedies as Support for Exit 362
The 2011 Legislative Clarifications 364
Political Obstacles to Substantive Equality 367
Lessons for Legal Challenges to Pornography 368

Conclusions 371
Challenging Inequality, Ideology, and Law 371
The Limits of Criminal Laws 380
The Potential of Civil Rights Laws 386
The Postmodern Critique of the Civil Rights Approach 390
Extended Implications 397

Notes 403
Index 521

Preface

This book began in 2006. As a graduate student in political science, then, with a particular interest in feminist theory, I pondered a challenging dissertation topic where contributions were needed. I had read scholars such as Catharine MacKinnon, Iris Marion Young, Carole Pateman, Dorothy Smith, and Nancy Hartsock, finding them more inspiring than the feminist postmodern turn at the time. Searching for opportunities to read graduate courses abroad, I wrote to Professor MacKinnon since she had impressed me the most. She graciously responded, and I eventually visited her at the University of Michigan Law School (Ann Arbor). She also became a (long-distance) dissertation adviser. We have since worked together within as well as outside academia.

In 2006, I sensed that the challenges posed by pornography constituted an amalgam of the most intractable, thorny, and adversarial conditions facing feminist politics. What was in the way of democracies addressing its proven harms? If that problem could be solved, it would be crucial for advancing women's rights and possibly offering lessons for other stubborn problems. These challenging questions inspired me to continue. Soon, a separate demand arose for informed international scholarship on Sweden's then recently passed prostitution law. The law criminalizes the purchasers of sex while supporting prostituted persons to leave the sex industry and permitting no sanctions against them. Few other Swedish academics were published in English about the theory and impact of this law at the time.

Several individuals and entities have contributed support to this work over the years. The English-language expression has been considerably improved by Lisa Cardyn, who applied her eye for detail and nuance with great care and devotion. She also contributed insightful, substantive comments in the process. Catharine MacKinnon provided crucial contributions from its earliest stages. Jonas Tallberg at Stockholm University, too, advised my dissertation, boldly perceiving the potential of this work while showing an exceptional level of continuing commitment and support.

Spending the academic year of 2016–2017 as a research fellow at Harvard University's Weatherhead Center for International Affairs opened up a new world of collaborators, among others Ana Catalano Weeks, whose comment on Chapter 2 improved it crucially. A year at the University of Michigan Law School as a visiting researcher in 2017–2018 further enabled me to work productively on this project, adding numerous new parts to the manuscript while rewriting, updating, cutting, trimming, and improving old ones. Concentrated work was made possible by the support of the Wenner-Gren Foundations (Sweden), the Sweden-America Foundation's Prins Bertil fellowship, and Helge Ax:son Johnssons Stiftelse. I particularly wish to thank my Wenner-Gren mentor, Professor Arne Jarrick, and Professor Britt-Marie Sjöberg, the CEO of Wenner-Gren Foundations. Additionally, the Stockholm University Department of Political Science provided postdoctoral office space in 2018–2019 and a creative academic atmosphere.

Many other scholars have provided encouragement and valuable comments over the years. These include, among others, Amy G. Mazur, R. Amy Elman, S. Laurel Weldon, Celeste Montoya, Ingrid Bego, Cheryl O'Brien, Melissa Farley, Peter Hovde, Carrie Doan, Kathleen E. Mahoney, Neil Malamuth, and Paul J. Wright. Law librarians Ann Chase, Jocelyn Kennedy, Sandy Zeff, and Lexis representative Elizabeth Arnkoff conveyed crucial knowledge and beneficial technical skills. Faculty, students, and staff at Stockholm University, Södertörn University College, Harvard, and Michigan have also contributed to this project's development. Olivia Björklund Dahlgren fastidiously double-checked a number of the citations at a late stage. The people at Oxford University Press, especially Lucy Randall, saw the potential for this book, wanted it published, and made it happen. Hanna Doyle assiduously guided me through the final preparations while Sindhuja Vijayabaskaran and her team at Newgen KnowledgeWorks provided nonintrusive yet meticulous manuscript editing.

Last but not least, I am forever indebted to my family. If anyone has, my wife, Marlene, sustained me through hard times and joys from the beginning throughout and to the end. My children, who have now grown older and become interested in politics on their own, are also sources of inspiration. My mother, Louise, has been a long-time supporter. My late dad, Bernard, although physically absent, provides inspirational memories.

I hope that this book will be helpful to scholars, teachers, students, policymakers, journalists, activists, and the survivors of the harms that pornography inflicts by offering answers about what can be done to stop them.

Stockholm, Sweden
December 2020

Credits

All translations throughout this book are my own unless indicated otherwise. Earlier versions of parts of this book appeared as "Rethinking Democracy: Legal Challenges to Pornography and Sex Inequality in Canada and the United States," *Political Research Quarterly* 63 (2010): 218–237; "Prohibiting Sex Purchasing and Ending Trafficking: The Swedish Prostitution Law," *Michigan Journal of International Law* 33 (2011): 133–57 (formally translated into Korean, informally into Hebrew and Italian); "Sweden's Prohibition of Purchase of Sex: The Law's Reasons, Impact, and Potential," *Women's Studies Int'l F.* 34 (2011): 449–74; "Assessing Evidence, Arguments, and Inequality in *Bedford v. Canada*," *Harvard J. Law & Gender* 37 (2014): 459–544; "Appraising the Impact of *Toward a Feminist Theory of the State*: Consciousness-Raising, Hierarchy Theory, and Substantive Equality Laws," *Law & Inequality: A Journal of Theory and Practice* 35, no. 2 (2017): 353–91; "The Politics of Legal Challenges to Pornography: A Comparative Analysis," *Wisconsin Journal of Law, Gender & Society* 35, no. 1 (2020): 1–41; and my doctoral dissertation in the Stockholm University Department of Political Science, *The Politics of Legal Challenges to Pornography: Canada, Sweden, and the United States*, Stockholm Studies in Politics 160 (Stockholm: Stockholm University, 2014) (limited series edition). A popularized report for Swedish women's shelter umbrella organization Unizon also includes brief selective parts of this analysis, published in Swedish and English. See "Pornography and Men's Violence Against Women," with a Preface by Catharine A. MacKinnon, in *Part 2,* Chaps. 1–4 in *Pornography and Prostitution: A Report on Exploitation and Demand,* edited by Unizon (Stockholm: Unizon, 2016), 31–108. Moreover, a Swedish anthology for a popular audience includes a scholarly chapter with a brief argument based on a similar but updated analysis. See "Pornografins koppling till prostitution och våld mot kvinnor: En analys av forskningsläget och rättspolitisk diskussion," in *Stora Porrboken*, edited by Nina Rung (Stockholm: Rebel Books, 2021), 41–51. Also, I have elaborated some of my insights here in several newspaper op-eds, opinion pieces in online media, and briefs and submissions to government bodies since 2006.

Introduction

The subject of pornography produces a marked divergence of opinion. Its critics raise concerns about sex inequality, sexual abuse, and exploitation, focusing on discriminatory harms against particular groups. Its defenders raise concerns about expressive and sexual freedoms, focusing on the dangers of regulation. Far more women than men oppose pornography. In Sweden, for example, national surveys from 1979 to 2012 found that a majority of women favored "banning all forms of pornography," while men held a "considerably" more negative view of that proposal.[1] A 2006 poll of young adults in Sweden aged 18–21 showed that 67% of women and 45% of men endorsed a "total ban on pornography," responses that were not associated with a respondent's position on a left-right ideological continuum.[2]

In the United States, the General Social Survey from the early 2010s found that about 43% of women and 23% of men believed there "should be laws against the distribution of pornography whatever the age."[3] An American survey from 2014 reported that only 23% of women and 35% of men considered it "morally acceptable" to consume pornography, though 39% of both sexes nonetheless opposed legal restrictions.[4] A survey of Americans aged 18–26 published in 2008 found that 53.1% of women disapproved of pornography consumption, while only 33.4% of men did so.[5]

Research also shows significant differences in levels of consumption between men and women. An anonymous self-administered representative population survey conducted in the United States in 2014 estimated that 46% of men and 16% of women aged 18–39 use pornography in any given week.[6] A similar Swedish survey conducted in 2017 estimated that among those aged 16–29, as many as 41% of males viewed pornography "intentionally" 3 times or more per week, while only 3% of females did the same; likewise, 24% of males viewed pornography 1–2 times per week, while 7% of females did the same.[7] The consumption decreased in the older age brackets. Still, among those aged 30–44, as many as 23% of men viewed pornography "intentionally" 3 times or more per week, while only 1% of women did the same; likewise, 21% of men viewed pornography 1–2 times per week, while

Pornography. Max Waltman, Oxford University Press. © Oxford University Press 2021.
DOI: 10.1093/oso/9780197598535.003.0001

3% of women did the same.[8] Several earlier studies found similar consumption frequencies.[9]

Most men seem to consume pornography in solitude, whereas women's consumption is more often initiated by others.[10] A Danish survey conducted in 2003 and 2004 with young adults aged 18–30 found that women who consumed pornography reported a weekly average of 21.9 minutes compared to 80.8 minutes for male consumers.[11] Some studies have also shown that consumption is more strongly associated with physiological sexual arousal in men, with women exhibiting a stronger negative affect in response to pornography than even their lower rate of arousal would suggest.[12]

Considering that roughly 1 in 5 of the young men who participated in the 2008 survey used pornography themselves at the same time they did not see it as "acceptable behavior," and roughly 1 in 5 women did *not* use it despite seeing it as "acceptable,"[13] the opinions might be even more polarized by gender if women had greater knowledge about pornography. Their expressed views, in other words, typically do not reflect direct experience.

Divisions of opinion similar to those prevailing within the bodies politic are manifest in political and legal views when democratic institutions have confronted the issue of pornography. This study inquires into the major political and legal challenges that the social "practice"[14] of pornography poses to modern democracies, and how three nations, in particular, have responded to those challenges. It devotes considerable attention to the impact of pornography on the realization of sex equality in each society. The arguments set forth rest on an evidentiary tripod: (1) an assessment of the empirical harms of pornography as they relate to gender-based violence, including prostitution; (2) a political theory of legal challenges to pornography; and (3) an analysis of both the obstacles legal challenges encounter and the potential means of overcoming them that is designed to test the theory against practice.

Assessing the Harms

The first part of the study analyzes the validity and reliability of a large body of social science literature and other evidence produced since the 1970s that principally measures harms inflicted on others that are demonstrably related to pornography consumption.[15] It draws on evidence produced by a variety of methods, such as laboratory experiments that control for causality by using control groups, naturalistic longitudinal or cross-sectional surveys that better control for ecological validity than experiments but, at least in the case of cross-sectional surveys, are themselves less able to sustain causal inferences. Also assessed are studies using qualitative methods, which, when juxtaposed with the findings of quantitative studies, can shed light on underlying causal mechanisms. These complementary sources converge to support the conclusion that pornography consumption is a causal factor that, independent of all others, contributes to sexual aggression[16] and attitudes supporting violence against women. This conclusion relies on, among other things, several published meta-analyses that together subsume about one hundred individual quantitative studies comprising experimental and nonexperimental data. Contrary to some studies that misleadingly control for moderating variables such as rape myths, promiscuity, and hostility toward women—variables known to be positively correlated to men's consumption of pornography—even men who are least predisposed to aggression are more likely to sexually aggress and adopt attitudes supporting violence against women if they consume more pornography.[17]

Other individual studies discussed in the course of this analysis show that pornography consumption amplifies attitudes supporting violence against women, supporting beliefs that "only bad girls get raped," "women ask for it," and "women who initiate a sexual encounter will probably have sex with anybody." Consistent with such rape myths, an individual experiment found that male and female college students exposed to close to five hours of common nonviolent pornography over a six-week period recommended significantly lower penalties for rape of a hitchhiker—on average five years imprisonment, in contrast to an average of ten years recommended by the control group.[18] Similar causal associations with attitudes supporting violence against women have been found in other long- and short-term experiments, with self-report surveys showing similar correlations in social context, thus suggesting the experiments have ecological validity.[19]

The first part of the book will assess evidence from specifically targeted groups, such as survivors of rape or domestic abuse, showing that abusers become more abusive when they consume more pornography. Also analyzed are studies of prostitution documenting the significant association between increased consumption and the number of women bought for sex, and men's propensity to coerce prostituted[20] women into more harmful and unwanted acts of the sort that other women often resist, including unsafe sex, violent sex, even, on occasion, gang rape. Survey responses and individual testimony provided both by men who purchase prostituted people (johns)[21] and by prostituted people themselves clarify causal mechanisms suggested by experimental research, demonstrating that abusers pinpoint specific pornographic acts they have tried to force those in prostitution to imitate. Other studies indicate that many younger men imitate, and want to imitate, what they see in pornography with their female sexual partners, including conduct that substantially fewer women want to imitate, such as penile "gagging" during oral sex, anal sex, ejaculating in women's faces and mouths, and "ass-to-mouth" (where a woman performs oral sex on a man immediately after penetrating her anally). Qualitative studies further indicate that the men imitating pornography, depicting, for example, anal sex, often pressure reluctant women into it despite realizing that it likely causes them pain.

The analysis of the studies on harms inflicted by pornography consumers triangulates evidence gathered by different methods and measurements in order to address concerns expressed in the literature regarding the validity of individual conceptual research frameworks. This is intended to facilitate an assessment of the extent of the challenge pornography poses to democratic societies and legal systems that purport to be responsive to the rights of their citizens to equal protection from systemic harms, personal security, and the redress of civil rights violations perpetrated on the basis of group membership.

In addition to assessing potential harms caused by consumers, the first part of the study examines evidence of harm inflicted during the production of pornography, addressing critics and contrary arguments regarding the existence and extent of such injuries.[22] Evidence of the profits and economic structure of the pornography industry is considered. Research and information suggesting that pornographers exploit the multiple disadvantages affecting those they use as performers, who are typically recruited from other forms of prostitution or populations sharing similar disadvantages, are also analyzed. Among the preconditions widely seen among those who enter the sex industry are extreme poverty, child sexual abuse and neglect, comparable abuses suffered in adulthood, homelessness, and discrimination based on sex, race, and ethnicity. This part of the study also considers whether the unequal position and lack of real or acceptable alternatives, as documented among those in the sex industry, are associated with coercion by pornographers to accept unwanted and physically dangerous acts in order to increase profits, as a range of evidence shows. Likewise, it asks whether the apparent power imbalance is associated not only with physical injuries sustained by those used to produce pornography but also with related psychological injuries manifest in such conditions as posttraumatic stress disorder (PTSD).

Other studies suggest that prolonged pornography exposure desensitizes consumers to common nonviolent pornography, making them look for more extreme and more dehumanizing[23] or violent materials to achieve and maintain arousal. This pattern is consistent with the increasing popular demand researchers have found for materials that include sexually aggressive acts against women such as gagging, choking, sadomasochism, and gang rape, as well as aggressive anal sex and degrading practices like "ass-to-mouth" and ejaculation in women's faces and mouths.[24] Tellingly, when Canadian researchers sought pornography for an experiment in the 1980s, they were unable to locate feature-length films that did not contain at least some violent, dehumanizing, or degrading material and consequently had to compile a series of excerpts from multiple sources instead.[25] Findings such as these are highly relevant in light of evidence, as revealed in a study with 854 prostituted persons in nine countries, that not only did two-thirds of the respondents exhibit symptoms of PTSD on a level comparable to treatment-seeking Vietnam veterans, battered women seeking shelter, and victims of rape and torture,[26] but the rate of PTSD symptomatology was also significantly higher among the half who reported prostitution in pornography than among the half who reported only off-camera prostitution.[27] A critical question in this regard is the extent to which the apparent demand for abusive materials creates economic incentives for pornographers that are even more harmful to the population needed to produce them. Could this demand further explain part of the exploitation, trauma symptoms, and abusive conditions in pornography production?

Part I also systematically engages opposing scholarly and popular views regarding methodology, theory, and conceptual validity and reliability. Consideration is given to the extent to which the results can be generalized from female to male "performers."

Implications for Equality

Gender-Based Violence as a Linchpin of Sex Inequality

An empirical analysis of the harms of pornography as a social practice exposes a number of potential implications for democracies concerning sex equality norms and policies. If a practice like pornography can be shown systematically to exploit vulnerable women and increase sexual aggression and attitudes supporting violence against women (e.g., the trivialization of sexual abuse and suspicion regarding the motives and veracity of those who report rape), it can readily be seen as impacting negatively on women's already unequal status compared to men. Indeed, "gender-based violence"—that is, "violence that is directed against a woman because she is a woman or that affects women disproportionately," including "acts that inflict physical, mental or sexual harm or suffering, threats of such acts, coercion and other deprivations of liberty"[28]—is internationally regarded as both a violation of human rights and a form of sex discrimination, such that states are obliged to provide adequate protections against them and remedies for those that occur, whether or not they are perpetrated by states or non-state actors.[29] The empirical prevalence of these harms has been found to be substantial cross-culturally, a fact that militates toward an international approach to the problem. For instance, according to the World Health Organization's 2013 estimates, the combined prevalence among females aged 15 years and older of physical and/or sexual violence by intimate partners, or sexual violence by non-partners, varied regionally from 27.2% to 45.6%, with an average of 32.7% among high-income countries.[30]

Although the measurements employed and the estimates they generate naturally differ, national studies show substantial rates of sexual violence and aggression against women in general. In a 1982 study of 930 randomly selected adult females in San Francisco, 44% reported having been victims of rape or attempted rape at least once in their lives, with fully half reporting multiple instances of victimization.[31] A study published in 2007 estimated that 18% of all American adult women had been raped (attempts were not counted); more precisely, 16% had experienced "forcible rape," and 5.0% had experienced rape that was facilitated by drugs and alcohol (i.e., incapacitated rape).[32] It also estimated that "forcible rape" had increased by 27.3% per capita since 1991.[33] Another American survey, this one from 2010, estimated that 44.6% of women experienced "sexual violence victimization other than rape" during their lifetime.[34]

Studies find that, among adults, young women are most often exposed to sexual abuse. For example, a 2012 Swedish prevalence survey of 5,681 female respondents found that during the prior 12 months, 10.3% of women aged 18–24 reported being "subjected to sexual abuse with elements of violence," which was defined to incorporate forcible, attempted, incapacitated, and defenseless rape, or exposure to some other form of sexual abuse perpetrated through physical violence.[35] As a comparison, only 3.4% of women of all ages reported the same for the prior 12-month period.[36] In a weighted survey of a representative sample of U.S. college women conducted in 1984–1985, as many as 53.7% of respondents reported being subjected to sexual aggression, which ranged from brutal rape to accepting unwanted sexual acts due to overwhelming "continual arguments and pressure," after age 14.[37] Among the full weighted sample, 15.4% reported rape and another 12.1% reported attempted rape.[38]

Scholars have seen gender-based violence as a linchpin of male dominance—one that produces, reinforces, and maintains a social system of gender-based hierarchy. For instance, on the basis of similar data concerning violence against women, including as it relates to pornography production and consumption, Catharine MacKinnon argues that the sexuality modeled for and available to women is imposed through a system of terror.

> Given the effects of learning sexuality through force or pressure or imposition; given the constant roulette of sexual violence; given the daily sexualization of every aspect of a woman's presence—for a woman to be sexualized means constant humiliation or threat of it, being invisible as human being and center stage as sex object, low pay, and being a target for assault or being assaulted. Given that this is the situation of all women, that one never knows for sure that one is not next on the list of victims until the moment one dies (and then, who knows?), it does not seem exaggerated to say that women are sexual, meaning that women exist, in a context of terror.[39]

Consistent with the pervasive intimidation and fear she describes, an empirical study estimated in 1991 that virtually all American women worried about being raped, two-thirds consciously so, effectively living in a state of terror, while the remaining third claimed not to worry, yet nonetheless took precautions, "sometimes elaborate ones," against rape.[40] MacKinnon further underscores the role of gender-based violence (or the fear of it) in women's lives, stating that "Sexuality is to feminism what work is to Marxism: that which is most one's own, yet most taken away."[41] This oppressive injustice was also recognized as such when, in December 1993, the United Nations General Assembly Declaration on the Elimination of Violence Against Women identified "violence against women" as "one of the crucial social mechanisms by which women are forced into a subordinate position compared with men."[42]

In Context of Other Indices of Sex Inequality

The analysis of men's violence against women as reinforcing women's subordination must be situated alongside and be informed by the knowledge that sexual violence takes place within a broader context of sex inequality and is enforced by an array of means, in addition to violence, that have a cumulative effect. Economic sex inequality is often popularly perceived to be diminishing around the world. Yet, despite the fact that women, as of 2011, comprised 40% of the labor force of the global economy, 43% of the agricultural labor force, and "more than half" of university students worldwide,[43] about the same time their wages were only between 70% and 90% of men's in a majority of countries.[44]

In 2009, it was predicted that women would, over time, be substantially underrepresented in "green jobs" that "reduce energy consumption and the carbon intensity of the economy, protect and restore ecosystems and biodiversity, and minimize all forms of waste and pollution," thus systematically excluding them from essential labor sectors of the future.[45] For instance, a minimum of 80% of such green jobs was estimated to come in the secondary sector, including construction, manufacturing, and energy production,[46] yet women comprised only 9% of the workforce in construction and 24% in manufacturing.[47] Likewise, women comprised roughly 20% of the energy industry workforce in industrialized countries, but were less than 1% in top management, 4% in decision-making positions, and 6% among technical staff (as distinguished, e.g., from administration and public relations).[48]

As of 2017, the U.S. Department of Labor reported that the median "usual weekly earnings" female-to-male ratio among full-time wage and salary workers was 82% and that this measure has ranged from 80% to 83% since 2004,[49] thus showing no measurable change in recent years. Explaining some mechanisms behind these actual and anticipated inequalities, economists have concluded that "employers see the worth of predominantly female jobs through biased lenses" and tend to pay lower wages than for comparable work undertaken by men,[50] thus contributing to sex discrimination.

A related measurement of economic inequality is the proportion of unpaid labor done by women relative to men. In "virtually every country," the Organization for Economic Co-operation and Development (OECD) reported in 2014, "men are able to fit in valuable extra minutes of leisure each day while women spend more time doing unpaid housework."[51] For instance, in Canada and the United States, females devoted just over 40 minutes per day to "care for household members" compared to about 20 minutes for males, while females spent approximately 130 minutes engaged in "routine housework" compared to about 80 minutes for males.[52]

Female underrepresentation in government is another important manifestation of gender hierarchy. As of November 1, 2018, women comprised only 24% of world parliamentarians.[53] After the U.S. 2018 midterm elections, women comprised 23.5% of the House of Representatives[54] and 23.23% of the Senate.[55] In Canada, women constituted 27% of the elected House of Commons and 45.7% of the non-elected Senate in December 2018.[56] In Sweden, women comprised 46.1% of Parliament, ranking it seventh in the world, following Namibia, Grenada, Mexico, Bolivia, Cuba, and Rwanda, in that order.[57] However, while over 40% of parliamentarians since 1994 have been women,[58] Sweden has yet to see a woman prime minister.

In addition to formal institutions of power, mainstream media wields considerable influence over the political agenda in most western democracies by influencing both the degree of popular pressure on politicians and the opinions of those who write, interpret, and apply laws. The nonprofit Women's Media Center reported no measurable change in women's representation in U.S. newsrooms between 1999 and 2014, when it varied from 36.3% (2013) to 37.7% (2006).[59] In broadcast news, in particular, the proportion of women anchors, field reporters, and correspondents fell from 32% in 2015 to 25.2% in 2016.[60] A 2017 study of "20 of the nation's top news outlets" found that women produced only 37.7% of news reports.[61] Regarding more subtle yet nonetheless culturally influential facets of American mainstream media, among the 250 top-grossing domestic films of 2015–2016, only 17% of "directors, writers, producers, executive producers, editors and cinematographers, combined" were women—the same proportion as in 1998.[62]

As this data suggests, by every significant measure of inequality, be it salaries, political participation, media representation, or unpaid labor, women's status renders them more vulnerable to being used in pornography production and less able to resist the harms caused by its consumers than men.

Implications for Democracy

Inequality is diametrically opposed to the democratic ideals of ensuring equality among citizens and enabling them to participate in self-rule to the extent they choose. Yet how likely is it that women's influence on decision-makers will equal that of men while women as a group are systematically underrepresented in legislatures, opportunities for advantageous employment, and the media? When they are relegated to performing more unpaid labor and enjoying less leisure time than men? When women live in constant fear of gender-based violence, including rape and sexual harassment, at the same time that such abuses are trivialized by their communities? Considering the circularity of these oppressive conditions, it is crucial to identify the obstacles to sex equality and the tools that may be employed to move toward the objective of sex equality.

Given that gender-based violence reinforces women's social subordination, as statistically documented and argued by numerous scholars and acknowledged by multiple international legal sources, gender-based violence vitiates women's potential to exercise substantively equal influence in democracies, despite being formally endowed with equal citizenship. The evidence of its harms also suggests that pornography is one of the linchpins of gender-based violence, which in turn is one of the linchpins of sex inequality. Presuming that the empirical evidence on pornography assessed in this study supports these hypotheses, are democracies acting in accordance with their own ideals when they fail to address the persistence of interlocking hierarchical systems of social dominance to which its production and consumption contribute? If democracies do not prevent or redress pornography's impact on women's equality in general, and on those exploited, harmed, and subordinated in its production in particular, is there a deficit of equality that needs to be remediated in theory and in practice? If so, how might present systems of democracy best proceed to overcome these problems? What conditions obstruct and enable legal challenges to the production and consumption harms of pornography, and what are the alternatives? By asking these questions, this study also seeks to shed light on other democratic challenges to hierarchical practices of social dominance.

Challenging Subordination: A Problem-Driven Theory

A problem-driven approach to theory fits here since, following the political theorist Ian Shapiro, this study starts "with a problem in the world,"[63] importantly pornography's role in reinforcing gender-based violence. Certainly, most theories were developed with a problem in mind, and the descriptions of many empirical problems are indirectly theory-laden.[64] However, to avoid inapposite theoretical and methodological assumptions about what is necessary to efficiently address pornography's harms, which in turn would conduce to erroneous conclusions about its legal politics,[65] this study undertakes a thorough and rigorous assessment of whether, and in what ways, pornography does indeed create harm, before further theorizing its role in democracies. In this sense, Shapiro's approach is distinct from one in which the problem analyzed is a "mere [artifact] of the theories and methods that are deployed to study it."[66] Likewise, a democratic theory that does not properly account for democratic practices as they occur in social reality will be of limited value in establishing future policy as it is not empirically problem-driven.

A problem-driven inquiry that aims to develop a useful political theory of legal challenges to pornography must ascertain how to take account of a number of critical democratic principles that are often posited in oppositional terms, centrally the tension between equality rights and expressive freedoms. This opposition is problematic in relation to such empirical realities as off-camera gender-based violence, including domestic abuse, rape, sexual harassment, sex trafficking/prostitution, and child pornography—abuse and exploitation that, when challenged, are usually not defended on the basis of freedom of expression, although they arguably have expressive dimensions. For the same reasons that pornography is exceedingly difficult to challenge politically and legally, scholarly analysis of the problem may produce theoretical contributions that prove pertinent to a broader set of political issues than would be the case with a less complex problem.

Moreover, to the extent that theories about challenges to hierarchical systems of social dominance are tested and found useful or wanting, this study contributes to the cumulative development of democratic theory. Conversely, to the degree that these problems can be resolved legally in democratic nations, equality will be promoted. And if systemic barriers impede their resolution, the egalitarian principles and premises of democracy will themselves be scrutinized and challenged.

An examination of the politics of legal challenges to pornography may provide a blueprint to guide studies of other complicated, seemingly intractable, social problems, for example, challenges to climate change that face strong "vested interests" or "problematic existing norms" that obstruct efforts to mitigate the emission of "so-called greenhouse gases" in the atmosphere.[67] Obstructions like these may be amplified in the interest of short-term profits or norms of environmentally unsustainable consumer behavior, which may be analogized to the obstacles that must be overcome for challenges to the pornography industry to succeed. That is, the pornography industry is sustained by consumers who demand its products and who have more power in democracies than do its victims, as the evidence adduced here will show. Consumers of pornography have a vested interest in the viability of the industry, notwithstanding overwhelming evidence that their consumption harms those exploited to produce it and the harms consumers inflict on others as a consequence of their pornography consumption. Consumer behavior and the norms of entitlement to these materials—which together constitute their vested interest in sustaining the industry—contributes to profits for pornographers.[68] A vicious circle of demand, profits, and harm is thus created. A qualified analogy with legal challenges to climate change might be made, for instance, to the ways those harms are typically contested and denied by those most responsible for producing them.[69]

This study is restricted to legal challenges to pornography and does not extend to those that may be mounted through other means, such as education. Given what the empirical evidence indicates are the harms of pornography—and given the history of the women's antipornography movement seen through the events analyzed here—the persistence and expansion of the pornography industry strongly suggest that nearly fifty years of efforts to educate the public have failed. Moreover, the evidence of harm underscores the failure to protect vulnerable populations and the pressing need for a remedy, which is the job of legal systems. Law can also be highly informative, often leading to both voluntary compliance and educational change. Finally, state action through law, including in response to social movements, is an essential focus of inquiry for the study of politics.

In order to explain what obstructs or enables legal challenges, it may be useful to consider the broader social and historical context (i.e., political and cultural changes, both spatially and over time) within which they are pursued. However, a narrower focus on legal challenges, where context is viewed as secondary, can produce more focused insights into the ways in which a limited set of legal and political factors affect legal challenges to pornography. Therefore, the main objective here will be to understand what systemic political and legal factors obstruct or enable them. If politico-legal research, for purposes of such analytical parsimony, is criticized for disregarding the influence of history on legal challenges, it should be acknowledged that when "history matters," it will often be reflected in law. Although the association between history and law is an empirical question, legal doctrines and jurisprudence arguably reflect broad historical debates and trends, as political decisions ultimately influence them, even when such decisions are polarized and contentious—a fact evident from the opinion surveys on pornography summarized previously, as well as from divisions of opinion within case law. In this sense, legal changes, and efforts to change the law, also offer a record of social history. That said, in studying what determines variations in legal doctrine over time, it is important to remain sensitive to secondary influences that may emerge from the social context within which legal challenges are attempted, and thus to draw upon sources beyond those that are strictly legal, such as media reports, accounts of social movement activists, or journalistic pursuits, as this study does.

Hierarchy Theory and Its Critics: A Key Summary

Hierarchy is the opposite of equality. Given the evidence that pornography contradicts equality by subordinating women to men through its impact on gender-based violence, democratic theory is called for that can explain the relevant aspects of social hierarchy and suggest how to counter illegitimate, antidemocratic hierarchy. Likewise, given that pornography has an instrumental role in perpetuating a hierarchical social system of sex inequality and male dominance, other theories addressing challenges to social dominance may be useful in demonstrating how pornography can be successfully challenged. For these reasons, this study reviews a coherent set of ideas and arguments set forth in a body of social and political theory developed by scholars such as Kimberle Crenshaw, Catharine A. MacKinnon, Jane Mansbridge, Ian Shapiro, Laurel Weldon, and Iris Marion Young.[70] The theories provide insight into how to successfully challenge both the harms of social dominance and inequality in general and certain of its specific features. They are collectively identified as "hierarchy theory"—an umbrella term consistent with MacKinnon's use of the term "hierarchy" to describe problems that her feminist theory addresses.[71] By adjusting, applying, and testing it on legal challenges to pornography, this theory will be refined throughout the analysis to follow. Ultimately, it will point to other problems where hierarchy theory may be effectively employed.

The foremost criticisms of hierarchy theory, which include proponents of both so-called postmodern approaches and more traditional political theories, will also be addressed.[72] Among the latter are versions of liberalism that are more suspicious of democratic intervention than interventionists, liberal and otherwise. The concepts of "negative" and "positive" freedoms can be useful in describing contrasting approaches within liberalism, notably those concerned with promoting individual liberty in a complex modern society characterized by intrinsic social interdependence among individuals, groups, and government institutions. Negative freedom may be figuratively described as the absence of obstacles to the desired action (e.g., a roadblock or a law prohibiting traveling), while positive freedom may be described as the capacity or potential for self-determination (e.g., access to food, health care, or literacy).[73] Within a politico-legal context, however, the corresponding negative and positive "rights" are more relevant.

James Madison, one of America's "Founding Fathers," expressed the viewpoint underlying negative rights when he argued for a system of government that would protect against majoritarian tyranny or the "violence of faction" that pursues interests "adverse to the rights of other citizens or . . . the community."[74] For fear of abuse of state power, negative-rights liberalism favors concepts such as the separation of powers, judicial review, federalism, bicameralism, and other checks and balances that include broad (if not absolute) expressive freedoms as a means to counter government power in general and suspect interventions in particular.[75] By contrast, the positive-rights position, which hierarchy theory supports, favors promoting equality by permitting government intervention as a means of making equality a social reality rather than an abstract ideal. For this purpose, hierarchy theory stresses the necessity that democracies recognize and represent the perspectives and interests of those social groups that are disadvantaged because of systematic structures of oppression. Conversely, democracies need to distinguish disadvantaged groups from those who are not disadvantaged. Acknowledging these substantive structures of discrimination would, this study contends, include identifying the harms associated with pornography that discriminate against women.

A key concept within hierarchy theory's account of equality is "substantive equality," which can be seen empirically in various legal approaches meant to eliminate discrimination and social dominance.[76] Consistent with the groundbreaking work of Catharine MacKinnon, who developed the concept, it requires that constitutional equality be more substantive in social, economic, political, and other tangible terms than the conventional Aristotelian equality concept of treating likes alike and unlikes unlike, which has historically prevailed in classic liberal constitutions.[77]

Canadian equality law expressly recognizes "substantive equality," rejecting the "sterile similarly situated test focused on treating 'likes' alike"[78] since it "does not assure . . . the elimination from the law of measures that impose or perpetuate substantial inequality."[79] In contrast to "formal equality," or the Aristotelian approach, it requires a more searching inquiry into the ramifications of a challenged law in its social, political, economic, and historical context. The Supreme Court of Canada thus rejects "the position that every distinction drawn by law constitutes discrimination," holding instead that Canada's equality guarantee "is designed to protect those groups who suffer social, political and legal disadvantage in our society."[80] Conversely, this approach does not restrict itself to recognizing discriminatory distinctions that are facial or de jure.[81] It also reaches consequences that are substantively disparate even if occurring under facially neutral laws (sometimes termed de facto discrimination or discrimination "in effect"), whether intentional or not.[82] Although substantive equality is particularly prominent in Canadian constitutional law, where the legal concept originated, its impetus and insights can variously be seen operating in the case law, statutes, and legislative history of all countries and jurisdictions studied here, as well as in international law.

With regard to representation, hierarchy theory suggests that democracies promote the autonomous organization and representation of historically subordinated groups' social perspectives and interests in the political processes, legal architectures, and regulatory frameworks that affect them—in this case, particularly those regulating pornography. Hierarchy theory recognizes that historically oppressed groups, including women subjected to men's violence or Black people in the United States, have needed to organize separately from social movements with a broader ambit, such as left parties or mainstream women's organizations. These historically oppressed groups have sought to prevent the articulation of their priorities, perspectives, and interests from being controlled or diminished by competing voices within more expansive movements with preferences that may differ from, or conflict with, their own. As a result of these adversarial conditions, disadvantaged minorities often develop an "oppositional consciousness"—a consciousness they will need to retain to generate knowledge that can contribute to sustainable political and legal policies that aim to alleviate their particular oppression.[83]

Unlike hierarchy theory, both negative-rights liberalism and the postmodern approach to legal challenges discourage the legal recognition and representation of socially subordinated groups, thereby rejecting substantive equality in law. However, each of these theories rests on ostensibly different reasons to explain strikingly similar positions. In essence, the postmodern argument is that attempts to recognize and represent vulnerable or subordinated groups' perspectives and interests in law will "discursively renaturalize" the subordination of these groups.[84] This effect, it is claimed, makes the law susceptible to being "misappropriated by the state" and reinstating the very injuries that such legal recognition was intended to rectify.[85] Instead, the postmodern approach suggests using contentless generic rights as abstract aspirational ideals, promoting the prospect of equality and freedom with no "corresponding entitlements."[86] From the standpoint of hierarchy theory, the postmodern position is beset with the same problems and thus prone to produce the same inadequate outcomes as classical liberalism. The negative-rights approach within classical liberalism tends to ignore such abuses of power by non-state actors as social dominance between or among social groups. Under classical liberalism, it is assumed that any attempt to intervene to redress abuses of power within the "private sphere" invariably risks the imposition of more severe governmental abuses. However, hierarchy theory, including intersectional scholarship,[87] suggests that the options available to challenge social dominance are highly circumscribed, making it incumbent upon theorists to take account of non-state actors—something that both liberal and postmodern theorists expressly refuse to do.

Methods and Research Design

Comparative Qualitative Case Studies

This study employs the comparative case study method to explain what obstructs or enables legal challenges to pornography's harms. Legal challenges usually materialize either through legislative or judicial means. The latter may include attempts to change the applications of laws by reinterpreting them or attempts to respond to legislative action by initiating a constitutional challenge. A legislative challenge may be subject to judicial challenge; conversely, a judicial challenge may be countered by legislative action.

In political science, a "case study" refers to "an intensive study of a single unit for the purpose of understanding a larger class of (similar) units."[88] The term "unit" is interchangeable with the term "case," and the "larger class" of such units is referred to as the "population" of units identified for comparison.[89] The units are here defined as nations, where the objective is to shed light on a "larger class" of nations where legal challenges to pornography may occur. This modus of inquiry is similar to the approach often relied on to study one or a small number of revolutions, elections, or political parties to understand them as a collective phenomenon.[90] In such contexts, empirical researchers attempt to control some of the preconditions to the phenomenon at issue, otherwise known as "independent variables," by strategically selecting specific national units for the in-depth case studies. Structured comparisons like these may increase the study's explanatory leverage.

Qualitative case studies can be imagined, figuratively in the quantitative sense, as analyzing multiple observations within each case/unit.[91] Yet the aim of qualitative case studies is "analytical generalization" rather than "statistical generalization."[92] The within-case methods used in comparative qualitative case studies may offer causal insights into particular cases—insights that will primarily be descriptive and ideographic. However, as the comparative-historical sociologist Matthew Lange has pointed out, within-case studies may afford more nomothetic, generalizable insights when applied to a larger number of cases, especially in structured small-*n* research designs.[93] One way to use the analytical leverage of multiple cases is to apply within-case methods in a systematic comparison of two or more cases following John Stuart Mill's methods of agreement or difference.[94]

A within-case analytical method in comparative studies that is useful in testing the explanatory power of theories, hierarchy theory included, is pattern matching. This method may be understood by visualizing the analytical stages of within-case qualitative analysis as being comprised of "primary" and "secondary" methods.[95] In the present study, the "primary methods" generate evidence mainly by using traditional means of analyzing case law, legislation, and constitutional obstacles and possibilities for legal challenges to pornography's harms while also gathering information about relevant historical contexts from varied sources. In addition, the "secondary methods" use this evidence and the analytical insights it provides to illumine more complex problems, such as the conditions likely to promote or obstruct these challenges.[96] In addition to pattern matching, researchers can use other qualitative techniques, such as causal narrative and process tracing, as "secondary" methods.[97] Pattern matching, which is sometimes referred to as the "congruence method,"[98] is the predominant approach used here. It tests whether data conforms to theoretically predicted patterns.[99]

Case Selection Framework

When using the qualitative comparative case study method, political scientists often invoke one of John Stuart Mill's classic logics of inquiry, the "method of difference" or the "method of agreement." These two case selection techniques have subsequently been renamed the "most similar systems design" or the "most different systems design."[100] The rationale for selecting cases within most similar systems dictates that the researcher relies on accumulated knowledge to compare two or more units that are "similar" in many theoretically *relevant* aspects of the independent variables but differ on the "dependent" variable to be explained. The most similar systems design's objective is to hold constant and rule out as many independent variables as possible while seeking to identify one or more remaining variables that may explain different dependent outcomes. However, unlike large-*N* comparisons, Mill's small-*n* comparative methods offer little insight *unless* combined with other methods, including within-case analysis such as pattern matching or process tracing.[101] As applied to qualitative social science research, Mill's methods are therefore appropriately understood as *selection techniques* to determine what cases/units to compare. Properly applied, they can afford vital explanatory leverage but cannot, in isolation, be considered a comprehensive method of inquiry.

This study adopts the most similar systems design as a means of strengthening the within-case findings from pattern matching across units. The units by which legal challenges to pornography will be analyzed are Canada, Sweden, and the United States. Although legal challenges to pornography in Canada and the United States have previously been compared,[102] a major contribution of this study is to do so systematically within an analytical field that incorporates a third country, Sweden. While their legal foundations and approaches differ, these units are similar insofar as they are western liberal democracies whose laws aspire to guarantee freedom of expression and sex equality. Each of these countries also condemns gender-based violence, sexual exploitation, and other forms of abuse by non-state actors that are nonetheless perpetrated within their jurisdictions and which substantial empirical evidence suggests are significantly exacerbated by pornography. The relevant independent dimensions that differ among them in terms of their particular legal challenges may be categorized according to three Weberian ideal types:[103] (1) balancing with substantive equality, (2) liberal regulations, and (3) obscenity law. Table I.1 outlines these dimensions.

Table I.1. Comparative Predominance of Legal Frameworks

Dimension/Ideal Type	Canada	United States	Sweden
1. Balancing with Substantive Equality	High	Low	Medium
2. Liberal Regulations	Low	High	Medium
3. Obscenity Law	Medium	High	Low

Note: Table I.1 describes the degree of adherence to each of the three dimensions and ideal-type conceptual legal frameworks in Canada, the United States, and Sweden.

Canada's constitutional framework is imbued with a robust balancing approach that promotes "substantive equality" to a far greater extent than the more classical liberal framework of the United States.[104] For example, the law of expression in America harbors an implicit presumption against promoting substantive equality through racial classifications, even when such classifications intend to prevent social discrimination by combating hate speech on racial grounds. Cross-burning was thus permissibly banned when it was characterized in race-neutral terms, such as prohibiting the "intent to intimidate,"[105] but not when those grounds were explicitly acknowledged, as in a prohibition on expression that " 'arouses anger, alarm or resentment in others on the basis of race, color, creed, religion or gender.' "[106] By contrast, Canada has a law that criminalizes the "wilful promotion of hatred" against "any section of the public distinguished by colour, race, religion, national or ethnic origin, age, sex, sexual orientation, gender identity or expression, or mental or physical disability origin."[107] Their Supreme Court upheld it against a constitutional challenge, finding on balance that the equality interests outweighed the expressive interests, among other things, because such hate propaganda denies these "members of identifiable groups . . . equal standing in society."[108]

Given that U.S. case law supports substantive equality only occasionally, and balancing approaches are less commonly employed there than they are in Canada, the United States exhibits a stronger "negative rights" approach, in the classical liberal sense. This situation is hypothesized to discourage explicit recognition of disadvantaged groups and non-state abuses of power in legal challenges to adult pornography. Consistent with hierarchy theory, these circumstances would be less favorable for mounting successful legal challenges to pornography than those obtaining in Canada.

However, there are significant exceptions that attenuate the distinctions between the United States and Canada with regard to liberal and balancing substantive equality regulations. For instance, American case law on group libel and sexual harassment in the workplace is more attentive to both substantive equality and the perspectives and interests of historically disadvantaged groups targeted by such practices than U.S. laws on adult pornography tend to be.[109] The balancing approach is thus more prominent in some areas than others. Yet as will become more evident further on, these instances where substantive equality is balanced against speech rights do not belong to a systemic construction in U.S. constitutional law in the manner in which Canadian constitutional law is structured around substantive equality. According to hierarchy theory, then, Canada is still hypothesized to afford more favorable conditions for legal challenges to pornography than the United States, where the concept of "negative rights" discourages legal recognition of socially disadvantaged groups. By discouraging the acknowledgment of certain elements of substantive equality, U.S. law is more consistent with classical liberal and postmodern approaches.

Until recently, Sweden has been considered sui generis regarding its 1999 criminal prostitution law, which asymmetrically targets those who buy or otherwise exploit someone for sex while decriminalizing and supporting those who are bought for sex, facilitating their exit from prostitution.[110] To date, documentation of the legislative history, impact, and potential of this type of prostitution law is most extensive in Sweden, where it originated and has been implemented and studied the longest. This unique data makes Sweden a "revelatory case"[111] within the population of similar units/cases that followed its legal approach to prostitution, beginning with Norway in 2009,[112] and continuing with Iceland in 2010,[113] Canada and Northern Ireland in 2014,[114] France in 2016,[115] Ireland in 2017,[116] and Israel in 2020.[117]

In the text of the original bill that creates the Swedish sex purchase law, Sweden's government acknowledges that prostitution is related to men's violence against women, which it deems unacceptable in a gender-equal society.[118] It rejects criminalizing prostituted individuals since "most often" they are "the weaker party exploited by others."[119] Instead, it endeavors to "encourage" them to seek assistance and escape prostitution, a stance that militates against "any form of sanction."[120] This law recognizes and addresses substantive inequality between purchasers and prostituted people. Such an approach is favored by hierarchy theory but is inconsistent with a postmodern approach that discourages both the substantive recognition of disadvantaged groups and the remediation of group-based harm through law. Whether its practical impact has been consistent with its intentions is a separate question, one that will also be taken up in the analysis to follow.[121]

Laws pertaining to the dissemination and possession of pornography are subject to Sweden's constitutional framework. Many forms of expression can be legally restricted only with support from a written exception in the constitution—a rule referred to as the "principle of exclusivity" since the constitution's fundamental laws are theoretically given "exclusive" jurisdiction over much expressive conduct.[122] Amending the fundamental laws requires two majority parliamentary decisions with one election in between and some other minor requirements.[123] However, general law in Sweden has also been applied to expression that is not explicitly regulated in the constitution, if the purpose of the general law is not to restrict the "free exchange of opinion, free and comprehensive information, and free artistic creativity"[124] that constitute the "meaning and purpose" of freedom of expression.[125] For instance, it is well established that fraud, blackmail, unfair competition (e.g., misleading advertising), forgery of banknotes, dishonest conduct, misleading information, and the illicit printing of money are not protected as freedom of expression, even though they are not explicitly enumerated in the fundamental laws.[126] The Swedish legal scholar Nils Alexanderson was one of the first, in 1907, to clearly outline the principles to which this doctrine has mostly since been applied.[127]

Although the "Alexander doctrine" has withstood many challenges, a significant change has taken place since the 1960s, as legal scholar Gunnar Persson noted: then, instead of inquiring into the purposes underlying the challenged general law, courts and legislatures began asking whether an activity by itself had anything to do with the purposes of the fundamental laws.[128] When a law was passed to restrict the dissemination and possession of child pornography, it was thus considered necessary to make a constitutional amendment since child pornography was regarded as "an abuse of the freedom of expression" that implicated expressive interests.[129] These conditions make it slightly more challenging to create new pornography regulation than in Canada, where the constitution balances expressive interests against substantive equality interests without assuming that one is the norm and the other an exception.[130] Maybe not unexpectedly, then, substantive equality and a harms-based imperative are recognized in Sweden's legislative history in its prohibition on disseminating violent pornography,[131] though not to the extent seen in Canada, where nonviolent dehumanizing materials are also prohibited on similar bases.[132] If categorizing Sweden's expressive regulatory framework in terms of substantive equality and classical liberal regulations, it occupies a middle-position compared to Canada and the United States (see Table I.1).

However, Sweden's prostitution laws are potentially applicable to pornography production since they would not directly prevent someone from disseminating pornography (nor, e.g., prevent someone from producing virtual pornography without real persons). The principle is similar to that which holds for laws that prohibit child labor or regulate the working environment. Such regulations are not set aside in film studios or newsrooms, even though the final product may be constitutionally protected. So far, there have been few, if any, successful attempts in Sweden to apply the prostitution laws in this manner. Nevertheless, there were legislative attempts along these lines pursued in the 1990s and 2000s that will be carefully scrutinized.[133]

Obscenity law is the third dimension of comparative interest. It has been the most common regulative framework for pornography in western democracies and other nations as well.[134] Rather than recognizing sex inequality, exploitation, or sexual abuse, obscenity law's objective historically was to protect standards of appropriate behavior and counter the perceived deterioration of established social structures by containing sexuality to committed, ordinarily marital (heterosexual) relationships.[135] Catharine MacKinnon suggests one of its purposes is to control that which "makes male sexuality look bad."[136] Whether or not it is effective in challenging the harms of pornography remains an open question, one that will be broached at various points throughout this study.

The United States has the most traditional obscenity law of the three nations. Whether it can be applied to specific pornography without interference by the First Amendment turns on the Supreme Court's decision in *Miller v. California* (1973). That case defined obscenity according to "(a) whether 'the average person, applying contemporary community standards' would find that the work, taken as a whole, appeals to the prurient interest . . . (b) whether the work depicts or describes, in a patently offensive way, sexual conduct specifically defined by the applicable state law; and (c) whether [it] lacks serious . . . value."[137] On its face, this law is not intended to promote substantive equality, although a few more recent criminal prosecutions have tacitly assumed as much.[138] Potential alternatives to obscenity law for regulating pornography in the United States are governed by constitutional doctrines that conform to a stricter liberal negative-rights framework than that seen in Canada.[139] In Sweden, adult pornography regulations have shed most elements of obscenity law since 1970.[140]

Canada occupies a middle position on obscenity (see Table I.1), having kept some facets of obscenity law, as manifest both in its use of criminal rather than civil rights law and reliance on community standards to mediate its legal adjudication.[141] However, its obscenity law differs from its U.S. counterpart in defining its target as "the undue exploitation of sex, or of sex and any one or more of the following subjects, namely, crime, horror, cruelty and violence."[142] It has been much more responsive to substantive equality concerns when courts have applied it and adjudicated the constitutional conflicts under Canada's balancing approach compared to similar challenges posed judicially in the United States and legislatively in Sweden.[143]

In conclusion, Canada, Sweden, and the United States are similar on several key measures of democracy, principally in recognizing the imperatives of sex equality, non-exploitation, and freedom of expression, and in their express commitment to combating gender-based violence. At the same time, they evince sufficient cross-variation on certain independent dimensions, including the regulatory frameworks hypothesized to impact the effectiveness of legal challenges to pornography, to make them suitable for both within-case analysis and cross-national comparisons.

Policy Output and Policy Outcome

Considering the many comparative research studies and governmental evaluations of the impact of its prostitution law, Sweden provides an unparalleled opportunity to test hypotheses and ascertain some of the theoretical implications of its approach in terms of *policy outcomes*, as distinguished from *policy outputs*.[144] Measuring and explaining the causes of change in policy or law (construed as a policy output) is relatively uncomplicated compared to distinguishing change in the empirical outcome of policy output changes.[145] For instance, those adult pornography statutes that have been enacted are inefficiently implemented for various reasons, as will become evident throughout this study. For similar reasons, public policy analysts generally agree that the adoption of a policy (or a law) by itself is "a poor predictor of its implementation."[146] However, unlike existing pornography laws, the evidence adduced here suggests that some prostitution statutes are enforced with considerable efficiency. This conclusion is based on several studies that rely on more precise measurements of the effects of legal change, for example, measuring the prevalence of prostitution over time in a selection of otherwise similar countries, only one of which has revised its prostitution law.[147]

Prostitution is also akin to pornography in the sense that those used in each industry are typically one and the same; moreover, the pimps and pornographers who profit from their abuse exploit them in similar ways.[148] From this vantage point, pornography production is a form of prostitution. The legislative objectives of Sweden's prostitution laws, namely the prevention of sexual exploitation, the provision of support to prostituted people who wish to leave the sex industry, and the promotion of sex equality, are as relevant in prostitution for pornography as they are in off-camera prostitution. While no country has thus far endeavored to apply substantive equality prostitution laws to pornography production, hence making it difficult to investigate empirically, some comparative insights can be gleaned by assessing the impact of the prostitution laws per se. If the reduction of sexual exploitation, the provision of support for those in prostitution, and the promotion of substantive equality were among their policy outcomes, that would suggest that similar legal challenges to pornography production might also prove effective.

Following John Gerring's approach to case selection, countries similar to Sweden, where prostitution has been documented since 1999, will be considered "informal units" in the comparative design.[149] Such a disposition is "warranted" when the relevant comparisons are "obvious or generally accepted."[150] Within Sweden and these informal units, there is data of the development over time of street prostitution, advertisements for indoor prostitution, and other information about prostitution—notably changes in the extent of abuse and exploitation perpetrated and the degree of safety experienced that can be related to the operation of different prostitution laws. This comparative data may provide measures to ascertain whether legal challenges made a difference in policy outcome, and, if so, how.

Alternative Selection

One may consider studying other countries than Canada, Sweden, and the United States. Alternative groupings surely exist. Yet no other combination of three appears to afford the advantages of the one employed here. Legal challenges of comparable magnitude posed in other countries that address the documented empirical harms while systematically relating those harms to gender-based violence, including prostitution, have been rare indeed. For example, although a civil rights law challenging pornography's harms was proposed by influential lawyers in Germany in the late 1980s, it was never subject to extensive legislative and judicial consideration, as were challenges pursued in Canada and the United States.[151] Likewise, there were recurrent reports in 2013 that the government in Iceland was considering establishing laws against "'violent or hateful'" pornography "through the use of web filters, blocked addresses and making it a crime to use Icelandic credit cards to access pay-per-view pornography," apparently sparked by concerns about gender-based violence.[152] While these proposals were bold and substantial, there has been no indication to date that any of them has been formally presented, far less passed, by the legislature.

Another example comes from the United Kingdom, where the major internet service providers require customers to take the affirmative step of turning off a filter in order to view pornography.[153] However, the policy is not comparable to the legal challenges included in this study that target all violent, degrading, and subordinating pornography irrespective of any filtering technologies that may or may not be utilized. Proposals requiring pornography websites to mandate viewer age verification are not comparable for analogous reasons: even if not lacking viable means of confirming viewers' attestations by digital identification, they would not prevent children from accessing internet pornography through alternative means such as social media, emails, and virtual private networks (VPNs), in effect, also enabling both adult consumers and the industry itself to proceed otherwise relatively unchecked.[154]

PART I

HARMS AND CHALLENGES TO DEMOCRACY

1
Supply, Demand, and Production Harms

The challenges of pornography and its harms entail claims of abuse, exploitation, and male dominance—discrimination, victimization, and subordination, primarily of women and children.[1] As with other political claims of dominance and subordination, where harmful hierarchical social practices seemingly exist for few reasons other than maintaining disproportionate distributions of power, the charges against the producers, disseminators, consumers, and other facilitators of pornography are typically contested ferociously by those they indict, including their apologists. The material interests and contrasting perspectives involved add to the confusion of observers trying to determine where they stand on the problem. Such polarized discourse makes assessing the empirical evidence key when responding to the outrage expressed by people engaged in fighting pornography's harms, the legal accountability they demand, and the political implications of the problem and its prospective solutions. Analyzing the extent of pornography's empirical harms is thus an essential first step to establishing sound law and policy.

Supply and Demand

Men and Women's Consumption

Social science research examining its associations to gender-based violence defines pornography minimally as "sexually explicit media that are primarily intended to sexually arouse the audience," or in similar terms.[2] Population-based surveys in the new millennium have collected data on how many had seen pornography at least once and their age of first exposure. In an American population-based survey with 2,227 persons aged 18–60 sampled in 2016, 94.1% of the men and 86.9% of the women reported having used pornography, the mean age of first exposure being 13.8 for men and 17.5 for women.[3] Among 688 Danish heterosexual adults aged 18–30 sampled

Pornography. Max Waltman, Oxford University Press. © Oxford University Press 2021.
DOI: 10.1093/oso/9780197598535.003.0002

in 2003 and 2004, whose educational attainment was slightly above average, 97.8% of the men and 79.5% of the women reported having watched pornography, the mean age of first exposure being 13.2 for men and 14.9 for women.[4] Similarly, among 477 boys and 400 girls randomly sampled in 2011 from a population of first-year high school students (median age 16) in a medium-size and small town in Sweden, 96% of boys and 54% of girls admitted having consumed pornography, the mean age for first "having searched actively" for it being 12.3 for boys and 13.8 for girls.[5]

Considering that occasional and accidental pornography consumption is widespread, survey instruments must distinguish at least occasional from systematic exposure in order to indicate the extent of potentially harmful effects, such as increases in sexually aggressive tendencies in consumers. Thus, an anonymous self-administered computer survey from early 2014 with a weighted probability sample of 5,165 noninstitutionalized adults in the United States, aged 18–39, estimated that 46% of male respondents and 16% of female respondents used pornography in any given week, with corresponding rates of 56% and 26% using in any given month.[6] The question asked was "When did you last intentionally look at pornography?"[7] When the same study increased its sample to 15,738 Americans aged 18–60, it was estimated that 43% of men and 9% of women reported "watching pornography in the past week," while 34% of men and 72% women reported *no* pornography use in the past year (if at all).[8] The youngest men were not necessarily the highest weekly consumers. Forty percent of the men aged 18–23 used pornography in the previous week, while 49% of men aged 24–32 and 48% of men aged 33–39 did so.[9] However, younger women reported more frequent pornography use than did older women, the corresponding frequencies being 19%, 19%, and 9%, respectively.[10] In a group spanning a broader age range, pornography consumption was reported to peak in men in their 20s and 30s, then to decline slowly, with about 35% of 60-year-old men still reporting pornography use within the previous week.[11] By contrast, women exhibited a stronger negative linear trend in which only 3% of those in their 50s reported viewing pornography in the previous week compared to 19% of those under age 30.[12]

The Public Health Agency of Sweden conducted a more detailed survey in 2017 with a random stratified sample of about 50,000 individuals aged 16–84.[13] It received a response rate of 31% that was weighted in the analysis to represent the Swedish population demographically.[14] The question asked was "Do you intentionally watch pornography?"[15] Among those aged 16–29, the survey estimated that 16% of male respondents watched pornography on a daily/almost daily basis, while only 1% of female respondents did so; 25% of males watched pornography 3–5 times per week, while only 2% of females did so; and 24% of males watched pornography 1–2 times per week, while only 7% of females did so.[16] Further, among those aged 16–29, 11% of males and 13% of females watched pornography 2–3 times per month, 11% of males and 25% of females watched pornography once per month or more seldom, and 14% of males and as many as 52% of females did *not* watch pornography.[17] The consumption was systematically less frequent in the older age brackets. Thus, among those aged 30–44 the survey estimated that, for example, 9% of men and 0% of women watched pornography on a daily/almost basis, 14% of men and 1% of women watched pornography 3–5 times per week, and 21% of men and 3% of women watched pornography 1–2 times per week.[18] When counting everyone, the survey estimated that 31% of the men and 73% of the women never watched pornography.[19]

Several previous population-based surveys conducted in various countries, including Norway, Sweden, Denmark, Hong Kong, and the United States, present individual frequencies of pornography consumption comparable to those set forth above, at least among men.[20] For instance, among the 688 heterosexual Danish adults aged 18–30, of those who had *ever* watched pornography, 38.8% of men and 6.9% of women reported watching it 3 times a week or more, 28.8% of men and 11.4% of women reporting a viewing rate of 1–2 times per week, 17.1% of men and 30.3% of women reporting a rate of 1–2 times per month, and 15.3% of men and 51.4% of women reporting a rate less than once a month.[21] Similarly, a survey published in 2008 based on a diverse sample of 813 American college students aged 18–26 found that 21.3% of males reported consuming pornography either "every day or almost every day" or "3 to 5 days a week," while only 1% of the women reported doing so.[22] Furthermore, 27.1% of male respondents reported using pornography 1 or 2 days a week, while only 2.2% of females reported doing so; 21.0% of males reported using it 2 or 3 days a month, while 7.1% of females reported doing so; 16.8% of males reported using it once a month or less, while 20.7% of females reported doing so; and 13.9% of males reported *no* use, while as many as 69.0% of females reported *no* use.[23]

Men and women's differences in consuming pornography appear even stronger when additional factors are taken into account. A large representative Swedish sample of 4,343 senior high school students (typically age 18) surveyed in the early 2000s reported that, among those using pornography, males used it significantly more often when alone than did females (84.6% vs. 29.3%), and females used it more often in company with others or with a partner.[24] Another Swedish study of senior high school students surveyed in early 2003 also found that substantially more men than women (75% vs. 19%) had *initiated* pornography use.[25] Similarly, the Danish survey of young heterosexual adults reported that the total time users spend masturbating with pornography was far higher for men than for women (48.2% vs. 8.7%); that many more men than women used it alone (79.6% vs. 29.5%); that fewer men than women consumed it together with a regular partner (17.8% vs. 34.2%); and that men on average spent more time per week with pornography than women (80.8 minutes as opposed to 21.9 minutes).[26] An American survey published in 2011 with 326 male and 456 female heterosexual college students enrolled in a lower-level psychology course at a public university in the Northwest found similar differences: 58.1% of men and 6.6% of women reported viewing pornography once per week or more; men were significantly more apt to consume it "alone, when not in a relationship, and when masturbating," compared to women, who more often reported viewing it together with a "dating partner."[27]

Although potential effects on female consumers should not be understated, research demonstrates that they consume considerably less frequently than men, and typically not in the same solitary way. Moreover, some studies show that pornography consumption is more strongly associated with physiological sexual arousal among men than among women, who, compared to men, exhibit stronger negative affect in response to pornography than even their relatively lower levels of arousal suggest.[28] Given that there is a positive causal association between, on the one hand, pornography consumption and, on the other, sexually aggressive behavior and the trivialization of violence against women,[29] it particularly concerns that reliable methods now document,[30] as this review suggests, that roughly half of young men aged 18–39 and many older men aged 40–60 consume pornography regularly, on a weekly basis.

The question of why some men do not use pornography—why they are not interested, or why they have stopped consuming it—has not been a significant focus of research so far. Moreover, a problem in existing research is the lack of uniformity in the measures of consumption. Some surveys ask respondents about the number of consuming days or hours per week/month/year, which is preferable to more imprecise measurements such as weekly versus monthly consumers.

Size and Economics

Would consumption frequency be reflected in the revenue size of the pornography industry? The American industry organization Adult Video News (AVN) estimated that annual revenue increased from $75 million in 1985 (during the so-called porn wars) to $12 billion in 2005—a 160-fold increase.[31] By contrast, *Time*'s movie critic and writer Richard Corliss provided a lower estimate in 2005, suggesting annual revenues from videos alone near $4 million.[32] Writing in the *New York Times Magazine* in 2001, Frank Rich estimated that Americans spent "between $10 billion and $14 billion annually" on pornography, when also considering "porn networks and pay-per-view movies on cable and satellite, Internet Web sites, in-room hotel movies, phone sex, sex toys and . . . magazines."[33] *Forbes*'s Dan Ackman asserted that Rich's numbers were inflated.[34] Yet Ackman himself appears to have conflated what people actually spend on pornography with what producers alone earned, excluding revenue from distributors and rental stores.[35]

Considering that about four in ten American men are weekly consumers and that U.S. pornography revenues alone may have been close to $14 billion in 2005,[36] another frequently cited 2006 estimate based on revenue from sixteen countries indicating that pornography raised a total of $97.06 billion may not be entirely unreasonable, even if its methods and sources are unclear.[37] If accurate, its revenues that year were greater than those of Microsoft, Google, Amazon, eBay, Yahoo!, Apple, Netflix, and EarthLink combined.[38]

The substantial criminal element within the pornography industry, thoroughly documented by the U.S. Attorney General's Commission on Pornography ("the Commission") as early as 1985, and the illicit nature of its activities, suggests that even the above figures are underestimations.[39] Certainly, lobbyists attempted to orchestrate a media storm to misrepresent and discredit the Commission's work in 1986.[40] However, since pornography is documented to have been produced under conditions such as war and genocide,[41] in connection with sexual murders,[42] and as part of pimping activities or sex purchasing in prostitution,[43] the Commission's conclusion that it is also the object of other criminal activities is hardly controversial. That said, legitimate corporations have become increasingly involved in the distribution of pornography since the 1980s.[44]

Despite occasional rumors to the contrary, profits overall seem not to have been undermined by the availability of free online pornography. Indeed, according to the journalist Benjamin Wallace, writing in 2011, some entrepreneurs profited by using "free" internet materials to stimulate the demand and propensity to pay among an increasing pool of consumers, while others saw their business models becoming less profitable partially because of the internet.[45] Similarly, media researcher Gail Dines concluded in 2012 that this "fierce competition" led to the weeding out of laggards, which ultimately consolidated the industry into "a few large firms" that were more professionally managed and had the ability to operate in multimarket segments.[46]

Considering that pornography consumption is sizeable, especially among men, and that there is an organized industry catering to and profiting from it, with indications of organized crime associations and links to prostitution, could the demand for pornography also contribute to an abusive and exploitative condition of its production? In order to broach this question, it will be useful to first look at what types of acts are being demanded by consumers, whether the resulting pornography is abusive, and to what extent market demand is being met by the industry. This will provide insight into what may be required of those being made to perform in pornography, hence to what extent production conditions may be deemed exploitative and abusive.

Consumer Desensitization

In 1986, the psychologists Dolf Zillmann and Jennings Bryant published an experiment looking at how consumer preferences are influenced by prolonged consumption, providing clues about underlying market dynamics.[47] Their experiment included 80 nonstudents with a mean age of roughly 35, and 80 college students with a mean age of roughly 22.[48] Half were exposed to nonviolent "commonly available pornography" for one hour per week for six weeks, and the other half to materials consisting of "sexually innocuous situation comedies taken from prime-time broadcast television."[49] Then, during a follow-up experiment undertaken the second week after final exposure on the pretext that there had been some delay, all subjects were given the opportunity to choose something to watch, in private, from a collection of pornographic and nonpornographic videos with clearly labeled contents.[50] After reviewing the subjects' selections, researchers found that the half exposed to common nonviolent pornography chose significantly and considerably more violent or extreme pornography, such as bondage, discipline, and sadomasochism (BDSM) and bestiality, than did those in the control group.[51] For example, on average exposed nonstudent men chose to spend over 13 minutes viewing pornography with violence or bestiality compared to 1 minute and 42 seconds for controls, 9 seconds viewing nonviolent pornography compared to over 3 minutes for controls, and 13 seconds viewing G-rated or nonpornographic R-rated materials compared to over 6 minutes for controls.[52] Contrary to popular perceptions that youths are more readily impacted, the effects that exposure to nonviolent pornography had later in increasing selection of violent or extreme pornography for viewing were significantly stronger among older nonstudents compared to students.[53] The exposure effects were also significant for females, though weaker than among males.

To determine whether their findings had ecological validity (i.e., reflected reality), Zillmann and Bryant interviewed employees in pornography stores who confirmed that their regular customers often changed their preferences from "common" pornography to less common or "unusual" material over time.[54] Similarly, a recent Belgian study surveying 434 adult men who conducted "online sexual activities," 99% of whom reported watching pornography, found that 49% of consumers also admitted to searching for sexual materials or being involved in online sexual activities they previously thought were uninteresting or "disgusting."[55] A 2016 review of research studies and clinical reports, including pertinent brain research, also found that pornography consumption increases demand for more "novel" and "extreme" materials.[56] Correspondingly, a Canadian study of 211 adult males published in 2015 found a significant positive correlation between higher self-reported frequencies of pornography consumption and the proportion that was explicitly violent.[57] Attesting to consumers' disinterest in other materials, when the Canadian psychologist James Check and his colleagues in the 1980s attempted to find sexually explicit videos that were neither violent nor dehumanizing or degrading in order to design an exposure experiment, they were unable to locate feature-length films that were exclusively nonviolent, non-dehumanizing, and non-degrading, and thus had to create edited excerpts themselves.[58]

Aggression and Subordination in Popular Pornography

Are the documented shifting preferences among consumers also affecting what pornographers produce? Clues are available in the content analysis published in 2012 by the sociologist Natalie Purcell based on 110 of roughly

250 of the "most popular, best-selling, critically acclaimed, and influential hardcore pornographic movies" over a 40-year period.[59] She found "arguably violent, abusive, and/or coercive encounters in nearly all" movies.[60] Hence, even during the 1970s, when sexually abusive presentations were not among the most frequent, "they were nonetheless indispensable elements in the popular pornographer's repertoire."[61] However, according to Purcell, the content of mainstream pornography has changed considerably since that time, especially in the new millennium, a factor of heterosexually oriented pornography's seeming domination by what she refers to as the "gonzo" standard—a genre of " 'reality-based' " as opposed to " 'fantasy-based' " pornography (meaning it presents no plot, only sexual activity).[62]

Reviews by fans and interviews with consumers suggest that "fantasy" is marketed for couples and is less violent and degrading than gonzo pornography, which is ordinarily consumed by lone men (who are the predominant consumers).[63] According to Purcell, many gonzo presentations such as "ass-to-mouth" sequences, where a woman is made to perform oral sex on a man immediately after he has penetrated her or another woman anally,[64] were "unheard of 20 years before."[65] In terms of previously unusual acts that are now typical, Purcell found that "nearly every" popular gonzo movie of the 2000s featured not only ass-to-mouths, but also throat sex, where a woman gags during penile penetration, and double penetration.[66] Purcell's analysis is, as we shall see, corroborated by the quantitative content analysis performed by Ana Bridges and her colleagues on a random sample of 50 of the 275 best-selling/most rented pornographic movies in the United States during December 2004–June 2005.[67]

Bridges and associates counted scenes rather than complete movies, as Purcell did. They found sequences with ass-to-mouth in 41.1% of all scenes in their sample.[68] Overall, they found that 88.2% of the 304 scenes examined contained physical aggression.[69] Although the most common form of physical aggression as a proportion of scenes was spanking (75.3%), which is arguably not the most aggressive act presented, "gagging" also occurred in 53.9% of scenes, meaning that "an object or body part, e.g., penis, hand, or sex toy, is inserted into a character's mouth, visibly obstructing breathing."[70] Other forms of aggression frequently seen in Bridges et al.'s sample were open hand slapping (41.1%), hair pulling (37.2%), and choking (27.6%). Verbal aggression was present in 48.7% of all scenes, of which 97.2% included dehumanizing name-calling, using terms such as "bitch" and "slut." The targets of both physical and verbal aggression in 94.4% of such scenes were women, who responded with apparent pleasure or indifference in 95.1% of cases.[71] Only 9.9% of all scenes included kisses, laughter, embraces, caresses, or verbal compliments, and even those scenes included an average of four aggressive acts.

Among the 304 scenes studied, 58.6% also presented men ejaculating into a woman's mouth, 3.9% onto a woman's face, with 12.2% containing multiple ejaculation sites.[72] Considering the meaning of these practices, qualitative interviews with 16 heterosexual male pornography consumers aged 19–32 in a large northeastern U.S. city, most white and relatively highly educated, revealed respondents' clear understanding that women they might encounter in reality would not appreciate ejaculation on the face or into the mouth.[73] Nonetheless, "the vast majority" of these men admitted finding such scenes arousing to watch.[74] The men also "by and large" recognized that varieties of such ejaculation were "male-centered and misogynistic."[75] Their interpretation is supported by a recent quantitative study of 1,880 heterosexual men and women in America, most of whom were relatively religious white college and university students from a city or suburb: 66.7% of the men reported having ejaculated on a woman's face or in her mouth, and 62.1% of the women reported having been subjected to it.[76] Yet while 59.6% of the men reported an interest in engaging in these acts, only 12.5% of the women reported a wish to try them.[77] Thus, when pornography presents male ejaculation on a woman's face or in her mouth—a practice that the vast majority of women studied rejected—it is intended to sexualize women's subordination to men, a message consumers clearly understand.

Notably, ass-to-mouth and verbal aggression were the only two out of nine different presentations that were significantly predictive of more physical aggression in Bridges and her colleagues' sample from 2004–2005.[78] Ass-to-mouth scenes were 8 times more likely to contain physical aggression and 3 times more likely to contain verbal aggression than average, both of which predominantly targeted females.[79] Such verbal aggression might also be accompanied, as Purcell observed in her sample, by male performers who often "point out how 'nasty' or disgusting the woman's act is . . . that she's licking 'shit.'"[80] The implicit degradation of ass-to-mouth is corroborated by other research based on consumers' online discussions, where comments posted by "fans" suggest they take particular pleasure from the obvious debasement, revulsion, and disgust that women display in films with ass-to-mouth.[81] As an analysis of the responses provided by the 1,880 U.S. respondents in the study previously mentioned shows, women seem to detest the practice of ass-to-mouth: while

13.6% of the men wished to try ass-to-mouth, only 0.5% of the women wanted to do so; moreover, while 7.2% of the men reported having tried it, only 1.9% of women reported partaking in this activity.[82]

Another change in mainstream pornography since the 1970s relates to fellatio. According to Purcell's content analysis, "contemporary pornographers have crafted several strategies for situationally transforming oral sex into a signal of women's filth and inferiority."[83] For instance, oral sex became "faster," "deeper," and "rougher," while women were "far less likely to control their heads or use their hands while fellating men" and "far more likely to have their throats penetrated." By contrast, in the 1970s, Linda Boreman, who played "Linda Lovelace" in the classic pornographic movie *Deep Throat*—and who was assaulted, threatened, and raped many times by her pimp as a means to make her perform in that and other contexts—required training in hypnosis to block her gag reflex.[84] Thus, she seemed to act like "a trained carnival sword-swallower."[85] Now, according to Purcell, many new movies featuring men penetrating women's throats are instead "filled with gagging, retching, choking, gasping, and—less often—vomiting."[86] They are commonly described in the terminology of pornography as " 'throat fuck,' 'face fuck,' and even 'skull fuck.' " The male performer sometimes holds the woman's nose in order to appeal to the consumers' sense of the woman's suffocation, amplifying the impression with "commands" such as " 'Deeper . . . till you can't breathe.' "[87]

Purcell maintains that pornographers increasingly attempt to capitalize "on the arousal-generating potential of taboo violation," and that the taboos they violate are "overwhelmingly . . . degrading and humiliating only for the women" involved.[88] While in the 1970s, the use of epithets such as "bitch" or "cunt" was generally limited to rape scenes, these became "more universally deployed in the 2000s," as were gestures traditionally associated with "hostility, such as wringing women's necks, holding their heads against the floor, or pushing fists and feet into their mouths." Similarly, heterosexual anal sex was still a "rarity" in mainstream pornography of the 1970s. By 2005, Bridges et al.'s content analysis found that 55.9% of all scenes included anal sex.[89] Five years later, in 2010, Purcell concluded that anal sex had become the "primary event," its "depth, speed, duration, and intensity" having increased considerably.[90] At the end of that period, she noted that anal scenes commonly occurred "without vaginal sex at all or with just a minute or two of vaginal sex followed by twenty minutes of anal penetrations."[91] Sometimes a woman's anus was stretched "to the point of 'gaping,' " which ventured "toward disfigurement or mutilation," as directors zoomed in while making gleeful exclamations.[92]

Popular opinion may be mixed on whether anal sex is harmful or degrading. However, although 28.2% of both men and women among the 1,880 U.S. young adults surveyed reported having tried anal sex,[93] many more men (45.3%) than women (8.1%) wanted to try it.[94] Corroborating this perception, a U.K. study, drawing on depth interviews conducted in 2010–2011 with a diverse group of 37 females and 34 males aged 16–18, found that a quarter of all subjects reported having had heterosexual anal sex, their initial experiences of which "were rarely narrated in terms of mutual exploration of sexual pleasure."[95] Unlike men, women "reported painful anal sex."[96] Notably, few men and only one woman in the sample "referred to physical pleasure"—the latter elaborating that the act was initially painful and something she tried only because of her partner's interest.[97] Another U.S. study based on interviews with 20 diverse adult women whose average age was 34 (*sd*=13.35) likewise found that 6 out of the 12 of those who had tried anal sex revealed that they "tried it willingly (though often reluctantly) only to discover their lack of enjoyment or too much pain," and a quarter of all 20 women had "overtly violent encounters with anal sex," many having been pressured into it.[98]

Although gonzo is not the only pornography made or viewed, multiple sources suggest that it is by far the most popular genre among male consumers—an observation consistent with research on viewer desensitization and the shifting preference for more extreme presentations that accompanies it. According to Purcell, popular gonzo movies now "[boast] an abundance of overt and unmistakably cruelty," where the violence is "*meant* to be violence, sex that is meant to do harm."[99] One common scenario involves 30–40 minutes of "gradual defilement" of a woman's "beauty."[100] In rougher movies she may be bruised while being "choked and throttled," mascara streaking down and her nose dripping with mucus, eyes irritated and red, ultimately having her face "sprayed" with semen, often amid mocking comments.[101] Materials of this kind are themselves evidence of abusive production conditions that suggest the need for further inquiry into both the preconditions for entry into the industry and potentially abusive off-camera production conditions.

Gay Male Pornography

Gay male pornography production is a vital subset of the sex industry. Inquiring into unsafe and potentially abusive conditions, a study of 302 randomly sampled internet videos from five large, relatively representative, free gay male pornography sites between April and July 2012 found frequent high-risk sexual behavior.[102] For instance, unprotected anal intercourse occurred in 34% of the videos compared to 36% showing anal sex with a condom (a statistically nonsignificant difference); rimming (oral–anal contact) occurred in 17% of the films viewed; and fully 99.5% of all oral sex presented was unprotected.[103] The study found no warnings or other attempts to promote safe sex,[104] which is consistent with findings from content analyses of heterosexually oriented internet and video pornography.[105] Conversely, a smaller British analysis of 125 gay male pornography scenes on "popular Web Sites and DVDs," sampled according to "viewing statistics, popularity ratings, and sales data," found that, among the 95 (76%) scenes containing anal sex, 47 (37.6%) showed unprotected anal intercourse.[106] Reflecting the popularity of unprotected anal intercourse, a survey of what was reputedly the biggest U.S. gay male pornography streaming site undertaken by the legal scholar Shannon Gilreath in 2008 found that "bareback movies"—meaning those featuring unprotected anal intercourse—"constituted the largest segment on the 'most watched' list."[107]

Does the supply of unprotected anal intercourse in gay male pornography reflect consumer preferences? In surveys with men who have sex with men and who report pornography consumption, 46% of respondents in a U.S. study reported that half or more of the online pornography they viewed during the prior 3 months included it.[108] Moreover, only 21% preferred that condoms be worn in pornography, with 33% preferring no condoms, and 46% reporting no preference. Concomitantly, 74% reported that pornography with unprotected anal intercourse "looked more natural," and 61% reported that it "was more arousing" than protected anal intercourse.[109] A similar U.S. survey reported that "typical" respondents viewed equal amounts of unprotected and protected anal intercourse in the prior 3 months, but slightly more were exposed to protected anal intercourse than unprotected.[110] Although 42.6% reported no preference, 40.2% preferred "bareback" unprotected anal intercourse, while only 17.2% preferred "safer sex" pornography.[111] A similar survey in Norway found that respondents reported viewing "slightly more" unprotected than protected anal intercourse in the prior 3 months; likewise, 39.4% reported no preference, 43.7% preferred no condoms, and only 16.9% preferred that condoms be worn in pornography.[112] To the extent it is taken into account by producers, a stronger expressed preference for unprotected compared to protected anal intercourse is likely to make production conditions more unsafe.

Regarding more direct physical abuse, the proportion of violent sex in the sample of 302 gay male pornographic movies discussed above was somewhat lower than the researchers expected. For example, only 10% of the videos showed BDSM.[113] That said, when sex and violence are fused, absent an overtly negative victim reaction it may not register as violent to some observers.[114] Furthermore, the British study of gay male pornography concluded that, while 37.6% of all scenes studied included unprotected anal intercourse, some were more likely to include it than others; thus, it was present in 68% of scenes presenting a "power-imbalance," like BDSM or "role play" with dominance and submission, 88% of scenes involving interracial sex, and 100% of scenes portraying intergenerational sex.[115] While the British study does not address whether the subordination noted was based on race or age, or whether the pertinent scenes were implicitly or explicitly violent, the higher proportions of unprotected anal intercourse may suggest subordination of the receiver, just as ass-to-mouth, "throat gagging," ejaculation on the face or in the mouth, and anal sex convey the inferiority and humiliation of women in popular heterosexual pornography.

Even if the supply of violent pornography is lower than nonviolent materials on websites catering to gay men, scholars such as Christopher Kendall and Shannon Gilreath have shown violence and domination—including sexual torture, BDSM, sexualization of stereotypical racial hierarchies, and references to subordinate males in feminized terms—to be prominent themes in gay male pornography.[116] An asymmetrically stronger demand relative to a lesser supply of abusive or otherwise extreme materials has been documented among consumers of heterosexual pornography.[117] Gay male pornography consumers might also begin to demand more abusive materials, especially if prolonged consumption desensitizes them and gradually changes their preferences, as has been observed among heterosexually oriented consumers. Such a dynamic would almost certainly affect production conditions adversely.

Contending Perceptions of Aggression

According to multiple studies, the well-documented desensitization evidenced among consumers appears to precipitate a greater demand for abusive and unsafe pornography. However, some researchers argue that the incidence of violence and aggression is overestimated. For example, in his study of a sample of what are purported to be the best-selling pornographic movies in Australia, Alan McKee found only 1.9% to be "violent."[118] Yet he applied a number of restrictive criteria in his definition of violent pornography, like requiring that violence provoke an explicitly negative reaction by the target.[119] By this definition, Bridges et al. would have found "aggression" present in only 12.2%, rather than 89.8%, of cases, since they defined aggression to include a target who expresses a neutral or positive reaction to the aggression.[120]

McKee himself alluded to earlier psychological studies,[121] which have actually found that exposure to so-called positive-outcome rape pornography (in which the female target initially resists but later expresses pleasure) caused both more aggression against women and more attitudes that trivialized and promoted violence against women than so-called negative-outcome pornography (in which the target displays a negative reaction throughout).[122] Nevertheless, he did not address the fact that his restrictive definition of violent pornography excludes categories known to produce even stronger negative effects among consumers. Instead, McKee defended his approach by claiming that, among other things, sadomasochism is "categorically different" from "positive-outcome rape" because the targets of the violence in the former never express displeasure before arousal, whereas those in the latter do.[123] However, against the background of the numerous experimental studies that have persuasively shown that exposure to nonviolent pornography is causally related to aggression against women and attitudes supporting violence against women,[124] it seems more reasonable to posit that sadomasochism might desensitize viewers and inspire more sexual aggression. Like much nonviolent pornography, it lacks a clear negative message, rather fueling the idea that women desire sexual pain. McKee has yet to present any empirical evidence to support his assertion that exposure to sadomasochistic pornography leads to less aggressive behavior among consumers than does positive-outcome rape (or other) pornography.[125]

A more recent study of changes over time in aggressive content undertaken by Eran Shor and Kimberly Seida tracked the number of "views" and the percentage of "likes" for different types of pornographic content during the years 2008–2016, using a sample of 269 videos uploaded to PornHub, one of the world's top free pornography websites.[126] Based on their sample, the authors claimed that aggression in pornography was less pervasive than other studies suggested, going so far as to maintain that it had actually decreased over the period examined. However, by sampling only one free website, the study likely overrepresented the preferences of novices or less frequent consumers compared to those of desensitized frequent consumers who demand more aggressive or extreme content—content likely easier to find on specialized websites, especially for pay. This bias was further amplified by the researchers' decision to sample only from PornHub's general categories, defined according to the ethnicity or sexuality of those made to perform, not from its aggressive categories that viewers interested in violent pornography would be inclined to select.[127]

Although the 269 movies included an "alternative" random subsample of 80 videos from PornHub with categories beyond the general ones, even that excluded heterosexual videos with more than two participants.[128] As the authors themselves remarked, "We would have likely found more aggression if we conducted a purposive sample on categories like 'double penetration' or 'bukkake,' but . . . our main purpose was to focus on the most watched content."[129] The flaw in their reasoning is that their study did *not* sample what was "most watched," only that which was most watched on PornHub—and even at that, it excluded categories where the increase in aggression over time would likely have been comparable to that found in previous studies. Shor and Seida made no reference to the study by Purcell, asserting that, to their "knowledge, no previous study has systematically examined the temporal tendencies in depictions of aggression."[130]

Recall that Purcell's sample of 110 was drawn from a list of roughly 250 films that fit criteria reflecting the "most popular, best-selling, critically acclaimed, and influential" pornographic movies from 1970 to 2010, such as having been included on industry top-selling/-renting lists and in reviews or lists compiled by "multiple respected" insiders and fans.[131] Both the sample gathered by Purcell and that by Bridges and her colleagues of the best-selling/most rented U.S. movies during December 2004–June 2005[132] thus provided measures of producers' most successful content. At least Purcell included films by all major producers, finding that they showed similar "aesthetics, techniques, and themes."[133] Moreover, for every decade considered, her content analysis reached a " 'saturation point' " where "virtually nothing" looked different. The movies were "so conventionalized" that Purcell was "confident" that they were similar to "much content in the larger universe of popular, heterosexual pornography."[134] By contrast, speaking of websites such as PornHub, she observed that "it is far more difficult to determine which free content is the most popular content or to track who is downloading what for free."[135] Indeed, in light of its sampling biases, Shor and Seida's study of PornHub cannot represent the general trends in pornography over time.

Production Harms

Preconditions of Abuse and Vulnerability

The conspicuous demand for violent and unsafe material along with the economic incentives thereby created raise questions about whom pornographers can recruit to perform in their productions—persons who may be subjected to considerable harm. Important research has underscored associations between pornography and prostitution. In a study published in 2004 involving 854 prostituted persons in nine countries with different laws, engaging in different forms of prostitution (both indoors and outdoors), 49% reported that pornography was made of them in prostitution.[136] Other studies have found similar percentages.[137] Confirming the associations to prostitution, a study published in 2017 where the participants were 271 female "adult film performers" in Los Angeles recruited at clinics proximate to the pornography industry found that 23% reported off-camera prostitution including "sex work, such as escorting in the past three months."[138] Considering that reporting prostitution could incriminate the industry, thus compromising respondents' source of income or safety, this proportion may be an underestimation. Unsurprisingly, a smaller 2009 study, drawing on interviews with 18 women who were used in pornography in Los Angeles, also reported that, while the actual frequency was "unclear," participants "worked as escorts" and had sex "off-camera in exchange for money or other favors."[139] Anonymous interviews with "johns" (i.e., clients) who buy prostituted sex further emphasize the associations between prostitution and pornography. For example, 60% of 103 johns in London and 49% of 113 johns in Chicago admitted that they "classified" or "thought of women in pornography" as prostituted.[140]

Given that the proportion of prostituted persons used in pornography is high, it is useful to compare the extent to which accounts provided by those used as performers in the industry are reflected in accounts from more general studies of prostitution. To the degree their realities converge, more comprehensive and inclusive legal challenges may be appropriate. The

U.S. Attorney General's Commission devoted an entire chapter of its *Final Report*—"The Use of Performers in Commercial Pornography"—to the subject.[141] Among other things, it found that the personal conditions among those used as performers and the preconditions to their involvement in pornography were generally similar to what researchers have learned about those exploited in prostitution.[142] The "performers" were often young, poor, and victimized by childhood abuse.[143]

The Commission's observations were more recently confirmed in a quantitative survey of performers published in 2011 that compared 134 female "performers," who were identified using American databases or internet websites advertising jobs in the pornography industry and contacted by email, with 1,773 demographically matched women from California.[144] Although researchers warned of underestimation given that online surveys risk excluding more vulnerable subgroups,[145] it was nonetheless found that those used as performers often had more difficult childhoods than women in the control group. Reflecting this pattern, 21% of performers compared to 4% of controls reported having been placed in a foster home by a government or court before age 18, which may indicate serious neglect or abuse; 37% of performers compared to 13% of controls reported having been victimized by "forced sex" before age 18; and 24% of performers compared to 12% of controls reported belonging to a household on welfare before age 18.[146] In addition, 34% of performers compared to 6% of controls reported having experienced domestic violence during the prior 12 months, and 27% of performers compared to 9% of controls had experienced "forced sex" as adults. These figures on abuse are all notable, particularly in light of the fact that rape is not only common but also liable to be grossly underreported or minimized by prostituted persons.[147] Unsurprisingly, then, those used as performers reported "significantly worse" mental health and higher rates of depression than did those in the control group.[148]

Financial adversity was also widespread among respondents. Thus, 50% of the performers said they had lived in poverty, defined as applying for food stamps, receiving public assistance, or not having "enough money to meet basic needs," in the preceding 12 months.[149] Consistent with the degree of impoverishment reported in 2011, the Commission reported roughly 25 years earlier that, "with striking regularity," pornography performers "speak of money and dire financial need as critical factors in their decision to model."[150] Similarly, extreme poverty is the most common reason for prostitution given by prostituted persons themselves in studies conducted all over the world—encompassing industrialized welfare societies as well as rural and urban developing societies.[151] The study of prostituted persons in nine countries in which 49% had been prostituted for pornography determined that the 75% of the 854 persons who also reported a need for "a home or a safe place," combined with the 89% who reported a wish to "get out of prostitution" and the 76% reporting a need for "job training," were responses suggesting that poverty and lack of alternative means of survival are critical obstacles for prostituted persons to get out of prostitution.[152]

In addition to economic immiseration, there is evidence from studies based on data from several countries indicating that 60–90% of prostituted persons were abused sexually (and a majority physically) in childhood.[153] As a general population comparison, the prevalence of child sexual abuse among women has been estimated to be three times lower in the United States, approximately 20–30% depending upon the study.[154] This may be juxtaposed to the 2011 survey of 134 women used as pornography performers where the prevalence of "forced sex" in childhood was nearly three times greater than the California controls (37% vs. 13%).[155] Notably, forced sex is a more restrictive definition of child sexual abuse, which, for instance, can otherwise be compelled through psychological pressure or abuse of authority without the use of force. Adult-child sex is thus often regarded as statutory rape regardless of force.

A Canadian study compared 33 female survivors of prostitution with 36 women in a demographically matched control group who had not been prostituted, all reporting child sexual abuse, and found that, on average, the sexual abuse sustained by survivors started earlier, occurred with much greater frequency and over a longer time period, involved more perpetrators, and demonstrated a "dramatic" variety and severity of assaults compared to the abuse experienced by the controls.[156]

Prostituted persons who have been subjected to child sexual abuse frequently state that it strongly influenced their entry into prostitution. One widely publicized study from the early 1980s involving 200 prostituted juvenile girls and adult women in San Francisco is telling: 60% of respondents reported being sexually abused before age 16, with 10 the mean age of first victimization;[157] of those, 47% reported that this abuse caused serious injury, including "broken bones, cuts, bruises, and concussions."[158] Seventy percent of the sample's child sexual abuse victims reported that it definitely affected their entry into prostitution, and a greater number strongly suggested as much in open-ended responses. One respondent reflected, " 'My brother could do it; why not everybody else? Might as well make them pay for it.' " These respondents were recruited informally without the assistance of official agencies through such means as "word of mouth," flyers, and advertisements, in order to increase "credibility" and avoid a biased sample of "arrestable" or "service-oriented" participants.[159] Even so, the findings are aligned with those of subsequent studies with prostituted persons undertaken in Canada, Sweden, the United States, and Korea.[160]

Considering their exposure to childhood sexual abuse, it is reasonable to postulate that many prostituted persons were runaways at one time.[161] This may also be manifest in the early ages of entry into prostitution. Forty-seven percent of the 854 participants in the nine-country study reported entering the industry prior to age 18.[162] In a sample of 222 adult women prostituted in the Chicago metro area, 61.7% said they entered before age 18, with 35% stating they had been prostituted before age 16.[163] Among the 200 prostituted women and teenage girls studied in San Francisco, as many as 78% reported beginning before age 18, 62% before age 16, and "a number" before the ages of "9, 10, 11 and 12."[164]

The low average ages of entry into prostitution are intelligible when considering that prostitution is one of few alternatives by which children can support themselves. Attesting to an absence of alternatives, respondents in the San Francisco study reported an "almost total lack of positive social supports, and . . . an extremely negative self-concept" at the time they entered prostitution.[165] The "primary picture" researchers drew from the evidence was of vulnerable teenage runaways who were exploited sexually "because they have no other means of support due to their young age, lack of education, and lack of the necessary street sense to survive alone."[166] Consistent with these findings, 75% of the 854 prostituted persons in nine countries also reported either current or past homelessness.[167]

Even in relatively strong welfare states like Sweden, studies conducted in places like the Gothenburg area, its second-largest metropolitan region, confirm strong links among childhood abuse and neglect, homelessness, and prostitution similar to what studies in other countries have shown.[168] Such links were also apparent in a representative survey of Swedish youth, including LGBTQ populations,[169] though the sampling procedures employed likely measured occasional, more often than systematic, prostitution.[170] A government inquiry also reported in 2004 that the number of Swedish children who were exploited sexually was still "considerable."[171] Certainly, it is easy for pornographers, like other pimps, to exploit at-risk youth. Tellingly, a 2014 synthesis based on the findings of eighteen sources (including research studies and reports by government and nongovernmental agencies) from the United States, Ireland, Spain, Germany, the Netherlands, Italy, Poland, Bulgaria, India, Nepal, and Cambodia, estimated that an average of 84% of prostituted women were under the control of third parties, including pimps and human traffickers, with no readily apparent regional or national differences.[172]

In addition to poverty and childhood abuse and neglect, social discrimination in the form of sexism and racism is associated with entrance into prostitution, from which many persons used as pornography performers are recruited. In the United States, African American women and girls are overrepresented in prostitution;[173] First Nation Aboriginal women and girls are overrepresented in Canada;[174] and in Sweden, the Council for Crime Prevention found that poverty and discrimination against minorities are key structural factors facilitating recruitment into sex trafficking to Sweden, Finland, and Estonia, with many women and girls belonging to minority groups such as the Baltic Russian-speaking minority and the Roma people in Eastern Europe, and the majority coming from the lowest socioeconomic strata.[175] Swedish surveys also indicate that foreign nationality predicts a higher vulnerability to prostitution among youth populations.[176]

International studies have long shown that johns, perhaps surprisingly, are usually well aware of the difficult social circumstances in which prostituted persons find themselves, even when they try to minimize their own role in promulgating the subjugation of those from whom they purchase sex.[177] For example, researchers interviewed 110 johns in Scotland, randomly sampled through advertisements, and found that 50% recognized that pimps victimize prostituted persons, "73% noted that women prostitute strictly out of economic necessity, and 85% acknowledged that women did not enjoy the sex of prostitution."[178] A similar study of 101 johns in Boston reported that 66% of those interviewed believed that "a majority of women are lured, tricked, or trafficked into prostitution,"[179] and 55% of 103 johns in London believed the same.[180] Similar responses came from 113 johns in Chicago, where 57% believed a majority of prostituted persons had experienced childhood sexual abuse.[181] Consistent with this relatively stable conception of reality, many johns are also well aware of the links between pornography and prostitution.[182] The shared knowledge among johns who regularly buy prostituted sex raises doubts about the disbelief regarding these conditions widely exhibited by non-buyers.

Abusive Conditions of Production

Similar to what pimps and johns do with prostituted people, pornography producers are apt to exploit social inequality and oppression in order to recruit those with few alternatives. Persons used as pornography performers, due to their difficult situations, likely lack strong bargaining power—a circumstance reflected both in the many harmful and degrading actions they accept as well as the frequency with which they are targets of physical aggression.[183] The varied evidence set forth below further supports such a conclusion.

A study published in 2009, including 18 women and 10 men who performed in pornographic movies produced in Los Angeles, provides useful information.[184] Six performers expressly admitted having been harmed during filming, and 6 more implied as much, citing common symptoms such as anal tears.[185] Some informants felt they had control over the performers with whom they had sex, while others said they were forced to endure violent sex simply to obtain work. As for health risks, the study noted that "[w]hile some female and male performers entered the industry with the intent to perform only with condoms, many found that they had to perform without condoms to get work."[186] In addition, respondents reported earning higher wages when they engaged in high-risk activities, including anal sex and sex with "multiple partners."[187]

Considering that a majority of prostituted persons cite poverty as the predominant reason for entering the sex industry, it is easy to see how the pornography industry can use money to coerce performers to participate in unsafe practices. Nevertheless, money is not always enough. The 1986 report of the Attorney General's Commission quoted the testimony of a Los Angeles man who asserted he appeared in over one hundred films and maintained that producers, directors, and photographers regularly " 'badger[d] or almost force[d] the girls into doing things that they would really rather not do,' " such as " 'a couple of sets where the young ladies have been forced to do even anal sex scenes with a guy which is rather large and I have seen them crying in pain.' "[188] Other witnesses described pornographers' use of violence in similar terms: one reputedly tortured women and young girls to the extent of inflicting permanent physical injuries in order to meet the publisher's demand for sadomasochistic photographs bearing a higher commercial value.[189] Those photographs happened to be published in a national publication that the Commission later acquired from an outlet in Washington, DC.[190]

During another public hearing in Minneapolis in 1984, a witness testified that she had been coerced into appearing in pornographic films as early as age 8 and recalled scenes involving numerous children.[191] In the 1990s, a Swedish government inquiry described police investigations of sex clubs (e.g., Pir 59, Roxy, and Kings Club) where groups of paying male guests could participate in the filming of pornography, coercing financially insecure young women to exceed the prostitution contract and endure situations resembling gang rapes, acts that were charged as "sexual exploitation" for lack of appropriate statutes.[192]

One well-known example illustrating the extent to which violence and coercion may be needed to compel women to perform in pornography is that of Linda Boreman, who performed as "Linda Lovelace."[193] Unless the viewer is able to discern the bruising on Boreman's body, there is no sign of violence in the movie,[194] in contrast to the "gonzo" films popular today. Other survivors have also offered public testimony about being covered in bruises throughout their time in the pornography industry.[195] Boreman's case is thus not unique but rather reflects the asymmetrical power relations in pornography as well as in other forms of prostitution.

The legislative history of the 1999 Swedish sex purchase law[196] includes remarks dating back to 1995 acknowledging that prostituted women are "commonly subjected to various forms of violations such as assault and rape" and that some johns believe that since they are "paying" they have "a right to treat the woman as they wish"[197]—a position evidenced in the documented violence of commercial sex. Among 200 prostituted women in Chicago, 21% reported having been raped over 10 times, a proportion mirrored in escort prostitution, street prostitution, and prostitution occurring in the women's own residence.[198] Among the 200 prostituted persons in San Francisco, 70% said that sex purchasers had raped or similarly victimized them "beyond the prostitution contract" an average of 31.3 times each.[199] And of 55 women survivors who had been prostituted in Portland, Oregon, 84% reported having been subjected to aggravated assault an average of 103 times per year, 78% reported having been raped an average of 49 times per year, and 53% said they had been sexually tortured an average of 54 times per year, frequently during the filming of pornography.[200]

Even though there is now substantial evidence that abuse occurs during pornography production, informants who are dependent on the industry to support themselves may nonetheless avoid discussing abuse and assault. An informant who reveals such information is, of course, vulnerable to reprisals, especially if her employer becomes the subject of an official inquiry. Furthermore, prostituted persons often have little confidence in researchers, journalists, social workers, law enforcement, doctors, and others outside the sex industry, which may also lead to underreporting of adverse conditions.[201] This lack of confidence is implied in the 2009 Los Angeles study, where even participants who exposed abusive and exploitative conditions were cautious in their responses. For instance, 16 of those interviewed described how agents or so-called "suitcase pimps" exploited and mistreated the women, yet few explicitly addressed their own experiences of such abuse.[202] A similar example is found in a London study where all of the women interviewed who were prostituted legally in apartments revealed that *other* women accepted unsafe sex with johns, often to earn enough to pay the high apartment rents and fees—yet none admitted doing so themselves, although several studies have determined this to be a widespread practice in legal brothels.[203]

Moreover, third-party profiteers in the sex industry, in both legal and illegal venues, often use force against prostituted persons, threatening them into silence to prevent them from reporting the abuse to outsiders. For example, the researcher Lenore Kuo reported that all of those she interviewed who were prostituted in legal brothels in Nevada appeared to be "more concerned with possible assault or abuse" by management than they were by johns.[204] Similarly, other researchers encountered or learned of various incidents and conditions during interviews in licensed Nevada brothels suggesting that women prostituted there were under strong pressure not to disclose information that could cast the brothels in a negative light.[205] Even the Supreme Court of Canada in 1992 recognized that pimps' threats made prostituted persons unlikely to testify about mistreatment.[206] In a report on human trafficking released almost twenty years later, the Royal Canadian Mounted Police likewise related accounts of witness intimidation that discouraged prostituted persons from speaking on the record against their exploiters.[207]

Mental Sequelae

Another objective measurement of abuse that is indicative of its severity, yet does not depend on direct testimonies, is posttraumatic stress disorder (PTSD). This is a psychological measure of harm to a person that may result from extreme violence, including sexual violence, or from witnessing it inflicted on others. The diagnosis is well-established and listed in the American Psychiatric Association's *Diagnostic and Statistical Manual.*[208] Diagnosing PTSD is relatively straightforward and generally uncontroversial since it is determined by a rigorously defined battery of questions that measure objective symptoms like hypervigilance, inability to concentrate or sleep, persistent nightmares, and self-inflicted harm.[209] Thus, it is not a slippery diagnosis such as those frequently applied in cases like that of the Norwegian mass murderer Anders Breivik, where one team of bona fide experts concluded that he had "a psychotic disorder" and was thus "legally unaccountable," and another determined he evidenced a "personality disorder" (marked by intense narcissism and pathological lying) that rendered him "legally accountable."[210]

The study of 854 prostituted persons in nine countries engaged in various forms of prostitution found that 68% met the clinical criteria for PTSD, on average at levels similar to those of treatment-seeking Vietnam veterans.[211] The severity of symptoms displayed by those in prostitution was also comparable to that seen among battered women seeking shelter, refugees from state-organized torture, and survivors of rape.[212] Crucially, the 49% reportedly used in pornography exhibited "significantly more severe symptoms" of PTSD than did the other 51%.[213] When controlling for other relevant predictors, such as child sexual abuse, rape, and physical assault, a statistical "ceiling effect" was reached whereby pornography was the only distinguishable predictor,[214] suggesting that those prostituted for pornography are in an even more dangerous situation than other prostituted persons. A similar association was found among 43 prostituted women in legal brothels in Nevada, where about half reported having been filmed in prostitution for pornography production. When life events triggered memories of past trauma, the respondents who reported being used in pornography also reported significantly higher levels of emotional distress compared to those who did not.[215]

Besides the specific associations of mental illness or distress with pornography production, general studies of prostituted persons in different parts of the world have analyzed whether the statistical correlation between prostitution and such symptoms is eliminated when controlling for other potentially relevant traumatogenic events or types of prostitution. In South Korea, a study of 46 women formerly prostituted indoors revealed significantly more intense symptoms of PTSD and disorders of extreme stress not otherwise specified when compared to a control group, even after researchers controlled for a history of childhood sexual abuse and despite the passage of an average of 573.12 days (range 16–2,190) since the participants left prostitution.[216] A study from Alberta, Canada, found that more months spent in prostitution was a significant predictor of poorer mental health among 45 prostitution survivors, even after controlling for, among other things, the severity of child sexual abuse before age 16 and separation from a biological parent for 5 or more years before age 12, and those associations persisted when 45 community controls were factored into the analysis.[217] In Zurich, Switzerland, where registered adult prostitution may be legal under certain circumstances, researchers studying violence and mental disorders among 193 prostituted persons concluded that indoor prostitution was "not generally associated with more safety" compared to street prostitution.[218] Overall, the "burden of sex work" (e.g., number of working days, number of johns seen per week, and motivation) over the course of just one year was found to negatively impact respondents' mental health in a manner "comparable to the rates developed during their whole previous lives."[219] In a study of 123 prostituted women in Mexico, no significant differences were found in the severity of PTSD depending on whether the prostitution occurred in brothels and massage parlors (n=44), strip clubs (n=54), or on the streets (n=25).[220]

Prostitution in itself seems to be a deeply harmful activity for those purchased for sex. This is entirely in keeping with the results of john studies. For example, 79% of 110 anonymous johns in Scotland and 48% of 113 anonymous johns in Chicago admitted to buying prostituted sex for which they feel uncomfortable asking their partners, or sex acts their partners refuse to perform, such as oral sex, anal sex, and sadism and masochism.[221] Put simply, as many survivors and some more forthright johns describe it, prostitution is "paid rape."[222] Moreover, pornography production distinguishes itself as being potentially more harmful than other prostitution.[223]

Another measure of the dangers of being prostituted is a greater likelihood of being the victim of a homicide. A 2004 study showed that in a population of 1,969 prostituted persons in Colorado Springs spanning the years 1967–1999, those within 3 years of first being observed in prostitution were 18 times more likely to be murdered than those in a comparable non-prostituted population.[224] Corroborating the high incidence of murder in prostitution, the final report of a Canadian inquiry published in 1985 quoted estimates from the city of Regina suggesting that, between violent death and drug overdose, mortality for prostituted persons might have been 40 times higher than the national average.[225] Consistent with that finding, women in prostitution are documented to be particularly vulnerable to victimization by serial murderers, who often target women (and men) who are prostituted, likely presuming a weak social support network that is disinclined to search for them when missing.[226]

Male Performers

Research and public inquiries indicate that those used as male performers are often treated differently than those used as female performers. For instance, they are not aggressed against in heterosexually oriented productions as often as females, and when they are, they exhibit a more negative response than women.[227] However, specialized health clinic surveys have found that male performers, like female, are subjected to unsafe sex and that sexually transmitted infections (STIs) are common within both populations. Thus in Los Angeles, 69.3% of 360 performers (271 female, 89 male) sampled at clinics proximate to the pornography industry reported *never* using condoms on set; only 6.4% reported *always* using them. Correspondingly, the prevalence of chlamydia and gonorrhea, the only STIs tested, was 24% (*n*=86/360).[228] Similarly, among 115 performers sampled in London, of whom 51% (59) where male, *every* performer reported having unprotected sex during filming, and 44 (29 men, 15 women) were found to have an STI.[229] A smaller survey also conducted in London found a similar prevalence of unsafe sex and STIs.[230] Male performers also face demands to use performance-enhancing drugs such as Viagra, undergo plastic surgery (e.g., penis extensions and hair implants),[231] and go on extreme diets, all of which carry additional health risks.[232] And though men typically have longer "careers" than women, they are on average paid less per scene.[233] However, since the women are often subjected to considerable abuse, they are understandably less willing to perform for similar pay as the men. Men are more likely to be abusers.

Certainly, some male performers may have freely opted to participate. For example, in the 1990s johns could pay approximately $10 at various "sex clubs" in Sweden to have sex on camera with prostituted women.[234] However, as early as the 1980s males in more expensive productions were under constant pressure to perform like "machine[s]," as a leading agent then described it:

> You have to get it up, get it in and get it off on cue. . . . For example, if you're working on location for a film shoot and staying at a motel for seven days, you have to cope with being in unfamiliar surroundings, getting irregular sleep and living on McDonald's and Kentucky Fried Chicken, and still be able to perform sexually no matter what else is on your mind.[235]

In the 1980s, the more organized sector of the commercial pornography industry dedicated to heterosexual materials generally appears to have relied on a minimal number of male " 'superstars' who 'end[ed] up in all the videos,' "[236] a pattern distinct from that prevailing among female performers. With respect to the small segment of men featured in "glossier, commercial 'X' rated material,"[237] the Attorney General's Commission found that many male "models" shared some demographic characteristics with prostituted women, for example, poverty or specific and urgent financial needs. To take just one example, Harry Reems—a well-known performer in pornographic films, including *Deep Throat*—reported that he " 'was making a whopping $76.00 per week [as a New York actor]' " and thus " 'needed to supplement' " his " 'income.' "[238] The financial straits Reems describes are corroborated by accounts from other men in the industry.[239] And, like women who moved between off-camera and on-camera prostitution, some male pornographic "models" reported transitioning to pornography from nude dancing or other modes of prostitution.[240]

As with heterosexually oriented pornography, the content of gay male pornography poses serious health hazards for those used as performers. Given that, who can pornographers recruit to appear in gay male materials? Examining the biographies of a number of gay male performers, Christopher Kendall identifies convergences with the familiar narrative of those entering female prostitution, including childhood abuse, being a teenage runaway with little education, or ejected as a youth by family members due to their sexuality, thus easy prey for those seeking new victims for exploitation in the sex industry.[241] Some of these performers were subsequently infected with AIDS.[242] Additionally, the nine-country study included male and transgender respondents in South Africa, Thailand, and the United States, and neither of those groups showed significant differences in PTSD symptoms compared to women in prostitution.[243] Data like this suggests there may be intrinsic inequalities in male and transgender prostitution that produce the forms of exploitation now well documented in female prostitution.

Although some sexually explicit gay male media may hypothetically be made with different *intentions*—such as being part of LGBTQ people's political identity struggles—when there is a demand for gay pornography, the risk for exploitation is inevitable. As Kendall argues, there is "little reason to believe that gay men driven by profit incentive will be any more motivated to protect the people whose abuse makes them more likely to be in pornography and who, as vulnerable, are easily exploited."[244]

The Myth of Alternative Production

Occasionally it is claimed that there exist "alternative," "home-made," "feminist," or "amateur" pornography, whose production is said to be characterized by non-coercive, even voluntary, circumstances. Yet to date, no one has presented credible empirical evidence showing anything of the kind, certainly not on a meaningful scale. For instance, the media researcher and philosopher Rebecca Whisnant sought, but could not find, evidence to support self-proclaimed feminist pornographer Tristan Taormino's assertions that her performers " 'decide who they have sex with, when, where, and what they do' " and "set their own pay rates,"[245] as opposed to having to abide by the market logic demanding more extreme violence and degradation that is documented by overwhelming evidence, including evidence derived from Taormino's own films and contradictory public statements.[246]

Additional information regarding female-directed commercial pornography is available in a comparative study of the best-selling/most rented pornographic movies in the United States from late 2004 through mid-2005 that examined 122 randomly selected female- versus male-directed scenes.[247] The analysis found that scenes directed by women contained similar rates of degrading and aggressive acts against women as those directed by men.[248] The authors concluded that regardless of the director's gender, "female targets almost always exhibited pleasure or indifference toward the aggression inflicted on them" and that "female-directed films did not offer an alternative construction of sexuality and gender roles from their male counterparts."[249] In fact, although female-directed scenes included a higher proportion of women than did male-directed scenes, after controlling for the gender of the main characters the female-directed scenes continued to show "significantly more woman-to-woman aggression" (27.9%) compared to male-directed scenes (12.6%).[250] These results are not unexpected in light of what research has found regarding consumer desensitization and the corresponding lack of demand for pornography presenting women as equal to men and sex as a mutual reciprocal activity.

Pornographers also seem to employ the notion of "amateur porn" as a marketing technique both to reach new consumers and to require existing customers to pay for new materials.[251] In their more candid statements, industry professionals have dismissed labels like this as mere ruses. Farrell Timlake, a website operator who uploaded sponsored clips free of charge as a means of attracting additional paying customers, dispelled any myths to the contrary in a 2011 *New York Magazine* article:

> Pretty much all the porn labeled "gonzo" and "reality" these days is a put-on, Timlake insists. In the Dancing Bear series, a male stripper wearing an enormous bear head performs for a bachelorette party until several fairly respectable-looking women suddenly lose control and start fellating him. "That stuff looks pretty real," he says. "It takes a minute, but where are there roomfuls of women willing to have sex with a guy?" Watch a few of them, and you'll notice the same women reappearing. Another series, Dare Dorm, claims to pay real college kids for tapes of campus orgies, but Timlake isn't buying it. "I can always tell, because most college kids can't afford as many tattoos as those people have."[252]

Evaluating the Evidence

A recurring problem in debates over research into the pornography industry in particular and prostitution in general is the proliferation of studies that convey an impression of industry conditions that is largely unproblematic—one with fewer abuses, less economic exploitation, and more satisfied participants. Studies like this may impede legal challenges to conditions actually extant. As occurs in the case of harms associated with the industry, here too informants may be deterred from exposing exploitative and abusive conditions to outsiders where doing so may lead to reprisals or other negative ramifications, especially when they are dependent on pornography, prostitution, or both to support themselves.[253]

Moreover, since the evidence here indicates that most women used as pornography performers are heavily traumatized, many with severe PTSD, some are also likely suffering severely from numbing and avoidance symptoms.[254]

As with prostitution survivors in general, such symptoms inhibit their ability "to recall and describe events and feelings associated with prostitution."[255] Thus, those who are most traumatized may also more likely minimize or omit abusive memories and situations than those less traumatized.[256] This bias can easily skew studies that attempt to measure various conditions within the industry; whether asking respondents to assess their "job satisfaction" or their exposure to abuse, there is a substantial risk that the most wounded individuals stay silent. It is hence incumbent upon readers to critically identify biased information that romanticizes or trivializes the harms of the sex industry lest self-interested narratives take hold at the expense of decades of empirical research.

One example of unreliable and potentially biased information may be found in a study undertaken by James Griffith and his colleagues comparing a group of 177 female "pornography actresses" in Los Angeles to a demographically matched control group.[257] According to the authors, the women used as performers ranked higher than the controls in both "self-esteem" and "quality of life";[258] by contrast, Corita R. Grudzen et al. concluded that performers were more likely than controls "to be depressed and to have significantly worse mental health."[259] Participants in the research undertaken by Griffith and his colleagues responded to a survey measuring their sexual behaviors and attitudes, self-esteem, quality of life (as defined by the World Health Organization), alcohol and drug use, and demographic information.[260] The questionnaire was distributed at a private health clinic run by the Adult Industry Medical Healthcare Foundation (AIM)—a Los Angeles organization supported by the pornography industry for the purpose, among other things, of conducting regular mandatory tests for sexually transmitted diseases. The study was thus conducted under the auspices of an industry-funded body that, in addition to having a direct conflict of interest, was the target of vocal public criticism. The *Los Angeles Times* reported that authorities went so far as to force the AIM clinic to close in December 2010 in part because of a lack of transparency and inadequate patient follow-up.[261]

Beyond those deficiencies, the performers studied by Griffith et al. reported having tried one of ten different drugs (from marijuana to ecstasy) during their lifetimes at rates approximately three to nine times higher than the control group; yet in the most recent six months, they reported a higher use of only one drug, marijuana, than the control group.[262] These responses are suspiciously muted, suggesting they may have been understated to avoid attracting the attention of law enforcement. Furthermore, in light of previous research, the positive health outcomes reported also raise concerns of bias: performers claimed better self-esteem, sexual satisfaction, and financial circumstances, more social support, a better quality of life, and more positive feelings than did the control group. Yet there are significant problems with the study's methodology. For example, despite mandatory monthly visits to the clinic where performers are encouraged to answer the questionnaire, the response rate was only 15%, which is even more noteworthy considering that it was administered over a four-month period, in theory giving each respondent four occasions to complete it.[263]

The authors admit that "[i]t is certainly possible that there was a self-selection bias such that those who chose to participate were different from those who chose not to participate."[264] Yet they performed no attrition analysis to assess how this bias might have skewed the results, notwithstanding their acknowledgment that "[t]his is an important methodological issue." Griffith et al. rationalize the publication of these unreliable and externally contradictory findings as a consequence of the high interest in the issue: "although there has been interest in the characteristics of pornography actresses for decades, there has been a lack of studies because of the difficulty in accessing this population."[265] This admittedly intense interest combined with the difficulties in accessing the target population should have made the researchers more reticent to uncritically report results that stand in sharp contrast to almost thirty years of research.

The risk of misleading readers is not insignificant. One example of this danger is manifest in a recent popular-science book on the pornography industry authored by Professor Shira Tarrant: without benefit of citations, she takes the findings of Griffith et al. at face value, failing to note their unreliability and potential bias except for a passing mention of the authors' failure to define child sexual abuse, a variable on which they assert no significant differences in reports between female performers and controls.[266] The sociologist Ronald Weitzer has referred to the same study, accepting its findings more uncritically than did Tarrant, failing to point out the unreliability of the conclusions regarding child sexual abuse,[267] despite the authors' terming it a "superficial (or limited)" measure.[268] Not defining child sexual abuse, or even offering illustrative examples, places actual and prospective respondents in the position of having to define their own subjective experiences as abusive or not, which risks underreporting.[269]

Credibility of Representation

A related issue in evaluating the evidence is how to assess the credibility of those claiming to represent prostituted persons and people used as pornography performers. Some organizations have been formed by "survivors" of this inherently exploitative industry, while others portray themselves as "sex worker activists"; both organization types claim to legitimately represent the interests and perspectives of prostituted persons and pornography performers, though further inquiry reveals that they have very different agendas. When organizations or individuals have associations with third-party profiteers such as pimps, brothel owners, pornographers, strip clubs, or escort agencies—parties that would be regarded as employers within a labor market framework—it makes those self-described representatives less credible.[270] Yet many "sex worker" organizations have conducted themselves as if either trying to conceal, or ignore, such obvious conflicts of interests.

For instance, a 2014 Justice Committee hearing in Northern Ireland's legislative assembly questioned a witness appearing under the pseudonym "Laura Lee," who claimed to represent "sex workers"; in her responses, she conceded that her organization included "managers," "pimps," and "those who control sex workers," including a large escort organization in the U.K. run by one Douglas Fox and his partner.[271] Fox led the so-called International Union of Sex Workers and presented himself as "an independent male sex worker," in spite of the fact that the escort agency he owns had been publicized as such by Channel Four on British TV and other media outlets.[272] A similar deception was perpetrated in Ireland, where a campaign known as "Turn Off the Blue Light" presented itself online as an "association of sex workers and others who care about the welfare of sex workers in Ireland . . . campaigning against calls to criminalise the purchase of sex."[273] However, according to the Irish press, the person behind the site as of 2011 was a man—a former Northern Ireland law enforcement reservist and convicted pimp.[274]

One of the earliest and best known of the so-called sex workers organizations is Call Off Your Old Tired Ethics (COYOTE), formed in San Francisco in 1973.[275] COYOTE supported "the repeal of all existing prostitution laws" and, instead of recognizing that the harms of prostitution are most often related to the intrinsically unequal exploitation of persons for sex, maintained that "most of the problems associated with prostitution are directly related to the prohibition of prostitution and the stigma [accordingly] attached to sex and especially sex work."[276] Norma Jean Almodovar, who has been the executive director of COYOTE in Los Angeles since 1984,[277] was a traffic officer in the 1970s and early 1980s but in 1984 was convicted of the third-party offense of "pandering" (i.e., promoting prostitution) and sentenced to prison.[278] Almodovar herself, unsurprisingly, claims that the conviction was a "set-up" by the Los Angeles Police Department, purportedly meant to deter her from revealing departmental corruption.[279] The founder of COYOTE, Margo St. James,[280] has served as an expert witness, testifying on behalf of pornographers.[281] She too was convicted of a third-party offense—running a "disorderly house" (i.e., a brothel)—in 1962, although in contrast to Almodovar, St. James appealed her conviction successfully.[282] Whether or not she ran a brothel, anyone profiting from prostitution would typically be in a position to exploit prostituted persons' vulnerability. The credibility of such a person to act as a representative of prostituted women as a group would be severely undermined by so blatant a conflict of interest.

Another well-known U.S. organization—the Sex Workers Outreach Project (SWOP)—has an agenda similar to COYOTE's. SWOP was founded by the late Robyn Few in 2003, a year after she had been convicted of conspiracy to promote interstate prostitution—a crime that also applies to third parties.[283] Maxine Doogan—a woman reportedly convicted for a third-party offense while running a prostitution escort agency in Seattle—led a comparable organization, the Erotic Service Providers Union, which initiated an unsuccessful ballot proposal to decriminalize prostitution in San Francisco in 2008.[284] Although termed a "union," which to an uninitiated reader might be meant to benefit prostituted people, its web page expressly makes clear that it includes "anyone who is . . . compensated for their support of someone else's erotic service."[285] Being compensated for supporting *someone else's* prostitution distinguishes third parties (e.g., brothel and strip club owners) from those who are, or have been, prostituted and those who buy them (i.e., johns).

In Sweden, the organization Rose Alliance supports a similar agenda as these U.S.- and U.K.-based organizations: "sex work" (i.e., prostitution) is regarded as "work" that "should be governed" by common labor laws.[286] Hence, the organization is "against" both the criminalization of "sexual services for compensation" transacted between "consenting adults" and the criminalization of "third parties."[287] Expectedly, Rose Alliance lists SWOP, along with comparable groups established elsewhere in the world, as "sibling organizations."[288] No information exists about third-party involvement in Rose Alliance. However, its co-founder, Pye Jacobsson, now president of the Global Network of Sex Work Projects and a self-described "former sex worker,"[289] was also a board member for a number of years in a smaller strip club in Stockholm where she both stripped and scheduled other strippers, though she claims not to have received compensation for being on the board.[290]

All in all, leading so-called sex worker organizations not only favor decriminalization of the entire sex industry, but many also appear to have organizational ties with third-party profiteers. Unlike "sex worker" organizations that advocate across-the-board decriminalization, survivor-led organizations are often abolitionists.

For instance, several survivor-led nongovernmental organizations such as Trisha Baptie's Educating Voices in Vancouver, Vednita Carter's Breaking Free in Minneapolis, Kristy Childs's Veronica's Voice in Kansas City, Tina Frundt's Courtney's House in Washington, DC, and Natasha Falle and Bridget Perrier's Sex Trade 101 in Toronto, describe themselves as "abolitionists" intending to raise funds for programs designed to assist those seeking to exit prostitution, all agreeing "that to end trafficking/prostitution we must address demand and focus on providing more choices and empowering recovery services for the victims."[291] Likewise, the South African activist Mickey Meji, who founded the survivor network Kwanele, which includes members who are or have been prostituted and those " 'in the process of leaving that life,' " states that their members " 'feel patronised by the use of the terminology "sex work" ' " because it normalizes what they " 'view as violence against women.' "[292] Consistently, while Meji agrees that prostituted persons "should be decriminalized," she maintains that "those who buy sex and those who sell women and girls (pimps and brothel owners) . . . must remain criminalized" and "should not be given a license to exploit a position of vulnerability caused by gender inequality, unemployment and poverty."[293] A similar network in Sweden is Prostituted Persons' Revenge in Society, which also advocates the criminalization of sex purchasers and third-party profiteers (in contrast to the Rose Alliance) along with the decriminalization and support of those being bought for sex.[294] The international survivor-led organization Survivors of Prostitution Abuse Calling for Enlightenment, the international survivor-centered Coalition for the Abolition of Prostitution, and the international Coalition Against Trafficking in Women support a similar agenda, including advocating for the criminalization of johns and third parties and the decriminalization and support of those being bought for sex.[295] The perspective of abolitionist organizations like these is demonstrably different from organizations such as SWOP and COYOTE, which promote regulated or deregulated prostitution that permits third-party profits.

Although SWOP, COYOTE, and similar organizations might provide some legitimate services to prostituted people, it may not be inconsequential that they also more or less explicitly recognize their ties with the profiteers of the sex industry. One possible reason is that such information could serve as marketing material, where acknowledging these ties implies to informed observers that the organizations can facilitate recruitment for various sectors of the sex industry, including pornography production.[296] In any event, with documented ties to third-party profiteers, using terms like "sex workers" and "unions" and the rhetoric of rights often associated with them is not unlike disingenuously presenting an employers' association as working in the interests of its employees. Such organizations are not legitimate "representatives" of prostituted people, whatever support they may provide. For these reasons, concerned observers should diligently inquire into how and by whom organizations claiming to represent prostituted people are operated before accepting their claims to representation.

Summary

Claims of abuse, exploitation, and dominance through pornography include claims of discrimination, victimization, and subordination. Empirical evidence corroborates and considerably strengthens their validity. Among other significant findings is strong evidence of pornography's integral association with prostitution: pornographers, like johns, pimps, and other third-party profiteers in prostitution, exploit the social vulnerability of those it recruits for use in pornography, as evidenced in the multiple disadvantages shared by the majority of prostituted people, such as severe poverty, childhood sexual abuse and neglect, homelessness, and discrimination on account of sex/gender, race, ethnicity, sexuality, or other social grounds. While these facts are well-documented with regard to females, quantitative studies of gay male pornographic content, health surveys of male and transgender persons used as pornography performers, and related qualitative investigations suggest that similar exploitative practices afflict these performers as well. Moreover, the nine-country study and two smaller studies found that roughly half of the respondents reported having had pornography made of them in prostitution.[297] Samples of women used as pornography performers also suggest that many are regularly prostituted off-camera as well.[298]

As a result of the abusive and vulnerability-producing preconditions to entering the sex industry, women used as performers in popular heterosexually oriented materials seem to lack the leverage necessary to avoid requirements common since the 2000s to perform unsafe or dangerous acts. These include "ass-to-mouth" penetration, being "gagged" by oral penetration to the point of choking, gasping, retching, sometimes vomiting, and being penetrated anally without protection and with such speed, duration, and intensity that some popular movies are reported to exhibit disfigured "gaping" anuses of female performers as directors zoom in and make gleeful "infantile"[299] comments. Such practices are usually accompanied by gender-based verbal dehumanization, embodied in slurs like "bitch" or "cunt." While such abusive materials were "unheard of 20 years before" in the most popular and influential movies,[300] studies of consumer desensitization help explain why content has become more aggressive and subordinating of women over time, and how that led consumers to demand more extreme materials. Producers go to great lengths to make harmful materials, including using violence and threats where monetary incentives are not enough. The empirical evidence shows no meaningful popular demand for materials that are neither violent nor dehumanizing.

Studies of gay male pornography have quantitatively mapped the prevalence of unsafe sex practices such as "barebacking," which seems to occur in half of all anal intercourse scenes in popular movies. A less systematic content analysis exists of potentially aggressive or subordinating conduct in gay male pornography than that available in the research of heterosexual pornography. However, qualitative accounts suggest a similar dynamic of dominance and subordination that is common in heterosexual pornography, including the sexualization of stereotypical racial hierarchies and references to subordinated males in feminized terms.

Sixty-eight percent of the prostituted persons in the nine-country study had PTSD on average, in the same range as Vietnam veterans seeking treatment, battered women seeking shelter, and refugees from state-organized torture[301]—symptoms intelligible in light of the abusive conditions of prostitution and the trajectories leading there. The PTSD symptoms were significantly more severe among the 49% of respondents who reported having been used in pornography than for the 51% reporting only off-camera prostitution.[302] These differences may be explained in part by the abusive pornography itself and the off-camera abuse often necessary to compel those used in pornography to perform the acts demanded of them (resorting to violence not generally visible in the marketed product). No empirical evidence exists to support speculation that conditions under female-directed, "feminist"-labeled, or "amateur" productions would be substantially different, much less non-coercive; rather, such claims are directly countered by evidence from quantitative comparative content analysis and other empirical studies and sources.

Some researchers reject the information about preconditions commonly leading to pornography performers' entrance into the sex industry and the health outcomes characteristic of the vulnerable populations in prostitution. However, like those claims promulgated in the study of Los Angeles performers, which was facilitated by organizations closely tied to the local pornography industry, they frequently employ unreliable methods and exhibit obvious conflicts of interest. Such claims, which diverge dramatically from those of reliable sources, may also be marred by researcher bias. Similar claims supporting decriminalizing johns and sex industry third parties are often voiced by individuals and entities claiming to represent "sex workers," their conflicting interests as profiteers from others' prostitution notwithstanding. By contrast, survivors among prostituted populations and pornography performers who have left the industry typically favor criminalization of third-party sellers and buyers, combined with decriminalization of, and support for, those exploited in prostitution and pornography so they can exit the sex industry. Survivors have no ongoing financial interest in commercial sexual exploitation, hence may reasonably be considered more reliable when expressing opinions about the relative harm of the conditions experienced. They are also basing their reports on firsthand experience.

The best empirical evidence available strongly supports the conclusion that pornography production is a harmful and abusive social practice of inequality based on sex that exploits multiple social disadvantages that render it tantamount to slavery. Yet pornography is consumed by a majority of young men, some indulging occasionally, others on a more or less daily basis. This pervasive male consumption buttresses a thriving multibillion-dollar industry that involves organized crime, exploits vulnerable populations with virtual impunity, and has consistently demonstrated the capacity to deploy new technologies to its own ends. While some women view pornography, they do so considerably less often than men do. Their consumption also differs in being more often initiated by a partner, women's solitary use being less frequent and of shorter duration than that of men, who further report spending more of their time with pornography engaged in masturbation than women do. Men's mass consumption of pornography is particularly concerning in light of the associations between increased pornography consumption and increased sexual aggression, greater support for attitudes promoting violence against women, and more frequent purchase of prostituted sex.[303]

2

Harm Caused by Consumers

The conditions of production demonstrate how pornographers exploit social vulnerability, inequality, and multiple disadvantages, perforce severe childhood abuse, which make it easier for them to control and further abuse their performers when catering to market demands for more extreme materials. In this light, the question arises whether such coercive conditions will be reflected in the behavior of consumers. If it is largely impossible to produce commercially viable pornography without exploiting or abusing people, will such actions transfer to consumers so that they also begin to exploit and abuse others? Will consumers also become more tolerant of similar sexual aggression in their communities?

Methods Assessing Effects from Exposure

Chapter 2 will explain how quantitative research focusing primarily on men's violence against women, in order to understand and explain the effects of pornography consumption on sexual aggression and its related attitudes, has triangulated[1] a number of related methods and measurement instruments to permit stronger causal inferences with ecological validity within the "normal" population (i.e., non-convicted and non-institutionalized individuals). Additionally, quantitative studies have also been made of populations especially targeted by gender-based violence, such as battered women or prostituted persons, along with studies of those doing the targeting and victimizing (e.g., johns and other perpetrators). Furthermore, qualitative research with similar populations has been conducted, enhancing the validity of the quantitative research by, for example, demonstrating causal mechanisms involved in the associations between pornography consumption and violence against women. Some research has attempted to analyze correlations between reported sexual crimes and the consumption of pornography with entire societies as the units of analysis, as opposed to population surveys where individuals are the units of analysis. However, as

Pornography. Max Waltman, Oxford University Press. © Oxford University Press 2021.
DOI: 10.1093/oso/9780197598535.003.0003

the analysis here will show, these "aggregated" methods are increasingly disfavored by scholars because of their many methodological pitfalls.

Experiments and Naturalistic Studies

The quantitative research on pornography and sexual aggression can be divided into two main methodological groups: laboratory experiments and nonexperimental naturalistic observational surveys. With a few exceptions, such research was first undertaken in the early 1970s. Experiments make it more likely that causal inferences can be made between pornography consumption and increased aggression or attitudes supporting violence against women since experiments can control whether a hypothesized cause temporally precedes its presumed effect through use of control groups. Crucially, by using control groups that are not exposed to pornography, the experimental method can rule out confounding, or third, variables (e.g., prior exposure to parental spousal abuse or abuse of alcohol or drugs) that may exist in social reality where they (rather than pornography) might be responsible for covariation between independent and dependent variables. Studies can also control for variables that moderate (increase or decrease) or mediate the effects of individuals' exposure to pornography.[2] These variables might include sex/gender, type of pornography, the extent to which the experimental design lessened inhibitions to be aggressive (moderators), or arousal or disgust (mediators). Moderators and mediators are sometimes referred to as "interaction effects" or "interaction terms" in statistical analysis.

When researchers introduce individual psychological differences such as sexually aggressive predispositions as moderators or ordinary controls in pornography consumption studies, experimental as well as nonexperimental, more caution is warranted by readers.[3] For instance, when researchers say they found that only sexually aggressive men will become more so by watching pornography, they seemingly ignore the fact that these three things (aggressive men, their aggressive behavior, and pornography) are not wholly independent of each other to begin with. Where studies show that more pornography consumption is associated with a more sexually aggressive personality, it might have taken months or years for the respondents to develop a more sexually aggressive personality. Put otherwise, when a person consumes more pornography he or she is developing a more sexually aggressive personality that, in turn, will more likely be "triggered" by watching more pornography than it might for someone who rarely consumes pornography. So if, by focusing exclusively on the present moment, researchers claim that only aggressively predisposed men are affected by pornography, they can easily elide the long-term perspective whereby consumption could increasingly affect aggression over time for more or less every user, even those who were not sexually aggressive initially.

In other words, although variables such as exhibiting an aggressive personality may moderate or otherwise influence consumption effects, the predispositions may themselves be a result of prolonged pornography consumption—the key causal variable for present purposes. When researchers who investigate the causal effect of pornography treat a disposition toward aggressive personality as if it were an independent factor causing aggression, whether it is perceived as a moderator or a control, they neglect to consider that the personality disposition may itself be a consequence of having consumed pornography over time, thus being a dependent, not an independent, variable. This statistical error, called "post-treatment bias,"[4] can lead to a serious underestimation of the real effects caused by consuming pornography.[5] The immediate risk is to mistakenly control away for some "consequences of the key causal variable"[6] of pornography consumption, thus underestimating its effect on aggression.

An analogous example of post-treatment bias would occur if someone studied the effect of sex discrimination on salaries while controlling for job type in a context where sex discrimination only occurs as a result of job segregation. A statistical model that controlled for job type in that scenario would show no mathematical effect of sex discrimination on salaries because it mistakenly controls away for some "consequences of the key causal variable"[7] of sex discrimination, leading to an underestimation of its total effect. A hypothetical example in pornography research would be to study the correlative relationship between consumption and sexual aggression while controlling for the moderation of rape myths—and studies show that pornography exposure increases rape myth acceptance.[8] As a moderator, rape myths will mathematically reduce this statistical model's measure of the effect of pornography on sexual aggression.

A more general weakness of experiments regardless of what variables are controlled for is that they are usually conducted in laboratories or teaching situations—not in the social world where "numerous factors interact and jointly impinge on the individual."[9] This means that their ecological validity needs to be corroborated through naturalistic studies (i.e., a method triangulation). Naturalistic quantitative studies can be divided into longitudinal and cross-sectional surveys. Cross-sectional surveys offer the advantage of ecological validity, which experiments do not, but may suffer from either potential "reverse causality" (i.e., more sexually aggressive persons might actively seek out pornography as a result of their preexisting aggressive predispositions) or from unmeasured independent third variables. These drawbacks make it more imperative that cross-sectional results are consistent with the experimental literature—a corroboration termed "between-method triangulation."[10] Longitudinal studies, in contrast, "address the reverse causation threat"[11] through temporality, controlling for whether increased pornography consumption predicts increased sexual aggression over time (or whether sexual aggression predicts increased use of pornography over time). They are especially useful when studying adolescents, whose sexual experiences generally exhibit greater variation over a shorter time span than those of adults. Hence, presuming they control for third/confounding variables and possible moderators/mediators, longitudinal surveys lend stronger support to causal inferences than cross-sectional surveys do.

When results conceptually "align" across experimental, longitudinal, and cross-sectional methodologies, the most persuasive between-method triangulation is demonstrated, thus providing "powerful evidence of a media effect."[12] Moreover, the hybrid quantitative and qualitative naturalistic studies reviewed here include surveys with johns (clients), of whom a majority report trying to imitate pornography. The johns' qualitative accounts detail how the pornographic materials they encountered inspired them to "imitate" specific acts of sexual abuse that they proceed to inflict on prostituted persons. If these johns were previously unaware of the abuse, imitating it only *after* seeing it in pornography, the sequential data from those studies further supports a cause-effect model.

Meta-Analysis

A meta-analysis increases the sample size by adding data from several studies into one overarching analysis, averaging the correlations across studies, reducing confidence intervals and sampling errors. Meta-analysis enables statistically significant effects to be estimated more accurately within a population.[13] Moreover, given that they include comparable studies covering the same phenomenon, posing similar research questions and using equivalent indicators, this methodology affords an advantage over "overly conservative" conventional literature reviews.[14]

For instance, imagine four different studies observing a .20 correlation between pornography exposure and subsequent aggression compared to controls, but two of the studies have samples of 50 subjects each and two have samples of 140 subjects each.[15] The smaller samples would not exhibit a significant association within confidence intervals, while the larger samples would. A typical "box count" literature review that does not report the direction of statistically nonsignificant results, apparently the predominant approach in psychology in the early 1980s, would have concluded that these four studies showed inconclusive results.[16] Hence, a rationale for meta-analysis is that conventional literature reviews may be misleading when only small samples are available, in turn leading to failure to detect an effect that is actually there; visible trends are thus falsely dismissed as a result of chance—a mistake referred to as a "Type II error" or "false negative." Indeed, researchers who conducted a meta-analysis of the pornography effect studies implied that a reason for earlier controversies in the literature may have been that many individual experiments lacked sufficiently large samples, making them susceptible to Type II errors.[17]

With proper and sufficient coding within the individual studies included in a meta-analysis, the known moderators can be controlled for—a procedure typically undertaken when there is an unexpectedly "weak or inconsistent" relation between independent and dependent variables.[18] When there are no known moderators, a meta-analysis can still facilitate tests that may indicate the presence or absence of undetected moderators in the average correlations,[19] though such tests have weaknesses of their own, the most significant of which will be considered below. If moderator tests find average correlations across studies exhibiting a "homogeneous" correlation, this is an indication that individual differences among subjects and observations are the result of sampling error; by contrast, a test finding "heterogeneous" correlations indicates the presence of potential moderators, implying a study of "apples and oranges."[20] When an individual study has coded for moderators, and comparisons of those moderator subcategories subsequently show significant statistical differences between them (e.g., men/women, violent/nonviolent materials), and the heterogeneity test also indicates homogeneous correlations *within* each moderator subcategory, that particular moderator may be particularly relevant for understanding the phenomenon being studied (i.e., harms caused by pornography consumers).[21] However, simulations have shown that the statistical power to detect heterogeneity and indicate unknown moderators becomes exponentially weaker and less reliable when a meta-analysis includes fewer studies, where the average sample sizes are smaller, and when "between-studies variation" is relatively weak.[22] A benchmark entails that a heterogeneity test with fewer than 20 studies, with average sample sizes of 80 or fewer, and with weak between-studies variation should be interpreted cautiously.[23]

On research topics other than pornography consumption effects, meta-analysis has sometimes evidenced "publication bias"; researchers and journals may not be interested in publishing studies that do not reject the null hypothesis.[24] Nevertheless, two recent meta-analyses of the associations between pornography exposure and "sexual aggression" or "satisfaction," respectively, tested for publication bias by comparing correlations of published and unpublished studies (e.g., dissertations), finding no significant differences.[25] Indeed, intellectuals and politically interested observers frequently defend the freedom to disseminate pornography, claiming that there are few (if any) negative consumption effects. Studies confirming the "null hypothesis" on this topic should thus enjoy favorable publishing conditions regardless of any publication bias identified in studies involving other topics.

Measuring Sexual Aggression, Experimental Predictors, and Attitudes

So far, most experiments where researchers studied the effect of pornography on behavioral aggression were conducted during the 1970s and 1980s.[26] In the more conceptually important experiments, researchers usually exposed one group of subjects to pornographic materials and another group either to control materials (e.g., comedies, documentary films) or to no media at all. Alternatively, participants have sometimes been exposed to different types of pornography. After exposure/control treatment, these groups have been statistically studied with respect to the effect of the pornography on subjects in the exposure conditions compared to controls. Considering ethical and legal concerns, sexual aggression does not seem to have been part of any officially sanctioned experiment, although self-reported measures are sometimes included. Researchers intent on making stronger causal inferences have therefore had to use more general indicators of aggression in the early days, including fictional negative evaluations, noxious noises, electric shocks, or the (indirect) withholding of rewards. Such tactics were often first used against the subjects in order to provoke them, as in mock performance-based exercises, with subjects later being given opportunities to ostensibly retaliate by meting out similar treatment to confederate subjects under varying levels of feigned tolerance for aggression.

Over time, researchers have become more interested in conducting experiments on attitudes that might reliably predict sexual aggression among individuals, especially since they might replace cumbersome aggression experiments with a simple attitudinal survey. The attitudes explored were described in varied terms, including "rape myth acceptance," coined by Martha Burt in 1981,[27] or the later umbrella term, "attitudes supporting violence against women" (ASV), which encompasses attitudes promoting or trivializing men's violence against women.[28] These attitudes reflect various perceptions and mindsets, including believing that it is usually only "promiscuous" women or those with a "bad reputation" who are raped; that a woman who initiates sex "would probably have sex with anybody"; or that women report rapes in order to take revenge on former boyfriends, and similar fallacies.[29] Other attitudes similar to rape myths include the perception that women are more sexually manipulative by nature than men; that men must use force because women say no to sex in order not to appear "loose"; and that women enjoy being raped.[30]

As the research developed, it was found that men who exhibited more ASV in anonymous surveys consistently reported (also after controlling for other factors) being significantly more sexually aggressive[31] and being significantly more likely to commit rape or otherwise force "a female to do something [sexual] she didn't really want to do" compared to what other men reported.[32] The men scoring higher on ASV were also significantly more aggressive toward women in laboratory experiments after controlling for other predictors.[33] One among a number of such experiments additionally collected self-reported data on sexual aggression, finding that men who were more aggressive in the laboratory reported being significantly more sexually aggressive in social contexts as well.[34] Men with similar attitudes (e.g., reporting a higher likelihood of raping than the average man) were also more aroused by pornographic depictions of sexual aggression, studies found.[35] Furthermore, such attitudes and associations were commonly found among convicted sex offenders.[36]

Over time, experiments on the harms caused by pornography consumers that measured general aggression were largely replaced by experiments measuring attitudinal effects. The reason seems to be that a sufficient number of experiments and naturalistic studies had identified the attitudes that significantly and substantially predicted male sexual aggression. Put otherwise, through the triangulation of methods, concepts, and measurement instruments, researchers could reliably show that it is possible to conduct studies to determine whether pornography increases men's sexual aggression simply by assessing the effect of pornography on attitudes that have been shown to predict such aggression. Lending further support to these conclusions, two meta-studies provided robust evidence in 1993 that attitudes predicted corresponding behavior in numerous situations apart from sexual aggression.[37]

Experimental Research

Some experiments have exposed subjects to pornography several times over a number of weeks (prolonged/long-term exposure), then taken a break for a few days, or even weeks, before measuring the effects;[38] others have measured the effects in a laboratory almost directly after the exposure (short-term exposure).[39] There is a widespread misapprehension that pornography exposure experiments have only been conducted on college students. However, several significant experiments have been conducted with younger nonstudents as well as with older adults with varying demographic characteristics and shown few differences, none of them critical, in how pornography exposure affects these groups compared to students.[40] Corroborating the ecological validity of such findings, a meta-analysis of naturalistic longitudinal and cross-sectional studies found no moderation by age when comparing adolescents with adults; there were no significant differences between the two groups in the association between pornography consumption and sexual aggression.[41]

To underscore, laboratory exposure experiments of general aggression are more complicated to design and execute than attitudinal experiments (e.g., the assessment of general aggression often required "acting" by confederates). The former were thus more important before researchers had mapped and validated attitudes that predicted more men's violence against women. Nevertheless, laboratory measures of general aggression are ecologically valid; for instance, they significantly predict self-reported sexual aggression against women.[42] Moreover, the elaborate design of these experiments has contributed to researchers' understanding of social situations in which the effects of pornography consumption and exposure will be stronger. Formerly, experiments were often conducted as a teaching tool presented to subjects as the actual experiment. A female graduate psychology student typically posed as a subject, though her role was actually to test the real subjects of investigation. Early research indicated that, in order to observe significant effects, social inhibitions that normally prevented men from displaying aggression toward women in public contexts had to be neutralized.[43] Inhibitions were lowered by, for instance, deliberate provocations from the confederate, followed by opportunities for the subjects to retaliate (e.g., meting out fictional punishments), sometimes two or more times in order for subjects to feel less awkward when aggressing. A summary of a few typical experiments will serve to illustrate these methodologies and identify their strengths and weaknesses. Following that, a meta-analysis of this body of experimental research will be discussed along with subsequent studies that shed light on how the results may be interpreted.

Early Critical Findings on Aggression

A study published in 1978 tested whether additional social inhibitions (i.e., psychological thresholds preventing aggressive behavior in public) influenced the effect of nonviolent pornographic and non-pornographic aggressive films on aggression.[44] Subjects wrote short essays on marijuana legalization that were reviewed by a confederate who provided a written evaluation and administered electric shocks on a 10-point scale (the greater the number of shocks, the poorer the rating). All subjects received a negative evaluation (9 shocks) and were then exposed either to films or control conditions involving no external stimulus for 3½ minutes. An ostensibly additional teaching tool experiment was then presented, where subjects could retaliate against the same confederate via electric shock or reward (small amounts of cash). In order to make subjects more comfortable aggressing (disinhibition), a second opportunity was afforded to repeat the same exercise ten minutes later. At the first opportunity for retaliation, the nonviolent pornography and a non-pornographic aggressive film produced significantly higher levels of aggression toward both male and female targets than the no-film condition. However, at the second opportunity for retaliation, the nonviolent pornography condition produced significantly and substantially stronger aggression toward both female and male targets compared to the first opportunity for retaliation. During the second opportunity, the men's aggression was also significantly stronger against female targets compared to males. These results indicate that social inhibitions were lower on the second occasion because no sanctions had resulted from the first acts of aggression.[45] Likewise, the effects of pornography consumption will likely be more salient where social inhibitions are weak or where women are perceived as legitimate targets, such as at home or in prostitution—situations illustrated more concretely in studies with both battered and prostituted women and with johns.

An experiment published in 1974 tested the persistence of aggressive effects after subjects were exposed to diverting media immediately after exposure to different types of film clips, including (1) a neutral control sequence from the movie *Marco Polo's Travels*; (2) an aggressive sequence from the boxing movie *The Champion*; (3) brutal lethal violence from the movie *The Wild Bunch*; and (4) nonviolent pornography with foreplay and intercourse, but no aggressive elements.[46] Since another study reported no "appreciable differences" in provocative or retaliatory laboratory aggression between electric shocks and "intense noxious noise,"[47] this experiment used noise through headphones. After exposure, subjects were shown a one-minute educational film about rivers with natural landscapes and rainfall. Only those who had previously been exposed to the nonviolent pornographic movie were significantly more aggressive in the subsequent experiment compared to controls.

In an experiment published in 1981 measuring aggression with an electric shock technique after a fictitious negative evaluation of essays about legalization of marijuana similar to what was used in the 1978 study, the subjects were exposed to films presenting either (1) control material consisting of a nonsexual talk show; (2) nonaggressive pornography with intercourse; (3) aggressive pornography showing a woman being bound and subjected to violence and aggression by two men, with a "positive outcome" where she smiles and stops resisting; or (4) aggressive pornography similar to the third option, but with a "negative outcome" suggesting that the woman suffered.[48] The two different endings in the aggressive pornography were reinforced by different introductory narrations. In contrast to the other two experiments thus far discussed, the nonaggressive pornography did not lead to a statistically significant increase in aggression toward women, although there was an observable tendency in that direction. However, the authors noted that their experiment seemingly provoked the control group subjects (but not those in the exposure groups) much more before exposure, unlike previous studies that had used the same non-pornographic movie; hence, controls aggressed more afterward than controls in the previous studies using the same movies, while the aggression exhibited by those in the exposure group was similar in all studies.[49] The authors also referred to the 1978 study, which gave subjects two opportunities for retaliation; as mentioned, social inhibitions and restraints were evidently reduced on the second occasion, when those exposed to nonaggressive pornography became more aggressive. The 1981 study noted that, unless a similar method of inhibition is used, the effect of nonaggressive pornography may not be apparent in laboratory experiments.

The comparisons among various earlier studies illustrate the difficulties of designing an efficacious experiment. Further highlighting these considerations, the 1981 experiment conducted a follow-up with male subjects and a female provocateur to compare the effects of both violent pornographic movies once again. When the subjects were *not* provoked, only the violent pornography with a positive outcome produced a stronger aggressive effect, but with provocations, both movies produced a stronger effect than what was observed among controls.[50] In the subsequent survey, the subjects reported that the woman in the "negative" movie suffered most; however, the men who were provoked perceived the woman in the negative movie as enjoying the situation more than those who were not provoked.[51] One interpretation of this finding is that men's anger toward individual women can desensitize them to women's suffering in general—a collective apportioning of blame that may become amplified in sexualized contexts.

Understanding Meta-Analysis on General Aggression

A 1995 meta-analysis of experimental studies on the effect of pornography exposure on aggression included experiments studying how pornography influenced a person to knowingly attempt to harm another person "either physically, materially, or psychologically."[52] Self-reported aggression and physiological arousal, among other things, were excluded. Thus a total of 33 experiments were included, with primary data from 30 distinct studies that together included 2,040 subjects.[53] In the first meta-analysis with a zero-order (raw) correlation of the 33 experiments, pornography exposure was found to lead to more aggression; however, the analysis showed heterogeneous correlation effects. Following its methodology, potentially moderating variables were controlled for. The analysis found that the only statistically significant moderators demonstrating internally homogeneous correlation effects were the three content categories—(1) violent pornography, (2) nonviolent pornography, and (3) nude or semi-nude pictures with no sexual activity.[54] By contrast, the sex/gender of the consumer or target, prior anger, media used (e.g., film, photography, or written pornography), and level of sexual arousal typically showed statistically significant associations as moderators, but mostly with heterogeneous correlations to aggression.

To reiterate, although the subcategories of the meta-analysis where the test indicated homogeneous correlation effects are particularly relevant, the heterogeneity test's statistical power within these smaller subgroups was below the recommended threshold,[55] especially for violent pornography or nude or semi-nude pictures without sexual activity.[56] Hence, there might be undetected moderators in the analysis. For example, different experimental designs may well have affected the strength of the relative effects among studies. Individual sexually aggressive personality characteristics may also moderate the effects, but such characteristics may also likely be caused by prolonged consumption over time. For such moderators, it is essential to be aware of potential post-treatment bias where moderators risk erroneously controlling away for what is actually a consequence of the key causal variable,[57] in this case, pornography.

Exposure effects were found for both (visibly) nonviolent pornography (r=.171) and violent pornography (r=.216), both of which significantly increased subjects' aggression against women compared to controls (p<.05).[58] The difference in the effect of violent pornography compared with nonviolent pornography was not significant. No distinction was made in the meta-analysis as to whether individual studies included strategies for countering social inhibitions or restraints on aggression in laboratories, for instance by allowing two opportunities for retaliation that have been shown to promote stronger aggression, and whether they used more or less sensitive instruments. The authors also remarked that there was "no information on the reliability of the behavioral measures" in the studies included, leading to an "inability to correct for attenuated measurement," essentially meaning that "observed effects are underestimates."[59]

A somewhat puzzling result of the meta-analysis was that exposure to nude or semi-nude still photographs, such as covers of *Playboy* or

Penthouse,[60] led to significantly less aggression ($r=-.137, p<.05$) compared to controls.[61] However, one experiment included in the meta-analysis used more sensitive measurement instruments, finding that subjects exposed to photographs in *Playboy* doled out electric shocks of longer duration than subjects in the control group, thus demonstrating the opposite result, albeit one that was only "marginally significant" statistically.[62] Other studies had found that the length of the electric shock was determined to be the product of less "cognitive mediation" than the intensity of the shock.[63] Even a marginally significant trend may be relevant when taking into account two later experimental studies with non-pornographic sexually objectifying print advertisements, and one with R-rated Hollywood movies—none of which contained violence. Nevertheless, all three studies found that the objectifying materials produced a significant increase in ASV compared to controls.[64] Similar statistically significant associations between experimental exposure to covers of non-pornographic, yet sexually objectifying, men's magazines, and a self-reported likelihood of raping ("rape proclivity"), were seen in a Spanish study published in 2015.[65] Another naturalistic study published the following year similarly found that past consumption of magazines such as *Maxim* and *Esquire*, which objectify women, were significantly "associated with stronger notions of women as sex objects"—notions that, in turn, mediated significantly stronger ASV.[66] As shown in other studies, pornography consumers also become considerably desensitized over time, seeking more extreme, dehumanizing, and violent material—a process to which nude photographs may contribute.[67] Given this, the validity and utility of the earlier studies of general aggression, specifically with respect to nude and semi-nude pictures, can, therefore, be called into question.

Attitudes Supporting Violence against Women (ASV)

By the 1980s, experimental and nonexperimental quantitative research among men showed that certain ASV, including "rape myths," significantly predicted more sexual aggression and violence against women as well as the trivialization of women's suffering.[68] ASV also predicted subjects' estimations of the likelihood that they would rape or otherwise force women to have sex with them if they could do so with impunity.[69] A similar attitude that has been measured in the pornography effects research is the relative trivialization of women's suffering in simulated rape trials, where the experimental subjects mete out a recommended sentence.[70]

A meta-analysis of 16 experiments comprising data from 2,248 subjects, measuring the effects of pornography on ASV, was published in 1995.[71] The meta-analysis included experiments using movies, written narratives, and audio recordings.[72] Despite the potentially moderating effect associated with differences in media formats, the meta-analysis demonstrated that the pornography produced an increase in ASV, with average exposure effects (r=.146) being homogeneous, providing no evidence for "a moderating condition."[73] The statistical power of the heterogeneity test was marginally weak, with 16 instead of the recommended 20 studies, but an average sample size of approximately 141, well above the recommended lower threshold of 80.[74] The test might have included undetected moderators, but if so, they were probably relatively weak.

When the researchers examined different content subcategories, significant differences were found among the average correlations of the three types of statistical comparisons within the 16 individual studies: (a) violent pornography compared to control groups (r=.112), (b) nonviolent pornography compared to control groups (r=.125), and (c) violent pornography compared to nonviolent pornography (r=.163).[75] As expressed in these figures, the *direct* comparison of the average effects of nonviolent compared to violent pornography found that the latter caused a greater increase in ASV. By contrast, in the *indirect* comparison between, on the one hand, effects of nonviolent pornography compared to control groups and, on the other hand, effects of violent pornography compared to control groups, a stronger average effect was found to result from nonviolent compared to violent pornography.

The three comparisons of effect correlations were presumptively homogeneous, but the statistical power of the tests did not rise above the recommended threshold with regard to the number of studies included, although average sample sizes well exceeded it.[76] The results of the heterogeneity analysis within subgroups should thus be interpreted cautiously, since they may include undetected moderators. Nevertheless, other studies assessed in the following discussion of individual differences and post-treatment biases suggest that past pornography consumption is, over time, one of the stronger moderators in amplifying adverse consumption effects, thus implying that pornography consumption by itself is the primary cause of increases in ASV, other moderators notwithstanding. Some of those experiments also found that different subgenres within both nonviolent and violent pornography increased ASV with slightly different strengths.

Why Nonviolent Pornography Feeds Violence against Women

Research conducted in the 1980s—a body of literature sometimes neglected in more recent reviews—highlighted psychological mechanisms that could explain why not only violent but also nonviolent pornography leads to aggression against women.[77] In various studies from that decade, men tended to categorize women according to stereotypical dichotomies like "whore-Madonna," "promiscuous-prudish," and sexually "permissive-nonpermissive."[78] In light of this evidence, Kenneth Leonard and Stuart Taylor's 1983 experiment examined associations among dichotomous conceptualizations, pornography consumption, and aggression against women: 30 of 40 men looked at a series of pornographic slides while a female confederate in an adjoining room ostensibly commented on the same images in one of three different ways: (1) sexually permissively (e.g., "I'd like to try that"), (2) neutrally (no comment), or (3) nonpermissively (e.g., "this is disgusting").[79] The 10 controls looked at neutral non-pornographic slides with no confederate commentary. After the four exposure conditions, an aggression experiment was conducted with four blocks of trials using electric shocks adjusted to each subject's perceptions of what was "definitely unpleasant"—a point set at 5 on a 5-point scale.[80] Subsequently, point 4 was set as 90% of the maximum, 3 as 80%, 2 as 70%, and 1 as 60%. Deliberately stronger provocations were used against subjects in each block, going from an average of 1.5 in the first block to 4.5 in the last block.[81]

Averaging the four blocks, Leonard and Taylor found that pornography-exposed males administered significantly higher electric shocks to women making promiscuous comments, with a mean shock intensity of 3.09, compared to 2.14 against women making no comments, and 1.80 against women making sexually inhibitory comments, while neutral image–exposed controls administered shocks with an intensity of only 1.77.[82] Even in the first unprovoked trials, when subjects had not yet received any shocks from the confederate, men exposed to the promiscuous-comments pornography condition imposed significantly higher shocks than men in the three other conditions. In all four blocks, only the results of the promiscuous-comments condition differed significantly from the others, with one exception: during the last block, pornography-exposed men also aggressed significantly more against women making no comments as compared both to those making inhibitory comments and to neutral-slide male controls.[83] These results are particularly noteworthy considering the relatively small sample size of 40 subjects, where only 10 could be assigned to each exposure condition.

Leonard and Taylor's experiment was later interpreted by the psychologists Dolf Zillmann and James Weaver as having promoted aggression through a psychological mechanism they termed "target devaluation" and "target depersonalization."[84] In Zillmann and Weaver's words, the male subjects probably thought along the lines of "'let the bitch have it,'" then projected such thoughts onto the women they perceived as being more promiscuous.[85] Stereotypical impressions of women's sexually permissive attitudes, combined with exposure to similarly suggestive pornography, thus made the men more inclined to perceive women as legitimate "prey." Several other experiments corroborate this psychological mechanism that dehumanizes women by showing how nonviolent pornography leads to attitudes that support or trivialize men's violence against women.

An illustrative short-term experiment by Weaver exposed male and female subjects to four different types of pornographic movies and one neutral control exposure condition in order to clarify the potential influence of the type of materials on subjects' relative trivialization of violence against women.[86] The dependent variable involved a simulated jury trial of "transgressive physical victimization of women," where "rape" was "the case of special interest" and subjects had to "sentence male offenders."[87] Within the control group that saw a non-pornographic movie, the men recommended a prison sentence of 823 months, and the women a sentence of 869 months.[88] Subjects exposed to a movie showing *female-instigated* heterosexual sex where the women were presented as promiscuous—and the movie did *not* contain either force or violence (e.g., *Lady on the Bus*)—recommended a significantly shorter sentence of 514 (males) and 515 (females) months.[89] Both male and female subjects who saw movies with *rape pornography*, in which men coerced and assaulted women, recommended shorter sentences than controls and, somewhat counterintuitively, women's sentences (503 months) were even shorter than men's (599 months).[90] Male subjects who had seen so-called "slasher movies" with *eroticized violence*, such as a naked woman who unsuccessfully offers sex in an attempt to avoid murder, recommended the shortest sentence, while the female subjects in this group recommended a longer sentence (481 and 671 months, respectively).[91] Those who had seen films with "consensual" sex where *romance* led to passionate sex (e.g., *Lady Chatterley's Lover*) recommended a shorter sentence compared to the controls, 775 months (males) and 719 months (females), respectively, but even when counted together these sentences were not significantly different from the controls' sentences.[92]

To understand more about how stereotypical categorizations of women as legitimate targets for sexual aggression are related to the trivializing effects of different pornography categories, Zillmann and Weaver administered a questionnaire both one week prior to and immediately after exposure where subjects reviewed different stereotypical descriptions of "wild and promiscuous" and "nice, virtuous girls," respectively.[93] Men exposed to either a film with *female-instigated* sex without violence or one with consensual *romance* sex rated the descriptions of stereotypical "nice and virtuous girls" of their own age as significantly more promiscuous than did controls.[94] Notably, among males, the romance category was one of the two that produced significant rating effects compared to the results of the sentencing experiment, where its effect trend was nonsignificant and comparatively weak. Female subjects, by contrast, tended to be most inclined to categorize stereotypical "virtuous girls" as more promiscuous after exposure to *rape* pornography, although the trend was not statistically significant.[95]

Zillmann and Weaver interpreted the rating and sentencing experiments as illustrating how the influence of pornography on perceptions of female promiscuity may influence their relative trivialization of rape, although the psychological mechanisms were slightly different for the women than for the men.[96] Importantly, other experiments with nonviolent pornography have corroborated these general consumption effects for both men and women. For instance, an experiment published in 1988 showed how male and female subjects who viewed common nonviolent pornography over six weeks for a total of around six hours were significantly more inclined, one week later, to perceive women as sexually promiscuous by nature and to accept male dominance and female submission, compared to a non-exposed control group.[97] Similarly, an experiment with male and female subjects published in 1982 showed that consumption of common nonviolent pornography over six weeks for a total of about five hours "produced visions of people doing more of anything pertaining to sex" that were significantly different compared to controls, for instance, leading exposed subjects on average to believe that about 29% of all adults have anal or group sex whereas controls believed that about 12% have anal or group sex.[98] This study also included a simulated rape trial where those exposed recommended on average of around five years' imprisonment—a statistically significant and far lower penalty than the almost ten years recommended by the control groups.[99] Exposure to pornography also significantly diminished support for "women's liberation," reducing it from 76.5 for neutral media controls to 38.6 for the five-hour exposure group on a 100-point scale, and significantly increased sexually callous attitudes that promote men's violence against women.[100]

These experiments with nonviolent pornography demonstrate, among other things, how pornography operates through certain psychological mechanisms that lead consumers to view women more as legitimate "prey" for sexual aggression, thus rendering them "targets" for abuse. Similar consumption effects have been found by other researchers, including the psychologist James Check, whose work strongly influenced Canadian courts in the 1980s. In Canadian case law, Check's three-pronged definition of pornography was adopted in *R. v. Wagner* (1985), which categorized pornography as (1) violent, (2) nonviolent but "dehumanizing or degrading," or (3) nonviolent "explicit erotica" that does not degrade or dehumanize.[101] Only the third category, "explicit erotica," was considered by the courts to be harmless.[102] To more precisely define dehumanizing/degrading pornography without violence, *Wagner* mentioned, inter alia, portrayals where "[w]omen, particularly, are deprived of unique human character or identity and are depicted as sexual playthings, hysterically and instantly responsive to male sexual demands."[103] Thus, the concepts of "dehumanizing" and "degrading" include stereotypical pornographic representations of women as exaggeratedly promiscuous—representations that research shows are particularly effective in trivializing and supporting men's violence against women, even without being overtly violent.

Some commentators erroneously argue that pornography cannot be defined in a way that is politically or legally useful. In a study inquiring into different pornography exposure effects using the three-pronged definition from *Wagner*, Check and his colleague Ted Guloien also addressed this misconception by asking whether materials classified accordingly were perceived similarly by their research subjects.[104] Their experiment included 436 participants residing in Toronto, of which 319 were nonstudents and 117 were college students.[105] Following the *Wagner* definition, they used three different pornographic videos that each totaled about 30 minutes, with three or four 5–10-minute scenes in each. Recall that these researchers had to splice fragments of different scenes from commercial pornography and sex education films in order to create a coherent "erotic" film without any dehumanizing or violent scenes, since no feature-length movie could be found that did not also include violence or dehumanization. Then, in the experiment's first part, they tested whether the three movies had been accurately categorized, finding that the subjects' ratings "generally conformed quite well" to their own three-pronged definition.[106] Violent pornography was consistently rated as comparatively "the least educational, realistic, and affectionate" and most offensive, aggressive, and degrading; by contrast, nonviolent but "dehumanizing" pornography was rated in between the violent and "erotic" categories, while "erotica" was rated the most educational.[107]

The next part of Check and Guloien's experiment studied the exposure effects of the three movies. Subjects were shown one type of films on three occasions over a 6-day period.[108] After 4–5 days, exposure subjects and unexposed controls were measured on a number of attitudes known to promote men's violence against women, including subjects' reported likelihood of *raping* or *forcing* a female into sex she did not want when they were certain not to be caught. These two conditions were measured on 5-point scales, where 1 meant "not at all likely," 5 "very likely," and any number of 2 or higher was interpreted as "any likelihood."[109]

On the *likelihood of raping* scale, only 9.6% of controls reported any likelihood, their reported average being 1.14. The violent pornography condition produced an average of 1.43, with 20.5% reporting any likelihood. The dehumanizing nonviolent pornography produced an average of 1.44, with 20.4% reporting any likelihood. And the erotica produced an average of 1.31, with 15.7% reporting any likelihood. Except for those in the "erotica" group, exposed subjects differed significantly from controls.[110]

On the *likelihood of forcing* a female to have sex scale, notably it was the dehumanizing nonviolent, rather than the violent, pornography that produced the strongest effect, with exposed subjects evidencing an average likelihood of 1.76, compared to 1.47 among controls. While the remaining exposure conditions resulted in a higher average than controls, only the dehumanizing nonviolent condition was significantly different from the controls. Similarly, higher percentages reporting any likelihood of forcing a woman to have sex were seen in all exposure conditions compared to controls, but none significantly so by conventional social science standards (p>.05), though the nonviolent dehumanizing condition came close (39.1% vs. 26.9%; p=.083).

As several studies have shown, the degree of violence in pornography is not in itself sufficient to explain why many consumers become more sexually aggressive or adopt attitudes more supportive or trivializing of men's violence against women compared to non-consumers. Many studies also lack the precision that more detailed experiments afford, for example, specifying to what degree the pornography shows dehumanization, degradation, or a representation of stereotypically "promiscuous" women. An emphasis on such portrayals, research shows, makes consumers even more inclined to perceive women as "legitimate targets" for sexual aggression, in turn feeding aggression and attitudes that support or trivialize men's violence against women. The psychological mechanisms that underlie as well as result from dichotomous categorizations of women as "whores" or "Madonnas" may help to explain why one experiment found that unambiguous presentations of "nymphomania" with a "total absence of coercive or violent action" nonetheless led to "the strongest trivialization of rape" compared to other pornography.[111] In the consumer's eyes, such presentations appear to objectify women and rob them of some of their human value.

Put another way, pornography *subordinates* women through its influence on consumers, thereby coming into conflict with democratic values since subordination on the grounds of sex/gender is a form of discrimination that is incompatible with sex equality. It is no coincidence that the American women's anti-pornography civil rights movement of the 1980s, led by the legal scholar and advocate Catharine MacKinnon and the late writer-activist Andrea Dworkin, included terms such as "graphic sexually explicit *subordination*"[112] in its definition of pornography when challenging it legally. The perception that only violent pornography fuels violence against women, contradicted by empirical evidence, must be abandoned. In order to combat the effects of pornography, it is of paramount importance to understand the extent to which women (or men in gay male pornography) are subordinated, dehumanized, and presented as legitimate targets for male sexual aggression. Such sexual objectification can clearly take place with or without violence—a fact implied in the meta-studies surveyed, where no substantial differences were identified in the measured effects of violent and nonviolent pornography.

Individual Differences and Post-Treatment Bias

To underscore, post-treatment bias is a well-known phenomenon in statistics and particularly relevant when researchers attempt to control for confounding, moderating, or mediating variables, which in the pornography effects research might include individual differences among pornography consumers. Yet scholars have noted that post-treatment bias "is assumed away in most models and decompositions,"[113] while studies including post-treatment bias are frequently published, even in leading journals, their problems still unacknowledged.[114] Check and Guloien's experiment analyzed a number of potential interaction effects, otherwise called moderators. One was monthly frequency of pornography consumption, where the complete sample comprised 241 respondents who reported consuming once or more per month (m=2), and 195 reporting consuming less than once per month (m=0.8).[115] Among the subgroup exposed to dehumanizing nonviolent pornography, the effects were significant and stronger with respect to the likelihood of raping among those reporting pornography consumption at least once a month compared to controls, but they were not significant among those who reported consuming pornography less than monthly.[116] However, this interaction effect with levels of past pornography consumption was not observed for subjects exposed either to violent pornography or nonviolent "erotica."[117]

Importantly, the interaction effect of levels of prior consumption with exposure to dehumanizing pornography is an ecological consequence of the key causal variable, pornography itself, related to the naturalistic (as distinguished from experimental) exposure. Indeed, longitudinal studies suggest that prolonged exposure predicts more sexual aggression among male adolescents, even after controlling for other relevant predictors and the reverse causation hypothesis.[118] Sexual aggression, to underscore, is a measure significantly associated with ASV like those measured by Check and Guloien, including the likelihood of raping and coercing sex. Therefore, their results should not be interpreted as if only those men consuming pornography more often are at risk of evidencing higher likelihoods after exposure to dehumanizing nonviolent pornography, considering that any of their low consumers could have started to consume pornography more often at any given time. Even if it might be implied by the variable of past consumption itself, Check and Guloien did not explicitly acknowledge that this interaction term is controlling for a consequence of the key causal variable of pornography, leading to a form of potential "ecological" post-treatment bias. Their study may also contain other interaction terms with similar problems of post-treatment bias.

Check and Guloien analyzed another interaction effect by measuring presumed moderating prevalence factors for aggression by classifying subjects on a 20-point scale for symptoms of *psychoticism* (0=no symptoms).[119] Psychoticism is not precisely what it might sound like at first blush. The concept was introduced and developed by Hans Eysenck in collaboration with his wife, Sybil Eysenck, in the late 1960s. They wrote that the term was "meant to suggest the hypothesis 'that there exists a set of correlated behavior variables indicative of predisposition to psychotic breakdown, demonstrable as a continuous variable in the normal population, and independent of [extraversion] and [neuroticism].' "[120] According to the American Psychological Association's 2015 *Dictionary of Psychology*, psychoticism refers to "a dimension of personality . . . characterized by aggression, impulsivity, aloofness, and antisocial behavior."[121] Check and Guloien, citing Eyseneck, reported that he had "made abundantly clear" that the scale "purports to reflect levels of psychoticism that extend into the normal, nonpsychiatric population."[122]

Though none of the subjects in Check and Guloien's sample of 436 men was classified above 8 on the 20-point scale employed, 186 subjects were nonetheless classified between 1 and 8 (m=2.9), and the remaining 250 fell between 0 and 1 (m=0.50).[123] The exposure effects were found to be statistically significant only among the 186 subjects scoring higher on psychoticism.[124] After exposure to violent pornography, these subjects reported a significantly higher likelihood of raping and forcing sex, and after exposure to nonviolent dehumanizing pornography they reported a significantly higher likelihood of raping and forcing sex compared to the controls scoring higher on psychoticism. A nonsignificant trend in the same direction was seen in the "erotica" category among subjects scoring high on psychoticism.

The study did not expressly consider whether psychoticism may be an outcome in part associated with increased naturalistic pornography consumption. We will therefore analyze some conditions in their study indicating that their interaction findings are inconsistent with other pornography effects studies, which consequently make it more important to check for post-treatment bias. Following that, we will look at similar naturalistic studies where data is more transparently reported, which will facilitate exposure of post-treatment bias and illustrate how post-treatment bias may be a recurring problem when researchers assume that "individual differences" are important. Finally, in light of this analysis, we will look again to Check and Guloien's Canadian study in conjunction with analyzing a similar experiment conducted more recently in Denmark and map out where and why post-treatment bias is likely to exist and how it minimizes the assessment of the harms of pornography.

When the 186 men scoring high on psychoticism in Check and Guloien's study were further divided into students and nonstudents, the effects of exposure to violent and nonviolent dehumanizing pornography were significant only for students.[125] Although student status is hardly an effect of pornography, it is possible that "psychoticism" might in part be a consequence of past pornography consumption, thus potentially constituting a post-treatment bias. We will return to psychoticism later. At this point, when exposure groups were subdivided on the basis of symptoms of psychoticism and student status, each exposure condition's subsample was effectively decimated roughly four times. Consequently, risks for Type II errors became considerably greater, meaning that nonsignificant effects might be real ("false negatives") even for nonstudents. One reason the meta-analytic method was developed was specifically to counter Type II errors of this sort. Indeed, in contrast to the student-nonstudent comparison, a meta-analysis of naturalistic longitudinal and cross-sectional surveys found no significant moderation on grounds of age, while differences in the association between actual sexual aggression and pornography consumption among adolescents and adults, respectively, were likewise insignificant.[126]

Moreover, it is not clear how sensitive Check and Guloien's measurements of self-reported likelihood of raping or forcing sex were as indirect indices of sexual aggression. The meta-analysis of 16 experiments conducted on 2,248 subjects found homogeneous effects of pornography on ASV.[127] Although its statistical power was not ideal for the heterogeneity test, it did not indicate any dramatic moderator effects even if undetected interactions were present.[128] The meta-analysis of ASV also included the dependent measures Check and Guloien used (likelihood of raping/forcing sex), and their 1989 experiment was included among the 16 examined.[129] Certainly their subjects appear to have been influenced by the pornography to quite varying degrees, some seemingly not at all, at least in terms of self-reported likelihood of being sexually aggressive. But their analysis was based on smaller subsamples, which increased the risk of Type II errors bespeaking a failure to detect an actual effect. In light of the meta-analysis, it can be hypothesized that, at least when including a broader set of measurement instruments, pornography exposure makes most individuals more or less likely to adopt ASV, even if individual predispositions would moderate this association.

Indeed, a large cross-sectional *naturalistic* study on the association between pornography consumption and sexual aggression published in 2000, based on a representative sample of almost 3,000 male college students in the United States from 1984 to 1985, found results lending ecological validity to the meta-analytic indications that most men, including those with low sexually aggressive predispositions, become to some degree more sexually aggressive in response to pornography consumption.[130] This survey of college males measured consumption by asking how often subjects "read" the magazines "*Playboy, Penthouse, Chic, Club, Forum, Gallery, Genesis, Oui,* or *Hustler.*"[131] Its measure of "sexual aggression" was based on a battery of questions, ranging from asking respondents whether and, where appropriate, how often they had violently forced someone into painful anal sex, to posing the same questions regarding their use of continual arguments and pressure to obtain sex unwanted by the other party.[132] After adjusting for moderators—a high, medium, or low predisposition for sexual aggression—consistent with the meta-analyses, the high-frequency consumers, even those with low predispositions, self-reported significantly more sexual aggression compared to low-frequency consumers.[133] Certainly, this self-reported difference was considerably smaller than it was among the most highly predisposed men, where differences in sexual aggression were "dramatic" between high and low consumers.[134] Yet the finding pertaining to less aggressively predisposed men is particularly noteworthy due to several methodological problems that bear closer analysis, especially the potential post-treatment bias caused by moderators that likely contribute to underestimating the correlations between pornography and sexual aggression.

The study used two latent constructs, Hostile Masculinity and Sexual Promiscuity, respectively,[135] to measure the moderating effect of a sexually aggressive predisposition; in turn, these constructs were used to classify subjects as having a high, medium, or low predisposition for sexual aggression, thus controlling for that factor. Hostile Masculinity signifies a "personality profile" that includes "(a) an insecure, defensive, hypersensitive, and hostile-distrustful orientation, particularly towards women, and (b) sexual gratification from controlling or dominating women"; Sexual Promiscuity signifies "a promiscuous, noncommittal, game-playing orientation towards sexual relations, which is statically predicted by certain early familial aggression and adolescent delinquency."[136] Hostile Masculinity is often measured in the literature by precisely those ASV that meta-analyses as well as other experimental and nonexperimental studies have shown to be significantly increased by pornography exposure.[137] Put succinctly, they are the same thing. Moreover, Sexual Promiscuity was measured by surveying age of first intercourse and number of sexual partners reported since age 14,[138] both of which are significantly affected by pornography: specifically, longitudinal studies have found that pornography consumption is a contributing factor in increasing the number of sexual partners and, among early pubertal adolescents, lowering the age of first intercourse.[139] This finding is also consistent with numerous cross-sectional studies.[140]

The 2000 study made a misguided selection of moderators that were then used to control for sexually aggressive risk levels—interaction variables that are already partial consequences of the key causal variable, pornography. These choices introduced post-treatment bias. Predictably, the study found significant "simple correlations" between pornography and Hostile Masculinity ($r=.17$, $p<.001$), between pornography and Sexual Promiscuity ($r=.17$, $p<.001$), and between pornography and the "cross product" of Sexual Promiscuity and Hostile Masculinity ($r=.21$, $p<.001$).[141] Similarly, a 2015 replication study undertaken in Canada with 211 adult men using more precise measures found a significant zero-order correlation between self-reported general pornography consumption and Hostile Masculinity ($r=.21$, $p<.01$); between violent pornography and Hostile Masculinity ($r=.25$, $p<.05$); between general pornography and Sexual Promiscuity, though non-significantly ($r=.10$, $p>.05$); and significantly between violent pornography and Sexual Promiscuity ($r=.17$, $p<.05$).[142] Moreover, a higher frequency of pornography consumption was significantly correlated with a larger consumed proportion of violent pornography ($r=.20$, $p<.01$),[143] thus corroborating studies that suggest frequent consumers need more extreme materials to be aroused.[144]

By including moderators that are positively associated with pornography, the 2000 and 2015 studies appear to control away for a consequence of its consumption that can soak up part of the effects otherwise attributable to pornography, thereby creating a recipe for minimizing the true extent of pornography's impact on violence against women.[145] A recently published meta-analysis by Christopher Ferguson and Richard Hartley makes precisely the same blunder by controlling for such variables in the data within the included studies, among which we find the 2000 study and others that included the latent constructs hostile masculinity and sexual promiscuity.[146] This disregard for treating variables as controls and moderators, despite their not being independent of the key causal variable, pornography, is done under the pretense of pursuing "the most conservative" estimation, "involving [the] greatest number of theoretically relevant controls."[147] The risk of post-treatment bias is considered nowhere. Earlier meta-analyses have first presented the raw average correlation between pornography and sexual aggression and other variables.[148] Such information may indicate post-treatment bias if the statistical model's moderators generate unlikely results. However, this was not done in the present meta-analysis, which claims that nonviolent (and possibly violent) pornography does not affect sexual aggression.[149] As will be shown, these conclusions are wrong.

Moreover, three other methodological problems in the study from 2000, which may also be present in other studies, seem to contribute to further underestimating the harms of pornography. First, the 2000 study measured pornography consumption with a 4-point subjective scale: "never," "seldom," "somewhat frequently," or "very frequently."[150] In order to answer accurately, respondents would have to know the population average. In light of taboos and controversies surrounding pornography, particularly in the 1980s, when the survey was conducted, many students were likely unaware of such an average. Thus, low consumers probably overestimated their consumption while high consumers underestimated it. Similar to other measurement errors in the literature, this tendency would support the observation that "the lower the reliability, the greater the degree of underestimation."[151]

Second, a common source of underestimation was missing data on some independent variables that were then replaced by the respondent average—a "conservative" method that typically reduces differences between groups, as the study's authors admitted.[152]

Third, in a parallel survey with female students drawn from the same cohorts, 54% of respondents reported victimization by sexual aggression, while only 25% of the men admitted to perpetrating it; yet these women reported experiencing a "virtually identical" number of the sexually aggressive acts that 25% of the men reported perpetrating, which raises the suspicion that the men did not "admit enough sexual aggression to account for the number" of incidents women reported (e.g., failing to accurately perceive a woman's resistance in a sexual situation).[153] Such measurement errors can also cause researchers to underestimate correlations between pornography consumption and sexual aggression where high pornography consumers are desensitized to sexual aggression and therefore less likely to perceive it as such, thus more prone to avoid reporting sexual aggression than low consumers. Indeed, pornography exposure increases attitudes trivializing violence against women.

All told, the sources of probable underestimation in the 2000 study notwithstanding, correlations between increased pornography consumption and increased sexual aggression were statistically significant among all groups of men.[154] This finding is especially striking considering likely post-treatment bias controlling away for some portion of the consequences of pornography consumption, a subjectively worded questionnaire underestimating differences in consumption, underreporting of sexual aggression by high-consuming men, and the replacement of missing data with sample averages. Regardless of these flaws, the study's results suggest that pornography consumption makes most men more sexually aggressive, albeit to varying extents.

The lessons on post-treatment bias from the 2000 and 2015 studies, respectively, raise concerns that similar problems of post-treatment bias may have compromised Check and Guloien's previous experiment. It, too, attempted to control for moderating psychological variables, there via psychoticism, but without reporting its correlation with pornography consumption (the 2000 and 2015 studies were more transparent in these respects). The political scientist Jason Seawright suggests that in such cases scholars should "search for moments in which control variables" in the statistical analysis "appear as causal steps connecting the treatment and the outcome."[155] Although the authors did not do so in 1989, it is possible to follow Seawright's suggestion retrospectively.

The 2015 edition of the American Psychological Association's *Dictionary* states that psychoticism is "characterized by aggression."[156] As mentioned, research dating back to the 1980s showed that both sexual aggression and general aggression toward women were significantly and positively predicted both by stronger ASV and by higher pornography consumption. Pornography, in turn, significantly predicted stronger ASV. Notably, Check and Guloien reported that the experimental exposure effects from nonviolent, but dehumanizing, pornography on subjects' self-reported likelihood of raping were significantly stronger for the subgroup reporting consuming pornography at least once a month compared to controls, but not for those consuming less than monthly.[157] Considering that pornography is demonstrably associated with attitudes that predict aggression against women, and that this association was confirmed by Check and Guloien's own data, their findings raise questions whether more frequent past consumption would also predict higher scores on psychoticism, considering that the latter is also associated with aggression. Including psychoticism as a moderator seems to make potential post-treatment bias more likely. By doing so, in the words of Gary King and Langche Zeng, the researchers may be "inappropriately controlling for the consequences of our key causal variable, and for most of the effects of it, thus biasing the overall effect."[158]

According to a "reverse causation" hypothesis, higher psychoticism scores could certainly predict greater "past" pornography consumption. Yet this review of numerous experimental and longitudinal studies suggests otherwise: more pornography consumption contributes to more sexual aggression and more ASV, irrespective of potentially "reversed" causal effects. Therefore, it seems more likely that pornography contributes to psychoticism and similar psychological characteristics, even if the opposite might simultaneously hold to some extent. Furthermore, considering that the average age of first use of pornography for masturbation is in early adolescence for boys,[159] and that some attitudinal and behavioral effects may become stronger over time, the number of years an individual consumes pornography might also be significant. Check and Guloien's moderator only measured current "frequency" (i.e., "times per months"), not frequency over time.[160] If extensive pornography consumption over time engenders negative personality traits such as psychoticism, more men than those who already score high on such measures would be at risk for becoming more sexually aggressive if they start consuming more pornography, especially if they start at a younger age. Check and Guloien's study did not consider these possibilities.

A more recent example of post-treatment bias may be seen in Gert Hald and Neil Malamuth's experiment with Danish subjects, published in 2015, where an interaction analysis similar to Check and Guloien's was undertaken.[161] Hald and Malamuth found significant, and considerable, effects on scales measuring ASV after about 25 minutes of exposure to nonviolent contemporary commercial pornography among men who scored lower on "agreeableness"—a subsample of 40.82%, including controls (i.e., 40 out of 98 men).[162] The average exposure/nonexposure difference in this subgroup was greater than one standard deviation, and thus regarded as large. Agreeableness is a personality dimension considered within the well-known "Five Factor Model" in psychology, where lower scores signify traits that, according to Hald and Malamuth, are "most clearly relevant to an exploitative approach to sexuality and conflict in relationships (e.g., antagonism, coldness, hostility, suspiciousness, disagreeability, unfriendliness, and self-interest)."[163] However, the authors admit that "some of the stratified analyses suffered from small cell sizes" (i.e., when subdividing into smaller subgroups based on agreeableness scores), hence limiting the measure's statistical power while increasing the "risk of Type II errors."[164] By implication, they acknowledge that similar associations might have held for a larger proportion of subjects than the 40.82% they found, had their sample been larger.

Hald and Malamuth also conducted a multiple regression analysis including the following independent variables: (1) agreeableness, (2) pornography consumption in the past year, (3) experimental pornography exposure, and (4) an interaction term encompassing experimental exposure and agreeableness. Significant positive associations with ASV were found for (1) lower agreeableness; (2) more past-year pornography consumption; and (4) the interaction of experimental exposure and low agreeableness.[165] In addition, the exposure effect on ASV was significantly mediated by sexual arousal, which is to some degree inherent to the activity "since pornography is designed primarily to activate . . . sexual arousal,"[166] and consumers would not likely continue watching pornography that failed to arouse them.

However, Hald and Malamuth did not report having controlled for the extent that past pornography consumption predicted agreeableness scores, just as Check and Guloien's study did not do so with regard to psychoticism. Lower agreeableness may be a partial consequence of pornography, the key causal variable. This is especially so when considering that the experimental studies examined here have demonstrated causal associations in that direction for variables like agreeableness—findings also supported by the longitudinal studies considered in this chapter. Moreover, the measure of "past" consumption was restricted to one year and did not include age of first exposure or longer exposure over time,[167] despite the possibility that persistent exposure might have a stronger effect on attitudes than short-term exposure.

If pornography consumption on average causes a decrease in agreeableness, but the model controls for lower agreeableness and its interaction with experimental pornography exposure as if agreeableness was a moderator and not a dependent variable like ASV, the model will necessarily evidence post-treatment bias.[168] By taking this approach, Malamuth and Hald are essentially controlling away for some consequences of the key causal variable, soaking up its effects with the risk of wrongly attributing a portion of them to agreeableness. Put differently, if agreeableness is affected by the "treatment" of pornography, it should have been designated as a "post-treatment" dependent variable. As with Check and Guloien's experiment and the other naturalistic studies reviewed here, many more men than those 40.82% already scoring low on agreeableness seem to be at "risk" for developing stronger ASV, should they start consuming more pornography in the future. That said, 40.82% is already a compellingly large proportion of men, given that their attitudes are so strongly influenced by exposure to merely 25 minutes of nonviolent commercial pornography.

Similar methodological problems also exist at the societal level, where anything from music videos to literary fiction is increasingly influenced by pornography, thus potentially mediating and masking its contribution to the "sexualization"[169] of society. This "mainstreaming" of pornography makes it difficult to distinguish various causes of sexual aggression and may therefore minimize pornography's impact. For instance, non-consumers may still be influenced by pornography through its influence on society, which in turn may make non-consumers' attitudes and sexually aggressive behaviors more like those of consumers. Differences between these two groups may then become harder to statistically discern.

Population-Based Naturalistic Longitudinal and Cross-Sectional Surveys

Naturalistic studies of the correlation between pornography consumption and men's violence against women that have been conducted with population samples, such as the large cross-sectional survey with almost 3,000 U.S. college students, may corroborate the extent to which effects demonstrated in laboratory experiments are manifest in social contexts. This triangulation of research methods is also useful in countering the criticism that laboratory experiments have low ecological validity.

Sexual Aggression, Attitudes Supporting Violence, and Post-Treatment Bias

A meta-analysis of the association between pornography consumption and sexual aggression published in 2016 was based on 20,820 subjects from 22 studies carried out in seven different countries.[170] A positive and significant association was found between pornography consumption and actual sexual aggression, leaving "little doubt" that more pornography consumption on average predicts more "actual acts of sexual aggression" by individuals than less consumption.[171] Several moderators were controlled for directly, and researchers found no interactions based on consumers' sex/gender, age, country of study, time of study (before and after the internet), or whether the study was cross-sectional, longitudinal, published or not.[172] Importantly, the longitudinal studies rejected the counter-hypothesis on reverse causation that would imply that correlations reflect aggressive individuals' pornography consumption conforming to their predispositions.[173]

Further findings showed that verbal sexual aggression predictably exhibited stronger average correlations (r=.30) with pornography consumption than did physical sexual aggression (r=.20), although both were significant.[174] A "marginally significant" (p=.07) stronger correlation was also found for "violent" pornography consumption compared to "general" pornography consumption. However, since no consumption frequencies are reported in the meta-analysis (e.g., hours/days per week/month), and considering that consumers often become desensitized and quickly move on to view more violent or dehumanizing materials, this marginally significant stronger correlation for violent materials might simply be an artifact of a higher frequency of consumption—a potentially confounding variable.

As recalled, ASV also significantly predict sexual aggression in individual men.[175] These measures triangulate with one another, expressing a similar underlying phenomenon. A meta-analysis of the naturalistic associations between men's pornography consumption and ASV published in 2010 corrected serious errors that marred the naturalistic findings of the meta-analysis from 1995.[176] The 2010 meta-analysis included nine studies that met the requisite quality criteria.[177] The sample consisted of 2,309 respondents and focused exclusively on males.[178] The resulting analysis concluded that increased pornography consumption significantly predicted an average increase in ASV (r=.18, p<.001).[179] When the average correlation between violent pornography and ASV (r=.24, n=1,394) was compared to that between nonviolent pornography and ASV (r=.13, n=1,617), the former was found to be significantly stronger than the latter (p<.001). Yet, to underscore, a higher frequency of pornography consumption seems to be a confounder that may partly explain these differences. This meta-analysis does not report specific consumption frequencies. Under these preconditions, it is impossible to disentangle to what extent increased consumption per se, rather than violent pornography consumption, is associated with the increase in ASV found among violent pornography consumers. The meta-analysis also found heterogeneous average correlations, both in combined correlations and in correlations for violent and nonviolent pornography separately. This heterogeneity suggests the existence of additional moderators that reduce or amplify the average associations. Such moderators might be reflected in the individual respondents' different frequencies of consumption, for which the study design did not control.

Another attitudinal study published in 2012 made an ill-advised attempt to control for moderators similar to the problematic personality characteristics considered in the survey of a representative sample of almost 3,000 male college students from the United States, using the same data.[180] As recalled, the 2000 study looked at pornography and sexual aggression,[181] while the 2012 study looked at pornography and ASV. The zero-order correlation in the 2012 study between more pornography consumption and stronger ASV was significant (r=.12, p<.001)[182]—a correlation roughly similar to that found between nonviolent pornography and ASV in the nonexperimental 2010 meta-analysis (r=.13, p<.001).[183]

When the same moderating predispositions were controlled for in estimating differences between individuals as in 2000, the 2012 study found a positive association between more pornography consumption and stronger ASV to be statistically significant only among the highest risk group, comprising 6.65% of all males (i.e., 185 of the 2,781 sample).[184] However, the vague and subjective wording of the survey measuring consumption, and the replacement of some missing data with sample averages[185]—as well as the statistical modeling and analysis of moderators in the 2012 study—were all based on the same questionable decisions that caused the probable underestimations and post-treatment bias observed in the 2000 study. Moreover, the later study contained additional methodological problems that conduced to further underestimating the effects of pornography consumption.

One of the two moderators used in both the 2000 and 2012 studies is based on attitudinal measures almost identical to those used in the 2012 study's dependent variable, ASV. That is, Hostile Masculinity was measured through the attitudinal scales of Negative Masculinity and Hostility Toward Women.[186] Unsurprisingly, previous studies have used literally the same ASV as indicators for Hostile Masculinity that the 2012 study employed as a dependent variable.[187] In contrast to the 2000 study, where the dependent variable was sexual aggression—not attitudes, as in the 2012 study—the 2012 study's inclusion of Hostile Masculinity led to an extreme emphasis on attitudes in both presumptively independent and dependent variables. Simply put, such a design is akin to asking, "Does hostility lead to hostility?" This suggests a strongly correlated and trivial, even tautological, association between Hostile Masculinity and ASV. Its addition to the study's statistical model seeming to make it even more susceptible to post-treatment and other bias, the measures in moderators and dependent variables in 2012 were not only both consequences in part of the key causal variable of pornography but also much more similar than they were in the 2000 study, where one was an attitude and the other a behavior. As a moderator, Hostile Masculinity will probably soak up considerable effects otherwise affecting the dependent variable, ASV, thus artificially minimizing the correlation effects of pornography on the latter.

The second moderator was "Impersonal Sex," which differs in name only from Sexual Promiscuity; this variable was used in the 2000 study and measures the age of first sexual intercourse and the number of sexual intercourse partners since age 14.[188] Because both Sexual Promiscuity and Hostile Masculinity are already significantly and positively associated with pornography, in addition to the tautological relationship between one moderator and the dependent variable, the study also introduced a potential post-treatment bias whereby moderators are partial consequences of the key causal variable, pornography. Their inclusion in the model is likely to minimize the effect correlations of pornography on the dependent variable.[189]

While the 2000 study and its 2015 Canadian replication explicitly reported significant simple correlations between pornography and Hostile Masculinity and Sexual Promiscuity,[190] those conclusions do not appear in the 2012 study. Absent knowledge of the other studies, this omission makes it more difficult for readers to discern potential post-treatment bias. Yet the 2012 study does report frequencies of consumption among the six risk groups for sexual aggression, where "risk" was determined by Hostile Masculinity and Impersonal Sex scores.[191] When we convert the reported number of respondents into percentages within each group in Table 2.1 here, it is easy to see a trend similar to that suggested by the reported correlations in the 2000 study.

That is, the four lower risk groups report never consuming pornography at exponentially higher rates than the moderate and high risk groups; conversely, moderate and high risk groups report consuming pornography somewhat frequently or very frequently at exponentially higher rates than the four lower groups. These differences are particularly notable considering

Table 2.1 Pornography Consumption and Sexual Aggression Risk Score

Consumption:	Never	Seldom	Somewhat Frequently	Very Frequently
Low Risk 1 $n = 180$	31.11% (56)	58.89% (106)	6.67% (12)	3.33% (6)
Low Risk 2 $n = 656$	19.82% (130)	61.74% (405)	16.62% (109)	1.18% (12)
Low Risk 3 $n = 378$	16.67% (63)	61.38% (232)	18.52% (70)	3.44% (13)
Low Risk 4 $n = 659$	12.29% (81)	66.92% (441)	18.51% (122)	2.28% (15)
Moderate Risk $n = 723$	10.37% (75)	61.69% (446)	22.41% (162)	5.53% (40)
High Risk $n = 185$	5.95% (11)	54.59% (101)	30.27% (56)	9.19% (17)

Data Source: Neil M. Malamuth, Gert Martin Hald, and Mary Koss, "Pornography, Individual Differences in Risk and Men's Acceptance of Violence against Women in a Representative Sample," *Sex Roles* 66, nos. 7–8 (2012): 435 tbl. 2 (percentages are rounded).

the subjective consumption measures used, which were criticized previously for underestimating group differences compared to more objective measures such as hours per week spent consuming pornography.

As Table 2.1 shows, the proportion of respondents reporting "never" consuming pornography ranged from 31.11% among the lowest risk men to 5.95% among the highest risk men in a linear trend. The non-linear trend of those reporting "seldom" consuming pornography is consistent with the linear directions charted for other risk groups, suggesting that when fewer men report never consuming pornography in the four lowest risk groups, more men report seldom consuming it (from 58.89% in Low Risk Group 1 to 66.92% in Low Risk Group 4). Then as the risk becomes greater, fewer men report seldom consuming (61.69% in the Moderate Risk Group, 54.59% in the High Risk Group), while more men report consuming somewhat and very frequently. Furthermore, those reporting consuming "somewhat frequently" ranged from 6.67% for the lowest risk men to 30.27% for high risk men in a mostly linear trend. Those reporting consuming "very frequently" ranged linearly from 1.18% for the lowest risk men to 9.19% for those at highest risk, with exceptions of linearity only for Low Risk Group 2 and Group 4.

Taken together, Table 2.1 illustrates that individuals predisposed to being at a higher risk for sexual aggression in the 2012 study were on average more likely to report consuming pornography at higher frequencies than men with lower sexually aggressive predispositions. This finding is consistent with those of previous studies. The differences in consumption frequency are particularly persuasive considering that the 2012 study's survey methodology likely underestimated the group differences.[192] Considering the direction of causality that the experimental and longitudinal studies suggest, the data drawn from the 2012 study cannot be taken as evidence that increased pornography consumption only (or primarily) predicts which men among populations at high risk for aggression will adopt stronger ASV. Rather, greater pornography consumption predicts stronger sexually aggressive predispositions, which in turn predicts stronger ASV. In other words, any man who consumes more pornography runs an elevated risk of adopting attitudes more supportive of violence against women—not only (or primarily) those already at higher risk for sexual aggression, as the study's flawed methodology would suggest.

Advantages of Longitudinal Research Designs

Because longitudinal data measures the effects of an increase in consumption over time—for instance, whether consumption predates sexual aggression—it can indicate causal effects, especially when controlling for previous sexual aggression. Longitudinal studies are therefore more persuasive than cross-sectional studies in supporting causal inferences and in rebutting the "reverse causation" hypothesis that presumes that individuals predisposed to sexual aggression will seek out and consume more pornography, hence that it is predisposition, not pornography, that causes aggression. Michele Ybarra and Richard Thompson have published one of the most comprehensive longitudinal studies undertaken with the objective of explaining the emergence of sexual aggression over time, relying on six waves of survey data (2006–2012) gathered from youths aged 10–21.[193] After adjusting for other relevant predictors, including previous sexual harassment perpetration, they found that those reporting previous violent pornography exposure (likely the more frequent pornography consumers) ran a significantly increased adjusted odds for later having first "kissed, touched, or done anything sexual with another person when that person *did not want*" it compared to those consuming no pornography.[194] The study added four more measures of sexual violence and aggression during the three last data waves extending from 2010 to 2012, also finding significant increased adjusted odds for youths who had consumed violent pornography to later commit a first "rape," act of "coercive sex," or "sexual harassment" compared to non-consumers, while the odds of committing "attempted rape" were elevated but nonsignificant.[195]

Another longitudinal study by Jane Brown and Kelly L'Engle, published in 2009, found that, when controlling for various relevant "baseline" predictors among 12- to 14-year-old boys in wave one, more general pornography consumption predicted significantly more sexual harassment perpetration after two years in wave two.[196] A third longitudinal study, this one also published in 2009 by Jochen Peter and Patti Valkenburg and relying on three data waves, found similarly significant results where more general pornography consumption at wave one led to stronger "notions of women as sex objects" at wave three, mediated at wave two by the extent that respondents "liked" pornography.[197]

Brown and L'Engle's longitudinal study on general pornography consumption noted that adding a third wave of data would establish "a causal sequence with more confidence" than was possible with the two waves they employed.[198] Accordingly, the fact that Ybarra and Thompson's study contained six waves of data on the "sexual assault" measure supports a stronger causal inference, making it worth looking into in some detail.

Ybarra and Thompson defined pornography as either violent or nonviolent, the latter further specified as involving "sexualized media (e.g., kissing, fondling, having sex)."[199] Notably, this definition of nonviolent pornography is considerably broader than most, including non-explicit presentations typically not regarded as pornographic (e.g., fondling without nudity or genital exposure).[200] Moreover, the indicator is compounded by only measuring consumption dichotomously, as involving either exposure or non-exposure,[201] which makes it impossible to distinguish low and accidental from high and systematic consumers directly. However, since previous research suggests that violent pornography consumers are also likely to be more desensitized high consumers who are less able to be aroused by nonviolent pornography,[202] violent pornography consumption is *indirectly* a good predictor of the effects of higher pornography consumption per se, which for policy purposes may be the more critical subgroup to study.[203]

Ybarra and Thompson also found that the two strongest predictors of the perpetration of a first sexually violent act were violent pornography consumption and prior exposure to parental spousal abuse.[204] Even when including both male and female survey respondents, violent pornography exposure significantly predicted "a fourfold increased odds or higher" of committing any of the four types of sexually aggressive acts after adjusting for other relevant predictors ("attempted rape" exhibited elevated but nonsignificant odds). Certainly, the confidence intervals were wide for some measures of sexual violence, suggesting a lack of precision due to the small perpetrator sample size.[205] However, fifty years of research, including experiments and naturalistic studies, supports the inference that the longitudinal data in this study represents substantial causal effects.

Targeted Groups, Perpetrators, Imitation

What does it entail, more concretely, when pornography consumers become more "sexually aggressive" than non-consumers? As a consequence of pornography consumption, what might doing "anything sexual with another person when that person did not want you to" mean in social reality? Detailed studies conducted both with specifically targeted groups and those who predate upon them, and accounts of imitating pornography provide additional clues while also corroborating and strengthening the ecological validity of studies previously considered.

Impact in Battered Women's Lives

Several surveys have been conducted with battered women. A study published in 2014 surveying 138 battered women aged 20–76 who were recruited voluntarily from 30 shelters throughout Quebec, Canada, found that 26.1% (n=36) reported at least one abusive incident related to their abusive partner's pornography use (other assailants were excluded from the analysis).[206] Of these 26.1%, 80.5% reported being forced to reenact specific pornography, 75.0% reported being forced to view pornography, and 27.8% reported being forcibly filmed or photographed by their partners during sexual activities. Depending on the measurement scales employed, the women reporting pornography-related incidents were about 12 or 20 times significantly more likely to be subjected to "severe sexual violence" ($p<.01$, $p<.001$) and about 10 times more likely ($p<.01$) to be subjected to "moderate sexual violence."[207]

Another study of 2,135 women seeking refuge in women's shelters in an American metropolitan area during the years 1998–2002 asked if the women's partners viewed pornography or utilized the sex industry in some other way (e.g., strip clubs), with over 40% giving an affirmative response.[208] Within this subgroup, the likelihood of reporting sexual violence was significantly higher (e.g., sexual abuse, marital rape, or stalking) than among the other women.[209] For instance, the prevalence of marital rape was 40.7% among women reporting that their partner used pornography or other parts of the sex industry compared to 23.0% among women who reported that their partner did not use the sex industry.[210] Women's accounts of male partners who utilized the sex industry also revealed significantly more controlling behavior, including threats, intimidation, minimization, denial, blaming, economic abuse, enforced isolation, and enforcing "male privilege," when compared to other women's accounts.[211] The authors note, though, that the proportion of variance explained was moderate in some instances and weak in others, suggesting the potential involvement of third variables, and that, in contrast to sexual violence and pornography, the differences in physical or emotional violence related to pornography consumption were insignificant.[212] However, one reason women seek refuge at women's shelters is likely that they are exposed to more aggression than the average woman, thus this study is almost inevitably reporting information about particularly aggressive men. Differences between pornography consumers and non-consumers might therefore not be as salient in the subsample as they are in the general population, which make those differences that are found particularly telling.

An earlier study of 271 women who had been subjected to male violence and participated in a New York support program during the years 1988–1991 asked participants about the length of their relationship with their abuser and his use of pornography and abuse of alcohol.[213] Thirty percent of the abusers were reported to have used pornography.[214] Forty-six percent of all respondents reported being abused sexually (as distinguished from other forms of abuse), and those whose batterers reportedly used pornography ran a 1.960 significant increase in odds of having been sexually abused after controlling for other predictors—odds comparable to women whose abusers reportedly abused alcohol.[215] When compared to abusers who did not use pornography or abuse alcohol, batterers that only used pornography ran a significantly increased odds of 3.584 of committing sexual abuse after controlling for other predictors.[216]

In another American study, this one involving 100 female survivors sampled from rape crisis centers in the Northeast in 1997 and 1998, 28% reported that their "abusers" used pornography; interestingly, 58% said that they did not know one way or the other.[217] Roughly 40% of the women claiming that their abuser used pornography also stated that "the pornography was part of the abusive incident"; 43% believed it "affected the nature of the abuse"; 21% believed it increased the "frequency" of the violence; 14% believed it increased the "level" of violence; 18% believed their abuser became more "sadistic" while using pornography; and, finally, in open, thus partially unsolicited, responses, five women reported being forced to participate in the making of pornography.[218] None of the study's participants believed pornography decreased either the frequency or the level of violence they experienced; by contrast, 12% of the total sample believed that pornography was imitated during the abuse, and a majority of those women believed their abuser imitated pornography in order to "victimize them."

An American study published in 1998, two years prior to Bergen and Bogel's, examined the connection between violent pornography and men's violence against women using an ethnically stratified sample of 198 women drawn from public medical clinics who had reported abuse a year prior to or during a pregnancy.[219] The study asked specifically about their abusers' use of "sexually violent scenes where a woman is being hurt," as distinguished from pornography in general.[220] The sample consisted of one-third each of African Americans, Hispanics, and white Americans. Among all of the women studied, 40.9% indicated that their abusers watched violent pornography, of whom a significantly higher proportion were white (58.7%) than either Hispanic (38.5%) or African American (27.1%).[221] The most severe violence was significantly more frequently reported by women who stated that their abuser "forced" them to "look at, act out or pose for pornographic scenes"—a group comprising 25.8 % of all 198 participants.[222]

In an earlier study of 87 self-identified battered women in a large city who, whether separated or cohabiting, pressed charges against their male partners at the district attorney's office, a similar association between violent pornography and sexual abuse was found.[223] Here, 40% (n=35) reported that their partners used violent pornography.[224] Of these 35 women, 26% stated that they had been "reminded" of the pornography during the abuse, 53% stated that their partners had shown them violent pornography and either "asked or forced them to reenact a scene" or asked them to pose for pornographic photographs, and 20% reported that their partner explicitly referred to violent pornography during the abuse. Rape was reported by 41% (n=36) of respondents, of whom 75% (n=27)[225] said their rapist used violent pornography. Given that there were only 35 violent pornography consumers in the total sample, only 15.69% (n=8) of the remaining 51 non-rapists could reportedly have consumed violent pornography. A difference between 75.00% and 15.69% is strongly significant even with these small samples (χ^2=27.559; *df*=1; *p*<.000). Since high consumers typically view more violent or dehumanizing/degrading materials, these findings also indicate that batterers consuming more general pornography might also more likely commit rape.

In a more qualitative study based on interviews conducted in 2003 and 2004 with 43 separating and separated battered women from a rural area in southeastern Ohio, and complemented by "back-talks" with 12 respondents in 2013, 24 reported that pornography was involved in their "estranged" partner's sexual assaults.[226] The women revealed a number of themes related to their abusers' pornography consumption, such as imitation of pornography, including with violence, comparing respondents to women in pornography, forcibly introducing other sexual partners, and filming sexual acts without permission.[227] In one example, a respondent explained how her ex-husband often imitated violent rape pornography with "degrading and foul language," noting how the experience was "forceful, nasty, demeaning . . . . just horrible."[228] He used martial arts skills to pin her down, refusing to release her until she was visibly "uncomfortable," or "worse than that," because, she eventually learned, he could not climax unless she appeared to be raped, such as when screaming " 'get off of me!' " or fighting with him. Toward the end of their relationship, when she tried to assume the role of rape victim more quickly, she stated that he "got off before he even got his pants down."

Decades earlier, witnesses from women's shelters had begun to publicly attest to the role pornography played in men's violence against women. For example, a founder and director of a program for sexual assault survivors in New York City testified in writing at a public hearing held in Minneapolis in 1983 that she was meeting an increasing number of throat-rape survivors, some reporting that their assailants referred to the pornographic movie *Deep Throat* prior to assaulting them.[229] In a similar public hearing conducted in Massachusetts in 1992, a women's shelter submitted written testimony describing the organization's practice of asking clients whether their abusers used pornography as part of their abuse, offering a "conservative" estimate that half of the abusers did so.[230] Furthermore, prosecutors with considerable experience in sexual abuse investigations, clinical psychologists treating both sex offenders and survivors, and representatives of women's shelters testified during the 1980s and early 1990s that pornography played a similarly important role in hundreds of cases of sexual abuse.[231] This information was supported with an abundance of testimony from ordinary women and girls given at public hearings and in other forums, recounting their abuse by men who forced, or attempted to force, them to imitate pornography.[232]

It is also notable that results from population surveys posing similar questions mirror those from surveys of battered women, although the proportion and severity of pornography consumption and sexual violence are not as great since general population surveys are not restricted to those seeking shelter, but may include respondents who have not been exposed to such abuse. Accordingly, a Canadian national survey from 1992 undertaken on college campuses with 1,835 women (median age 20) and 1,307 men (median age 21) found that 8.4% of the 1,638 women who were dating at the time reported being "upset" by dates' pressuring them to imitate pornography.[233] The sociologist Diana Russell asked a similar question of a representative sample of 930 women of diverse ages in San Francisco in 1977, where 89 women (9.6%) reported being upset by someone attempting to get them to enact something they knew came from pornography.[234] The 1992 Canadian campus survey found that as many as 22.3% of the women reporting sexual abuse also reported being upset by attempts to make them imitate pornography, yet only 5.8% of the women who did not report sexual abuse said they had been upset by such attempts.[235] Even among the male students, as many as 6.8% admitted having "upset" dating partners by attempting to make them imitate pornography. Moreover, these "upsetters" were also significantly more likely than "nonupsetters" to admit having committed forcible sexual victimization after high school (9.3% vs. 2.4%).[236] Given the probability that some men did not realize that they upset their dating partners with such attempts, these numbers may be underestimations.

Cross-sectional surveys and other evidence from battered women on the association between abuse and pornography offer more substantive information on the ensuing harms in naturalistic contexts, lending support to the causal evidence produced by longitudinal studies and providing ecological validity to evidence derived from experiments. However, perhaps the most compelling naturalistic evidence of harm can be found in studies with prostituted persons and "johns" (clients).

Evidence from Prostituted Persons

Among the 200 prostituted women and girls from San Francisco discussed earlier, where researchers used strategies meant to avoid oversampling from "arrestable" or "service-oriented" populations in order to gather more representative data,[237] a large number of respondents spontaneously disclosed that violent johns made references to pornography during their abuse.[238] Similar reports of johns forcing, or attempting to force, women to imitate pornography are also found in later studies, including the nine-country study where 47% of 802 persons sampled in various types of prostitution (brothels, streets, escorting, strip clubs, etc.) reported being upset by attempts to compel them to imitate pornography.[239] The final report of the Swedish government's Prostitution Inquiry, issued in 1995, also incorporated descriptions by social workers in Gothenburg of johns who, not infrequently, pointed to images in pornographic magazines in order to convey their expectations to those from whom they were seeking to buy sex.[240]

In San Francisco, many of the 200 prostituted females spontaneously described having been exploited in pornography before age 13.[241] In a subgroup of 60% who reported having been sexually abused in childhood, 22% also offered unsolicited accounts of the perpetrating adult's use of pornography before the abuse, which, for instance, had the objective of legitimating their actions and persuading the child to submit to their wishes, or to arouse themselves in advance of the abuse. Similar accounts of childhood abuse involving pornography have been given by non-prostituted women and experts on sexual crimes.[242]

In American public hearings, survivors of prostitution have, at least since the 1980s, testified to johns' pervasive references to pornography they wanted prostituted women to imitate.[243] A woman in Minneapolis who represented a group of prostitution survivors explained: " 'Men witness the abuse of women in pornography constantly, and if they can't engage in that behavior with their wives, girlfriends, or children, they force a whore [*sic*] to do it.' "[244]

Among the 200 prostituted persons in San Francisco, 73% provided specific information about rapes committed against them.[245] Researchers gathered 193 such case reports, in which 24% of respondents spontaneously averred that their rapists consistently referred to pornographic materials.[246] Interviewees commonly referred to rapists' first mentioning pornography they had seen or read, and then suggesting that the prostituted woman or girl not only enjoyed being raped, but also enjoyed being victimized by other extreme violence. Furthermore, in 19% of the 193 San Francisco rape cases interviewees reported attempting to stop their rapist by saying things like, "Calm down, I'm a hooker. Relax, and I'll turn you a free trick without all this fighting."[247] Contrary to the respondents' expectations, their attempts had the opposite effect in "every single case"; the men usually started yelling, their violence in all cases leading to more serious injuries than in cases where the woman had not mentioned her prostitution. Moreover, in 12% of the 193 rape cases where those victimized disclosed their prostitution, the disclosure prompted "overt" pornography-related comments by the rapists, and in most other cases among the 19% revealing their prostitution, the rapists made "indirect references" to pornography.

Consistent themes in the perpetrators' reactions to the prostitution disclosure included (1) becoming more aggressive in their language; (2) becoming markedly more violent; (3) saying they had seen prostituted persons in pornography, the majority naming specific materials; and (4) after vaginal rape, further sexually assaulting the woman in a way the women in the pornographic materials referenced were said to enjoy.[248] For example, one rapist verbally attempted to link pornography to his victim, reportedly stating, "I know all about you bitches, you're no different; you're like all of them. I seen it in all the movies. You love being beaten."[249] Another respondent reported that her perpetrator made similar statements: "he had seen whores [*sic*] just like me in (three pornographic films mentioned by name), and told me he knew how to do it to whores like me. He knew what whores like me wanted."[250]

The words and actions of these rapists are similar to the psychological mechanisms exhibited in experiments with normal (non-institutionalized/non-convicted) men discussed in connection with the exposure effects of common nonviolent pornography, where exposed subjects were significantly more likely to categorize women according to binary stereotypes (e.g., "Whore vs. Madonna") than controls. Pornography thus led to the objectification of women, where women were dehumanized and perceived as more legitimate "targets" for sexual aggression. In laboratory experiments, this mechanism, among other things, seems to have contributed both to more general aggression against female actors and greater trivialization of rape in simulated trials compared to controls. The San Francisco study suggests how these mechanisms work in a social context. For instance, when an assailant is informed that his female victim is prostituted, this knowledge seems to buttress his stereotypical view that prostituted women (who by necessity have more sex, thus making them "promiscuous" in his view) are legitimate targets of his aggression. Moreover, perpetrators associated this stereotype with pornography, which in turn seemingly justified increasing the violence against the woman. Pornography thus appears to have inspired the assailant to subordinate the prostituted woman, making her a legitimate target of aggression—as when he reportedly said to his target that he "knew what whores [*sic*] like me wanted." The mechanisms revealed in interviews with prostituted women who were raped and physically assaulted by johns provide a triangulation of methods and evidence, corroborating the ecological validity of psychological experiments with naturalistic observations.

When Catharine MacKinnon and Andrea Dworkin advanced a civil rights definition of pornography in the 1980s as "the graphic sexually explicit subordination of women,"[251] the behaviors documented in San Francisco were among the objects of their legal challenge.[252] Indeed, evidence so far suggests that pornography systematically contributes to women's subordination by objectification, sexual aggression, violence, and attitudes trivializing such acts—reasons why MacKinnon and Dworkin considered pornography to be a systematic practice of sex discrimination that violates women's civil rights and runs contrary to democratic values of equality.[253] The following studies with johns show similar associations consistent with the evidence found in experiments, longitudinal and cross-sectional population studies, and information gathered from battered women and prostituted persons.

Evidence from Johns

Research suggests that many johns want to imitate pornography. Studies asking johns about the issue directly corroborate the accounts of prostituted women. For instance, 71% of 133 johns interviewed in Cambodia[254] and 52% of 101 johns in Boston[255] acknowledged that they imitated pornography with prostituted women. Many men in a similar study in Chicago likewise described reenacting pornography with prostituted women.[256] A man in Boston explained that, when people with whom he wanted to do this refused, he began purchasing sex from prostituted persons.[257] Other comments by Boston johns explaining why they bought sex included "'If my fiancée won't give me anal, I know someone who will.'"[258] Responding to a similar question, a john in Scotland stated that "'[s]ome guys watch a lot of pornography and expect their partners to perform certain acts. They'll either pressure their partner to a certain point or then go and get what they want.'"[259] Similar responses were also found in a London study.[260]

Researchers in Boston, Chicago, Scotland, and London probed the issues further in Cambodia—the last study in a series of questionnaires and interviews with johns.[261] The Cambodian questionnaire was improved and refined to capture more details about the association between pornography and violence against women. As the researchers stated: "For the Cambodian study, based on existing research and local reports, 40 additional questions on pornography use were included along with 28 questions about men's experiences with gang rape (*bauk*), and questions about their and their families' experiences under the Khmer Rouge."[262] The intent to imitate pornography conveyed by individual johns' responses was expressed directly in this study: "'Whenever I went for sex, I'd like to try new styles I had seen in sex movies'"; "'We want to try to follow what we see in the pornographic movies'"; "'I copied those styles from sex movies and tried them all.'"[263] Reflecting on his imitation of anal sex with a prostituted woman, a Cambodian john elaborated on how he "'fucked her asshole like it was in the sex movie.'"[264] This individual account becomes more intelligible when triangulated with other studies, such as one from India with 684 johns, where those who had consumed pornography in the past month ran a significantly increased adjusted odds ratio of 4.49 to have had anal sex with a prostituted woman compared to the others.[265]

Since evidence suggests that a majority of prostituted persons are in a vulnerable position without real and acceptable options, they have little leverage and are thus less likely than other women to reject demands to imitate pornography. This power imbalance is corroborated by accounts from johns who admit that no one else wants to perform the sex they want with them: 79% of 110 of the anonymous johns in Scotland randomly sampled through advertisements[266] and 48% of the 113 johns in the similar Chicago study[267] acknowledged buying sex that they felt uncomfortable requesting from their other partners, or in which others simply refused to engage. Chicago johns most commonly mentioned that such sexual conduct included anal sex (27%), followed by oral sex (7%), but also group sex, sadomasochism and dominance, and other conduct.[268] Reflecting johns' wish to imitate pornography, heterosexual anal sex is frequently depicted in the most popular mainstream genre.

A number of studies have found a significant and substantial association whereby johns who consume more pornography are more likely to buy more sex than are johns consuming less pornography. This association was reported among 110 johns in Scotland (r=.26, p=.006),[269] 133 johns in Cambodia (r=.39, p<.0001),[270] and 97 johns in Boston (r=.29, p=.004).[271] Likewise, strongly significant associations were found in a study of 1,672 johns arrested in the United States, which were also compared to national male population samples who did not buy sex.[272] Thus, 74.0% of 927 repeat offenders reported consuming "X-rated videos" during the prior year, while only 28.7% of 2,430 non-johns reported doing so, and 74.3% of the repeat offenders reported buying "any sexually explicit books" during the prior year, while only 15.0% of non-johns reported doing so.[273] A study of 11,219 migrant workers in southern India found similar associations, adjusted to account for socio-demographic factors. Migrant workers who reported consuming pornography exhibited a significant increased adjusted odds ratio of 4.2 of buying sex compared to non-pornography-consuming migrant workers.[274]

Although the correlations between pornography consumption and buying sex are based on cross-sectional data, which may technically suffer from reverse causation or confounding variables, a between-method triangulation indicates that this data should be interpreted in light of the causal narratives provided by johns and prostituted women alike describing how pornography inspires the john to buy more sex, especially when other partners refuse to imitate it. The experimental and longitudinal studies that demonstrate and support the existence of a causal effect by which pornography makes consumers more sexually aggressive should also be taken into account. In light of the triangulation of methods and sources, it is conceptually consistent to regard laboratory aggression and ASV to be indirectly associated with the type of sexual behavior these johns' other sexual partners often refuse, and which impels johns to buy sex from prostituted persons—persons with little leverage to deny their wishes since they rarely have other viable options for survival.

Responding to the question asked at the outset of this chapter, it seems that the studies with johns in particular suggest that injuries inflicted on women used as performers in contemporary pornography will actually impact consumers' sexual proclivities, leading them to exploit and abuse other people and inflict the same injuries. Indeed, johns are not only more often frequent pornography consumers, but they also seem to consume more unsafe and subordinating materials. In the Boston study comparing 101 johns with 101 non-johns, researchers found that johns reported masturbating significantly more to a greater variety of pornographic genres than non-johns, including to scenes depicting multiple men penetrating a woman, anal sex, group sex, and groups of men ejaculating on a humiliated woman's face.[275] Recall that these acts are all commonly presented in the most popular contemporary pornography.

Considering that johns want to imitate pornography and many of their partners are unwilling to do so, how will prostituted persons fare if they are expected to comply and have few or no alternatives for survival? Clues to the answer to this question may be found in the Cambodian study, with its refined and improved questionnaire on pornography-related issues. Its 133 johns were recruited through a "snowball sampling" technique, yielding an average age of 34 from a range of 19–57.[276] Forty-one percent of respondents acknowledged having participated in gang rapes; of these, 17% reported participating in gang rapes more than ten times, 19% six to ten times, 42% two to five times, and 28% only once.[277] Crucially, 93% of all johns interviewed in Cambodia reported having seen gang rape in pornography, and regarding the imitation of gang rapes and other pornographic conduct, those who reported committing such acts "often" referred to their wish to do so *after* they had viewed it in pornography.[278] Some explained further: "We all collectively want to try, after watching a sex movie that shows gang rape/bauk"; "We had watched Thai sex movies about gang rape/bauk . . . [and] we wanted to follow their style"; "'I was drunk and wanted to try bauk like in the movie.'" These statements demonstrate a causal narrative, a temporal sequence of "before" and "after" pornography exposure. As such, the sequence exhibits similarities to experiments assessing the impact of short-term pornography exposure. While subjects' inhibitions and restraints on aggressing against women were lowered by the provocations in the experiments, they are lowered in the context of prostitution due in part to the extreme power imbalance between johns and prostituted women, which seemingly amplifies the effects of pornography exposure.

One respondent elaborated on the role of pornography in gang rapes, describing how participants "'took turns to have sex'" and "'used different styles that [they] saw in the movie.'"[279] Another john explained that "'[s]ometimes the woman changes her mind when she sees how many people are waiting at the place. If that happens, my friends threaten and force her, sometimes beating her.'"[280] In yet another case, a john stated that his

" 'friends beat [their victim] and forced her to do all that they wanted; sometimes [his] friends threatened her with death should she not follow what they say.' "[281] Further, another john stated: " 'we bet on who was strong enough to prolong the sex. Anyone who could not prolong would be called the loser.' " A great deal of violence and force is clearly required to imitate pornography and gang rape prostituted women. Considering that the johns show no concern for the women's physical or mental health, it is noteworthy that one of them reported that after a gang rape one woman " 'was in so much pain' " that he " 'was afraid she had died.' "

Bearing in mind the penchant for imitating pornography that johns commonly admit to, the allegation made by 38% of the Cambodian johns that "Western sex videos" were predominantly to blame for gang rapes might not be entirely inaccurate.[282] Although this claim certainly elides their own responsibility for a malicious and egregious atrocity, profoundly harmful in immeasurable ways, it is notable that *every* john in this study who admitted participating in gang rape also claimed that their fathers and grandfathers had *not* done so.[283] Their claims were supported by statistical analysis: younger johns were significantly more likely than older johns to report engaging in gang rape.[284] As pornography movies have become more available—first on VHS, then CD-ROM, DVD, and now the internet—the current generation's ready access to and potentially more frequent use of pornography may have made previously relatively uncommon forms of sexual violence and abuse, such as gang rape, more prevalent. Again, this hypothesis has been supported by statistical analysis: among the 82 johns who consumed pornography weekly or more often, 50% reported having committed gang rape, while only 27% of the 51 johns who used pornography less frequently reported having committed gang rape.[285] Furthermore, of the 81 johns who consumed pornography at least weekly, 22% (18) reportedly still perpetrated gang rape, while among 51 who used pornography less frequently, only 6% (3) reportedly still perpetrated it.[286]

To uninitiated readers, the gang rapes reported in Cambodia might appear to be extreme global outliers. However, that is not necessarily so. Recall that the Cambodian survey was the last in a series of similar studies undertaken in other locations, the questionnaire being subsequently improved and its precision enhanced mainly in order to document the association of gang rape with pornography. Since then, no similar studies seem to have been conducted with an appropriate instrument and follow-up questions. Frankly, we therefore do not know how typical Cambodian johns are globally.

Although more research will be needed to answer this question, gang rapes similarly incited by pornography in which women were practically unable to refuse sex have been stated or implied in accounts from, among other places, the United States and Sweden. Especially pertinent here are the conclusions set forth in the final report of the Swedish Prostitution Inquiry indicating that the police had investigated a number of so-called sex clubs, where pornographic movies were produced with crowds of paying male guests. In those situations, financially distressed women were forced to perform sexual acts to which they had not agreed in advance—sometimes involving, among other things vaginal, oral, and unprepared anal intercourse, with more than ten men.[287]

Similarly, in the United States, in the mid-1980s a prostituted woman testified at a public hearing of the Attorney General's Commission's in Washington, DC, where she described how her pimp took her to "stag" parties with hundreds of men where pornographic movies were shown and followed by sex with prostituted women, the films "most often" setting the tone for the type of acts the women were expected to perform.[288] Although this source does not say whether or not gang rapes occurred, from what we know about prostitution and pornography, the situations she described are surely conducive to such conduct, especially considering the numerical advantage of johns over prostituted women. In the more recent Chicago study, although gang rapes are not explicitly referenced, two situations it describes are also conducive to their perpetration. One john thus reported that he and his friends bought a woman for sex in Las Vegas and subsequently ejaculated " 'on her face at the same time, like in the porn movies.' "[289] Another Chicago john described a holiday in Cuba with friends where a "travel agent" was paid to arrange for women to stay in their apartment for three days in order to clean and "perform" the "sex acts requested by the man and his friends."[290]

Even if evidence about gang rapes in other countries is less plentiful, expressions that "emphasized" the "pleasure" of being able to assert "their dominance over women" in prostitution were openly expressed by several johns in Scotland.[291] These resemble themes that 54% of the johns in Cambodia who admitted gang rape expressed when acknowledging that power over and violence against the victim was "important" for them.[292] For johns in Scotland and Cambodia alike, the demonstrable subordination of women was plainly desired. Moreover, in Cambodia, not only did johns ignore the women's suffering, but they also took "pleasure in deliberately inflicting harm."[293] One of them spoke of a friend who had admitted that "'he felt happy'" after having participated in gang raping a prostituted woman, who "'screamed loudly because she was probably hurt a lot.'" It may be for similar reasons that a john in Scotland acknowledged that prostitution afforded men the "'freedom to do anything they want in a consequence-free environment.'"[294] The implicit message is that nowhere besides in prostitution can johns perpetrate with impunity. Whether accurate or not, admissions like this one suggest that there are obstacles and consequences preventing them from imitating pornography with other women that are not present in prostitution. Indeed, there is no disagreement between these johns' accounts and the public hearing testimony offered by many who have been exploited in the industry, such as the Minneapolis woman who, speaking on behalf of a group of survivors of prostitution, affirmed that men purchase sex in prostitution when they cannot reenact abusive pornography with their partners or children.[295]

Assuming, arguendo, that johns have a stronger propensity toward sexual aggression in the first place than other men, regardless of pornography use, even by their own accounts the johns would not have performed the acts they did, such as gang rape, anal sex, or other "styles," had they not first seen those acts in pornography. The sequential ordering and outcome of these events suggest more than a mere correlational association. That is, the sex that johns imposed on prostituted women through various forms of coercion would likely not have been the same without pornography, granted otherwise potentially abusive. In this sense, pornography shapes social reality, and brutally so for prostituted persons.

Returning to the issue of triangulation of methodologies, while it is generally thought that surveys and interviews cannot control for causal associations like experiments can, the johns' reported chain of events with respect to imitating acts they have seen in pornography are consistent with the associations found in numerous experiments with pornography on the causes of violence against women. The sequencing of events johns have reported is also consistent with the causality demonstrated by the longitudinal population studies on sexual aggression. These experiments and longitudinal studies suggest that high pornography consumption causes more sexual aggression than low consumption, including nonviolent pornography consumption that causes consumers to increasingly perceive and act on women as legitimate targets of sexual aggression. Johns who viewed more pornography bought more sex and admitted imitating what they had seen, including sexually aggressive behaviors. Certainly, more imitation per se is not necessarily indicative of more aggression per se, and none of the experiments and longitudinal studies measured "imitation" directly. Yet, since the 2000s, johns' imitation of mainstream pornography, which includes aggressive conduct such as gang rape, gagging, sadism, and dominance, has arguably demonstrated more frequent imitation of sexual aggression compared to what was evidenced with respect to the relatively less aggressive mainstream pornography from the 1970s or 1980s.[296] In this sense, studies with johns complement experiments and longitudinal studies, highlighting details on the causal mechanisms with which the associations between pornography consumption and sexual aggression documented in more general population studies are played out in specific social settings such as prostitution. In this context, it is particularly worth examining a number of general cross-sectional population studies of men (and women) that ask to what extent subjects imitate or wish to imitate similar contemporary mainstream pornography. These studies may indicate whether the causal mechanisms found among johns are present among men in the general population.

Imitation in Population Surveys

A study of 384 heterosexual men in Germany had three primary objectives: first, to assess respondents' interest in watching aggressive or subordinating behaviors presented in popular mainstream pornography, materials that authors label "gonzo," including, for example, "ass-to-mouth," penile "gagging," and ejaculation on the face or in the mouth; second, to find out to what extent the men imitated, or wanted to imitate, such conduct during sex; and, third, to determine the statistical associations between the men's reported interest in watching gonzo and their reported imitation or wish to imitate such conduct.[297] The men were recruited in 2011 and 2012, either via advertisements at university departments (or units) of psychology, psychiatry, gender and sexology, or via individual German sexologists or a German gender studies group blog.[298] The mean age was 32.12. Interest in watching gonzo was measured by presenting four popular gonzo movie titles and their synoptic descriptions from DVD covers or reviews, then asking respondents how "interested" they were in viewing them on a 9-point scale (1=not, 9=very). The average interest score was 3.24 (*sd*=2.22). The survey also measured average pornography consumption for masturbation on an

8-point scale (1=never, 8=daily or almost daily), which yielded an average of 6.21 (*sd*=1.48).[299]

As many as 66.1% of the men reported having "tried" and 17.9% reported that they "would like" to try ejaculating on a woman's face or in her mouth; the 16.0% who neither had tried nor wanted to try reportedly expressed "no desire to try" it.[300] Furthermore, 72.2% reported that a partner had performed oral sex on the respondent while kneeling (i.e., "penis worship") and 19.1% wanted to try the same; 26.4% had tried sexually dominating a partner in sadomasochism and 19.1% wanted to try the same; 24.2% reported they had "inserted their penis so deeply into a partner's throat it caused her to gag" (gagging) and 11.8% wanted to try the same; 12.1% reported having "anally penetrated a partner then inserted their penis directly into her mouth" (ass-to-mouth) and 12.4% wanted to try the same; 18.1% reported choking and 6.1% wanted to try the same; 23.7% reported pejorative name-calling during sex (e.g., "slut" or "whore") and 6.75% wanted to try the same.

After controlling for age, student status, viewing pornography with a partner, relationship status, and religiosity, the German study found a significant positive correlation between reported interest in popular gonzo pornography and "wanting to try" or "having tried" 12 of 14 acts common in gonzo—the exception being choking and face slapping, where nonsignificant correlations were nevertheless in the same direction.[301] Moreover, significant positive correlations between more pornography consumption in general, and having tried or wanting to try 9 out of 14 gonzo behaviors, were also found after adjusting for control variables. Further, all remaining nonsignificant correlations were positive, indicating potential Type II errors. When considering that gonzo seems to be the most popular genre among male consumers,[302] the associations between general pornography consumption and imitation of gonzo also make sense.

A U.S. population study much like the German survey offers additional insights into women's experiences and attitudes regarding the behaviors depicted in popular pornography.[303] This survey used a convenience sample of 1,883 heterosexual women and men, most of whom were fairly religious white college and university students living in a city or suburb, whose average age was 22.55 (*sd*=7.95).[304] Pornography consumption was measured by whether it was or was not for masturbation, but the consumption reported was overwhelmingly for masturbatory purposes, both among male and female consumers, the latter in much lower numbers.[305]

In terms of imitation, 28.2% of the men as well as 28.2% of the women reported having tried anal sex, but many more men (45.3%) than women (8.1%) wished to try it.[306] A smaller number of these young men reported having tried ass-to-mouth (7.2%), and far fewer women (1.9%); by contrast, considerably more men (13.6%) compared to very few women (0.5%) wished to try it. In contrast, ejaculation on a woman's face or in her mouth was reported by as many as 66.7% men and 62.1% women; yet while 59.6% of the men also wanted to try it, only 12.5% of the women did. The qualitative U.S. study interviewing 16 young male pornography consumers discussed previously found that, by and large, they saw ejaculation on the face or in the mouth as expressing women's subordination to men, and realized that women did not appreciate it[307]—a belief confirmed by the fact that notwithstanding a majority of women in this survey had experienced it, a very small female proportion compared to the much larger male proportion wanted to have semen ejaculated on their face or in their mouth. Along similarly gendered lines, although 26.9% of men and 19.7% of women reported name-calling during sex (e.g., "slut," "whore"), men were significantly more likely to want to try it than were women (13.1% vs. 5.4%).[308] Moreover, as many as 15.9% of men reported choking their partner with their hands during sex, while only 3.8% of women reported doing so, and 5.7% of the men indicated they wanted to try it compared to merely 2.0% of women.

Those men and women who reported consuming more pornography for masturbation were also significantly more likely to report imitating aggressive behavior (e.g., choking or hair-pulling), more degrading or uncommon behavior (e.g., ass-to-mouth or facial ejaculation), and more target behavior (e.g., being choked or having hair pulled) seen in popular pornography movies.[309] In addition, similarly significant associations were found between more pornography consumption and greater interest in imitating aggressive, degrading/uncommon, or target behaviors.[310] Women were more likely to engage in target behaviors, while men were more likely to engage in aggressive or degrading/uncommon behaviors—a finding consistent with the "pornographic script" in which males subordinate women and treat them as targets of physical and verbal aggression and degradation.[311]

As with heterosexual anal sex, which appears frequently in popular pornography, 28.2% of both sexes reported trying it, but many more men (45.3%) wanted to try it compared to women (8.1%). These sex/gender differences can be further explained in light of a qualitative U.K. study on youth sexuality conducted in 2010–2011, which sampled a purposively diverse group of 130 respondents aged 16–18.[312] Nine focus group interviews and 71 individual depth interviews were conducted with 37 of the females and 34 of the males.[313] About a quarter of respondents in the depth interviews reported anal heterosexual experiences, with the authors observing that "[i]nitial anal sexual experiences were rarely narrated in terms of mutual exploration of sexual pleasure. Women reported painful anal sex."[314] They further noted that "few of the men and only one woman . . . referred to physical pleasure," the latter respondent explaining how she initially did not want to try anal sex, but did so because her partner was interested in it.[315] Yet even then she acknowledged that the anal sex was painful, although subsequent attempts were reportedly less so. The researchers also remarked on the perception "taken for granted by many" of their respondents, whereby women typically did not want to perform anal sex and thus needed "to be either persuaded or coerced" into it.[316] Moreover, the interviews revealed that even in "seemingly communicative and caring partnerships, some men seemed to push to have anal sex with their reluctant partner despite believing it likely to hurt her." By contrast, some men reportedly avoided anal sex for the same reason.

Another qualitative U.S. study undertaken in a large southwestern city was based on interviews with 20 demographically diverse adult women whose average age was 34. Here, too, women's experiences of anal sex were similar: for instance, 6 out of 12 respondents had reportedly tried anal sex "willingly (though often reluctantly) only to discover their lack of enjoyment or too much pain."[317] Furthermore, a quarter of the sample had "overtly violent encounters with anal sex," many being pressured into it by partners who had discussed it with male friends or wanted to imitate pornography they had viewed.[318] Accordingly, a 41-year-old bisexual Latina respondent believed her boyfriend wanted to "mimic" pornography performers, while a 23-year-old white heterosexual woman offered a more detailed description of her ex-boyfriend becoming "obsessed with acting out fantasies he saw in pornography: 'He watched a lot of porn, so he wanted to try every little single thing out there that had to do with anything that he'd seen. It went from ropes and gags to meeting people on Craigslist to having sex with couples to anal sex.' "[319]

Likewise, in the U.K. study the "main reasons given for young people having anal sex were that men wanted to copy what they saw in pornography, and that 'it's tighter' "—that is, tighter in the sense of being "better for men . . . while women were expected to find anal sex painful, particularly the first time."[320] However, without further elaboration, the U.K. researchers claimed that "[t]he 'pornography' explanation [of imitation] seems partial at best," maintaining that "young people only seemed to see this as motivating men, not women." These researchers ignored the many studies showing that a very low percentage of women compared to men regularly view pornography, especially while masturbating.[321] Hence, their respondents' claim about pornography as the "motivation" for imitating anal sex seems perfectly accurate with regard to men, but not women. By contrast, their claim to the contrary narrowly focuses on causal mechanisms that seem to mediate the men's underlying wish to imitate pornography, namely the "competition between men; the claim that 'people must like it if they do it' (alongside the seemingly contradictory expectation that it will be painful for women); and—crucially—normalisation of coercion and 'accidental' penetration."[322] Actually, the respondents' perception that "people must like it if they do it" would, if anything, be associated with consumption of pornography, where most women are presented as enjoying anal sex. Considering the totality of the pornography effects research paradigm, pornography involving anal sex most likely contributes to men's persistence in imitating it, despite women's resistance.

A more recent American survey study with a weighted probability sample of 2,227 persons aged 18–60 (mean 42.4) corroborates the prior studies regarding imitation, including also among the subpopulation of men who have sex with men.[323] The study, published in 2020, found a significant positive association between on the one hand more frequent pornography consumption during the past year and a greater range of pornography accessed during one's lifetime, and on the other hand engaging in various "dominant and target" sexual behaviors.[324] The dominant behaviors against a target included, among other things, trying anal sex without asking, ejaculating on another person's face, choking someone during sex, and pressuring someone into doing something sexual that they did not wish to do.[325]

A crucial finding of the studies on pornography imitation summarized here was that men consuming more pornography were more likely to imitate or try to imitate behaviors shown there than those consuming less pornography. The behaviors surveyed were often aggressive and subordinating to women, who mostly lacked the desire to imitate them. While these population surveys were cross-sectional, which as a method usually does not provide measures of causal direction on its own unless it is implicit in the variables themselves, there is more than ample evidence in related studies from which inferences about causal directions can be drawn. Related studies include experiments and longitudinal surveys controlling for other relevant predictors, and the direct testimony from johns addressing their desire to imitate the pornography they have most recently seen when purchasing women for sex, the enactment of which frequently involved violently coercing vulnerable women into tolerating becoming the targets of subordinating, degrading, and aggressive sexual acts. Corroborating testimony was provided by prostituted and battered women, many of whose assailants imitated pornography during the abuse. Hence, a triangulation of the evidence and methods from all types of studies thus far considered coherently corroborate the causal direction: pornography consumption comes first, imitation later. Interpreted accordingly, the more general population studies discussed demonstrate that heterosexual pornography popular among high-consuming men is a causal contributor in their performance of violent, coercive, subordinating, and painful acts against women in their lives, whether in or outside of prostitution.

Unreliable Methods

Some researchers have attempted to draw conclusions on the association between pornography consumption and men's sexual aggression against women based on the number of *reported* sex crimes. However, national crime statistics are obviously influenced by many more variables than influence any single individual. For instance, while pornography is one variable likely to influence both individuals and a society's aggregated crime statistics, variables such as the resources and reliability of law enforcement, or demographic factors such as number of single-person households, proportion of young people, poverty levels, and so on, are only impactful at the societal level. When so many variables are included in aggregated studies that it is difficult to tease out which ones are responsible for changes in the measures of outcome (e.g., crime reports), the result is termed " 'causal overdetermination,' " which occurs where there are two or more "*sufficient* and *distinct* causes for the same effect."[326] Another problem with aggregated studies is known as the "ecological fallacy," which refers to the risk of drawing conclusions from the wrong units of analysis, for example, making erroneous generalizations about individuals or groups on the basis of data about the larger society.[327] The problems of causal overdetermination and ecological fallacy are further exacerbated in longitudinal studies with aggregated data that attempts to understand the association of pornography consumption and reported crimes over long periods of time. Such research designs have been expressly criticized in the literature for, among other things, deploying "overly simplistic explanatory models."[328]

Crime reports—it should also be noted—do not necessarily reflect the actual *prevalence* of sex crimes. Consider the population-based studies which found that pornography consumption leads individuals to trivialize men's violence against women. Such an effect might discourage victims from reporting sexual crimes they do not believe will be taken seriously; the same result might occur if those victimized themselves minimize the abuse due to the wider influence of pornography. Indeed, the first of these tendencies was evidenced in an American population study from 2006 showing pervasive nonreporting among rape victims who did not believe that the sexual crimes perpetrated against them would be taken seriously. For instance, among adult women whose responses suggested they had de facto been raped, 44% said that one of the main reasons they did not report their rapes was fear of "bad treatment" by the criminal justice system.[329] In addition, 63% said they did not want their "family" or "others" to find out about the incidents. This study further found that only 37% of female college students correctly identified the abuse as rape, despite the fact that the other 63% also provided behaviorally specific responses consistent with criteria for rape.[330] The college women who did correctly identify their experience as rape were almost 10 times more likely to report it than those who did not. Apparently, attitudes and perceptions of sexual crimes may be more important than the actual crimes in determining the number of crimes *reported*.

To draw inferences from the aggregated association between pornography consumption and reported crime, the researcher must obviously control for many more independent variables and potential sources of error compared to the relatively parsimonious methods described previously. A few recent studies, like Ferguson and Hartley's meta-analysis on the relationship between pornography and sexual aggression, whose statistical model included control variables with post-treatment bias, also rely on aggregated data on reported rapes and arrests.[331] In order to critically evaluate the aggregated methods approach and its potential contribution to cumulative knowledge, it will be useful to examine examples of more and less persuasive studies in greater depth.

Aggregated Comparative Cross-Sectional Studies

The sociologists Larry Baron and Murray A. Straus statistically compared the associations between potential determinants of rape and the rate of reported rapes to the police within each and every one of the fifty U.S. states during the years 1980 to 1982.[332] Their study was replicated with refined measurements by Joseph E. Scott and Loretta A. Schwalm for 1982.[333] Both studies found, after controlling for relevant alternative predictors, a significant and substantial positive correlation between the per capita number of pornographic magazines circulated and the number of reported rapes.[334] Accordingly, Baron and Straus' structural equation model, reduced to those six predictors (including pornography) that were significant ($p<.05$), found a direct correlation ($r=.599$) between pornography and rape reports, with the model as a whole accounting for 83% of "state-to-state variation" in reported rapes when adjusting for degrees of freedom.[335] Baron and Straus' (and Scott and Schwalm's) control variables were based on prior research on the social determinants of rape, including the proportion of each state's population that was urbanized, the proportion of young adults (aged 18–24), proportion of men and women aged 15–24, economic inequality or poverty, alcohol consumption, the status/relative equality of women, the proportion of single males over age 15, proportion unemployed, proportion of African Americans,[336] proportion of murders, robberies, and aggravated assaults, and the sale of non-pornographic magazines (both general magazines and magazines with "macho" themes, e.g., guns, hunting, and sport).[337] Other state-level indicators controlled for by Baron and Straus (and to some extent by Scott and Schwalm) related to latent constructs hypothesized to be important: (1) cultural support for violence, measured by, for instance, laws authorizing use of corporal punishment in schools, public executions, and the circulation of generally violent media; (2) social disorganization, measured by proportions of divorces, single-headed households, secularism, ratio of tourists to residents, and geographical mobility; and (3) sex equality, measured by indices of the number of women in state political assemblies, secularism, and other legal, economic, or social indicators.[338]

Since reported rapes always underestimate the actual incidence of rapes, often dramatically so, Baron and Straus controlled for whether this was a problem among states within America. They reviewed prior research confirming that the *relative* differences among states' rape reporting statistics corresponded to the relative differences among their estimated *prevalence* of rape.[339] Although the prevalence studies Baron and Straus relied upon have also been found to underestimate rape incidence,[340] they are an acceptable control given that the percentage of underestimation is relatively similar throughout the United States. Both Baron and Straus' and Scott and Schwalm's studies were further reinforced by the fact that the per capita ratio of sales of pornographic materials and rapes reported were several times higher in some states than in others,[341] producing considerable statistical differences with stronger correlative power to support making robust conclusions. In contrast to longitudinal and cross-national aggregated studies, Baron and Straus and Scott and Schwalm compared fairly similar sub-national units, which gave them the advantage of controlling for substantial cultural and social differences and changes occurring over time that might otherwise have impacted the propensity to report sexual crimes, thus avoiding many, if not all, problems typical of overdetermination.[342]

Scott and Schwalm argued that they selected magazines more appropriately in their replication study than did Baron and Straus,[343] yet the results attained by the two studies were nonetheless similar. Notably, when controlling for the other known predictors of rape, greater circulation of pornography significantly predicted (r=.54, p<.05) more reported rapes.[344] Their multiple regression analysis found that 64% of the total variance in reported rapes could be accounted for by the eight most relevant variables, while only 47% of the variance could be accounted for by the remaining seven variables when pornography circulation was excluded from the model.[345] In addition to pornography, only two other variables significantly predicted reported rapes: the proportion of the population living below the poverty line and the proportion urbanized. An additional controlling analysis that excluded Alaska from the regression, which per capita had the largest proportion of reported rapes and highest circulation of pornographic magazines, yielded no significant changes of betas (β), regression coefficients (r), or explained variance (R^2).[346] Moreover, an alternative hypothesis that rape could be predicted by a general "subculture of violence," presuming that the correlation between pornography magazine circulation and rape reports was an artifact of such a confounding variable, was not empirically supported: in contrast to the fairly strong correlation demonstrated between pornography and reported rapes (r=.54, p<.05), the much weaker correlations observed between pornography and rates of aggravated assault (r=.12), robbery (r=.15), and homicide (r=.15) were statistically nonsignificant.[347] If pornography consumption was merely an expression of a "subculture of violence," as alternatively predicted, such nonsexual violence would likely have significantly predicted rape reports in a manner substantially similar to pornography.

Causal Overdetermination in Aggregated Longitudinal Studies

When considering the more complex models employed in the state-by-state comparisons, including many more potential predictor variables than the population studies, crime reporting may easily be a strongly overdetermined phenomenon. The same methodological problems are exacerbated in longitudinal studies, where societal changes over time introduce additional potential confounders. A 2011 study undertaken in the Czech Republic covering the period from 1971 to 2007 exemplifies this approach.[348] The authors assumed that if pornography consumption became more prevalent over time, particularly since 1989,[349] that trend could also explain changes in the reporting of sex crimes over time. The study's temporal design claimed by implication to demonstrate causal, not just correlational, associations as yielded in the state-by-state comparisons undertaken in the U.S. Surprisingly, then, the authors of the Czech study claim that their data shows that more pornography consumption does not lead to more sex crimes, thus contravening the entire pornography and sexual aggression research paradigm presented here. Yet interpreting trends in rape reporting over the 1971–2007 period in the Czech Republic—or, for that matter, the trends of reports of sexual abuse of children and "lesser sex crimes"[350]—is a far from straightforward endeavor.[351]

First, despite the study's conclusions, official Czech rape reporting rates increased demonstrably beginning in 1989, when pornography supposedly became more available, and reached an exceptionally high level of about 900 rape reports in 1990, after which the number of annual rape reports remained just below 750 until 1998.[352] Rates of rape reporting stabilized during the period 1999–2007 at between 500 and 750 cases annually, which was roughly the same rate evidenced during 1971–1989. The authors refer, however, to an increase in the male population aged 15–64 that implies a 15.5% de facto decrease of reported rapes per capita.[353] Given that this decrease in reporting took place over a 35-year period that included rapid and sweeping technological, social, economic, cultural, and political change, this relatively small change may be attributable to many other variables. Notably,

Czechoslovakia experienced the Velvet Revolution, the transition from communism to capitalism and liberalism, as well as a separation into two states, the Czech Republic and Slovakia, in just a few tumultuous years. From this perspective, a 15.5% reduction in the proportion of crime *reports*—not to be equated with crime *prevalence*—may certainly harbor (to borrow an expression) many "sufficient and distinct causes for the same effect."[354]

It is already suspicious that the Czech study makes no mention of the numerous studies previously conducted showing that pornography promotes both violence against women and the attitudes that trivialize it, particularly a tendency among both men and women to recommend less severe penalties for rape. Such conditions might well depress rape reporting. Recall the American population survey, where roughly half of the women who said they had been raped avoided reporting it to authorities out of fear of "bad treatment" by the criminal justice system, and where college women who failed to correctly identify their rape as such were almost ten times less likely to report it to authorities compared to those who accurately identified their rape as rape accordingly.[355] In light of persistent underreporting, one hypothesis is therefore that the initial rise in rape reporting seen in the Czech Republic between 1989 and 1998 reflected an actual increase in rape prevalence that was partially due to increased pornography consumption—not simply an increase in the inclination to report. The subsequent reduction in reporting after 1998 could then also be a partial byproduct of increasing attitudes that trivialize rape, which pornography slowly engendered with its increasing availability even among those victimized by rape after 1989. Hence, an increasing proportion of those raped might have considered it less useful to report the crime after 1998, particularly if sanctions were likely to be minimal and trials taxing due to a growing cultural tendency toward trivialization and disbelief.

In contrast to the lack of control for trivialization due to pornography consumption in the Czech longitudinal study, the American state-by-state comparisons controlled for such problems by comparing the relative differences among states' rape *reporting* with the relative difference in rape *prevalence*. The Czech study does not incorporate prevalence studies that could confirm whether proportional variance in official crime reporting over time is aligned with proportional variance in prevalence over time. Neither did the Czech study make comparisons with analogous data from Slovakia or other neighboring post-communist countries in Eastern Europe, which could either have supported their conclusions or provided rival hypotheses.

Obviously, indirect comparisons with U.S. studies from the early 1980s are inadequate considering that the Czech Republic during the 1971–2007 period was a very different society than the United States in 1980–1982.

The Czech study does, however, refer to a dramatic increase in reports of nonsexual crimes, such as robbery, willful battery, or robbery-related "murders," from 1989 onward.[356] This increase, admittedly, as the authors state, says something about "comparative markers of social change."[357] Yet it is never explained how this "social change" pertaining to *nonsexual* crimes is related to the reporting frequency of *sexual* crimes—whether positively, negatively, or otherwise. Hence, the statement about social change appears to be merely perfunctory and lacking in substance, offering no meaningful support for the study's conclusions. Broaching the problem from a strictly substantive perspective, a reasonable counter-hypothesis would be that the dramatic increase in the reporting of robbery, assault, and murder after 1989 precipitated a considerable increase in the workload of police forces nationwide. Such a dramatic increase in the reporting of other crimes could discourage rape reporting if women had cause to believe not only that their rapes would be trivialized (partially due to increased pornography consumption in society), but also that their reports would not be prioritized when the police were overwhelmed with reports of other crimes in a rapidly transforming post-communist society. This scenario is quite plausible considering that rapes are notoriously difficult to investigate and successfully prosecute even in robust criminal justice systems such as exists in the United States.[358]

The Czech longitudinal study did not attempt to control for any alternative demographic predictors of rapes like those that have predicted more rapes or rape reporting in the United States, and which were controlled for in the American state-by-state comparisons (e.g., unemployment rates, proportion of single residents and/or single-parent homes, economic decline, urbanization, and city size).[359] Furthermore, the Czech study was unable to control for cultural changes over a 35-year period that likely introduced unknown predictors—a problem that did not impair the American studies since they compared 51 similar sub-national units during the same two years. In comparison with the American studies, the Czech study is at best considerably less reliable, at worst completely misleading.

Compared to the more parsimonious scientific methods employed in experiments and general population surveys on individual subjects or specific surveys of vulnerable or abusive groups like those discussed earlier, the aggregated methodology—especially in longitudinal studies—must control for many more alternative predictors. Thus, the latter's statistical modeling, by necessity, must be much more nuanced if it is to come close to approximating the reliability of studies based on individuals as the primary unit of analysis. All in all, even though well-conceived aggregated studies have seemingly controlled for relevant alternative predictors (e.g., the American state-by-state comparisons), these studies nonetheless seem to be "carrying coals to Newcastle." It seems by far more fruitful to refine the population-based surveys and control for more easily identifiable predictors using well-designed questionnaires (e.g., unburdened by vague frequency measurements, post-treatment bias, or tautological variables). The aggregated method has been used to present not only unreliable but also potentially misleading claims to suggest that increased pornography consumption over time would contribute to fewer sex crimes, contradicting more or less the entire pornography and sexual aggression paradigm. This fact implies that readers who come across aggregated studies in this field should exercise particular caution.

Summary

This chapter set out to answer the question of to what extent pornography consumption contributes to gender-based violence. Evidence shows it invariably does, and substantially so—a conclusion corroborated across several relevant indices and various methodologies, measuring different, but statistically and significantly, related concepts such as sexual aggression and ASV. The analytical review set forth here draws upon experimental and nonexperimental psychology, including meta-analysis as well as individual studies, with key conceptual contributions from qualitative as well as quantitative data, general population samples, and samples of particularly abusive or targeted groups. Further, it critically reviews other methods, such as studies relying on aggregated data (e.g., crime reports). The conclusions are robust and statistically significant, showing that consumption of pornography in all the forms the market typically demands contributes to substantially more gender-based violence and to an array of attitudes that minimize, trivialize, or normalize it.

More detailed psychological experiments suggest that it is not primarily the level of aggression or violence in pornography that determines the measure of such outcomes as rape or rape myths. Instead, the extent to which these materials objectify, dehumanize, degrade, or present women as sexually indiscriminate do. Such a finding is empirically consistent with legal conceptualizations first articulated in the 1980s that challenged pornography presenting "graphic sexually explicit subordination of women," for example, in positions of servility or implied promiscuity.[360] Although certain classes of pornographic materials may produce stronger effects than others, similar effects can be observed across the board in significant measure in all pornography demanded by a nontrivial number of consumers, be it violent or nonviolent. The increase in behavioral aggression to which pornography use contributes is mirrored by comparable increases in ASV—two empirically and statistically associated indices.

Nonexperimental surveys conducted in naturalistic contexts consistently corroborate the experimental results: pornography consumption in population-based samples of males significantly and substantially predicts increased sexually aggressive behavior and more ASV, even after controlling/adjusting for other relevant predictors that may moderate its effects. Longitudinal studies are noteworthy since they lend more support to causal inference while also strengthening ecological validity in tandem with numerous cross-sectional studies.

The research designs employed in some studies unconvincingly attempt to isolate attitudinal or behavioral moderators that would supposedly show that only a subpopulation of men is substantially likely to be affected by pornography consumption. When looking closer at some of the correlations reported between variables and at the differences apparent between and among groups in light of other experimental and longitudinal research, their own data suggests—contrary to their conclusions—that, on average, men are more likely to adopt those very moderating personality characteristics or behaviors that promote sexually aggressive behavior and attitudes if they consume more pornography. In other words, *any* man who consumes more pornography, especially over more extended periods, seems to run an elevated "risk" of becoming more sexually aggressive and adopting attitudes trivializing gender-based violence—not just those already at higher risk of sexually aggressing as a consequence of specific personality characteristics. These particular studies failed to control for post-treatment bias since the moderators were either partial consequences of the key causal variable pornography or, where no data was reported, could be suspected to be so based on their underlying attitudinal concepts. In lay terms, these biased studies understated the effects of pornography on sexual aggression and similar behaviors by erroneously presuming that factors that in actuality are outcomes of pornography consumption, not underlying causes, were responsible for much of the documented increase in sexual aggression that pornography causes.

The findings from population studies with normal (i.e., non-institutionalized and non-convicted) men are corroborated by studies of populations that have either been significantly exposed to gender-based violence (i.e., battered or prostituted women) or are responsible for such abuse (i.e., batterers or johns). Importantly, surveys and qualitative interviews with johns and prostituted women alike exhibited a causal narrative consistent with the temporality shown in experimental and longitudinal research findings: johns often imitate specific kinds of sexual aggression, degradation, and humiliation with prostituted women that they have seen in pornography, and the imitation happens *after* they have seen it. That is, even if these johns might already be more sexually aggressive than non-johns—a condition in itself exacerbated by pornography consumption—the imitation itself would not happen without first viewing pornography. A between-method triangulation indicates that the aggressive outcomes demonstrated in experiments and longitudinal studies, which gain ecological validity in cross-sectional surveys, also overlap with the sexual abuse inherent in johns' imitation of aggressive or degrading pornography with prostituted persons. From johns' accounts, it is also evident that their other sexual partners often refuse to engage in these acts, or the johns feel uncomfortable even asking them. Instead, johns prefer to exploit prostituted women, whom evidence shows are typically in such a vulnerable position that they will either submit directly, or if not, they can be more easily coerced into such sex by johns, who rarely face official or social sanctions. Consistent with these observations, studies from several countries using different types of samples find that more pornography consumption significantly and substantially predicts a higher likelihood of buying prostituted sex.

Quantitative data reported from studies with battered women, corroborated by numerous testimonies and affidavits from individuals in public hearings, shows that batterers who use pornography are significantly and substantially more likely to sexually aggress, coerce, control, and abuse women than batterers who do not use pornography and to imitate pornography during their abuse similar to how johns tend to behave toward women in prostitution. Cross-sectional studies with normal population samples also confirm that many young men, in some cases possibly a majority, have imitated pornography with their partners (e.g., ejaculating on women's faces/ in their mouths). Many men also wish to imitate pornography, usually much more so than women, including conduct such as anal sex, ass-to-mouth, gagging, or derogatory name-calling (e.g., "slut" and "whore"). Although these are cross-sectional studies, a between-method triangulation suggests similar causal relationships when interpreting them in light of the causal effects exhibited in experiments and longitudinal surveys, and in light of interviews with johns and prostituted women that revealed conceptually similar causal narratives. In addition, qualitative studies on anal sex practices indicate that many men, even in ostensibly caring relationships, motivated mainly by the wish to imitate pornography, pressure reluctant female partners into anal sex despite realizing it would likely be painful for them.

Aggregated cross-sectional and longitudinal studies of pornography consumption and reported sexual crimes, where entire societies serve as the primary unit of analysis, appear considerably more unreliable and problematic than studies where individuals are the primary unit of analysis. The reporting rates of sexual crimes are demonstrably "overdetermined" by a number of disparate social factors apart from pornography consumption, including unemployment rates, the number of single residents and/or single-parent homes, economic decline, urbanization, and city size, to name but a few. Moreover, aggregated studies are typically compromised by inadequate measurements of sexual aggression, a consequence of their dependence on unreliable official crime reports rather than relatively more reliable prevalence surveys.

In addition, using official reports as the dependent variable does not take into account that exposure to pornography, as shown in experimental studies (and ecologically validated in nonexperimental studies), causes individuals on average to develop more ASV, including minimization, trivialization, and normalization of sexual aggression. Thus, increased pornography consumption promotes attitudes that dissuade victimized women from reporting sexual abuse to officials and others. This phenomenon could make it look as if pornography consumption reduces the prevalence of sexual crimes (as distinguished from reducing reports), although, in reality, it does the opposite. While some aggregated studies have attempted to control for problems with official reports by comparing them with prevalence surveys in studies that supported the findings from the methods discussed, other aggregated studies did not control accordingly, thus rendering their contrary conclusions unconvincing. The many methodological pitfalls associated with this aggregated paradigm, and particularly some of its more unreliable findings, suggest that it provides few insights that cannot be gained through more parsimonious and reliable research methods.

The trivialization of violence against women that pornography contributes to, making its consumers minimize and ignore the effects that the research has documented is flowing from its consumption, likely fuels the public resistance to acknowledging the harms of pornography. Yet compelling evidence, much of it adduced here, documents that pornography consumption contributes to more gender-based violence and attitudes that support, trivialize, and normalize it. For example, exposure to pornography makes normal men more likely to rape their dates, pester their partners with sexual demands, such as imitating aggressive or degrading pornography, which is unwanted, and trivialize or minimize sexual abuse as jury members. Men who consume more pornography are also statistically more likely to buy women for sex, to make prostituted women imitate pornography, even when it is violent, unhealthy, degrading, or traumatizing, and possibly more inclined to participate in gang rapes of prostituted women. These findings effectively refute the hypothesis that pornography consumption is merely a "symptom" mediated by other underlying phenomena or that other factors moderate most of its effects. Pornography produces effects that are significant, substantial, and independently contribute to the severe harm its consumers do to women.

3
Democracy and Hierarchy

Previous chapters showed that pornography is a social practice that contravenes equality by exploiting multiple disadvantages and contributing to gender-based violence. Additionally, the chapters demonstrated intricate links between exploitation in pornography production and prostitution. The harms engendered by pornography disproportionally affect certain groups of women (and some men) more severely than others. This fact will have to be accounted for when examining the politics surrounding legal challenges to pornography. In democracies, political efforts to contravene practices that promote inequality and violence against disadvantaged groups have historically been institutionalized by establishing new legal rights or implementing laws designed to protect their members. This trajectory makes sense when considering that legal structures provide stability, continuity, and predictability, all of which are important in promoting empowerment and affording protections against oppression, which may otherwise be subject to the whims of political majorities or other decision-makers.

By comparing pornography to analogous problems of social hierarchy and inequality where groups are subordinated, exploited, or abused (e.g., redlining, unequal pay, or domestic abuse), this chapter will set forth a political theory of what would make legal challenges to such practices more successful generally, and particularly with respect to pornography. Since the objective is to build a theory by which efficient legal challenges to social hierarchies based on domination may be mounted, the result will be labeled "hierarchy theory"—derived in part from the scholarship of Catharine MacKinnon, who frequently uses the term "hierarchy" to describe the problem her feminist theory addresses.[1] It is used here as an umbrella term comprising several elements drawn from various theorists' works with the potential to inform solutions to problems like pornography, where harmful, yet politically contested, practices disproportionately affect disadvantaged groups.

In order to develop a theory of successful legal challenges to pornography that can be applied to other harmful hierarchical practices, this chapter first outlines the politico-legal obstacles to such a project, including in democratic

Pornography. Max Waltman, Oxford University Press. © Oxford University Press 2021.
DOI: 10.1093/oso/9780197598535.003.0004

theory where we find both justification and criticism of key concepts and ideas on which modern democratic political systems are founded.

Substantive Inequality in Democratic Theory

Early democracies distinguished themselves, in theory, from autocracies and monarchies by positing a proportional decision-making process among persons regarded as citizens or their representatives. Ancient systems are sometimes idealistically portrayed in terms of "equality." However, they did not exhibit many of the political rights, freedoms, and protections of later liberal democracies. For instance, women, children, and slaves were legally excluded from the public sphere in Greece, even though their politically unrecognized domestic work was "directly linked" to the "achievements of classical democracy."[2] Furthermore, according to both republican Rome and Athenian democracy, it was every citizen's duty to participate actively in politics; collective public decision-making could exert a substantial impact on the private sphere, with "claims of the state" being "given a unique priority over those of the individual citizen."[3] There was relatively little constitutional separation of executive, legislative, and judicial powers—a situation enabling rash, impulsive, and irreversible decisions (e.g., expulsion or execution of opponents) during a society's intemperate moments, including collective euphoria.[4] Notwithstanding these dangers, in his *Discourses* (ca. 1513–1519), the early modern political theorist Niccolò Machiavelli tends to favor this brand of democracy over elite authoritarianism, contending that the inclusion of a broader proportion of the population in governance would, for various reasons, produce stability and better judgment, notably because various factions would be forced to cooperate and compromise.[5]

All liberal political theorists did not share Machiavelli's optimistic view of democracy. For instance, in *On Liberty* (1859), John Stuart Mill argues that the masses do not adequately appreciate socially productive contributions by individual eccentric "geniuses" due to the pressures of conformity and concomitant intolerance of individual diversity; in his view, diversity is a major engine of human progress.[6] However, nurturing one's individuality was more often a prerogative of the privileged classes than of the masses during Mill's era. Indeed, in *On Liberty*, Mill expresses a fear that greater equality might counteract diversity, hence obstruct progress:

> As the various social eminences which enabled persons entrenched on them to disregard the opinion of the multitude, gradually become levelled; as the very idea of resisting the will of the public, when it is positively known that they have a will, disappears more and more from the minds of practical politicians; there ceases to be any social support for nonconformity—any substantive power in society, which, itself opposed to the ascendancy of numbers, is interested in taking under its protection opinions and tendencies at variance with those of the public.[7]

Here, Mill is indirectly defending substantive inequality, arguing the "ascendancy of numbers" and "practical politicians" constitute an equation that reduces the incentive for progress. Consistent with his view of the relationship between progress and inequality, Mill's *Considerations on Representative Government* (1861) outlines a representative democracy that includes a franchise graded by wealth and education.[8] Yet it ignores the fact that a critical cause of inequality, namely discrimination, is also opposed to diversity and progress; precluding opportunities based on class, sex, race, ethnicity, or sexuality, among other grounds, hardly promotes progress, far less diversity, in any meaningful way.[9]

However disagreeable, Mill's thoughts on social equality are not merely philosophical; they are related to a theme common among early liberal contract theorists interested in restricting government power and protecting private property—both foundations of modern liberal democracy. John Locke, for instance, spoke in 1690 of his fear of a government using power "arbitrary and at pleasure," inherently contrary to the public's interest, thus violating an implicit social contract distinguishing society from a "state of Nature," where no one is subjected to the rule of others or the rule of law.[10] Thomas Hobbes, an earlier contract theorist, was willing to invest power in the hands of a sovereign ruler, which, according to Locke, was tantamount "to think[ing] that men [*sic*] are so foolish that they take care to avoid what mischiefs may be done them by polecats or foxes, but are content, nay, think it safety, to be devoured by lions."[11] Locke's writings appear to favor a restricted role for the government, concerned primarily with protecting life, liberty, and private property.[12] Other early liberals advanced various checks and balances to control the government, so it could not easily change the status quo even with legislative majorities' consent. For instance, Charles Montesquieu (1748) proposed an executive veto and a bicameral legislature's house of "nobles," the latter to be empowered to reject initiatives from the house representing the "people."[13]

Moreover, Mill and other liberals emphasize that expressive rights are fundamental means for preventing government abuse of power by enabling independent and informed value judgments, for example, making different views available to the public so that "the deliberative forces should prevail over the arbitrary."[14] As such, expressive rights are critical in preventing despotism, corruption, and tyranny as they allow dissident political opponents to be heard. Expressive freedoms are thus often associated with reason and enlightenment. Nonetheless, in an age of mass communication and complex postindustrial societies, liberal democracies have tried to develop various regulative approaches for dealing with harmful expressions. Core liberal arguments to this end and the conflicts raised by promoting free expression while simultaneously attempting to avoid its harms also emerge in Mill's *On Liberty*. There, he argues that free expression and other freedoms, rights, and liberties are essential for the development of progressive societies; restrictions, therefore, are only legitimate to the extent that the rights of one would harm those of another: "The object of this essay," Mill writes, "is to assert one very simple principle. . . . [T]he only purpose for which power can be rightfully exercised over any member of a civilized community, against his [*sic*] will, is to prevent harm to others."[15] This principle leads Mill to conclude that "[a]cts, of whatever kind, which, without justifiable cause, do harm to others, may be, and in the more important cases absolutely require to be, controlled by the unfavourable sentiments, and, when needful, by the active interference of mankind [*sic*]."[16]

Mill's rhetoric implies that adjudicating between liberty and harm is uncomplicated. However, when applying his ostensibly "very simple" principle in a social context, he implicitly introduces a conceptual distinction between *direct* and *indirect* harm—a more complicated principle still grappled with within liberal jurisprudence:

> An opinion that corn-dealers are starvers of the poor, or that private property is robbery, ought to be unmolested when simply circulated through the press, but may justly incur punishment when delivered orally to an excited mob assembled before the house of a corn-dealer, or when handed about among the same mob in the form of a placard.[17]

One may argue that, regardless of Mill's attempted distinction, circulating an opinion in the press that corn-dealers are responsible for starving the poor could incite an angry mob (perhaps many mobs). Doing so may, in turn, cause danger, destruction, and death equally as severe as when circulating the opinion on a placard. If not outright rejected by Mill, he nonetheless deems the hypothetical effect of opinions circulated through the press as an insufficient cause for public intervention. Hence, when more realistically recasting his "simple principle" as involving a balance between competing interests, Mill chose liberty of the press over the prevention of harm.

Likewise, when Mill confronts the complications presented in empirical settings where substantial damage may ensue from society's toleration of indirectly harmful practices, he succumbs to the fear of potential excessive regulation. For example, he concedes that unregulated access to fermented liquors entails costs, damages, and injuries to society and its members—harms that one of his contemporaries described as "social disorder" and a "profit from the creation of a misery" that he and others were allegedly "taxed to support."[18] Yet Mill opposes regulating fermented liquors on the basis of such harms because, he implies, any regulation of that sort could legitimize a "monstrous" principle that, in the name of preventing harm to others, might be invoked to disproportionately infringe upon the freedom of expression and other liberties.[19] His fear, and rejection, of this supposedly "monstrous" principle has since been referred to as the "slippery slope"[20]—an argument suggesting that future decision-makers would be unable to distinguish particular facts consistent with a general principle of harm, whether willfully or not. That is, it is presumed difficult to decide what the dangerous (as opposed to benign) indirect causes of harm would be.

A more complex, yet related, concern with public abuse of power was voiced by the American "founding father" James Madison (1787), who feared "factions" within modern governments—that is, certain groups of citizens, whether majorities or minorities, who could become "violent" in their struggle to control the government in pursuit of interests "adverse to the rights of other citizens or the permanent and aggregate interests of the community."[21] Certainly, many political regimes representing only "factions" of the population, left or right, have used government powers to torture and deprive opponents of life, liberty, and property. However, as the political theorist Robert Dahl noted in 1956, "in the absence of certain social prerequisites, no constitutional arrangements can produce a nontyrannical republic."[22] One of Dahl's examples was the Supreme Court of the United States, popularly perceived at the time as protecting democratic freedoms and rights, despite consistently having obstructed congressional efforts to protect and extend such rights to African Americans.[23]

Yet constitutional politics can be improved by new inventions. Much has happened since Dahl's remarks in 1956—even more since the time of Mill, Madison, Montesquieu, and Locke. The early liberals' thoughts were likely shaped by their experiences as white men with priorities that are not reflective of other social groups. Belonging to a privileged class among men, they had little need for protection of liberty and life in the private sphere, such as protection against violence based on their sex. However, like all men, their class of men needed a "social contract" to protect them from arbitrary intrusions by other men into their private sphere, shielding them in particular from an intrusive state acting on behalf of factions likewise comprised of white men. Construing protections against private actors as less significant than public actors is inadequate as a conception of politics. This point is frequently made in feminist political theory,[24] emblematized in the phrase "the personal is political," which was commonly heard during the women's movement of the 1970s. The example of pornography—its exploitative abuse, its fueling of consumers' violence against women—is instructive: although official abuse of power was the predominant interest among early liberal theorists, state actors (e.g., southern courts before racial desegregation) and non-state actors (e.g., pornographers or domestic batterers) are similar in that the abuses they have perpetrated have been tolerated within many populations. Moreover, both cases of abuse of power typically target a distinct social, political, religious, ethnic, or national group on the basis of their group membership, whether de jure or de facto. Tolerance for gender-based violence, for example, permits a group selected based on their gender, most often women, to be targeted.[25] Likewise, pornography targets groups based on certain multiple disadvantages, including poverty, child sexual abuse, youth, sex/gender, race, and homelessness. Still, the abuse of power envisaged as dangerous in classic liberal theory typically pertains to government power, meaning its conceptualization of freedom rejects all but minimal authority for states to intervene in non-public spheres. This point of view is increasingly losing ground.

The New Rights Approach

The concepts of "negative" and "positive" freedoms usefully describe contrasting approaches to freedom and liberty within modern liberalism in complex societies with intrinsic social interdependencies connecting individuals, groups, and government institutions. Their roots have been traced back to the philosopher Immanuel Kant (1724–1804),[26] yet were more systematically articulated by Isaiah Berlin in the 1950s and 1960s. These theorists conceptualized negative freedom as the absence of tangible obstacles to individual actions (e.g., a roadblock or a law prohibiting travel), and positive freedom as the capacity or potential for self-determination (e.g., access to food, health care, or literacy).[27] The two concepts, although limited to freedom and liberty, are related to the legal concepts of negative or positive "rights" within liberalism: the former generally disfavoring government interventions, the latter more inclined to view such interventions as instruments of emancipation.[28]

An empirical example of negative rights can be seen in judicial responses to legal action against child abuse. The Supreme Court of the United States expressed the quintessential negative-rights approach in the 1989 case of *DeShaney v. Winnebago*, which rejected civil rights actions on behalf of an abused child against government social workers and local officials for failing to appropriately intervene in a case of domestic violence that was known to them and eventually resulted in the child sustaining permanent brain injuries and crippling disability:

> Like its counterpart in the Fifth Amendment, the Due Process Clause of the Fourteenth Amendment was intended . . . . to protect the people from the State, not to ensure that the State protected them from each other. The Framers were content to leave the extent of governmental obligation in the latter area to the democratic political processes. Consistent with these principles, our cases have recognized that the Due Process Clauses generally confer no affirmative right to governmental aid, even where such aid may be necessary to secure life, liberty, or property interests of which the government itself may not deprive the individual.[29]

In *DeShaney*, the U.S. Supreme Court took the position that the Constitution and its implicit social contract primarily (or even exclusively) protects the individual's right to be free from government encroachment or abuse, rather than protecting the right to be free from such excesses by other individuals. In contrast to this widely contested decision, which has not been overruled,[30] comparable situations involving abuse by non-state actors reviewed by the highest courts of other countries as well as supranational bodies have supported a conception of positive rights encompassing the entitlement to affirmative government intervention against similar abuses of power.

For instance, in 2001, South Africa's Constitutional Court reviewed a case where government officials received ample evidence and warnings of a severe threat to a woman's safety by a man already suspected of having raped her; nonetheless, officials failed to intervene by arresting or subjecting him to enforced institutionalized care.[31] Following the government's inaction, he broke into her residence and inflicted additional injuries on her, including knife wounds, and was eventually sentenced to prison for attempted murder and other offenses.[32] In contrast to the U.S. case, the South African Constitutional Court considered the government liable for failing to take "positive action" to prevent the woman's injuries, recognizing that "'in certain well-defined circumstances [there exists] a positive obligation on the authorities to take preventive operational measures to protect an individual whose life is at risk from the criminal acts of another individual.'"[33] The European Court of Human Rights has also reached conclusions affirming government obligations to intervene in domestic violence cases.[34]

A possible corollary to the South African and European courts' position on positive rights implies that government abuse of power is merely one of several ways that individuals or factions may illegitimately exercise power. When negative rights enable such private abuse, it may simply mean toleration of privatized terror. Another corollary in the context of prostitution and pornography is that inequality may itself be a form of power; economic inequality can lead to exploitation when a person is vulnerable to starvation, homelessness, poverty, or severe social exclusion on account of their socioeconomic position. The state does not need to be directly involved for this power to be exercised, though in terms of the state's legal architecture (e.g., strong protections of private property and weak mandates for redistribution of wealth) it might be involved in its dynamics. Correspondingly, it may be inevitable under conditions of sex inequality that certain women will lack sufficient social power to avoid exploitative relations with men, as the evidence on pornography production and social inequality suggests. From this vantage point, inequality and gender subordination are circumstances making individuals particularly vulnerable to abuses of power by non-state actors. As recognized by the United Nation's Declaration on the Elimination of Violence Against Women (1993), violence against women is among the "crucial social mechanisms" that force women into positions of subordination relative to men.[35] Women may also fear men's violence, hence accept an exploitative situation that is not physically abusive. Thus there is a reciprocal relationship between gender-based violence and sex inequality.

The classic liberal public/private dichotomy has been slowly replaced by a more nuanced view of power reflected in current international human rights law.[36] Gender-based violence is now regarded as a violation for which states are obliged to provide adequate protections and remedies, regardless of whether states or non-state actors commit the violation.[37] International law exhibits a similar, if less definitive, position against pornography as it does against gender-based violence more generally. An essential step in this direction was taken in 1992 by the Committee on the Elimination of Discrimination Against Women (CEDAW), the U.N. monitoring body for the implementation of the Convention on the Elimination of All Forms of Discrimination Against Women. That year, CEDAW identified "pornography" as a practice that "contributes to gender-based violence"[38] and held that states parties were obliged to "take all legal and other measures . . . including . . . civil remedies and compensatory provisions"[39] to fight gender-based violence. This step was extended in 2000 when the U.N. Human Rights Committee issued a General Comment on the interpretation of the International Covenant on Civil and Political Rights (ICCPR) as it pertains to balancing the interest in women's equality to men with the competing interest in freedom of expression. Here, the Human Rights Committee followed the CEDAW Committee's view of pornography and thus held that, since "pornographic material which portrays women and girls as objects of violence or degrading or inhuman treatment is likely to promote these kinds of treatment of women and girls, States parties should provide information about legal measures to restrict the publication or dissemination of such material."[40]

Positions against pornography analogous to those expressed under CEDAW and ICCPR have also been voiced, or reiterated, independently in other international and regional instruments. States parties agreed in the U.N. 1995 Beijing Declaration that "[i]mages in the media of violence against women . . . including pornography, are factors contributing to the continued prevalence of such violence."[41] The African Union's 2005 Protocol on Women's Human Rights urged states to "take effective legislative and administrative measures to prevent the exploitation and abuse of women in advertising and pornography."[42] Similar human rights resolutions have been passed against pornography under the auspices of the European Union where, in 1993, the European Parliament (the only democratically elected pan-European body), in a non-binding resolution, stated that it was "convinced that pornography is a systematic practice of exploitation and subordination based on sex that disproportionately harms women and contributes to inequality between the sexes, existing power imbalances in society, female subordination and male domination."[43] Again in 1997, in a resolution on "discrimination against women in advertising," the European Parliament called for "statutory measures to prevent any form of pornography in the media and in advertising and for a ban on advertising for pornographic products and sex tourism."[44] Likewise, these positions on pornography have been introduced into some domestic laws, as when the Supreme Court of India adopted the CEDAW Committee's understanding of sexual harassment, including showing pornography at work, which they have subsequently applied in case law.[45]

However, existing laws and policies in modern democracies are woefully ineffective in addressing most of the substantial de facto harms from pornography—a situation recognized after gender-based violence became a more prominent public concern in the 1970s. Within the women's movement, organizations were formed to take concrete actions, like picketing outside pornography stores and organizing marches and rallies.[46] For instance, when the movie *Snuff* (as the title suggests, it presented a woman's murder and dismemberment as erotic entertainment) was released in the United States in 1976, it ignited vehement feminist opposition to pornography in both Canada and the United States. Women picketed, demonstrated, and committed civil disobedience against the film.[47] In 1977, a small women's organization called Women Against Violence Against Women picketed outside a screening of *Snuff* in Canada,[48] and another group calling itself Wimmin's Fire Brigade took credit for bombing three video stores in 1982 that were part of a pornography chain in the Vancouver area.[49] The feminist anti-pornography movement had an impact on public discourse that at times seems to have affected legal outcomes in, among other things, Canadian case law.[50] Yet, relative progress notwithstanding, none of these movements, whether in the United States, Canada, Sweden, or elsewhere, succeeded in creating effective legal challenges with sustainable outcomes. The question is why.

Hierarchy Theory

Consciousness-Raising

Those harmed by pornography can be seen as one population within a larger group of populations harmed by politically contested practices that disproportionately affect disadvantaged groups. It will be useful to compare those impacted by pornography with similar groups that have historically amassed the necessary evidence, knowledge, and social mobilization required to articulate political objectives that could then be translated into laws designed to diminish, and ultimately end, their subordination. Catharine A. MacKinnon's seminal work, *Toward a Feminist Theory of the State* (1989), provides insights into this process. It scrutinizes the obstacles that begin at the level of knowledge production, noting how conventional epistemology (the predominant theory of how to acquire valid scientific knowledge) presumes neutrality, objectivity, and detachment of the observer.[51] However, MacKinnon observes that it was when women came together in consciousness-raising groups, where they were not inhibited by men's interruptions, challenges, disbelief, and objections, that the complex and multifaceted reality of gender-based violence, including sexual harassment, domestic violence, child sexual abuse, rape, and other previously hidden practices, was finally named as such and recognized as a public policy concern.[52] The fact that it took the concerted efforts of movement activists to effectively reveal abusive situations necessarily calls the conventional ideal of a point-of-viewless observer into question. This arguably essential lack of neutrality has been reified by the #MeToo movement, driven primarily by women who have come forward to speak out against previously unknown perpetrators of gender-based violence.

Following MacKinnon, consciousness-raising has been employed as a method that "inquires into an intrinsically social situation, into that mixture of thought and materiality which comprises gender in the broadest sense."[53] As members of a specific group that is widely exposed to gender-based violence, women may be endowed with knowledge that is less accessible to other groups.[54] Yet this is not to say that the men who contribute to gender-based violence and sexual exploitation somehow lack knowledge. Rather, it is recognition of its harm that is hidden or ignored.[55]

Along with the consciousness-raising practices of the late 1960s and early 1970s, feminist scholars started asking different questions than conventional researchers did, such as: What role does pornography have in women's subordination? How is abortion linked to women's position of vulnerability and inequality to men? Why does the law privilege the rapist's state of mind—that is, what the perpetrator thinks he is doing—over how his behavior harms his victim? As MacKinnon has explained, the traditional perspective on pornography either treated it as obscene and unsuitable for public consumption or celebrated it as a mark of sexual liberation. Rarely was it called exploitation of vulnerable women, inspiration to rape, and a cause of systemic gender discrimination.[56] Likewise, abortion was typically framed either as a woman's private choice or as an irresponsible act of feticide. Conservatives did not call it a consequence of unequal conditions that diminished women's bodily autonomy, and the left did not recognize how abortion or the use of contraceptives could stigmatize women as sexually available, thus targeting them for rape.[57] MacKinnon also noted that like many other crimes, a criminal mind (*mens rea*) was typically a requirement for conviction under rape laws.[58] Yet the degree to which pornography fuels men's feelings of sexual entitlement and rape myths (e.g., believing women desire coerced sex) will inversely affect the possibility to prove such criminal intent to rape to the point of making the rapist's perspective the law.[59]

MacKinnon further demonstrated that many of the purportedly neutral and objective presumptions underlying U.S. law and policy were, in fact, expressive of the point of view as seen from a position of dominance within a system, whether left- or right-wing, that subordinated women. This dominance, masquerading as neutrality in law and objectivity in scholarship, is what MacKinnon often refers to as objectification as a scientific method.

> If the sexes are unequal, and perspective participates in situation, there is no ungendered reality or ungendered perspective. . . . In this context, objectivity—the nonsituated, universal standpoint, whether claimed or aspired to—is a denial of the existence or potency of sex inequality that tacitly participates in constructing reality from the dominant point of view. Objectivity, as the epistemological stance of which objectification is the social process, creates the reality it apprehends by defining as knowledge the reality it creates through its way of apprehending it.[60]

Facing the consequences of her analysis, *Toward a Feminist Theory of the State* accounted for a large body of empirical research on gender-based violence and its determinants that had emerged clearly by the time of the book's publication—footnoted, for example, in chapters analyzing sexuality, rape, and pornography laws.[61] Much of that research could not have been done without feminists taking women seriously and asking the questions. Similarly, many of the studies described here regarding the relationships between prostitution, pornography, and gender-based violence were published by the early 1980s, when researchers would likely have been aware of and possibly influenced by the feminist anti-pornography movement. Politics and knowledge are thus intertwined.

Without oppressed groups practicing some form of consciousness-raising, producing their own knowledge as a foundation for further political mobilization, their capacity to effectively challenge their oppression through legal means would have been highly circumscribed. As history demonstrates, particularly regarding violence against women, other groups cannot be relied on to do it for them. This circumstance was confirmed by the political scientists Laurel Weldon and Mala Htun. They examined why some governments make progressive policy changes to combat violence against women, while others do not.[62] Their study compared seventy nations over a thirty-year period representing a range of political systems, from democratic to authoritarian, and with diversity in the services available to those victimized by violence against women, the extent of relevant legal and administrative reform, how well the needs of more vulnerable female populations were addressed, and whether professionals were trained and prevention programs adopted to support victims.[63] By far the strongest predictor of progressive policies on this issue was the relative prevalence and strength of an autonomous feminist movement that could draw attention to gender-based violence.[64] By contrast, the proportion of women in government, the presence of "left" parties, and higher levels of national wealth or modernization were negligible predictors of progressive policy changes, often statistically insignificant.[65] Moreover, the autonomous feminist movements were found to "predate" progressive policy changes "by a long period of time."[66] This chain of events suggests that movements pressured governments to legally challenge violence against women, which in turn influenced government policy.

Echoing MacKinnon's writings on consciousness-raising, Weldon and Htun explain that when "women come together to discuss their priorities as women, the problem of violence comes to the fore."[67] This group dynamic is a key reason why "the issue of violence against women was first articulated by and diffused from women's autonomous organizing,"[68] and not by political parties, religious groups, or presumptively generally progressive organizations such as Amnesty International and Human Rights Watch.[69] An empowering politics for disadvantaged groups would thus, at a minimum, support their self-organization.

Group Representation

As distinguished from broader social movement theory, political theorists have explored potential changes within established political systems that could empower disadvantaged groups with more surgical precision. Iris Marion Young identifies and suggests remedies to systemic problems within democratic decision-making processes that exacerbate inequality and amplify social hierarchies. For instance, in referring to Jane Mansbridge's seminal work on New England town meetings, Young notes that women, Black people, working-class, and poor people did not participate to the same extent as men, whites, or members of the middle and educated classes; hence, the former groups' perspectives and experiences were not accounted for to the same extent as the latter's.[70] Furthermore, she observes that, while single mothers and older people had difficulty attending the meetings, white middle-class men did not; additionally, the latter generally took their "authority" for granted and were better trained to speak persuasively.[71] Amy Gutman's work on community control of local schools shows analogous dynamics at work: increased democratic participation increased racial segregation in many American cities, because, as Young explains, the more privileged white people were better able to articulate, thus more efficient in promoting, their "perceived interests" over Black people's "just demand for equal treatment in an integrated school system."[72]

Apparently, without strong autonomous representation of disadvantaged groups, deliberative and participatory forms of decision-making, which on their face might appear to promote public access to the legislative process, in fact tend to elevate the interests and perspectives of more privileged groups.[73] Hence, since existing legislative forums are more likely to favor existing power relationships, political activists fighting inequality often eschew them, choosing to rely instead on actions outside established decision-making procedures.[74]

If public decision-making forums disfavor disadvantaged groups, including those harmed by pornography, a politics challenging similar harms will begin by strengthening their self-organization. Recall that the history of political, social, economic, or cultural subordination shared by such groups often creates an "oppositional consciousness"[75] reflecting their perspectives and interests and how they conflict with those of more privileged groups. Following Young, a "perspective" in this sense implies common bases for discussion that do not determine the outcome, while an "interest" is more suggestive of common and specific goals.[76] Accordingly, a perspective among sex industry survivors might incorporate the view that pornography is a sexually exploitative and abusive expression of inequality. Yet this perspective does not by itself set forth a policy that will address pornography most effectively. By contrast, an "interest" would be expressed in more concrete terms, for example, encompassing the policy goal to abolish prostitution and support those victimized by it.

The priority of articulating the perspectives and interests of particularly disadvantaged groups may differ from, and sometimes be in direct conflict with, other progressive groups' preferences, including more generally oriented feminists. Therefore, like Weldon and Htun reasoned regarding survivors of violence against women, the consciousness-raising process and the mobilization necessary to translate the perspectives and interests of sex industry survivors into policy and law "cannot be developed in more generally focused organizations or in settings where [their] group concerns must be subordinated to other sorts of imperatives."[77] Given this and related factors, Young suggests providing more solid public support for the "self-organization" of disadvantaged groups on the rationale "that they gain a sense of collective empowerment and a reflective understanding of their collective experience and interests in the context of the society."[78]

Given Young's essential support for grassroots social movements and the knowledge that historically disadvantaged groups are inadequately represented within established public decision-making institutions, her proposal for mechanisms that oblige decision-makers to account for these groups' perspectives makes sense.[79] In the case of pornography, the evidence demonstrates that its consumption contributes to harming prostituted and battered women in particular. Therefore, states could legally mandate that decision-makers, under specified circumstances, give special consideration to legal briefs or other submissions by legitimate organizations[80] on behalf of these groups. Additionally, laws could require that vital decisions and policies affecting them account for the potential consequences to these groups explicitly.

Young has also advocated for political quotas for members of disadvantaged groups—not necessarily in parliamentary assemblies, but also in decision-making bodies with issue-specific and narrower mandates—a less controversial form of political quota.[81] One could imagine such quotas being established for commissions preparing relevant legal reforms or institutions that interpret laws applicable to disadvantaged groups. In light of the compelling harms that pornography causes to prostituted and battered women, Young's proposal to extend veto power to groups representing those most vulnerable on public decisions immediately affecting their interests appears warranted.[82]

One rationale for supporting more assertive representation for disadvantaged groups in the forms Young envisaged is that it compels more privileged groups to reckon with social facts and circumstances they are unaware of, whether by accident or design.[83] Another is that the invocation of notions of the "common good" in public deliberations frequently favors the self-interests of the privileged,[84] whereas the affirmative representation of less favored groups militates against the former's interest being "masked as an impartial or general interest."[85] For example, the harms of pornography are often framed as an issue of free expression, with absolute freedom conceived as promoting the common good, whatever the empirical reality may be.[86] In such situations, quotas for groups that are particularly harmed by pornography would balance this skewed perspective. More specifically, insofar as they are better situated to anticipate the effects of policies and ideals that affect them, absolute expressive freedom prominent among them, their representation would contribute to public knowledge, especially during policy deliberations.[87] In addition, greater representation of disadvantaged groups is needed to counter the interests of groups that benefit from the persistence of existing inequalities and exploitation.[88] Pornography's consumers, producers, distributors, and other business profiteers all have vested interests in maintaining the status quo; the representation of those who are exploited and harmed by this state of affairs could effectively disrupt it.

The theory of power and hierarchy articulated by the political scientist and legal scholar Ian Shapiro complements Young's perspective. He argues that there are essentially two forms of hierarchy within democracies: one, such as a teacher "requiring a student to do her homework," is associated with legitimate "power"; the other, such as a teacher "taking advantage of his powerful position to engage in sexual harassment of her," is associated with "domination."[89] Shapiro follows in Machiavelli's footsteps, where democracy is viewed as a means of countering relationships of domination, in contrast to Jean-Jacques Rousseau's view of democracy as a vessel for delivering the "general will that reflects the common good."[90] Shapiro thus argues that "democracy is better thought of as a means of managing power relations so as to minimize domination."[91] Consistent with Young, he observes that deliberative politics is insufficient on its own in a society with inequalities caused by social domination. However, if groups subjected to social domination are "strengthened" in deliberative processes where their "basic interests" are threatened, it can be countered.[92]

Although Shapiro agrees with Young that supporting disadvantaged groups in public deliberations can increase public "wisdom," he maintains that challenging domination by shifting the "bargaining power" in their direction is a sufficient objective in itself that requires no further rationalization in terms of added learning.[93] Consistent with Young's concept of veto power,[94] Shapiro also argues that similar means be afforded to groups to "appeal, delay, and in extreme cases even veto" public decisions to the extent that they "are vulnerable to the powers of others because they have basic interests at stake in a given setting."[95] Those groups shown to be most severely harmed by pornography are indeed "vulnerable" to the extent that their vital interests are at stake in its regulation. To Shapiro, the distinction of a group that is under domination relative to groups that are not dominated is particularly important, since "[u]nless we limit rights of delay to those whose basic interests are threatened, we privilege the status quo, making it impossible for government to prevent domination."[96] Extending veto rights to any group whose interests are threatened, even where the only threat posed would entail a potential loss of privilege, is more consistent with liberal negative rights disfavoring public interventions than positive rights favoring progressive interventions.

Jane Mansbridge observes that a "history of dominance and subordination typically breeds inattention, even arrogance, on the part of the dominant group and distrust on the part of the subordinate group."[97] In such a context, when men and women have conflicting interests, and women's interests have been historically unarticulated, women's greater political representation promotes equality.[98] Pornography presents a conflict of interests prone to heighten distrust between the sexes since it exploits sex inequality and breeds gender-based violence. Without more robust substantive equality and political representation of those women who are targeted, their perspectives and interests are likely to be disregarded. Mansbridge further contends that where dominant populations "have ever" intentionally thwarted or criminalized attempts among oppressed groups to represent themselves, or where there is a "history of strong prejudice" against them, those oppressed have a strong case for "affirmative selective representation."[99] As many nations traditionally regarded prostituted persons as criminals, a fact that made it difficult, if not impossible, for them to represent themselves publicly, they seem entitled to affirmative representation.

When considering the groups most harmed by pornography, it is essential to note that a greater representation of women, in general, may create an illusion that deliberation is improved and that domination of those most harmed by pornography is countered. However, it is difficult to know how women generally would represent those particularly harmed by pornography. Compared to women overall, prostituted and battered women are more likely to be subjected to the worst of pornography's harms—both those to which producers subject performers (who are often recruited from among prostituted persons), as well as those caused by consumers (e.g., increased sexual aggression and coerced imitation of pornography). The presence of multiple disadvantages, such as race and poverty, may also increase exposure to such harms, elevating the risk of being exploited in prostitution and pornography. Likewise, race may render some populations more vulnerable to sexual aggression, including sexual harassment,[100] which is amplified by greater pornography consumption.[101] Race (or class) may also be a factor that reduces public concern for those victimized, the severity of the abuse notwithstanding.[102]

Given the characteristics of those more likely to be exposed to the harms of pornography, women in legislatures may not share their perspectives and interests. Furthermore, their constituents may not provide them with the necessary information and incentives to seek insight into the harms of pornography. Put otherwise, female politicians, in general, may lack the social "consciousness" essential for mobilizing the interests and experiential knowledge of the groups harmed and may lack a political rationale to represent them. These problems may be more intense when politicians or other decision-makers who ostensibly represent disadvantaged groups receive their constituents' uncritical support.[103] For these reasons, facilitating the self-organization of distinct social groups that share a history of subordination caused in part by pornography will be critical to mounting a successful challenge to ongoing domination.

The legislative arena is often built upon the cooperation and coexistence of men and women, which by design is not conducive to the social mobilization of "oppositional consciousness" found in autonomous organizations challenging social domination as evidenced in violence against women or the production and consumption of pornography. An effective strategy to empower those victimized would thus account for the fact that a general descriptive representation of women in legislatures or other decision-making fora may sometimes be counterproductive, offering pro-pornographers false legitimacy through symbolic gender representation.[104]

Intersectionality

The theory of multiple structures of social oppression elaborated by Kimberle Crenshaw—the law professor who popularized the political and legal concept of intersectional discrimination[105]—can be applied to the problem of legally challenging pornography. Among other things, Crenshaw analyzed how "Black women are marginalized in the interface between antidiscrimination law and race and gender hierarchies,"[106] using the metaphor of a basement filled with different people to illustrate the problems of intersectional discrimination:

> Imagine a basement which contains all people who are disadvantaged on the basis of race, sex, class, sexual preference, age and/or physical ability. These people are stacked—feet standing on shoulders—with those on the bottom being disadvantaged by the full array of factors, up to the very top, where the heads of all those disadvantaged by a singular factor brush up against the ceiling. Their ceiling is actually the floor above [on] which only those who are *not* disadvantaged in any way reside. In efforts to correct some aspects of domination, those above the ceiling admit from the basement only those who can say that "but for" the ceiling, they too would be in the upper room. A hatch is developed through which those placed immediately below can crawl. Yet this hatch is generally available only to those who—due to the singularity of their burden and their otherwise privileged position relative to those below—are in the position to crawl through. Those who are multiply-burdened are generally left below unless they can somehow pull themselves into the groups that are permitted to squeeze through the hatch.[107]

Crenshaw's basement metaphor illustrates the obstacles confronting those exploited or harmed by the pornography industry who seek to influence policy in democracies. Sex industry survivors are burdened with what Crenshaw would describe as a number of additional "but for" factors that preclude their protection under singular categories of legal disadvantage. For instance, many survivors describe their daily experiences as tantamount to paid rape, regardless of whether they are bought for sex in legal or illegal venues.[108] Even some johns use similar terms to describe prostitution.[109] Much of the abuse endured by those victimized might have constituted legal rape "but for" the fact that they were *paid* for sex. Yet these people tend to enter prostitution due to multiple disadvantages that create coercive circumstances essentially forcing them into the sex industry, often precisely to get the money to survive, whether in prostitution on- or off-camera. However, those in prostitution cannot use a rape law that is premised explicitly on the use of physical violence or threats or which requires evidence of such to legally establish nonconsent—an approach commonly seen in the law of rape.[110] In addition, those in prostitution are frequently not regarded as raped even when apparently forced by violence or threats and de facto robbery (when the buyer fails to pay).[111] This situation may be exacerbated by widespread bigotry in society and among members of the judiciary. Most existing laws against sexual abuse and exploitation, including laws against rape, sexual coercion, torture, and assault, have been similarly ineffective in the domain of pornography. They were simply not intended to adequately address the daily exploitation and harm the industry entails for those used in the production of pornography.

Put otherwise, the multiple disadvantages of those exploited in the sex industry are far too numerous to be comprehended by a one-dimensional social theory or redressed by a simplistic legal concept of victimization. To reiterate, this population has typically been subjected not only to severe poverty but also to the disadvantages accruing from early child abuse and neglect, running away from home, homelessness, and insufficient education and job training. Such conditions often lead them to engage in criminal behavior just to survive, thus compounding their problems with the stigma and obstacles resulting from having a criminal record. Considering Crenshaw's concept of intersectionality, the dominant political and legal systems have not adequately recognized, far less remediated, the problems typically plaguing the lives of prostituted people. The multitude of causes underlying their disadvantage makes it virtually impossible for them to "squeeze through"[112] the narrow needle's eye of the law that might otherwise afford them some restitution.

The difficulties confronting decision-makers seeking to address intersectional disadvantages frequently lead to what Crenshaw describes as a situation analogous to a traffic accident at an intersection where multiple vehicles collide, an individual is harmed, but ambulances and doctors refuse to intervene unless the person responsible for the injuries is both identified and covered by medical insurance.[113] An analogous situation prevails with prostituted people, who, beyond being frequently deprived of necessary treatment, support, or even recognition as crime victims, have historically been regarded as responsible for the abuse and sexual exploitation perpetrated on them. For instance, despite that the overwhelming majority of those in prostitution wish to escape it,[114] many have been additionally burdened by criminal fines and sometimes jail time because of being prostituted, and by the practical and public victim-blaming that attends being labeled a criminal under the laws of many nations, which is sometimes as severe as or more severe than what is directed toward the pimps and profiteers who exploit them.

Crenshaw argues that if law, rather than addressing singular disadvantages in seriatim, began addressing intersectional disadvantages and "the needs and problems of those who are most disadvantaged[,] restructuring and remaking the world where necessary, then others who are singularly disadvantaged would also benefit."[115] Conversely, a democratic theory that addresses the problems of groups that are multiply disadvantaged and situated at a complex nexus of conflicting democratic rights and freedoms—which people prostituted in pornography have been under existing law and legal interpretations—could also benefit other groups disadvantaged in less complex situations. Crenshaw's basement metaphor thus implies that when prostituted people "'enter'" and crawl through the top hatch, "'we all enter.'"[116] The concept of intersectionality entails that legal strategies to address the harms of pornography should include those groups that have been most severely disenfranchised, burdened by distinctions that historically excluded them from protection and restitution under the law. Those exploited in pornography and other forms of prostitution belong to this group. Legally unprotected upon reaching the age of majority, the abusive treatment they endure has been disregarded as an unexceptional feature of paid sex or similarly rationalized in a manner that perpetuates inaction under existing laws, distinguishing it from how domestic abuse or rape would be facially addressed. Thus the pernicious consequences precipitated by being used daily for numerous unwanted sex acts are not legally cognized as equal to one instance of rape outside of prostitution.

As presently written, distinctions in the legal conception of gender-based violence fail to comprehend the coercive circumstances and abuse present in pornography and prostitution, rather minimizing them. Consistent with a hierarchy theory of group representation, those who have experienced such abuse are better situated to conceptualize what would be required to successfully challenge these conditions than those who have not.[117] Hence, pornography-related abuse survivors' perspectives must be taken into account, grounding the choice of strategies when formulating legal challenges—legislative, judicial, or otherwise. Considering the barriers confronting outsiders seeking to gain access to and reliable information from people currently being exploited in the sex industry,[118] exited survivors' perspectives may often be the most reliable sources available. While many, if not most, remain vulnerable, survivors are not in the same position of dependency on the sex industry as many of those currently being exploited. Those directing survivor-led organizations are experienced organizers and are gaining greater influence over public opinion.[119] In contrast to the sex industry itself, these groups lack the incentive to produce misinformation calculated to increase profits from others' sexual exploitation.

Postmodern Theory

An alternative approach critical of hierarchy theory is promulgated by a group of scholars that may be denoted "postmodernists." They question the usefulness of legal rights for challenging male dominance per se. Perhaps the best-known exponent of this position is Judith Butler, who more or less rejects the notion that legal challenges to hate speech or the harms caused by pornography may emancipate subordinated groups such as women, people of color, or sexual minorities:

> Consider that hate speech is not only a production of the state . . . but that the very intentions that animate the legislation are inevitably misappropriated by the state. . . . It will not simply engage in a legal discourse on racial and sexual slurring, but it will also reiterate and restage those slurs, this time as state-sanctioned speech.[120]

Butler's account seems to assume that pornography can be equated with hate speech in a legal context. From that dubious surmise, Butler claims that Catharine MacKinnon "argues that pornography ought to be construed as a kind of hate speech and that it both communicates and enacts a message of subordination."[121] In fact, nowhere does MacKinnon equate hate speech and pornography, though she opposes both on different grounds.[122] Likening pornography to hate speech disregards it as a social practice that relies on sexual exploitation to arouse consumers sexually; by contrast, a "text" or a "speech" by the Ku Klux Klan can be published or spoken without exploiting anyone, with sexual arousal being at most a potential side effect.

Butler concludes her argument by considering to what extent "the state produces and reproduces hate speech" (and, presumably, the injuries associated with pornography), stating that "[t]he only question that remains is: How will that repetition occur, at what site, juridical or nonjuridical, and with what pain and promise?"[123] Beyond a general skepticism toward law, she articulates no conclusive position.[124] This reluctance to take a political stance is consistent with the systematic tendency in her work to employ skeptical questions and multivocal sentences, even near the end of her argument where one would expect more decisive claims, which force readers to arrive at any such conclusions by process of deduction.[125]

The political scientist Wendy Brown develops a similar position as Butler's in *States of Injury: Power and Freedom in Late Modernity*, where she asks: "When does legal recognition become an instrument of regulation, and political recognition become an instrument of subordination?"[126] She further describes the problematic of abstract personhood assumed under gender-neutral liberal rights based on the presumption of a similitude among individuals without regard to class, race, or other social particularities. For instance, Brown approvingly reiterates Marx's "criticisms of bourgeois rights," pointing to the contradictions between a liberal "illusory politics of equality, liberty, and community in the domain of the state," and a substantive politics characterized by "the unequal, unfree, and individualistic domain of civil society."[127] Drawing upon Marx, Brown's critique is not unlike the one expressed here regarding the liberal concept of "negative rights."[128] Indeed, in Brown's terms, such negative rights may quickly "become an instrument of subordination."[129]

In her further rendition of Marxism, Brown suggests that liberal "bourgeois" forms of rights "legitimize by naturalizing various stratifying social powers in civil society, and they disguise the state's collusion with this social power, thereby also legitimating the state as a neutral and universal representative of the people."[130] Again, her statement is not unlike the criticism advanced in this chapter, which argues that the liberal concept of negative rights misrepresents the role of the state as a neutral arbiter protecting freedom when, in fact, it often acts, as Brown would put it, in "collusion" with "social power,"[131] thereby protecting the private abuse of women by men through a politics of toleration.

Likewise, Brown criticizes the "analysis of abortion proffered by liberal legal and political theorist Bruce Ackerman, an analysis that does not once mention gender, women, or the constitution of gender through regimes of sexuality and reproductive work."[132] She maintains that even Ackerman's "grammar . . . suppresses the fact that it is women who have abortions, that conception and abortions occur at the site of women's bodies, and that this site is the effect of the very social powers (of women's subordination) making abortion a political issue in the first place."[133] In a separate but related piece, Brown notes that framing abortion rights as emanating from a " 'constitutional right to privacy' "[134] neglects the substantive inequality at issue: "grant women formal legal equality, and grant them limited abortion rights on the basis of privacy, and watch the analytic disappearance of the social powers constitutive of women's unfree and unequal condition as reproductive workers. Instead, watch the public debate for decades whether or not a fetus is a person."[135] Here, Brown's rhetorical question—"How does a liberal discourse of generic personhood reinscribe rather than emancipate us from male dominance?"—seems amply justified,[136] not least when considering that coercive circumstances and lack of choices often precipitate abortions.[137] Yet that is precisely why democratic theorists like Young argue for recognizing particularized group rights, including group veto power for women on reproductive rights policy.[138]

The approaches to group rights and representation advanced by proponents of hierarchy theory are fundamentally opposed to the abstract "bourgeois" or "generic" rights criticized by Brown. Hierarchy theory advances group rights built from knowledge generated by historically subordinated groups' direct experiences and social consciousness. By contrast, the liberal negative rights criticized by Brown are abstract and supposedly universally applicable to all of humanity. However, upon closer inspection, it is apparent that they derive primarily from the experiences, perspectives, and political imperatives of privileged, presumptively white men. In many ways, the "postmodern" feminist critique of rights identifies the same essential problem as scholars relying on hierarchy theory. However, these two schools of thought reach different conclusions on how to address it.

For instance, in her critique of MacKinnon, whose work on sexual harassment and pornography incisively deploys the concept of group rights against harmful hierarchical practices,[139] Brown alleges that such rights are "abetting rather than contesting" social dominance and "discursively renaturaliz[ing]" social powers; "rights must not be confused with equality nor legal recognition with emancipation," she rhetorically concludes.[140] Brown apparently says that just as "liberal discourse . . . reinscribes rather than emancipates us from male dominance,"[141] group rights intending to counter such domination do the same. According to this critique, the "positive" representation of historically disadvantaged groups' perspectives and interests would theoretically produce the same results in practice as those assertedly resulting from the fundamentally opposed "negative" concept of rights embodied in liberalism. Recall that "negative rights" were criticized for their implicit grounding in privileged men's general interest in being protected from the arbitrary abuse of state power—a concept of rights that unduly downplays other abuses of power such as domestic violence and labor exploitation, thus reinscribing existing hierarchical social relations.

Butler reaches a similar endpoint through a different line of argument when she alleges that laws intending to combat group-based injuries arising from conditions of dominance (e.g., hate-speech regulations) would produce counter-intentional results by being inevitably "misappropriated" by the state.[142] Butler does not propose any legal alternative, concluding instead that the "only question" is when and where the state will "repeat" the injury of the hate speech it seeks to regulate.[143] By contrast, Brown suggests a legal alternative in *States of Injury* consisting of "empty signifiers":

> If rights figure freedom and incite the desire for it only to the degree that they are void of content, empty signifiers without corresponding entitlements, then paradoxically they may be incitements to freedom only to the extent that they discursively deny the workings of the substantive social power limiting freedom. In their emptiness, they function to encourage possibility through discursive denial of historically layered and institutionally secured bounds, by denying with words the effects of relatively wordless, politically invisible, yet potent material constraints. . . . It is, rather, in their abstraction from the particulars of our lives—and in their figuration

of an egalitarian political community—that they may be most valuable in the democratic transformation of these particulars.[144]

Put succinctly, Brown advances a concept of rights without "content" that nevertheless "incites" the desire for freedom and figures an "egalitarian political community," but does not identify any particular grounds so as not to "renaturalize" their oppression. Taking her concept of rights at face value, any positive rights, including protections against the discriminatory impact of facially neutral laws, where the grounds of sex/gender, race, or sexuality are recognized to identify disadvantage and promote equality (e.g., affirmative action), will by definition be incapable of serving as "empty signifiers without corresponding entitlements." Brown's concept of abstract equality rights may be compatible with protections against facial discrimination by law or "negative rights" against state interventions that might otherwise contradict formal equality; however, they will be incompatible with substantive equality rights where discriminatory grounds are identified. Put otherwise, Brown disfavors doing anything against the discriminatory impact of laws that are facially but not practically neutral. Somewhat incongruously, then, Brown adopts the same universalizing posture that she previously criticized for failing to address the substantive inequality underlying women's subjection to male dominance in sexuality and reproductive work.[145]

Brown's seemingly contradictory positions on rights invite the question of how abstract rights, encouraged "through discursive denial" but absent claims of "entitlement," can possibly challenge any "potent material constraints,"[146] such as gender-based violence or sexual exploitation. This question may be answered by looking at the underlying ontological assumptions of power, social dominance, and sex inequality in postmodern theory. These assumptions are expressed indirectly, for instance, when Butler criticizes the putative approach of MacKinnon (who advocates recognizing and remedying inequality through the extension of group-based rights) and others with whom Butler disagrees. Subsuming her opponents under the rubric of "Gender theory," Butler contends that their scholarship "misunderstands the ways in which that asymmetrical relation between the sexes is installed through the primary workings of language, which presuppose the production of the unconscious."[147] According to Butler, such an "analysis of gender . . . tends toward a sociologism, neglecting the symbolic or psychoanalytic account by which masculine and feminine are established in language prior to any given social configuration."[148] Butler here emphasizes language as the foundation of sex inequality. Brown seemingly assumes the same role for language, preferring rights against dominance that "encourage possibility through discursive denial . . . by denying with words" otherwise "relatively wordless" material inequalities.[149]

Brown's postmodern political strategy relies on language and abstract equality rights that "deny" inequality, and it rejects concrete rights that do not deny but instead identify and challenge substantive inequality. In opposing multidimensional forms of dominance and discrimination that cover practices ranging from reproductive politics, childrearing, and discriminatory pay at work to sexual exploitation, pornography, and media stereotypes, Brown and Butler advocate, if not a linchpin linguistic theory of inequality, then a theory in which language is the leading site for progressive, or "subversive," resistance. Indeed, Brown employs an arguably obfuscatory poststructuralist vocabulary to imply that MacKinnon lacks insight into the linguistic realm, relying on a theory said to be "at odds with poststructuralist insights about . . . social subjects who bear some capacity for subversive *resignification*."[150]

Locating social dominance primarily in the workings of language—as distinguished from the organization of sexuality, labor, housework, reproductive politics, or gender-based violence—carries with it the danger of being "totalizing" to the extent that it reduces social complexity to accommodate a singular linchpin theory that only recognizes resistance to power when it occurs in the linguistic domain.[151] The empirical evidence on pornography does not suggest language to be particularly constitutive of its harms. The gender inequality that pornography has been documented to promote is the product of its impact on violence against women, effectuated through the exacerbation of attitudes supporting violence against women and the sexually exploitative conditions of its production. None of these three elements appears to be dependent per se on the "primary workings of language," even though language is often the vehicle by which attitudes and demands are communicated. Neither does empirical evidence suggest that language is the underlying phenomenon producing these effects. As a harmful *social practice* of inequality based on sex that exploits and produces multiple social disadvantages, it is counterintuitive to interpret pornography primarily, even secondarily, as a sort of linguistic game. In this sense, Butler and Brown are indeed correct in asserting that those who advocate group-based rights as a means of opposing sex inequality base their theory on a "sociologism" that does not recognize "language" as the predominant cause for social dominance. Contrary to Butler's and Brown's theories, hierarchy theory centers on society and social conditions. Language occupies a position on par with several important factors that are neither diminished nor amplified by the others.

Crenshaw has criticized theories that conflate "the power exercised simply through the process of categorization" with the "power to cause that categorization to have social and material consequences," dismissing them as forms of "vulgar constructionism."[152] Vulgar constructionism challenges only the "categorization" of, for example, de jure sexist stereotypes of submissive women, or sexism, but fails to challenge their "social and material consequences," for example, the de facto sexual exploitation of women, sexism, or women's submission.[153] According to Crenshaw, vulgar constructionism holds "that since all categories are socially constructed, there is no such thing as, say, Blacks or women, and thus it makes no sense to continue reproducing those categories by organizing around them."[154] The disavowal of group politics imbues Butler's and Brown's skeptical postmodernism. For instance, when Brown claims that institutionalizing rights based on the social consciousness of historically subordinated groups will "discursively renaturalize" social powers rather than "discursively deny" them,[155] she is reflecting the position of vulgar constructionism by which group rights will simply "continue reproducing" social categories such as Blacks or women.[156] By contrast, Crenshaw sees such "vulgar constructionism" as distinguishable from legitimate constructivist critiques that "leave room for identity politics."[157] Brown's and Butler's politics do not leave much room for identity politics based on historically oppressed groups' oppositional consciousness. Indeed, Brown effectively dismisses the legal codification of subordinated groups' perspectives and interests by conceptualizing rights as "empty signifiers without corresponding entitlements."[158] Her "discursive denial" of "potent material constraints" suggests a denial of the constraints of group-based oppression and with it a denial of a politics that could effectively challenge that same material reality.

The claims of postmodern theory regarding legal challenges to pornography and its harms are also sweepingly broad. After all, a "renaturalization" of women's subordination or a "misappropriation" of laws and legal discourse may, if taken seriously, occur in many contexts far removed from pornography statutes themselves. As the postmodern account would have it, a discourse on women's equality within a legal challenge to pornography could be misappropriated to support international military interventions in non-western religiously conservative societies, putatively as a means to promote gender equality if men in the latter were perceived as more patriarchal and sexist than westernized men. Similarly, a discourse on gender-based violence situated within such a challenge could be misappropriated by democratic majorities to support racially discriminatory and otherwise arbitrary domestic interventions among vulnerable minority or religious groups, including overzealous surveillance of families. In theory, powerful public institutions can misappropriate nearly anything, including civil rights laws targeting distinctions based on race and any prohibitions against rape, sexual harassment, domestic violence, or child abuse. This position fails to consider, among other things, what is to be done with respect to those victimized by legally prohibited practices.

In addition to its overbreadth, which amounts to a reductionist anti-state position assumed within a void bereft of understanding of unequal social status, the explanatory power of postmodern theory as applied to legal challenges to pornography is very difficult to verify empirically. For instance, to the extent that it matters what governments say to motivate their military or racially discriminatory actions for purposes of evaluating pornography laws, it raises the question of how many instances of government speech would need to be analyzed to refute or verify the postmodern hypothesis that pornography laws can inferentially contribute to gender "renaturalization" elsewhere in society. Although postmodernists have not targeted them, similar problems would arise, for example, in considering equal pay laws. In these respects, the implications of Butler's and Brown's postmodernism amount to what the methods literature refers to as "stretching the theory beyond all plausibility by adding numerous exceptions and special cases" that must be controlled for, which in turn creates a theory that is "invulnerable to disconfirmation."[159] Additionally, none of the postmodern critics has offered an alternative approach to the real production and consumption harms of pornography unburdened by the problems they say exist. The underlying normative posture appears to be that women's situation should not be improved by government action and that their needs—perhaps with isolated exceptions—should not be responded to or taken into account in determining public policy.

Because the claims of postmodern theory are so difficult to confirm or rebut empirically, being essentially conjectural, there can be no systematic test of its approach to pornography analogous to the comparative case study design employed in testing hierarchy theory.[160] Hierarchy theory, by contrast, can be tested, here by combining qualitative within-case methods that include pattern matching and a small-*n* comparison of Canada, Sweden, and the United States.[161] The animating question is to what extent institutionalizing the perspectives and political and legal interests of historically subordinated groups, particularly prostitution survivors and battered women, is likely to redound in progressive policy change. To the extent it does, it supports hierarchy theory.

Summary

This chapter sets forth several theories that may shed light on the obstacles and possibilities for undertaking successful legal challenges to pornography, gender-based violence, and sexual exploitation in modern democracies. It identifies barriers in the solutions early liberals offered to the dangers of public abuses of power, including the separation of governmental powers and circumscribed public mandate for intervention in social or putatively private affairs—a constitutional politics based on a cramped conception of liberty and democracy. The harms attending pornography production and those perpetrated by consumers are overwhelmingly caused by non-state actors, though effectively tolerated by public powers.

Addressing the problems, contemporary democratic theories—here collectively termed "hierarchy theory"—suggest that recognizing those disadvantaged groups that are particularly victimized by pornography's harms provides indispensable grounding for substantive policy and legal challenges. Theories of political representation and intersectional discrimination highlight the confluence of multiple disadvantages related to pornography production survivors' perspectives and interests and those most exposed to the consumers' harmful behaviors, making them best situated to ground efficient legal challenges. By contrast, the singular theories of disadvantage that currently inform most laws against gender-based violence and sexual exploitation exclude them from protection, support, or restitution. Prior research shows that disadvantaged groups are more efficient in generating the knowledge needed to improve their condition within autonomous organizations, as opposed to participating in more general organizations with priorities that may conflict with or inhibit their agendas.

An alternative theory is suggested by "postmodern" accounts that, contrary to hierarchy theory, hold that democracies should refrain from recognizing vulnerable or subordinated groups in legal or policy processes. Its proponents contend that anti-pornography or hate speech laws will inevitably be misappropriated by the state, which will ultimately replicate the very injuries the laws were intended to remediate.[162] Instead, a postmodern approach suggests using generic rights devoid of content as abstract aspirational ideals of equality and freedom, allowing for their reification without "corresponding entitlements."[163] However, a critique of the postmodern position from the viewpoint of hierarchy theory suggests that it leads to the same problems identified in the classic liberal concept of "negative rights," where the law largely ignores abuse by non-state actors. Without acknowledging historically obscured abuse by recognizing the social groups concerned, there is little possibility of challenging it under law, hierarchy theorists would argue. An intersectional critique similarly charges the postmodern position with being a form of "vulgar constructionism" that leaves no room for "identity politics" among groups with a shared condition of social oppression that would benefit from the legal recognition that postmodernism denies them.[164]

A significant question that emerges is to what extent recognizing the grounds of social dominance in legal challenges to pornography's harms has led to progressive legal change and impacted gender-based violence and sexual exploitation. A related question is to what extent the absence of recognition has affected progressive policies and harms from pornography.

PART II

THE UNITED STATES

4

The Anti-pornography Civil Rights Ordinances, 1983–1991

In the late 1970s, radicals within the women's movement began to articulate a more forceful critique of pornography. The feminist critique of pornography entered the public sphere before it was conceptualized and presented as a legal challenge. The first significant legal move came in Minneapolis in 1983. Residents of the Central and Powderhorn Park neighborhoods in Minneapolis—who at that time were generally poor and working class, predominantly people of color (i.e., Black, Native American, and Southeast Asian), and some political activists who had been living there since the 1960s—were disproportionately exposed to "adult establishments" such as pornography theaters and stores.[1] Patrons were drawn from throughout greater metropolitan Minneapolis–St. Paul and were emboldened to sexually harass women and children and solicit random pedestrians for prostitution. Faced with higher crime rates, women reported persistent fears that they and their children were vulnerable in their own neighborhoods.[2]

Local activists, who had fought against pornography businesses since the first stores and theaters opened in the 1970s, noted that city elites' vigorous support for civil liberties in defense of pornography did not prevent them from using zoning laws and other available means to effectively prohibit these establishments from being sited in their own predominantly white, relatively affluent areas.[3] This substantial cohort of visitors to these de facto red light districts could thus return to the protected zones where they lived; disadvantaged populations living in the exposed areas could not.[4]

Due to a number of local social and political trends and events that were coalescing at the time, Catharine MacKinnon and Andrea Dworkin were invited to address the Minneapolis City Council's Zoning and Planning Committee on October 18, 1983, about the problems posed by pornography.[5] Dworkin rejected the idea of using zoning laws to ameliorate the situation, arguing that it would simply shift the sources of contention to someone else's backyard, thus "'permit[ting] the dissemination of materials that

Pornography. Max Waltman, Oxford University Press. © Oxford University Press 2021.
DOI: 10.1093/oso/9780197598535.003.0005

uphold the inferior status'" and "'the exploitation of live women.'"[6] Professor MacKinnon continued their presentation, suggesting that, rather than zoning pornography, the city should be "'taking a civil rights approach.'"[7] She urged that listeners "'consider that pornography as it subordinates women to men is a form of discrimination on the basis of sex. You already have an ordinance against sex-based discrimination in this city. You have the jurisdiction to make laws against forms of discrimination.'"[8]

Mindful that previous attempts to challenge pornography in Minneapolis had failed, the City Council decided to hire MacKinnon and Dworkin to hold public hearings and develop a civil rights approach to address the harms of pornography.[9] The major players who worked most intensely to pass the anti-pornography civil rights ordinance that emerged, estimated to number somewhere between fifty and two hundred city-wide, included neighborhood activists, local politicians, and a larger group of anti-pornography activists, among whom were battered women and students, some having taken a course on pornography offered at the University of Minnesota by MacKinnon and Dworkin during the fall 1983 term.[10] During the legislative process, additional calls went out to the city's network of community organizations, including women's shelters, rape crisis centers, social workers, and other groups seeking potential witnesses for the hearings.[11] Individual survivors who had been exploited and abused through the production of pornography and harmed by the consumers provided powerful testimony in support of the ordinance.[12] Consistent with hierarchy theory's emphasis on group representation, the Minneapolis ordinance came into existence in significant part due to the experiences of people who had been directly affected by the documented harms of pornography. By the same token, opposition was expressed throughout the hearings.[13]

A brief outline of the chronology of the major anti-pornography ordinances underscores some of the political stakes involved. The first ordinance was passed by the Minneapolis City Council on December 30, 1983; however, it was vetoed on January 5, 1984, by Mayor Donald Fraser, who had already made up his mind and did not attend the hearings.[14] An identical ordinance was passed on July 13, 1984, and once again vetoed by Mayor Fraser.[15] A similar anti-pornography ordinance was passed in Indianapolis in 1984 but invalidated by the Seventh Circuit Court of Appeals without having been tested.[16] After Indianapolis, the ordinance resurfaced again as a voter-initiated law in Cambridge, Massachusetts. There, the political scientist, then graduate student, Amy Elman and the journalist, then student,

Barbara Findlen, with the help of other activists, almost succeeded in passing it by a referendum.[17] But first, they had to sue the Cambridge City Council, which, in contravention of existing law, refused to put the ordinance on the ballot;[18] it was included only upon the order of the State Supreme Court.[19] The ordinance was ultimately defeated, 42% to 58%.[20] A similar referendum succeeded in Bellingham, Washington, in 1988, when it garnered the support of 62% of voters.[21] However, after being challenged in court again, the still unused ordinance was invalidated by summary judgment in federal district court, citing the Seventh Circuit's 1985 decision.[22] It appears that the plaintiffs avoided appealing the decision for strategic reasons, assessing the Ninth Circuit Court of Appeals as constituted at the time to be adverse to their interests and possibly expecting that other challenges would be brought in federal courts elsewhere in the near term.[23] Attempts to pass the ordinance were also made in Los Angeles, California (1985), and in the state of Massachusetts (1991), but they too were unsuccessful.[24]

Evidence, Equality, and Representation

Recall that hierarchy theory suggests that a successful challenge to the social dominance of pornography's beneficiaries by the multiply and intersectionally disadvantaged groups that are subordinated by its practices is best founded upon laws that recognize substantive inequality among people as opposed to treating all groups and individuals as formally equal. Moreover, these laws should be drafted with the perspectives and interests of the disadvantaged at the center, thereby promoting substantive equality. By promoting substantive equality through recognition of disadvantaged populations victimized by pornography and by representing their perspectives and advancing their interests with precision, the anti-pornography civil rights ordinances instantiated this theory of hierarchy.

Substantive Equality and Perspective

The Minneapolis City Council found pornography to be "a systematic practice of exploitation and subordination based on sex which differentially harms women."[25] This conclusion is in keeping with the evidence analyzed in Part I. The Council also determined that pornography is "central in creating and maintaining the civil inequality of the sexes" and that the "bigotry and contempt" that pornography "promotes," including the "aggression it fosters," will "harm women's opportunities for equality of rights" in a number of spheres.[26] Thus, in the Council's words, pornography promotes "rape, battery and prostitution and inhibit[s] just enforcement of laws against these acts."[27] Violence against women, partly fueled by pornography, is indeed widespread in society, creating systematic fears and worries among women,[28] which the Council acknowledged further "contribute significantly to restricting women from full exercise of citizenship and participation in public life, including in neighborhoods."[29] Put briefly, the effects of pornography acknowledged by the Council negatively impact women's substantive equality to men because pornography promotes social practices and attitudes that subordinate women, including gender-based violence, while trivializing the harms they engender.

In order to promote substantive equality, hierarchy theory suggests that laws should represent the perspectives of disadvantaged groups that are affected by social dominance.[30] One way to operationalize this insight is to incorporate the perspective of the relevant groups into legal definitions of the problem that a law is meant to remedy. The legal definition of pornography set forth in the Minneapolis ordinance accordingly reads:

> (gg) *Pornography.* Pornography is a form of discrimination on the basis of sex.
>
> (1) Pornography is the sexually explicit subordination of women, graphically depicted, whether in pictures or in words, that also includes one or more of the following:
>
> (i) women are presented dehumanized as sexual objects, things or commodities; or
>
> (ii) women are presented as sexual objects who enjoy pain or humiliation; or
>
> (iii) women are presented as sexual objects who experience sexual pleasure in being raped; or
>
> (iv) women are presented as sexual objects tied up or cut up or mutilated or bruised or physically hurt; or
>
> (v) women are presented in postures of sexual submission; or
>
> (vi) women's body parts—including but not limited to vaginas, breasts, and buttocks—are exhibited, such that women are reduced to those parts; or

(vii) women are presented as whores by nature; or

(viii) women are presented being penetrated by objects or animals; or

(ix) women are presented in scenarios of degradation, injury, abasement, torture, shown as filthy or inferior, bleeding, bruised, or hurt in a context that makes these conditions sexual.

(2) The use of men, children, or transsexuals in the place of women in (1) (i–ix) above is pornography [under] . . . this statute.[31]

This definition focuses on the "explicit subordination of women," a practice antithetical to substantive equality and, therefore, reflective of the experiences of those who have been subordinated through pornography. Subordination may, among other things, be manifest in the form of dehumanization or degradation, or in violence against women—concepts that appear in the ordinance. The ordinance's definition of pornography is thus consistent with those developed by social science research in light of the categories of pornography that were proven harmful.[32] Yet degradation and dehumanization are not always understood to be the opposite of social equality. By contrast, the term "subordination" as employed in the Minneapolis ordinance is more clearly antipodean as well as being more consistent with the concept of antidiscrimination law.

There is conceptual coherence among the ordinance's definition of pornography, the types of acts consumers demand, the abuse and subordination inflicted on the women expected to reproduce them, and the acts of abuse or subordination inflicted on women because of its consumption. The definition is, therefore, consistent both with social reality and with the *perspective* of pornography survivors. It was the world's first legal definition to explicitly adopt the perspective of survivors while simultaneously being corroborated by the triangulation of social science evidence and experiential accounts from its consumers. By contrast, the definition of actionable material under U.S. obscenity law established in *Miller v. California* (1973) turns on "(a) whether 'the average person, applying contemporary community standards' would find that the work, taken as a whole, appeals to the prurient interest, (b) whether the work depicts or describes, in a patently offensive way, sexual conduct . . . and (c) whether [it] lacks serious . . . value."[33] *Miller* ignores the fact that pornography creates its own "community standard" by desensitizing consumers, a sizeable subpopulation, leading them to demand materials they would previously have regarded as "offensive," with the market adjusting accordingly. These mechanisms render the obscenity law ineffective. It was for such reasons that the United Nation's Rapporteur on Violence Against Women in 1994 referred to the Minneapolis definition as a "major breakthrough" distinct from prior approaches that "fail to address the issue that most pornography represents a form of violence against women and that the evidence shows that it is directly causative of further violence against women."[34]

An experiment published in 1993 tested the applicability of an antipornography ordinance similar to the one passed in Indianapolis in 1984, comparing it both to existing U.S. obscenity law and to another definition of pornography drafted by the law professor and legal theorist Cass R. Sunstein.[35] Law students were asked to use the three definitions to categorize five sexually explicit texts and one photograph that ranged from, on one hand, materials such as *Hustler*'s photograph *Beaver Hunters* and the pornographic novel *Story of O* to, on the other hand, a sexually explicit scene in Andrea Dworkin's work of "feminist fiction," *Ice and Fire*.[36] Assuming the first two categories should be covered, but not the third, the Indianapolis definition was determined to be more reliable than the other two. U.S. obscenity law was considered overbroad and vague, while Sunstein's definition was unable to sensibly categorize and order the materials.[37] The Indianapolis definition was particularly easy to apply when its definition was qualified to cover materials "whose dissemination in context would tend to subordinate women."[38] Indeed, the legislative history of the definition made clear that it was reliant on such a finding, for instance in the documentation coming from the testimonies and written submissions of survivors, researchers, and other public authorities and experts attesting to the harms that ensue from pornography and situating it within the context of male dominance, gender-based violence, including prostitution.[39]

The ordinance's definition incorporates social science evidence from psychological experiments, including those examined earlier that found it was primarily the degree of objectification, dehumanization, and degradation, along with the portrayal of women as sexually indiscriminate, not the aggression and violence in pornography, that determined outcomes with respect to such phenomena as rape myths. These findings are consistent with the ordinance's conceptualization of nonviolent pornography as the "graphic sexually explicit subordination of women" who are, among other things, "presented dehumanized as sexual objects, things or commodities" or "in postures of sexual submission."[40] Several experimental studies have found that sexist advertisements and R-rated movie scenes portraying "women as sexual beings," or "sexually objectifying" women, or presenting women's principal function as appearing "erotically enticing" to men produce similar attitudes supporting violence against women.[41] Yet these non-pornographic categories, which do not contain "sexually explicit subordination" and thus are not classified as "graphic," are *not* covered under the Minneapolis ordinance. To underscore a crucial point too often lost in the contemporaneous debates, the ordinance only covers provable harms that fall within specifically delineated categories that run the gamut from purportedly nonviolent objectification,[42] to dehumanization and/or degradation,[43] to more violent pornography.[44]

MacKinnon reports that the conceptualization of the harms in the ordinance substantially reflects the accounts of women who shared their own experiences of pornography with Dworkin, often in conjunction with the latter's public speeches.[45] Dworkin's book *Woman Hating* (1974), which included an incisive critique of pornography, had by that time already been published. Dworkin thus writes that when she and MacKinnon were hired to draft the ordinance, she was able to draw on what she had learned directly from survivors.[46] In addition, many accounts that corroborated the validity of the ordinance were placed on the record in the public hearings preceding its passage. There, numerous survivors attested to their personal traumatic experiences of sexual abuse despite the risks, including compromising their anonymity, that coming forward entailed.[47]

In sum, the perspective of the ordinance builds on the perspectives of people disadvantaged and harmed by pornography and converges with the feminist theory and practice of consciousness-raising.[48] In this sense, the results of the legislative deliberations were revolutionary: the legislators sided with the position of the "oppositional consciousness" of pornography survivors, who belong to historically disadvantaged and typically marginalized groups, and who were seeking to generate efficient knowledge and organize to challenge their oppression.[49]

Representing Interests

Hierarchy theory suggests that laws should represent the interests of disadvantaged groups oppressed by social dominance to promote substantive equality.[50] The concept of civil rights law is essential in this context. The American civil rights movement's legacy implies that civil rights laws should share common and specific political objectives in order to elevate the social status of disadvantaged groups. Such objectives stand in stark contrast to the partiality behind the façade of gender-neutrality typical of obscenity laws, where pornography is cast as an offense against the prevailing community standards rather than against survivors of pornography's harms—survivors who are overwhelmingly female. As the next subsection on legal causes of action demonstrates, the Minneapolis ordinance was a law against sex discrimination that gave survivors the right to initiate a claim, in contrast to obscenity laws that extend that right to the state. The drafters' intention was to make the creators and disseminators of pornography directly accountable to the survivors harmed by their actions through civil damages and injunctions, not to seek imprisonment or fines payable to the state as is ordinarily the case under criminal laws.[51]

Moreover, unlike traditional criminal laws, the civil rights approach avoids the higher burden of proof associated with criminal penalties. Rather than requiring proof "beyond a reasonable doubt," a "preponderance of the evidence" standard is employed that diminishes one barrier to effective legal action. The civil rights approach also bypasses prosecutors and law enforcement officials who, along with publicly appointed victim's advocates, ombudsmen, attorneys general, and other public authorities, may have different priorities and be unaware of survivors' perspectives. Since pornography consumption is widespread among men in contemporary society—a result of which is heightened trivialization of sexual abuse—it is also likely that many within the criminal justice system are less willing or able to be representatives of survivors' perspectives and interests.

A civil rights law providing for damage claims and giving survivors the right to initiate action also offers a means of raising public awareness of the problems of pornography, particularly through court testimony provided by survivors. Until such a law exists in a form that the courts uphold, survivors' relative public silence about pornography-related harms will likely persist. Absent monetary or injunctive incentives, those victimized by pornography have little reason to speak publicly about their experiences since doing so may well expose them—at least prior to the #MeToo movement—to the prejudice and contempt commonly directed toward those who disclose sexual information, including information about abuse, in public.

Causes of Action

There were four causes of action under the Minneapolis ordinance.[52] The first cause of action pertained to dissemination, which was referred to as "trafficking in" pornography:

> (1) *Discrimination by trafficking in pornography.* The production, sale, exhibition, or distribution of pornography is discrimination against women by means of trafficking in pornography.[53]

Under this subsection, any woman could employ the ordinance "as a woman acting against the subordination of women."[54] Men or transsexuals could also take action, provided they were injured "in the way women are injured by" pornography.[55] Exceptions were available for public libraries as well as college and university libraries, public and private, for purposes of study, although "special display presentations" were regarded as sex discrimination.[56]

The cause of action against "trafficking" in pornography, which empowered "any woman" or similarly subordinated person to sue for discrimination resulting from the circulation of specific materials, was potentially the most effective, and contentious, part of the ordinance. Even if producers, distributors, sellers, and exhibitors would only have to pay small sums of money to each successful plaintiff, they faced a potentially endless stream of similar lawsuits that cumulatively could prove quite costly. The trafficking subsection thus advances substantive equality by representing the interests of survivors, and those of "any" woman suing under the law, and increasing their monetary power vis-à-vis pornographers and men in general. This law has the potential to reduce the subordination of women by deterring distribution for consumption as well as its production.

The second cause of action provided remedies for those exploited in the production of pornography:

> (2) *Coercion into pornographic performances.* Any person, including transsexual, who is coerced, intimidated, or fraudulently induced (hereafter, "coerced") into performing for pornography shall have a cause of action against the maker(s), seller(s), exhibitor(s) or distributor(s) of said pornography for damages and for the elimination of the products of the performance(s) from the public view.[57]

The subsection of the ordinance on "coercion" allows for the most direct action against production harms, allowing compensation for those injured in the form of monetary support for their escape. Although it is geared specifically toward the pornography industry rather than off-camera prostitution, this cause of action is similar to Sweden's substantive equality prostitution laws. Recall that producers typically draw the people used in the materials from socially disadvantaged populations similar to those exploited in other forms of prostitution. In order to show "coercion" or exploitation of coercive circumstances under this cause of action, a plaintiff's lawyer could compare to what extent a client's situation relative to evidence of vulnerability, exploitation, and coercive conditions is similar to those shown in numerous studies of prostituted people analyzed previously, including high rates of PTSD, physical evidence of injury, childhood abuse and neglect, poverty, and a history of persistent discrimination.

As a specific law against production harms, but with similarities to other laws against sexual abuse, the coercion provision meticulously enumerates impermissible defenses similar to the way some rape laws "shield" plaintiffs from being questioned about their prior sexual history, style of dress, or other attributes that may evoke discriminatory attitudes among jurors or judges (i.e., rape myths). The objective of enumerating these impermissible defenses was to discourage resort to common stereotypes that generally divide women into dichotomous categories like deserving or undeserving of aggression, promiscuous or prudish, whores or madonnas, and so on. The ordinance thus stated:

(2) Proof of one or more of the following facts or conditions shall not, without more, negate a finding of coercion;
  (i) that the person is a woman; or
  (ii) . . . is or has been a prostitute; or
  (iii) . . . has attained the age of majority; or
  (iv) . . . is connected by blood or marriage to anyone . . . related to . . . the pornography; or
  (v) . . . has previously had, or been thought to have had, sexual relations with anyone . . . ; or
  (vi) . . . has previously posed for sexually explicit pictures . . . ; or
  (vii) that anyone else . . . has given permission on the person's behalf; or

(viii) that the person actually consented to a use of the performance that is changed into pornography; or

(ix) . . . knew that the purpose . . . was to make pornography; or

(x) . . . showed no resistance or appeared to cooperate actively . . . ; or

(xi) . . . signed a contract, or made statements affirming a willingness to cooperate . . . ; or

(xii) that no physical force, threats, or weapons were used . . . ; or

(xiii) that the person was paid or otherwise compensated.[58]

Although the comprehensive list of impermissible defenses above may appear unnecessary, some of the provisions reflect the fact that many of the women exploited within mainstream pornography production are parties to legal contracts—even though some wish to escape an environment in which they endure immense harm. Such conditions attest to the necessity of these defenses. The theory underlying the enumerated list is similar to the theory of intersectionality: legal challenges to pornography production are complex because they must account for the multiple disadvantages facing people harmed in its production. Such disadvantages are implicit in the defenses against common prejudices articulated in the subsection above, specifically that women in pornography have chosen to be there despite evidence to the contrary (e.g., poverty and lack of other options). Hence, this cause of action is consistent with a substantive equality approach that acknowledges intersectional discrimination and represents survivors' interests in addressing the ensuing disadvantages.

The third cause of action provided remedies for those forced to view pornography:

(3) *Forcing pornography on a person.* Any woman, man, child, or transsexual who has pornography forced on him/her in any place of employment, in education, in a home, or in any public place has a cause of action against the perpetrator and/or institution.[59]

This cause of action, which is directed not at pornographers per se but against those directly responsible for forcing pornography on others, reflects the authors' recognition that people forced to look at pornography, particularly women and children, receive a message that they belong to a group that society systematically subordinates. This can amplify victims' fear of men's violence, including rape, which nearly all women feel to some extent.[60] Forcing pornography on someone is thus a form of sexual harassment, and in this sense, the third cause of action serves as a sexual harassment law that extends beyond the workplace.

Although the ordinance has not yet been upheld in its entirety in any jurisdiction, judicial interpretations of sexual harassment law since 1991 have recognized that forcing pornography on someone through its display in the workplace can constitute sexual harassment. In *Robinson v. Jacksonville Shipyards*, a female shipyard employee sued her employer for sexual harassment because of "extensive pervasive posting of pictures depicting nude women, partially nude women, or sexual conduct and the occurrence of other forms of harassing behavior perpetrated by her male coworkers and supervisors."[61] The federal district court found that the display of these predominantly nude or seminude *Playboy*-type images[62] in the workplace "clearly has a disproportionately demeaning impact on the women."[63] It subsequently required the employer to create and enforce a sexual harassment policy, noting that "the First Amendment guarantee of freedom of speech does not impede the remedy of injunctive relief."[64] *Robinson* has been largely followed by courts deciding subsequent cases where the question has not been whether or not pornography in the workplace is actionable, but rather how pervasive it must be to constitute sexual harassment and whether additional conduct is needed.[65]

Robinson cited two earlier Supreme Court precedents that regarded the elimination of sex discrimination against women as a compelling state interest—not only at work, but also more broadly in terms of removing "barriers to economic advancement and political and social integration that have historically plagued women."[66] In the first of these two cases, *Roberts v. United States Jaycees* (1984), the Jaycees claimed that being required to admit female members would violate its First Amendment rights, and the U.S. Supreme Court admitted that it "may impair the ability of the original members to express only those views that brought them together."[67] Nonetheless, the Court held that a voluntary organization whose members lack any other distinctive characteristics, yet excludes women, is engaging in "invidious discrimination" that "cause[s] unique evils that government has a compelling interest to prevent—wholly apart from the point of view such conduct may transmit."[68] Put otherwise, sex equality was deemed more compelling than freedom of expression. *Robinson* adopted a similar balancing approach, weighing the interest in preventing sexual harassment against permitting pornography in the workplace and ultimately siding with equality rather than expression.

Adult pornography forced on employees in the workplace is thus effectively or potentially regarded as unprotected expression. In this specific area, U.S. law now relies on the balancing substantive equality framework of pornography regulation rather than the liberal framework—a position more consistent with hierarchy theory than with liberal "negative rights" and postmodern approaches to social dominance. Likewise, the cause of action afforded by the Minneapolis definition against "forcing" pornography on someone is consistent with hierarchy theory since it was intended to promote substantive equality, prevent discrimination, and provide disadvantaged groups with economic compensation for their losses, both tangible and intangible. This cause of action furthers the interest of pornography survivors, much like U.S. sexual harassment law furthers the interests of those being forced to view pornography at work.

The fourth cause of action provided remedies for those harmed because of specific pornographic materials (as opposed to being discriminated against through "trafficking" in pornography generally):

> (4) *Assault or physical attack due to pornography.* Any woman, man, child, or transsexual who is assaulted, physically attacked or injured in a way that is directly caused by specific pornography has a claim for damages against the perpetrator, the maker(s), distributor(s), seller(s), and/or exhibitor(s), and for an injunction against the specific pornography's further exhibition, distribution, or sale.[69]

This "assault" provision would impose a stringent evidentiary standard for proving causality, requiring a showing by a preponderance of evidence that "but for" the pornographic materials at issue, the harm would not have occurred. However, a number of studies discussed earlier contain accounts by johns suggesting that they are able to identify specific pornography that inspired them to perpetrate offenses, including gang rape, anal sex, violent rape, and physical assault. Likewise, johns' causal narratives describing the sequence of events leading from consumption to perpetration are corroborated by information reported by prostituted women regarding their experiences both during assaults, when abusers referred to specific materials, and in other situations where an abusive man alluded to particular pornography. Moreover, a number of quantitative studies with battered women in

North America found that many were forced by their partners to reenact elements depicted in specific pornography they had viewed. Along the same lines, a rape case discussed at a national conference of U.S. women judges in 1986 involved six adolescent boys who gang-raped a juvenile while reenacting a specific scene from a pornographic magazine.[70] Similarly, a founder of a rape crisis program in New York City attested in a letter to the Minneapolis City Council in November 1983 that she had encountered an increasing number of survivors of throat rape, some of whom reported that their perpetrators explicitly used the term "deep throat," which was coined in the pornographic movie by that title, prior to their assault.[71] Likewise, at the Minneapolis ordinance's public hearing in December 1983, a survivor testified that "most of the scenes" that her former husband made her reenact were "the exact scenes that he had read in the magazines"—which provided a model he followed "like a textbook."[72] Given that the materials referenced in these cases satisfy the ordinance's definition of pornography, under a preponderance of evidence standard, the plaintiff must also show that the assailant consumed the associated items before the assault and that there is behavioral consistency between its content and the perpetrator's conduct. Based on these examples, evidence sufficient to meet this burden does not appear difficult to obtain.

The cause of action involving "assault or physical attack" is also consistent with hierarchy theory in that it represents the survivors' interest in obtaining compensation for harms to which specific pornography contributed. Furthermore, it may equalize some substantive inequalities of power, at least economic, between victims and their assailants. Finally, the threat of potential lawsuits may well deter the production and dissemination of pornography generally and in turn promote substantive equality among men and women by reducing sexual aggression and diminishing attitudes supporting violence against women caused by pornography, and reducing the sexual abuse and exploitation typically needed to produce popular pornography.

Summary Analysis

The political scientist Jane Mansbridge has argued that the political representation of women's perspectives promotes equality in contexts involving conflicting interests and "mistrust" between the sexes, and where women's interests have historically not been articulated.[73] Pornography presents a situation marked by conflicting interests, mistrust between the sexes, and inadequate representation of the groups most marginalized in the political process where their interests could have been articulated. Yet groups of men who were never victimized by pornography have long articulated their interests, as men, drafting obscenity laws that are ineffective in preventing the harms of pornography. If the anti-pornography civil rights ordinances had survived, they would have integrated survivors' perspectives on pornography's harms into law for the first time, and further promoted the interests of women by providing legal causes of action to contest a social practice that demonstrably subordinates them as a social group.

Sexual harassment law in the United States incorporates the ordinance's cause of action concerning the "forced" viewing of pornography, where it is sufficiently pervasive or integral to another form of harassment. However, this law is tailored to the workplace, with possible applications in educational and other public settings. It is not applicable elsewhere in society, most assuredly not in the "private sphere." By contrast, the causes of actions afforded by the ordinance covered a broader range of multiply disadvantaged groups that are often most grievously harmed by pornography, including those exploited and abused in its production. Those with a cause of action under the ordinance need not be "singularly" disadvantaged (e.g., as children and those violently forced into pornography) to avail themselves of its potential benefits.[74] The ordinance took great care in enumerating impermissible defenses to the cause of action against harms sustained in production, ensuring that intersectionally and multiply disadvantaged people would not be barred from using it because they had been "paid" during the abuse, "signed a contract," had "previously posed" for pornography, or were prostituted off- as well as on-camera.[75]

The ordinance would have created an opportunity for those subordinated by pornography to deter and significantly diminish, possibly wipe out, the circulation of materials documented to be harmful. Its civil rights structure, including the precise definition of actionable content and its tailored causes of actions, would have elevated the power of historically disempowered people over their oppressors. In these respects, the ordinance is a substantive equality law.

Public Responses and Ideological Clashes

During the Minneapolis City Council hearings on the ordinance, many sides were presented and legislative deliberations suggested that something akin to a sense of emergency prevailed in terms of the harms presented.[76] A critic of the hearings, the political scientist Donald Alexander Downs, who neither attended nor had complete transcripts of the hearings,[77] nevertheless alleges that they were orchestrated by anti-pornography activists and marred by "one-sidedness."[78] Yet, at the first session, held on December 12, 1983, two critics spoke directly after those invited by the Council were finished, and the second session started off with seven critics of the ordinance testifying in seriatim—five from the city's own Civil Rights Commission and two gay rights activists.[79] Moreover, the third and final session was open for comments from anyone and concluded with a written note stating that no more speakers had requested time.[80] Considering that Downs himself recognizes American politics to be "notoriously beset by special interests and pressure groups," making it at best inconsistent to criticize the Minneapolis hearings as unbalanced—not the least since "widespread" judicial review "encourages" legislatures to take constitutional risks[81]—his critique appears misplaced.

Downs also claims that "[m]any knowledgeable leaders expressed strong reservations about the lack of deliberation, the one-sidedness, and the surreal sense of moral emergency that prevailed" when the anti-pornography ordinance was on the agenda in Minneapolis.[82] Considering that more leaders within the City Council voted for the ordinance than voted against it, the scope and significance of these reservations appear exaggerated. Had it not been for the mayor's successive vetoes, the ordinance would have become law.[83] Furthermore, the deliberations were not, as Downs maintains, one-sided.

In addition, by using terms like "moral emergency" to describe the cross-partisan support for the ordinance, Downs alters the conceptualization of harm as employed by the supporters and sponsors of the ordinance. The latter, whether feminists, liberals, or conservatives, generally framed pornography as a problem of sex discrimination against women. For instance, in conservatively dominated Indianapolis, site of the second attempt to pass an anti-pornography ordinance, the *Indianapolis Star* cited its Republican sponsor, Beulah Coughenour, and a public prosecutor who indicated in March 1984 that they were planning "a municipal ordinance that would define pornography as a form of sexual discrimination," and that it would be "aimed towards protecting the civil rights of women."[84] The prosecutor further stated that "'[a]s long as it is a question of morality, there will never be a limit [of sexual violence]. The question is one of harm.'"[85] Thus these supporters did not see the ordinance as a matter of "morals," but rather as a matter of sex discrimination, civil rights, and harm. Following the political scientist Giovanni Sartori, to conceptualize the ordinance's support as emanating from a perceived "moral emergency," as Downs does,[86] is at best "conceptual stretching" (i.e., "vague, amorphous conceptualizations")[87] and at worst deliberately misleading. This misappropriation of meaning suggests that some critics, like Downs, may not understand the ordinance.

The public response to the Minneapolis ordinance also reflected different democratic ideals among its critics relative to its supporters. For example, Downs contends that complex problems such as pornography require democratic "deliberation" that follows the practice of "consensus politics"—a decision-making style he claims would otherwise "have been typical of Minneapolis."[88] However, this deliberative theory is at odds with other strains within democratic theory, especially hierarchy theory. Following the political theorist Ian Shapiro, deliberation is not appropriate in every social conflict of interest.[89] Where there is substantive inequality, a demand for consensus will effectively create a right for the privileged to "delay, appeal, or veto" the disadvantaged group's proposal,[90] thus creating obstacles to any attempt to challenge social dominance. Shapiro explains:

> In reflecting on when it is appropriate to require deliberation, we should attend to the kind of interest at stake. . . . To fix intuitions, think of South Africa's white minority before the democratic transition. They stood to lose vastly more than nonwhites (who in fact stood to gain) from the planned transition, because they had vastly more resources, status, and power than nonwhites. For the whites the costs of leaving were in this sense greater, but it does not follow that they should have been entitled to rights of delay, appeal, or veto in virtue of that fact.[91]

The politics of pornography can be seen as precisely such an issue wherein opposing and unequally powerful interests are at stake, like many issues under apartheid. As the evidence here has demonstrated, men are the overwhelming consumers of pornography, yet, despite that, women are disproportionally subject to its harms, while men have power over its harm to women "by virtue of the decision-making procedure."[92] Therefore, what result would Downs' requirement for deliberation and "consensus politics" lead to in a situation where, as has been asserted throughout, women in general and pornography survivors, in particular, have much to win, and male consumers—and many non-consuming men—have much to lose? In a hierarchical relationship between two or more groups with opposing interests in protecting or dismantling that same hierarchy, Downs' "consensus politics" would not counter social dominance, but would rather protect the status quo.

Reflecting the contemporaneous critics of the ordinance, Downs further implies that American legislatures' engagement with anti-pornography activists—many of whom had been raped and tortured[93]—risked threatening the "perspective and civility required by healthy public life."[94] As an alternative, he introduces the concept of "public virtues," defined in terms of "self-restraint, reasonable tolerance, and perspective."[95] Accordingly, a theoretically virtuous politics requires "democratic elitism," whereby elites protect "civil liberty" from infringement by mass politics "when people at large fail to exhibit the virtues of a tolerant society."[96] This democratic ideal is reminiscent of the liberal ideal of "negative rights," as conceived by Charles de Montesquieu, James Madison, and John Stuart Mill, among others. Recall that those theorists preferred legislative and judicial checks and balances on democratic decision-making, with a primacy of "negative rights" (e.g., unrestricted speech) over "positive rights" (e.g., substantive equality) that limit the sphere for democratic intervention against non-state actors' abuses of power, as opposed to state abuses of power. Such "virtues" may limit the options of disadvantaged groups that have less access to established decision-making than do more privileged elites.

As demonstrated by the political hierarchy theorist Iris Marion Young, among others, where there is substantive inequality politically, socially, and culturally, "formally democratic processes often elevate the particular experiences and perspectives of the privileged groups, silencing or denigrating those of oppressed groups."[97] The concept of "public virtue" does not contain any mechanism to counter existing substantive inequality and oppression as do those favored by hierarchy theory and incorporated into the civil rights approach to pornography established to promote the interests of disadvantaged groups.

A related critique of an asserted lack of "restraint" concerns the forms of political expression employed by anti-pornography activists during the Minneapolis deliberations. For instance, critics complained about activists' booing and hissing at hearings and were critical of such unorthodox lobbying tactics as approaching politicians in public restrooms.[98] Other tactics that aimed to heighten awareness of the "reality of pornography" and "its harms to women," and which may have been perceived as unorthodox, included dumping piles of pornography outside city hall.[99] In an action undertaken at a public City Council session, twenty-four women were arrested and convicted of "disturbing the peace," and in yet another, a woman poured gasoline over her head and set herself on fire in a bookstore in a manner reminiscent of Buddhist monks and Norman Morrison—a man who committed suicide outside the Pentagon during a 1965 protest against the Vietnam War.[100]

Criticizing the anti-pornography activists in Minneapolis for being disorderly or exhibiting "incivility"[101] fails to acknowledge that the interests of pornography survivors' have been systematically silenced under law, suppressed in political processes, and distorted or ignored in the media.[102] The personal risks to which these activists exposed themselves also illustrate their substantive exclusion from traditional politics. For instance, many were stigmatized in their communities, terrorized, and compelled to leave their homes after testifying about their experiences of rape, abuse in prostitution, and sexual harassment in a context permeated by pornography. Among these witnesses was a woman whose testimony was published as pornography in *Penthouse Forum* without her consent, and several others who were sexually harassed through the mail and telephone calls.[103] It is not a coincidence that these women, many of whom had been severely abused, were uncompromising in their approach to lobbying. Their social circumstances left them few means of exerting influence besides those that were comparatively revolutionary. Perceived as revolutionary, they were readily dismissed as illegitimate.

The Minneapolis City Council was similarly criticized by politicians, civil servants, staff, and the American Civil Liberties Union for bypassing the standard procedures involving lengthy deliberations with other government offices and officials.[104] The mayor rationalized his veto in part by deploying this argument.[105] But, after his first veto, he pursued a more elitist and detached legislative approach that was less susceptible to activist influence. Even Downs notes that a new task force was set up in order to "reinstitute the search for consensus that normally prevailed in Minneapolis."[106] Unsurprisingly, the leading sponsor of the original ordinance, Councilwoman Charlee Hoyt, reported that she was opposed to the creation of the new task force, which she perceived as a tactic to diffuse interest in the issue, co-opt supporters, and water down the resulting legislation.[107] As Hoyt expected, the task force proposed zoning and opaque cover laws, changed "women" to "persons" in the ordinance's pornography definition, narrowed the definition of pornography to depictions of violence, and eliminated the trafficking provision that previously held disseminators liable.[108]

Watered-down proposal notwithstanding, a newly elected thirteen-member Council, acting democratically with regard to procedure, rejected the task force's proposal in favor of a reworked MacKinnon-Dworkin ordinance by a vote of seven to six.[109] After lengthy deliberations favored by the ordinance's critics, the mayor vetoed the ordinance a second time, and the Council failed to muster enough votes to override the veto.[110] The decisions, including the mayoral vetoes, suggest that issues like pornography and apartheid are too pressing and too unequal for Downs' ideals of deliberative consensus and public restraint to produce a fair outcome. As Shapiro's critique of deliberative politics suggests, when there is a relationship distinguished by hierarchy and oppression, requiring consensus in decision-making will simply obstruct substantive social change.[111]

Much of the contemporaneous criticism of the anti-pornography civil rights movement was expressed as *proceduralism* ostensibly unrelated to the substantive issues at stake. However, further analysis has revealed this proceduralism to be *ideological*, as in the democratic ideals of consensus-making discussed above. Downs' factually ill-founded critique of the legislative proceedings as "one-sided" is yet another example. Its logic implies that there is always more than one side that is equally relevant to decision-makers' consideration. As during apartheid, where one side was actually right and the other wrong, this assumption may itself simply be wrong. From this vantage point, the criticism of one-sidedness may be construed as an attempt to depoliticize the civil rights ordinance rather than confront the substantive choices presented to the legislature.

A critique of the hearings' alleged one-sidedness has also been articulated by the Canadian scholar Dany Lacombe, who argues that the "rigidity" of anti-pornography feminists "cannot allow for the plurality of subject positions that women occupy" nor recognize "differences" and the "fluidity of political identities."[112] Lacombe's assertion that there are "differences" in women's "subject positions" relative to pornography implies that a non-trivial number of women enjoy being used in pornography—a claim unsupported by empirical evidence. The dismissal of anti-pornography feminists' legitimate political views as "rigid" and lacking in awareness of "differences" also reveals her own unwillingness to situate herself in the "position" of those victimized because of pornography. Contrary to her contention, pornography could be seen precisely as a practice that circumscribes social and cultural "fluidity and difference" among women, while affirming their role as sexual objects for men's use through the promotion of hierarchical gendered stereotypes. This conclusion is supported by the well-documented popular demand for graphic dehumanizing and aggressive materials that subordinate women.

Lacombe also seems to assume that there is an almost endless variety of "subject positions" that women occupy, making an anti-pornography civil rights approach meaningless for women as a group. This position is similar to that of the postmodern "vulgar constructionism" criticized by Crenshaw, which alleges "that since all categories are socially constructed, there is no such thing as, say, Blacks or women, and thus it makes no sense to continue reproducing those categories by organizing around them."[113]

Lacombe and Downs do not seem to understand hierarchy. Their critiques avoid confronting substantive issues in the social practice of pornography, such as the relative hierarchical positions of one group vis-à-vis the other—the inequality that substantive equality opposes. Although they do not deny gender as a structure that systematically subordinates women to men, the forms of decision-making and policy positions implicitly favored by their critique contain no institutional mechanisms or legal rights to counter the entrenched hierarchy. Downs' proceduralism and demands for consensus in decision-making, and Lacombe's apparent unwillingness to endorse a politics responsive to the shared reality of women subordinated by pornography, constitute a rejection of hierarchy theory, which holds that in order to promote substantive equality democracies should recognize disadvantaged groups and support their perspectives and interests—a theory on which the ordinance was founded.

Judicial Responses and Ideological Clashes

Representation and Ripeness

The civil rights approach to pornography, as conceived in the Minneapolis anti-pornography ordinance, was codified in a similar ordinance in

Indianapolis in 1984.[114] However, it was immediately challenged in federal court by a group of publishers, book distributors, trade associations, and nonprofit organizations in *American Booksellers Ass'n v. Hudnut*.[115] Their challenge came before any of the ordinance's causes of action had an opportunity to be employed. On May 9, 1984, the court issued a temporary injunction barring the use of the ordinance until the case was decided.[116] Since the Indianapolis mayor had already ordered his administration to await the outcome of the case before enforcing the ordinance, the parties did not contest the order.[117] In effect, these decisions meant that the litigation was shaped by parties who were not directly affected by the ordinance. There were, most glaringly, no pornographers and no survivors involved. In 1989, another district court faced a challenge to a similar civil rights ordinance passed by voter initiative in Bellingham, Washington. Writing as amici, sex industry survivors urged the court to consider that "prostitution" for pornography "is not an hypothesized condition," like "pondering whether 'Leda and The Swan' might be considered pornography under the ordinance,"[118] as was literally done in *Hudnut* four years earlier.[119] In their brief, they lambasted the *Hudnut* decision as a "fantasized future law suit, brought by some unidentified party, before an as-yet nameless judge."[120]

Notably, a seller and exhibitor of pornography, I.S.S.I. Theater, Inc., did attempt to intervene as a plaintiff in the Indianapolis case during the judicial proceedings, submitting that "[n]one of the plaintiffs . . . alleges that it sells or exhibits materials dealing with sex, much less specializes in the sale or exhibition of such materials as do intervenors. Consequently, intervenors have a greater and more immediate interest in the litigation."[121] I.S.S.I. Theater, Inc., disappeared from the proceedings shortly thereafter, suggesting strategic coordination with the other plaintiffs to dissociate the lawsuit from the considerably less legitimate commercial sex industry. Indeed, in the litigation's aftermath, lawyers representing I.S.S.I. Theater, Inc., filed an unsuccessful motion seeking $7,903 in attorneys' fees from the City of Indianapolis for what the court regarded primarily as a review of the other plaintiffs' filings "and discussing strategy—all to ensure that their clients' interests were being protected."[122] MacKinnon and Dworkin have noted that these pornographers had no difficulty defining pornography while arguing that they were "specializing" in the materials targeted by the ordinance, calling into question charges that the ordinance was overbroad or vague in its definitions.[123]

The challenge to the Indianapolis ordinance was eventually appealed and settled in the Seventh Circuit, but denied a hearing in the U.S. Supreme

Court.[124] The Supreme Court summarily affirmed the circuit court's decision on direct appeal without hearing arguments, reading briefs, or offering an opinion—a route that has been generally impermissible since the passage of congressional legislation in 1988; for this reason, *Hudnut* is technically binding only within the Seventh Circuit's jurisdiction.[125] Moreover, it is unclear for what, specifically, a summary affirmance is precedential, not least since no reasons are given.[126] Chief Justice Burger, joined by Justices Rehnquist and O'Connor, dissented from the majority's summary affirmance and wanted to hear arguments,[127] indicating that they may have reviewed the case differently than the court below. The *Hudnut* opinion has nevertheless not been challenged in any of the other twelve circuits, though it could be.

Judicial review of anti-pornography civil rights ordinances has so far been undertaken without any plaintiff having been granted the opportunity to use their causes of actions; thus no one has attested to the harms of specific pornography in pursuit of a civil action against an alleged perpetrator when the ordinance's constitutionality has been tested. Unlike the legislatures and voters that passed the ordinance, the judiciary has had no opportunity to confront directly the real harms that producers and consumers cause. The Seventh Circuit defended its decision not to abstain from deciding the case before a plaintiff filed suit under the ordinance, despite criticism that the absence of directly affected parties meant it was not ripe for adjudication: "Deferred adjudication would produce tempered speech without assisting in resolution of the controversy. . . . Abstention is appropriate when state courts may clarify the meaning of a statute, thus sharpening the constitutional dispute and perhaps preventing an unnecessary constitutional adjudication. This statute, however, is all too clear."[128] Apparently, the author of the opinion, then Circuit Judge Frank H. Easterbrook,[129] viewed the statute as sufficiently clear to him, and clear to the parties that were *not* the most affected, to conclude that these parties might need to "temper" their speech unless the controversy was immediately decided.

When considering other ideological dimensions of how the terms of judicial review were set here, a requirement for "consensus" similar to that envisioned by Donald Downs and his informants would also allow the community at large, whose interests are even less affected than those of the parties to the case, to have a say in formulating official policy on pornography. If widening the circle of parties accordingly, the opportunity to exercise influence is extended to the point that it can effectively (in Shapiro's words) "delay, appeal, or veto" democratic decisions.[130] Hierarchy theory suggests that this may create a situation where disadvantaged and oppressed groups become hostage to their oppressors "by virtue of the decision-making procedure."[131] In the legal challenges to the anti-pornography ordinances, such a dynamic is evident to the extent that other parties, including consumers[132]—but not survivors and those they opposed (i.e., producers and distributors)—could be given the de facto (if not de jure) power to veto the ordinance. This adjudicative situation can reinforce hierarchy for similar reasons it would in a legislative forum. An analogy can be made to global warming: wealthy countries have disproportionally caused global warming, while poor countries have contributed virtually nothing to the problem, but the latter often have most to lose; however, what if wealthy countries were provided front seats at the global climate policy negotiation table, with poor countries relegated to the back seats? Such terms would likely lead to poor countries paying for "decades of profligate Western consumption."[133] From this point of view, American courts amplified social hierarchy when judging the civil rights ordinance as ripe for a constitutional challenge, even though the affected disadvantaged groups had not yet used it to sue anyone.

The Constitutional Review

Law has been conceived as "a system of enforceable rules governing social relations and legislated by a political system," while ideology has been referred, "in a general sense, to a system of political ideas."[134] However, the law may be more or less ambiguous and afford more or less latitude for ideological interpretation. The more the law is regarded as "settled" rather than open to interpretation, the more difficult the obstacles will likely be to change it in order to challenge the harms of pornography. Hence, a key question is whether the Seventh Circuit's reasons were more ideological than legal.

The Seventh Circuit initially accepted the legislature's findings regarding harm, at times acknowledging Indianapolis' understanding that pornography is a social "practice"[135] and, as such, encompasses more than mere depictions or ideas; the court averred that "pornography is not an idea; pornography is the injury,"[136] and that "we accept the premises of this legislation."[137] However, the court does not consistently adhere to these premises throughout the opinion; instead, it substitutes them for its own definition of pornography as "[d]epictions of subordination"[138] rather than as a form of subordination itself. The substitution of "subordination" with "depictions" makes the argument appear more superficially logical when the court later casts pornography as "speech," and the ordinance as a form of discrimination against viewpoints, thus allegedly impermissibly infringing on free speech, although this later change of modality is inconsistent with the ordinance's intentions and the court's initial premises.

Indeed, the Seventh Circuit concedes that "[d]epictions of subordination tend to perpetuate subordination," which "leads to affront and lower pay at work, insult and injury at home, battery and rape on the streets."[139] The court furthermore approvingly quotes "the language of the legislature." It allows that " 'pornography is central in creating and maintaining sex as a basis of discrimination' "; that it constitutes " 'a systematic practice of exploitation and subordination based on sex which differentially harms women' "; and recognizes that the " 'bigotry and contempt it produces, with the acts of aggression it fosters, harm women's opportunities for equality and rights [of all kinds].' "[140] These acknowledgments notwithstanding, the court argues that the evidence of pornography's "insidious" power as a practice of subordination—even if "pornography is what pornography does"—by itself suggests why it should be constitutionally protected:

> Yet this simply demonstrates the power of pornography as speech. All of these unhappy effects depend on mental intermediation. Pornography affects how people see the world, their fellows, and social relations. If pornography is what pornography does, so is other speech. Hitler's orations affected how some Germans saw Jews. . . . None is directly answerable by more speech, unless that speech too finds its place in the popular culture. Yet all is protected as speech, however insidious. Any other answer leaves the government in control of all of the institutions of culture, the great censor and director of which thoughts are good for us.[141]

However, speech, including depictions, cannot constitute subordination in the same sense that pornography can. The court's analogy equating pornography with "orations" is misleading because speech does not necessitate exploitation even when it is hateful, racist, or anti-Semitic. For instance, Hitler's orations did not require the exploitation and abuse of Jews to produce any of its effects, a circumstance contrary to what popular pornographers typically need to do when relying on real performers. Hence, the court does not appear to conceptualize the ordinance accurately, superficially accepting its definition of pornography while continuing to equate it with "other speech."

Furthermore, in arguing that the harm "simply demonstrates the power of pornography as speech," the court turns an accepted principle of First Amendment law on its head. Harm, generally speaking, is a measure of whether or not there is a compelling or heightened government interest in regulation. For example, the Supreme Court upheld the criminalization of child pornography in *New York v. Ferber* (1982) on the grounds that the resulting harms were compelling and that "the evil to be restricted so overwhelmingly outweighs the expressive interests, if any, at stake, that no process of case-by-case adjudication is required."[142] *Ferber* was later used to support the criminalization of possession, as distinct from distribution, of child pornography.[143] Notably, Indianapolis did not target possession, only distribution, and did not use criminal, only civil, means, in pursuing damages.[144] If the *Hudnut* logic of harm was to be accepted as a fundamental principle, it would effectively invert the tiers of scrutiny by tacitly holding that the more compelling or substantial the harm, the more protected such harmful expression becomes. Clearly, this does not comport with U.S. free speech law.

Mill's Distinctions

In defending its decision to strike down the ordinance, the Seventh Circuit further reasons that the "ideas of the Klan may be propagated," "Communists may speak freely and run for office," and the "Nazi Party may march through [the streets of] a city with a large Jewish population," citing three well-known cases.[145] One rationale common among the three cases cited is that John Stuart Mill's liberal distinction between *direct* and *indirect* harm was utilized. For instance, *Brandenburg v. Ohio* (1969) permitted Klan speech based on the distinction between "mere advocacy" and "incitement to imminent lawless action."[146] *Brandenburg* protected televised Klan speech that advocated lynching and other terroristic acts against specific vulnerable groups through statements such as "this is what we are going to do to the n——ers," "bury the n——ers," "send the Jews back to Israel," and "we intend to do our part."[147] Hate-filled expressions like these have precipitated genocides, pogroms, and the same type of acts advocated in *Brandenburg*, even if not as overtly as someone "falsely shouting fire in a theatre and causing a panic."[148] One example of what the "indirect" outcome of the prolonged dehumanization of a racial group may look like under conditions of racial inequality and white supremacy, in which *Brandenburg* speech forms an integral part, are the massacres that were euphemistically labeled "race riots" in East St. Louis, Illinois, in July 1917. At that time, white mobs, including law enforcement officers and other public officials, systematically murdered Blacks and terrorized members of the African American community by engaging in such atrocities as throwing children into a fire, evidently for amusement.[149]

Yet, courts have never strictly adhered to the "clear and present danger" standard in adjudicating First Amendment cases, but instead have developed numerous exceptions to balance competing government interests against expressive interests, even when the harms are only indirect in the sense conceived by Mill and manifest in *Brandenburg*. For instance, obscenity, fighting words, and potentially group libel are unprotected and can be regulated under a rational review standard.[150] Similarly, regulations of child pornography can withstand strict scrutiny review if the government employs narrowly tailored means to further a compelling interest.[151] These conditions indicate that the Seventh Circuit, had it so chosen, could have carved out an exception for the Indianapolis ordinance under a number of theories. It could have severed some parts of the ordinance, for example, the "trafficking" provision that is more sweeping, or the "assault" provision that would be more difficult to apply, while retaining the "coercion" or "forcing" provisions that are narrower in their scope. Indeed, the provision against "forcing" pornography on someone is already applied under federal law governing sexual harassment in the workplace, at least since *Robinson v. Jacksonville Shipyards* was decided in 1991, several years after the Seventh Circuit's decision in *Hudnut* (1985). These facts suggest that the Seventh Circuit ignored a number of theories in support of the ordinance.

Strict Scrutiny: Equality as a Compelling Interest

There are three main routes by which the ordinance could have survived expressive challenges, which follow different standards of judicial review: strict scrutiny, intermediate scrutiny, and rational review, respectively. The most demanding is strict scrutiny, in which the ordinance is presumptively invalid. Here, the government must show that its means employed are "narrowly tailored" to further "a compelling interest" to prevent harm.[152] The ordinance's definition of actionable materials is of particular interest. While the Minneapolis ordinance had nine sub-definitions of pornography, at least one of which was required for further action, the Indianapolis ordinance was limited to six sub-definitions that were somewhat differently worded:

> (q) *Pornography* shall mean the graphic sexually explicit subordination of women, whether in pictures or in words, that also includes one or more of the following:
> (1) Women are presented as sexual objects who enjoy pain or humiliation; or
> (2) Women are presented as sexual objects who experience sexual pleasure in being raped; or
> (3) Women are presented as sexual objects tied up or cut up or mutilated or bruised or physically hurt, or as dismembered or truncated or fragmented or severed into body parts; or
> (4) Women are presented being penetrated by objects or animals; or
> (5) Women are presented in scenarios of degradation, injury, abasement, torture, shown as filthy or inferior, bleeding, bruised, or hurt in a context that makes these conditions sexual; [or]
> (6) Women are presented as sexual objects for domination, conquest, violation, exploitation, possession, or use, or through postures or positions of servility or submission or display.
>
> The use of men, children, or transsexuals in the place of women in paragraphs (1) through (6) above shall also constitute pornography under this section.[153]

Law students participating in the 1993 experiment described earlier indicated that this definition was not overbroad or vague: these future lawyers were able to apply it to real pornographic materials without being stymied by overbreadth or vagueness—especially when compared to existing U.S. obscenity law and an alternative definition by the legal scholar Cass Sunstein, both of which performed significantly worse.[154]

Furthermore, materials that would *not* fit the ordinance's "sexually explicit" requirement, including sexist advertising or R-rated movie scenes, have also been shown to increase attitudes supporting violence against women in psychological experiments.[155] Although such attitudes significantly predict sexual aggression among normal men,[156] the definition omits materials of this kind, further suggesting that the ordinance is not overbroad, but narrowly tailored to accomplish its ends.

Notably, the four causes of civil action set forth in the ordinance do not include such broader or more severe criminal sanctions that are typically applied for child pornography crimes. Indianapolis' causes of actions also include a number of limitations not present in the Minneapolis version: (i) a prohibition against applying the "trafficking" provision on " 'isolated passages or isolated parts' ";[157] (ii) an exception making damages unavailable under the "trafficking" provision where respondents neither " 'knew [n]or had reason to know' " that materials constituted pornography under the ordinance;[158] (iii) an exception under the "assault" provision in which " 'a seller, exhibitor or distributor' " would not be liable for damages unless a plaintiff proves that the respondent "knew or had reason to know" that the materials were "pornography"; (iv) and a complete exemption under the "trafficking" provision for materials where women " 'are presented as sexual objects for domination, conquest, violation, exploitation, possession, or use, or through postures or positions of servility or submission or display' "[159]—a limitation referred to as the "*Playboy* exception" since it exempted centerfold-type materials.[160]

However, despite the Seventh Circuit's acknowledgment of the harms, thereby tacitly endorsing the premises of the Indianapolis ordinance,[161] the court does not appear to have considered the gravity of the harms "compelling" enough to withstand strict scrutiny. Compared to the Supreme Court, which upheld a law against child pornography in *Ferber* three years before *Hudnut*, noting that literary, artistic, political, or scientific value of such materials were " 'irrelevant to the child' " that is abused as a result of its production or its consumption,[162] the Seventh Circuit rhetorically asks why an "other value" should matter with regard to adult pornography: "It is irrelevant under the ordinance whether the work has literary, artistic, political, or scientific value. . . . [A]s one of the principal drafters of the ordinance has asserted, 'if a woman is subjected, why should it matter that the work has other value?' "[163] The opinion's silence on the question implies that the court believes the answer to be self-evident. Apparently, the court cannot conceive that preventing prostituted women from being gang-raped by johns imitating pornography, or preventing women from being abused by intimate partners under similar circumstances, would be a more compelling interest than any potential artistic, literary, political, or scientific value.

Partly because the Seventh Circuit does not perceive any compelling interest in upholding the ordinance against freedom of expression challenges, it expresses no opinion on whether the ordinance is overbroad or vague.[164] It takes this position with respect to an ordinance that is more narrowly tailored than comparable regulations of obscenity; does not reach any materials that do not cause the harms it seeks to combat, even excluding some materials that fit this description; and has been successfully applied to real pornographic materials in an experiment conducted with law students.

Although it discusses *Ferber* in other contexts, the Seventh Circuit never addresses the fact that children and adults are the same people, only at different points in time. Evidence presented early on in this analysis indicated that at least half of those prostituted begin before age 18, and a majority of people used for sex in prostitution, from which pornographers often draws the persons used in the materials, have also experienced sexual abuse in childhood, sometimes severely so. Adult pornography production thus takes advantage of prior child sexual abuse and neglect, as well as prostitution, which together contribute a vulnerable population from which to recruit. As they grow older, many prejudices begin to operate more harshly against these children, including timeworn rape myths, such as "only bad girls get raped," which further impede justice and make it difficult to escape sexual exploitation. Only those who receive effective intervention that enables them to escape the commercial sex industry before age 18 will be shielded from the production harms affecting adults exploited in pornography. Many vulnerable children will never be protected from these prospective harms or be afforded an effective remedy for prior childhood abuse unless the conditions endured by adults are effectively addressed by law. For these reasons, using an intersectional approach that takes account of multiple disadvantages is far preferable. It would benefit not only adults but also the children whose disadvantage is more easily identifiable, increasing their protection and rights should they need them later.[165]

Because the U.S. legal landscape has changed somewhat since the Indianapolis ordinance was challenged, children exploited in pornography are now entitled to pursue civil damage awards as well as criminal restitution, even from consumers—the contested issue not being liability itself, but its extent.[166] The civil rights approach to the harms of pornography is, by this move, incorporated into federal law with respect to children. One rationale for extending liability from producers to consumers articulated in public discussions was that children exploited in pornography production reported serious psychological problems, some feeling haunted by the circulation of their images, not knowing who had already seen them or who might see them in the future.[167] Similar difficulties were reported by adult pornography survivors in testimony before the 1985 U.S. Attorney General's Commission on Pornography.[168] Likewise, a more recent Nevada study found that women in legal brothels felt that pornography that had been made with them there defined and stigmatized them, circulating as a permanent record of their prostitution.[169] The addition of consumer liability for harms occasioned by child pornography is far more sweeping than was ever imagined in Indianapolis. Although the ordinance contained no criminal sanctions, and consumers were never its targets, it was not upheld under strict scrutiny. By contrast, the federal legislature and the judiciary apparently concluded that the child pornography law, which provides considerably broader sanctions and damage claims, is narrowly tailored to achieve its intended purpose.

A few years after the *Hudnut* decision, the *Robinson* court held that sex discrimination was a "compelling state interest" when pornography was forced upon a woman in her workplace—a practice now actionable as sexual harassment under federal law if it is sufficiently pervasive.[170] As mentioned, *Robinson* cited two Supreme Court cases, one of which, *Roberts v. United States Jaycees* (1984), was decided over a year prior to *Hudnut*,[171] and which supported *Robinson*'s position that there is a "compelling governmental interest" in eliminating sex discrimination against women and removing "barriers to economic advancement and political and social integration that have historically plagued women."[172] Arguably, pornography is such a barrier to equality for women. *Roberts* acknowledged that requiring a voluntary all-male organization to accept women "may impair" the original member's free expression.[173] Still, it determined that sex equality was more important than free speech.[174] *Roberts* should have been known to the *Hudnut* court. Yet nowhere does *Hudnut* recognize that sex discrimination can be a compelling competing interest, which could have been used to support the ordinance against expressive challenges.

It is symptomatic that sex equality has so far only trumped freedom of expression in areas where the women affected are least socially disadvantaged, such as the workplace and voluntary associations. By joining male voluntary associations, perhaps these women have, in MacKinnon's words, already "achieved a biography that somewhat approximates the male norm, at least on paper."[175] Although they are "the least of sex discrimination's victims," when these women "are denied a man's chance, it looks the most like sex bias."[176] Women joining organizations such as the Jaycees are unlikely to be multiply disadvantaged to the same extent by childhood abuse, extreme poverty, and race discrimination as women in prostitution typically are. As MacKinnon would predict, a non-substantive equality approach to pornography, which U.S. law to date has been, does not promote the equality of those "*least* similar, socially, to those whose situation sets the standard against which their entitlement to equal treatment is measured," but restricts itself to women who are " 'similarly situated' " to men.[177] The workplace and voluntary organizations are likely contexts where men also have less trouble imagining how discrimination would negatively impact a person of any gender, race, ethnicity, or sexuality. By contrast, men generally lack similar experiential frameworks for reflecting on discriminatory effects in other social contexts, such as being victimized, stigmatized, or discriminated against because of pornography. Unfortunately, MacKinnon points out, when "the lack of similarity of women's condition to men is extreme because of sex inequality, the result is that the law of sex equality does not properly apply."[178]

Following MacKinnon, the narrowness of existing equality law also relates to the problem of intersectional discrimination. Crenshaw argues that equality law, even in the employment context, needs more " 'bottom-up' approaches, those which combine all discriminatees in order to challenge an entire employment system."[179] However, such approaches "are foreclosed by the limited view of the wrong and the narrow scope of the available remedy." Her reasoning is also applicable in settings outside the workplace, including among groups particularly harmed by pornography that are often also subjected to other disadvantages. Following Crenshaw, then, the group of prostituted persons, "which, because of its intersectionality, is best able to challenge all forms of discrimination," is, unfortunately, "essentially isolated and often required to fend for themselves" under existing equality law. She suggests that women, in general, should "accept the possibility that there is more to gain by collectively challenging the hierarchy, rather than by each discriminatee individually seeking to protect her source of privilege within the hierarchy."[180] Similarly, challenging pornography might produce more collective gains than protecting individual women's sources of privilege within a male supremacist society saturated by pornography would.

Like MacKinnon's approach, intersectionality, as Crenshaw conceives it, suggests more meaningful and substantive equality than the current impoverished, restricted, and narrow equality law. Indeed, the selectivity by which substantive equality is mandated in some spheres, but not in others, may itself be seen as discriminatory. If a more inclusive sex discrimination law against pornography covered situations where women are most unequal to men, it would, in Crenshaw's terms, place "those who currently are marginalized in the center."[181] Such a strategy would be "the most effective way to resist efforts to compartmentalize experiences and undermine potential collective action" on behalf of women's equality.

Consistent with MacKinnon's and Crenshaw's theories, the 1985 Attorney General's Commission on Pornography indeed found that pornography could be seen as already covered under a more expansive reading of Title VII sex discrimination law. Among other things, the Commission maintained that Title VII protected workers "from having to prostitute themselves to supervisors or submit themselves to sexual intercourse or harassment to keep their jobs."[182] Furthermore, it noted that the law required that such acts be "unwelcome," a requirement the Commission regarded as easily satisfied since "the overwhelming factor motivating the sexual conduct of pornographic models is financial need, certainly not a desire to have sex with the partner assigned to him or her for the scene"[183]—a finding consistent with many more recent sources of evidence. Thus, the Commission argued that "much of the commercial production of pornography runs afoul of Title VII," and that "Title VII embodies a principle that should not be strangled by technicalities: no one in this country should have to engage in actual sex to get or keep his or her job."[184] On a similar theory, then, the ordinance's "coercion" provision could have sustained a legal challenge by using Title VII.

Regardless of discrimination, as mentioned, the Seventh Circuit implied that "other" literary, artistic, political, or scientific "value" is more important than pornography's harms.[185] A related argument that other values matter more was also presented by one of the two amici curiae supporting the suit against Indianapolis: the so-called Feminist Anti-Censorship Taskforce (FACT), whose brief was co-signed by the Women's Legal Defense Fund and eighty individuals, mostly academics.[186] The FACT cohort feared that the ordinance might stop some women from appropriating "for themselves the robustness of what traditionally has been male language,"[187] further arguing that women had a right to enjoy " 'a rape fantasy.' "[188] These so-called fantasies are often experienced as "paid rape"[189] by the women typically recruited to portray them in pornography—women who tend to be vulnerable, often prostituted off-camera, and subjected to serious abuse in the course of pornography production. For FACT, protecting the fantasy was evidently more important than protecting the women who are effectively raped.

By virtue of being women, the "feminist" amici behind FACT's brief were demographically similar to those harmed by pornography, at least superficially. Hence, their arguments warrant extra scrutiny. For instance, the FACT cohort invoked a particular doctrine under the Fourteenth Amendment's Equal Protection Clause to stress that gender-based classifications are discriminatory per se. In their view, the ordinance "assumes and perpetuates classic sexist concepts of separate gender-defined roles which 'carry the inherent risk of reinforcing stereotypes about the "proper place" of women and their need for special protection.' "[190] FACT's allegation implies a conflation, in Crenshaw's terms, of "the power exercised simply through the process of categorization" in law with the "power to cause that categorization to have social and material consequences."[191] Elaborating "stereotypical" categories in civil rights legislation may be necessary to identify the materials and the sex industry survivors and others subjected to discrimination who are harmed by pornography. Ironically, when FACT suggests public education and support for female survivors of men's violence,[192] they are acknowledging stereotypically gendered perpetrators and victims, if not explicitly identifying them as such. Yet FACT fails to recognize how pornography reinforces these very categories. Similarly, the Canadian scholar Dany Lacombe does not recognize that it is pornography—not the civil rights approach—that reinforces female stereotypes.[193] Such postmodern theory has yet to explain how an abstract formal equality doctrine prohibiting any legal recognition of gendered reality can change it.

In 1992, the Supreme Court of Canada responded to proposals similar to those previously offered by FACT[194] when it was asked to substitute law with other non-mandatory measures, such as public education about pornography's harms, "counselling rape victims to charge their assailants," or "provision of shelter and assistance for battered women, campaigns for laws against discrimination on the grounds of sex, [and] education to increase the sensitivity of law enforcement agencies and other governmental authorities."[195] The Court rejected substituting the law with such reactive policies that do not target pornography directly, finding it "noteworthy that many of the above suggested alternatives are in the form of *responses* to the harm engendered by negative attitudes against women. The role of the impugned provision is to control the dissemination of the very images that contribute to such attitudes."[196]

When advocates are more concerned with the neutral application of abstract gender-equal laws than they are with legally recognizing an unequal social reality, as exemplified in a substantive equality approach, it will likely only benefit those women already protected from the worst harms of pornography.[197] Adopting an intersectional approach to substantive inequality, rather than addressing singular disadvantages such as those mentioned by FACT—for instance, lacking the "robustness of . . . male language" or missing " 'a rape fantasy' "[198]—Crenshaw suggests that the pursuit of equality should begin by addressing multiple disadvantages among "those who are most disadvantaged," from which "others who are singularly disadvantaged would also benefit."[199]

FACT also implied that the anticipated chilling effect on pornography dissemination, as defined by the ordinance, was comparable to "constrictions" that silence the speech of sexual minorities.[200] However, the ordinance barred lawsuits under the "trafficking" provision against "isolated passages or isolated parts."[201] That exception clearly permitted the expression of irony, literary criticism, and other valuable forms of cultural and political expression by, for example, minorities seeking to highlight sexual or other oppression, even using expression similar to what was otherwise targeted by the ordinance, such as presenting women "as sexual objects who experience sexual pleasure in being raped."[202] FACT betrayed no awareness that the opportunity for the selective use of pornography was available under the ordinance. Moreover, just as democratic ideals of deliberative consensus and negative rights are criticized for being blind to substantive inequality and the power disparities underlying it, comparing the restriction of a social practice of subordination such as pornography with restricting potential forms of expression by sexual minorities seems equally blind to power and disempowerment. Pornography consumers do not masturbate in large numbers to expression that critically scrutinizes the heteronormativity of postmodern industrialized societies. The documented popular demand is rather for presentations of sexual aggression against (or the degradation of) women, such as gagging, gang rape, "ass-to-mouth," and verbal aggression. Yet FACT's analogy stage the two practices as if they were substantively equal and comparable when they are not. Restricting minorities' legitimate speech is not analogous to restricting sexual exploitation and the presumed freedom to promote violence and discrimination against other minorities, such as prostituted persons. The first is ideally an expression promoting equality; the others are social practices of subordination and oppression.

Intermediate Scrutiny: Viewpoint Neutrality

After dismissing the Indianapolis ordinance as lacking a compelling state interest, arguably wrongly so, the Seventh Circuit continues to review the First Amendment's doctrine that covers subjects constituting an "important or substantial governmental interest."[203] Here, the "viewpoint neutrality" doctrine attempts to distinguish regulations or applications based on whether they are content-based or viewpoint-based (the latter being more suspect) in order to determine whether the suppression of speech is impermissible. It has, for example, been invoked to reverse tort liability awards in order to protect admittedly "hurtful"[204] anti-gay picketing at military funerals on the rationale that "any distress occasioned . . . turned on the content and viewpoint of the message conveyed, rather than any interference with the funeral itself."[205] Another case invalidated a law requiring that all profits from books describing actual crimes be paid to their victims, the Court opining that such a law could "effectively drive certain ideas or viewpoints from the marketplace."[206] The doctrine's implicit philosophy seems to be that the state should not restrict the expression of nonconforming viewpoints, such as those of dissident leftists, while authorizing those that are orthodox or mainstream, or vice versa. It is shaped by twentieth-century American attempts to suppress or protect left-wing oppositional speech.[207]

Recall that the Seventh Circuit acknowledges that pornography " 'is a systematic practice of exploitation and subordination based on sex which differentially harms women,' " and that "pornography is not an idea; pornography is the injury."[208] Yet the court later represents the ordinance as a form of "thought control," claiming that it "establishes an 'approved' view of women, of how they may react to sexual encounters, of how the sexes may relate to each other."[209] This characterization equates pornography, as defined by the ordinance, with political protests, dissident commentary, or subversive literature. Hence, despite initially rendering pornography a "practice," the Seventh Circuit refers to the ordinance as if it regulated "depictions," "viewpoints," or "speech."[210] If the ordinance gave a cause of action to sue people who disseminate the "viewpoint" that women are of less human worth than men, should be subordinated sexually, or enjoy being raped, this would indeed be correct. However, the ordinance does not regulate these things, regardless of how much people might want it to. Neither does it regulate expression that is not graphic, explicit, and sexually subordinating as pornography provably is. The fact that "other speech" also "does" things, as *Hudnut* notes,[211] does not change the fact that *only* pornography does what it does. Only pornography can be subject to a cause of action under the ordinance—not "other speech."

Assuming, arguendo, that the ordinance implicates the dissemination of "viewpoints" on certain subjects, including whether women should be sexually subordinated, it could still be sustained under the viewpoint neutrality doctrine. In *United States v. O'Brien* (1968), the Supreme Court sustained a law that prohibited burning one's draft card on the rationale that even if such conduct could be considered "symbolic speech," it would impact public administration negatively regardless of its associated political viewpoint.[212] Under *O'Brien*, if the law's "governmental interest" is identified as conduct like prostitution or rape rather than the suppression of free speech—thus targeting the subordinating practice rather than the viewpoint that subordinating practices should be legal—the law can be regarded as "unrelated to the suppression of free expression" if "the incidental restriction on alleged First Amendment freedoms is no greater than is essential to the furtherance of that interest."[213] Perforce, the Indianapolis ordinance is narrowly tailored to its objectives, particularly when compared to current laws against obscenity.

Moreover, in *Perry Educ. Ass'n v. Perry Local Educators Ass'n* (1983), the Supreme Court held that the exclusion of certain speech from a particular venue or forum may be permissible if there are "substantial alternative channels" for that speech.[214] Hence, if the ordinance's application to pornography would cause unintended restrictions on free speech, for instance, suppressing the view that women should be sexually subordinated, there are numerous alternative venues for expressing those perspectives in the age of global mass media. Indeed, the most reactionary views on women's rights, including the opinions that women should be sexually abused and degraded, or that they are biologically inferior to men, can be expressed and reach a considerable audience without the coercion, force, assault, or trafficking that attend pornography. Thus, the ordinance does not incidentally restrict "alleged First Amendment freedoms" more than is "essential"[215] to furthering its interest in preventing the sex discrimination, exploitation, and abuse caused by the production and dissemination of pornography.

Notwithstanding *O'Brien* and *Perry*, the Seventh Circuit continues to equate the ordinance's definition of pornography, which it initially acknowledged being a "practice" of subordination, with political "viewpoints" about women. This misrepresentation of the ordinance is starkly revealed when the court of appeals attempts to explain why the cause of action for "coercion into pornographic performances"[216] could not withstand scrutiny. That provision did not target dissemination, far less consumption, directly. The coercion provision would have been a substantive equality law similar to Sweden's law against sexual exploitation in prostitution, asymmetrically targeting those who exploit and subordinate while providing relief and remedies to those exploited and subordinated. Assuming again, arguendo, that pornography is protected speech, this provision, at most, raise the same First Amendment issues as *O'Brien*. There, the criminal obstruction of public administration, not the "symbolic speech," constituted the offense. Likewise, the coercion provision only targets certain conduct that occurs in the course of pornography production, such as paying someone vulnerable to exploitation for sex. Pornographers can still produce almost identical materials without using real people, which would raise no liability issue under this provision.

Some state and federal courts have already recognized pornography to include prostitution when pornography performers are recruited to have sex for money; in that situation, the pornographer is viewed as a third party, or buyer, in the prostitution transaction, which is not protected by the First Amendment. For instance, the Tenth Circuit held in *United States v. Roeder* (1975) that a man transporting a woman across state lines for the purpose of producing pornography violated the Mann Act, the court remarking that the "First Amendment does not constitute a license to violate the law."[217] Similarly, in *People v. Kovner* (1978) the New York Supreme Court upheld the conviction of a pornography producer for "promoting prostitution" and other offenses associated with the production, promotion, and sale of pornography, noting that, "[w]hile First Amendment considerations may protect the dissemination of printed or photographic material regardless of the manner in which it was obtained, this protection will not shield one against a prosecution for a crime committed during the origination of the act."[218]

With no controlling federal case, other courts have reached determinations contrary to *Kovner* and *Roeder* as to whether the First Amendment protects pornography production.[219] For example, in the California case of *People v. Freeman* (1988), state courts refused to apply prostitution laws to pornography based on an interpretation of statutory language rather than the First Amendment.[220] Justice O'Connor, acting as Circuit Justice, thus denied certiorari for lack of jurisdiction, concluding "that the state court's statutory holding is independent from its discussion of the First Amendment and was not driven by that discussion."[221] O'Connor further noted "that the State has a strong interest in controlling prostitution within its jurisdiction and, at some point, it must certainly be true that otherwise illegal conduct is not made legal by being filmed."[222] This view has been echoed in Supreme Court cases on animal cruelty, child pornography, and labor picketing.[223] Thus, in *United States v. Stevens* (2010), a case involving animal cruelty, the Court stated that "'[i]t rarely has been suggested that the constitutional freedom for speech and press extends its immunity to speech or writing used as an integral part of conduct in violation of a valid criminal statute.'"[224]

In spite of the distinctions drawn by the Supreme Court and state and federal courts between targeting non-expressive coercive conduct during production versus targeting the dissemination of the expressive material itself, the Seventh Circuit defends its decision to strike down the cause of action against the use of coercion in pornography production on the ground that it is "not neutral with respect to viewpoint."[225] The court thus argues that "a state may make injury in the course of producing a film unlawful independent of the viewpoint expressed in the film."[226] However, the Seventh Circuit neglects to mention the fact that there are already numerous "independent" laws against "injury," if not specifically geared to the film industry. It ignores the reasons why these laws (e.g., criminalizing prostitution and rape laws) are rarely applied to adult pornography production. Recall that general laws against sexual abuse are often inapplicable to pornography production because of the multiple disadvantages commonly experienced by performers, including being forced by a history of childhood abuse and neglect, discrimination, poverty, and lack of other alternatives, to accept the injury when being paid—conditions that are difficult to legally address and exist exclusively in the sex industry. When these people lack the necessary resources to overcome their "position of vulnerability,"[227] having "no real and acceptable alternative but to submit to the abuse involved,"[228] international law has since 2003 defined the third parties who profit from their sexual exploitation as human traffickers. Yet because laws against sexual abuse do not address abuse that is "paid for," and prostitution and trafficking laws are not yet effectively applied to this category of victimized people, those subjected to abusive sexual exploitation in the pornography industry are mostly without remedy.

In contrast to existing laws, the ordinance's coercion provision would have provided persons used as pornography performers with an unambiguous remedy. The ordinance acknowledged that the ubiquity of rape myths and trivialization of sexual exploitation and abuse would make it difficult for prostituted women to use other laws against coercion and abuse in pornography retroactively, thus added the impermissible defenses referenced earlier for those reasons. For instance, alluding to plaintiffs' previous prostitution or sex with defendants is not a permissible defense under the coercion provision. Only a law against pornography production, prostitution, or other sexual abuse would require a similar list of impermissible defenses, which is rarely seen in general laws against "injury in the course of producing a film . . . independent of the viewpoint expressed in the film."[229] That it is impermissible to infer anything from such superficially adverse facts as a plaintiff's prior performance in pornography, technical consent, receipt of payment, or apparent cooperation[230] also sheds light on the fact that the "injury" attending the production of a pornographic film occurs not only "in the course of producing" it, as the court's narrow understanding suggests. Rather, the foundation for the injury is established by the surrounding constraints that enable pornographers to recruit a "consenting" population of performers at all.

When shoehorning the civil rights ordinance into a misplaced doctrine of viewpoint neutrality, the Seventh Circuit also reasons that "a book about slavery is not itself slavery, or a book about death by poison a murder."[231] But pornography is *not* like a "book about slavery." In fact, rather than being a "book" about it, the evidence presented previously suggests that pornography *is* a form of slavery for the women (and some men) who perform in it. That is why a specific civil rights law that recognizes this form of slavery from the perspective of those most affected is necessary to end it. Arguably, to invalidate the coercion provision with reference to viewpoint neutrality is inconsistent with *O'Brien*, where the defendant expresses an antiwar viewpoint and is nonetheless convicted for burning his draft card.[232] Accordingly, *Kovner* and *Roeder* apply prostitution and anti-trafficking laws on pornographers while citing *O'Brien*,[233] finding no violation of viewpoint neutrality. The Seventh Circuit should recognize that under *O'Brien*, the "governmental interest" underlying the ordinance's cause of action against coercion in pornography, perhaps more than any other of its causes, "is unrelated to the suppression of free expression," and that "the incidental restriction on alleged First Amendment freedoms is no greater than is essential to the furtherance of that interest."[234]

The viewpoint neutrality doctrine derives from a body of law that, unlike more recent child pornography and sex discrimination laws, was largely carved out of cases arising during the Red Scare (1920s) and McCarthyism (1950s) and the 1960s and 1970s anti–Vietnam War efforts.[235] The First Amendment, among other things, protected social activists, intellectuals, and other dissident minorities from being arbitrarily censored or otherwise persecuted by the U.S. government, partially as a means to ensure that, in Justice Brandeis' words, "the deliberative forces should prevail over the arbitrary."[236] When the Seventh Circuit applies this doctrine to pornographers, they turn the law on its head: the court protects pornographers as if *they* are the marginalized, oppressed groups or intellectual dissidents being persecuted by the U.S. government. Evidence suggests instead that pornographers—who partake in the profits of a multibillion-dollar industry—walk almost literally over dead women's bodies in order to provide millions of young American men with graphic new images of women's sexual subordination as masturbation materials.

The Seventh Circuit is thus protecting *not* marginalized groups, as originally envisioned under the viewpoint neutrality doctrines, *but* the mainstream population of consumers and pornographers that exploit, abuse, and subordinate the marginalized. This misuse of the viewpoint neutrality doctrine is akin to what Karl Marx and Friedrich Engels refer to as "ideology" when introducing the *camera obscura* analogy, which represents an inverse image of material reality—an ideology derived not from "empirically verifiable" facts, but from the statements, conceptions, and imaginings of that reality.[237] Dominant ideologies tend to support dominant groups' perspectives and interests. Here, the Seventh Circuit inverts the actual power relations characterizing pornography production: corporations that exploit vulnerable populations for sex are portrayed as marginalized underdogs, while women and children victimized by producers and consumers are equated with powerful government censors. By contrast, the Indianapolis ordinance would codify a substantive equality perspective in law that draws on the empirical evidence in a manner consistent with the unequal material reality experienced by survivors of pornography's harms.

Rational Review: Alternative Balancing

Another potential route to sustaining the ordinance would be to argue that pornography, as defined under the ordinance, is sufficiently analogous to low-value speech (e.g., "fighting words"),[238] obscenity,[239] or group libel[240] to sustain the same standard of review. This legal theory was raised by Indianapolis and is superficially recognized by the Seventh Circuit.[241] Unprotected expressions like these are not regarded as contributing to the vibrant and robust public discourse that the First Amendment protects.[242]

A "legitimate objective" is sufficient to regulate expression of this sort under rational basis review, where "the law need not be in every respect logically consistent" so long as "there is an evil at hand for correction, and that it might be thought that the particular legislative measure was a rational way to correct it."[243] The regulation of obscenity on the internet was upheld in 2005 under this standard by the Third Circuit Court of Appeals, which followed previous Supreme Court obscenity decisions, such as *United States v. Orito* (1973), holding that "Congress could reasonably determine such regulation."[244]

Indianapolis invoked the Supreme Court's group libel decision in *Beauharnais v. Illinois* (1952),[245] which upheld an Illinois law against group libel that proscribed "any . . . publication or exhibition [that] portrays depravity, criminality, unchastity, or lack of virtue of a class of citizens, of any race, color, creed or religion" that might expose people to, among other things, "contempt, derision, or obloquy."[246] Substantive considerations involving the relationship between groups and equality were present in *Beauharnais*' reasoning, even if it did not explicitly invoke the Fourteenth Amendment's Equal Protection Clause. For instance, the Court noted that group defamation affects the status of individuals relative to the group, thus by extension affecting their relative equality: "a man's [*sic*] job and his educational opportunities and the dignity accorded him may depend as much on the reputation of the racial and religious group to which he willy-nilly belongs, as on his own merits."[247] Put otherwise, group libel contributes to discrimination against disadvantaged groups.

The type of expression covered under the Illinois law could pertain to matters of public policy, such as crime or immigration, which are arguably closer to the type of speech regarded as being encouraged and protected by the Constitution than is pornography as defined under the ordinance. Yet the Supreme Court upheld Illinois' group libel law against First Amendment challenge, balancing expressive freedoms against centuries of "exacerbated tension between races, often flaring into violence and destruction,"[248] and concluding that Illinois was not "without reason in seeking ways to curb false or malicious defamation of racial and religious groups" that would " 'deprive others of their *equal right* to the exercise of their liberties.' "[249] Thus, the Court's conclusion came by way of a balancing test where equality rights outweighed expressive freedoms.

Note the difference between balancing sex equality against expressive interests under strict scrutiny in sex discrimination cases and balancing similarly under rational review by applying the analogy with low-value speech, obscenity, and group libel cases. Under strict scrutiny, the government would argue that combating pornography is a compelling interest; under rational review, it would argue that pornography is unprotected because it does not contribute to the liberal values protected by the First Amendment. In terms of the level of scrutiny applied to the government interest, the group libel analogy has one advantage over the sex discrimination theory in that the latter requires narrowly tailored legislation. Obscenity, as observed previously, has been found to be a more vague and overbroad concept than what was articulated in the ordinance,[250] yet it has been sustained under the First Amendment.

The Seventh Circuit's only direct response to the argument that *Beauharnais* supports the ordinance is found in a footnote. There, it is briefly claimed that the court's own decision in *Collin v. Smith* (1978) and other cases, such as the Supreme Court's decision in a defamation suit brought by a public official in 1964 (*New York Times v. Sullivan*), had by implication "washed away the foundations" of *Beauharnais*.[251] Absent Supreme Court review in *Collin*, the invalidation of an ordinance enacted to prevent a Nazi march in Skokie, Illinois, was allowed to stand—an ordinance that used language similar to the group defamation law upheld in *Beauharnais*.[252] Yet this denial of certiorari is not enough to infer that *Beauharnais* is superseded; after all, the Court provided no explanation for its denial of certiorari.[253] Crucially, the Supreme Court has continued to distinguish *Beauharnais* as an example of unprotected expression, usually in a string of citations, but still without indicating that it has been superseded or is otherwise legally infirm. For instance, the Court in 2010 distinguished *Beauharnais*' group libel from such protected expression as depictions of animal cruelty.[254] Moreover, contrary to the Seventh Circuit's allusions regarding *N.Y. Times v. Sullivan*, the Supreme Court has distinguished that holding on defamation of "public persons" from the holding in *Beauharnais* to support their decision on child pornography, determining that group libel and child pornography deserved less First Amendment protection than the defamation of public figures.[255] This interpretation is consistent with the Court's decision to limit the reach of the *New York Times* libel standard to public figures; as maintained in *Gertz v. Robert Welch, Inc.* (1974), "private individuals" are more vulnerable to the injury of defamation, and "the state interest in protecting them is correspondingly greater."[256]

Since Indianapolis advanced a novel theory with no direct precedent, the Seventh Circuit should have considered more seriously to what extent

Beauharnais was relevant in the constitutional review of the ordinance. Instead, it asserted in a footnote that pornography "must be an insult or slur for its own sake to come within the ambit of *Beauharnais*," providing no citation.[257] The wording of the statute upheld in *Beauharnais* directly refutes that interpretation: to reiterate, the Illinois statute prohibited a publication or exhibition that "portrays depravity, criminality, unchastity, or lack of virtue of a class of citizens."[258] Such expression can take many forms, with insults and slurs likely the least potent and persuasive in portraying the purported "depravity" or "criminality" of an identified group. Nowhere are there insults, slurs, or expressions analogous to those referenced in the quoted statute, nor does the opinion itself suggest so. The Supreme Court chose not to sever parts of the Illinois statute, or to rewrite it to correct for overbreadth, vagueness, or other feature deemed unconstitutional. The statute was sustained in entirety.

Indeed, the Seventh Circuit admits that the Supreme Court "sometimes balances the value of speech against the costs of its restriction, but it does this by category of speech and not by the content of particular works. Indianapolis has created an approved point of view and so loses the support of these cases."[259] However, the ordinance does not create "an approved point of view." It regulates a *practice* of subordination, not *viewpoints* endorsing subordination. Nowhere does it prevent someone from expressing the viewpoint that women are second-class citizens who should be sexually subordinated, whether such statements are made in television, newspapers, books, or elsewhere.

Assuming, for the sake of argument, that the ordinance *implicitly* created an "approved point of view" that sex discrimination is wrong. By the same token, then, the statute the Supreme Court upheld in *Beauharnais* implicitly created the approved point of view that discrimination against groups " 'of any race, color, creed or religion' " is wrong.[260] Nonetheless, rather than being abrogated because it "created an approved point of view" based on the "content of particular works" it targeted (i.e., defamation of groups on the basis of their race, color, creed, or religion), *Beauharnais* has continued to be cited by the Supreme Court as an example of unprotected expression. Certainly, *Beauharnais* has not been accorded a place of prominence by the Court, which has never invoked it in support of an analogous law. Yet its recurrence in various opinions suggests that it is still good law.

Another inaccuracy in the Seventh Circuit's opinion is its rendering of First Amendment law as statically adhering to a finite list of established categories of speech. As recalled, *Hudnut* claims that the Supreme Court only balances the value of speech "by category of speech and not by the content of particular works."[261] Again, *Beauharnais* disproves the point. Group libel was a category of expression that did not exist in First Amendment doctrine until that decision, where the Supreme Court conceded that, although "[n]o one will gainsay that it is libelous falsely to charge another with being a rapist, robber, carrier of knives and guns, and user of marijuana," the "precise question" of whether such libelous statements could be proscribed when "directed at designated collectivities" as opposed to individuals was not answered.[262] "We cannot say . . . that the question is concluded by history and practice."[263] Although there were "authorities" who suggested that libelous statements against groups were "crimes at common law," the Court described them as "dubious."[264] Nonetheless, it accepted Illinois' analogous reasoning on the notion that the discrimination suffered by members of social groups through group libel was similar to that suffered by individuals in the case of personal libel insofar as the former's status depends as much on the group's reputation to which they "willy-nilly" belong as on their "own merits."[265] This logic can likewise be applied to social groups subordinated by pornography.

Beauharnais invented a new category of unprotected speech that, contrary to the Seventh Circuit's claim, had to be based on the "content of particular works," such as materials that were similar to the leaflet defaming the Black community in Chicago circulated by the White Circle League of America, Inc., which was thus subject to the indictment. Just as *Beauharnais* invented a group libel category by analogy, then, the Seventh Circuit could have taken the same approach as a means of sustaining the ordinance. If the creation of new categories of unprotected speech under the First Amendment was impossible, as implied by the Seventh Circuit, the law could not change regardless of the gravity of the conditions presented. Likewise, the notion that the ordinance is not viewpoint neutral because it does not conform to preexisting categories, thus purportedly making it unconstitutional, fails to acknowledge that some unprotected categories were conceived in situations analogous to those surrounding the anti-pornography civil rights movements in Minneapolis and Indianapolis. Unprotected expressive categories under the First Amendment are ultimately based on politics, viewpoints, and sometimes ideology. For instance, obscenity is, by law, defined according to the contemporary community standards test.[266] Yet this test is impliedly a measure of the majority's viewpoint, which is hardly viewpoint neutral, at least not relative to the minority's point of view. The difference from the ordinance's definition of pornography, which was supported by a majority of legislators or voters where it was passed, is that the concept of obscenity has endured for centuries and thus been supported by more courts and legislatures.[267]

Obscenity law implies that the viewpoint neutrality doctrine is really a consensus test: expression deemed unprotected by sustainable legislative majorities, judicial decisions, or both, is the only one exempt from constitutional protection, whether or not it amounts to viewpoint discrimination. It is at this juncture that the notion of consensus, used by Downs' informants to criticize the Minneapolis legislature,[268] partially merges with the liberal concept of negative rights. Without a strong public consensus, there is no opportunity for democratic action against non-state abuses of power; hence the status quo, according to the concept of negative rights relative to legislative activism, will not be disturbed. Such a democratic regime creates serious obstacles to oppressed minorities who wish to change their situation—especially prostituted persons, a group that fits the description of "discrete and insular" minorities who face "prejudice," thus should be protected under the Fourteenth Amendment's Equal Protection Clause since the Supreme Court issued its famous dicta in *United States v. Carolene Products Co.* (1938).[269] Indeed, the impermissible defenses under the ordinance's cause of action for "coercion into pornographic performance" previously discussed would have protected such groups from various prejudices.

As shown, the current democratic regime in the United States substantially prevents majorities from taking action against non-state abuses of power, as evidenced in the cases of the anti-pornography ordinances passed in Minneapolis and Indianapolis. In light of the difficulty inherent in mounting legal challenges to sex discrimination, the Seventh Circuit's concluding remarks that "[f]ree speech has been on balance an ally of those seeking change," and "[w]ithout a strong guarantee of freedom of speech, there is no effective right to challenge what is,"[270] appear disingenuous. Certainly, free speech enabled advocates in both cities to persuade legislatures to pass laws that would effectively have promoted the substantive equality of specific groups. Yet the legislation was invalidated on the Seventh Circuit's notion that the same expression and social practices that harmed those groups must be protected in order to preserve the freedom of those harmed. Rather than serving as "an ally of those seeking change," this application of freedom of speech seems not only legally wrong but also functionally an ally of those seeking to maintain the status quo.

Summary of Analysis

Law has been conceived as "a system of enforceable rules governing social relations and legislated by a political system," while ideology has been referred, "in a general sense, to a system of political ideas."[271] The Seventh Circuit Court of Appeals had numerous legal theories to choose from had it wanted to save Indianapolis' civil rights ordinance from constitutional challenge, suggesting that its decision to invalidate was based more on *ideology* than on *law*.

First, when considering other Supreme Court cases that permitted limitations on expressive freedoms when balanced against the compelling interest of preventing sex discrimination, the ordinance furthered the similarly compelling interest of combating sex discrimination, including sexual exploitation and gender-based violence—interests that could have been upheld under *strict scrutiny*. Federal law today proscribes pornography at work as a form of sexual harassment, if sufficiently pervasive, on the same rationale, finding it weightier than the associated expressive freedoms. In addition, the ordinance used a more "narrowly tailored means" than related laws regulating obscenity. The ordinance relied on a definition of actionable materials that was successfully applied by law students in an experiment, in contrast to obscenity law, which was judged overbroad and vague. The ordinance reached only those materials that provably caused harm, converging with social scientific research and experiential accounts from survivors. The Indianapolis ordinance's definitions and causes of action were additionally limited by restrictions on the broader sub-provisions and required more to show knowledge on the part of the defendant than the previous Minneapolis definition. Child pornography law, by way of contrast, encompasses a broader set of targets, which includes consumers as well as distributors, and provides similar civil remedies as afforded by the ordinance. At least one cause of action under the ordinance that was invalidated has since become law through judicial construction: forcing pornography on someone at work is now proscribed under federal sexual harassment law. Here, hierarchy theory on substantive equality and intersectional discrimination suggests a problem in that pornography, like other forms of sex discrimination, has primarily been made actionable in social contexts where women are most equal to men—for instance, at work, in civic organizations, or during childhood. By contrast, hierarchy theory supports the notion that law should develop from the bottom up, providing relief to those who are most disadvantaged, like prostituted people who are exploited and abused because of pornography. If so, the less disadvantaged women who are more equal to men would also benefit, for instance, by reducing the discriminatory attitudes and sexual aggression heightened by pornography.

Second, the Indianapolis ordinance, at least parts of it, could have been sustained under *intermediate scrutiny*, considering that it furthered the "substantial or important governmental interest"[272] to prevent sex discrimination and provide remedies to those victimized by pornography. According to the so-called viewpoint neutrality doctrine applied by the Seventh Circuit, the ordinance arguably targeted only underlying conduct that subordinated people and was, therefore, "unrelated to the suppression of free expression." Put otherwise, the ordinance did not proscribe the expression of viewpoints in newspapers, television, or books that women should (or should not) be sexually subordinated, exploited, or do (or do not) enjoy being raped. According to this standard of review, if "the incidental restriction on alleged First Amendment freedoms is no greater than is essential to the furtherance" of the governmental "interest," a law may be upheld. The means employed by the ordinance were narrowly tailored, and there were ample alternative venues for expressing the incidentally restricted view that women should be sexually subordinated. However, the Seventh Circuit drew a misplaced analogy to political or dissident speech, failing to appreciate that the ordinance regulated a practice, not a view, of subordination. The Court even suggested that suppressing "Hitler's orations" or "a book about slavery" could be equated with regulating pornography. However, unlike most pornography, such speech does not depend upon exploitation. Rather than being "a book about slavery," pornography is slavery itself. Taken together with the fact that other courts have applied prostitution laws directly to pornography producers (*e.g.*, *Kovner* and *Roeder*), the Seventh Circuit's analogies suggest that its decision not to save the coercion provision—which did not target dissemination or consumption, only the conditions of production—was based more on ideology than on law.

Third, the ordinance could also have been sustained under *rational basis review*, requiring only a "legitimate" interest in preventing sex discrimination. Here, the argument would have been that pornography is analogous to other unprotected categories of expression, such as group libel, obscenity, or "fighting" words. The Seventh Circuit erroneously dismissed this approach on the presumption that the Supreme Court only balances such expression against equality according to predefined categories that are not based on expressive content of particular works. In fact, the Supreme Court created a new category in a 1952 group libel case at the same time it explicitly recognized that neither "history" nor "practice" had previously commanded that such expression be denied protection. The determination of what was included in the category had necessarily to be made on the basis of the content of the relevant expression. The interests considered in that case were also similar to those of Indianapolis, as both the Illinois group libel law and the Indianapolis ordinance were intended to prevent discrimination against members of disadvantaged social groups. It is particularly notable that Illinois' group libel law also targeted speech that the First Amendment was originally understood to protect, including policy discussions on topics like crime, immigration, and religious practices. By contrast, the Indianapolis ordinance targeted graphic sexually explicit subordination that is more similar to obscenity than to policy discourse and is thus further removed from the type of expression originally protected under the First Amendment—expression that was within the ambit of the Illinois statute, but not the Indianapolis ordinance. If group libel could be created as a new unprotected category of expression by analogous reasoning, the Seventh Circuit could similarly have created a new category for Indianapolis using analogous laws with interests and purposes similar to those mentioned. By contrast, if courts could only sustain a new law with reference to existing categories, legal change would be difficult, if not impossible.

5

Federal Responses, 1984–2014

The civil rights anti-pornography movements in Minneapolis and Indianapolis had gathered enough public momentum by 1985 to produce widespread national debate. The Attorney General at the time was William French Smith, who was appointed by then President-Elect Ronald Reagan in 1981.[1] In 1985, Smith established the Attorney General's Commission on Pornography (the "Commission"), which was tasked "to determine the nature, extent, and impact on society of pornography in the United States, and to make specific recommendations to the Attorney General concerning more effective ways in which the spread of pornography could be contained, consistent with constitutional guarantees."[2]

Civil Rights Challenges (1984–1992)

Attorney General Smith's Commission (1985–1986)

The Attorney General's Commission has conducted what is likely the single most extensive investigation to date of the harms caused by the production and consumption of pornography. It is partly on account of its many unique and high-quality sources that it is cited in a number of places throughout this book. A common misconception among critics of the Commission is that it was the work of Edwin Meese III, the Attorney General appointed by Reagan later in 1985. In actuality, it was William French Smith who selected the Commission's members and defined its scope of inquiry.[3] Although Meese had announced the Commission's formation after Smith created it,[4] thereafter he was unresponsive to its needs, ignored its recommendations, and ridiculed it by publicly receiving its *Final Report* under a semi-nude statue of the Spirit of Justice.[5]

The Commission's *Final Report*, published in July 1986, devoted a full chapter to "performers," providing numerous interviews and systematic readings on the subject, including such varied sources as the industry's

Pornography. Max Waltman, Oxford University Press. © Oxford University Press 2021.
DOI: 10.1093/oso/9780197598535.003.0006

own publications and interviews with performers and others used in different forms of pornography.[6] Similarly, the public testimony of numerous witnesses, among them producers, performers, and law enforcement personnel, was systematically collected.[7] The Commission acknowledged that the evidence "taken as a whole, supports the conclusion that the pornography industry systematically violates human rights with apparent impunity."[8] Moreover, it observed that the "most powerless citizens in society are singled out on the basis of their gender—often aggravated by their age, race, disability, or other vulnerability—for deprivations of liberty, property, labor, bodily and psychic security and integrity, privacy, reputation, and even life." Notably, by acknowledging multiple grounds of disadvantage, including gender, age, race, and disability, the Commission adopted what was later termed an "intersectional" approach to pornography's harms.[9] The Commission's findings are also consistent with the findings made here.

The Commission implicitly questioned the Seventh Circuit Court of Appeals' decision to invalidate the Indianapolis anti-pornography civil rights ordinance by proposing similar legislation themselves, largely following the model of the local ordinances drafted by Catharine MacKinnon and Andrea Dworkin.[10] The Commission pointed out that the Supreme Court, in such groundbreaking decisions as *Brown v. Board of Education* (1954),[11] which ended de jure racial segregation in public education, and *Muller v. Oregon* (1908),[12] which sustained laws against what the Court determined to be excessive working hours, relied on social science and other empirical evidence similar to that used by the Indianapolis legislature to construe its ordinance.[13] Elaborating on the Seventh Circuit's decision, the Commission noted that "[m]ost of the evidence that establishes the fact that pornography subordinates women and undermines their status and opportunities for equality comes from [such] extra-judicial sources, studies and individual accounts."[14]

In addition to the Commission's points, it is also worthwhile to compare the Seventh Circuit's treatment of *Beauharnais v. Illinois* (1952) with the Supreme Court's decision in *Brown v. Board of Education* (1954). Recall that the Seventh Circuit neglected to mention that the Supreme Court did create a new category of unprotected speech in *Beauharnais*, which neither "history" nor "practice" had previously commanded.[15] In *Brown*, the Court made a similar maneuver in rejecting established doctrine despite the absence of preexisting categories from which to draw; rather, *Brown* relied on empirical evidence.[16] However, the Seventh Circuit's analysis and remarks, for example, that " 'pornography' is not low value speech within the meaning of these cases"[17]—cases that included group libel (*Beauharnais*), obscenity, and fighting words—suggested the Seventh Circuit would only sustain laws that relied upon preexisting doctrinal categories. If the Supreme Court had followed the Seventh Circuit's approach, the *Brown* decision as we know it would have been impossible insofar as racial segregation in southern schools was widely perceived to be perfectly consistent with the doctrine of "separate but equal" established under the Fourteenth Amendment's Equal Protection Clause. Before May 17, 1954, the law of the land was *Plessy v. Ferguson* (1896), which held that, although the "object of the [Fourteenth] [A]mendment was undoubtedly to enforce the absolute equality of the two races before the law . . . it could not have been intended to abolish distinctions based upon color, or to enforce social, as distinguished from political equality, or a commingling of the two races upon terms unsatisfactory to either."[18]

Not until the attorneys representing the *Brown* plaintiffs successfully challenged *Plessy*'s interpretation did de jure educational segregation end. As the Court in *Beauharnais* had done regarding group libel two years earlier, the *Brown* Court realized that although preexisting doctrines "cast some light, it is not enough to resolve the problem with which we are faced. At best, they are inconclusive."[19] In deciding *Brown*, the Court went beyond traditional categorical thinking and looked at relevant empirical evidence. It found that, for African American children, racial segregation in education "generates a feeling of inferiority as to their status in the community that may affect their hearts and minds in a way unlikely ever to be undone."[20] The Court even quoted from a lower court decision upholding *Plessy*, where that lower court itself acknowledged that " 'the policy of separating the races is usually interpreted as denoting the inferiority of the negro group. A sense of inferiority affects the motivation of a child to learn . . . [and] deprive[s] them of some of the benefits they would receive in a racial[ly] integrated school system.' "[21]

In contrast to the *Brown* Court, in *American Booksellers Ass'n v. Hudnut* (1985), the Seventh Circuit observed that pornography causes "affront and lower pay at work, insult and injury at home, battery and rape on the streets,"[22] yet chose to invalidate the ordinance nonetheless. In this respect, its decision is similar to the approach taken by the lower court cited in *Brown*, which sustained *Plessy* despite acknowledging that racial segregation in education imposed a sense of "inferiority" on African American children and negatively affected their ongoing education compared to those attending racially integrated schools.

Similar to *Hudnut*, then, social reality did not fit preexisting legal categories in *Brown*. Yet the Supreme Court decided on the empirical evidence rather than on precedent: "Whatever may have been the extent of psychological knowledge at the time of *Plessy v. Ferguson*, this finding [that segregation is harmful and inherently unequal] is amply supported by modern authority [n.11]."[23] The Court then footnoted the work of a number of social scientists, including the American psychologist Kenneth Clark and the Swedish sociologist and economist Gunnar Myrdal, the author of the classic study *An American Dilemma*.[24] Consequently, *Plessy* was overruled and racial segregation in education was deemed "inherently unequal."[25] Likewise, the empirical evidence reviewed here overwhelmingly shows that pornography is an "inherently unequal" practice of subordination. This politico-legal situation is not unlike recognizing racial segregation in education as a practice of subordination while still feeling "compelled to rule against" African American plaintiffs challenging that subordination,[26] presumably based on *Plessy*'s framework that relied on formal equality to protect racial discrimination. That is basically the approach taken by the Seventh Circuit when it rejected the civil rights ordinance because it did not conform to a preexisting category, serious harms notwithstanding.[27] The Seventh Circuit's theory of precedential reliance would have made a decision like *Brown* impossible and left *Plessy* undisturbed.

The Attorney General's Commission, in contrast to *Hudnut*, *Plessy*, and similar cases upholding the status quo, engaged the perspective and interests of those victimized by pornography. Not only did it devote an entire chapter to "performers" and another to "victim testimony," but it also endorsed the antipornography civil rights ordinances: "The civil rights approach, although controversial, is the only legal tool suggested to the Commission which is specifically designed to provide direct relief to the victims of the injuries so exhaustively documented in our hearings throughout the country."[28] Although the Commission noted that the Indianapolis ordinance had been declared unconstitutional in a summary affirmance by the Supreme Court, it nonetheless supported the ordinance, albeit with the caveat that "proponents . . . must attempt to fashion a definition of pornography which will pass constitutional muster," and a recommendation that it provide "an affirmative defense of a knowing and voluntary consent to the acts."[29] The Commission's suggested affirmative defense was in tension, however, with the ordinances' impermissible defenses, which addressed situations where vulnerable people knowingly "consent" to being bought for sex in prostitution or pornography due to, among other things, economic desperation and lack of alternatives.[30] But except for this suggestion, the Commission showed little or no deference to the Seventh Circuit or the Supreme Court's summary affirmance. Instead, it underscored its support for the ordinances while concluding that when pornography is trafficked in, forced upon someone, or contributes to an assault it "constitutes a practice of discrimination on the basis of sex" and "[a]ny legal protections which currently exist for such practices are inconsistent with contemporary notions of individual equality."[31]

The P.R. Campaign against the Commission

The response to the Commission's *Final Report* was predictable for a country known for its powerful interest groups that routinely exert tremendous influence on public opinion. The press dubbed the Commission the "Meese Commission"[32] despite that Attorney General Smith was responsible for its creation.[33] By associating the *Final Report* with Meese, critics seemingly intended to delegitimize it, because Meese was unpopular in many quarters, indeed "almost universally despised."[34] The machinations behind the scenes, which can explain much of the hostile media response, were revealed by contemporaneous journalists and others.[35] A month before the *Report*'s release, the Media Coalition was committed to paying Gray & Company, then Washington, D.C.'s largest public relations firm, up to $900,000 for "a strategy designed to further discredit the Commission."[36] This strategy was revealed in written communication between Gray and their client, which was subsequently leaked.[37] The Media Coalition was an interest group funded primarily by publishers and distributors, including *Playboy* and *Penthouse* (either directly, or indirectly through a parent corporate entity).[38] Gray's budget was more than twice the Commission's $400,000.[39] According to investigative journalist Susan B. Trento, "much" of this budget was covered by *Playboy*, and some by *Penthouse*.[40] Gray advised its client to attempt to persuade the Attorney General, the White House, and the leadership of both political parties that the *Final Report* was "so flawed, so controversial, so contested and so biased that they should shy away from publicly endorsing the document."[41]

Observers have noted that some of Gray & Company's baseless claims were promulgated so successfully that they were treated as "conventional wisdom" in most media coverage of the *Report*.[42] This misinformation included the assertion that "[t]here is no factual or scientific basis for the exaggerated and unfounded allegations that" pornography "is in any way a cause of violent or criminal behavior"[43]—a claim clearly refuted even by the evidence available at the time. On June 22–24, shortly before the Commission published its *Report*, the U.S. Surgeon General held a workshop for two dozen independent researchers and experts—mostly professors, a few of whom had criticized the Commission[44]—which issued a conference report on August 4 that "summarized the consensus" among the group "regarding the nature and extent of evidence about the effects of pornography."[45] Notably, this group did not have access to the Commission's full report, which included new evidence from several public hearings with adult survivors, producers, and others with experience either with the pornography industry, the harms linked to it, or both. Five "consensus statements" were nonetheless agreed upon:

(1) "Children and adolescents who participate in the production of pornography experience adverse, enduring effects."
(2) "Prolonged use of pornography increases beliefs that less common sexual practices are more common."
(3) "Pornography that portrays sexual aggression as pleasurable for the victim increases the acceptance of the use of coercion in sexual relations."
(4) "Acceptance of coercive sexuality appears to be related to sexual aggression."
(5) "In laboratory studies measuring short term effects, exposure to violent pornography increases punitive behavior toward women."[46]

Its conservatism notwithstanding, and the statement's acknowledged links, among other things, between pornography's presentation of sexual aggression as "pleasurable" and real sexual aggression, the media sided with Gray & Company's manufactured claim that there was "no" evidentiary basis that pornography harms women. For instance, the *Chicago Tribune* ran an unsigned editorial on July 13, 1986, falsely maintaining that the Commission made "some dubious connections between sexually explicit material and violence" and that its policy proposals "drew attention to the unconvincingness of the empirical data that some pornography can cause sexual violence in those who read or watch it."[47] Similarly, the *Toronto Star*, criticizing the Commission in a piece on September 27, 1986, erroneously claimed that "there's no evidence pornography causes rape or any other vicious behavior."[48] A more tendentious piece run in the *Washington Post* on July 14, 1986, claimed that the Commission's "conclusions and recommendations" ranged from "preposterous" to "unconstitutional, with numerous local stops in between,"[49] while an unsigned editorial in the *New York Times* published on July 2, 1986, erroneously stated that "[t]he Meese commission's connection of pornography and crime outruns its own evidence."[50] These newspapers' representation of the evidence of harm as "dubious," "unconvincing," and "preposterous" stands in sharp contrast even to the admittedly conservative "consensus" among researchers at the time. Far from being independent and critical, much of the mainstream media was effectively manipulated by powerful lobbyists, and thus failed to uphold fundamental principles of responsible journalism in a well-functioning democracy.

Gray's P.R. campaign had also disseminated the claims that the Commission's work "infringe[s] on all our rights," that it was orchestrated by "religious extremists," and further contended that if "this campaign against one segment of publishing is successful . . . small, extremist pressure groups will step up their efforts to impose their narrow moral and social agenda on the majority'"[51]—notions echoed in such venues as *Time* magazine and the *Los Angeles Times*, which cast the conflict as one between religious conservatives and secular liberals, systematically ignoring the feminist perspective.[52] These claims were also wrong. For example, the anti-pornography civil rights ordinances never gave anyone the right to sue based on the expression of extreme sexual opinions about women; as previously noted,[53] it directly targeted demonstrably subordinating practices, not viewpoints. Moreover, contrary to the P.R. campaign's statements, the commissioners represented a broad spectrum of political views, reported to include three liberals, four conservatives, and four "middle of the roaders."[54] Some of the Commission's members even had the courage to change their views significantly during the course of investigation based on the empirical facts they confronted. For instance, Dr. Park Elliot Dietz, who initially held a liberal position that was tolerant of pornography, wrote a personal statement later included in the *Final Report* (with which some other members concurred), stating, among other things, that pornography "is used as an instrument of sexual abuse and sexual harassment."[55] He considered the situation of those used as performers and the effects of consumption on society while urging the nation not to tolerate pornography, but instead to "strike the chains from America's women and children, to free them from the bonds of pornography, to free them from the bonds of sexual slavery, to free them from the bonds of sexual abuse, to free them from the bonds of inner torment that entrap the second-class citizen in an otherwise free nation."[56]

Congressional Attempts (1984–1992)

In spite of the negative media response to the Attorney General's *Final Report*, and the obstacles to passing and successfully defending the anti-pornography civil rights ordinances on local and state levels, similar ideas continued to generate interest among American politicians. For instance, Senator Arlen Specter (R-Pa.) introduced the Pornography Victims Protection Act in 1984, a bill that was later introduced in the House as well by Representative Sedgwick "Bill" Green (R-N.Y. 15) in 1986.[57] The proposal contained a civil ground for adults and children who had been coerced into making pornography, which was defined as the "visual depiction" of "sexually explicit conduct,"[58] to recover damages from producers.[59] It also offered shields against judicial gender bias that could not negate a finding of coercion, such as whether the plaintiff previously had been prostituted, had at some time had consensual sex with the defendant, had previously posed for pornography, had consented, had signed a contract, or had been paid.[60] These shields resemble the impermissible defenses that were originally proposed in the Minneapolis ordinance.[61]

The Pornography Victims Protection Act did not propose a similarly narrow and subordination-based definition of pornography as set forth in the Minneapolis and Indianapolis ordinances. Still, because the congressional bill only targeted production, not distribution, far less consumption, harms, it should not have raised First Amendment concerns. As recalled, some American courts had already applied prostitution laws against third parties or buyers on pornographers, finding no bar under the First Amendment to proceeding against the underlying non-expressive criminal conduct.[62] Although some courts had not followed suit, it can be argued that the proposed legislation would have met the *O'Brien* standard since the legislative interest in combating sexual coercion in pornography production is "unrelated to the suppression of free expression," and "the incidental restriction on alleged First Amendment freedoms is no greater than is essential to the furtherance of that interest."[63] Compared with the Indianapolis subordination-centered definitions and their subcategories, the bill's broad definition of actionable materials as visual "sexually explicit conduct"[64] might have been perceived as a strategy to avoid repeating a judicial challenge such as that presented in the Seventh Circuit, where the Indianapolis coercion provision was invalidated as not "neutral with respect to viewpoint,"[65] however questionable that decision may have been. Yet despite being reintroduced in the Senate and the House through 1987, this bill failed to obtain enough support to pass.[66]

Another congressional attempt to pass a civil rights law against pornography occurred in 1989 when Senator Mitch McConnell (R-Ky.) introduced the Pornography Victims' Compensation Act.[67] This bill centered on harms caused by consumers and offered civil remedies from producers, distributors, exhibitors, and sellers of specific materials where plaintiffs could prove by "a preponderance of evidence"—the same standard employed by the Minneapolis and Indianapolis ordinances—that the specifically identified pornography was a "proximate cause of the offense, by influencing or inciting the sexual offender to commit the offense perpetrated against the victim."[68] The bill did not have a companion measure in the House.[69]

Initially, the Pornography Victims' Compensation Act appeared similar to the assault provision in the Minneapolis anti-pornography civil rights ordinance.[70] However, as deliberations moved to the Senate Judiciary Committee, the bill's original approach was watered down in the course of the events that followed. In one revision, a provision was struck that treated offender testimony as admissible evidence.[71] This provision was sometimes referred to as the "Bundy Bill," usually by critics who speculated that it would encourage leniency toward the defendant relative to the disseminator.[72] The nickname referred to the notorious serial killer Theodore R. Bundy, who testified in his final interview before the execution that "his gruesome killings of women were inspired by hard-core pornography."[73]

Although the bar against "offender testimony" was removed in a subsequent revision,[74] several other substantial restrictions and exceptions were inserted instead,[75] of which two departed considerably from the Minneapolis model. First, Senator Howell Heflin (D-Ala.) added an amendment requiring a criminal conviction of the offender of the sexual crime before a civil suit could be filed against a commercial disseminator of the specific pornography that potentially contributed to the offender's conduct.[76] Second, Senator Specter added an amendment requiring that producers and disseminators of these materials first be "criminally convicted for violating obscenity or child pornography laws prior to the commencement of the civil action" against them.[77] By contrast to Senator Specter's amendment, which tied the civil action to obscenity or child pornography laws, the initial versions of the bill had defined pornography as that which is "sexually explicit," and had also included various sub-definitions to specify the meaning of the term, with some elements similar to the Minneapolis ordinance's subordination approach that centered on explicitly violent and coercive materials.[78]

An additional restrictive amendment proposed by Senator Joseph R. Biden (D-Del.), the Chair of the Judiciary Committee, who now serves as President of the United States, went even further, only to narrowly miss the majority needed to pass (7–7).[79] Senator Biden wished to require that plaintiffs only be allowed to sue under the bill if the producer or disseminator of the material alleged to have substantially caused the sexual offense not only had first been convicted under obscenity laws but continued to disseminate the same obscene material before providing it to the sex offender.[80] Put differently, in the words of Senator Strom Thurmond (R-S.C.): this amendment presumed a perpetrator "foolish enough to commit the identical criminal act twice."[81]

Likely at this point, being tied to the vagueness of obscenity, the difficulties of proof it presents, and its imperviousness to the claims of victims, the bill would have become a dead letter even without Senator Biden's amendment.[82] Although the Senate Judiciary Committee voted to favorably report a revised bill without the Biden amendment by a vote of seven to six on June 25, 1992,[83] the full Senate took no action thereafter.[84] As recalled, the bill also never had a House companion.[85] Whether or not the bill was purposefully opposed later, the bill's original supporters in and outside Congress may have lost interest at this stage.

In contrast to the congressional approach, the Attorney General's Commission took a more proactive stance, proposing the civil rights ordinances mostly unaltered.[86] The commissioners were appointed for a year to study the problem of pornography. Members of Congress are in a far different position. Given the varied interests competing for their support, it is unlikely that many looked beyond the evidence exposed through hearings and in consultation with staff, constituents, professional lobbyists, and other policy stakeholders. This lack of focus provides another reason why, as hierarchy theory hypothesizes, stronger representation of disadvantaged and affected groups in the political process would improve outcomes, presuming, that is, that their perspectives and interests are not drowned out by the cacophony of opposing interest groups and competing issues on the agenda.

Obscenity Law in the Twenty-first Century (2002–2014)

Since the congressional attempts to pass civil rights legislation against pornography were obstructed, adult pornography in the United States has largely been unchallenged as a civil rights violation outside the confines of sexual harassment in the workplace. Absent civil rights legislation and the application of existing prostitution and trafficking laws to pornography production, the only direct route remaining to challenge the harms of pornography legally is obscenity law. Considering that the concept of obscenity is neither victim-centered nor concerned with sex discrimination, this, as observed earlier, is a dubious route. However, in light of the dearth of alternatives, it is important to examine its contemporary application more closely.

A New Approach to Violent, Aggressive, and Degrading Materials

After the turn of the twenty-first century, the Department of Justice renewed its efforts to pursue the producers of adult and child pornography in tandem. Observers described the approach as "'trying to set boundaries as to the acceptable realm of adult material'"[87]—an approach that diverged from that undertaken during the Clinton era, when obscenity charges often served as proxies for increasing the prosecutorial leverage, "piled onto other counts, like child pornography, to enhance a prison sentence or encourage plea bargains."[88] This initiative was begun during the Bush administration and continued under President Obama.[89]

The focus of the new prosecutions of adult pornographers was perhaps most evident in the congressional testimony of Mary Beth Buchanan, a U.S. Attorney for the Western District of Pennsylvania. During a 2003 hearing, she did not focus on "prurient interest" or lack of other "value,"[90] but instead on violence against women. Among the materials her unit was intent on prosecuting were representations of the "brutal rape and killings of three women" who are "hit, slapped, and spit upon."[91] Buchanan further alluded to production harms, referencing a letter from a woman who reported that her adult daughter had been exploited by pornographers, after which she was "reduced to an anorexic drug addict with severely compromised mental and physical health."[92] Buchanan also emphasized that "it is important to recognize that adults, as well as children, are often victims of pornography."[93]

In her congressional submission, Buchanan further maintained that "[o]bscenity, by its very nature, reduces human beings to sexual objects."[94] Sexual objectification had not previously been a discernible element of American obscenity law, unless it could be classified as appealing to "prurient interests" or otherwise being patently "offensive" to community standards.[95] Community standards today might also be more accepting of sexual objectification than they were in the 1980s and 1990s, considering that pornography consumption may have expanded with its increased accessibility on the internet. However, it is much more rare for women than men to consume pornography on a regular basis. Given that women comprise half the population, the community standard could potentially be reshaped to include at least violent and degrading pornography, and possibly be extended to sexual objectification per se. Buchanan's equation of obscenity with sexual objectification is consistent with common presentations in mainstream pornography. Her interpretation thus corresponds to a more empirically sound argument for pursuing criminal obscenity laws against pornography that provably make consumers cause harm to others and typically requires exploitation of detrimental social conditions. Without a civil remedy, however, this legal approach is less direct than the civil rights ordinances.

The First Trials

The first major federal case against a well-known pornography producer under the Department of Justice's new approach was *United States v. Extreme Associates, Inc.* (2005).[96] The government's brief presented content similar to what was described in Congress two years earlier. Accordingly, a video entitled *Forced Entry* showed three women being "abused and degraded throughout graphic portrayals of forced sex acts," and raped and murdered.[97] Among other videos referenced was one that presented women being subjected to "sex acts with multiple partners while a bowl . . . is filled with various bodily liquids," where at the "conclusion of each vignette, the women drink the concoction." Additional materials cited presented sexual abuse "between adult males and females dressed to look like minor children." Furthermore, the prosecution presented internet "video clips," one of which showed "men urinating directly into the mouths of women and a woman having sex with multiple men, marketed as a 'gang bang.'"

None of the parties disputed that Extreme Associates, Inc., "maintained a website through which it engaged in the business of producing, selling, and distributing *obscene* video tapes, DVDs, and computer files in interstate commerce."[98] Hence, the obscenity indictment itself was not disputed, but its constitutionality was. In the Federal District Court for the Western District of Pennsylvania, the defendants successfully argued that obscenity law "as applied" was unconstitutional; however, the decision was reversed by the Third Circuit Court of Appeals, and the Supreme Court subsequently denied certiorari.[99]

One of the district court's central rationales for invalidating the obscenity law had been that developments in privacy law allegedly superseded it. A purportedly analogous case was invoked, *Lawrence v. Texas* (2003),[100] where a statute prohibiting sodomy was held to violate adults' rights to liberty and privacy, including gay people's right to engage in consensual sex. The district court attempted to cast pornography (or rather, "obscenity") as analogous to privacy—that is, equating obscenity with consensual sex between gay people, thereby assertedly raising the standard from rational review to strict scrutiny:

> First, we find that after *Lawrence*, the government can no longer rely on the advancement of a moral code, *i.e.*, preventing consenting adults from entertaining lewd or lascivious thoughts, as a legitimate, let alone a compelling, state interest. Second, we find that, as applied to the particular circumstances of this case, the laws are not narrowly drawn to advance the government's two asserted interests: 1) protecting minors from exposure to obscene materials; and 2) protecting unwitting adults from inadvertent exposure to obscene materials. . . .
>
> . . . .
>
> The *Lawrence* decision . . . . can be reasonably interpreted as holding that public morality is not a legitimate state interest sufficient to justify infringing on adult, private, consensual, sexual conduct even if that conduct is deemed offensive to the general public's sense of morality.[101]

The district court's analogy to consensual gay sex is particularly misleading. Sexual activity engaged in by two willing participants is, by definition, antipodal to the typically coercive circumstances that are documented to be pervasive in the production of pornography. Moreover, to identify the government's interest in pursuing obscenity litigation as only a means of protecting "minors" or "unwitting adults" from involuntary exposure ignores the underlying government interest on which these prosecutions were premised, as demonstrated, for instance, in U.S. Attorney Buchanan's congressional testimony two years earlier. The district court, among other things, ignored the consumers' sexual aggression and the exploitation and sexual abuse of prostituted women that is associated with pornography. Although later reversed, the objections raised at trial were very similar to those that have historically been raised against obscenity law: that it aims to promote "morality" rather than to advance more compelling state interests (like preventing sex discrimination, sexual exploitation, and abuse). Similar arguments were propounded in Sweden over thirty-five years prior to the *Extreme Associates* litigation. In support of repealing obscenity laws, a Swedish lawyer, who had defended pornographers in obscenity trials,[102] contended in 1969 that the consumption of these materials was "private business" of no government concern.[103] Indeed, except for a prohibition against public exhibition of pornography "meant to be offensive to the public,"[104] the obscenity laws were repealed a year later. Not until 1989 was there a new criminal law against the dissemination of violent pornography in Sweden,[105] a law that has since been ineffective.

The Third Circuit Court of Appeals rejected the district court's invalidation of the obscenity law as applied, including the latter's reliance on *Lawrence* for the proposition that obscenity law unconstitutionally infringed on privacy rights.[106] However, the reversal was made on doctrinal, not empirical, grounds. The Third Circuit did not say, for example, that obscenity causes sex discrimination, therefore making its suppression a compelling governmental interest. Instead, it held that because a case concerning the privacy violation inherent in sodomy statutes is not "directly" controlling for obscenity law, such a case does not entitle a lower court to overrule the Supreme Court's obscenity decisions; hence, only the Supreme Court has the authority to overrule its own decisions on obscenity.[107] Moreover, the Third Circuit held that the internet does not change the legal fact that privacy rights and liability under obscenity laws are controlled by different lines of precedents.[108] Indeed, *Lawrence* did not raise First Amendment issues; it was not a case about commerce, as *Extreme Associates* was, nor was it about obscenity, save for an offhanded remark by three dissenters that equated sodomy laws with "laws against bigamy, same-sex marriage, adult incest, prostitution, masturbation, adultery, fornication, bestiality, and obscenity . . . laws based on *moral* choices."[109]

Before *Extreme Associates* was reversed on appeal, the case drew the attention of a number of legal commentators whose observations appeared in law review articles that cast the case as a wholesale assault on obscenity law in the age of the internet.[110] Even though the case was ultimately reversed, these initial reactions underscore the fragility of obscenity law. Considering that Extreme Associates, Inc., produced among the most violent pornography on the market—pornography that should readily be seen as violating community standards—the case trajectory leaves unresolved the question of whether obscenity is a sound and effective means of protecting against the empirically documented harms of pornography. Although obscenity laws may deter some pornographers from abusively exploiting persons as performers, the lower court's first response to the facts of the case suggests that obscenity law provides precisely the tenuous foundation for evaluating relevant facts for which it has been criticized, perforce in a modern democratic context where constitutional imperatives framed in the moral language of prior centuries are typically viewed with suspicion.

Some Well-Known Producers in L.A. Imprisoned

After the Third Circuit reversed the decision in *Extreme Associates*, the couple behind the company, Rob Zicari and his wife, Janet Romano, signed a plea agreement on July 1, 2009, sentencing each of them to prison for one year and one day.[111] Their defense attorney, H. Louis Sirkin, claimed in a media interview that the decision " 'obviously' " caused a " 'ripple effect on the adult industry' " and was " 'devastating' " to the defendants, ruining them financially, causing them to lose " 'their home,' " even blacklisting them in " 'their industry.' "[112] Whether or not his statements about a "ripple effect" on the industry should be taken seriously, the results of another high-profile case prosecuted at around the same time make Zicari and Romano's punishments seem lenient. A 2007 Department of Justice press release identified the next major suspect to be targeted as a "nationally-known director, producer and star of films featuring acts such as anal penetration, urination, insertion of an entire hand into a vagina or anus, vomiting, and severe violence towards the female performers participating in the acts."[113] This description applied to the Los Angeles–based pornographer Paul F. Little (a.k.a. "Max Hardcore"), who, after a jury trial in June 2008, was sentenced on October 3, 2008, in *United States v. Little*, to forty-six months in prison for multiple obscenity offenses.[114] Little was released on July 19, 2011.[115]

The Obama administration continued the obscenity prosecutions initiated under President Bush. The Los Angeles–based pornographer Ira Isaacs, for example, was first brought to trial in 2008.[116] After overcoming some procedural hurdles, a federal district court jury found him guilty in 2012.[117] Isaacs was sentenced to four years in prison, three years of supervised release, and fined $10,000 for having produced, sold, and distributed obscene materials that showed, among other things, women being used for sex with animals or with human bodily waste.[118] The Ninth Circuit upheld the sentence in its entirety in 2014.[119] During a 2012 congressional hearing, the *Los Angeles Times* reported that U.S. Attorney General Eric Holder "touted Isaacs' prosecution as 'a major case' and called it 'an example of what we are doing' with respect to adult obscenity."[120]

The U.S. Department of Justice filed the last of the high-profile cases in 2008, this one against the well-known pornographer John Stagliano, "widely deemed the originator of plotless 'gonzo' porn."[121] Stagliano is recognized as a major producer and distributor and has been "honored" by the pornographic film industry "with several awards."[122] Prospective jurors were shown materials that included "urination, use of enemas and bondage,"[123] as well as so-called ass-to-mouth and repeated racial slurring against Black male performers.[124] The parties differed as to whether the urination was real or simulated, and whether that distinction (and likewise the distinction between anal milk enemas and anal excretion enemas) was relevant for determining obscenity.[125] Because Stagliano also distributed a wider range of videos that were indistinguishable from other mainstream pornography, it has been posited that the government's other contemporaneously successful prosecutions involving some of " 'the most extreme stuff' " showed that its intent in targeting Stagliano was to be more assertive and " 'put pressure on the entire industry.' "[126]

In July 2010, however, a federal district court in the District of Columbia dismissed the case against Stagliano on "technical grounds" even before defendants "began their defense,"[127] which meant that no judgment was rendered as to whether the movies themselves were protected by the First Amendment.[128] Nevertheless, the government had some success in a separate decision in the Stagliano case that upheld the constitutionality of the federal obscenity statutes. This district court, which falls under the D.C. Circuit's jurisdiction, went beyond the reasons set forth by the Third

Circuit in *Extreme Associates* when it dismissed Stagliano's similar challenge: the district court in Washington, D.C., criticized the defendants for having "conjured up an alternative theory" like "alchemists of old," attempting to invoke "evolving developments in the Supreme Court's substantive due process jurisprudence" in order to challenge the obscenity law's constitutionality.[129] The court concluded that "possession and use of obscenity are hardly analogous to the sexual acts that the *Lawrence* Court found to be so instrumental to the relationships of homosexual persons"; furthermore, it reasoned that a "purported privacy right to obtain or distribute obscenity does not remotely approach the fundamental liberty interests implicated in *Griswold v. Connecticut*, and *Eisenstadt v. Baird*, where . . . the right to obtain contraceptives" was upheld by the Supreme Court.[130] Hence, the court dismissed defendant's alternative theory "that *Lawrence* and its predecessors created a so-called right to sexual privacy so fundamental and so sweeping that it includes the right to obtain, as well as the correlative right to distribute, obscene materials in the public marketplace."[131]

Results, Potential, and Limitations

What are the practical results of these recent federal anti-pornography obscenity prosecutions? The veteran pornography performer William Margold, acting as spokesman for a trade organization, told a journalist reporting on the *Extreme Associates* case in 2009 that it " 'could have been a lot worse.' "[132] He had suspected that the government's indictment of Zicari and Romano could have turned into " 'the quintessential witch hunt of all time and used them as the sacrificial lamb.' " Yet Margold did not think other producers " 'would learn from the sentence' " they received. " 'Unless it happens to you,' " he explained, " 'you don't learn much.' "[133] He had "warned Mr. Zicari when he flaunted his movies in a 2002 PBS 'Frontline' special that he was going to be prosecuted." Nevertheless, Margold maintained that the trade had been affected: " 'There are certain things you just don't do anymore—denigration and degradation,' " he said. " 'We have to comply with what society feels is comfortable.' "[134] Obviously, it is not in the interest of industry representatives to say otherwise.

Nathalie Purcell's book-length content analysis of 110 of the 250 most popular, best-selling, critically acclaimed, and influential hardcore pornographic movies from 1970 through 2010 contradicts Margold's account.[135]

Purcell found that "many contemporary pornographers" in the 2000s met consumers' desensitization by "amping up overt expressions of hostility, anger, and contempt in their movies" toward women.[136] Under the circumstances, prevailing community standards might not object to what Margold recognizes as "denigration and degradation" of or violence against women. Indeed, two studies from the United Kingdom and the United States discussed previously, both published in 2014, indicate that most women who engage in heterosexual anal sex reject it and regard it as painful. Still, their male partners pressure them to do it, often seeking to imitate pornography.[137]

By 2010, anal sex had become the "main or primary event of nearly every sex sequence" in Purcell's sample of pornography movies over time[138]—a finding roughly contemporaneous with the sentencing of Zicari, Romano, and Little and the indictment of Isaacs and Stagliano. The predominance of anal sex in heterosexual pornography likely desensitized the community setting the standards to abusive anal sex, especially among men who consume pornography. In Purcell's words:

> As every gonzo pornographer began to feature anal sex, it became routine and lost its edge as a taboo act. Contemporary fans and viewers have a hard time thinking of anal sex as painful, difficult, or special in any way when every woman in porn is doing it. Twenty-first-century pornographers have responded by increasing the depth, speed, duration, and intensity of anal sex performances.[139]

Other indicators of desensitization to painful anal sex were reported in the previously mentioned study with 1,880 American students published in 2016, which found that although 28.2% of both men and women in this sample reported having tried anal sex,[140] only 8.1% of women, compared to 45.3% of men, wanted to try it.[141] This gender disparity makes sense insofar as men comprise the overwhelming majority of pornography consumers. In other words, neither the industry nor its primary consumers seem to recognize the heterosexual anal sex in contemporary pornography as often being abusive.

Notably, neither the couple at the center of the *Extreme Associates* case, nor Little, Isaacs, or Stagliano, were prosecuted solely for producing or distributing depictions of aggressive anal sex—or for other practices commonly seen in pornography, such as ass-to-mouth, gagging, or verbal aggression. As previously recounted, each of these cases involved further extreme conduct, for example, sexual murders, urination, bestiality, sex with human waste, or severe violence against women. If they set the standard for future cases, much of the abuse and degradation that is essential to mainstream pornography will be left outside the law's purview. By contrast, the anti-pornography civil rights ordinances had the necessary precision to reach the subordination that is commonplace in mainstream pornography, while not capturing non-subordinating sexually explicit materials that may simply offend community standards.

Even if individual prosecutors today may be driven more by the incentive to prevent harm to individuals, community standards are conceptually more consistent with the consensus approach suggested by the opponents of the Minneapolis anti-pornography civil rights ordinance.[142] Additionally, the initiative to use obscenity law is currently in the hands of the government, not civil plaintiffs, which creates distance from those harmed, thereby empowering the state rather than survivors. By contrast, hierarchy theory emphasizes enhancing the direct representation of substantively disadvantaged perspectives and interests, which could empower survivors injured by producers or consumers to influence legal applications directly. Such an approach is embodied in the proposed civil rights ordinance's trafficking provision, for example, where "any woman" or similarly subordinated person would be empowered to file a civil lawsuit and seek damages for discrimination based on the circulation of specific materials.[143]

It is notable that in addition to the high-profile federal cases, there have also been local obscenity prosecutions in some states since the 2000s as well as other federal cases.[144] The local cases typically targeted brick-and-mortar retailers that sell a broader swath of materials than the "extreme or fringe content."[145] Jennifer M. Kinsley, who has been a regular counsel for the defense in obscenity cases, notes that despite prosecuting "even mainstream adult-oriented" pornography retailers, there is "no evidence" that the local cases "have quelled the demand for sexually explicit materials in communities where obscenity charges are filed."[146] Instead, she asserts, "even in the wake of ongoing state prosecutions, online pornography has flourished, both in quantity and profit." Her conclusion is consistent with the analysis made here; criminal obscenity law is not an effective tool in suppressing the consumption of pornography.

Still, there is no legal impediment that would prevent a legislature from incorporating civil remedies that include damage awards into existing obscenity laws, for instance, as the Senate Committee on the Judiciary proposed in 1992.[147] Creating specially trained juries to decide obscenity cases might also be an alternative that would standardize procedures and draw on a uniform knowledge base. Such juries would stand out in contrast to general juries that decide many different matters and whose knowledge about pornography's harms may vary considerably, from highly prejudiced to entirely open-minded. This "civil obscenity law" would be a hybrid. It has conceptual limitations related to the meanings ascribed to "contemporary community standards," "prurient interests," and "serious" value.[148] Yet it would provide a means for survivors who are better able, more committed, or both, to file civil actions. Certainly, the law on its face would be inconsistent with modern conceptions of human rights and freedoms, which the civil rights ordinances were not. Nevertheless, like other obscenity laws manifesting the same inconsistency, it might nonetheless pass constitutional muster.

So far, obscenity laws have survived rational basis review, requiring only a showing of a legitimate governmental interest. However, the use of the least rigorous standard of review may be their Achilles heel. For instance, whereas challenging whether forcing pornography on someone at work can constitute sexual harassment was found to be supported by the "compelling interest" of preventing sex discrimination,[149] obscenity laws provide no similarly compelling or substantial interest to prevent appeals to "prurient interests" that offend community standards and lack serious value.[150] The arguably vague legislative objectives underpinning obscenity laws could embolden pornography's apologists to ignore overwhelming empirical evidence to the contrary and claim that since obscenity law facially protects no compelling or substantial interests, pornography's harms are neither compelling nor substantial. Indeed, this was the crux of the argument pursued, albeit unsuccessfully, by the defendants in the *Stagliano* and *Extreme Associates* cases. In this sense, in particular, the anti-pornography civil rights ordinance is more consistent with reality than is obscenity law.

PART III
CANADA

6

Legislative Attempts, 1983–1988

The most direct legal tool available in Canada for targeting pornography and its associated harms is obscenity law. The Commonwealth's definition of obscenity as set forth in *R. v. Hicklin* (1868) defined obscenity as that which could potentially "deprave and corrupt the mind" of persons so predisposed.[1] *Hicklin* was superseded in England by case law in 1954.[2] Further, it was replaced by statute in Canada five years later,[3] with Parliament's passage of a law defining obscenity as "any publication a dominant characteristic of which is the undue exploitation of sex, or of sex and any one or more of the following subjects, namely, crime, horror, cruelty and violence."[4] In accordance with this modification, the Canadian Supreme Court in *Brodie v. Queen* (1962) supplanted the prior *Hicklin* test with this new definition based on the Criminal Code and decided that the "contemporary standards of tolerance" test would determine its application.[5] However, the community standards test was not mandated by the legislation per se. As mentioned in previous chapters, the interpretation of community standards is largely driven by the consensus as to what breaches acceptable standards, which in turn is affected by the level of pornography consumption in those communities. The test has therefore received criticism for allowing pornography to contribute in setting its own standard of tolerance.

The Canadian law professor Kathleen Mahoney has observed that, until the early 1980s, the meaning of "undue exploitation of sex" was usually understood to imply only that the degree of explicit sex was significant for determining the presence or absence of obscenity.[6] The additional elements, "crime, horror, cruelty and violence," were "largely ignored by the courts."[7] The divergence from the earlier *Hicklin* definition was not as important as it could have been, its primary impact being that explicit sex became the focus of what was obscene rather than, as under *Hicklin,* one possible target among others with a supposed "tendency . . . to deprave and corrupt" the minds of persons so inclined.[8] *Hicklin* did not enumerate other potentially pertinent elements such as "cruelty and violence."

Pornography. Max Waltman, Oxford University Press. © Oxford University Press 2021.
DOI: 10.1093/oso/9780197598535.003.0007

Feminist opposition to pornography was ignited by the 1976 release in both Canada and the United States of the movie *Snuff*, which presented the murder and dismemberment of a woman as erotic entertainment. Although Canadian courts did not find *Snuff* obscene, in 1977, the organization Women Against Violence Against Women picketed outside a Toronto theater where the movie was playing.[9] Another group calling itself Wimmin's Fire Brigade took credit for bombing three video stores in 1982 that were part of a pornography chain in the Vancouver area.[10] Although "most women's organizations" in Canada did not endorse the actions of the Brigade, they nevertheless "sympathized with the group's frustration at not being able to get the police to lay obscenity charges."[11] The inadequacy of judicial enforcement of obscenity laws in the face of the rapidly growing pornography industry thus became a source of widespread discontent among women's organizations in the late 1970s and early 1980s.

The Fraser Committee (1983–1985)

The Special Committee on Pornography and Prostitution, appointed by the liberal federal government in 1983, marked the "culmination" of the intense and diversified public pressure that had persisted since the mid-1970s to change, improve, or abolish existing obscenity laws.[12] It was colloquially referred to as the "Fraser Committee," after its chair, Paul Fraser, and its final report was delivered in February 1985.[13] Around the time of the Fraser Committee's appointment, there was a consensus among virtually all critics that the Canadian obscenity law was "too broad and too vague."[14] Anti-pornography activists noted that the relevant section of the Criminal Code was not only prone to permit "violent" and "degrading" pornography, but also that "non-violent, non-degrading sexual material" was sometimes found obscene.[15] The statutory requirement that obscenity should be primarily concerned with the "undue exploitation of sex" also implied that there was an acceptable "due exploitation" of sex.[16] Some critics argued that even violent sex could be classified as "due," thus inferring that the code should change to prevent lapses of this kind.[17]

The Fraser Committee investigated the harms of both prostitution and pornography, although it did not connect the two as systematically as others did. The U.S. Attorney General's Commission on Pornography noted that the Fraser Committee did not investigate the conditions of pornography production, nor otherwise examine the associations between off-camera and on-camera prostitution.[18] Nevertheless, members of the Committee asserted in their report that they knew "that the relations between the producers of violent pornography and the actors in it are often such that there is little or no respect for the rights and physical welfare of the latter."[19] Their decision not to study the issue might have been rationalized by their assumption that most pornography sold in Canada originated abroad.[20] Yet even if predominantly of external origin, the domestic consumers and distributors would have contributed to a commercial demand that we now know fuels abuse and exploitation during pornography production. The only way for the Committee at the time to ensure that they had addressed such a concern would have been to study the production itself, whether domestic or foreign.

Vulnerability, Legal Distinctions, Intersectionality

The Fraser Committee solicited a wide variety of viewpoints from throughout Canadian society during their investigation. Diverse opinions were regularly expressed during the Committee's public hearings as well as in closed sessions held across twenty-two city or town centers where numerous organizations and individuals, including some prostituted women, presented their views, often complemented by written submissions. Those in favor of regulation included many women's organizations, churches and church groups, community organizations, educational associations, representatives of law enforcement, those holding elected office, even some men's groups that were specifically organized against pornography. Among their opponents were civil liberties groups, some professional associations (notably, librarians), media, publishing, and related associations, as well as gay rights organizations.[21]

The Committee collected substantial testimony and other documentation showing that women and children were generally harmed in prostitution, including contemporaneous sociological research indicating that many prostituted people were subjected to incest or sexual abuse as children. Similarly, research and testimony from social workers and associated professional organizations stressed that a large proportion of prostituted persons had been teenage runaways. Many groups and individuals stressed the correlation between women's subordination and their low status in society and the phenomenon of prostitution. For instance, several groups pointed out to the

Committee that women in Canada earned only 60% of what men earned, and that 75% of all minimum wage workers were women. Some said that pornography served as a "cause and contributor" to prostitution. As noted in the final report, which reiterated these observations, pornography "reinforces the view that women are sexual objects for men's pleasure," and "the prostitute [*sic*] is the most available person to engage in the sexual acts portrayed in pornography. One promises, the other delivers."[22]

These Committee conclusions are now well-documented in numerous research studies and complementary sources. Although persons used as pornography performers are typically drawn from those who are prostituted or vulnerable to exploitation in prostitution, at the time, Canada nonetheless criminalized prostituted persons (as well as third-party profiteers and johns) in a number of venues at the time.[23] Simply put, Canada penalized prostituted people themselves for what evidence shows is a form of rank sexual exploitation.

The Committee noted that community associations, law enforcement agencies, and civic organizations "were anxious to force prostitutes from the streets of their cities" but "said very little when it came to a discussion of the root causes of the phenomenon of prostitution."[24] Although that remark is implicitly critical of these latter groups, in their proposed legal approach the Committee did not side with the women's groups and others who wanted the law to acknowledge the multiple disadvantages inherent in the coercive circumstances that pushed women into prostitution:

> We are of the view that as a general rule, the adult must accept responsibility for his or her actions. We heard during the public hearings that adult women, in particular, who become involved in pornography or prostitution should be seen as victims, whether of the economy or patriarchal social structure, or of abuse directed at them during early years. We have sympathy with this point of view, and do not think that it would be out of place as a consideration in sentencing the individual case. However, we do not accept it as a principle upon which to structure criminal law.
>
> In contrast, it is our view that children should be regarded as vulnerable, and in need of society's protection, when dealing with the issues of pornography and prostitution. Children would thus be seen as victims or potential victims of people engaged, or wanting to engage, in these activities.[25]

The passage quoted above suggests that, after having been subjected to sexual abuse and incest, then forced to run away from home during childhood or adolescence—then confronting the challenge of procuring basic sustenance, managing school, and obtaining professional skills under dire, likely impoverished, circumstances—those in prostitution should be regarded as "responsible" for being prostituted, often by pimps, upon reaching the age of majority. This reasoning places blame squarely on the victim for her (or his) own victimization. Since the impact of childhood abuse is almost invariably seen across the life course, unless the rights of adults in pornography are strengthened and enforced, sexually exploited children can never count on society to provide them meaningful justice or protection. The Fraser Committee's conclusions reinforce the rigid divide between children and adults to the detriment of both groups.

Approaching legal reform from an intersectional perspective has the capacity to address the multiple disadvantages that affect both children and adults.[26] Here, a comparison with the Fraser Committee's American counterpart, the Attorney General's Commission on Pornography, is striking: the latter focused much attention on "performers," devoting a whole chapter to the preconditions and harms of participation in pornography production.[27] It found that people in pornography where "exploited under conditions providing them a lack of choice [and] coerced to perform sex acts against their will," and further noted that multiple disadvantages, such as "age, race, disability, or other vulnerability," apart from gender, had primed them for abuse.[28] The Commission recommended the civil rights anti-pornography ordinances as a means of challenging the harms of pornography,[29] which could have given the survivors an unambiguous remedy. The Fraser Committee's view that adults in prostitution should be held criminally responsible for their own circumstances reflects a contrary approach.

Constitutional Substantive Equality

The Fraser Committee's final report referred to the "great interest" in Canada surrounding the civil rights anti-pornography ordinances, particularly the trafficking provisions through which any woman or other person in a similar situation could sue pornographers and distributors for sex discrimination provided the materials at issue were within the stated ambit.[30] When mentioning the ordinance's assault provision that would have enabled plaintiffs who suffered harm caused by specific pornography to sue its producers, the Fraser Committee cited consistent evidence from Canadian women's shelters in support of such a remedy, including testimony that male partners of clients sometimes required them to participate in (or be subjected to) acts depicted in pornography.[31] The Committee also said that its "attention" had been "drawn" to reports of violent sex crimes where the perpetrator had been found with "a supply of violent pornography."[32] More recent research discussed earlier corroborates these observations.

Wherever the Fraser Committee conducted a hearing, they were presented with extensive samples of the content of contemporary pornography, often accompanied by complaints regarding the failure of existing laws to stop its circulation.[33] These materials were described as suffused with misogyny, racism, degradation, coercion, violence against women,[34] which sounds quite like the aggressive, dehumanizing, and debasing content that recent scholarly studies have shown to be popular. Moreover, "many briefs" to the Committee provided detailed accounts of the harms caused by consumers.[35] The "concern of most" of these briefs was "that pornography degrades women, robs them of their dignity as individual human beings and equal partners within a relationship and treats them as objects or possessions to be used by men; that male violence against women is treated as socially acceptable and viewers are desensitized to the suffering of others"; and that these outcomes will strongly and negatively influence children and families.[36] Several submissions reportedly included references to both "academic research studies, many of which were from the United States," as well as experiential accounts that the Committee termed "local anecdotal evidence."[37]

Many studies available at that time suggested that pornography was causally linked to attitudes supporting violence against women, sexual aggression, and the sexual exploitation of people in prostitution[38]—evidence that has grown exponentially since. The extant sources provided sufficient evidence for the Committee to conclude that the consumption harms of violent pornography "lower the status of women and thus contravene their right to equality,"[39] and point to the equality guarantees in section 15 of the Canadian Charter of Rights and Freedoms (the "Charter")[40] to support stronger regulations.[41] Justification for limiting freedom of expression that might otherwise protect pornography under the Charter's section 2(b) could be found through one of two routes: either balancing the Charter's section 15 equality rights against section 2(b) expressive freedoms, or, if balancing alone proved insufficient, invoking section 1 to support "reasonable limits"[42] on freedom of expression that are demonstrably justified.[43] The Committee made an argument analogous to one set forth in the case of *R. v. Keegstra*, where the trial court in 1984[44] upheld a provision in the criminal code barring protection of hate propaganda against a freedom of speech challenge.[45] The Supreme Court of Canada reached the same conclusion in reviewing *Keegstra* five years later, although it also relied on the Charter's section 1 that "guarantees the rights and freedoms set out in it subject only to such reasonable limits prescribed by law as can be demonstrably justified in a free and democratic society" to sustain the hate propaganda provision[46]—not primarily section 15 on equality and section 27 on multicultural heritage, as the trial court had done.[47]

Recommended Legal Definitions

The Fraser Committee's proposed definition of pornography did not frame it as a contravention of women's right to equality, despite members' perception that constitutional equality imperatives supported a law against it. Instead, it defined pornography in gender-neutral terms that focused on an assessment of the depiction of sexual explicitness, violence, and certain body parts or sexual practices, including whether it presented "lewd" acts or the "lewd exhibition of the genitals."[48] Although this definition did not expressly refer to obscenity or indecency, it did not recognize the role of pornography in reinforcing gender inequality, an omission for which obscenity law has also been criticized.[49] By contrast, the civil rights ordinances would have defined pornography as the graphic sexually explicit subordination of women (or of men and transgender persons who were similarly presented) and required further specification under various sub-definitions in accordance with that approach; in these respects, the ordinances were drafted to conform both to social scientific findings and experiential accounts exposing the links between pornography and gender-based violence; they were, moreover, narrowly tailored to reach only materials provably harmful. Like obscenity law, the Fraser Committee's body-parts approach was more concerned with sexual explicitness per se than with sexual subordination, and had less of a connection to the Charter's equality imperatives that were assertedly recognized by the Committee than the civil rights ordinances would have had.

The Committee recommended that pornography laws be organized according to a "three-tier system," by which the first tier would be reserved for the "most serious criminal sanctions," "less onerous" sanctions would apply to the second tier, and no criminal sanctions would apply to the third tier, apart from cases of sexual exposure to children, unsolicited exposure, or exposure without warning.[50]

The first tier included child pornography and other materials that, in various ways, condoned or normalized "sexual abuse of children" and that had been produced by physically harming participants.[51] Notably, the Committee did not discuss the evidence required to prove physical, as opposed to simulated, harm to participants.[52]

The second tier included adult pornography, but only those categories presenting "sexually violent behavior, bestiality, incest or necrophilia."[53] Since the criminal sanctions would be less severe than they would be at the first tier, the defenses of "artistic merit and educational or scientific purpose" would be permitted for these materials.[54] By contrast, the invalidated Indianapolis ordinance did not include artistic or other similar defenses but did bar lawsuits under the "trafficking" provision that targeted "isolated passages or isolated parts,"[55] thus shielding pornography that was used in literary irony, political criticism, and comparable contexts.

The third tier encompassed all adult nonviolent pornography apart from the few exceptions included in tier two. However, no criminal sanctions were recommended for these materials except for regulations relating to time, place, and manner of display, performance, or accessibility.[56]

Once again, the Indianapolis ordinance was more nuanced, providing a sixth sub-category of "graphic sexually explicit subordination of women" where women were presented "as sexual objects for domination, conquest, violation, exploitation, possession, or use, or through postures or positions of servility or submission or display."[57] This included a greater range of conduct, from the patently violent to the suggestively subordinating, when compared to the Fraser Committee's second tier that required sexual violence, bestiality, or necrophilia. In this respect, the Committee's recommendations were significantly more limited than the range of materials actionable under the Indianapolis ordinance, which targeted mainstream pornography. The extent to which materials dehumanize or present women as stereotypically submissive or sexually indiscriminate beings can also be more critical than violence in inspiring sexual aggression and heightened attitudes supporting violence against women in consumers. Thus, the Indianapolis ordinance was more consistent with scientific evidence indicating that it is not primarily the level of aggression or violence in pornographic materials that affects aggressive outcomes, as the Fraser Committee's three tiers would imply, but the subordination they authorize and reflect.

The fact that people are often abused in the second tier category that included violent pornography seems to have been employed as an additional rationale for criminalizing and deterring "commercial dealings" in it, apart from countering the "message" that such materials generally conveyed.[58] However, although the first tier covered materials where abuse perpetrated in the course of production was purportedly prohibited, there was no indication of the means by which any such abuse could overcome a defense asserting that the contents were simulated. As the U.S. Attorney General's Commission on Pornography noted in 1985,[59] abuse can also occur off-camera in producing materials that are superficially nonviolent—a fact glossed over by the Fraser Committee, which avoided inquiring into the conditions of production, entirely eliding the question of how to distinguish real harm from simulation. That said, the Committee's recommendation for a law against abuse in pornography production indirectly acknowledged that special laws are needed in certain situations to prevent physical abuse effectively. The corresponding cause of action for coercion in pornography under the Indianapolis civil rights ordinance enumerated impermissible defenses meant to shield plaintiffs from common prejudices, like "only bad girls are raped," and other attempts to avoid liability based on plaintiffs having ostensibly "consented" by accepting money or signing a contract.[60] Without specifying what defenses were impermissible, a law against harmful exploitation in pornography production would be hard to enforce—especially under a criminal standard of proof "beyond a reasonable doubt."[61] If a civil rights ordinance had been recommended instead, proof on a "balance of probabilities" would have sufficed in Canada.[62] But the Fraser Committee advocated a criminal law, not a civil rights law.

Civil Rights versus Criminal Law

The Fraser Committee noted that an American federal district court had invalidated the anti-pornography civil rights ordinance on First Amendment grounds, and opined that the ordinance would receive more favorable judicial treatment in Canada.[63] The Committee stressed that "equality of women is a strongly protected value" under the Charter, which would support a decision to sustain the ordinance.[64] Yet despite the Committee's overall determination that the ordinances in major parts would likely survive a constitutional challenge in Canada, it did not recommend a civil rights approach.

In explaining its reasoning, the Committee likened the civil rights ordinances' "action for damages and injunctive relief which may be brought by any woman complaining of trafficking in pornography" to the conferral of "a private cause of action to restrain or redress a public wrong" that "has not, until now, been a prominent feature of Canadian law."[65] Additionally, because an action of this sort "ordinarily" necessitated the Canadian "Attorney General's permission," it was recognized as an executive decision not to be second-guessed by the courts at the preliminary stage. The Committee hence acknowledged that the civil rights approach would put some traditional state power to initiate legal action into the hands of women instead. This shift of power was rejected on the assumption that "a lot of the interest" in this approach "really derives from Canadians' dissatisfaction with the administration of the criminal law relating to pornography." Given this essentially unproven presumption about the true reasons for the public's interest, the Committee preferred "to address directly the deficiencies in the criminal law rather than create a new form of civil action." Because the premises for preferring criminal over civil rights law were so unarticulated, it implies that the Committee believed that tradition militated against adopting a new legal mechanism, however promising—a fundamentally conservative argument.

The Committee also advocated the use of existing human and civil rights laws rather than recommending "that a separate pornography-related offence be added to human rights codes at this time."[66] Apparently, members believed that the equality-related provisions already incorporated into Canadian human rights law would be applicable, notwithstanding the fact that these statutes had never been used in relation to the harms caused by pornography consumers or its production harms. In reaching this conclusion, they reviewed a body of largely, if not exclusively, analogous domestic human rights law, maintaining that pornography could be challenged as a human rights violation under these varied cases, statutes, and regulations, though none of them made any mention of pornography.[67]

Unlike the approach taken by the Committee, various international human rights instruments *explicitly* define pornography as a violation of women's human rights. For example, in 1992, the monitoring body of the Convention on the Elimination of All Forms of Discrimination Against Women identified "pornography" as a practice that "contributes to gender-based violence," gender-based violence itself being a violation of women's equality, thus obliging states parties to "take all legal and other measures . . . including . . . civil remedies and compensatory provisions"[68] to stop it. Similarly, under the International Covenant on Civil and Political Rights, the U.N. Human Rights Committee in 2000 held that, since "pornographic material which portrays women and girls as objects of violence or degrading or inhuman treatment is likely to promote these kinds of treatment of women and girls, States parties should provide information about legal measures to restrict the publication or dissemination of such material."[69] Under the 1995 Beijing Declaration and Platform for Action adopted at the United Nations' Fourth World Conference on Women, states parties agreed that "[i]mages in the media of violence against women . . . including pornography, are factors contributing to the continued prevalence of such violence."[70] Consistent with these positions, the African Union's Protocol on Women's Human Rights in Africa promulgated in 2005 urged states to "take effective legislative and administrative measures to prevent the exploitation and abuse of women in advertising and pornography."[71]

None of these international human rights instruments meant to advance women's equality advised, as the Fraser Committee did, that pornography could be omitted on the premise that it was implicitly covered. Like the careful enumeration of grounds for discrimination found in general equality laws, express recognition of discriminatory practice is the surest way to avoid future interpretive uncertainty. The only counter to this argument is provided by postmodernists, who are inclined to favor laws avoiding facial recognition of disadvantaged groups on the questionable theory that their inclusion reinforces social dominance by renaturalizing stereotypical categories of oppression.[72] That the Committee did not invoke postmodern theory in rejecting the inclusion of distinct offenses under human rights regimes that would target pornography indicates that members simply thought such specificity to be unnecessary—a striking contrast to key international instruments that reflect an obverse conception of the best means of redress.

Concluding Analysis

The Fraser Committee argued that its recommendations on how best to approach the problems presented by pornography constituted "a rational, fair and realistic balancing of the interests involved."[73] However these proposals are evaluated, they were never adopted. Considered critically, it is unclear for whom the Committee's recommendations represented "a significant advance."[74] Certainly, the recommendations did advance beyond the long standard method of assessing obscenity through resort to the contemporary community standards test, and in this respect offered a more reliable legal definition of pornography. Otherwise, its emphasis on "sexually violent behavior, bestiality, incest, or necrophilia"[75] is not significantly different from obscenity law. Sex and violence had been incorporated into the criminal code since the mid-1950s, when Canadian law defined obscenity as "the undue exploitation of sex, or of sex and any one or more of the following subjects, namely, crime, horror, cruelty and *violence*."[76] Crucially, the Committee's definition of pornography contained no explicit recognition of *subordination*—a key element in the civil rights approach to pornography.

Likewise, notwithstanding the "enthusiasm" of supporters of the civil rights approach,[77] the recommendations for further criminal enforcement did not "advance" from prior conventions. In contrast to the civil rights approach, with the exception of advocating criminalization of pornography made through abuse, the Committee's proposals did not promote substantive equality or the perspectives and interests of survivors of production and those directly harmed by consumers. Indeed, even that singular recommendation lacked crucial impermissible defenses that were integral to the civil rights ordinances, which would have precluded defenses based on common biases that persons used as performers who "consent," are "paid," or have previously been prostituted are not harmed by performing in pornography. Without their preclusion, it would be difficult to prove "beyond a reasonable doubt" that people used as pornography performers are harmed in the course of production. Generally speaking, legal counsel are not social scientists with extensive knowledge of the documented harms of pornography. Even if they were, absent the incorporation of impermissible defenses, public and professional incredulity—most consequentially among jurors and judges—could result in the dismissal of these essential facts and insights.

Similarly, unlike the substantive equality prostitution law that criminalized johns and third parties while supporting and decriminalizing prostituted persons that was adopted in Sweden in 1998 and in modified form in Canada in 2014,[78] the Fraser Committee's insistence that adults in prostitution must take responsibility for their actions under existing criminal law betrays no awareness of hierarchy theory. Analyzed from the latter perspective, prostitution is understood as a substantially unequal practice in which, consistent with overwhelming empirical evidence, people are usually bought for sex under coercive circumstances, including poverty and the lack of realistic alternatives for survival. Thus, it appears that the Committee's approach was "fair" to none but those in favor of the status quo.

Parliamentary Bill C-114 (1986–1987)

The Fraser Committee's *Special Report* did not lead to immediate legislation after its submission in February 1985. However, when the Progressive Conservative government replaced the Liberal government that initially appointed the Fraser Committee, conservatives introduced parliamentary bill C-114 in 1986 in an attempt to reform the pornography laws.[79] Bill C-114 did not follow the Fraser Committee's recommendations to criminalize only violent materials, but instead relied on a body-parts approach that defined and criminalized pornography more broadly. It included four sub-definitions, the most comprehensive of which, "pornography," encompassed "any visual matter showing vaginal, anal or oral intercourse, ejaculation, sexually violent behaviour, bestiality, incest, necrophilia, masturbation or other sexual activity."[80] The proposed legislation also contained specific provisions against "degrading" and "violent" pornography, as well as "pornography that shows physical harm."[81] Even though its ambit was considerably broader than that of the Fraser Committee, for reasons explained below, bill C-114 neither considered pornography as a social practice of subordination, as the civil rights ordinances did, nor apprehended sex inequality and discrimination against women as a necessary prerequisite for making pornography and a consequence of its consumption.

For instance, the concept of "degradation" is not the equivalent of "subordination"; neither inequality nor subordination must be per se degrading in the ordinary sense of the word. Indeed, bill C-114 defined "degrading pornography" as "any pornography that shows defecation, urination, ejaculation or expectoration by one person onto another, lactation, menstruation, penetration of a bodily orifice with an object," or that treats a person as "an animal or object."[82] With the possible exception of treating someone as an object, it is difficult to see how, outside of a context of subordination, practices such as "ejaculation" or "menstruation" would promote sex inequality or be per se degrading. Recall that the Minneapolis City Council found pornography to be "a systematic practice of exploitation and subordination based on sex which differentially harms women"; thus, the ordinance defined pornography broadly as "the sexually explicit subordination of women, graphically depicted."[83] Research analyzed earlier indicated that it is presentations of women's subordination that are most productive of harmful effects, not any "other sexual activity," whether or not degrading, as the more expansive definition in bill-C114 implied.

Certainly, research suggests that there is very little popular demand for adult heterosexual pornography that does not subordinate women. However, an expansive definition like that provided in bill C-114 will be vulnerable to criticism on that ground. Although the bill provided educational, scientific, and artistic defenses, it targets an unduly broad swath of materials, many of which would not be considered pornography under the civil rights ordinances. If the primary objective is to prevent the creation and circulation of materials that cause harm, then the artistic defense is unavailing. An artistically adept graphic sexually explicit presentation that subordinates women might simply provoke more intense consumer reactions, thereby promoting greater sexual aggression and attitudes supporting violence against women than would a work of lesser quality.[84] Indeed, recent studies with johns in several locations worldwide found that most of them seek to imitate pornography, some even if it necessitates abusing prostituted women severely.[85] Materials of lower quality may rather be less appealing as sources of imitation. Hence, although bill C-114 might have exerted a more pronounced chilling effect on a broader set of benign sexually explicit materials than the civil rights ordinance, the artistic defense would permit provably harmful materials that the civil rights ordinances would not have protected from liability. The result of these two features of bill C-114 was to provide a definition that was so capacious that it created significant loopholes for harmful materials.

Furthermore, bill C-114 provided only for criminal measures, with no civil recompense or opportunity for survivors or those otherwise affected to make use of the law. The authority to use and apply it would have resided solely with prosecutors. A legal approach more consistent with hierarchy theory would favor empowering survivors and others directly affected to influence the application of the law, once codified, as they are likely to have stronger incentives to pursue legal action than other groups.

Bill C-114 drew criticism from several quarters, most notably from those primarily interested in protecting civil liberties.[86] The position of the "women's groups and feminist organizations" that weighed in was ambiguous; while some thought the bill was " 'extremely puritan and totally unacceptable' " because it did not differentiate between subordinating and non-subordinating materials, others believed it was important to take advantage of what they saw as a strategic opportunity to legislate against pornography.[87] These groups sought to improve the legislation by replacing its focus on "sexual explicitness" with a focus on "dominance and power imbalance."[88] Basing her analysis on interviews, news reports, and public statements, Dany Lacombe argues that, in drafting the legislation, the Progressive Conservative government "lost track of feminists' concerns about the harm pornography causes to women's rights to equality," and that the work had been dominated by negotiations within the conservative caucus.[89] Her account seems reasonable when considering the plain text of the bill. It was not designed to challenge subordination, but to prevent exposure to sexually explicit content that lacked artistic, scientific, or educational merit. To underscore, the artistic defense could exonerate misogynist and subordinating material that promoted sexual aggression and attitudes supporting violence against women, while material that was harmless by those measures could be targeted.

Bill C-114 was abandoned and never debated in Parliament after Minister of Justice John Crosbie was moved to the Department of Transport and replaced by Ramon Hnatyshyn. According to Lacombe, in his new post, Hnatyshyn gave serious consideration to the public discontent surrounding bill C-114 and was interested in trying to improve it.[90]

Parliamentary Bill C-54 (1987)

The next response by the Department of Justice came in 1987 with bill C-54.[91] This legislation started out by defining sexually explicit material that would *not* be subject to criminal sanction, labeling it "erotica," which was defined as "any visual matter a dominant characteristic of which is the depiction, in a sexual context or for the purpose of the sexual stimulation of the viewer, of a human sexual organ, a female breast or the human anal region."[92] By its terms, "erotica" would only be subject to time, place, and manner regulations, including for exposure to minors, with summary penalties for violations.[93] The next element, "pornography," was also subject to criminal sanctions. It was defined as "any visual matter that shows" (i) child pornography; (ii) the infliction of bodily harm, or attempting to cause harm "in a sexual context"; (iii) sexually violent conduct, including any conduct where "physical pain is inflicted or apparently inflicted on a person"; (iv) degrading activity occurring "in a sexual context," including treating a person "as an animal or object," "bondage," penetration with an object, and defecation, urination, or ejaculation "onto another person, whether or not the other person appears to be consenting," or "lactation or menstruation in a sexual context"; (v) "bestiality, incest or necrophilia"; and (vi) "masturbation or ejaculation not referred to in subparagraph (iv), or vaginal, anal or oral intercourse."[94] Additionally, non-visual materials containing "any matter or commercial communication that incites, promotes, encourages or advocates any conduct referred to" in the above sub-paragraphs, except (vi) and (iv), were proscribed.[95]

A closer look at bill C-54 suggests that it attempted to appease several constituencies. For instance, the distinction between non-visual and visual materials afforded greater protection to written works since non-visual items falling within category (vi) would be protected. Those who drafted the legislation seemingly assumed that visual materials were more likely to engender harm.[96] Yet this assumption finds no support in the literature. To offer just one example, studies have found that audiotaped portrayals of rape induce similar harmful exposure effects as visual pornography.[97] It may be that the provision is a symbolic concession to those holding conservative views of obscenity law, where sexual matters, to the extent they are more pronounced in visual than non-visual forms, are regarded as "obscene" and "off-stage."[98] Similarly, the distinction between "erotica" and "pornography" appears to be a concession to women's groups that argued that legislation should " 'allow for an appreciation of healthy adult sexuality,' "[99] and to some liberal groups that were against restricting sexually explicit materials per se. However, when scrutinizing these concessions in conjunction with other deficiencies in the proposed legislation, it appears that C-54 may be more misguided than its predecessor, C-114.

The Canadian journalist Susan Cole and others, for example, criticized bill C-54 for defining "erotica" as "the depiction of human genitalia" without more specificity, and as such hinging on "male experiences with so-called girlie magazines" that were simply "a milder form of pornography."[100] Indeed, it used a body-parts approach to define "erotica" as encompassing explicit presentations with no actual, only simulated, sexual conduct.[101] Yet the definition made no reference to equality, mutual pleasure, or the positive choices of participants. As Mahoney states, presentations "of a woman's body which humiliate, ridicule or present the female in a demeaning, unequal context could not only be saved by the bill C-54 definition; they would acquire the positive label of 'erotica.' "[102] Several other depictions proscribed under the bill were also set forth as enumerations of sexual practices without regard to subordination (e.g., "vaginal, anal or oral intercourse").[103] This definitional approach contrasts with that of the anti-pornography civil rights ordinance, which was narrowly tailored to reach provably harmful materials.

Cole also criticized the proposed legislation for failing to consider "women's experience . . . that erotica and pornography can stand in contradiction, and are not simply matters of degree," and cited an article by Gloria Steinem to support her point.[104] That is, bill C-54 could have defined erotica as "a mutually pleasurable, sexual expression" guided "by positive choice," as Steinem had done previously.[105] Steinem's definition made clear that materials that "subordinate," which would have been actionable under the Indianapolis ordinance, would not have been protected as "erotica" under bill C-54 if they included nonviolent acts where women were "presented as sexual objects for domination, possession, or use, or through postures or positions of servility or submission or display."[106] Hence, bill C-54 suffered from the same deficiencies as bill C-114; neither recognized that the subordination in pornography makes consumers more likely to behave harmfully and adopt attitudes supporting violence against women, whether or not presentations are also dehumanizing, degrading, or violent. Bill C-54 could have protected nonviolent but subordinating, objectifying, dehumanizing materials, or materials presenting women as stereotypically promiscuous that have been proven harmful.

Bill C-54 further defined "pornography" to reach materials that both could and could not be harmful, which in each category included those that were explicitly violent or physically harmful or otherwise extreme (e.g., penetration with objects, defecation, urination, or ejaculation, lactation, or menstruation in "sexual context," and those that presented explicit sexual acts instead of simulated conduct such as "masturbation or ejaculation . . . or vaginal, anal or oral intercourse."[107] Such a definition would have encompassed a wider range of materials than those that are provably harmful, including educational and scientific materials that present ejaculation, safe sex, or masturbation. This situation made medical, scientific, educational, and artistic defenses necessary, which, like the precursive legislation, were also included in bill C-54,[108] with an exception carved out for child pornography and pornography presenting infliction of bodily harm. By contrast, the civil rights ordinances were narrowly tailored to reach only harmful materials, making the inclusion of medical, scientific, educational, and artistic defenses unnecessary. Absent clear opposition to subordination, a judicial interpretation of artistic merit under such a statute could find violent or degrading pornography protected from liability, especially given that consumers and community standards have become desensitized to pornography and more accepting of what may objectively be regarded as violent or painful sexual acts over time.

For instance, Mahoney remarked that since bill C-54's criminalization of portrayals of " 'masturbation or ejaculation . . . or vaginal, anal or oral intercourse' " had no "reference to a context" of subordination that could have evaluated such conduct,[109] it neglected both that some sexually explicit presentations may be beneficial, and that harm must be "demonstrated" to justify restrictions.[110] She concluded that such a law rather "reflect[s] . . . the conservative moralist view that any explicit sexual portrayal which sexually stimulates the viewer should be prohibited."[111] In addition, women's organizations demanded a better conceptualization of bill C-54's definitions and urged the government to explore civil remedies as well.[112] As happened with bill C-114 and the Fraser Committee's recommendations, bill C-54 only included criminal measures and provided nothing for survivors of pornography's harms that would have empowered them to initiate use of the law to further their own interests. Similarly, bill C-54 did not attempt to change prostitution laws nor acknowledge that persons used as pornography performers are routinely exploited.

Responses to Bill C-54 (1987–1988)

When Minister of Justice Hnatyshyn presented bill C-54 to the public on May 23, 1987, the *Toronto Star* quoted him as saying at a press conference that bill C-54 was the result of consultations with various groups that represented a " 'broad consensus in Canadian public that there is no place for portrayals of child pornography, sexual violence and degradation in a sexual context.' "[113] However, its sweeping definitions of pornography, along with its contradictory exceptions, suggest that the public response by the various groups on all sides that had tried to change the pornography laws since the time of the Fraser Committee would be overwhelmingly negative. Indeed, Lacombe describes how the Canadian Civil Liberties Association "largely orchestrated" a protest against the bill by librarians—a seemingly unconventional alliance—by soliciting the opinion of a well-known criminal lawyer, Edward L. Greenspan, "concerning the potential vulnerability of library personnel to Bill C-54."[114] Greenspan had been representing defendants in obscenity trials since as early as 1983.[115] In his letter to librarians, Greenspan claimed that the consequences of the proposed legislation would be to make library staff and board members criminally liable for distributing pornography, and with it a possible ten-year prison sentence for distribution of "many" purportedly "important artistic and educational works" that included "passages that may 'encourage'" sex between children or between children and adults because the bill provided no artistic or educational defenses.[116]

The Toronto Public Library Board decided that twenty-eight of thirty-two public libraries in Toronto would close on December 10, 1987, in protest against bill C-54.[117] When Sheryl Taylor-Munro, a trustee of the Board, explained her decision, she contended that bill C-54 was "'a clear threat to a first-class library system,'" and that the government had essentially portrayed librarians as "'no different than child pornographers.'"[118] She further maintained that it went "'against everything'" that librarians believed in, "'things like open access to information and freedom of speech.'"[119] When then Minister of Justice Hnatyshyn responded to the librarians' protests, he tried to assure them that the target of the legislation was "'hard-core pornography,'" not librarians.[120] However, because other conservative MPs had defended the bill in ways that implied the need for some "reorganization" of libraries in order to keep some works away from youthful populations, the distrust of librarians was exacerbated and they continued to protest.[121]

According to Lacombe's account, many people within the Department of Justice felt that the librarians' "revolt . . . singlehandedly killed the legislation."[122] Yet her analysis of contemporaneous parliamentary debates suggests that the librarians' revolt had not been as important as some in government perceived it.[123] There had also been protests by other groups, such as writers and artists, who, in 1987, exhibited works by Matisse and other luminaries covered in brown paper, portraying bill C-54 as a concerted attempt at censorship that would prevent public discourse on such legitimate subjects as HIV-AIDS.[124] Given the defenses available for medical, scientific, educational, and artistic purposes, and the additional permissible expressions of "erotica" that were incorporated into the bill's definition, this critique seems exaggerated. That said, it is also worth contemplating why artistic and educational considerations should ipso facto be prioritized over pornography's harms, including discrimination and sexual violence against women.

The Progressive Conservative government had a majority in the House and could easily have pushed bill C-54 through, but it chose not to.[125] As events unfolded, criticism erupted from within the conservative caucus, as well as from the women's anti-pornography movement, which had been reservedly supportive. Both conservatives and feminists variously noted that the bill was internally inconsistent and marred by overly broad exceptions and definitions.[126] This analysis suggests that the librarians were not solely responsible for the bill's fate. Religious and conservative organizations that were initially supportive withdrew their support when another lawyer, hired in March 1988 by the Inter Church Committee on Pornography, reported finding "numerous loopholes" that could "drastically liberalize an apparently conservative law."[127] This interpretation stood in direct contrast to Mr. Greenspan's, which may have exaggerated the criminal liability that could be assigned under the bill. Although Greenspan's legal opinion encouraged librarians to protest C-54 as a form of overzealous censorship, liberalization was suggested by the text of the bill itself. Recall that its capacious definition of "erotica," together with the artistic defenses set forth, certainly created loopholes that would protect provably harmful materials.[128]

Comparative Analysis

By comparison, the civil rights challenges to pornography mounted in the United States retained their conceptual precision and support of those harmed through several years of attempted legal reform. The Canadian political challenges during the same period were seemingly controlled by moderate liberals on the Fraser Committee and by conservatives in Parliament; at the same time, their proposals were neither sufficiently precise and substantive nor widely supported by the groups harmed. In 1995, the sociologist Kirsten Johnson concluded that Canadian "feminist strategies for reform of obscenity law have shown a lack of strategy."[129] In support of her conclusion, another contemporaneous observer noted that "most of the submission to the Fraser Committee 'provided an emotional purge for all women who are sickened by the extent of violent and degrading pornography, but few attempted to address the specifics of law reform.' "[130] Yet there were individual exceptions, such as the law professor Kathleen Mahoney, who wrote critical academic articles on legal reform during the period the Fraser Committee was active and Parliament was considering new legislation.[131] Nonetheless, the fact that bill C-54 offered virtually no meaningful improvements compared either to the Fraser Committee's first recommendations or to bill

C-114 suggests that the feminist anti-pornography movement lacked either influence over the legislative deliberations or sufficient focus to exert the desired impact.

In contrast to events in Canada, the more visible and vocal civil rights anti-pornography activists in the United States managed not only to define legal challenges more clearly but also to facilitate passage of civil rights ordinances in several local legislatures (including also by local referendum), albeit they were eventually invalidated through a combination of judicial resistance and executive veto. Certainly, in terms of end results, the U.S. activists were no more successful than their Canadian counterparts, but they seem to have emerged from the struggle better positioned to pursue future political and legal attempts to counter the harms wrought by pornography. Indeed, during the Canadian battle, there were numerous references to the trailblazers in the United States, and particularly to the civil rights approach they innovated. Although some believed that the legal architecture of the United States was less suitable for challenges to pornography than that of Canada, structural conditions do not necessarily influence actions taken at the executive or legislative levels, where actors are driven less by constitutional imperatives than judicial actors are bound to be. Considering the lack of informed legislative action in Canada, it is not surprising that around the time of the second failed parliamentary attempt to modify the nation's pornography laws the focus shifted to the courthouses, where the influence of the feminist anti-pornography movement's discourse could be seen among members of the judiciary, who had begun reinterpreting existing obscenity laws in more progressive ways.[132]

7
Judicial Challenges, 1982–2019

As mentioned earlier, Canada's criminal obscenity law has, since 1959, covered the production and dissemination of "any publication a dominant characteristic of which is the *undue* exploitation of sex, or of sex and any one or more of the following subjects, namely, crime, horror, cruelty and violence."[1] Here, it will be shown how Canadian courts during the 1980s incorporated notions of sex inequality, including the concepts of dehumanization, degradation, and, to some extent, subordination, while rejecting freedom of expression challenges to the application of obscenity law.[2] Although this development was likely driven in part by contemporary social movements and the discourse surrounding them, judicial change seemingly accelerated after the adoption of the Canadian Charter of Rights and Freedoms in 1982 (the "Charter"), especially when section 15's equality guarantee took effect upon the expiration of its quarantine provision in 1985.[3] At that point, all cases entering the legal system were to be considered in light of the newly enshrined equality guarantees.

The Charter's section 15, subsection 1 reads: "Every individual is equal before and under the law and has the right to the equal protection and equal benefit of the law without discrimination and, in particular, without discrimination based on race, national or ethnic origin, colour, religion, sex, age or mental or physical disability." Moreover, rather than identifying gender-blind or race-blind classifications as the equality standard, the Charter's section 15, subsection 2 expressly supports affirmative substantive equality law: "Subsection (1) does not preclude any law, program or activity that has as its object the amelioration of conditions of disadvantaged individuals or groups including those that are disadvantaged because of race, national or ethnic origin, colour, religion, sex, age or mental or physical disability." According to the Supreme Court of Canada, section 15(1) is "aimed at *preventing* discrimination on grounds such as race, age and sex," while section 15(2) is "aimed at permitting governments to *improve* the situation of members of disadvantaged groups that have suffered discrimination in the

Pornography. Max Waltman, Oxford University Press. © Oxford University Press 2021.
DOI: 10.1093/oso/9780197598535.003.0008

past.... affirming the validity of ameliorative programs [or laws and activities] that target particular disadvantaged groups, which might otherwise run afoul of section 15(1) by excluding other groups."[4]

In addition, section 28 of the Charter guarantees that, "[n]otwithstanding *anything* in this Charter, the rights and freedoms referred to in it are guaranteed equally to male and female persons" (emphasis added). The "anything" referenced could be the expressive freedoms provided in section 2(b), which states that "[e]veryone has the . . . freedom of thought, belief, opinion and expression, including freedom of the press and other media of communication." As established, pornography made with real people generally exploits their inequalities and other material disadvantages, particularly those of vulnerable women, often subjecting them to abusive or degrading treatment. There is also ample documentation showing that consumers become more sexually aggressive and adopt more attitudes supporting and trivializing violence against women. The harms of pornography are exposed in sex-based hierarchical treatment, which may compromise women's right to free expression, impeding women from exercising such rights on an equal basis with men.[5] Given that section 28 of the Charter guarantees all freedoms "equally to male and female persons," and pornography demonstrably impedes women's enjoyment of their expressive freedoms on an equal basis with men, then that section can be invoked to protect the regulations of pornography at issue from expressive challenges under section 2(b).

A critical constitutional preference that may distinguish Canada from the United States is apparent in section 1 of the Charter, which "guarantees the rights and freedoms set out in it subject only to such reasonable limits prescribed by law as can be demonstrably justified in a free and democratic society." This recognition that rights and freedoms may be reasonably limited constitutes a more explicit acknowledgment that no rights or freedoms are absolute than anything afforded by the U.S. Constitution, where limitations are not expressly incorporated into the text itself but are instead the product of judicial interpretation.[6] Combined with its strong equality guarantees, Canada's balancing constitutional architecture appears favorable to a positive-rights approach that can enable government interventions, given that their purpose is to improve the situation for disadvantaged groups. In light of the U.S. experience, analysis of the legal challenges to pornography in Canadian courts will further reveal the significance of its constitutional architecture.

Substantive Equality in Obscenity Law (1980s)

In *R. v. Doug Rankine Co.* (1983), the Hon. Stephen Borins, an Ontario County Court judge, announced that the contemporary community standards test used to adjudicate the concept of obscenity would rest on the presumption that "degradation, humiliation, victimization and violence in human relationships" were untenable.[7] Judge Borins concluded that "films which consist substantially or partially of scenes which portray violence and cruelty in conjunction with sex, particularly where the performance of indignities degrade and dehumanize the people upon whom they are performed, exceed the level of community tolerance."[8] In the words of the law professor Kathleen Mahoney, this opinion marks the first time that Canadian law has addressed pornography "from the point of view of the victims of the sexual abuse, rather than of the sensibilities of the observers."[9] However, the equality guarantees contained in sections 15 and 28 of the Charter were not cited, although concepts related to substantive equality, such as dehumanization, degradation, humiliation, and victimization, were mentioned.[10] *Rankine* is nevertheless important, particularly given that the law up to that point had been concerned almost exclusively with explicit sex—often so classified under a decidedly permissive standard—and rarely considered the presence of violence and cruelty, though these characteristics were listed in the criminal code and had begun to appear in Supreme Court dicta and dissenting opinions in the 1970s.[11] Before *Rankine*, courts evidently had difficulty cognizing that sexual violence against women, often patently apparent in the materials under review, was not experienced as "sex" by those it victimized.[12] Mahoney's observations suggest that, prior to *Rankine*, many courts, often heavily male-dominated, were likely to have viewed sexual violence as synonymous with sex in no small measure because "certain male perceptions of violence can exclude the consideration of female reality."[13]

One year after *Rankine*, the Manitoba Court of Queen's Bench further developed obscenity law in *R. v. Ramsingh* (1984) to include degradation and dehumanization, whether or not violence was present.[14] Judge Mr. Patrick Ferg held that "where violence is portrayed with sex, or where there are people, particularly women, subjected to anything which degrades or dehumanizes them, the community standard" is "exceeded" even if the offending materials are viewed in a "private home." His opinion criticized the indicted pornography for its sexual objectification, dehumanization, and propagation of the rape myth that women "secretly" desire pain and force in sex.[15]

In contrast to *Rankine*, the defendant in *Ramsingh* not only appealed the application of the law but challenged its constitutionality under the Charter's freedom of expression guarantee in section 2 (b). Relying on section 1 of the Charter, the Court resolved the challenge in favor of the government, finding that obscenity law was a "reasonable limit prescribed by law as can be demonstrably justified in a free and democratic society." Although the arguments in *Ramsingh* that favored sustaining the obscenity law did not explicitly refer to any of the sex equality guarantees contained in sections 15 and 28, the idea that pornography asymmetrically harmed women as a group, thus denying them substantive equality, was plainly implied. For instance, when the Manitoba judge asserted that the regulation of "pornography qua obscenity" resulting in restrictions on freedom of expression was "demonstrably justifiable," he added that "women of this country, quite legitimately," had "a right to demand that some limitation be imposed by government on freedom of pornographic expression."[16]

One reason why constitutional equality was not invoked may have been that section 15 was not in force yet.[17] It may also have been a consequence of the prosecution's omission of the concept of equality in their briefs, and the apparent absence of interveners meant that it was not raised by others involved in the case. Certainly, the review took place in a lower court and was not yet of national interest, but the lack of any mention of constitutional equality may ultimately have been a function of the framework of criminal law itself. Under the criminal law, survivors of pornography-related harms were not, as they would have been in the Minneapolis civil rights ordinance, empowered to initiate legal proceedings.

The exclusion of survivors' views and experiences from judicial deliberations may be one reason why *Deep Throat*—one of several pornographic films prosecuted in *Ramsingh* that "without hesitation" were found to have exploited sex—was not among those found to be obscene.[18] Yet its lead performer, Linda Boreman, had by that time testified in public hearings, even taking and passing a polygraph test, about how she was tricked into joining the cast by a violent pimp, then threatened, battered, and raped, sometimes on a daily basis, to compel her to continue.[19] Though her performance in *Deep Throat* was coerced, *Ramsingh* did not consider such production harms. Reaching instead for artistic defenses, Judge Ferg first concluded that, although all the movies evaluated were "generally [of] good" quality in terms of "colour" and "camera work," some had no redeeming artistic qualities beyond technique. On this point, the court claimed that *Deep Throat* was distinguished by its "fairly well developed story lines" that lent it "some merit," praising it as "a satirical, very humorous contemporary statement upon the sexuality of the 60's and 70's" in which the "actors and actresses played their roles well." Judge Ferg could thus "not describe" *Deep Throat* "as the least bit offensive."[20]

As Mahoney and others have argued, an artistic defense is counterproductive to a law against harmful pornography.[21] Certainly, off-camera coercion and production harms have never been the concerns of obscenity law, but even if they had considered consumer-generated harms, *Ramsingh* missed the mark on *Deep Throat*. To wit, clients in programs for sexual assault survivors, particularly survivors of throat-rape, have reported that their assailants referred to the movie *Deep Throat* prior to their assault.[22] Similarly, studies undertaken in various locations of battered women, prostituted women, and johns, respectively, report that men forced them to imitate specific pornography that they had seen.[23]

Apparently, there was not sufficient knowledge of the harmful effects of pornography for the Manitoba court to accurately ascertain the impact of *Deep Throat*. It is difficult to chide prosecutors and judges for their lack of knowledge; after all, none were experts on sexual aggression, and the literature was still in its nascency. The *Ramsingh* decision demonstrated why a civil cause of action on behalf of those victimized by pornography like *Deep Throat*, as proposed under the civil rights anti-pornography ordinances, would have been preferable to relying on criminal law. Because a civil cause of action would likely be initiated by individuals or groups with significant knowledge and strong incentives to present persuasive evidence, it would almost certainly better inform, educate, and sensitize participants in the judicial system to seriously consider gender-based violence and sexual exploitation. Indeed, ambitious prosecutors looking to add to their tally of wins may seem like an effective antidote to misinformed courts. However, considering among other things the public resistance engendered by those in support of pornography, careerist prosecutors can be discouraged and choose to prioritize other crimes. Making the process more accessible to the survivors would, therefore, strengthen incentives for bringing more cases and improve the likelihood of success independently of the prosecutors.

The standards for obscenity were further developed one year after *Ramsingh* in *R. v. Wagner* (1985), where Judge Mr. Melvin Earl Shannon of the Alberta Court of the Queen's Bench rejected the argument that dehumanization must be related to explicitness, as implied in some prior decisions, holding instead that "it is the message that counts, not the degree of explicitness."[24] The court adopted the three-pronged definition of pornography articulated by the Canadian psychologist Dr. James V. P. Check, which distinguished (a) sexually explicit materials with violence; (b) sexually explicit materials without violence, but dehumanizing or degrading; and (c) explicit erotica. Categories (a) and (b) were deemed obscene, while (c) was not. Check's expert testimony convinced the court "that social harm does result from repeated exposure to obscene films" as so defined. Regarding the films specifically reviewed in *Wagner*, Judge Shannon found that most of them "fall into the category of non-violent but degrading and dehumanizing, with some episodes in the sexually violent class."[25]

As previously observed, psychological experiments employing Check's definition were both conceptually valid and corroborated by studies using similar concepts.[26] Hence, the Canadian definition of obscenity since *Wagner* has become more consistent with social science research, whereas U.S. obscenity law continued to proscribe pornography that "appeals to the prurient interest."[27]

Referring to Dr. Check, who testified in the case that violent or degrading and dehumanizing pornography contributes to sexual aggression and "less receptiveness to" women's "legitimate claims for equality and respect," the court was "convinced" that "the Crown has demonstrably justified the need for" the obscenity law "and the reasonable limitations it places on freedom of expression."[28] Here, the *Wagner* court relied on the same constitutional analysis as had recently been set forth in *Ramsingh*, balancing competing legal interests under section 1. Yet the court did not explicitly cite any Charter equality guarantees, a decision that appears inconsistent with its explicit acknowledgment of pornography's contribution to sex inequality and sexual aggression—social practices that are in direct conflict with the equality objectives enumerated in sections 15 and 28. Again, *Wagner* was a criminal case where no plaintiffs or interveners represented those actually harmed by pornography—people who might have been inclined to invoke the legal right to equality, which is more tangible and robust than community standards.

Like *Ramsingh*, which did not scrutinize the conditions in which pornography is produced, *Wagner* variously minimized and ignored production harms. To cite one example, with no evidence beyond viewing the movie *Greenhorn*, which contained gay male pornography, Judge Shannon assumed that "[a]ll of the participants" in *Greenhorn* were "willing, consenting adults" and that "no one" was "degraded or dehumanized"; thus the movie qualified as "erotica."[29] However, off-camera abuse can be difficult to discern merely from the materials presented in court and the presumptive consent of the performers involved. In other passages of the opinion, Judge Shannon referred to a movie in which one woman who appeared in a scene of bondage was said to be in pain—a characterization implying coercion and abuse, although it could be acting—and proceeded to describe the following scene where a man was "squirt[ing] semen in her face," to which Judge Shannon remarked that she seemed "to like that."[30] Yet the scene by itself provided no evidence from which to draw such an inference. The first scene of pain could also have led Judge Shannon to assume a more critical stance toward positive emotions expressed by the persons used as performers.

Remarks like these, within the context of *Wagner*'s generally superficial analysis, support the argument for a civil rights rather than a criminal law approach to pornography. That is, unless pornographers are held directly accountable to survivors through civil liability or survivors have another incentive to testify, those well-suited to provide insight will not be present in the courtroom to correct prejudice and misguided beliefs regarding the reality of pornography. Under current criminal pornography statutes, survivors could expose themselves to the sort of contempt and stigma that commonly attaches to those revealing personal sexual experiences, even abusive ones, in public settings. The #MeToo movement may have broken down some of those barriers, but its impact on the application of pornography and prostitution laws has yet to be seen.

The Canadian obscenity law's approach to the harms caused by consumers continued to develop after *Wagner* was decided when the Supreme Court of Canada, in *Towne Cinema Theatres, Ltd. v. R.* (1985), addressed the question of whether a trial court had "applied the proper test" for obscenity.[31] In an attempt to clarify the relationship between community standards of tolerance and the Criminal Code's "undue exploitation of sex" requirement, the Court observed that community standards had

> never been seen as the only measure of such undueness; still less has a breach of community standards been treated as in itself a criminal offence. There are other ways in which exploitation of sex might be "undue." Ours is not a perfect society and it is unfortunate but true that the community may tolerate publications that cause harm to members of society and therefore to society as a whole. Even if, at certain times, there is a coincidence between what is not tolerated and what is harmful to society, there is no

necessary connection between these two concepts. Thus, a legal definition of "undue" must also encompass publications harmful to members of society and, therefore, to society as a whole.[32]

On the one hand, *Towne Cinema* recognized that the contemporary community standards test was inadequate since it was relativistic and could accommodate empirically harmful materials. On the other hand, after the Court's plurality related "undue exploitation of sex" to sexually violent and dehumanizing materials by noting that no person "should be subject to the degradation and humiliation inherent" in pornography[33]—a view approved by the concurring justices[34]—it contradicted itself, opining of degrading and dehumanizing materials, "[i]t is not likely that at a given moment in a society's history, such publications will be tolerated."[35] Having previously recognized that theirs was "not a perfect society and it is unfortunate but true that the community may tolerate publications that cause harm," the suggestion that it was unlikely that "such publications will be tolerated"[36] seems plainly illogical.

Moreover, at the outset, the *Towne Cinema* Court assumed that "undue exploitation of sex is to be assessed on the basis of community standards" while noting that community standards had "its origins in" *Brodie v. The Queen* (1962), the first Supreme Court obscenity case following the introduction of Canada's 1959 obscenity law.[37] From a substantive equality perspective, it would have been preferable to abandon community standards entirely. The Court itself recognized that "[e]ven if certain sex related materials were found to be within the standard of tolerance of the community, it would still be necessary to ensure that they were not 'undue' in some other sense, for example in the sense that they portray persons in a degrading manner as objects of violence, cruelty, or other forms of dehumanizing treatment."[38] In light of their own critique, the Court could have applied Check's three-prong dehumanization test as the sole determinant of obscenity. Like the civil rights ordinances, it recognizes substantive inequality, and thus promotes the perspectives and interests of those directly harmed.

By retaining community standards as one of the tests available to determine undue exploitation of sex, the Court also retained the internal conflicts between a test that recognized harm and a test that could ignore it. After *Towne Cinema*, what remained were three competing tests that could be used to interpret "undue exploitation of sex": (1) the community standards test; (2) the violence, degradation, and dehumanization test; and (3) the "internal necessities" test, which provided a defense for serious purpose and artistic merit.[39]

The progressive obscenity cases discussed so far did not enter into explicit constitutional balancing with the support of the Charter's section 15 and 28 equality guarantees. Although section 15 did not formally take effect until April 17, 1985,[40] there was no such restriction on the application of section 28, which was invoked in the 1985 obscenity case of *R. v. Red Hot Video Ltd.* There, the British Columbia Court of Appeal unanimously dismissed a constitutional challenge contending that the prevailing obscenity law, among other things, was vague, uncertain, overbroad, and therefore not a reasonable limit on expressive freedoms sustainable under sections 1 and 2(b) of the Charter.[41]

Red Hot Video followed *Wagner* in viewing violent as well as nonviolent but dehumanizing and degrading pornography as obscene unless literary, artistic, political, or scientific defenses applied. In one of the two resulting opinions, both concurring in the outcome, Judge Anderson rebutted the restrictive view that such pornography was "not a threat to society" except when it falls "into the hands of children." By contrast, Judge Anderson stated that materials of this kind "constitute a threat to society because they have a tendency to create indifference to violence insofar as women are concerned" and "exalt the concept that in some perverted way domination of women by men is accepted in our society." In this context, Judge Anderson asserted that determining whether obscenity law is a reasonable limitation on expressive freedoms under section 1 should not be decided "in a vacuum but should have regard to the provisions of the Charter as a whole, including section 28," which guarantees that " '[n]otwithstanding anything in this Charter, the rights and freedoms referred to in it are guaranteed equally to male and female persons.' " Furthermore, Judge Anderson reasoned, "[i]f true equality between male and female persons" was to be realized, Canada could not "ignore the threat to equality resulting from the exposure to male audiences of the violent and degrading material described [in *Wagner*]." Judge Anderson also noted that "such material has a tendency to make men more tolerant of violence to women and creates a social climate encouraging men to act in a callous and discriminatory way towards women." Hence, as of 1985, a judicial opinion had concluded that violent, dehumanizing, or degrading pornography infringes women's right to equality under the Canadian Charter.[42]

Consolidation and Progression in *R. v. Butler* (1992)

Representation of Perspectives and Interests

After the second unsuccessful parliamentary attempt to pass a new pornography law in 1988,[43] representatives of the anti-pornography movement in Canada were able to intervene in *R. v. Butler*, a criminal obscenity case that reached the Supreme Court in 1992.[44] It involved an owner and an employee of a Manitoba pornography store, both convicted of obscenity by two lower courts based on some of the merchandise sold there, who challenged the constitutionality of the statute under section 2(b) of the Charter.[45] Several parties were granted intervener status when the case reached the Supreme Court: four provincial and one federal attorney general, and four non-governmental organizations, two on each side. Among the latter four, the Canadian Women's Legal Education and Action Fund (LEAF) and the Group Against Pornography defended the law, while the Canadian and British Columbia Civil Liberties Associations and the Manitoba Association for Rights and Liberties argued that the law impermissibly infringed freedom of expression.[46]

LEAF's *factum*, the Canadian analogue to a U.S. amicus brief, addressed the constitutional issues by submitting that pornography is a practice of sex inequality that disproportionally harms women.[47] Their position was largely accepted by the Court in sustaining the law.[48] By contrast, as Catharine MacKinnon has observed, the prosecution never raised a defense of the obscenity law on sex equality grounds.[49] This circumstance lends support to hierarchy theory's hypothesis that groups disadvantaged by social dominance are best suited to recognize, articulate, and represent their own perspectives and interests.[50] It also serves as a reminder that criminal law, as opposed to civil rights ordinances like those discussed here, provides fewer institutional mechanisms for self-representation by disadvantaged groups. Groups such as those that intervened in *Butler* had not pursued a similar course of action in any of the criminal obscenity cases that preceded it.

It is worth noting that LEAF's intervention in the case was facilitated by the federal Court Challenges Program, which was cut for about two years by the Canadian government just after *Butler* was decided.[51] The program had provided funds for women, poor people, "visible minorities and other disadvantaged groups" to hire lawyers and intervene in important constitutional litigation.[52] Because the Canadian Charter was itself relatively new and section 15's equality guarantee had only been in force since 1985, many groups were critical of the government's decision to cut the program when it did. In the words of Shelagh Day of the Canadian National Action Committee on the Status of Women, the program had provided "'disempowered groups . . . a little bit of control over the way very important issues were being argued in the court.'"[53] The program received new funding in 1994 and continued to operate until September 2006, when most of its funding was cut again.[54] However, the program was eventually reinstated on February 7, 2017.[55]

Following political theorist Iris M. Young, a policy like the Court Challenges Program would amplify the representation of disadvantaged groups' perspectives in decision-making bodies, confronting more privileged groups with perspectives they might not otherwise encounter, which in turn undermines social dominance.[56] Additionally, those directly harmed in the production or by the consumers of pornography, such as women or prostitution survivors, are likely better situated to foresee the effects of pertinent policies than other groups, and should, therefore, be duly represented during public deliberations to ensure that any decisions that emerge are well-informed. Their representation would, moreover, serve as a counterweight to groups that stand to benefit from the status quo, especially consumers, producers, distributors, and third-party profiteers. Consistent with Young, the Court Challenges Program might have provided particularly favorable conditions to a legal challenge to pornography in Canada. For this reason, a closer look at the arguments set forth by LEAF, the only women's group participating in the judicial deliberations, is warranted.[57]

The materials seized at the Manitoba store were described in LEAF's factum in detail; among other things, they presented women (some appearing to be children) as being raped, exhibiting a range of reactions to the abuse.[58] On one side of the spectrum was resistance, screaming, and attempts to run away; on the other were positive displays, including enjoyment. Other materials presented sex involving superiors and subordinates, such as "employer on employee, priests on penitent, doctor on nurse, and nurse on patient." Women were shown having sex with other women to gratify the desires of a male audience. Some were presented as "sexually insatiable." Women were "simultaneously or serially penetrated in every orifice by penises or objects," on occasion "gagging on penises down their throats." Materials showed women licking men's anuses. Women were "bound with rings through their nipples, and hung handcuffed from the ceiling." Materials showed men who ejaculated on women's faces and into their mouths. The women in these situations were "referred to and described" using terms such as "pussy," "cunt," "split beavers," "hole," "bitch," and "dyke meat." Moreover, a "small number" of the items seized in *Butler* presented men who sexually aggressed against other men in ways analogous to male aggression against women, incorporating such abuses as men "gagging on penises down their throats" and men ejaculating into other men's mouths or urinating on other men.[59]

In short, the type of materials seized in *Butler* was similar to what was documented as being in popular demand in content studies undertaken in the 2000s.[60] The seized materials also satisfied the definition of "graphic sexually explicit subordination of women" under the Indianapolis anti-pornography civil rights ordinance, including its relevant subcategories of violent and ostensibly nonviolent materials.[61] Politicians in American jurisdictions where civil rights ordinances were proposed connected *Butler*-style pornography with women's social subordination more broadly, and consequently defined it as sex discrimination that was actionable as such.[62] This argument was also made by LEAF in its defense of the existing obscenity law.[63] Counsel thus resurrected the legal theory the organization had used when it intervened in a prior hate propaganda case, *R. v. Keegstra*,[64] with some modifications introduced to account for the differences between pornography and hate propaganda. LEAF essentially advanced a three-level theory where only the final level would consider balancing under section 1 of the Charter necessary.

Indeed, even after the adoption of the Charter, the Court had continued to recognize that rights and freedoms were subject to limitations and balancing prior to any section 1 analysis.[65] Section 1 thus created a two-tier analysis, where an initial balancing test assessed whether the challenged law was sustainable without the invocation of section 1. If not, a section 1 inquiry was undertaken. LEAF defended the sufficiency of the first two levels on the rationale that protecting pornography under section 2(b) before engaging section 1 ran the "risk" of "not only dignifying a vicious traffic" in sexual subordination but also "eroding" expressive guarantees for other forms of expression in favor of a "policy-oriented" approach under section 1 that would permit more indiscriminate suppression of legitimate expression.[66]

Accordingly, LEAF's first-level argument drew from the Supreme Court's previous statements in *Irwin Toy Ltd. v. Quebec* (1989) and other cases where it had been remarked in dicta that violence and threats of violence would be unprotected by section 2(b) because that "form" of expression was impermissible.[67] LEAF thus stipulated that some of the materials seized at Butler's store were outside the bounds of expressive protection under section 2(b) because they had been produced through coercion and abuse and therefore constituted a violent form of expression.[68] Moreover, the consumers' sexual aggression and attitudes supporting violence against women to which pornography contributes were cast as "threats of violence," at least regarding materials that combined violence and sex.[69]

In addition, LEAF submitted that, since physical violence was inflicted on "real people" to produce some of the pornography seized in *Butler*, such materials were appropriately placed in a category accorded less protection than hate propaganda. Indeed, hate propaganda "does not require violence against real people" to be produced. Furthermore, LEAF argued that "the mass marketing" of abuse as "sexual entertainment" was "no more worthy of protection as expression than are the assaults themselves." LEAF also made an analogy to how the U.S. Supreme Court addressed child pornography, noting that dissemination and possession of child pornography were unprotected in part because their production is regarded as inherently abusive, not only on account of the power imbalance between children and adults but also because distribution and possession contribute to the expansion of the market in child pornography, in turn perpetuating the abuse.[70] By this logic, at a minimum, the production and distribution of abusive adult pornography likewise contribute to a market for materials whose promulgation is reliant upon further abuse, and, as such, would lose protection under section 2(b) on LEAF's rationale.

Notably, the *Irwin Toy* Court had stated that when the *purpose* of a law was not to restrict attempts to convey "meaning," the law required less support from section 1 so long as its restrictions on expression were an incidental effect caused by that purpose.[71] This position was, in some respects, similar to the American doctrines that permit regulation of the underlying conduct[72] or the "secondary effects"[73] of speech. LEAF's position held that, when applying obscenity law to pornography that was made through coercion, the objective was to prevent sexual abuse—not to suppress the "viewpoint" that women should be sexually abused. For the sake of argument, it is not necessary to unduly exploit presentations of explicit sex for communicating statements with a meaning that endorses sexual abuse. Put otherwise, it is the violent and threatening "form" of expression that the law proscribed, not its "meaning." That said, LEAF distanced itself from the "position that pornography has no meaning," instead submitting that "all social practices, however invidious, have meaning."[74]

Following *Irwin Toy*, even if an incidental effect resulted from the application of obscenity laws that restricted defendant's "attempts to convey a meaning," the burden remained on the defendant—not the government—to show how the challenged "activity" would have promoted "at least one" of the underlying liberal values of section 2(b): (1) "seeking and attaining truth," (2) "participation in social and political decision-making," and (3) recognizing that "diversity in forms of individual self-fulfillment and human flourishing ought to be cultivated in an essentially tolerant, indeed welcoming, environment not only for the sake of those who convey a meaning, but also for the sake of those to whom it is conveyed."[75]

It can hardly be argued that coercing anyone into performing pornography would constitute an attempt to seek and attain the "truth." Much coercion and abuse also occur beyond the view of the cameras; thus, the purpose is more aptly described as an attempt to hide, not reach, the truth. In a similar vein, pornography has generally made no meaningful attempt to "promote" participation in social and political decision-making. Lastly, if pornography would be regarded as "human flourishing," LEAF submitted, it was "at women's expense."[76] Indeed, pornography's well-documented production harms and injuries caused by its consumers suggested that pornography did not contribute to a "welcoming environment" for anyone but those who intended to engage in or profit from sexual subordination.

In its second level of the argument, LEAF maintained that unlike the hate propaganda litigated in *Keegstra*, laws regulating pornography were protected by section 28's guarantee that all rights and freedoms in the Charter apply "equally to male and female persons."[77] As previously mentioned, Judge Anderson of the B.C. Court of Appeal had engaged in a similar balancing with section 28 in 1985, but under section 1 rather than section 2(b).[78] In contrast to his analysis, LEAF argued that the plain language of section 28 suggested that the defendant had to "demonstrate" that the pornography in question did "not limit women's rights before the protection of section 2(b)" could be "claimed."[79] Indeed, the strong terms of section 28 "guarantee[d]" equal rights, and pornography seriously eroded those rights for women by its contribution to gender-based violence and attitudes supporting and trivializing violence against women. LEAF's reading of section 28 implied that a higher level of scrutiny must be applied to any claims to protect expression that undermine equality rights,[80] which would have raised a presumption against protecting pornography rather than against restricting the right to produce and distribute it. In this part of their factum, LEAF also noted that research published since the Fraser Committee issued its special report in 1985 showed that nonviolent but dehumanizing and degrading pornography produced effects comparable to those of violent materials[81]—a position similarly consistent with more recent findings.

Because the Canadian Charter supports substantive equality,[82] LEAF maintained that its equality guarantee focused "on eliminating the disadvantage of historically subordinated groups," and therefore was "not neutral on practices that promote inequality, but rather [had] a constitutional commitment to ending them."[83] Keeping in mind that pornography is particularly harmful to those who are multiply disadvantaged, such "disadvantaged individuals or groups" were either expressly included in the discriminatory grounds enumerated in section 15 (e.g., sex, age, or ethnic origin),[84] or related or analogous to those groups. This logic is manifest in *R. v. Turpin* (1989), where the Supreme Court describes those meriting protection under section 15 as having been subjected to "stereotyping, historical disadvantage or vulnerability to political and social prejudice,"[85] disadvantages that prostituted persons and battered women arguably suffer, including victim-blaming, trivialization of their abuse, and criminalization. The Charter, therefore, seemed to cast a presumption against those who would challenge laws that promote substantive equality and the elimination of such historical disadvantage, which would support upholding a law against pornography on equality grounds rather than reverting to the indiscriminate policy-oriented balancing under section 1 that LEAF criticized for dignifying pornography as meriting some degree of constitutional protection.[86]

LEAF's third level of argument addressed situations in which the Court would reject the contention that equality interest outweighed the expressive interests of pornography under section 2(b). Here, LEAF submitted that the same analysis it had proffered under levels one and two were perforce applicable under the more relaxed section 1 balancing standard,[87] which "guarantees the rights and freedoms set out" in the Charter "subject only to such reasonable limits prescribed by law as can be demonstrably justified in a free and democratic society."[88] The test that had been introduced by the Supreme Court in *R. v. Oakes* (1986) specified that the "objective" of identifying an acceptable limit on rights and freedoms had to be " 'of sufficient importance' " and "at a minimum" relate to an objective of "pressing and substantial" significance.[89] Further, the chosen legal means had to be "reasonable and demonstrably justified."[90] In concrete terms, this meant that the adopted measures must (1) not be "arbitrary, unfair," or "irrational," but must instead be "rationally connected to the objective"; (2) "impair 'as little as possible' the right or freedom in question"; and (3) where limiting "effects" on a Charter right or freedom are presented, must be proportional to the identified objective.[91]

LEAF's factum stressed that the harms of pornography provided a pressing and substantial objective for legal regulation in that they contribute to sexual abuse, victimization, coercion, aggression, and attitudes endorsing or trivializing such behaviors against women.[92] It further contended that pornography promoted "systemic discrimination against women through systematic bias and subordination," which eventually affected the "status and treatment" of women who did not "directly" experience pornography-related abuse.[93] Given that, a prohibition on pornography would promote equality and thus be rationally connected to the objective of preventing harm and discrimination—an objective supported by sections 15 and 28, so far as the obscenity law was interpreted consistent with the Charter's equality guarantees rather than outmoded moral preoccupations with offensiveness and explicitness.[94] Hence, LEAF underscored that the "*Wagner* line of authority," which unlike other Canadian interpretations of obscenity law identified real harms, employed the appropriate standard.[95]

As an implicit response to the *Oakes* test, which demands proportionality between means and ends with only minimal impairment of expressive rights, LEAF submitted that "[w]hen interpreted to promote equality," the obscenity law was "neither vague nor overbroad." Additionally, it asserted that the state's pressing and substantial interest in "eliminating systemic social subordination" provided a clear guide to interpretation and constrained "any potential overreach in the statutory language." Quoting a Supreme Court decision from 1986, LEAF also reminded the Court that the Charter should not be made to serve as a vehicle for those with greater privilege " 'to roll back legislation which has as its object the improvement of the condition of less advantaged persons.' "[96] Here, LEAF implied that if rolling back the existing manner of regulating pornography by striking down the obscenity law under section 1 were to affect disadvantaged populations harmed by those materials adversely, it would be contrary to the manner in which the Charter was meant to be used.

Balancing Substantive Equality under Section 1

The Supreme Court did not adopt LEAF's first two levels of arguments that violent, dehumanizing, and degrading pornography was without expressive protection under section 2(b). Instead, it took the position that the obscenity law sought "to prohibit certain types of expressive activity" and thus infringed section 2(b) of the Charter.[97] Nonetheless, the Court saved the obscenity law under section 1, and did so unanimously,[98] with a majority opinion on behalf of seven justices delivered by Justice John Sophinka, and a concurrence supported by two justices delivered by Justice Charles D. Gonthier.

When analyzing the reasons for sustaining the obscenity law as a reasonable limitation on freedom of expression under section 1, Justice Sophinka invoked the imperative of sex equality. Building on cases handed down since *Rankine*, the *Butler* Court conceded that "degrading or dehumanizing materials place women (and sometimes men) in positions of subordination, servile submission or humiliation," and further recognized that these materials "run against the principles of equality and dignity of all human beings."[99] The notion that "the appearance of consent" should determine whether or not a work unduly exploited sex, thus rendering it legally obscene, was flatly rejected. In the words of the Court, "Sometimes the very appearance of consent makes the depicted acts even more degrading or dehumanizing." This position militated against allowing prejudicial assumptions about consent to affect juridical consideration as occurred in *Wagner*, where Judge Shannon assumed that the materials at issue constituted "erotica" that was neither dehumanizing nor degrading in light of the apparent consent of the participants.[100]

Justice Sophinka concluded that degrading or dehumanizing materials "fail the community standards test" not because they offend "morals," but because they are "perceived by public opinion to be harmful to society, particularly to women."[101] Although the opinion did not go so far as to say that these conclusions were "susceptible of exact proof," it asserted that a "substantial body of opinion" supported them, at which point the Court cited the U.S. Attorney General's Commission on Pornography's *Final Report* and other public inquiries undertaken in Australia, New Zealand, and Toronto. Justice Sophinka found it "reasonable to conclude that there is an appreciable risk of harm to society in the portrayal of such material."[102] The Court further reiterated its established position that "the overriding objective" of the obscenity law was "not moral disapprobation but the avoidance of harm to society," and that "criminalizing the proliferation of materials which undermine another basic Charter right may indeed be a legitimate objective."[103]

Contrary to LEAF's argument, the Court found that the obscenity law infringed on expressive freedoms in section 2(b) of the Charter. Yet the Court asserted that promoting equality was more important than protecting pornography, which enabled a balancing of constitutional interests that sustained the law under section 1 in the following terms:

> The infringement on freedom of expression is confined to a measure designed to prohibit the distribution of sexually explicit materials accompanied by violence, and those without violence that are degrading or dehumanizing. As I have already concluded, this kind of expression lies far from the core of the guarantee of freedom of expression. It appeals only to the most base aspect of individual fulfilment, and it is primarily economically motivated.
>
> The objective of the legislation, on the other hand, is of fundamental importance in a free and democratic society. It is aimed at avoiding harm, which Parliament has reasonably concluded will be caused directly or indirectly, to individuals, groups such as women and children, and consequently to society as a whole, by the distribution of these materials. It thus seeks to enhance respect for all members of society, and non-violence and equality in their relations with each other.
>
> I therefore conclude that the restriction on freedom of expression does not outweigh the importance of the legislative objective.[104]

The Court here recognized that, by preventing the distribution of some pornography, the government was promoting equality by preventing the aggression and discrimination its distribution would otherwise contribute to. This exemplifies a substantive equality approach to obscenity law meant to advance the interests of disadvantaged individuals and groups harmed by pornography.

From a comparative perspective, the Indianapolis ordinance's definition of pornography was conceptually very close to the violence, dehumanization, and degradation standard effectively adopted in *Butler*. In fact, the two legal definitions were based on similar findings that have been corroborated repeatedly. The *Butler* decision can thus be broached as a hypothetical decision by the Seventh Circuit Court of Appeal that would have sustained the Indianapolis ordinance under a strict scrutiny standard.[105] In that scenario, a compelling governmental interest to prevent sex discrimination would outweigh the First Amendment interests protective of pornography. Indeed, when the Supreme Court of Canada sustained the obscenity law as applied to violent and dehumanizing materials, there was no need to invoke any exceptions like those employed under intermediate scrutiny—for example, "viewpoint neutrality,"[106] proscribing an underlying conduct (e.g., burning draft cards),[107] or targeting not "content" but "secondary effects."[108] The Supreme Court of Canada simply balanced equality against expressive interests, without assuming ipso facto that freedom of expression was the norm, equality the exception, as had been the case under the more liberal regulations applied in Sweden and the United States. These comparative conditions support the hypothesis that Canada's substantive equality architecture was an important independent contributor to its successful legal challenges to pornography. It is possible that a constitutional framework of this kind is more consequential than other social variables, for example, popular opinion and the strength and focus of the women's movement, in mounting a successful legal challenge to pornography.

However, the *Butler* decision was limited to the criminal law that was litigated in that case. The Canadian law after *Butler* was thus very different from the anti-pornography civil rights ordinances proposed in United States, which would have empowered those harmed rather than prosecutors. Although the *Butler* case supported the comparative hypothesis that legal architecture matters, it did so only in the limited sense that architecture may enable or obstruct legal challenges. Legal architectures do not perform miracles by themselves, like churning out civil rights ordinances. For that to occur, activists and legislators must act. While *Butler* refined and reinforced the equality- and harms-based constitutional standard for regulating pornography, it did not by itself create a more efficient remedy, but rather facilitated the passage of anti-pornography civil rights legislation by Canadian legislatures at a later date.

Butler's Remaining Problems

In *Butler*, the Court tried again to resolve the conflict between the competing internal rationales apparent in the tests of harm, community standards, and artistic defenses. Justice Sophinka acknowledged that previous cases had failed "to specify the relationship of the tests one to another," and that this failure raised "a serious question as to the basis on which the community acts in determining whether the impugned material will be tolerated."[109] While he then reiterated Check's test of violence, dehumanization, and erotica established in *Wagner*,[110] Justice Sophinka concluded that the test reliant on a community standard of tolerance should mediate the determination of harm:

> Some segments of society would consider that all three categories of pornography cause harm to society because they tend to undermine its moral fibre. Others would contend that none of the categories cause harm. Furthermore there is a range of opinion as to what is degrading or dehumanizing. See *Pornography and Prostitution in Canada: Report of the Special Committee on Pornography and Prostitution* (1985) (the Fraser Report), vol. 1, at p. 51. Because this is not a matter that is susceptible of proof in the traditional way and because we do not wish to leave it to the individual tastes of judges, we must have a norm that will serve as an arbiter in determining what amounts to an undue exploitation of sex. That arbiter is the community as a whole.
>
> The courts must determine as best they can what the community would tolerate others being exposed to on the basis of the degree of harm that may flow from such exposure.[111]

This facet of Justice Sophinka's opinion may be read as conceding that, even when there is harm "flowing" from "such exposure," if the community tolerates others' exposure to the materials—that is, tolerating "the degree of harm that may flow from such exposure"—then those materials should not be judged obscene. By this move, community standards were made a Trojan horse inside a harms-based substantive equality approach to obscenity.

In order to break down the problematic assumptions that led the Court to elevate community standards as the "arbiter" of obscenity, it is first necessary to address the contention in the passage above that "some segments of society" believed pornography was not harmful and that harm could not be proven "in the traditional way." Here, Justice Sophinka downplayed an earlier statement in which he maintained that "a substantial body of opinion" holds that the "portrayal of persons being subjected to degrading or dehumanizing sexual treatment results in harm, particularly to women."[112] Although he also noted that such evidence was "not susceptible of exact proof," his precise meaning was difficult to discern because "exact proof" implied a very demanding standard rarely or never reached in the social sciences. Indeed, the

U.S. Attorney General's Commission on Pornography, which was also cited approvingly,[113] noted in its *Final Report* that "[w]henever a causal question is even worth asking, there will never be *conclusive* proof that such a causal connection exists, if 'conclusive' means that no other possibility exists."[114] The Commission further stated that "all too often, the claim that there is no 'conclusive' proof is a claim made by someone who disagrees with the implications of the conclusion."

As shown earlier in this analysis, there is overwhelming evidence demonstrating that both pornography production and its impact on the behavior of consumers are harmful. Much of this evidence was already available in 1992, when *Butler* was decided.[115] Furthermore, Justice Sophinka's opinion repeatedly recognizes that the legislature is entitled to a " 'reasoned apprehension of harm' resulting from the desensitization of individuals exposed to materials which depict violence, cruelty, and dehumanization in sexual relations," and that Parliament thus had "reasonably concluded" that the distribution of violent, dehumanizing, and degrading pornography causes harm.[116] This reasonable apprehension of harm led the *Butler* Court to adopt the view that there was "a sufficiently rational link between the criminal sanction, which demonstrates our community's disapproval of the dissemination of materials which potentially victimize women . . . and the [legislative] objective."[117] There is no reason offered to explain why, when applying the law, a decidedly rational determination of harm should be subject to the whims of different "segments of society"[118] when potentially desensitized or overprotective community standards would mediate it.

Justice Sophinka further contended that it was not possible to apply the violence, dehumanization, and degradation test judiciously because of an asserted "range of opinion as to what is degrading or dehumanizing."[119] This was supported by a pinpoint citation to the Fraser Committee's report, which distinguished between "merely sexually explicit" materials and materials presenting "sexual exploitation and degradation of its participants, with portrayal of men as aggressors and women as subordinate."[120] On the same page, the Committee followed up with the observation that "[p]ractically speaking, there can be no real dividing line between the two, since interpretation of a particular image depends to such a great degree on shades of meaning and implication, and on what a particular viewer brings to it." This relativistic claim has been disproven by psychologists who systematically applied the definition in an experiment published roughly three years before *Butler*, where the definition was effectively employed to distinguish among different categories of pornography available on the market and their effects on consumers;[121] it was also intelligible to a heterogeneous sample of 436 men drawn from Toronto, who applied the definition "quite well" when called upon to rate materials along dimensions related to violence, degradation, and non-dehumanizing "erotica," thus corroborating the researchers' own classifications of the materials under consideration.[122]

Given that the degradation and dehumanization test was shown to be reliable, Justice Sophinka's opinion appears overly skeptical. Unfortunately, he went further, suggesting that violent pornography could on occasion be non-obscene and that degrading and dehumanizing pornography was not necessarily obscene, although it might be if the harm was "substantial":

> [T]he portrayal of sex coupled with violence will *almost always* constitute the undue exploitation of sex. Explicit sex which is degrading or dehumanizing *may be* undue if the risk of harm is substantial. Finally, explicit sex that is not violent and neither degrading nor dehumanizing is *generally* tolerated in our society and will not qualify as the undue exploitation of sex unless it employs children in its production.[123]

In post-*Butler* cases discussed later in this chapter, the formulations "almost always" and "may be" have supported acquittals in lower courts, where materials that were demonstrably violent and/or dehumanizing and degrading were prosecuted. Arguably, Justice Sophinka modified Check's three-pronged definition in a manner that made it more ambiguous, despite its having been accepted by some lower courts after *Wagner* without modification. For example, although *Wagner* ostensibly referred to contemporary standards, it assuredly concluded that "the contemporary Canadian community will not tolerate either of the first two classes" (i.e., violent or dehumanizing pornography), but will "tolerate erotica no matter how explicit it may be."[124] This statement implied no case-by-case ambiguity as to whether degrading or dehumanizing pornography would be judged obscene.

Ultimately, there is no need for a community standard test under Canada's obscenity law. Yet, as *Butler* and its progeny demonstrate, the courts have continued to rely on it for no good reason, beyond, perhaps, habit, tradition, and resistance to change. One reason why *Butler* did not reject community standards may simply be that none of the parties or interveners argued that it should have. If the opinion had stated clearly that the obscenity law was sustained on the basis of the constitutional right to sex equality set forth in sections 15 and 28 of the Charter, as Judge Anderson did in *Red Hot Video*,[125] community standards could have been construed as unconstitutional because they enable the application of the obscenity law contrary to the equality guarantees mandated under the Charter, and contrary to expressive freedoms. That is, community standards could tolerate materials that promote sex discrimination while prohibiting materials that promote equality, such as safe sex education or critical accounts of sexual abuse. A test so vague that it can invert constitutional principles of equality is likely not to survive judicial review, even though the obscenity law otherwise could be sustained without it.

Albeit speculative, the possibility that community standards might result in outcomes inconsistent with sex equality may have dissuaded the Court from recognizing, with formal citations to both section 15 and section 28, that the law is supported by these fundamental elements of the Charter. Although equality was clearly and repeatedly identified in *Butler* as an objective supported by the law, in contrast to Judge Anderson's opinion in *Red Hot Video*, Justice Sophinka never cited the Charter's formal equality guarantees. In this sense, *Butler* is also distinct from *R. v. Keegstra*, where section 15 on equality and 27 on multicultural rights were explicitly invoked to uphold the law against hate propaganda under section 1 against a section 2(b) challenge.[126]

Moreover, *Butler* never engaged LEAF's argument that some of the materials seized in Manitoba amounted to violent and threatening forms of expression that must be assessed in light of section 15 and 28 equality guarantees when section 2(b) expressive guarantees are considered, thus that there was no need to resort to the less discriminating balancing mandated under section 1. When the Court analyzed the obscenity law's position under section 2(b), it only addressed the positions presented by the litigants in the lower courts along with those of the intervening Attorney General of British Columbia,[127] who argued that *Butler* pornography was physical activity without meaning. The Manitoba Court of Appeal, for instance, interpreted *Irwin Toy* as supporting the conclusion that the impugned materials conveyed no "meaning," only "sexual stimulation,"[128] in contrast to LEAF's contention "that all social practices, however invidious, have meaning."[129] Furthermore, the appellate court, contrary to LEAF's posture, did not view the purported expressive protection in light of the sex equality rights embodied in section 15 or 28, or state that the pornography under review was a violent or threatening form of expression. Instead, it took the view that these materials furthered none of the underlying liberal values of section 2(b): "There is nothing of the quest for truth in the materials before the court. They add nothing to the democratic process. They are the antithesis of individual self-fulfillment and human flourishing."[130]

Recall that LEAF was the only one of the eight interveners that directly represented women's interests—this where the very essence of the case concerned women's interests as a social group subject to systematic discrimination. Considering that women are the predominant target of the harms of pornography, when a large organization representing Canadian women advanced claims about sexual violence contained in the prosecuted pornographic materials that no other party or intervener advanced, those claims should have been accorded greater judicial weight than they were. As Mahoney noted with respect to the line of cases that preceded *Rankine*,[131] courts seemed to have significant difficulty grasping the fact that sexual violence against women is not experienced as "sex" by its victims. Hence, despite its legacy in sustaining an equality and harms-based obscenity law, *Butler* still exhibited some of the bias inherent in "male perceptions of violence" that "can exclude the consideration of female reality."[132]

If the relatively limited representation of survivors of gender-based violence in the *Butler* criminal litigation was one of the reasons for the opinion's bias, a more affirmative representation of the interests of disadvantaged peoples could have been institutionalized by design through an anti-pornography civil rights law similar to those proposed in the United States. Such a law would have reversed the order of interests represented. Recall that in *Butler*, the interests included not only the criminal defendant and the prosecution, but also five government interveners and four nongovernmental organizations (NGOs).[133] However, three of the NGOs were unaffiliated with the perspectives and interests of either women or prostitution survivors, and two argued that the obscenity law infringed upon freedom of expression.[134] According to a contemporaneous observer, the second NGO supporting the law, Group Against Pornography, was not a women's organization at all, but rather a group that embraced "a conservative critique of pornography and, although not exclusively religious, organize[d] extensively through churches."[135] An anti-pornography civil rights law would only empower those directly harmed to bring a lawsuit, although interveners might attempt to join the litigation at a later date. Had *Butler* been litigated under civil rights laws, LEAF would likely have represented the plaintiff that sued the pornographer—one of the two primary parties that the Supreme Court had to consider. In such a scenario, it is possible that provincial and federal attorney generals would not even have been granted standing to intervene. That said, it is still notable that courts since *Rankine* chose to adopt some of the arguments and discourse from the women's anti-pornography movement, even if others were ignored. *Butler* is no exception in this regard: it advanced the notion of pornography as a form of sex discrimination.

Post-*Butler* Law (1993–2019)

After *Butler*, many activists in the national women's anti-pornography movement might reasonably have expected that materials similar to those litigated in *Butler* would be successfully prosecuted in the future. Neither were these expectations met, nor did *Butler* lead to a new era in which the spread of pornography was countered. The following analysis explains this development, focusing on published decisions in major obscenity trials that centered on adult pornography films.

R. v. Hawkins (1993), Nonviolent Dehumanizing Materials Non-Obscene

In 1993, the Court of Appeal for Ontario heard five cases together on appeal, indexed as *R. v. Hawkins*, where a key issue was determining whether nonviolent pornography was at once dehumanizing or degrading and also obscene.[136] Detailed descriptions of the nonviolent materials seized from sellers and distributors are available in the trial court opinions, which include frequent representations of men ejaculating onto women's faces, into their mouths, and over their bodies, and of anal intercourse.[137] Women are generally cast as sexually insatiable and constantly looking for sex with strangers, be they burglars, hitch-hikers, neighbors, or coworkers, often in groups or with other women, the court designating the latter as "lesbian" scenes.[138] These are the same types of materials that had previously been prosecuted in *Butler*.[139] In *Hawkins*, the Court of Appeal for Ontario first concluded that the nonviolent materials lacked artistic qualities, hence were unprotected by the "internal necessities" test.[140] The next question to be decided was whether the materials were " 'degrading or dehumanizing' " and whether they created "the substantial societal risk of harm required by *Butler*" to be deemed obscene.[141]

The *Hawkins* Court noted that *Butler* "did not define 'degradation or dehumanization,'" but instead took the position that there is a "range" of opinions "as to what is degrading and dehumanizing," thus making "'the community as a whole' the norm by which to determine whether material is degrading or dehumanizing and whether a substantial risk of harm is created by such material."[142] Again, looking to *Butler*, *Hawkins* stated that violent pornography "'will almost always'" be obscene, "'[e]xplicit sex which is degrading or dehumanizing may be undue if the risk of harm is substantial,'" and "'explicit sex'" that is neither will "'generally'" be tolerated unless it involves children.[143] On these premises, *Hawkins* found that the prosecution had not shown beyond a reasonable doubt either that the materials were dehumanizing or degrading, or, if so, that they would necessarily be harmful.[144]

The prosecution argued that the nonviolent pornographic materials at issue in *Hawkins* would "cause 'attitudinal harm' in the sense that, among other things, they encourage unrealistic and damaging expectations."[145] However, the court referred to the Ontario Film Review Board that had approved the distribution of films of this kind, which, while by no means juridically dispositive, was "plainly relevant to the question of community standards of tolerance, and supportive of the trial judge's conclusion."[146] The "fact" that a provincial review board, "composed of a cross-section of citizens," did not consider the films prosecuted "to be either degrading or dehumanizing" was "clearly" regarded as "evidence of contemporary Canadian standards of tolerance that a trial judge must weigh in objectively."[147] As anticipated in the reading of *Butler* set forth previously, community standards became increasingly important in judging obscenity, *Towne Cinema*'s (1985) indications to the contrary notwithstanding.

Hawkins never decisively determined whether the nonviolent movies it was tasked to evaluate were dehumanizing or degrading. The court instead emphasized that, "[u]nder the *Butler* test, not all material depicting adults engaged in sexually explicit acts which are degrading or dehumanizing will be found to be obscene."[148] Indeed, *Butler* only stated that such materials "*may be* undue if the risk of harm is *substantial*."[149] This phrasing practically mandated that subsequent courts inquire into the nature and magnitude of harm in every case that came before it, even when presented with incontrovertible evidence of dehumanization. *Hawkins* thus concluded that the question of whether the harm is "substantial" must, just "[l]ike any element of a criminal allegation . . . be proved beyond a reasonable doubt and that proof must be found in the evidence adduced at trial." Here, *Hawkins* distinguished between a legislative finding of harm on "a reasonable basis" in the context of justifying a law under section 1 of the Charter, as opposed to finding that specific materials create a "substantial risk of societal harm . . . when a person is on trial." In this analysis, *Hawkins*' nonviolent materials were found to be non-obscene.[150]

As in every obscenity trial thus far mentioned except for *Butler*, survivors, including those represented through women's organizations, were not directly represented in *Hawkins*. The court's composition was notable considering that *Hawkins* was a major post-*Butler* obscenity trial that encompassed five discrete cases, all reaching the highest provincial court in Ontario. From a democratic perspective, the analysis set forth here on the United States suggested that criminal law was an inadequate model for informed decision-making when the outcome would affect disadvantaged groups whose perspectives and interests were not directly represented. As observed with respect to pre-*Butler* decisions, bias and erroneous assumptions about the relative harms of pornography were often prevalent in criminal trials. Indeed, the *Hawkins* Court thought none of the materials before it bespoke "a lack of consent on the part of any of the participants"[151]—as if "consent" would render the materials less harmful in the hands of consumers, or meaningful consent and off-camera abuse were so readily discernible. As shown previously, similarly harmful attitudinal and behavioral changes have been tracked among those exposed to pornography where performers appear to have consented; indeed, the harm may be more severe when the appearance of consent is combined with violence or graphically explicit sexual subordination.[152]

Another misconception about the harms caused by consumers was on display in a description of nonviolent pornography offered in a lower court's examination of the *Hawkins* matter, which assumed that, as long as women were portrayed as active and assertive rather than passive objects of sex, the materials were harmless. A judge described a movie that both parties agreed was representative of the materials seized accordingly:

> I simply make the point that throughout, it is the women who take the lead in inducing the sexual activity with the men. Throughout, the impression is deliberately created that it is the women who are the dominant sex and, indeed, that they at last are asserting their equality, if not their superiority.

> And, not surprisingly, the male participants seem to be delighted with this new found assertion.
>
> It would be quite wrong for me to say that there is even a hint of humiliation or degradation of one of the sexes and it would be just as wrong for me to say that collectively they are dehumanized or demeaned or that there is any tendency to do so.[153]

However, a psychological experiment published about three years before *Hawkins*' appellate review documented that nonviolent pornographic movies presenting women as indiscriminately initiating sex, in *Hawkins*' terms being "assertive," induce among the highest rates of trivialization of sexual violence, even when compared to those that are more violent.[154]

The fundamental error of *Hawkins* was to interpret the nonviolent materials presented—materials it found to contain no "humiliation or degradation"—out of context. Pornography does not exist in a gender- and power-neutral vacuum. It is, after all, mostly men, not women, who consume it regularly. To underscore, pornography exists in a society characterized by entrenched inequality between the sexes where male sexual aggression against women is a systemic condition.[155] In a context of male consumption and female subordination, presentations of sexually indiscriminate women who compulsively seek out strangers for all forms of sex, anal included, and women who allow men to ejaculate on their faces, in their mouths, and all over their bodies[156] will likely conduce precisely to what the prosecution referred to as "unrealistic and damaging expectations"[157] for women. Indeed, recall the study involving 1,880 heterosexual U.S. college and university students that shed light on the detrimental impact of such expectations.[158] Researchers found that, although 66.7% of the men reported having ejaculated on a woman's face or in her mouth and 62.1% of the women reported having been subjected to it, only 12.5% of the women reported a wish to try it, yet as many as 59.6% of the men still wanted to do it.[159] Several other studies discussed previously demonstrated that the more pornography men consume, the more likely they were to imitate or attempt to imitate it, including with unwilling women.

Looking back at the definitional experiment, law students found it easier to apply the Indianapolis ordinance's subordination-based definition of pornography, which is conceptually similar to the Canadian dehumanization and degradation standard, when the phrase "whose dissemination *in context* would tend to subordinate women" was added.[160] They apparently understood that context matters. Tellingly, when the Canadian psychologist Check, along with his associates, attempted to find complete pornographic movies that did not include dehumanizing or degrading scenes for an experiment, they were unable to do so, and instead had to assemble excerpts from multiple exemplars.[161] Given this, it would be surprising if the many nonviolent materials litigated in the *Hawkins* case would have been deemed wholly devoid of dehumanizing and degrading elements by Check and his colleagues, or that they would have been so rated by their experimental subjects whose evaluations along these axes were similar to those of the researchers.[162] That same study further revealed that the "strongest and most pervasive" effects ensued from nonviolent, not violent, dehumanizing materials.[163] Put otherwise, the evidence suggests that *Hawkins*' finding that the harm engendered by the nonviolent materials was not "substantial" was factually wrong, regardless of community standards.

The case law does not indicate that the problematic claims made in the *Hawkins* litigation regarding the nonviolent pornography's supposed harmlessness were adequately countered by the prosecution, for example, through reference to studies measuring harm. Extrapolating from studies like those invoked by LEAF in *Butler* regarding nonviolent pornography,[164] *Hawkins*' contention that materials of this kind were not harmful could easily have been rebutted if an appropriate intervener had been present. Again, a civil rights model would enable and empower such interveners, even reversing roles, making them the primary parties, while governments would assume the role of interveners in cases presenting broader policy implications.

R. v. Erotica Video (1994), Nonviolent Dehumanizing Materials Non-Obscene

Later obscenity cases that considered nonviolent pornography movies in Canada followed the approach taken in *Hawkins*. In *R. v. Erotica Video Exchange Ltd.*, decided in December 1994 by the Alberta Provincial Court, one video store was convicted for selling and renting out violent pornographic movies, but two others that sold and rented out nonviolent, but concededly "degrading and dehumanizing," pornography were acquitted.[165] The court largely dismissed expert testimony provided by the psychologist James Check, whose expertise was previously relied on in *Wagner* and other pre-*Butler* decisions to establish the three-pronged violence and dehumanization test, casting him as "more of an advocate than an academic or social science researcher."[166] However, the court quoted another researcher, Berl Kutchinsky, who had referred to aggregated data based on longitudinal official crime reports from West Germany that were said to indicate that the association between " 'pornography and rape' " was " 'more than weak.' "[167]

Actually, Kutchinsky's 1971–1984 data showed an increase in reported sexual coercion accompanied by a reduction in reported rapes.[168] However, as recalled,[169] interpretations of the relationship between pornography consumption and reported sex crimes over time must be broached with extreme skepticism, for unlike controlled psychological experiments or naturalistic surveys of individuals, aggregated crime statistics are causally overdetermined by numerous social phenomena, including changes in urbanization, proportion of young men, victims' propensity to report, law enforcement efficiency, the prioritization of offenses, legal changes, and shifts in culture.[170] Kutchinsky's work and similar longitudinal studies have since the 1970s been sharply criticized by scholars in the field for being unreliable.[171] This should have cautioned the court against relying on it in *Erotica Video*. The longitudinal research, in particular, is susceptible to facile deductions, both because there are typically several potentially sufficient and distinct causes for the same effect present in such studies and because any interpretation of this data invariably requires "inappropriate" generalizing about individual behavior based on what is observed in society at large, meaning "drawing conclusions from the wrong units of analysis."[172]

That the Alberta Provincial Court relied on Kutchinsky's research is especially concerning considering that the court made a point of relegating Check to the status of "advocate."[173] Check's research relied on a triangulation of experiments and naturalistic surveys undertaken with individuals,[174] which is known to be far more reliable than Kutchinsky's aggregated longitudinal methodology. Moreover, the court's presumption that researchers should not be "advocates" reflects a fundamental misperception that social scientists are generally neutral with respect to the policy positions their research favors. As the Canadian criminologist Christopher Nowlin remarked, the characterization of Dr. Check in *Erotica Video* reflected a "mistaken belief" among Canadian judges that "some experts, when they appear in court as academics, social science researchers, or literary professionals are not 'advocates.' "[175] Indeed, scientific disengagement does not require neutrality regarding research impacts, which often constitute a less obvious form of advocacy that is supportive of the status quo.

The apprehension expressed previously that the *Butler* decision afforded opportunities for interpretations permissive of nonviolent pornography was evidently warranted. After *Hawkins* and *Erotica Video Exchange*, Canadian legal databases available on Lexis, Westlaw, and CanLII contain no reported obscenity trials centering on adult pornography that include nonviolent but dehumanizing or degrading movies (i.e., where obscenity was not just added to other charges), although it is, of course, possible that unreported cases may exist.[176]

R. v. Jorgensen (1995), "Un-knowingly" Selling Violent Obscenity

Butler stated that violent pornography "will almost always constitute the undue exploitation of sex."[177] A video store operator who sold and rented out violent pornography in one of *Hawkins*' five appeals, the "Jorgensen-Scarborough" appeal,[178] was later acquitted in the Supreme Court of Canada.[179] Writing for a nearly unanimous court (8–1) in *R. v. Jorgensen*, Justice John Sophinka, who also wrote the majority opinion in *Butler*, pointed to a statutory mens rea requirement that sellers must "knowingly" offer products that are obscene in order to be liable.[180] Similar to other post-*Butler* decisions, no interveners were represented in the case—only the prosecution and defendants.[181] This situation is, of course, wholly inadequate from a democratic perspective since the disadvantaged groups whose interests are most directly affected by the harms caused by consumers and producers were not represented.

Jorgensen emphasized the Criminal Code's statutory language that divided the crime of obscenity into two subsections—one addressing producers and distributors, the other sellers, exhibitors, and advertisers.[182] According to the latter, anyone "who *knowingly*, without lawful justification or excuse, (a) *sells*, exposes to public view or has in his possession for such a purpose any obscene [material]" is liable.[183] The phrase "knowingly, without lawful justification or excuse" was not included in the section of the statute pertaining to producers and distributors.[184] Thus, *Jorgensen* reasoned that since this phrase was included in the Criminal Code since 1892, then rendered inapplicable by omission to producers and distributors in a 1949 amendment, a distinction was implied between the two categories.[185] The Court stated that "a seller of pornographic material may include among her merchandise magazines, books and a myriad of other products," and that it would be difficult to gather sufficient information about potential criminal content from distributors and producers who, it surmised, would "not likely" be "inclined to scare off buyers by telling them his or her product can potentially subject the potential purchaser to criminal liability."[186] This problem was not seen as restricted to sellers with "a myriad of other products" apart from pornography, but it would also affect sellers specializing in pornography. Indeed, by the terms of post-*Butler* law, pornography that included dehumanizing and degrading materials need not per se be judged obscene. The Supreme Court differentiated between sellers who knew that their materials presented "exploitation of sex" and those who knew "that the exploitation of sex is undue."[187]

The Crown objected to the requirement that it "prove beyond a reasonable doubt the retailer's knowledge that the materials being sold have the qualities or contain the specific scenes which render such materials obscene in law." It submitted that proving knowledge of violent sex "would effectively make prosecution impossible" because, among other things, "retailers will simply choose not to view their videos thereby escaping conviction." From this vantage point, when sellers have "consciously" chosen to operate in the "regulated and financially profitable field" of pornography, they are well aware of the fact that their products may contain obscenity but proceed nonetheless "in spite of this risk." The Crown further stated that the "retailer who has not viewed the film is thus as morally blameworthy as someone who has viewed the film" and "should be held responsible for the social harm caused when the pornography that they sell crosses the line into obscenity."[188]

The Court responded that prosecutors should find other evidence suggesting a mens rea: for instance, continued dissemination despite warnings that certain materials violate the statute, keeping a "separate selection" category in stores or special lists of materials available "on request only," and other similar circumstantial evidence would suffice to show a knowing state of mind.[189] Furthermore, willful blindness alone would not always be sufficient: "If the retailer becomes aware of the need to make further inquiries . . . yet deliberately chooses to ignore these indications and does not make any further inquiries, then the retailer can be nonetheless charged under s. 163(2)(a) for 'knowingly' selling obscene materials."[190] This last example relies heavily on others to actively monitor the available supply of pornography and warn retailers that transgress the boundaries of "obscenity," rather than relying directly on the retailers' incentives to avoid criminal charges. Barring irrational behavior on the part of retailers who might choose to continue selling obscene products after being put on notice, it is hard to imagine that any prosecution could be successful under these conditions. For practical purposes, the mens rea requirement transformed a criminal law into a framework for reviewing retailers' supply of movies either at public expense or through voluntary efforts.

Moreover, the Court stated that it was "quite properly not suggested that there is any constitutional impediment" preventing Parliament from amending the obscenity law to eliminate the "knowing" requirement from the determination of seller, exhibitor, and advertiser liability.[191] However, to date, no such amendment has been passed. Recall that legislative attempts to reform pornography laws in the 1980s resulted in two inadequate parliamentary bills that no party or group endorsed. For the Court to assume the feasibility of legislative action on this divisive issue seems naïve, if not disingenuous. As proponents of hierarchy theory have implied, highly placed public representatives rarely share the social perspectives and interests of those most affected by the harms contributed to by pornography. That is why it is vital to support the autonomous organizations involved. Such interventions have contributed significantly to successful political challenges to gender-based violence generally, where other factors, such as the number of women or left-leaning parties in government, did not.[192] The absence of any similar interveners in *Jorgensen* also suggested there was little public support for such a change. Alternatively, the public cuts to the Court Challenges Program between February 1992 and October 1994,[193] which supported intervention, may have reduced their numbers, *Jorgensen* being an example of the consequences of defunding.[194] Consistent with the prosecution's criticism, legal databases show no obscenity prosecutions against Canadian sellers in any reported judicial opinions since *Jorgensen*.[195]

R. v. Price (2004), Violent Pornography Not Obscene

In contrast to the absence of cases brought against sellers, a provincial court in British Columbia filed suit in 2004 against a man for producing and distributing over the internet (alternatively possessing for this purpose) eleven pornography videos, mostly involving bondage, discipline, and sadomasochism (BDSM).[196] The defendant's company made the videos available to paying subscribers "through various websites" controlled by the company or by other contractors.[197]

The materials prosecuted presented, among other things, a man who verbally abused a woman and then forced her to bend backward over a toilet while he urinated into her mouth. When her mouth overflowed, the man "punished" her by scrubbing the toilet bowl with her head. The judge observed that this woman was "obviously" not consenting. The "remaining ten" movies presented scenes of BDSM that were largely similar; eight contained a "subservient" female and two a "subservient" male. The "subservient parties" were presented "as being under duress to participate," not as "consenting." Among other things, the movies presented women confined in small cages, whipped with "canes, crops, switches or cat o' nine tails," being burned with hot wax from burning candles all over their bodies, including the breasts and genitals, and having electric shocks applied to many parts of the body, including the genitals. Similarly, weights, clamps, mousetraps, and other torturous devices were attached to various body parts, genitals among them. Some showed the use of small-gauge needles to pierce multiple body parts, including genitalia, which was sometimes accompanied by "minor amounts of bleeding." These implements were removed in the end, accompanied by the pouring of alcohol as "disinfectant" before and after insertion of needles. Furthermore, various forms of restraints and entrapment were visible, such as straps, hoods, gags, and tied ropes, that were applied over hands, feet, and heads, respectively. In one movie, a man urinates into the face of the woman after "a combination of a variety of" the practices described in the ten remaining movies had been performed. In one of them, a woman did the same to a man. Some subjects "shriek[ed] and writhe[d] continuously," others "merely wince[d] or twist[ed] in discomfort," while some, "after being asked, expressed pleasure."[198]

An expert identified as "Dr. Mosher" testified that the BDSM behaviors presented in the Eleven Videos "were part of normal and appropriate human sexual behavior" and that "about 10 percent" of North American adults either practiced or were aroused by BDSM. Similar claims were made by a retired police officer hired by the defense to attend various BDSM events in British Columbia and gather corroborating accounts of BDSM. Another witness, described as a thirty-year-old mother with a teenage daughter, testified that she enjoyed participating in "all manifestations of BDSM activities including those portrayed in the Eleven Videos."[199]

Addressing the scene in which a man scrubbed a toilet bowl with the head of a patently unwilling woman, Mosher claimed it was "part of the BDSM culture but acknowledged the video portrayed extreme violence and an uncommon BDSM fantasy." Mosher deemed none of these BDSM practices demeaning or dehumanizing but instead maintained that they were pleasurable to many and performed with the consent of all parties involved. Yet nowhere did the court's opinion explain how this supposed "consent" could be validated; nonetheless, the judge believed that the "form of consent envisioned" by Mosher met the requirements for consent under Canadian law. The *Price* Court thus concluded "that despite what is portrayed, the subservient parties in all Eleven Videos consented to the taking part in the procedures," and that any "indication of fear, pain or lack of consent portrayed by the subservient parties" was "merely play acting." This assertion stands in direct contradiction to the judge's observation regarding a man's use of a woman's head to scrub a toilet bowl, where "[t]he woman is obviously not consenting."[200]

However, none of the other persons used as performers in the Eleven Movies had testified or been interviewed. A thorough review of the literature yields no persuasive studies or other tangible evidence suggesting that pornography production, in general, does not exploit multiple disadvantages, such as extreme poverty, child sexual abuse, or discrimination based on race, sex, ethnicity, or similar grounds in order to compel performers to tolerate abusive acts.[201] The evidence presented in *Price* is inadequate to justify rejecting an analogous conclusion regarding the Eleven Videos. There is not enough basis on which to presume "consent" or "play acting"; the movies may suggest either that performers were actually abused, consenting or not, or that they acted as if they were abused. To infer any conclusion in this regard (except regarding the movie involving the toilet bowl) is impossible on the basis of the testimony and other evidence considered by the judge, which referred only to BDSM culture in general and offered no specific information about any of the Eleven Videos' performers.

Another expert called by the defense in the *Price* trial, "Dr. Fisher," offered testimony about the harms caused by adult pornography consumers that completely contradicted the myriad social science studies, meta-analyses, and other evidence analyzed here. The "thrust of Dr. Fisher's opinion was that exposure to diverse forms of pornography does not (a) cause attitudinal harm"; (b) does not "cause anti-social attitudes towards men or women"; (c) "does not cause sexual aggression"; (d) does not "cause people to act in an anti-social manner"; and (e) does not "cause the mental or physical mistreatment of women or men." The only data invoked in the opinion to support these claims lacked specific citation, but was said to have been drawn from official sex crime reports compiled in different countries over time (i.e., longitudinal data), on which basis Dr. Fisher claimed that the internet had had no discernible impact on attitudes supporting violence against women. Fisher further relied on official U.S. and Canadian crime reporting statistics showing a decline in "reported sexual assaults" from 1994 to 1999, "while the Internet 'was rolled out.'" However, during cross-examination, it was revealed that reports of forcible rapes in the United States had actually increased during 2001 and 2002. Nonetheless, the judge declared that "no evidence" had been presented to "contradict" Dr. Fisher's testimony on the matter.[202]

Yet, to underscore, interpreting the type of aggregated longitudinal data that relies upon official crime reporting, as seen in *Price* and earlier in *Erotica Video*, has been found to be a perilous venture. It is associated with serious methodological problems, notably "causal over-determination" (where there are several sufficient and distinct causes for the same effect) and the "ecological fallacy" (generalizing about individuals based on data from society at large).[203] The more controlled sub-national comparisons of specific years, where alternative independent variables that may change over time are thus held constant, have demonstrated a substantial and significant positive correlation between higher rates of pornography circulation and reported rapes.[204] Moreover, quantitative experiments show a causal effect from pornography exposure that, when triangulated against longitudinal and cross-sectional naturalistic surveys and other qualitative data, demonstrates that pornography consumption contributes to gender-based violence.[205] In addition, Dr. Fisher's claim that officially reported rapes have declined over the years is virtually meaningless when, based on more reliable social survey data, actual rapes are estimated to have increased. The 2006 U.S. study discussed at the outset of this volume estimated that the prevalence of "forcible rape" of women had increased 27.3% per capita since 1991 and that the proportion of women reporting the crime to law enforcement rose from 16% in 1991 to 18% in 2005.[206]

The lack of evidence presented by the prosecution in *Price* can be compared with LEAF's 1992 *Butler* factum, which included numerous citations to the latest social science research available at the time.[207] The posture of the case, with only prosecutors representing the perspectives and interests of those directly harmed by pornography, implies that the Crown's incentive may have been inadequate to rebut, by using more accurate research, the more unreliable claims made by the defendant. As hypothesized by democratic theorists, and shown empirically with regard to other political challenges to gender-based violence,[208] the autonomous women's movement's strength has been vital to successful progressive change. Perhaps not coincidentally, then, when the Canadian Court Challenges Program supported the legal intervention of autonomous organizations representing the perspectives and interests of disadvantaged groups in Canada,[209] one of their interventions presented more compelling evidence in the *Butler* trial. *Price* was decided in the first court of instance; thus, it was likely never seen on the radar of the women's anti-pornography movement. However, by choosing not to appeal the case, the Crown precluded future interventions by other affected parties.

In the end, *Price* did not accept Dr. Fisher's opinion, the essence of which was that pornography causes no harm to adults. Instead, it recognized that Fisher "simply contradict[ed] Parliament's reasonably based concerns as found by *Butler*." Therefore, the claim that violent pornography conduced to no harm was not considered "in determining the charges." Indeed, the judge was inclined to agree with the prosecution, remarking that "there is strong evidence simply from the content of the Eleven Videos themselves by which I may infer a risk of harm and that Canadians would have no tolerance for other Canadians viewing this material."[210]

Despite judicial and prosecutorial agreement on the issue of harm, the judge claimed that among "the three tests for undueness, considered in *Butler*, the most important [was] the community standard of tolerance test." He then noted that *Butler* had required that standards must be "contemporary" and account for social changes. With apparent regard to contemporaneous community standards, *Price* initially acknowledged "at least seventy websites" readily available elsewhere on the internet with similar materials, which provided "in many cases identical . . . [or] even more extreme examples of BDSM activities than shown in the Eleven Videos." Moreover, mainstream movies that contained sexual violence with more elaborate plots and artistic pretenses, such as *American Psycho*, *I Spit on Your Grave*, *Rape Me (Baise-Moi)*, *Irreversible*, and *Henry: Portrait of a Serial Killer*, were purported to show even more violence, while being less sexually graphic, than those comprising the Eleven Videos.[211] From these conditions, the court inferred a community standard by which the Eleven Videos were not obscene at the same time it recognized that the movies were objectively harmful:

> Canadians, for better or for worse, tolerate other Canadians viewing explicit sexual activity coupled with graphic violence which is more or less indistinguishable from the Eleven Videos.
>
> This evidence of tolerance . . . leaves me with a reasonable doubt that the contemporary Canadian community would not tolerate other Canadians viewing the Eleven Videos on the basis that harm would flow from watching the Eleven Videos.[212]

The *Price* Court thus found that, even when harmful, community standards may obviate a determination of obscenity if society regards the resulting harm to be tolerable. This outcome was foreshadowed in the *Butler* Court's statement on community standards. Indeed, *Price* cited both *Hawkins* and *Butler* for the proposition that harm must be proven in every case, even with respect to violent pornography, and concluded that "even if sex and violence are portrayed together, it remains open to the Court to find that the evidence does not establish beyond a reasonable doubt the portrayals exceed Canadian standards of tolerance and that the harm component has been established."[213] Although *Price* was never appealed, and there is a strong case to be made that it was wrongly decided, it cited Supreme Court precedents. *Butler* gave community standards a prominent role before *Price* when *Butler* stated that "courts must determine as best they can what the community would tolerate others being exposed to on the basis of the degree of harm that may flow from such exposure."[214] *Price* did that. Despite recognizing the harm associated with the Eleven Videos, *Price* held that the pervasive social presence of similar materials justified legal tolerance when interpreting what constituted "undue exploitation" of sex—a position that left an admittedly harmful condition without a legal remedy. In this fashion, *Price* illustrated what can happen when community standards determine how obscenity laws are applied, a state of affairs that persists in the United States.[215]

R. v. Smith (2002–2012), Violent Pornography Obscene

In *R. v. Smith* (2012)—an obscenity case litigated over a ten-year period, including trials with two different juries and judges—the Ontario Court of Appeal upheld the conviction of a producer and distributor of violent pornography that presented explicit sex, if not actual sexual activity.[216] A retrial was ordered in 2005 because of errors in the jury instructions.[217] However, the only difference in the outcome was that the second trial imposed a lower penalty: the initial sentence of Can$100,000 and three years probation was reduced to Can$28,000, two years probation, and 240 hours of community service.[218] *Smith* did not investigate conditions of production—only harms caused by consumers. That said, written notes from a conversation with a law enforcement officer, later contested by the wife of the defendant, indicated she had told the officer that the defendant hired and used prostituted women to produce audiovisual materials in his home, forcing his wife and children to remain in the basement during filming.[219] The wife's retraction notwithstanding, it is well established that pornographers typically recruit performers among prostituted populations, as recalled, exploiting their lack of alternatives and other vulnerabilities.

Two types of materials were prosecuted in *Smith*: (1) audiovisual presentations of simulated lethal violence against semi-nude and nude women in an explicitly sexual context, albeit without sexual activity such as "intercourse or fellatio," and (2) written short stories presenting "brutal rape and killing or sexualized killing of women in the most graphic terms" that "reinforce the myth that women enjoy being raped; that they enjoy their victimization."[220] As stated on a website maintained by the producer, his purpose was " 'to show beautiful women getting killed.' "[221] Nude or semi-nude women were presented being "shot, stabbed, stalked, executed by bow and arrow, or shown in combat with swords and knives" by a man "portrayed as being competent and a successful individual who can silence women with his violence, leave them on sexual display, and walk away without consequence." The women were depicted as "easily manipulated" and sometimes "complicit in the violence"; that is, being rendered as " 'bad women' by being sexually loose, or attempting to use their sexuality to control men, violence against them is portrayed as being justified."[222]

The prosecution called two witnesses: Dr. Neil Malamuth, probably the most widely published psychologist on sexual aggression and pornography exposure in the world at the time, and Dr. Peter Collins, a psychiatrist and expert in sexual deviance and paraphilia.[223] The defendant called two university scholars in literature and film studies, only one of whom, Dr. Barry Grant, a film studies scholar, was named by the court.[224]

Dr. Malamuth testified that exposure to the impugned materials could increase attitudes supporting violence against women, such as the myth that women "actually enjoy being raped, controlled or dominated in violent ways," and could increase the risk of sexual aggression. Dr. Malamuth (and Dr. Collins) "pointed to certain features" of the materials, such as placing women in "submissive positions," "the use of 'sexy' women," and a combination of nudity and dominance of women to support their opinions. The defendant's experts submitted evidence "about materials with sexual content combined with extreme violence that were available in the community," apparently attempting to demonstrate tolerant community standards. Dr. Grant also submitted that there was a distinction between pornography showing sexual acts and so-called sexploitation films showing nudity and that these genres could merge, seemingly in an attempt to say that the indicted materials were not pornographic enough to constitute obscenity. He further claimed that the defendant's new "skin-rippling technique" would be appreciated by "aficionados of horror and exploitation films," which gave the materials "artistic merit."[225]

The constellation of experts for the *Smith* prosecution was stronger than in *Price*, which seemingly had no researchers on its side. The prosecution's experts in *Smith* focused on the harm component of *Butler*'s tripartite test of obscenity (i.e., violence, dehumanization, and their effects). The defense may have surmised that expert testimony on community tolerance would suffice against expert testimony on harm. Yet it is equally plausible that it was difficult to find experts willing to go on record defending materials presenting violent death in a sexual context as harmless, even if simulated. Notably, the first conviction in *Smith* occurred in Ontario about seventeen months before the *Price* acquittal in British Columbia.[226] Considering their opinions, the expert testimony, and supporting evidence regarding harm or alleged harmlessness, the two cases could not have been more different: *Smith*'s prosecutors relied on a well-known psychologist with published experiments and naturalistic studies undertaken with individuals;[227] *Price*'s defense relied on unreliable aggregated longitudinal data derived from official crime reports. Likewise, their analysis of community standards diverged markedly. The ready availability of materials similar to those at issue was taken as evidence of community tolerance for pornography presenting male violence against women in *Price*.[228] By contrast, although both the prosecution and the defense in *Smith* agreed that women were "the invariable targets of sexualized violence in the horror genres," and the court itself recognized that the defendant's materials "always" targeted women,[229] it did not find them tolerable regardless of their community appeal. The 2002 trial court offered the following explanation:

> These are not victimless crimes. The undue exploitation of sex and violence directed at women is a poison in our society. It comes to us increasingly in films, literature and on the Internet. It has become acceptable and increasingly graphic entertainment. It has the power to change our perceptions, our attitudes towards each other. It may even prompt us to act on these negative attitudes. And then to justify ourselves. This poison threatens to overrun our conviction that the individual has dignity and worth.[230]

The *Smith* courts were apparently aware that the graphic sexually violent and explicit subordination of women, including in "submissive positions,"[231] was popular, thus tolerated by a meaningful proportion of the community. But unlike *Price*, which regarded community toleration as a mitigating circumstance, *Smith* regarded the popularity of the material as a toxic "poison" to society. Furthermore, when explaining why a psychiatrist's expert testimony about paraphilia, which can entail arousal to sexual abuse, was relevant for assessing community tolerance, the 2012 appellate opinion in *Smith* implied that community standards were a proxy for measuring the strength of harm, not the strength of tolerance for pornography: "The . . . testimony was directed to explaining paraphilia and the effect that exposure to [the defendant's] material . . . has on those who have a paraphilia. This evidence was necessary to establish an evidentiary foundation for the community standards test, which the jury would have to apply to render a verdict."[232] In other words, evidence of risk for sexual aggression was part of the foundation of community standards.

The Future of Community Standards: *R. v. Labaye* (2005), *R. v. Katigbak* (2011)

Two Supreme Court cases on indecency and child pornography, respectively, provide an additional indication that legal developments in Canada may be moving toward a reduction in the influence of the community standard of tolerance test, particularly with respect to a moral, as opposed to a harms-based, community standard. In *R. v. Labaye* (2005),[233] the Supreme Court set aside the conviction of a so-called swingers club in Montréal for having violated the prostitution-related crime of "keeping a 'common bawdy-house' for the 'practice of acts of indecency.' "[234] Lower courts had invoked "community standards" along with "harm" when they determined "indecency." The

Supreme Court criticized the concept of community standards, noting that members of a "pluralistic society" hold divergent views that make it difficult to discern the relevant "community," concluding "that despite its superficial objectivity, the community standard of tolerance test" has "remained highly subjective in application." By contrast, the Supreme Court stated that "[h]arm or significant risk of harm is easier to prove than a community standard." It further elaborated that "harm must be shown to be related to a fundamental value reflected in our society's Constitution or similar fundamental laws. . . . Autonomy, liberty, equality and human dignity are among these values."[235]

Chief Justice McLaughlin, writing for the majority, discussed obscenity and indecency interchangeably while assuming that the "notion of harm" recognized in *Towne Cinema* (1985) demanded that obscene materials must "have a harmful effect on others in society" apart from violating community standards, a harms-based concept that McLaughlin meant "had been implicit in Cockburn C.J.'s definition of obscenity in *Hicklin* [1868]."[236] The equation of harm as understood in *Towne Cinema* and in *Hicklin* was arguably only apt in the superficial sense that any obscenity law presumed some form of "harmful effect on others." The relevant issue should rather be what counts as harm—not that harm was counted per se. Yet Chief Justice McLaughlin concluded that, after *Butler* and subsequent cases, "the community standard of tolerance was determined by reference to the risk of harm."[237]

Perhaps Chief Justice McLaughlin inferred that the community standards concept had become a proxy for harm after *Butler*, as appears to have been the case in *R. v. Smith* in 2012. If so, she presumably meant harm to constitutional or similar fundamental values, rather than harm to moral values. Two Canadian criminal justice and sociology scholars, Richard Jochelson and Kirsten Kramar (formerly Johnson), appear to have been interpreting *Labaye* in this way when they claimed that the Court "abandoned the community standards of tolerance test for undue exploitation of *Butler*, replacing it with a more abstract test for risk of harm and harm."[238] However, the *Labaye* Court's firm reliance on the explicit language of *Butler*, which it quoted approvingly, did not suggest an interpretation of community standards different from that employed by most courts that have decided obscenity cases since 1992. In its view, "courts must determine as best they can what the community would tolerate others being exposed to on the basis of the degree of harm that may flow from such exposure."[239] As mentioned previously regarding the original *Butler* opinion, this passage suggests that even if harm was "flowing," the community might tolerate others' exposure to the materials, thus persuading courts not to judge them obscene. This happened in *Price*.

The *Smith* litigation (2002–2012) also mentioned community standards, at least in earlier instances. For example, all three tests of obscenity appear to have been operative in 2005 given that the Ontario Court of Appeal in *Smith* accepted (1) evidence by behaviorists on harms caused by consumers; (2) "evidence about materials with sexual content combined with extreme violence that were available in the community"; and (3) the opinions of literature and film experts regarding artistic merit.[240] If community standards had indeed been replaced by a harms-based test after *Butler* (1992), as *Labaye* implied in 2005,[241] the evidence of community standards presented in *Price* in 2004 and *Smith* in 2005 would have had no place in assessing obscenity. That said, *Labaye* itself, if not *Butler* before it, may be seen as expressly recognizing that the relativistic notion of community standards should not be used as the measure of harm, which should be measured by objective evidence. In this sense, perhaps *Labaye* came close to replacing community standards with a violence, dehumanization, and degradation test in practice, if not entirely in name.

After *Labaye* was decided, a 2011 Supreme Court opinion on child pornography, *R. v. Katigbak* (2011), cited *Labaye* in its discussion of obscenity law, concluding that "the *Labaye* interpretation is applicable in the present appeal. . . . Relying on the moral views of the community would be as unworkable for child pornography offences as it is for obscenity charges. . . . Instead, the courts must ask whether the harm is objectively ascertainable and whether the level of the harm poses a *significant* risk to children."[242] The Supreme Court then ordered a retrial in part because "the Court of Appeal had erred . . . by relying on a community standard of tolerance test to determine if the risk of harm posed was 'undue' when . . . '*society would find* that risk of harm inappropriate, unjustifiable, excessive or unwarranted in the circumstances of the case.' "[243] The "correct approach" would have been to "assess whether the accused's activities pose a significant risk of harm to young persons."[244]

Considering that *Katigbak* pertained to child pornography, not obscenity—just as *Labaye* pertained to indecency, not obscenity—the influence of these two opinions on future obscenity cases has yet to be seen. The strongly worded rejection of the concept of community standards of tolerance in *Katigbak* indicates, however, that the Supreme Court may be inclined to reject community standards in future obscenity cases. If so, that would leave only two tests for assessing obscenity: (1) the violence, dehumanization, and degradation test, and (2) the artistic "internal necessities" defense.

Gay Pornography after *Butler*: *Little Sisters v. Canada* (2000)

The analysis has thus far illustrated how legal challenges against pornography are successful when they recognize substantive inequality and represent the perspectives and interests of those harmed. By contrast, legal challenges are liable to be unsuccessful when they fail to recognize disadvantaged groups and their interests, a pattern that also appears to be tied to the inadequate presentation and consideration of evidence in court proceedings and a decided preference for relativistic community standards. A logical corollary is that misattribution and misuse of the Canadian obscenity law are more likely to occur when disadvantaged groups are inadequately recognized and represented. Most laws are flawed or present opportunities for misuse, whether minor or serious. For instance, in *Little Sisters Book & Art Emporium v. Canada* (2000), the Supreme Court conceded that customs authorities had "systematically targeted" a gay and lesbian bookstore in British Columbia under regulations that prohibited the importation of obscenity into Canada.[245] Officials had "wrongly delayed, confiscated, destroyed, damaged, prohibited or misclassified materials." General interest and other traditional bookstores did not encounter targeted inspections of this kind. However, other "small bookstores with specialized inventory or clientele," including a "women's" and a "feminist" bookstore, had been similarly targeted for selective customs inspections. Moreover, customs officials lacked the training necessary to classify obscenity and the time to perform this task, conditions that, in turn, likely contributed to the misapplication of the regulation.[246]

Although the application of customs' administrative practices may indeed have discriminated against gay and lesbian people's freedom of expression and access to information, it does not appear to have occurred as a consequence of any excessive recognition of substantive inequality that may be imputed to *Butler*. Selective enforcement can easily occur under any regime of pornography regulation, especially when adequate safeguards are lacking—just as much, if not more, under a traditional obscenity law oblivious to harm and equality.[247]

Arguments made in the Supreme Court of Canada also highlight the need to address and better situate the most directly harmed groups to challenge the harms of pornography legally. Two interveners in *Little Sisters* pursued different arguments in this regard: one intervener—LEAF, which had intervened with some success in *Butler*—pursued an argument in opposition to the one it set forth in *Butler*. As the Court noted, "intervener LEAF took the position that sado-masochism performs an emancipatory role in gay and lesbian culture and should therefore be judged by a different standard from that applicable to heterosexual culture."[248] LEAF was described as further submitting that "by definition, gender discrimination is not an issue in 'same-sex erotica,'" apparently assuming that same-sex pornography did not cause harm to gay and lesbian people.

By contrast, the second intervener in *Little Sisters*—Equality Now, an international human rights organization—"took the view that gay and lesbian individuals" had "as much right as their heterosexual counterparts to be protected from depictions of sex with violence or sexual conduct that is dehumanizing or degrading in a way that can cause harm."[249] Equality Now maintained that sexually explicit media that promoted sexual aggression and trivialized abuse may harm people belonging either to a minority group or to the majority. The gay and lesbian context did not constitute a pertinent difference. Just as not all women are equally harmed by pornography and may not be equally interested in opposing it, neither are all gay men and lesbians. To effectively address any minority (as in the *Little Sisters* context) or majority group (such as in the *Butler* context) so harmed, it was necessary to adopt an intersectional perspective capable of accounting for multiple disadvantages and differential vulnerabilities. An intersectional approach would encompass subordination within minority groups, between majority and minority groups, or within majority groups.

Although the evidence of the harms of same-sex pornography is less systematic than it is of heterosexual materials, as recalled, evidence suggests that a similar dynamic involving multiple disadvantages prevails among male performers, who tend to be exploited by pornographers to produce gay materials in a manner that poses dangers to performers. Furthermore, Dr. Malamuth, who testified in *Smith*, also testified in *Little Sisters*, where the Supreme Court accepted his testimony from the trial court that "'homosexual pornography may have harmful effects even if it is distinct in certain ways from heterosexual pornography.'"[250] The Court concluded "that the attempt to carve out of Butler a special exception for gay and lesbian erotica should be rejected," having stated that the "non-violent degradation of an ostensibly willing sex slave is no less dehumanizing if the victim happens to be of the same sex, and no less (and no more) harmful in its reassurance to the viewer that the victim finds such conduct both normal and pleasurable."[251]

Even though customs officials selectively misused the law to target gays and lesbians, the case of *Little Sisters* suggests that this fact does not diminish the likelihood that challenges to pornography are more successful than otherwise when groups that are particularly affected by its harms are recognized and represented. Indeed, customs officials as a group are not among those collectively affected by pornography's harms. If survivors of pornography-related harms would consult with customs authorities analogously to LEAF's intervention in *Butler*, where LEAF provided the Court with accurate evidence and arguments, customs' application of the law may well be adequate.

Comparative Analysis

Canada's constitutional framework for regulating pornography sustained its harms-based criminal law against challenges on expressive grounds. Unlike the more traditional liberal approaches in the United States and Sweden, which emphasize negative rights, there was no need in Canada to invoke exceptions such as viewpoint neutrality or "low value" speech to save the law. When the imperative of substantive equality was balanced against free expression, the harms engendered by violent or dehumanizing pornography outweighed its expressive value. From a comparative perspective, the Canadian Charter's strong emphasis on substantive equality enabled a more robust defense against those seeking to dismantle the law. However, several unnecessary conditions persist that severely hamper Canada's pornography law.

When courts continue to rely on contemporary standards of tolerance rather than the more objective violence/dehumanization test, it enables the normalization of sexual abuse to influence the adjudication of harm. This problem was starkly exhibited by the decision in *Price* (2004), which took widespread dissemination of materials presenting sexual violence against women as an indicator of community tolerance of admittedly harmful pornography. By this token, the more successful the commercial pornography industry is in making sexual entertainment out of subordination and violence against women, the more permissible of such abuse the community standards will become. Such a pernicious test can effectively legalize the sexual subordination of historically disadvantaged groups to the degree their subordination is entrenched in society. Rather than promoting substantive equality, this perpetuates subordination. Arguably, it violates the Charter's equality guarantees. Hence, the violence/dehumanization test should replace community standards as the primary method of determining undue exploitation of sex, qua obscenity.

The pornographers' defense lawyers have energetically appealed major indictments made in Canada after *Butler* (1992). Their efforts contributed to narrowing the law's reach and made further public litigation exceedingly difficult. Expectedly, as Canadian law professor Janine Benedet observed, a dwindling number of prosecutions of adult pornography has accompanied the increasingly permissible obscenity law, particularly since 1996.[252] In 2015, she had counted all reported and unreported court decisions on obscenity as well as news reports of arrests and convictions since *Butler*. During the period 1998–2012, she found fewer than ten newspaper reports of arrests, of which some involved obscenity charges that were ancillary to other charges. Likewise, during the same period, she merely found three judicial decisions and one jury verdict involving pornography that was alleged to be violent or degrading to women, with only one conviction (the *Smith* case). In contrast, with a simple search on legal databases, she found 283 separate cases of child pornography charges with a final verdict between 1993 and 2012. Indeed, Canadian law enforcement has shifted resources that were previously devoted to investigating obscenity charges to child pornography offenses.[253]

As of November 2019, no reported judicial obscenity decisions on adult pornography appear on Lexis, Westlaw, or CanLII since the 2012 *Smith* case was decided, except ancillary to other charges.[254] The Crown appears practically to have deserted all attempts to apply the obscenity law. Because of the structure of criminal law, the Crown must bring cases for other organizations to be able to intervene and provide accurate evidence of the harms (as LEAF did back in 1992). The lack of opportunity to influence the law has been a constant since the mid-1990s, whether the Court Challenges Program—which funded test litigation based on the Charter's sex equality guarantees[255]—was inoperative or not. Considering the meager prosecutorial activity, the fact that such funding was unavailable between September 2006 and February 2017[256] may not have had much of an impact on obscenity cases anyway. However, if Canada passes an anti-pornography civil rights law, it would enable those directly hurt by pornography who have the strongest incentives to initiate legal action on their own—with or without government assistance. In that scenario, the government would be ascribed a secondary role, if any, much like that of the interveners under the current regime. The civil rights ordinances share similar definitional terminology as the existing Canadian harms-based law, so should, therefore, likely be constitutional under *Butler*. There are currently no alternative fora for those hurt by pornography to address the problem and take legal action in a meaningful way. Thus, only if such a law exists will we know the true extent of the harms caused by pornography.

PART IV
SWEDEN

8

Challenging Production, 1993–2005

Prostitution is usually understood as a social practice where money is paid for sex. Given this understanding, it appears inconsistent that prostitution with persons who are paid for sex in front of a camera is not legally or politically seen as prostitution, while most other prostitution is. If pornography production was legally treated as prostitution, laws against the purchase of sex or third-party exploitation would still not target the resulting pornographic materials directly. Put otherwise, laws targeting production conditions do not evoke the same concerns regarding freedom of expression as laws directly targeting distribution or possession. Indeed, almost any form of pornographic content can be made using virtual media techniques. It is not, therefore, necessary for pornographers to purchase real people to perform sex acts in order to exercise their expressive freedom, particularly since doing so oftentimes involves subjecting performers to exploitative and abusive circumstances. Even assuming that expressive protections are available for the pornographic materials themselves, there is no compelling reason why its production should be insulated from the standards imposed on similar conduct under prostitution and human trafficking laws.

As mentioned earlier in this volume,[1] Sweden is a jurisdiction that may afford better prospects than Canada and the United States for mounting a successful challenge to pornography production with prostitution or trafficking laws due to its broad substantive equality approach to prostitution since 1999. An investigative report from 2019 indicates a significant commercial pornography production in Sweden, where producers exploit people of similar backgrounds as those used in prostitution who also often have direct experience with off-camera prostitution.[2] In addition to its sex purchase law, Sweden, like most countries, has ratified the United Nations' Protocol to Prevent, Suppress and Punish Trafficking in Persons, commonly referred to as the "Palermo Protocol," which entered into force on December 25, 2003.[3] Under the Protocol, trafficking can be "the recruitment, transportation, transfer, harbouring or receipt of persons, by means of the threat or use of force or other forms of coercion, of abduction, of fraud, of deception,

Pornography. Max Waltman, Oxford University Press. © Oxford University Press 2021.
DOI: 10.1093/oso/9780197598535.003.0009

of the abuse of power or of a position of vulnerability . . . for the purpose of exploitation."[4] A "position of vulnerability" has been further defined as "any situation in which the person involved has *no real and acceptable alternative* but to submit to the abuse involved."[5] According to the Protocol, consent is irrelevant in all such situations.[6]

Sweden's Criminal Code includes a *trafficking law* modeled on the Palermo Protocol with a maximum penalty of ten years' imprisonment.[7] Chapter 6 of the Criminal Code also incorporates *procuring laws*, which target anyone who "promotes or in an improper way financially is exploiting a person who has temporary sexual relations in return for payment," the maximum penalty for "normal" procuring being four years in prison.[8] Between procuring and trafficking is the crime of *gross procuring*, with a minimum penalty of two years' imprisonment and a maximum penalty raised by Parliament from eight years to ten years on July 1, 2018, the last amendment essentially making it equivalent to human trafficking in terms of penalties.[9] The anti-procurement laws create a more comprehensive legal framework for addressing sex trafficking, which is necessary in light of the higher evidentiary burden established by the anti-trafficking law to avert the prospect of many pimps and other exploiters never being brought to justice by, for instance, intimidating witnesses or hiding incriminating financial ties demonstrative of trafficking.[10] A comparison of the Swedish Council for Crime Prevention's crime statistics on 388 Swedish convictions of third parties in prostitution during the 2002–2019 period is telling: only 19.07% (74) among them were convictions for human trafficking.[11] Convictions for gross procuring comprised 21.65% (84), and normal procuring comprised 59.28% (230). Note that the category of human trafficking convictions also includes persons convicted for human trafficking for other than sexual purposes.

The 1993 Prostitution Inquiry

The idea of applying prostitution laws to pornography production was proposed by the Swedish government in the 1993 Prostitution Inquiry,[12] which otherwise culminated in the sex purchase law passed by Parliament in 1998.[13] The lead commissioner of the Inquiry, the former Supreme Court Justice Inga-Britt Törnell, candidly acknowledged that women who "participated" in the production of pornography were "often" used in prostitution as well, the result being that pornography "in reality" was "prostitution on camera."[14]

Moreover, she noted that women's on-camera humiliation would be "documented and repeated for a long time"—a comment highlighting harms that compound those accruing from prostitution off-camera. Consequently, Commissioner Törnell suggested extending existing criminal procuring laws to cover "anyone that promotes or in an improper way is profiting from someone else who, due to production of pornographic pictures or films, is remunerated for having temporary sex that includes intercourse or is characterized by a gross violation."[15] In addition, she suggested that those promoting or profiting from the transactional sex of another should also be liable where "bodily contact does not occur," as, for example, in "sexual posing."[16]

Commissioner Törnell observed that, although pornographers could be regarded as sex purchasers or accomplices to that crime, their activities were "primarily a promotion of or profiteering from a weaker party being exploited for temporary sexual relations—that is, a form of procuring."[17] Moreover, she recognized that the evidence of production harms was substantial, the harms themselves being just as severe as those affecting individuals prostituted off-camera. Those used as performers in pornography were "not infrequently" reported to be "subjugated to a treatment that profoundly violates them," leading the Inquiry to conclude that the opportunities for them to "protect themselves against those running the businesses were often very limited." These conditions often amounted to what would have been classified as a "gross crime," had they been manifest in off-camera procuring. According to Sweden's Criminal Code at the time, when determining whether an incident of procuring was gross, "special consideration" had to be given where it "involved ruthless exploitation of another person," among other things.[18]

Commissioner Törnell submitted that one could not "motivate a penalty for the traditional procurer but consider the pornography industry's . . . actions as lawful," not least since traditional pimps could be regarded as neither more harmful nor more "devastating for the exploited persons" than a pornography producer was likely to be. The Commissioner further maintained that anyone dismissing extended liability for pornography-based procuring would, logically speaking, have to defend dismissing procuring as a crime entirely. Her assessment of the exploitation and abuse in pornography production is still relevant today, especially in the light of the accumulated research and knowledge examined earlier. As for the wording of the procuring statute, Commissioner Törnell admitted that it "may appear to cover" the pornography industry's actions. Yet with no citation or explanation, she claimed that it was "clear that the legislator only considered making procuring criminally liable in the form of the profiteering from someone else's prostitution in the sense that the latter has temporary sex with 'customers' who pay to be sexually stimulated." Furthermore, she asserted, again offering no explanation, that the statutory language of the procuring provision was "not considered to cover the actions of the sex film producer when he pays others to have sexual relations with each other." The Commissioner went on to declare that the statute as written was more applicable to "the sex club owner who promotes someone else's temporary sex for remuneration by permitting or contributing to the occurrence of private posing."[19]

In the end, the Commissioner's audience was left with no indication of what, exactly, in the procuring provision's wording or otherwise supported the distinction she drew between these assertedly intended and non-intended applications. The relevant procuring provision reads: "A person who promotes or improperly financially exploits a person's engagement in temporary sexual relations in return for payment shall be sentenced for *procuring*."[20] Contrary to what Commissioner Törnell implied, it does not distinguish procuring as necessitating " 'customers' who pay to be sexually stimulated."[21] Rather, the provision refers only to two people: (1) one who promotes or exploits and (2) one who has "temporary sexual relations in return for payment."[22] The provision makes no distinctions among customers, performers, prostituted persons, or others. Put otherwise, an individual's involvement in "temporary sexual relations" says nothing about whether the purchased sex is conducted with a customer, a performer, a consumer (viewer), or a paying third party (producer) who is also performing, or anyone else. On its face, the provision thus appears applicable to pornography production that promotes or exploits those engaging in temporary sex for remuneration, and therefore requires no amendment.

The procuring provision's direct application to pornography production is supported by the Supreme Court's 1979 decision upholding its extension to cover newspaper advertisements for prostitution.[23] There, a newspaper editor was convicted for procuring because he approved publications of advertisements for prostituted women. That case underscores how the procuring provisions have historically been applied to areas not originally set forth in the legislation's history. The court of appeal dismissed the objection that its application to advertisements was implicated neither in the statutory language nor in its original or subsequent legislative history, which included a government report released as late as in 1976.[24] The case shows that it may be irrelevant whether a particular activity or result, such as pornography production or newspaper advertisements, had previously been perceived or considered in the legislative history. Omissions such as this one plainly did not prevent Swedish courts from applying the procuring provision to prostitution advertisements. Likewise, the omission of any mention of pornography production would not prevent the application of the law in that domain given that doing so is conceptually sound.

In any event, Commissioner Törnell did recommend an amendment to the criminal code that would extend procuring laws to pornography production.[25] In that connection, she also maintained that freedom of expression would not be infringed because her proposal did not "criminalize the production of the image/film," only "the underlying conduct" of procuring. She compared the proposed amendment to a "case where someone films an assault that he instigated himself—a condition that does not bar a conviction for liability for complicity in the assault, the provisions on freedom of expression notwithstanding." The proposal was also likened to a contemporaneous provision against child sexual molestation that was applied in the pornography production context.[26]

The 1998 Government Demands Further Inquiry

The 1993 Inquiry's suggestion that pornographers be viewed as procurers was not included in the associated government's 1998 omnibus bill on violence against women that included the sex purchase law. There, in one short paragraph, it was claimed that the 1993 Inquiry had not sufficiently considered the consequences of its proposal to freedom of expression and freedom of the press; hence, the issue was sent back for further review by a new commission of inquiry.[27] In 1998, the government appointed a committee comprised of members from all political parties in Parliament to undertake a thoroughgoing review of all sexual crimes in the criminal code (the "1998 Sexual Crimes Committee"). In the Committee's charter instructions, the Cabinet and the Ministry of Justice acknowledged the seeming inconsistency that the existing procuring law, which proscribed the promotion and improper exploitation of sex for money, was not applied to "a person that is paying another person to participate in pornography movies . . . despite that his incentive often is financial gain."[28] The new committee was instructed to investigate how the procuring law could be extended "in some other way" than Commissioner Törnell had proposed in 1995, although the government did not specify what was deficient, if anything, about her proposal.[29] Nonetheless, as a "starting point," the government instructed the Sexual Crimes Committee that its "proposals should not cause infringements in the constitutional regulations of freedom of the press and expression," and that it was "not the task of the Committee to propose a general prohibition of pornography,"[30] such as a law against its dissemination.

The Charter of the 1998 Sexual Crimes Committee, which circumscribed the potential recommendations members could make regarding pornography policy, gives the impression that the Cabinet and the Ministry of Justice were predisposed against extending procuring laws to pornography production. However, outside pressures may have forced them to take some action, if only symbolic. Recall that Laurel Weldon and Mala Htun's longitudinal study of seventy nations found that initiatives for more progressive and capacious policies against gender-based violence predominantly came from autonomous feminist organizations.[31] There were many minority motions on this issue raised in Parliament during the Committee's three-year tenure (1998–2001), which, in light of their detailed analysis of pornography's harms, might be seen as expressions of such pressure. A further examination of some of these proposals sheds light on the perspectives underlying them.

One motion was submitted in 1998 by six MPs from the Left Party, including one who was appointed to the Sexual Crimes Committee.[32] It proposed extending the Committee's Charter to include a comprehensive review that would "analyze pornography from a gender-political perspective, and from this analysis propose further measures with special emphasis on preventing harmful effects on young people."[33] The motion made it to a floor vote on February 16, 2000, with 49 MPs in support, 251 against, and 49 abstentions.[34] Another motion submitted by two Green MPs in fall 2001 demanded the appointment of a government inquiry to review the evolution of pornography, including its cultural, demographic, economic, and criminal dimensions, as well as its prevalence and distribution.[35] The motion noted that pornography had become "cruel exploitation of female children and young women in the name of profit."[36] It further called for an investigation of the views of "different researchers on the associations between pornographic film, rapes, and other sexual violence."[37] A motion submitted by two MPs from the Center Party the previous fall recognized associations between pornography consumption and the increase of rapes, "often brutally executed," with its proponents appealing to Parliament to take action that would "reduce the possibility to 'spur' people to . . . rape women (and men)."[38] Similarly, three Social-Democratic MPs submitted two largely identical motions during the fall of 1999 and 2000, noting a "probable" connection in some situations between "the use of pornographic movies and making use of sexual slurs, sexual harassment, and sexual assault," and urging the government to consider additional restrictions on television broadcasts of pornography.[39] The scope of these motions was sometimes broader, including international politics. For instance, a Social-Democratic MP submitted a motion in the fall of 2000 stressing that the European Union, "which should prioritize gender equality," needed to investigate the export of pornography to developing countries and recognize its harmful impact, particularly in countries confronting serious AIDS challenges.[40]

Earlier motions may have been more strongly worded. For example, a Christian Democratic MP submitted a motion in fall 1998 asserting that pornography was a multibillion-dollar industry that presented women and girls as "objects" and "slaves" for men; that it was "complicit in the oppression of women"; that it was a "threat against the security" of women and girls; that its production involved filming and photographing acts of sexual abuse that in turn encouraged "rape, incest, abuse, torture, and murder of women and girls"; and that it "suggested that women enjoy rape and abuse."[41] The motion also stated that it had been "found" that pornography provided a "manual for abuse" for rapists and other perpetrators[42] and called for a government "inquiry that could outline a strategy" to address all of these negative effects.[43] Similarly damning, two nearly identical motions submitted in 1997 and in 1998, and signed by ten and eight Left Party MPs, respectively, stated that "[c]ontempt for women is the essence of pornography, the presentation of a woman as an object, a sub-human creature that even enjoys violence and torture, which mirrors this contempt."[44] Moreover, it was asserted that "the pornography industry" was "the largest cause of an increase in the sexualized violence in the community."[45] Contemporaneous laws against violent pornography in Sweden were also denounced as "completely toothless."[46] The motions thus urged the government to, among other things, carefully review new legislation pertaining to pornography that was "degrading" to women and restrict access to such materials while awaiting the outcome of the review.[47]

The parliamentary motions cited so far were not the only ones that sought to challenge pornography on legal grounds during this time. Regardless, the majority dismissed all of the measures advocated by minority MPs. Consistent with these power dynamics, the Sexual Crimes Committee did not investigate the extent to which adult pornography leads consumers to harm women and children.[48] It recommended that the procuring laws not be extended to cover pornography production. From the perspective of its members, while the purpose of "protecting those who participate in pornographic pictures and movies" was not meant to undermine the constitutional right to produce and disseminate printed matter per se, the "actual restrictions" that resulted from extending the procuring provision were allegedly so significant that a constitutional amendment to the laws regulating freedom of the press and expression was needed—an amendment it recommended the government not pursue.[49] After receiving the Committee's report, the Cabinet and the Ministry of Justice dropped the issue entirely during its 2004–2005 term, when it compelled Parliament to pass a bill remedying the problems that had to that point been apparent in the criminal code's chapter on sexual crimes.[50] The Committee's opinion, which claimed that applying procuring laws to pornography production was unconstitutional, merits further scrutiny. To what extent was that opinion grounded in *law*, and to what extent was it an *ideological* position with limited legal basis?[51]

The 1998–2001 Committee's Dismissal

The Committee's final report in 2001 acknowledged that one could argue that the fundamental laws do not alter the fact that the "production and the dissemination of printed matter and other media . . . are subject to the same legal rules as other similar activity, for example, comparable business activity."[52] The Committee went on to explain:

> General restrictions that have nothing to do with the expected content are not regarded as a violation of the fundamental laws. For example, the Working Environment Act's regulation that criminalizes the use of child labor can also be applied to the production and dissemination of images and films. From this vantage point, it could be claimed that the legislation on sexual crimes constitutes such legal rules that hold generally, and that actual limitations that follow from these rules do not violate the fundamental laws.[53]

By its reasoning, using procuring laws against pornographers did not constitute a direct restriction on the freedom to produce or disseminate pornography because the restriction would only "follow indirectly from other . . . legislation with another purpose."[54]

The Indirect Standard

After acknowledging seemingly valid rationales for applying the procuring laws to pornographers, the Committee objected and sought to invoke an analogous argument on "indirect" media restrictions said to have been entertained in considering legislation relating to media concentration, antitrust, and bankruptcy law.[55] It remarked that two previous government committee reports on media concentration and antitrust law maintained that both case law and legislative history suggested that indirect restrictions were permissible as long as they did not "in practice" make the freedoms to print, publicize, and disseminate "illusory."[56] In a footnote, the Inquiry further observed that the Media Concentration Committee of 1999 allowed that "it could not be ruled out that the Competition Act's regulations on the acquisition of companies are nullified" by the fundamental laws on freedom of expression.[57] Since legislative history carries relatively strong legal weight in Sweden, these reports warrant closer examination to determine whether they support the Committee's conclusions.

First, nowhere did the cited reports on media concentration and antitrust law invoke "case law," as the Committee claimed.[58] Quite the contrary, the 1999 report stated that, except for a contemporaneous precedent decided in 1998 regarding the right of an editor-in-chief to refuse to publish an advertisement, there was *no* settled doctrine on how to resolve constitutional conflicts between antitrust law and freedom of expression in the context of media concentration.[59] The 1999 report even encouraged the Swedish Competition Authority to continue with their antitrust litigation in order to make the law more predictable.[60]

Second, the two government reports contained lengthy discussions of legal scholars' contrasting ideological perspectives regarding the indirect expressive restrictions that the application of competition law would impose on media businesses.[61] One contended that the danger was that media monopolies rather than democratic intervention would stifle diversity, thus limiting citizens' free exchange of opinions and the availability of comprehensive information that the constitution intends to protect.[62] Put otherwise, media concentration can contribute to citizens' freedom of expression becoming "illusory." This is inconsistent with the reasoning of the Sexual Crimes Committee, which described the reports as concluding that applying competition law to prevent media monopolies either infringes upon expressive freedoms per se, or infringes on media corporations' freedom of expression.

The perspective that the Committee ignored, which favors government intervention in the market by applying competition law on media corporations, is consistent with the concept of "positive rights" as opposed to "negative rights." By contrast, the Committee's implicit perspective was more consistent with the latter, whereby freedom of expression is seen as best served by precluding government intervention against the monopolization of the media out of fear of government abuse of power. A positive rights approach to substantive equality and freedom of expression would be more willing to consider the research showing that pornography promotes gender-based violence and discriminatory attitudes toward women and that these effects silence women's voices in the public arena relative to men's.[63] In other words, if making pornographers liable to procuring prevents sexual exploitation, it would also indirectly promote equal enjoyment of freedom of expression for women.

The 1980 Media Concentration Inquiry report acknowledged that a more rigid textual interpretation of the law might indirectly promote media monopolization, and therefore proposed a constitutional amendment to clarify that the application of competition law to media companies should not be seen as restricting freedom of expression.[64] Although its proposal did not pass, the subsequent government committee on media concentration stated in their 1999 report that "[s]uch a far-fetched interpretation of the constitutional regulations" in favor of media monopolies would not only jeopardize media competition but also jeopardize "the practical means for making use of freedom of speech."[65] The 1999 report further argued that this negative rights-leaning interpretation would be "irreconcilable" with statements made in Parliament by the Standing Committee on the Constitution.[66] Although those statements were not legally binding, the 1999 report concluded that they showed why "no one" could "know with certainty" how the law would be interpreted before the issue had been litigated or otherwise resolved.[67]

If the 1998 Sexual Crimes Committee would have considered more fully the content of the reports it chose to cite, it might have arrived at a different conclusion, one in which the application of procuring laws to the production of pornography would be consistent with the purpose of freedom of expression to promote a diverse, vibrant, and democratic public discourse. Through its analogy to antitrust law, the Committee attempted to show that a conflict of interests between equality and speech is inevitable when in reality, it is not. Indeed, the Committee relied on sources that could just as readily support the contrary view. In fact, the legislative history of media concentration law does not provide a negative rights defense for media monopolies like those the Committee sought to invoke when it argued that pornography production is insulated from regulations that apply to other business activities. The Committee's reference to these reports was thus misleading.

In an additional effort to support its argument, the Committee referred to a government bill from February 1980 that prohibited insolvent persons from operating private businesses.[68] Before that bill was finalized, the Council on Legislation (an advisory, non-binding parliamentary body composed of Supreme Court justices) objected that if those deemed insolvent were authors, freelance journalists, troubadours, or photographers, and made daily use of the constitutional rights associated with their professions, the new law could constitute a constitutional infringement.[69] Although the government responded to the Council by adding a waiver to protect expressive rights for such individuals,[70] the waiver's legislative history was considerably more cautious than the Sexual Crimes Committee, which did not refer to all relevant pages,[71] presented it to be.

For example, in 1980, the government doubted whether its proposal, even without the waiver, "in reality" entailed "any infringement of rights protected by the constitution."[72] It further reasoned that the proposal did not constitute a direct attack on constitutional rights since its objective was "to make it possible to intervene against business persons of all kinds, which through their activities have committed grossly unlawful conduct, often in the area of white-collar crime."[73] It was also assumed that the waiver had no "great practical importance" since it applied only to the business activities of individuals—not to individuals "acting on behalf of legal entities . . . regardless of whether the activities fall within the area protected by the constitution or not." The government moreover considered that "there would be reasons to discuss . . . the waivers anew . . . if it would be found that the waivers caused practical troubles."[74]

The Sexual Crimes Committee mentioned neither the cautionary remarks made by the government nor the actual limitations on the waivers to the bankruptcy law. It merely stated that "special regulations" were introduced so that prohibitions against conducting businesses while in bankruptcy "would not apply to the constitutionally protected business activity."[75] Considering that the waiver only applied to the personal business of individuals—not to individuals representing businesses—the Committee's statements distorted the legal landscape and mislead its readers as to the meaning of the legislative sources it invoked to buttress its conclusions.

Child Molestation versus Child Pornography Analogy

Further into its arguments, the Committee contended that the Prostitution Inquiry's 1995 report, which proposed extending the procuring laws to cover pornography production, had assumed a legal theory "similar" to that discussed in "the debate on whether the child pornography crime should be removed from the constitution."[76] In that debate, it was suggested that child pornography did not need a constitutional exemption from expressive protection since other crimes committed through expressive means, such as printing counterfeit money, did not require exemptions for the law to apply.[77] Here, the Committee impliedly referred to the "Alexanderson doctrine,"[78] which had indeed been invoked in the child pornography context. To reiterate, that doctrine holds that general law can be applied to expression that is not explicitly regulated in the fundamental laws, insofar as the purpose of the general law is not to restrict the cultural, social, or political aspects of free expression.[79]

Yet the debate surrounding the child pornography law presumed that whatever doctrine was preferred, it would target not just production, but dissemination and possession as well. A close reading of the terms employed in the child pornography law elucidates why the Committee's reference to Alexanderson was misplaced: the statute targets the dissemination or possession of materials that "portray children in pornographic images" and describes illegal activity in such terms as "disseminating," "transferring," "exhibiting," "acquiring," "offering," "facilitating dealings in," "possessing," or "viewing such an image."[80] Completely absent from the provision are words addressing the conditions of production, such as "exploiting," "molesting," "procuring," or "pimping." It was therefore not entirely surprising that the government rejected the Alexanderson doctrine during the debate, insofar as it believed that the child pornography law targeted "presentations that are considered an abuse of the freedom of expression in the same way as, for example, the unlawful portrayal of violence or agitation against a population group."[81] By contrast, the procuring law would not affect the production of virtual or simulated pornography—much less would it affect those attempting to express opinions regarding sexual matters. Thus, the child pornography law impinges far more substantially on expressive interests that the procuring law would do.

By failing to acknowledge the expressive differences between child pornography and procuring, the Committee mixed apples and oranges. This became even more apparent in the paragraph that appeared next in its analysis, where it referred to a 1984 government bill that amended the crime of sexually molesting a child under age fifteen. According to the Committee, that bill provided a "typical example" of molestation without actual body contact that was also to be covered under the law—namely, the exploitation of a child in order to produce a pornographic image.[82] Here, the Committee directly addressed harmful conduct perpetrated during production. It continued its description of the 1984 bill, noting that it stated that if the offender's intent was also to disseminate an image made through the molestation of a child, that offender should be convicted under *both* the sexual molestation *and* the child pornography provisions.[83] If, however, there was no intent to disseminate the image, liability would be limited to child molestation.[84] Yet the Committee did not draw the corollary conclusion. That is, a pornographer who promoted or exploited a performer's participation in temporary sex for money could also be convicted for either one or two crimes under Swedish law: *only* for the procuring, or—if the pornography was violent—for *both* procuring *and* the "unlawful portrayal of violence."[85] Indeed, the unlawful portrayal of violence has been recognized as an abuse of freedom expression in the fundamental laws since 1988, which (at least on paper) covers expressive conduct "whereby a person portrays sexual violence or coercion in pictorial form with intent to disseminate the image, unless the act is justifiable having regard to the circumstances."[86]

Rather than recognizing the similarity between how the child molestation and procuring crimes relate to constitutionally regulated crimes, the Committee merely described the 1984 bill's statements about child molestation, noting that a crime listed in the constitution could be committed "in those cases where such media covered by the constitution had been used."[87] It provided no analysis of whether that fact supported or refuted its conclusion that procuring laws could not be applied to pornographers. Indeed, nowhere did the bill state that a conviction for molesting a child while producing pornography would be impossible absent a constitutional exemption for child pornography.[88] Furthermore, the 1984 bill was drafted before the constitutional amendment delegating child pornography to general law was passed. This means that child pornography was not exempt from constitutional protection in 1984—only that it was enumerated among the constitutional "crimes against freedom of the press," along with the unlawful portrayal of violence and other such expressive crimes.[89] Assuming, arguendo, that the Committee believed that child molestation perpetrated during pornography production could only be prosecuted in 1984 because the dissemination of child pornography was also constitutionally proscribed as a crime against freedom of the press, then procuring during the production of violent pornography must also have been prosecutable on the same rationale, without resort to constitutional amendment. Yet, the Committee did not acknowledge this logical corollary.

Expressive Content and Underlying Crimes

The Committee made one last effort to argue its position, claiming that the previous Prostitution Inquiry's proposal to use the procuring law had wrongly presumed that "one can disregard the use of constitutionally protected freedom of expression when it has only been used as part of an otherwise criminalized conduct ('the underlying conduct')."[90] Here, the Committee referred to the Swedish legal scholar Hans-Gunnar Axberger's interpretation of the two-pronged distinction between "expression that was criminal per se" and expression that was criminalized "only as a part of criminal conduct that in its entirety had been criminalized," such as fraudulent advertisements.[91] As the late Gunnar Persson, another Swedish legal scholar, observed, the second prong of Axberger's distinction seemed to be the same as Alexanderson's "model" of constitutional interpretation.[92] Certainly, Axberger recognized the doctrine as mainstream but contended that the second prong derived from "tendencies of exercises in conceptual jurisprudence" that he criticized as "disconnected from the legislation," lacking "purpose," and ultimately "irrelevant."[93] Instead, he maintained that the legislative history supported a single interpretative model, where expressive activity was to be determined only "by a comparison between a presentation's content and the purpose of the freedom of the press"—hence, *regardless* of whether the presentation "was part of a larger set of conduct that as a whole could not be characterized as an expression." Therefore, he rejected the second prong of Alexanderson's test, arguing that whether an expression was constitutionally protected or not should "only" be determined by "the expression's content—and the purpose, the function, which could be derived from it—compared to the interests that the freedom of press is sought to protect."[94]

Persson has criticized Axberger for not having identified any specific support within the constitution's legislative history to validate his interpretive model.[95] Persson further asserted that Axberger's theory is unsustainable:

> Axberger's reasoning is inconsistent with reality. This is clearly seen if we look at those examples that have generally been accepted as exemptions from being exclusively regulated by the Freedom of the Press Act. How can you discern from the content that it is an attempt at fraud? How can you see that it is a case of swindle, only by looking at the content? How can you see that it is a crime of forgery, only by looking at the content?[96]

Persson concluded that Alexanderson's model of interpretation was supported by the legislative history, whereas Axberger's model was not: in Persson's view, the law must "assess what sort of crime had been committed—not whether the content showed this or not."[97] Yet the Sexual Crimes Committee referred to Axberger's controversial theory that the Alexanderson doctrine was "disconnected" from legislation and obsolete, thus serving no policy purpose.[98] Moreover, the Committee never demonstrated how Axberger's theory would be applied to procuring. Procuring is not an expression by itself, such as a fraudulent advertisement. By itself, it has no expressive "content." The Committee, therefore, seemed to be implying that no legal action could be taken if a procuring crime could not be easily inferred by viewing the "content" of a pornographic image or movie. But it would be irrational for pornographers to reveal anything within "the content" of their products to imply that they were paying performers for temporary sex. This fact alone shows the absurdity of Axberger's theory and the Committee's attempt to invoke it. Besides endorsing the naïve assumption that content by itself, rather than the underlying criminal conduct, is relevant for assessing a crime committed in part by expressive means, the Committee ignored that the procuring law did not criminalize the dissemination of pornography. Procuring is not comparable to child pornography or pornographic advertisements. It is better likened to the molestation of a child or unlawful coercion—that is, crimes that occur off-print, and which may not be discernible to the viewer. These crimes are unnecessary for producing pornography or running a media corporation, although they can certainly increase their profitability. Neither Axberger's nor Alexanderson's theories were construed to distinguish non-expressive crimes such as these. Rather, their theories have primarily been used to determine when *disseminating* printed media or other means of expression may be subject to legal action.

Assuming, arguendo, that at least the Alexanderson doctrine would apply to the procuring for pornography images or movies, the procuring law would not be purposed to infringe citizens' "free exchange of opinion, free and comprehensive information, and free artistic creativity" that is protected by the constitution.[99] Instead, its purpose would be to prevent sexual exploitation, abuse, and the promotion of sex equality. Put otherwise, procuring is not about freedom of expression. Indeed, there are alternative ways to produce pornography that do not involve procuring (e.g., virtual animations). According to the Alexanderson doctrine, procuring could thus be regulated without the "exclusive" constitutional rules otherwise applicable to expressive activity accorded greater protection. However, considering that procuring is more analogous to child molestation, unlawful coercion, unfair competition, and white-collar crime than it is to crimes committed by the use of expressive media or other expressive means like fraudulent advertising or printing counterfeit money, the Alexanderson standard of review should not be necessary at all. Nevertheless, by invoking Axberger's unpersuasive theory that only the content of expression can reveal a crime, the Committee seemed to assume that procuring could not be detected as the crime it is "without amendments to the constitution," amendments it recommended be rejected.[100]

The Seriousness of Expressive Infringement

In its conclusion, the Committee acknowledged that the "extension of the liability for procuring is intended to protect those who participate in pornographic images and films and certainly has another purpose than to suppress the rights to produce and disseminate [constitutionally protected expression]."[101] At this point, the Committee, which seemed to rely on its previous arguments, claimed that the "actual infringements" were "so serious" that they conflicted with the constitutional freedom to print and disseminate expression and information. However, a procuring law would not prevent pornographers from disseminating pornography with simulations of sexual conduct; even less would it prevent the dissemination of materials produced by virtual techniques, drawing, or writing. Hence, the pornographer's right to print and disseminate expressive media would not be rendered "illusory," as the Committee implied.[102] Given the alternatives available to using live performers for sex when making pornography, the procuring law would not remove any "serious" constitutional protection from "presentations characterized as pure entertainment," which some legal sources have likened to nonviolent pornography.[103]

Moreover, if the Committee saw pornography as making a more substantial contribution to public discourse than "pure entertainment"—perhaps offering an outlet for reactionary or radical views about gender, sex, and sexuality—the procuring laws do not target those who disseminate "opinion," "comprehensive information," or "artistic creativity"[104] that is protected by the constitution. There are numerous alternative media venues available for these purposes, including newspapers, magazines, books, motion pictures, and the internet. The procuring law only applies to someone who "promotes or improperly financially exploits a person's engagement in temporary sexual relations in return for payment."[105]

Finally, let us assume that, although the procuring law does not technically make the pornographers' right to create and disseminate expressive materials "illusory," the consequences for free expression of allowing it to be employed for prosecutorial purposes would remain "serious." If this theory is grounded in law, the law presumably also takes account of similar situations where the "indirect consequences" of prosecuting criminal conduct integral to otherwise protected expression seriously infringe expressive freedoms. A hypothesis can be deduced to test this theory: whenever someone has been convicted for criminal conduct that was integral to producing materials otherwise protected by freedom of expression, it weakens the theory underlying the Committee's conclusion. Such a test will reveal the extent to which the dismissal of the prior Prostitution Inquiry's proposition was or was not grounded in ideology as opposed to law.[106]

Case Law Rebuts Committee's Theory

One example that clearly speaks against the Committee's theory is a widely known Swedish case in which an artist was convicted of *violent resistance* and *dishonest conduct* under the Criminal Code in the performance of an artistic project that was otherwise legal and protected under the fundamental laws' expressive protections (the "artist's case").[107] These two crimes are not explicitly exempted from protection under the fundamental laws.[108] Hence, the situation is analogous to one in which a person engages in criminal conduct, for example, procuring, purchase of sex, or human trafficking, as an integral means of producing otherwise lawful nonviolent pornography.

On January 21, 2009, the artist staged a psychotic episode and suicide attempt on a public bridge. That conduct led to intervention from the police and mental health care providers, who apprehended and restrained her with straps, to which she admitted violently resisting by kicking, shouting, writhing, and flailing about. Her actions were filmed by a third party for the planned art film production. The District Court subsequently convicted her under the Criminal Code for violent resistance against a public servant and dishonest conduct. The court concluded that the fact that "the violent resistance was filmed for the purpose of showing the video to the public does not entail that the Freedom of Expression Act is an obstacle in the way for a regular criminal law trial of the [proscribed] conduct."[109]

The artist's case has been reported and discussed extensively in Swedish mainstream media. Had the constitutional issues been decided in a manifestly erroneous fashion, it would almost certainly have been appealed. In contrast to the 1998 Sexual Crimes Committee's reasoning, the court in the artist's case found no indirect restriction on constitutional rights that would make them "illusory"[110] by applying general law to conduct integral to the production of constitutionally protected expression. Indeed, the court acknowledged that the artist's purpose was to raise public awareness of compulsory treatment to which people with psychiatric disorders are vulnerable; that factor only mitigated her sentence by reducing the number of daily fines imposed to fifty.[111] Fifty is the same number of daily fines that were imposed on johns in a typical sex purchase in over 85% of the cases decided during the first ten years of Sweden's sex purchase law.[112]

The artist's case can be contrasted with another notorious case in which a Swedish tabloid newspaper published photos of neo-Nazis posing outside the homes of three well-known public figures.[113] The photos were accompanied by headlines like "Death Threat against Chief of Police," showed armed individuals covering their faces with balaclavas, and, in one case, posing with a tear gas gun pointed at the mail delivery slot of an apartment door.[114] Lower courts convicted the neo-Nazis for unlawful threats; the Supreme Court overturned the convictions.[115] At that time, making an unlawful threat was not enumerated in the fundamental laws as a crime against freedom of expression.[116] Even the district court acknowledged that taking threatening photographs outside a public figure's home is not a crime in itself.[117] Nevertheless, demonstrating a "complete disregard" of whether such images would come to the attention of those targeted could have constituted an unlawful threat in a different situation.[118] However, the Supreme Court considered the factor that the journalist wanted a visual representation of the neo-Nazi organization about which he had written an article. In this context, publishing the photographs at issue was integral to a constitutionally protected "journalistic activity" that also protected the neo-Nazis in their capacity as "informants."[119]

The artist's case, by contrast, was not about restricting the right to disseminate constitutionally protected materials that in themselves might constitute a crime under general law. The artist's case is thus not analogous to those situations, such as fraudulent activities or misleading advertisements, where the Alexanderson doctrine is needed to successfully prosecute expressive conduct that is integral to a broader pattern of criminal conduct that has little to do with the objectives underlying constitutional freedom of expression. Her crime was judged under a more relaxed constitutional standard because the subject of the prosecution was never her movie, but her conduct during its production. Hence, the artist's case suggests how the provisions on procuring might be applied to pornography production where someone "promotes or in an improper way financially exploits a person who has temporary sexual relations in return for payment,"[120] never mind that the right to disseminate pornography remains unrestricted.

Other examples of cases that do not comport with the Sexual Crimes Committee's reasoning include several involving sexual crimes that were filmed, sometimes with express artistic aspirations. Yet the perpetrators were nonetheless convicted under general law and sentenced with no mitigating circumstances applied. For example, in 2009, a court of appeal convicted a man of *gross violation of a woman's integrity*[121] and *gross rape* over a period of several years, a number of the sexual assaults having been filmed.[122] The court found the defendant's argument that the women had consented to the sexual acts, including filmed group sex, irrelevant since his "repetitive and almost routine abuse" of the women constituted a real threat that they would be abused if they refused, a circumstance effectively nullifying any expressed consent.[123] Similar situations have been documented in pornography production where pimps, in addition to exploiting the vulnerability of people used as performers, physically abuse women as a means of coercing them to smile and express consent in the films.[124]

The defendant also had artistic ambitions, evidenced, for instance, by the injured women's testimony that he did not want the films in which they appeared to include violence.[125] Accordingly, he deleted the first version of a film depicting group sex because one of the women "cried all the time" while the other sat on the edge of a bed and looked sad.[126] He proceeded to force them to make a new film in which they were directed to smile and look happy.[127] Such a film can be disseminated with constitutional protection because "presentations characterized as pure entertainment and without cultural value, even pornography," have been construed to be covered by the protection of freedom of expression.[128] Despite this, unlike the artist's case, the defendant did not invoke constitutional protection even for the purpose of mitigating his sentence. Neither did the defense point to any possible dangers of setting a precedent that would permit indirect restrictions on pornography production. However, the courts did note a number of other points of dubious significance that might have mitigated the sentence. For example, they did not accept the prosecutors' contention that the rapes between 2002 and 2008 had been perpetrated "more or less daily."[129] According to the courts' calculations, they only took place "several times a week," and the courts noted that one of the two women was not raped at all during 2004 when she was pregnant.[130] If details such as these were deemed worthy of the courts' time, had it appeared reasonable, it is likely that the defense lawyer would have cited impermissible "indirect restrictions" on freedom of expression in the same way the 1998 Sexual Crimes Committee did to shield pornography producers against procuring charges. However, this argument was not made.

Another appellate court heard a similar case in which a man had been tried for filming coercive sexual acts twice with his wife that he claimed (contradicting his wife's testimony) constituted consensual role-playing. However, the appellate court did not find the man's testimony credible, and in 2009 convicted him of rapes for the acts caught on camera, reversing the district court's acquittals.[131] As in the other appellate case, the defendant regularly produced pornographic movies; he even referred to the other films he had made with the injured woman in support of his claim that the two films presented voluntary role-playing.[132] Although this defendant produced sexual materials suggestive of artistic aspirations with some regularity, in contrast to the artist's case, he did, at no point, invoke freedom of expression as a mitigating circumstance.

In addition, the courts of appeals have handed down a number of decisions where individuals used cell phone cameras to film sexual activity that was later subject to criminal prosecution.[133] As in the two cases discussed here, the defendants did not raise freedom of expression in support of either acquittal or sentence mitigation, nor did they do so while objecting to the forfeiture of their cell phones, although they protested unsuccessfully on other grounds (e.g., that they had not intended to use the films for criminal purposes, or that the content was of a "private nature").[134] The only constitutional interest raised was private integrity, not freedom of expression.

The cases considering filmed sexual crimes, violent resistance, and dishonest conduct show that there is no legal barrier to applying sanctions against criminal acts that are conducted as an *integral means* of producing otherwise constitutionally protected materials. A similar general distinction was recognized in 2015, when the Swedish Supreme Court upheld convictions of journalists and editors at one of the two largest national tabloids for unlawfully purchasing and possessing a semi-automatic gun, although the purchase was made only to illustrate an article that described what was perceived as the increasing availability of illegal weapons in Sweden.[135] The trial court noted that "no one" was "made liable for the *publication* of the information about the unlawful possession of the weapon."[136] A distinction, however, between, on the one hand, the illegal weapons case, and on the other hand, the artist's case and the filmed sexual crimes is that only the illegal weapons case expressly relied on a special provision in the fundamental laws on freedom of expression,[137] which states that, fundamental law notwithstanding, general law may govern "liability under penal law and liability for damages relating to the manner in which an item of information has been procured."[138] The Supreme Court noted that the legislative history of this provision enumerated unlawful coercion among other crimes that could be committed with the "intent to procure information."[139] There are similarities among unlawful coercion, human trafficking, and procuring for sex in the sense that the latter also operates on a continuum of coercion, whether physical, economical, or otherwise.

It may be argued that pornography, by being legally regarded as "pure entertainment" devoid of cultural value,[140] is not "an item of information" as contemplated by the fundamental laws' provision that the Supreme Court relied on in the illegal weapon case. Yet it may also be argued that the lower cultural value placed on such entertainment as compared to news reporting about illegal weapons should be accompanied by a lower threshold for using general law to regulate it. In the illegal weapon case, the Supreme Court balanced the value of the expressive material against the harms of the illegal conduct integral to its production: first, when stating that, although the issue of the news article was of general interest, the relative ease of buying firearms could have been presented differently;[141] second, when concluding that the "publication interest" did not support accepting (as opposed to declining) an offer to buy an illegal firearm.[142] Given that pornography is recognized as having lower cultural value than news reporting on illegal arms, an argument can be made for extending the constitutional provision concerning the manner in which "information" is procured to cover "pure entertainment," perforce when a crime such as procuring or human trafficking is committed in the production of pornography, regardless of a slightly inapposite use of the term "item of information." Moreover, as in the artist's case involving violent resistance and dishonest conduct, no liability would attach to the dissemination of the resulting expressive material, thus further limiting the impact on free expression.

Law, Ideology, and Representation

The current state of the law suggests that crimes such as violent resistance and dishonest conduct can be proscribed when the conduct is filmed in the production of artistic works, even if penalties for conviction are low. Similarly, sexual coercion, which is contained within the same sexual crimes chapter of the criminal code as prostitution laws, may be proscribed when filmed under artistic pretensions. Given these conditions, there is no compelling reason why other laws, such as the law against procuring, cannot be likewise applied. Considering the inconsistencies in the Sexual Crimes Committee's argument and the contradictory case law examined here, the Committee's dismissal of the proposed extension of the procuring laws to cover pornography production appears to be driven more by ideology than law. The evidence set forth indicates that the Committee selectively applied the ideological concept of liberal negative rights that disfavors government intervention against non-state abuses of power. This, in turn, released pornographers from liability under criminal laws that would have targeted relevant non-state conduct in the way that other media producers are targeted. The Committee's position is based less on predictable legal rules adopted democratically in accordance with established political processes, and more on the political precept that democratic institutions should not intervene in the production of pornography.[143] The analysis set forth in these pages suggests that there is no absolute constitutional obstacle that prevents the Swedish judiciary from using existing procuring laws to take legal action against sexual exploitation in the pornography industry. Nor is Parliament or the Cabinet and the Ministry of Justice precluded from clarifying legislation in this area.

Considering that the constitution by no means prevents legislative action per se, the analysis also raises the question of why parliamentarians' calls for more proactive measures to address the harms of pornography legislatively did not win the support of the majority during the Committee's tenure, 1998–2001.[144] This is particularly significant in light of the fact that women then constituted 42.7% of MPs—an unprecedentedly high proportion.[145] In September 2002, women's representation in Sweden's Parliament climbed even higher, reaching 45.3%, setting what was at the time a global record.[146] Nevertheless, no new legal efforts were undertaken to challenge pornography. Therefore, despite ample evidence that pornography subordinates women to men,[147] having a substantial cohort of female legislators is likely not enough to redress the problem. The relationship of this circumstance to the differential harms of pornography among different groups of women bears underscoring. Those who are multiply disadvantaged (notably battered and prostituted women) are often the most extensively exposed. Since women are not equally harmed, the presence of a more substantial proportion of women in a legislative body does not ipso facto mean that female legislators will represent the perspectives and interests of those most injured by pornography. Additionally, those whose oaths of office demand otherwise are inclined to act in their own self-interest and may be better able to empathize with those like themselves. Again, these conditions support the work of hierarchy theorists like Iris Marion Young who contend that marginalized groups (including women heavily exposed to the harms of pornography) need special political representation—if not in the national Parliament, then at least in lower political bodies, including trial courts, that govern the application of laws that could affect the harms of pornography.[148]

9
Substantive Equality Prostitution Law, 1999–2019

Absent applying prostitution laws to pornography, the policy impact of which could be empirically investigated, it is essential to understand the outcome of the Swedish prostitution laws. Contrary to many other jurisdictions around the world where the regulation of prostitution (as distinct from trafficking) is classified among crimes against morality, decency, or the public order, often resulting in the criminalization of both the prostituted person and the john, since 1999 Sweden has, in addition to third parties, only criminalized those who buy prostituted people, *not* those being bought: "A person that . . . obtains themselves a temporary sexual relation in return for payment, shall be sentenced for *purchase of sexual service* to a fine or imprisonment for at most one year."[1] From January 1999 to July 1, 2011, the maximum penalty was imprisonment for six months.[2] When passing the first version of the law, Parliament accepted the Cabinet's conclusion that "it is not reasonable also to criminalize the one who, at least in most cases, is the weaker part who is exploited by others who want to satisfy their own sexual drive," which further emphasized that it is "important in order to encourage the prostituted persons to seek assistance to get away from prostitution, that they do not feel they risk any form of sanction because they have been active as prostituted persons."[3] By legally acknowledging the inequality between purchasers and prostituted persons in its asymmetrical criminalization, a substantive rather than formal equality approach characterizes Sweden's sex purchase law. However, the question is whether it subsequently reduced sexual exploitation, supported prostituted persons, and promoted substantive equality. The answer can provide valuable insight into the likelihood that similar legal challenges to pornography production would be successful.

A contrary approach to Sweden's prostitution laws treats prostitution as a symmetrical social practice tantamount to a job that is legal in some (if not all) forms, and therefore subject to regulation. The assumption here is that it is possible to prevent exploitation and harm and improve workplace safety,

Pornography. Max Waltman, Oxford University Press. © Oxford University Press 2021.
DOI: 10.1093/oso/9780197598535.003.0010

specifically with respect to health issues that disproportionately affect those engaged in commercial sex. Johns are regarded as customers, prostituted persons as service providers, and third parties—including brothel owners, managers, "escort agencies," and so on—may lawfully profit from the prostitution of others. For instance, a Nevada statute permits counties with populations under 700,000 to enable third parties, through a county licensing board, to profit from businesses that use "natural persons" for the purpose of prostitution, as long as they are not minors.[4]

Irrespective of the legality of prostitution, a symmetrical treatment of the parties involved is inconsistent with hierarchy theory. Laws based on presumed interparty symmetry do not recognize prostituted persons as members of severely disadvantaged groups, which johns are ordinarily not. Policies that legalize johns and third-party profiteers should, given the insights of hierarchy theory, produce more harmful social consequences to disadvantaged groups than laws like Sweden's.

Evidence from Legal Prostitution

Proponents of the legalization approach to prostitution have claimed that brothel owners, managers, escort agencies, bodyguards, drivers, and other third parties involved in prostitution would improve the safety and well-being of prostituted people if they could operate legally.[5] Yet prostitution is an inherently unequal social practice. Additionally, third parties are driven by profits, and johns are primarily concerned with their presumed right to buy sex in whatever form they wish despite widespread awareness of the coercive circumstances under which prostituted persons typically live.[6] Given this, the claims of proponents of legalized prostitution warrant further scrutiny.

Prostituted people in Victoria, Australia, for instance, have reported that legalization there led to increased competition to secure johns and more frequent demands for unsafe sex or for sexual practices not commonly sought (most notably a shift in demand from oral sex to anal sex).[7] A government study also found that some johns regard condoms as "unacceptable," and if denied unsafe sex in one brothel will simply seek it in another.[8] In keeping with their quest for profits, not all brothels in Victoria insist on safe sex.[9] Nonetheless, women prostituted in legal venues have reported that if they want "to get booked," they "have to do these things,"[10] one admitting (despite incriminating her brothel) that there was "no option" *not* to engage in unsafe sex.[11]

In New Zealand, a government committee reported in 2008 that the "majority" of prostituted people and other informants, including also brothel operators, believed that the Prostitution Reform Act of 2003 that legalized some forms of prostitution could do little to curb the violence perpetrated against women in the sex industry.[12] Similarly, a German federal government report in 2007 concluded that reforms legalizing certain forms of indoor prostitution have generally "not been able to make actual, measurable improvements to prostitutes' social protection," and that "hardly any measurable, positive impact has been observed in practice" regarding "working conditions" for prostituted persons.[13] Further, the government determined that the reforms did "not recognisably" improve prostituted individuals' "means for leaving prostitution," and that there were no "viable indications" that it "has reduced crime"; to the contrary, the government lamented that legalization "has as yet contributed only very little in terms of improving transparency in the world of prostitution."[14]

A 2013 feature article in *Der Spiegel*, a German weekly similar to *Time* magazine, was more critical in its reporting on the subject. Among those interviewed was a social worker with over twenty years of experience working with prostituted women, who said that a decade of legalization had made the conditions of prostitution considerably worse than before.[15] *Der Spiegel* further reported that legalization made it more difficult for law enforcement to uncover abuses in the sex industry because they are "hardly able to gain access to brothels anymore"; at the same time, the reforms contributed to an influx of poor foreign women into prostitution in Germany. In addition, the increased supply of prostituted people heightened competition and contributed to such detrimental trends as declining prices, intensified demands for harmful sex, including flat rates at brothels that afford unlimited time for sex, in some instances sex of any kind, anal, unprotected, and so-called gang-bangs prominent among them. The reported increase in demand for dangerous sexual practices after legalization in Germany is consistent with reports from Victoria, Australia.

Mirroring the experience of prostituted people in other countries, testimony from Nevada, where legal brothels exist, indicates that johns and pimps there are given to demand unsafe sex. For example, johns were said to bribe prostituted women there frequently not to use condoms.[16] In 2002, Lenore Kuo, a professor of women's studies and philosophy, collected accounts of women prostituted in Nevada's legal brothels attesting that measures meant to protect them, "especially the requirement of condoms, were regularly disregarded for an additional fee and that brothel management made no serious effort to prevent this."[17] Kuo also allowed that the "impression" she gained from her visits and interviews "was that the overarching focus of brothel management was the satisfaction of its customers," and that "[l]ittle interest was shown in the well-being of the workers."[18] Another woman who recounted her experiences of being prostituted there affirmed in a 1989 article that denizens of the brothel "were strictly forbidden to use condoms unless the customers asked for one, as it took maximum pleasure away from the paying customer"—a statement essentially consistent with that made almost twenty years later by another prostituted woman interviewed in a legal brothel in Nevada.[19] These accounts are striking in their consistency with those derived from Victoria, Australia.

Several other respondents have reported that beatings and rapes of prostituted women occurred regularly in legal brothels in Nevada and were covered up by management as long as the perpetrating john paid for the sex as agreed.[20] Evidence like this suggests an exploitative dynamic where little concern is shown for the prostituted person. Indeed, among Farley's sample of forty-five women in legal brothels in Nevada, 57% told interviewers that they gave part or all of their earnings to someone other than those controlling the legal brothel, and half believed that at least half of the women there were controlled by outside pimps.[21] Beyond those who own and manage these enterprises, it appears that exploitative third parties are also instrumental in controlling legalized prostitution in Nevada. A multilayered coercive structure may be necessary to ensure that business runs smoothly since johns around the world acknowledge that they routinely solicit prostituted women for the kind of sex others would refuse them, including sexual acts they have seen in pornography.[22] If unsafe, degrading, and abusive sex were truly prevented, as opposed to being controlled by pimps, it is reasonable to posit that business might decrease dramatically.

The demand for abusive sex is likely an important reason why brothel management and other third parties often encourage unsafe sex, are uninterested in intervening to protect women from violent johns, cover up violence after it has been perpetrated, and may have been unable to stop it even if they wanted to.[23] Moreover, the legalization of some prostitution does not eliminate illicit forms from the market, including child prostitution.[24] Accounts from Victoria, Australia, and Nevada indicate that pimps regularly move prostituted women and minors between venues where sexual commerce has been legalized and where it has not both in response to changes in the loci of demand and in order to launder money, avoid law enforcement scrutiny, and maximize profits, recognizing that third parties find minors easier to control and johns are willing to pay more to have sex with them.[25]

The evidence further suggests that neither legalization nor decriminalization lessens the stigma of prostitution for women. As the New Zealand Prostitution Law Review Committee reported in 2008, "[d]espite decriminalization, the social stigma surrounding involvement in the sex industry continues."[26] For many prostituted persons in the Netherlands, getting social security by registering with authorities and paying taxes is not a realistic option, especially if they have school-age children or other relatives who are unaware of their involvement in the sex industry and are unwilling to risk exposure.[27] Similarly, the German federal government's 2007 report found that, though possibilities "to create the legal framework" for social insurance have been available, "few" prostituted persons have "made use of this option."[28]

Some have contended that the legalization of prostitution, especially with respect to third parties, promotes the safety and well-being of those in prostitution. For example, in *Canada v. Bedford* (2013),[29] a Canadian trial court cited five studies that either purported, or which the court claimed purported, to support their decision to invalidate laws that targeted third parties.[30] However, none of these studies reliably controlled for potential bias in subjects' interview responses.[31] For example, in one of them—a study of legal brothels in Nevada[32]—the authors acknowledged having gained access to respondents through the Nevada Brothel Association, brothel attorneys, and brothel management.[33] These same sources, however, regularly deny entry to other researchers.[34] Nevertheless, the trial court did not question why all forty of the prostituted women interviewed claimed they felt protected, only one said she had experienced violence, or the managers and brothel owners saw "themselves as protecting women from violence on the streets by providing a legal alternative."[35] These observations stand in stark contrast to the findings of other studies and reports based on data from Nevada.[36] If prostituted people reported unsafe sex, drug use, management abuse, and exploitative conditions to outsiders, including government agencies, it might well jeopardize the continued legality of the very brothels on whose continued existence they are financially dependent.

Another British study on legal indoor prostitution in London apartments cited by the trial court gave a very different impression than the one that emerges from its own summation.[37] The court erroneously claimed that the London study "found that working in a flat was safer" and that unsafe sex was less frequent compared to the streets,[38] despite the fact that the article made it clear that the study had no control group from the streets against which comparative claims could be validated.[39] The study itself actually reported that women prostituted in flats had to sexually service approximately ten men per day before they even began to earn any money for themselves; the average number of johns per week was 76, with many seeing between 20 and 30 men a day, some up to 50 as a means to cover the substantial expenses incurred by the apartment establishments.[40] The women were first required to pay the daily rent, a receptionist's fee, a fee for advertising, utility bills, and so on, none of which were necessary on the street; as a result of these assessments, some days yielded no net earnings.[41] All of the women interviewed said that unsafe sex was often practiced at these apartments, and also acknowledged being frequently asked to perform unprotected sex, usually in exchange for more money.[42] However, since the interviewer was an official health care practitioner and this sort of information was bound to incriminate the brothels where they were prostituted, no woman admitted outright to have accepted such an offer.[43] Yet the expenses these women were required to pay simply to break even created a strong incentive to accept unsafe sex—something for which many johns willingly pay more. In addition, several respondents reported incidents of assault, rape, and robbery in the flats, where the authors found that the women had "to develop their own protective strategies" and that any role that the "maid" (i.e., receptionist) could "play in containing actual situations of violence" was decidedly "minimal."[44] None of these factors was mentioned in the trial court's summary.

The Canadian courts also misinterpreted data from two surveys that (apart from failing to account for the glaring problem of brothel respondents' propensity to underreport criminal activities) did not control for alternative predictors of the supposedly more frequent abuse found on the streets compared to brothels.[45] For instance, a New Zealand study stated that 41% of 78 prostituted women in the streets, as opposed to 21% of 225 women prostituted indoors, reported having been physically assaulted.[46] Likewise, in the U.K., 81% of 115 women prostituted outdoors reported at least one violent experience at the hands of a john, while 48% of 125 women indoors reported experiencing violence.[47] However, both studies also noted that those involved in street prostitution were younger, less experienced, and reported more drug use than women prostituted indoors.[48] These conditions likely exposed street-prostituted women to men who were more abusive and prepared to take advantage of the relative inexperience and vulnerability of younger women.[49] However, neither of the studies cited by the court controlled for whether current age (as opposed to age upon entering prostitution) or experience were confounding variables that might explain the variance in violence between the two venues.[50] Contrary to the trial court's misrepresentation,[51] neither of these studies was able to show whether it was the indoor environment per se that reduced violence in prostitution, or whether other confounding factors might explain that finding.

A study of prostituted women in Chicago reached very different conclusions. Researchers there found that 21% of women in both escort, street, and residential prostitution all reported having been raped over 10 times in prostitution,[52] thus further illustrating the difficulty of distinguishing venues based on the prevalence of violence. Indeed, the well-known nine-country study referenced throughout this analysis found high rates of PTSD symptomatology among prostituted people.[53] The researchers responsible for the Mexican sample obtained sufficiently large venue subgroups to enable intranational comparisons among 123 prostituted women, 44 in brothels and massage parlors, 54 in strip clubs, and 25 on the street, and identified no statistically significant differences in PTSD severity.[54] Nor were significant differences found between these three groups in the length of time in prostitution, childhood sexual and physical abuse, rape in prostitution, the number of types of lifetime violence, and the percentage of respondents saying they wanted to escape prostitution.[55] A Swiss study of 193 prostituted people, some legally, also determined that the "burden of sex work" (number of working days, number of johns seen per week, etc.) and mental health did not generally differ across venues, but were instead correlated with other factors, such as particular vulnerabilities associated with immigration, lack of support, high debts, and drug use, all of which may increase the exposure of prostituted people to "open violence."[56]

By rejecting the contention that buying people for sex should be permitted, whether indoors, outdoors, or elsewhere, the Swedish Parliament in 1998 tacitly recognized that it is impossible to both fight gender inequality and maintain prostitution as a viable option for women lacking options and resources. As long as prostitution is seen as nothing more than an alternative form of "work," principally for women, a substantial group of multiply disadvantaged people will remain trapped in sexually exploitative conditions that are tantamount to slavery from which they can rarely escape. Prostitution, as such, is antithetical to social equality. Like apartheid, prostitution cannot coexist with social equality. From the perspective of hierarchy theory, then, reducing the number of individuals in prostitution is imperative to the promotion of substantive equality. The Swedish law to be further explored below has accomplished not only such a reduction but also reduced the demand for prostitution.

The Impact of the Swedish Prostitution Law

Comparing Prostitution Prevalence in Scandinavia over Time

The 1993 Prostitution Inquiry estimated that there were 2,500 to 3,000 prostituted women in Sweden at that time, at least 650 of whom were prostituted on the streets.[57] In 1998, one year before the new law took effect, the number of women involved in street prostitution was estimated to be 726.[58] A Nordic study published in 2008 concluded that approximately 300 women were prostituted on the streets in Sweden, while roughly 300 women and 50 men were advertised for prostitution online.[59] In 2014, it was estimated that between 200 and 250 women were prostituted on the streets in Sweden, with no evidence of an increase in indoor prostitution.[60]

Comparable methods have been used to approximate the population of prostituted persons in Denmark and Norway when the new law had been implemented in Sweden, while prostitution remained legal in the other two countries. At that time, tallies of advertisements and those on the streets indicate that the population of prostituted women in Denmark increased from 3,886 in 2002 to 5,567 between June 2006 and July 2007.[61] Approximately 1,415 women were prostituted on the streets at the end of the period.[62] Thus, about eight years after the Swedish sex purchase law entered into force, the total number of people in prostitution was roughly one-tenth that of Denmark, a fact all the more remarkable considering that the total population of Sweden at the time was 9.2 million whereas that of Denmark was only 5.4 million.[63] Thus female prostitution in Denmark was almost sixteen times larger per capita than Sweden's.

A so-called sex workers organization in Denmark (SIO) claimed that Reden, an NGO that worked with prostituted women through outreach programs, had overstated the magnitude of the problem when it reported that 1,200 individuals were engaged in street prostitution in Copenhagen, SIO saying that the police had estimated that they were only 200.[64] Yet estimates of indoor prostitution, including, for example, "clinic prostitution" (i.e., massage parlors), which alone accounted for 3,278 people,[65] were not based on information from Reden.[66] Even presuming that the numbers on the streets were substantially overreported, as suggested by SIO, Denmark's total population of prostituted females at the time was still estimated to be about thirteen times larger per capita than Sweden's. This considerable difference indicates that regardless of how Copenhagen street prostitution was counted, the differences in laws contributed to a much higher prevalence of prostitution in Denmark compared to Sweden, where it decreased during the same period.

A similar trend was observed in Norway—which had an overall population of about 4.7 million people in 2007[67]—where sex purchasing was legal until 2009.[68] As in Denmark, but in contrast to Sweden, the number of people prostituted in Norway during the early 2000s increased, mainly due to an influx of foreign women onto Norwegian streets.[69] In 2007, there were thus 2,654 women prostituted there, 1,157 of whom were on the street.[70] This population was over nine times larger per capita than that observed in Sweden the same year. Although the numbers from Denmark, Norway, and Sweden are necessarily approximations, they provide compelling evidence of differential prevalence rates that cannot be readily dismissed.

In its 2010 assessment, the Swedish government also acknowledged having received "information that people who are involved in street prostitution also make contact with sex purchasers through advertisements via the Internet."[71] Therefore, it concluded that existing estimations of the extent of prostitution based on the two most visible venues might be misleading.[72] Correspondingly, Charlotta Holmström, an author of the 2008 Nordic study, acknowledged that since a number of studies show that people are often prostituted in more than one arena, some of the estimated 600 women prostituted on the streets and indoors in Sweden may have been counted more than once.[73] Yet she also allows for the possibility that some may have been missed due to the manner in which the social work related to these estimates was undertaken.[74] However, no information, empirical evidence, or other data show that there has been a more decisive move from street to the internet or other variants of indoor and allegedly "hidden" prostitution in Sweden than has been observed in other countries.[75]

Indeed, considering the need to be visible to attract potential johns, it is hardly likely that any measurable degree of prostitution would go undetected.[76] This is supported by a 2008 report published by the Swedish

National Board of Health and Welfare, where researchers found that johns in Sweden regularly demanded "novelty," citing informants stressing that women who were new to the market were "more desirable" and that "[n]ew pictures and advertisements garner the keenest interest on the Web."[77] Such dynamics make it all the more imperative for those in prostitution to be highly visible in order to attract new johns. Thus, any "unknown prostitution"—a seemingly oxymoronic concept[78]—would not substantially affect the relative differences among Swedish, Danish, and Norwegian estimations of the prevalence of prostitution.[79]

Corroborating Evidence of a Prostitution Decrease and Increased Safety

The apparent reduction in the scale of prostitution in Sweden after 1999 is also corroborated by other sources. For example, the National Criminal Investigation Department stated in 2002 that Swedish law enforcement received information from a number of informants that third parties were displeased with the decline in the prostitution market in Sweden since 1999.[80] The Department thus reported that this sentiment was echoed by multiple prostituted women during interrogations, by law enforcement in the Baltic countries on "several occasions," by police and social workers, by information from other Nordic countries, and in intercepted telephone conversations between international traffickers and their pimp counterparts in Sweden.[81] Among the reasons cited for their displeasure were such mundane realities as the need to calm johns' fears of getting caught in the act and the corollary need to conduct prostitution more discretely than in countries like Denmark, Germany, the Netherlands, and Spain.[82] Instead of johns simply lining up at a brothel or on the streets, prostituted women in Sweden may have to be escorted to individual johns, thus reducing the number of transactions and with it third-party profits.[83] In order to "carry on" indoor prostitution furtively, those orchestrating prostitution must avoid staying too long in any one location, thus creating the need for "several premises."[84] Securing access to multiple apartments or other suitable locations obviously makes the entire enterprise more expensive and complicated; nevertheless, this has been a "necessity" for third parties since at least 2002, one that was confirmed by nearly every preliminary investigation of procuring and trafficking conducted at the time.[85] Consequently, while European police raids have commonly found 20–60 prostituted women caught up in criminal pimping activities, raids in Sweden typically involve relatively small clandestine brothels where authorities rarely find more than 2–4 prostituted women on the premises.[86]

In tandem with changing legal conditions affecting the potential criminal liability of johns, the safety of prostitution in Sweden has also changed. As described earlier in this analysis, johns often demand harmful sex that others would refuse them, including insisting that prostituted women imitate abusive and degrading pornography in potentially dangerous ways.[87] Although women were victims of attempted and completed murder in prostitution prior to the new law,[88] since 1999, no woman has been murdered in Sweden while being prostituted or in direct proximity to her prostitution. In contrast, in Germany, at least 73 completed homicides and 43 attempts committed against prostituted persons by purchasers or other people in the prostitution milieu have been reported from the time prostitution was legalized in 2002 up to December 2020.[89] Several such murders have also been perpetrated in New Zealand since prostitution was decriminalized in 2003.[90] Swedish reports from 2005 and 2011 drawing on interviews with female, male, and transgender people in prostitution address some of the factors that may account for this remarkable difference in murder rates.[91] These informants described johns as being more careful since they can be reported simply for purchasing sex by an aggrieved party, notably a prostituted person who is not similarly liable—a circumstance that these respondents said gave them bargaining power they could leverage to ensure their safety, security, and personal integrity.[92] The National Board of Health and Welfare evidenced a similar dynamic when referring to an informant who knew "several" prostituted women that "dared to file rape complaints" against johns as a result of the new prostitution law, which was seen as "a source of strength and support" in those situations.[93] Other survivors have also told government investigators that the law empowered them by shifting the stigma of prostitution to johns.[94]

As has been established, legal prostitution not only contributes to the prevalence of prostitution but also makes it demonstrably more harmful by increasing competition, suppressing prices, and raising johns' expectations for more harmful and unsafe sex with the tacit approval of third parties. This is practically inevitable considering that third parties are motivated by the profits derived from johns—not by the needs of those in prostitution, whose vulnerability provides them little leverage. Granting that Sweden's law could be improved, it has already reduced the hierarchical distance between prostituted people and johns, increasing the former's substantive equality in contrast to that of people prostituted in countries that permit buying sex, enabling johns to behave as if there is nothing to stop them from treating those they buy as they choose, even if that means committing murder. Given the modest number of convictions obtained under Sweden's law, its impact is all the more impressive. Table 9.1 presents convictions in Sweden from 1999 to 2020 in cases where sex purchasing was the defendant's primary crime.

Considering the fluctuations in convictions over time, they may, to some degree, be dependent on the government's priorities. For example, in 2010 substantial funds were allotted to the government's action plan against "prostitution and trafficking," and a major case of organized pimping in the northern province (*landskap*) of Jämtland was exposed—two factors that contributed to a spike in crimes reported to the police, customs authorities, and prosecutors' offices that year.[95] Although reports cannot, of course, be equated with convictions, a large number of convictions shown in Table 9.1 for the years 2010–2012 is likely associated with the dramatic increase in reports. In 2010 there were 1,277 sex purchases reported, with 765 reported in 2011.[96] The highest number of annual reports prior to that was in 2005, when 460 crimes were reported; during the period 2012–2020, the lowest number reported was 523 (2015), and the highest 1,055 (2020).[97] That said, because enforcement of the law is dependent on public priorities, an increase in reports and convictions is not necessarily related to an increase in the prevalence of sex purchasing.

Table 9.1 Convictions of Sex Purchasers 1999–2019 in Sweden

Year:	*1999*	*2000*	*2001*	*2002*	*2003*	*2004*	*2005*	*2006*	*2007*	*2008*	*2009*
Number:	10	29	38	37	72	48	94	108	85	69	107
Year:	*2010*	*2011*	*2012*	*2013*	*2014*	*2015*	*2016*	*2017*	*2018*	*2019*	*2020*
Number:	336	450	319	238	260	282	270	194	279	269	418

Source: Brottsförebyggande rådet (Nat'l Council for Crime Prevention), Nat'l Criminal Statistics Database, Sweden (2020) [https://www.bra.se]. The numbers include district court sentences, orders for summary judgment, and waivers of prosecution, but neither appeals nor cases where defendants were simultaneously convicted for a crime with a higher penalty.[278]

Consistent Patterns of Attitudes and Sex Purchasing

Public support is also essential to make the law more sustainable, efficient, and effective. At least eight population surveys measuring support for the sex purchase law have been conducted in Sweden since 1996. Their results are presented in Table 9.2.

A clear majority has been in favor of the law since 1999, with estimated support between 63% and 76%. These numbers contrast sharply with the results of a survey conducted in 1996, before the law was implemented, when only 33% supported the law and 68% were against it.[98] There have been some fluctuations over time, though, including in men's support that seemingly weakened after 1999. However, since 1999 a minority, estimated to be between 15% and 21%, has opposed the law. Notably, women's support ranged from 79% to 85% between 1999 and 2017, whereas that of men has ranged from 50% to 70% (Table 9.2).

Table 9.2 Percentages for/against the Sex Purchase Law (Sweden)

Year of Survey:	1996	1999	2002	2008a	2008b	2011	2014a	2014b
All (for/against) (%)	33/68	76/15	76/–	71/18	63/–	65/21	63/–	72/16
Women (for/against)	45/55	81/–	83/7	79/12	—	80/8	—	85/–
Men (for/against)	20/80	70/–	69/20	60/27	—	50/34	—	60/–
No Opinion/Response	—	9	–/–	11	—	14	—	12

Data as reported by the following sources: for 1996, see Sven-Axel Månsson, "Commercial Sexuality," in *Sex in Sweden: On the Swedish Sexual Life 1996*, ed. Bo Lewin, Kerstin Fugl-Meyer, and Folkhälsoinstitutet (Stockholm: Nat'l Institute of Public Health, 2000), 249; for 1999, 2002, and 2008a, see Jari Kuosmanen, "Attitudes and Perceptions about Legislation Prohibiting the Purchase of Sexual Services in Sweden," *Eur. J. Soc. Work 14*, no. 2 (2011): 252–253; for 2008b, see Niklas Jakobsson and Andreas Kotsadam, "Gender Equity and Prostitution: An Investigation of Attitudes in Norway and Sweden," *Feminist Economics 17*, no. 1 (2011): 38; for 2011, see Gisela Priebe and Carl Göran Svedin, *Sälja och köpa sex i Sverige 2011: Förekomst, hälsa och attityder. Delrapport 1 ur Prostitution i Sverige* (Linköping: Linköping Univ. Electronic Press, 2012), 27 tbl. 1.6 [https://perma.cc/YBQ3-EHDV]; for 2014a, see Sofia Jonsson and Niklas Jakobsson, "Is Buying Sex Morally Wrong? Comparing Attitudes Toward Prostitution Using Individual-Level Data Across Eight Western European Countries," *Women's Stud. Int'l F.* 61 (2017): 61, 62 tbl. 2; for 2014b, see Länsstyrelsen Stockholm [a], *Prostitutionen i Sverige 2014: En omfattningskartläggning*, by Endrit Mujaj and Amanda Netscher (Stockholm: County Administrative Board, 2015), 27 [https://perma.cc/2ML4-6LMR]; and Länsstyrelsen Stockholm [b], Prostitutionen i Sverige 2014: Bilaga 2; Fördjupad metodbeskrivning, tillvägagångssätt och resultat, by Endrit Mujaj and Amanda Netscher (Stockholm: County Administrative Board, 2015), 14 tbl. 2 [https://perma.cc/V5UX-YV8V]. All percentages are rounded to the nearest whole number. Separate data for men and women, neutral opinions, nonresponses, and percentages for and against are included where reported.

Charlotta Holmström and May-Len Skilbrei, co-authors of a synoptic study of the Swedish sex purchase law, note that three of the attitudinal surveys conducted in 2008 and 2011 also asked whether "the sale of sex" should be criminalized.[99] Since just over half of participants responded affirmatively, with two studies finding that roughly two-thirds of women did so,[100] Holmström and Skilbrei argue that "while there is great support in the population for criminalization as a tool to combat prostitution, the intended message behind the law—that prostitution is demand driven and a form of violence against women—does not seem to resonate."[101] Yet they do not acknowledge that the more comprehensive 2011 survey also asked respondents whether they agreed that "[p]rostitution is an expression of men's power over women," to which 77.2% of the women and 51.4% of the men in the stratified web panel of 5,071 participants responded affirmatively.[102] Similarly, 83.5% of female respondents and 80.6% of male respondents agreed that "[s]ale of sex arise[s] due to social and economic problems."[103] In these two questions, the government's view of prostitution as a form of sex inequality related to men's violence against women[104] resonated more clearly among those surveyed.

In 2010, the Swedish National Council for Crime Prevention offered a theory that an unknown number of respondents asked only "Should the sale of sex be prohibited by law?" may have interpreted the question to apply to procuring and human sex trafficking rather than prostitution.[105] The Council pointed to a 1996 survey that used more detailed and gender-specific language in posing a similar question that yielded different responses: "*A woman accepts money* for a sexual contact. Should the woman's action be regarded as being criminal?"[106] Here, only 42% of women wanted to criminalize the prostituted woman.[107] In contrast, as many as 66% of women surveyed in 2008 and 65.4% in 2011 endorsed criminalizing "the sale of sex"—percentages that were underestimated compared to 1996 since the later surveys reported the percentage of respondents with "no opinion" in the totals (13.2% in 2008, 16% in 2011).[108] Because these questions have not been rephrased to reflect their intended meaning more aptly, it is difficult to know how many of these women support the law, in Holmström and Skilbrei's words, due to "a greater reliance on law and punishment" per se[109] than due to a legislative intent to fight sexual exploitation, abuse, and gender inequality.

The publicity, the debates, and the many discussions about prostitution encouraged both by the legislative activity prior to 1999, and the law's early implementation may have influenced the substantial increase in support for criminalizing johns that followed (see Table 9.2). The strong support the law has enjoyed since 1999 is also consistent with the declining market for prostitution in Sweden. A 2014 population survey of eight European countries asking whether it is "morally justified or morally wrong to pay for sex," with options ranging from 0 for "'completely justified'" to 10 for "'entirely wrong,'" and whether "it should be prohibited to buy sex" (yes/no), found similar correlations among attitudes, laws, and the prevalence of prostitution.[110] The survey indicated that people regard it as being significantly less justifiable and more egregious to buy sex in countries where it is criminalized than where it is legal, including after controlling for such individual variables as cohabitation, education, income, religion, living in the capital, and right/left political views.[111]

Moreover, in countries with large legal brothel industries, like Germany and the Netherlands, only 16% and 19% respectively favor criminalizing the johns. Where neither brothels nor sex purchasing was legal, and no sanctions were imposed on prostituted people, as in Norway and Sweden, 53% and 63% respectively favored criminalizing johns. In the remaining four countries where sex purchasing was permitted in smaller venues, support for criminalizing johns fell somewhere in between: 24% in Denmark, 25% in Spain, 28% in France, and 34% in the U.K.[112]

Regarding Swedish data about men's reported experience of ever having purchased sex—if only once, including abroad—six population surveys have reported surprisingly different results over time, suggesting that this measure, which shows a downward trend, is not very useful. In 1996, a paper survey sent to 5,250 men and women and yielding 2,810 responses found that 12.7% of men[113] reported having bought sex at least once.[114] In 1999, a telephone survey of 1,000 men and women found that just above 5% of men reported having done so.[115] In 2008, a paper survey sent to 2,500 men and women that garnered 1,134 responses found that 7.6% of the men (9.2% when inconsistent replies are included) reported having done so.[116] In 2011, a stratified web survey with 5,071 participants found that 10.2% reported having done so,[117] while a similar survey conducted in 2014 with 1,001 participants found that 7.5% reported purchasing sex on at least one occasion.[118] Lastly, in 2017, a paper survey sent to 50,000 individuals aged 16–84, yielding a 31% response rate, estimated that 9.4% of men had bought sex at least once.[119] Notably, 80% of these purchasers reported buying sex abroad, and 33% buying in Sweden.[120]

Considering that the proportion of the male population would be largely the same in 1996 and 2008 except those deceased, the decline in the proportion of men "ever" having bought sex from 12.7% to 7.6% in merely 12 years appears to reflect a substantial overestimation. These reliability problems have been acknowledged both by me and others.[121] Granting I may have been insufficiently clear in this regard in my previous publications, Holmström and Skilbrei nevertheless inadvertently misrepresent these findings in conjunction with their discussion of my assertion that caution is not called for simply because anonymous surveys ask respondents about prior criminal conduct, which studies have shown does not lead inexorably to underreporting.[122]

Surveys of the most recent incidences and frequencies of sex purchasing may be more useful than surveys counting single incidents of sex purchasing that might have occurred many years earlier. A government-commissioned report noted in 2015 that the Swedish surveys have thus far been inadequate in this respect, providing circumscribed data that reveals no clear trends.[123] However, a comparative population survey asking respondents in Denmark, Norway, and Sweden about sex purchasing during the prior six months is, if not dispositive, indicative that other sources of information on the associations between laws and prostitution markets and the behavior of johns in the Nordic countries accurately reflect reality.[124] There, an internet-based survey conducted in August 2010 of 12,252 men and women yielded a fairly even response rate across the three countries of 6,164 (50.3%).[125] Statistically significant differences (p=.002) were found in Denmark, where 2.63% of male respondents reported having purchased sex in the prior six months, as well as in Norway and Sweden, where 1.71% and 0.56% respectively reported having done so.[126] Specifically, the survey in Denmark, where buying sex was legal, reported a proportion of men purchasing sex during the previous six months that was 4.7 times greater than shown by the survey in Sweden, where buying sex was criminalized in 1999. Conversely, the survey in Norway, where buying sex was criminalized in 2009, reported a proportion between the two others (3.1 times higher than Sweden's). Although these are not exact measures, the national differences found are consistent with other evidence presented here, suggesting that the law has reduced prostitution in Sweden relative to that of other nations.

Unwarranted Skepticism

Some scholars question whether extant knowledge is sufficient to infer that Sweden's law contributed to a smaller prostitution market relative to that of other Scandinavian countries. Skilbrei and Holmström claim that "[a]ll in all it is difficult to say something conclusive about the relationship between prostitution law and the size and composition of the prostitution market."[127] They provide a few examples suggesting that some prostitution in Sweden started to occur beyond the radar of police and social workers, thus implying that what is presently known about the law's effect is inadequate. For instance, in 1999, prostitution was reportedly occurring in taxi cabs, while some prostituted women were using their own cars to transport johns to apartments where sex was purchased.[128] However, prostitution in taxis was regularly reported in Stockholm when the 1993 Prostitution Inquiry was collecting information, years before the new law took effect.[129] Moreover, the Inquiry included an in-depth interview with a prostituted woman who described using her own car to "pick up clients," which enabled her to "choose" her johns.[130] She explained that " 'if someone appears weird, he will have to get out of the car.' "[131] Skilbrei and Holmström thus omit information contradicting their implication that taxi prostitution and women picking up johns with their own cars first occurred in 1999. Furthermore, they say nothing about the prevalence of these forms of prostitution in other countries, or whether the women involved advertised or made contact with taxis or johns where street prostitution was known to occur, making it likely they would have been included in prevalence estimates for those venues. Absent cross-national or longitudinal data, or any information regarding the means of communication by which the purchase of sex was arranged, their isolated observations provide no meaningful insight into the efficiency and effectiveness of Sweden's law.

Skilbrei and Holmström also refer to prostitution reportedly having occurred "along roads outside smaller Swedish cities."[132] Here, too, without information as to the extent of roadside prostitution elsewhere in Scandinavia or in Europe, this observation is practically meaningless. In addition, more substantial Swedish legal cases decided between 1999 and 2008 involving third parties charged with trafficking or procuring foreign women are discussed, implying that the prevalence of foreign prostitution was higher than the government's 2008 assessment suggested.[133] However, in isolation, these cases provide little insight into the law's efficiency and effectiveness; some basis for comparison to neighboring countries is needed. Beyond legal prostitution, other observers have deduced that large criminal trafficking operations were much more common in other European countries at that time.[134] With nothing more than a pinpoint citation to the government's evaluation, Skilbrei and Holmström recount the case of 13 Estonian women "where contact was established in a pizzeria,"[135] implying that there was no internet or other advertising involved notwithstanding the fact that the page cited explicitly mentions that their prostitution was advertised on the website *Sekreterarakademin*.[136] Furthermore, that same page says only that one defendant unsuccessfully claimed to have socialized with, but not bought sex from, one prostituted woman whom he met at a pizzeria a week earlier.[137] Hence, contrary to the impression conveyed by Skilbrei and Holmström,[138] nothing in the evidence they set forth suggests that the 13 women were trafficked through a pizzeria.

Swedish criminalization is also said to have contributed to more prostitution in the Danish capital, Copenhagen, as well as in Norway, where more Swedish johns were reportedly seen after 1999.[139] Yet, unless the number of sex purchases would have been the same in Sweden but for those johns who traveled abroad since 1999, this information alone does not indicate that the Swedish law was inefficient and ineffective. Similarly, although prostitution in Sweden may have been advertised on Danish websites,[140] it does not follow that studies assessing prostitution in Sweden have underestimated its extent; advertising "directed at residents of Sweden" was included,[141] apparently regardless of the websites' origins.

Skilbrei and Holmström further maintain, "Waltman bases his conclusions on governmental reports on the consequences of the Law on very weak grounds,"[142] citing two of many sources marshaled while unfortunately assuming, incorrectly, that the National Criminal Investigation Department's report from 2003 "only" presents "an incident where police in surveillance material in a trafficking case overheard traffickers complain about lack of clients in Sweden" as evidence that the law has made Sweden "a less attractive country for traffickers."[143] As mentioned, the claim that traffickers regarded Sweden as a weak market was supported by a number of sources of evidence, including interrogations of prostituted women, information received "on several occasions" by law enforcement agents in the Baltic States, information from almost all preliminary investigations, and intercepted telephone conversations.[144] These sources cannot reasonably be described as "an incident."

Another skeptical researcher, Jay Levy, cites the high number of sex purchases reported to the police in 2010 in contending that, "[a]lthough this may not indicate an actual increase but only an increase in detection, these statistics certainly do not support an assertion that levels of prostitution are declining."[145] Actually, on their own, those numbers cannot reveal whether sex purchasing increased or decreased. Recall that the high number of reports in 2010 was related to the government's exceptionally large allocation of funds through its action plan and a sizeable case of organized pimping in northern Sweden that same year.[146] Levy further references various individual informants in Sweden along with scattered remarks from English-language publications that express doubt that the law had any effect within Sweden,[147] apparently assuming observations of this kind substantiate his claim that there is "no robust evidence that the criminalization of the purchase of sex has succeeded in its abolitionist ambition to decrease levels of sex work in Sweden."[148] Yet he completely ignores the well-known comparisons of prostitution advertisements and street prostitution in Scandinavia during the early years of Sweden's law and omits much of the other corroborating comparative data discussed here.[149] These comparisons conduce to a systematic and controlled analysis of the prevalence, attitudes, and behaviors related to Swedish prostitution in juxtaposition to neighboring countries, which strongly suggests that prostitution would have been considerably more extensive and unsafe than it is today had Sweden not changed its law in 1999.

With all of the indices and observations converging to support the conclusion that the Swedish law has reduced prostitution while also making it less harmful, the skepticism expressed by scholars like Skilbrei, Holmström, and Levy recalls the political scientist Giovanni Sartori's analogy of "the man [*sic*] who refuses to discuss heat unless he is given a thermometer," as distinct from "the man who realizes the limitations of not having a thermometer and still manages to say a great deal simply by saying hot and cold, warmer and cooler."[150]

The Importance of Specialized Exit Programs

When Sweden's law was passed, there had been specialized public social work organizations with roots dating back to the late 1970s that provided support for prostituted people in Malmö, Stockholm, and Gothenburg.[151] The national government adopted an action plan against prostitution and human trafficking for sexual purposes in 2007, which included evaluating the work these organizations do with the purpose of further developing it.[152] The task of conducting the evaluation was given to the National Board of Health and Welfare, which in turn commissioned researchers affiliated with Linköping

University who started working on the evaluation in 2009 and released their results in a 2012 report.[153]

Among other things, the evaluation report discusses a clinical study involving 34 subjects who, upon entering a treatment and support program in one of these units, exhibited mental health problems that were "considerably" more severe on all measures compared to a large clinical study of patients in Sweden with a range of psychiatric diagnoses and substance abuse problems.[154] The symptoms evinced by the prostituted women were also higher than or in line with those of women who had sought group therapy as a treatment for the effects of childhood sexual abuse,[155] thus further demonstrating the severity of their conditions. In this respect, those in the program are similar to the global population of prostituted people, of whom two-thirds in a nine-country study with 854 respondents reported PTSD symptoms at levels comparable to those of treatment-seeking Vietnam veterans, survivors of state torture, and battered or raped women.[156] Moreover, when screened prior to entering the program, participants in the Swedish study reported an average of 11.6 "potentially traumatic experiences" during childhood (*sd*=3.8),[157] with 85% reporting emotional abuse, 76% being beaten or injured, 67% being sexually abused, 76% being hospitalized, 61% being beaten or injured by adult family members, and 58% being bullied.[158] As a comparison, studies from a variety of countries show that between 60% and 90% of prostituted people say they were abused sexually (and a majority physically) in childhood.[159]

Twenty-six clients were still in treatment at a follow-up one year later (the eight dropouts reported significantly higher use of drugs).[160] Of those remaining, 80% had left prostitution completely, while 20% reported being prostituted less often and wishing to reduce its role in their lives further.[161] Those still in prostitution were significantly older and had been prostituted for a significantly longer period of time than the others.[162] Over 90% of all respondents said that the counseling sessions had "been a support" for their own decisions to exit prostitution, and a majority reported higher self-esteem and improved quality of life.[163] A greater number of respondents were living alone than had been the case a year earlier, with a majority reporting that the counseling sessions had supported their efforts to end destructive relationships and improve others.[164] Additionally, more were working or studying (*n*=18, 72%) than previously (*n*=13, 52%), although this difference was statistically nonsignificant.[165] However, a majority reported that counseling had positively affected these activities, and respondents were also statistically significantly more satisfied with their work or studies at the follow-up than before.[166]

The report also includes a post-evaluation study of clients who had ended their treatment on average three years earlier, where interviews "reveal that accurate type of support had been a necessity to survive."[167] The importance of "the specialized unit, the importance of a supportive relationship to a specialized treatment professional, and the recognition from the fact that others with the same type of problems have contact with the units" were reportedly paramount.[168] It further concludes that the survivor interviews "illustrate negative experiences of speaking about prostitution at other health care services"—a situation made worse by difficulties gaining access to the specialized units when they lived in another municipality.[169] Calls for greater accessibility were also voiced in the government's 2010 evaluation of the law when survivors and those who remained in prostitution noted that specialized care and treatment was insufficiently available across the country; several also reported having encountered other professionals in the social services sector that lacked the requisite knowledge to provide them with appropriate support.[170]

As a control, researchers conducted a third set of interviews with 11 women and girls aged 15–25 who had been prostituted through online venues and had not been recruited from the specialized units' treatment programs.[171] These respondents also emphasized the need for specialized units. For example, all of them "could describe meetings with social services, the judicial system, or the psychiatry programs where they felt overrun, misunderstood, and that they had not been given an opportunity to tell that they had sold sexual services."[172] Tellingly, all respondents "had been involved in the social welfare services and/or child psychiatry programs, but had rarely revealed that they sold sexual services."[173] Instead, these survivors reported that their contacts with non-specialized agencies left them feeling as if they were the ones who were "in the way, that they took up someone's time if they talked, that the people in their proximity reacted with despair," and that nonspecialists "did not know how to handle the situation when a young person confessed" to her involvement in prostitution.[174] When youngsters did attempt to discuss it, psychologists are said to have replied that they lacked the competence necessary to counsel them.[175] Accounts like these contrast sharply with those of respondents who had participated in programs offered by the specialized units, further demonstrating the need to expand specialized programs and make them accessible to all who need them.

Unlike the more recent French prostitution law that is partially modeled after Sweden's, Swedish prostitution laws do not regulate social work directly. France's law also provides a fund for initiatives to prevent prostitution and support and reintegrate those seeking to exit it, which is financed both by the state and by funds derived from assets seized from convicted third parties.[176] France also prioritizes those trying to exit prostitution in access to public housing, provides a tax debt waiver, financial aid (if they are ineligible for basic social welfare or financial assistance ordinarily available to asylum seekers), and can provide temporary or permanent protective residence permits to foreigners.[177] Under France's law, an agency comprised of national and local government representatives, health professionals, and organs of civil society is also created in every *département* (county) that is responsible for addressing the needs of those victimized by prostitution.[178]

Because Sweden's prostitution laws do not regulate public assistance, social work, and social welfare with the same specificity as those enacted in France, special public support for prostituted people may be unduly dependent on the vicissitudes of political decisions regarding resource allocation, as seen in the case of the three specialized units evaluated in 2012, or on the eligibility of prostituted people for assistance that is legally guaranteed for members of other groups (e.g., foreign or domestic crime victims, those with mental disorders, and the unemployed). Illustrating the precariousness of the resources available for exit programs not guaranteed by law, a widely criticized municipal reorganization of Stockholm's specialized unit supporting prostituted persons was undertaken in 2017, where vital services were transferred to less specialized social work and health care units, raising concerns about the potential impact on their quality and accessibility.[179]

Symptomatic Misinformation about Sweden's Law

Commercial sex, including pornography and prostitution, is a powerful industry supported by a spectrum of apologists, among whom are researchers and social commentators who may, in turn, influence public opinion and policymaking irrespective of the accuracy of their claims. Recall that the 1985 U.S. Attorney General's Commission on Pornography was surrounded by false rumors planted by a public relations firm, which were parroted in the media until they became so-called conventional wisdom.[180] Likewise, unfounded rumors were internationally circulated about Sweden's law early on, many attributed to the Swedish prostitution commentator Petra Östergren, including an unpublished English-language piece she wrote that was accessible online from 2003 or 2004.[181] Academics outside of Sweden have cited her piece approvingly,[182] as have NGOs like the Sex Worker Education and Advocacy Taskforce, which promulgated her claims to the South African Law Reform Commission in 2009 but referred to no published research from Sweden.[183] Östergren argued, inter alia, that "[a]ll of the authorities say that there is no evidence that prostitution was lower overall" since before the law, and that "hidden prostitution had probably increased."[184] However, none of the reports she cited had been published more than two years after the law took effect. Data before and after the law, as well as comparative data from the other Nordic countries and related corroborating evidence discussed here demonstrate that Östergren's claims were incorrect.

Östergren maintained that women in street prostitution faced harsher conditions after the law's enactment with, among other things, more frequent demands for unsafe sex and a larger proportion of violent johns.[185] However, to reiterate, women in legal prostitution have reported that legalization increases competition and demands for unsafe and dangerous sex acts. There is ample evidence not only corroborating their observations but also, as recalled, showing that Sweden's law encourages johns to be more cautious in their encounters with prostituted people at the same time it contributes to a safer environment, conclusions that are perhaps most powerfully demonstrated by the absence of prostitution-related murders commonly seen under legalization. Indeed, even Levy acknowledges that the "overall levels of exploitation and violence in sex work are relatively low in Sweden."[186] Although some informants told him that the law contributed to lower prices and less safety for some, others asserted that their security was enhanced by the law, which heightened johns' fears of being reported, thereby rendering them more cautious and in turn enabling women to charge them much higher prices than elsewhere in Europe.[187] Consistent with these developments, the Swedish National Board of Health and Welfare declared that its 2000 report—which Östergren used to substantiate her conclusions—is "not valid anymore."[188] Indeed, the Board first expressed doubts about her claims in 2003:

> While *some* informants speak of a more risk-filled situation, *few* are of the opinion that there has been an increase in actual violence. Police who have conducted a special investigation into the amount of violence have not

found any evidence of an increase. Other research and the responses of our informants both indicate a close connection between prostitution and violence, regardless of what laws may be in effect.[189]

Additionally, in a 2007 report, the Board noted that opinions among prostituted women varied, with some still preferring the street over restaurants, nightclubs, and the Web.[190] In the words of one informant, "making contact online" is much like "'buying a pig in a poke.'"[191] Another woman said that screening johns online or by telephone was more difficult than meeting face to face and therefore harder to reject an unwanted john after he had arrived for an arranged date than would be the case on the street.[192] Although Östergren may have been correct in saying that some purchasers stopped testifying against traffickers once their actions were criminalized,[193] the Gothenburg Police nonetheless reported having "received anonymous tips from clients who suspect human trafficking."[194]

Östergren also argued that cohabitation is difficult for prostituted people, the implication being that their partners may be charged with pimping under procuring laws; however, she neither cited nor mentioned any actual cases, relying exclusively on hypotheticals.[195] Similarly, Jay Levy and Pye Jakobsson have claimed that "[t]here are also reports of the police reporting sex workers to their landlord," allegedly "forcing an eviction."[196] They, too, offer no evidence, even less citations, from specific cases, and none of their informants seems to have personally experienced eviction.[197] However, some hotels seem to have enforced a no-prostitution policy, and there are reports about landlords evicting tenants when the premises are used for prostitution.[198] Yet these reports do not suggest that prostituted persons are evicted simply for being in prostitution, nor that their partners are charged with pimping.

Along with some of their informants, Levy and Jakobsson also criticize the specialized support programs in Stockholm and Gothenburg, which oppose the distribution of free condoms and other safe-sex materials on the streets (so-called harm reduction) on the theory doing so would indirectly promote prostitution.[199] Yet they elide the fact that johns often prefer unprotected sex and pressure prostituted people to provide it regardless—conditions that, as recalled, are systematically documented in legal prostitution and further suggested by information and informants from Sweden that they themselves cite.[200] Distributing free condoms to prostituted women certainly seems innocuous, but Levy and Jakobsson provide no evidence that it would reduce unprotected sex, seemingly intent on portraying prostitution as safer than it actually is.

For many years, few people outside of Sweden seemed to know how Östergren selected her sample of twenty prostituted women to which she frequently refers. She hinted at the answer in her book published in Swedish in 2006, where she admitted she did not attempt to contact or conduct interviews with "sellers of sex" who had "primarily bad experiences of prostitution."[201] Rather, she intentionally sought out women with "completely different experiences," contending that negative reports were "the only ones heard in Sweden."[202] Similarly, her 2003 master's thesis referred to interviews with fifteen female "sellers of sex" of whom "most . . . have a positive view of what they do."[203] Thus, when she mentioned "informal talks and correspondence with approximately 20 sex workers since 1996" in her English-language piece,[204] she was apparently referring to respondents who were selected precisely because of their positive views of prostitution as an institution. When writing that "[m]ost of the sexworkers I have interviewed reject the idea that there is something intrinsically wrong with their profession,"[205] she ought to have observed standard scholarly practice and informed readers that her choice of interviewees was tendentious, inclusion and exclusion being determined by prospective subjects' perspectives on prostitution.

Both activists and scholars outside of Sweden have repeatedly cited Östergren's piece in English (omitting those in Swedish) in tandem with other sources of biased information without acknowledging the problems they present. Jane Scoular, for instance, refers to "Östergren's interviews with women, who reported experiencing greater stress and danger on the streets" after the 1998 law took effect,[206] but without mentioning the admitted bias marring the selection of interviewees. Furthermore, Scoular advanced a number of claims in 2010 that diverge from a substantial body of research promulgated in the years before her article was published. To take just one example, she alleges that no Swedish report "has provided a straightforward comparison" before and after the law's enactment.[207] She proceeds to contradict that claim, writing that "the consistent message across a number of evaluations and sources . . . is of a temporary reduction in street sex work, leading to the displacement of women and men into more hidden forms of sex work and the worsening of conditions for those who remain on the streets."[208] Among the five citations Scoular provides to support these claims are two reports published just one year after the law was enacted and another published only two years after its introduction.[209] Moreover, referring to no specific page therein, she cites two of the National Board of Health and Welfare's reports quoted above,[210] which, in contrast to her conclusions, express serious doubts about purportedly worsening conditions.[211] Yet Scoular expresses no compunction about deriving her principal conclusion from plainly biased information, namely that "apparently contrary legal positions produce similar results on the ground . . . in part, due to law's involvement in wider forms of governmentality that operate to support a wider neo-liberal context."[212]

Ronald Weitzer, in turn, cites one of Scoular's pieces alongside the work of an unpublished author to support his assertion that "[i]ndependent assessments indicate that Sweden's law has not had the salutary effects claimed by advocates."[213] In the same way, Janet Halley and her co-authors cite Östergren's unpublished English-language piece and that of another activist in contending that prostitution became more covert and dangerous after the law took effect.[214] They maintain that "it is *clear* that the reform made the life of the remaining sex workers (local and migrant) *much* harder."[215] Further, they second-handedly cite a 2001 Swedish "administrative report" from the city of Malmö and "others" (presumably reports) they say were quoted in a Norwegian government report from 2004,[216] yet they omit the subsequent more authoritative National Board of Health and Welfare report discussed here that reached a different conclusion.[217] The Canadian scholar Emily van der Meulen similarly claims that "the criminalization of clients . . . leads to an increase in violence and stigma," relying only on Östergren's and other unpublished pieces from Sweden and the Norwegian report,[218] omitting substantial Swedish research produced since 1999 showing, as remembered, that the law's empirical impact on prostitution has been quite the opposite—producing more safety and less stigma while reducing the prevalence of prostitution compared to places where buying sex is legal. In a brief comment, John Lowman, too, tellingly refers only to Östergren's unpublished piece in misleadingly asserting that Sweden's legal approach "exposes prostitutes to harm."[219] The Swedish government's 2010 evaluation, of course, found that claims that the law exacerbated the conditions of prostitution were baseless,[220] a conclusion consistent with the numerous reports and research examined in this study. The fact that sources of biased information from Sweden have so often been uncritically cited with no acknowledgment of their flaws, particularly from those outside the country, is indicative of the support that the commercial sex industry receives from its apologists among academics, journalists, and others in civil society.

Potential of a Swedish Civil Rights Approach

Interpretative Problems under the Law

Until those victimized are compensated and enabled to leave the sex industry, a thorough remedy of their situation will not be practicable. Toward this end, the law could be further strengthened consistent with its intent. Contrary to the implication of much of the biased commentary about the Swedish statute, very few critics analyze the case law it has engendered. Liability for civil damages under the sex purchase law would, if implemented by judicial interpretation, put the onus for much of the harm where it belongs: on the johns who take advantage of the power imbalance in prostitution to purchase other people for sex, contributing to their suffering, denying their humanity, and violating their rights to equality and dignity. Civil liability under the sex purchase law would bear similarities to the cause of action for "coercion into pornographic performance" under the proposed Minneapolis antipornography civil rights ordinance.[221] It would recognize substantive inequality and the perspectives and interests of those harmed in commercial sex more concretely than a criminal law granting the government the right to fine or jail johns or pornographers.

Civil proceedings are often intertwined with criminal proceedings in the Swedish legal system, although they can be separately initiated or conducted at a later date.[222] The right to present damage claims and have them judicially assessed under the Swedish Code of Judicial Procedure usually follows by default where there is a person considered to be the party "against whom the crime was committed or who was affronted or harmed by it."[223] The person harmed is then referred to as the "injured party" (*målsägande*),[224] and her or his claims are partially represented by the prosecutor and by the victim's legal counsel.[225]

In 2001, the Swedish Supreme Court, in a cursory opinion consisting of four sentences, affirmed lower court rulings that interpreted the protected interest under the sex purchase law in the context of determining the penalty for a man who had purchased a woman to perform oral sex on him in a parked car.[226] The district court and the court of appeals differed on the applicable level of penalty, but both argued that the "consent" of the prostituted individual suggested that the crime committed is "primarily" against the "public order" rather than against the individual as a "person."[227] The implication was that the victim would not willingly consent to a crime against her- or himself as a person. However, neither the legislative findings[228] nor the contemporary research on the sex industry[229] documents the conditions of freedom required for the "consent" on which these courts relied to be meaningful. Indeed, the courts betrayed no awareness of the overwhelmingly fictional nature of the prostituted person's alleged consent; to underscore what should be uncontroversial, no legitimate consent is possible when an agreement is extracted through the exploitation of someone's desperate position, lack of options, or abuse history, all well-known antecedents of prostitution.

The district court remarked that the prosecutor had only called the woman in the capacity of a witness[230] rather than as an injured party. This, along with the fact that no damages were sought, also implicates prosecutors in the interpretation of sex purchasing as a more or less "victimless" crime.

In 2007, some applications of the law were improved when an appellate court convicted johns who bought sex from a prostituted woman through a third party and imposed conditional sentences and fines in recognition of the presence of coercive circumstances and other factors that justified a higher penalty than imposed in the previous Supreme Court case.[231] That said, the johns were not ordered to pay any damages. One rationale for raising the penalty was the fact that after a completed sexual act, a john introduced an acquaintance when the prostituted woman was, in the court's words, "in such a subordinate position against the two men that it must have appeared as a near-impossibility for her to refuse the other man intercourse, or to otherwise affect the situation"—a condition that the defendants "understood and exploited."[232] The woman was thus understood to be in a situation in which genuine consent was impossible. In prostitution, this is typical. Yet she was not regarded as an injured party, nor were damages deemed warranted as a consequence of the exploitation and victimization she experienced. Thus, it appears as if the judicial system does not yet regard prostituted people as being victimized by johns, the empirical evidence notwithstanding.

An additional effect of the Supreme Court's 2001 decision was to establish sex purchase as a crime of low judicial priority, although that position was slightly altered by the court of appeals' decision in 2007. The district court in the 2001 case had argued that a crime directed primarily against the public order merited a lower punishment per se than crimes against persons.[233] Although the penalty assessed was slightly higher on appeal, the john was subject only to monetary fines.[234] Consequently, the government reported in its 2010 evaluation that several law enforcement officers told the evaluators that "many times more" offenses of the sex purchase law would be reported if the law's enforcement was "prioritized"; prosecutors agreed with this assessment and attributed the situation to the low penalties assigned to the offense.[235] A corresponding problem noted by anti-trafficking police in Gothenburg is the law enforcement's long-standing preference for evaluating success in terms of the number of convictions won and the total jail time assessed.[236] Factors like these may explain why the National Human Trafficking Rapporteur Kajsa Wahlberg suggested in 2010 that a "higher penalty would perhaps also make the police prioritize these crimes more."[237] However, despite the inclusion of prison terms in 1999 and the increase in the maximum penalty in 2011, a 2016 government report stated that it is still "very unusual" for any john to be punished by more than fines.[238] The deficiencies in the law's application are not, of course, an argument against criminalizing the purchase of sex, but rather an argument for applying the law more rigorously as a crime primarily against the person, not the public.

Civil Remedies as Support for Exit

Under the Swedish Criminal Code, "fines accrue to the State."[239] This differs from civil damage awards that presumptively go directly to those harmed. Moreover, in contrast to France's law, which uses assets seized from convicted third parties to provide partial funding for social services for prostituted people,[240] there is no mechanism in place in Sweden to redirect fines collected from johns to support the needs of prostituted persons. Thus, johns are not individually accountable for the harms accruing to those from whom they purchase sex. To the extent that the government has provided assistance to those in prostitution under the public budget, it has been a political decision—not a legal obligation. In its referral response to the government evaluation's 2010 report,[241] the National Board of Health and Welfare likewise implied that clear and consistent legal recognition of prostituted people as injured parties would lend support to the position that they should be covered under the Social Welfare Service Act's provision for "Crime Victims," which mandates that Local Social Welfare Boards afford further "support and help" to those "subjected to crime."[242] This provision is not an individual right, but one that can only be invoked against the welfare boards as a whole.[243] But if those in prostitution were recognized as crime victims, support for exiting the institution would be based less upon politics than upon law. Concomitantly, public support for extending assistance to those in prostitution would thus be less dependent on the vicissitudes of political majorities.

The government's evaluation concluded that "a consequence of the Swedish view on prostitution is that it is not possible to make any distinction between so-called voluntary and involuntary prostitution."[244] Yet, contrary to decisive statements like this one and the cumulative evidence of the coercive circumstances underlying prostitution in general, law enforcement officers have occasionally expressed the view that women involved in domestic prostitution often meaningfully consent, while foreign women, commonly aligned with third-party profiteers, are often seen as coerced.[245] Sweden is thus still dealing with some of the myths about consensual prostitution that prevail worldwide. Additional judicial decisions emblematic of similar assumptions appeared in 2007 in the Stockholm Administrative Court of Appeal, which gave tax authorities permission to tax an apparently exited prostituted woman based on her presumptive unreported past income.[246] As the complainant pointed out, by the decision's own logic, "prostituted persons, in order to be able to pay taxes, are coerced to continue."[247] Even jurisdictions like Nevada, which has legalized prostitution in some counties in spite of its harms, have refused to make conditions worse by taxing the abuse.[248] Considering the Swedish legislature's acknowledgment that johns know, or should know, that their purchase of sex is "destructive" to the prostituted person,[249] and the imperative to support those seeking to exit prostitution,[250] the Stockholm Administrative Court of Appeal's decision is contrary to the law's intentions. Furthermore, the fact that the coercive circumstances, such as financial desperation and a lack of viable options, are common precursors to prostitution, makes it dubious that the threat of taxation will do much to deter prostitution. Instead, any such attempt seems like public exploitation of those mired in prostitution. By contrast, the prospect of civil damages would offer an incentive for prostituted people to testify against johns and, in turn, deter more sex purchasing.

In identifying the injured party as the one harmed or affronted by the crime,[251] the Swedish Code of Judicial Procedure is effectively mandating that any ambiguity in the law be resolved through an inquiry into its conception of the interests that the law is meant to protect. Judicial experience in this regard suggests that it would behoove any country considering a version of the Swedish law to avoid defining prostitution as the purchase of "a sexual service."[252] That said, the phrase has never been invoked by a Swedish court when interpreting the law's protected interest. However, the word "service" tends to minimize the harms of prostitution in light of that the evidence that the institution is per se abusive to the person being bought, or, at a minimum, sexually exploitative of vulnerable people, hence not simply a "service" like any other on the market. A more appropriate statutory definition is the "purchase of a person for sex," which clearly indicates that prostitution is neither an ordinary service for taxation purposes nor primarily a crime against the public order.[253]

The 2011 Legislative Clarifications

Although the government's 2011 reading of the law, which followed upon the recommendations of its evaluation, stated that some cases of sex purchase might be at once a crime against a person and a public harm (i.e., because prostitution promotes sex inequality), it decided that the issue of whether both are protected interests had to be assessed in *each and every case*.[254] This assessment is highly significant insofar as it influences what legal support may be available to a prostituted person intending to claim damages. A more thorough study of how these assessments could be improved might have conduced to an increase in the minimum standard for support. As with the Swedish prostitution laws against third parties, when there is only a conviction for normal procuring and no injured party is acknowledged by the court, the result is not only to exclude damages but also to negate legal rights and entitlements to health care, housing, and temporary or potentially permanent residence permits that convictions for trafficking and gross procuring would allow.[255] It is factors like these that make many foreigners staying in Swedish women's shelters reluctant to testify about sex trafficking and risk expulsion if prosecutors are unsuccessful in securing convictions for more serious charges.[256]

More recently, the Swedish National Rapporteur on human trafficking found that a civil society initiative in the EU provided considerable support in 55 of 86 cases where predominantly women and some girls were suspected of having been trafficked for prostitution in Sweden in 2017, even though no police reports had been filed.[257] Notably, though, among the 31 remaining cases where police reports were filed, only 12 preliminary investigations were initiated, and only 6 led to charges for procuring (3) or human trafficking (3).[258] Hence, there seem still to be considerable obstacles for prostituted persons to vindicate their legal rights fully. Indeed, some critics of Sweden emphasize that its migration laws are applied in ways that can deny residence permits to prostituted persons and that the housing laws prevent women from pursuing indoor (as opposed to street or escort) prostitution.[259] Admittedly, these applications contradict the intent to target only the pimps and johns, not the prostituted persons. However, the critics rarely acknowledge that the situation could be improved by treating all cases of sex purchasing and procuring as crimes against persons rather than as crimes against the public order, which would further incentivize those victimized to report crimes perpetrated against them and ensure more reliable public support than civil society alone can afford.

According to the charter of the Swedish government's 2008–2010 evaluation, the legal standing of prostituted individuals under the law was to have been investigated.[260] Yet the ensuing report provided no systematic review of the literature on preconditions to and harm perpetrated within prostitution, which could have made it easier to ascertain the injured party entitled to claim damages.[261] It did take account of more recent findings regarding conditions in Sweden, such as the strong association between being prostituted and having a history of child sexual abuse, neglect, or serious mental health problems.[262] Overall, however, the research review was comprised mainly of studies on the extent of prostitution in Sweden and the judicial application of the law—not preconditions or conditions of those being prostituted. Consequently, when it endeavored to identify the law's protected interests, and thereby the legal standing of prostituted people, it provided an extensive discussion of legal doctrines and scholarship on the abstract concept of a protected interest instead of empirical evidence of prostitution's harms.[263] To the extent that it concentrated on doctrinal literature that is indifferent to the injuries sustained by those in prostitution, the evaluation was not asking the right questions.

Certain questions, particularly those concerning entrenched social discrimination and inequality, cannot be adequately addressed by existing doctrines, perforce when they themselves are part of the problem. As the U.S. Supreme Court recognized in its groundbreaking decision in *Brown v. Board of Education* (1954), while existing doctrines "cast some light, it is not enough to resolve the problem with which we are faced. At best, they are inconclusive."[264] Rather than foregrounding doctrine, the Court turned instead to empirical evidence.[265] As the high court acknowledged in *Beauharnais v. Illinois* two years earlier, neither "history" nor "practice" had previously regarded group libel as unprotected expression, but it nonetheless decided to create a new doctrinal category.[266] Although the Swedish government's evaluation similarly concluded "that neither legal text nor doctrine gives any clear and unambiguous answer to the question of who is an injured person" under the sex purchase law,[267] it did not outline a new doctrine as did *Brown* and *Beauharnais* but left it for Swedish courts to resolve. Even after receiving the evaluation, the Cabinet, the Ministry of Justice, and the Parliament could have taken a more proactive stance in recognizing the purchase of sex primarily as a crime against the person bought, making any other interpretation an exception to the rule. Today, the issue remains in a state of limbo, dependent on the views of the judges, prosecutors, and law enforcement officials.

According to the Swedish Code of Judicial Procedure, the prosecutor is responsible for proffering information in the summons application regarding any potentially injured parties.[268] The prosecutor is also usually obliged to represent any such party.[269] In addition, either the prosecutor or law enforcement, depending on who initiated the preliminary investigation, must whenever possible recognize and represent the injured party before the summons application is submitted.[270] Yet it is reasonable to be skeptical that either entity will suddenly begin recognizing prostituted individuals as injured parties without a more decisive push from the Cabinet, the Ministry of Justice, or the legislature.

Recall that there were also problems with Canada's application of its criminal pornography statute, which, like Sweden's, was premised on the promotion of substantive equality. Canadian prosecutors often presented insufficient evidence, while judges frequently expressed prejudicial assumptions that were not adequately rebutted or confronted. By contrast, a Canadian government program that supported "court challenges" by disadvantaged groups facilitated the intervention of a well-organized women's organization in the *Butler* case (1992), presenting a compelling selection of evidence and arguments. However, if the government had not chosen to prosecute, then there could not have been any such intervention. Indeed, the criminal law framework seems ill-suited to representing the perspectives and interests of those harmed in the sex industry. Criminal law is usually dominated by the police, prosecutors, expert witnesses, and defense attorneys. This circumstance suggests that Sweden should strengthen the civil rights of prostituted persons, either by providing a more definite statement regarding their status as the primary injured parties that should be summoned by courts or by establishing a law or program, preferably building upon survivors' legitimate autonomous organizations, specifically designed to ensure that their perspectives and interests are adequately represented in legal proceedings.

Political Obstacles to Substantive Equality

Neither the 2010 evaluation nor the government bill circulated the following year contemplated enhancing support for damage awards in *all cases* brought under the sex purchase law. Granted, the specific amount available may still have to be judicially assessed on a case-by-case basis. However, given the qualifications that accompanied the proposal of the government and its evaluation to raise the maximum penalty to one year in prison, any change in that direction can be obstructed. According to these caveats, the raise "is not meant to change the choice of sanction for all sex purchase crimes," and if "there isn't any aggravating circumstance the penalty level would, for many sex purchases . . . *still stay* on daily fine-level."[271] Here, it should be noted that the current practice of handing out daily fines, as opposed to imprisonment or conditional sentences, was established when courts interpreted the crime primarily as one committed against the public order. Therefore, when the government indicated that many defendants could (even should) be similarly sentenced in the future, it seemingly accepted that the law was not primarily meant to redress crimes against persons, but rather crimes against the public order.

However, the evaluation's own statement that the sex purchase law "is more of a crime against a person than a crime against the public order, even if its background has elements of both," appears inconsistent with its position that many sex purchases would "still stay on the daily-fine level" after its proposed amendments were effectuated.[272] Thus, the sex purchase law may prove to be more responsive to damage claims if prosecutors or prostituted people themselves simply started to claim damages under it. The fact that no prostituted person has been awarded damages under the sex purchase law since its enactment suggests, however, a need for more robust legislative or judicial support for such an eventuality to be realized.

For purposes of damages, the empirical evidence shows that the coercive circumstances typically preceding entry create a situation that is both profoundly challenging and intrinsically unequal, which johns freely exploit.[273]

By purchasing sex from people compelled by a fundamental lack of choice to accept it, johns compound the harms sustained by those in prostitution even without engaging in additional aggravating conduct. Given this, purchasing a prostituted person for sex should be recognized as a violation of that individual's right to humanity, equality, and dignity—a crime primarily against the person her- or himself, not the public interest.[274] It has been argued that since the realization of these civil rights would deter potential johns, they infringe the right of a hypothetical category of people who are not harmed by doing so to "sell sex." However, someone who was bought for sex and did not her- or himself suffer harm as a consequence would likely not seek damages from a john. Even if this were insufficient to deter some johns, any legislature or judiciary should be capable of fairly balancing the rights, interests, and imperatives at stake. When weighing the interests of those being harmed and exploited in prostitution and their need for support to exit, the arguments favoring the hypothetically unharmed prostituted person appear strikingly imbalanced and detached from the documented realities of prostitution.

Lessons for Legal Challenges to Pornography

If the Swedish procuring laws were applied against those promoting or exploiting those paid for sex during pornography production, the impact might be similar to what has been seen in Sweden since the passage of its prostitution laws in 1999. It would not be difficult for law enforcement or attorneys representing injured parties to gather sufficient evidence to employ the procuring laws accordingly. Just like other pimps and traffickers, pornographers must make their products visible to attract distributors and consumers. The nature and extent of pornography production could be ascertained much as Swedish law enforcement has done in the cases of human sex trafficking and sex purchasing—for example, by receiving "information through Internet surveillance, physical surveillance, tip-offs from the public at large and other sources."[275] Similar methods of approximation were discussed earlier with respect to prostitution advertisements and the number of prostituted persons on the streets of Scandinavia. There, a downward trend in prostitution was seen in Sweden after it criminalized sex purchasing, while the opposite was exhibited in Norway and Denmark when it was permitted. Other evidence, including observations by law enforcement, prostituted persons, and social workers, corroborated these trends.

Even if some production were to persist in Sweden after the procuring laws were applied to pornography, those responsible would likely face greater peril than those in countries where it is legal. They would have to protect themselves from being apprehended by law enforcement or sued by injured parties who were exploited in their productions, just as pimps and johns have had to do in Sweden since 1999. Producers and their associates would also likely act more cautiously if persons used as pornography performers, like those prostituted off-camera, were able to report them for a crime and potentially sue them for civil damages while facing no criminal consequences of their own. This situation would be quite different from what obtains in countries that permit pornography production, where people used as performers are regularly pressured to tolerate more abusive and unsafe sex in order to satisfy consumer demand.[276] This, again, closely resembles the situation confronting prostituted persons in legal prostitution.

Although applying prostitution laws against pornography producers would not criminalize consumers, information about the harms of pornography could be disseminated in conjunction with these new legal applications, in turn potentially impacting popular attitudes and perceptions to favor more effective measures against consumption. Remember that opinion surveys showed that public support for the Swedish sex purchase law increased almost immediately following its passage, which may well have been an effect of public discourse at the time. Support for criminalizing sex purchasing is also strong in Norway, which passed a corresponding law in 2009, whereas support for such a law is considerably weaker in Denmark, Germany, and the Netherlands, where sex purchasing is legal and far more prevalent.[277] A similar shift in public views of pornography production might, for instance, recognize that it would not exist absent the demand. Such a perspective could pave the way for civil rights laws against the dissemination of pornography, targeting consumption more directly, efficiently, and effectively than laws directed toward production alone. Extending the law accordingly would make Sweden even more of a model for the world.

Sweden could also strengthen the rights of prostituted people such that they are recognized as injured parties in all cases, including in the production of pornography, with the attendant right to seek civil damages and support as crime victims, allowing them to obtain residence permits, housing, and health care. A civil rights approach along these lines would promote the substantive equality and related interests of those harmed by pornography more vigorously than criminal law. By empowering survivors rather than the state to initiate claims under the law, it would also enhance the incentives for members of the bench and bar to apply the law more frequently and effectively, in keeping with its original intent to support those in prostitution.

Conclusions

Compelling evidence demonstrates that pornography contributes to gender inequality. It is implicated in pervasive abuse that disproportionately affects populations suffering from multiple disadvantages, including poverty, childhood abuse, and race and gender discrimination. Almost fifty years of social science research show that pornography fuels sexual aggression and attitudes supporting violence against women and the demand for prostitution. Among its effects, consumers often wish to imitate pornography with reluctant partners, thus increasingly buy prostituted women who are disadvantaged and lack options. In its production, pornographers typically exploit populations similar to those used by pimps and traffickers, who, among other things, suffer from severe poverty, a history of childhood abuse and neglect, and mental illness. Whether directly or indirectly, producers, therefore, rely on some form of coercive social circumstances in order to make persons used as performers comply with the demands of the market, which frequently include abusive treatment. Given the egregiousness and irrefutability of these harms, existing democracies fail to embody their own ideals of equality when they allow them, and the system of social dominance that sustains them, to go unchecked and unremedied.

Challenging Inequality, Ideology, and Law

The most difficult hurdle that legal challenges to pornography must overcome is the purported conflict with freedom of expression typically raised by those resisting change. Yet this analysis demonstrates that many opponents only profess to rely on *law*, when, in fact, their positions are grounded in *ideology*[1] furbished with persuasive rhetorical devices. That said, different constitutional frameworks also impact on the potential success of legal challenges, and not superficially so. As an analysis of various democratic and feminist theories centering on challenging hierarchies (hierarchy theory) predicted, constitutional frameworks that balance evenly between conflicting interests

Pornography. Max Waltman, Oxford University Press. © Oxford University Press 2021.
DOI: 10.1093/oso/9780197598535.003.0011

while exhibiting robust support for both "positive rights" and substantive equality are conducive to mounting successful legal challenges to pornography. Less evenly balanced classic liberal frameworks that are more supportive of "negative rights"[2] and less supportive of substantive equality are, in turn, less receptive to challenge. These distinctions are partly explained by the fact that countries with constitutions that permit balancing substantive equality evenly against expressive rights generally have courts that are more apt to undertake an objective analysis to determine whether particular forms of expression and speech promote or obstruct substantive equality, and thus warrant positive public intervention. This constitutional approach contrasts with one in which expression and substantive equality are unevenly balanced in order to preserve a negative-rights approach, which is thought to protect against the public abuse of power by limiting governmental intervention. The latter often ignores that extending protection to more absolute freedoms against public intervention tends to enable private abuses of power. For instance, absent traditional exemptions or exceptional circumstances, the law under a negative-rights regime may treat all expression as formally equal by requiring "viewpoint-neutral" regulations even if doing so will reinforce substantive inequality, an eventuality exemplified in race and sex discrimination. The threshold for legally challenging pornography under classic liberal constitutions is ordinarily higher than it is under more evenly balancing systems.

This study also learned that a legal challenge must address the role of all critical and intersecting sources of inequality and disadvantage that attend a socially oppressive practice such as pornography if it is to be successful. This is consistent with the intersectional theory of discrimination, as originally articulated by Kimberle Crenshaw.[3] For instance, in contrast to more narrow and superficial formal equality approaches that require content neutrality in expressive regulations, balancing frameworks geared toward substantive equality may be better suited to assessing the complex ways that multiple disadvantages (e.g., race, sex, ethnicity, sexuality, mental or physical disability) may intersect in the context of expressive harms—grounds that are often enumerated in the constitution that supports them. With such clear mandates, the relevant laws are more attentive to the perspectives and interests of those most harmed by pornography. This intersectional approach also counters the problematic distinctions between children and adults that are often set forth in pornography and prostitution laws. Here, the evidence that many (maybe most) of the adults exploited and abused in the sex industry have been trapped in similar destructive circumstances as children cannot be ignored as it is under laws that criminalize or neglect these same people when they reach adulthood. Approaching the problem intersectionally constitutes a tacit acknowledgment that the only efficient way to address the injuries sustained by children is to extend the safety net of rights and guarantees of support into adulthood. Instead of compartmentalizing the harm, taking account of disadvantages beyond age ultimately enhances the rights and protections of everyone.

One empirical question considered is the extent to which traditional obscenity law may be employed in challenging pornography. This is an important question bearing in mind the constitutional doctrines that have thus far been less than amenable to other means of direct regulation. Seen through the lens of hierarchy theory, obscenity law was predicted to be unreliable, vague, and vulnerable to misuse. However, in the United States, producers and distributors of demonstrably harmful materials that are violent, dehumanizing, and degrading were targeted. Both the Bush and Obama administrations utilized traditional obscenity law for these purposes, even though it is not expressly aimed at materials of this kind and embraces a contemporary community standard of tolerance. Yet the indicted "obscenity" constituted pornography of the most extreme variety, presenting such acts as murder, urination, bestiality, sex with human waste, or severe violence against women as sexual entertainment. The prosecuted materials were thus emphatically not including the more prevalent abusive and degrading conduct, such as ass-to-mouth, gagging, or aggressive anal sex accompanied by the derogatory verbal aggression against women that is now commonplace in mainstream pornography. This key exclusion illustrates the limits of an approach to pornography regulation based on desensitized contemporary community standards.

In contrast to criminal obscenity laws, the empirical analysis of legal challenges indicates that a stronger civil rights framework would amplify the perspectives, interests, and knowledge of survivors of the pornography industry and others harmed by it. Criminal obscenity laws were found to discourage those harmed from seeking to influence the development of the law and privilege the perspectives of law enforcement, prosecutors, and the consensus of the public at large, the views of whom were not encouraged, in some instances not permitted, by those legal frameworks to be informed by the expertise and experience of survivors.

The findings of this study regarding the importance of constitutional frameworks are well illustrated by the relative ease with which Canada's harms-based substantive equality pornography law survived constitutional challenges on expressive grounds. It proscribes violent and dehumanizing sexually explicit presentations. In this regard, Canada stands in stark contrast to conceptually similar legal challenges pursued in the United States, where the obstacles were significantly stronger and a harms-based substantive equality law was rejected. Crucially, in *R. v. Butler* (1992) the Canadian Supreme Court held that even if "obscenity" (the Canadian law used the term, though not in reference to a traditional obscenity law) was deemed constitutionally protected expression, the law's restrictions on freedom of expression did not outweigh the importance of the legislative objectives of preventing harm and promoting equality.[4] This is all the more significant given that "obscenity" is not categorically exempted from expressive protections in Canada as it is in the United States.[5] To the contrary, the Canadian Charter of Rights and Freedoms made it possible for pornographers, their distributors, and select others to challenge the law on the grounds of free expression. But because obscene materials were found to cause harm and undermine equality—as distinct from U.S. law, where they have traditionally been unprotected—obscenity, as defined in Canadian law, lost its constitutional protection in the balance against competing interests.

A legal challenge similar to that pursued against the Canadian harms-based equality law was mounted in the United States in *American Booksellers Ass'n v. Hudnut* (1985).[6] There, a civil rights anti-pornography equality ordinance that, like the Canadian law, targeted violent, degrading, and dehumanizing materials, but defined them differently—as "graphic sexually explicit subordination" accompanied by at least one additional sub-definition—was successfully challenged on expressive grounds. In both the Canadian and American cases, substantive equality was evaluated against expressive freedoms. Only in Canada was a harms-based equality law, and a criminal law at that, found constitutional.

A detailed intra-country analysis lends further support to the predictive capacity of hierarchy theory. This is exemplified in the relative strength of women's anti-pornography movement. Although the women's anti-pornography movement had been relatively weak in Canada, the legal discourse of harm surrounding the Canadian challenges was more powerful than it was in the United States. This outcome is consistent with the heightened constitutional support for substantive equality seen in Canada. For instance, the analysis of legislative proposals in the United States during the 1980s and early 1990s revealed that many local politicians and some U.S. senators adopted the ideas of the women's movement against pornography with little apparent hesitation. By contrast, the proposals put forward by Canadian federal public inquiries and the Parliament during the same general period suggest that the Canadian women's anti-pornography movement wielded less influence on legislators than its American counterpart. Rarely, if ever, did those in government accept the ideas expressed by the Canadian movement; instead, they proposed traditional strategies, such as relying on criminal prosecution and sentencing. Likewise, the government unsuccessfully advanced sweeping legal definitions of pornography that focused on explicitness per se, not the narrower form of graphic sexually explicit subordination of women that empirical research shows contributes to sexual aggression and attitudes supporting violence against women. Hence, contemporaneous observers in Canada suggested that the women's anti-pornography movement was less concerned with the law than the analogous movement in the United States. Canadian "feminist strategies for reform of obscenity law" were said to be hampered by "a lack of strategy."[7] It provided a forum that enabled " 'an emotional purge for all women who are sickened by the extent of violent and degrading pornography' " rather than one single-mindedly dedicated to " 'the specifics of law reform.' "[8]

After *Butler*, it was clear that some version of the civil rights anti-pornography law would be constitutional in Canada, yet none has been introduced, leaving pornography's victims dependent upon the good offices of the criminal justice authorities. As pornography law after *Butler* was nonetheless more supportive of their position than what prevailed in the United States after *Hudnut*, the relative weakness of the Canadian movement bolsters the hypothesis that weighing substantive equality more heavily in balancing of constitutional interests, ceteris paribus, proportionally increases the probability that a legal challenge to pornography will be successful.

Lacking a balancing constitution expressly committed to substantive equality, the U.S. Court of Appeals for the Seventh Circuit chose to shoehorn the civil rights anti-pornography approach into the First Amendment viewpoint neutrality doctrine that has traditionally regulated political speech (or so-called secondary effects). Yet the civil rights ordinances did not regulate "viewpoints." No one was targeted for expressing a point of view, even one as extreme as advocating that women (or men) should be subordinated sexually. The ordinances specifically targeted the actual subordination that pornography enabled through its production and dissemination. They were, in other words, narrowly tailored to reach only the use of coercion in the production of pornography, or the circulation and exhibition of materials proven to cause harm. There was no analogous requirement in Canada that the legislature must draft a pornography law according to such liberal precepts as viewpoint neutrality. Moreover, unlike in the United States, judicial review in Canada did not require that its corresponding statute have to conform to legal categories traditionally recognized as unprotected, such as low-value speech, fighting words, or defamation. Categories like these were invoked by the *Hudnut* Court in rejecting the proposition that a harms-based equality approach to pornography merited a separate category, notwithstanding the fact that this had been done with respect to group libel in *Beauharnais v. Illinois*[9] and child pornography in *New York v. Ferber*.[10]

The same doctrinal straightjacket that the Seventh Circuit applied in *Hudnut*—emphasizing negative rights, that is, freedom from government intervention—was applied when Sweden's government dismissed legal challenges to the *production* of pornography on grounds that were more strictly ideological than legal. There, attempts had been made to make the executive and legislative branches take action. If they had been successful, Sweden would have ratified amendments confirming that its procuring laws against profiting from or promoting the prostitution of others also covered pornography production.

The constitutional architecture for regulating the dissemination of expression in Sweden rested on a liberal framework that had become more demanding since the 1960s. It started to require constitutional amendments each time Parliament passed new laws regulating the *distribution* of materials. But when laws concern only the conditions of *production*, there is no explicit constitutional requirement that an amendment must precede a general law before it can be applied to conduct that is otherwise integral to the production of expressive materials. For instance, a serious artist was convicted for violent resistance and dishonest conduct after staging a suicide attempt, even though her conduct was integral to the production of a movie intended to contribute to the public debate on Sweden's treatment of people with mental illness. Her case received extensive media coverage and involved the form of protected expression most vital to liberal democracies: participation in public discourse on political, social, and cultural issues. Yet her conduct was not free from legal liability simply because it was integral to the production of otherwise protected expression. Journalists and editors at a tabloid newspaper were likewise convicted for unlawfully purchasing and possessing a semiautomatic gun in a case ultimately decided by the Supreme Court; the fact that the purchase was made only to illustrate an article that described the assertedly increasing availability of illegal weapons in Sweden—an article that itself was never subject to legal action—was immaterial.[11] Similarly, several criminal cases against sex offenders who filmed their abuse with video cameras or cell phones, sometimes based on purported artistic ambitions, were decided without any defendant raising a freedom of expression defense. Neither was any sentence mitigated on account of expressive purpose. Thus, there is no apparent legal, as distinct from ideological, rationale for granting pornographers carte blanche to violate sex crime statutes in producing (otherwise potentially protected) expressive materials.

The legislative objectives of the Swedish prostitution and trafficking laws are intended to prevent the sexual exploitation of vulnerable people suffering multiple disadvantages and to counter sex inequality in society. These purposes are as valid in the context of pornography production as they are in off-camera prostitution. A 2001 Swedish government inquiry admitted that the application of procuring laws to pornography production would not "directly" target the distribution of expressive media. Indeed, it used much the same logic in concluding that no constitutional amendment was necessary for child molestation to be a crime when it was photographed or filmed by a pornographer, irrespective of bodily contact. Nonetheless, the same inquiry claimed that charging pornographers for profiting from or promoting the prostitution of others under procuring laws would indirectly infringe on their expressive freedoms. However, given the artist who was convicted for violent resistance and dishonest conduct, the newspaper employees who were convicted for illegally purchasing a gun, and the constitutional application of the criminal code to filmed sexual offenses, the inquiry's position appears to be compelled by ideology, not law. It should be challenged in courts.

The ideologically clouded conception of the legal issues raised when pornography is challenged has lent undeserved support to the pornographers, not just in Sweden. Legal defenses of pornography often cast those who exploit vulnerable populations for sex as political underdogs and dissidents—a position reached by misapplying legal doctrines derived from different empirical contexts, such as the infamous prosecutions for left-wing political views during the Red Scare (1920s), the McCarthy era (1950s), and the protests against the Vietnam War (late 1960s–1970s). With such analogies, those victimized by the production and consumers of pornography are effectively equated with government censors. This inverts reality, turning the power and inequality of men over women, pornographers over prostituted persons, upside down. Here, Karl Marx and Friedrich Engels' analogy of the "*camera obscura*," where the dominant ideology represents an inverse "upside-down" image of material reality,[12] is particularly apt.

Even though opponents often do their best to present the law as "settled," thus less amenable to change than it actually is, the legal challenges to pornography undertaken in the United States, Canada, and Sweden leave much room for improvement, notably in the provision of more effective remedies. Even the most complex legal architectures, seemingly inhospitable to substantive equality, provide numerous routes for challenges. Thus, within the constitutions characteristic of systems dominated by the liberal concept of negative rights, there remains much potential for legal challenges to pornography—challenges that would further the perspectives and interests of those harmed, albeit not as readily as "positive rights" jurisdictions.

If less overtly than the flawed analysis of the constitutionality of applying procuring laws to pornography proffered by the 2001 Swedish inquiry, the Seventh Circuit's analysis of the Indianapolis civil rights antipornography ordinance in *Hudnut* nonetheless prematurely precluded a number of options for sustaining the law without running afoul of the First Amendment. For instance, *Hudnut* presumed that under the more relaxed constitutional standard of *rational basis review*, the Supreme Court would only balance interests competing with free expression within predefined categories of speech, and not on the basis of their "content." However, in other progressive cases decided under this standard, such as *Beauharnais v. Illinois*, the Court did create new categories based on the very content they proscribed.[13] Following the Seventh Circuit's reasoning, not only would *Beauharnais* have been impossible, but the groundbreaking decision in *Brown v. Board of Education* (1954)[14] would also have been precluded because it did not rely on existing doctrinal categories, even diverging from precedent. The *Hudnut* Court accepted the evidence showing that pornography causes gender-based violence and discrimination against women in virtually all spheres of society, conceding that it was "consistent with much human experience."[15] Nonetheless, *Hudnut* took the position that preexisting doctrine barred legislators from granting women (or analogous others) the right to sue those responsible for the resulting harms.

Similarly, at the time *Brown* was decided, no prior doctrines or legal categories suggested that racial segregation in education was unconstitutional,[16] even in the face of psychological and other empirical evidence of harm.[17] If *Hudnut*'s reasoning had been applied then, racial segregation, resting on the doctrine of "separate but equal" given the Supreme Court's imprimatur in *Plessy v. Ferguson*, would still be law.[18] By analogy, there is much that can be done to challenge the harms of pornography—harms proven to be of compelling magnitude by the evidence examined here.

In the United States and Sweden, the liberal concept of negative rights is a more prominent feature of their respective legal architectures than it is in Canada. But contrary to the arguments set forth by defenders of the status quo, the obstacles to mounting a successful challenge to pornography remain more ideological than legal. That said, Canada's constitutional framework clearly presents fewer obstacles for legal challenges to pornography than those of the United States and Sweden. The obstacles in Canada are, therefore, more *political* than they are *legal*. That is, although there is a constitutional harms-based equality law against pornography production and distribution, recognition of which no ideology prevents, its remedies and potential applications can only go so far without further legislative action, an outcome which has thus far been politically precluded. A civil rights antipornography law, as yet unproposed, would almost certainly be constitutional under *Butler*. Under Canada's current pornography law, those harmed by pornography, whether they have been exploited in its production or injured by its consumers, have no right to compensation for damages. The impact of the law is also circumscribed by reliance on criminal law, where the burden of proof is higher than it is under the corresponding civil law. Perhaps most importantly, Canadian law has been stymied by courts' attachment to the concept of "community standards of tolerance" when interpreting harm, notwithstanding its inherent conflict with equality.

Canada moved away from its earlier preoccupation with "morals" and "decency" when its obscenity law was reinterpreted in the 1980s. There is nothing to prevent the courts from abandoning the community standards test in favor of one that is more firmly equality-based and more objective in its evaluation of dehumanization and degradation. Canada is, after all, partway there. The related decisions on indecency in *R. v. Labaye* (2005)[19] and child pornography in *R. v. Katigbak* (2011)[20] suggest that the role of community standards has already been weakened, such that it now serves more or less as a proxy for evidence of harm to equality and other constitutional values.[21] However, given that *Labaye* is a prostitution case under a statute that no longer exists, and the strong public consensus that child (but not adult) pornography is indefensible—not to mention the scarcity of obscenity cases since 2005—it is impossible to know to what extent *Labaye* will apply to subsequent cases of obscenity in Canada, and thereby to distinguish new from previous post-*Butler* cases. Nevertheless, social science experiments suggest that a harms-based standard can be reliably applied by lay people, including law students, to distinguish sexually explicit content that is harmful from that which is not.[22]

The Limits of Criminal Laws

Sweden's prostitution law that asymmetrically criminalizes johns and decriminalizes prostituted persons was hypothesized to illustrate the potential for more efficient challenges to pornography production since it is expressly based on a substantive equality rationale. After the passage of the 1999 sex purchase law, the prevalence of prostitution declined dramatically compared with Sweden's Scandinavian neighbors, where prostitution increased during the same period. In Denmark and Norway, estimates from around 2007 suggested that there were roughly ten times more prostituted people per capita than in Sweden. Moreover, prostituted people, survivors, informed observers, and other sources show that prostitution did not become more dangerous, unsafe, or more hidden than elsewhere. Rather, the fact that the law criminalized those taking advantage of multiply disadvantaged populations redistributed some of the power previously wielded by johns. A number of prostituted people now report having a bargaining advantage over johns, who in turn know they can be reported for mistreating the person they purchased, or attempted to purchase, for sex, while the prostituted person faces no corresponding legal jeopardy. This is in stark contrast to conditions prevailing in countries like Germany and New Zealand, where prostitution is legal. Women are occasionally murdered there in conjunction with their prostitution—something that has not occurred in Sweden since the new law was enacted. Furthermore, sex traffickers face complicated and costly hurdles not present elsewhere where sex purchasing is legal in Europe when they take steps to reduce the risk of being detected; consequently, their profits decrease.

All the positive legal consequences that have reduced prostitution and made it less dangerous would likely also be manifest if the prostitution law, including the provisions against procurement, were applied to pornography production in Sweden. Extending the statute accordingly would make Sweden even more of a global model, reducing the exploitation and abuse of those appearing in pornography while encouraging greater caution among any remaining producers.

Certainly, the Swedish substantive equality prostitution law has been successful in reducing prostitution, and the exit programs do provide support—support that should arguably be expanded—for those in prostitution to leave the institution. However, the judiciary has continued to interpret the law traditionally, regarding prostitution as a more or less "victimless" crime directed primarily against the public interest, absent more serious charges like gross procuring or human trafficking. Judges seem to perceive the law as mainly intended to prevent sexual exploitation on an aggregate level and such secondary effects as criminality and drug dealing, at the same time it promotes sex equality in general. A 2001 Supreme Court case practically dismissed the notion that a prostituted person could be the "injured party" who could claim damages for sexual exploitation by a john. Yet empirical evidence overwhelmingly shows that those bought for sex are typically in a state of heightened vulnerability, with no real alternatives to prostitution.[23] Apart from their desperate material circumstances, this situation is evident, inter alia, in the extremely high rate of mental illness found among prostituted people. A substantial proportion of them exhibit symptoms of PTSD on a level equal to that displayed by treatment-seeking Vietnam veterans and battered women seeking shelter.[24] Under these traumatogenic conditions, it is reasonable to posit that the humanity, equality, and dignity of those in prostitution are violated every time they are bought for sex. None of this empirical evidence was taken up by the Swedish courts around 2001 or later, when they determined that buying sex is primarily an offense against the public. To be fair, it is likely that the relevant legal actors were unaware of these facts while these cases were being adjudicated.

The Swedish government in 2011 clarified the law, stating that a prostituted person can bring a damage claim as an "injured party" against a john. But qualification for injured party status must be determined on a case-by-case basis before the question of damages is reached. This creates a double procedural presumption against the prostituted person that does not exist for victims of most other sexual offenses in Sweden. As yet, there have been no reports of a successful civil suit by a prostituted person against a former john in Sweden in law reports, legal databases, or in the scholarly literature that did not also involve other criminal grounds such as rape.[25]

The rationale submitted by the Swedish courts early in the new millennium for not recognizing prostituted people as being victimized as a consequence of being purchased for sex was that they "consented" to the financial agreement. However, as in Crenshaw's intersectional approach, it is vital to keep in mind that those in prostitution are burdened by disadvantages beyond gender. Moreover, prostituted people frequently lack education, job training, and a documented employment history, often as a direct result of their prostitution. They are consequently forced to engage in prostituted sex—sex that those not laboring under these, or similarly disadvantaged, circumstances would regard as rape—often simply to survive. Their "consent" to this treatment, as it has been regarded by Swedish courts, is purely fictional, typically lacking any meaningful basis in fact. Indeed, some forthright johns have described prostitution as "paid rape"—a view shared by many prostitution survivors. Unfortunately, as Catharine MacKinnon demonstrates in more general terms, the law is rarely made from the perspectives and interests of the multiply disadvantaged. More often, equality protections are available only for those who are most "similarly situated" to those who are not disadvantaged by discrimination—that is, people who are *least* in need of legal remedies.[26]

It is further apparent that multiple disadvantages and the problems that arise in seeking to address their intersections often make prostitution and pornography laws inadequate to the task of representing the perspectives and interests of those most directly harmed. This situation stands in contrast to sexual harassment law in the United States, where the display of pornography in the workplace may, under certain circumstances, be regarded as contributing to sex discrimination. Women at work are often more "similarly situated" to men than they are in other contexts. "But for" the display of pornography at work, these women would thus have been closer to a position of sex equality. It seems comparatively easy for men to recognize that harassment and discrimination are significant causes of workplace dysfunction. By extension, it is likely less difficult to persuade members of the judiciary and the public at large of the need for effective laws against it than it would be to persuade the same audiences that the display and consumption of pornography in private increases gender-based violence and attitudes trivializing violence against women in a manner that must be addressed.

Although some of the worst of pornography's harms arise in settings other than the workplace, notably in the context of prostitution and domestic abuse, there are few effective laws to redress them. It is here that those harmed (usually women or children) are the least "similarly situated" to men, and would, therefore, be most in need of equality protections. Yet, they are afforded no remedy, while often those who have a lesser disadvantage or injury are. To use Crenshaw's analogy, the situation is not unlike that of a person injured by a multiple-car accident who is left without a remedy if it is impossible to assign responsibility for all injuries to one person.[27] Put otherwise, there is no good reason that the complexity of multiple disadvantages and intersectional discrimination alone should make it harder to provide legal redress.

Returning to Sweden, it is notable that prosecutors and other law enforcement personnel who are responsible for reporting at the initial stage, whether or not there are any civil damage claims to be tried in a criminal trial, have not recognized prostituted persons as injured parties under the sex purchase law. No one has yet taken on the responsibility of representing the perspectives and interests of those most directly harmed by the offense: prostituted people. To represent them would necessitate a thorough review of accurate evidence showing why their "consent" was fictional and why buying sex constitutes an offense against their humanity, equality, and dignity. A similar lack of apparent interest and commitment was seen in Canadian criminal pornography trials both prior to and after *Butler*. There, prosecutors frequently failed to present persuasive, up-to-date social science findings showing the harms engendered, much as occurred in Sweden under the sex purchase law. They also failed to argue the constitutional equality interests at stake that recognize that those harmed by pornography belong to disadvantaged groups that merit consideration under the Canadian Charter of Rights and Freedoms. Not surprisingly, a number of ill-informed opinions were promulgated by judges who themselves had not been provided with accurate and comprehensive evidence on which to base their assessments. This, however, is unavoidable when none of the parties at trial represents the interest of those most harmed.

Criminal laws typically give the initiative to prosecutors and others in law enforcement, even when amended and reinterpreted to account for equality and harm, as Canada's obscenity law and Sweden's prostitution laws have been. These parties are naturally less interested in, or at least less cognizant of, the perspectives and interests of people harmed by pornography than such persons themselves. In contrast to survivors, criminal justice authorities are professionals who are less likely to have experienced sexual exploitation in pornography. Some have surely felt the impact of gender-based violence and other harms that ensue from pornography consumption, but that applies to any female in the general population. Yet the evidence suggests that, with rare exceptions, the harmful effects of pornography experienced by those outside the sex industry pale by comparison to those typically endured by prostituted people.[28] Those in prostitution are oftentimes doubly exposed, through the sexual exploitation that is pervasive in pornography production, and the harm caused by the consumers, for example, by johns forcing them to imitate acts depicted in specific materials.

Here, too, there are exceptions. One of them may be seen in the United States, where federal prosecutors in recent years have targeted producers and distributors of violent, dehumanizing, and degrading materials within the limits of obscenity law.[29] They have also pursued their cases despite the relative weakness of American obscenity law on issues of equality and harm, particularly in comparison to Canada, leaving them little legal basis on which to invoke equality rights. Modest exceptions notwithstanding, the general trend that emerges from the legal challenges examined here is clear: unless affirmatively addressed by policies or otherwise, criminal laws emphasize the perspectives, priorities, and interests of the government, which tend to be consistent with those of socially dominant groups, while civil rights laws prioritize the perspectives, priorities, and interests of survivors and others directly harmed by pornography and prostitution, who are typically members of socially subordinated groups. Indeed, despite the last recent uptick in federal obscenity prosecutions, U.S. law affords no civil remedies at all, such as money damages or support for those harmed by pornography who are seeking to extricate themselves from the industry. The only options upon conviction are incarceration, forfeiture, or fines selectively imposed on pornographers.

Additionally, obscenity law is governed by the ambiguous and inegalitarian "community standard of tolerance" test, which may lead to very different outcomes depending on how the community views sexual subordination. Recent American efforts to combat adult pornography have targeted more extreme materials, which is likely one factor contributing to their relative success. A case filed against a mainstream producer was dismissed in

2010 on technical grounds,[30] leaving the reach of this approach somewhat unclear. Even there, some more extreme fringe materials were used to support the indictment amid otherwise unexceptional pornography, once again demonstrating the limits of the community standards approach.[31] Also telling is an obscenity decision handed down in British Columbia in 2004 that invoked community standards to support the acquittal of a producer of abusive sadomasochistic pornography under *Butler*.[32] The case was hampered by inadequate evidence and the absence of an intervening party representing prostitution survivors or others who had actually been harmed in the production or by the consumers of the challenged materials.[33] However, a 2012 case in Ontario reached a very different conclusion. There, a producer-distributor of materials that depicted no sexual activity—only explicit sexualized renderings that combined sex and lethal violence against women—was convicted.[34]

The mixed results ensuing from the criminal law framework of obscenity law, even in its modified Canadian form that partly accounts for subordination and harm, epitomizes its unreliability as an arena for mounting successful challenges to pornography. Certainly, the message to producers, driven by an unvarnished profit motive, is unclear. The Supreme Court of Canada's related decision on indecency in *Labaye* in 2005, and on child pornography in *Katigbak* six years later, may have weakened the role of community standards. The post-*Butler* obscenity decisions should nonetheless discourage legislatures and courts from continuing to rely on community standards of tolerance, especially when they are permitted to mediate the determination of harm. Inequality is, by definition, often tolerated in unequal societies. Employing community standards accepts the popular consensus regarding what is and is not harmful. Yet the perspective that emerges is largely determined by the powerful, not concrete evidence and the perspectives of survivors of the harms of pornography.

The problems of relying on criminal law and the benefits of a more survivor-centric approach are apparent when comparing the seminal *Butler* decision with post-*Butler* law. The Courts Challenges Program, which provided support to disadvantaged groups to intervene in constitutional cases, likely facilitated a women's organization's intervention in *Butler*, namely, the Women's Legal Education and Action Fund. Once there, the organization presented an original and well-conceived sex equality argument that incorporated references to current social science in support of a harms-based obscenity law being challenged on expressive grounds. Since *Butler*, however, the pornographers have appealed major obscenity convictions, mostly with success and with the effect of narrowing the law's reach. Combined with the fact that the Crown all but stopped applying the obscenity law to adult pornography, there have been few occasions for progressive interventions since then. If Canada had an anti-pornography civil rights law unrestricted by the criminal approach to obscenity, by contrast, those directly hurt by pornography could initiate legal action without having to wait for the government or anyone else to make that decision.

A similar pattern suggesting that enabling the representation of the perspectives and interests of disadvantaged groups is key to success can be seen in legislative challenges. For instance, several American legislatures proposed theoretically and empirically sound civil rights challenges to pornography that were strongly influenced by the women's anti-pornography movement. By contrast, their Canadian counterparts failed to propose any effective legislation during the same period under the influence of a women's anti-pornography movement that was seemingly weaker. In other words, the strength of the representation afforded in practice had a significant impact on the policy output. This finding is consistent with the literature on general challenges to gender-based violence. Pertinent here is the sizeable cross-national comparison of seventy countries with panel data since 1975, which suggests that the strength of autonomous feminist social movements was by far the most significant factor in increasing the likelihood that effective policies relating to violence against women would be adopted.[35] It proved more important than the percentage of women in government, national wealth, the ratification of relevant international laws, and the involvement of left-wing parties.[36] Likewise, representation of the perspectives and interests of those most harmed by pornography in the politics of social movements is here shown to be essential to undertaking effective legal challenges and achieving real legal change.

The Potential of Civil Rights Laws

As an alternative approach to criminal law that would better address the intersectional character of pornography and prostitution's harms, the civil rights approach to pornography as sex discrimination, originally conceived by Catharine MacKinnon and Andrea Dworkin, was attempted in several U.S. jurisdictions, with parts of the ordinance proposed on the federal level.

The evidence showing how the criminal approach is improved with input from those more directly affected, as in the Canadian Supreme Court *Butler* case in 1992, implies that a victim-centered survivor-driven law would provide a more effective challenge. In MacKinnon and Dworkin's civil rights approach, the initiative to use and apply the law is accorded to those harmed, who are able to sue for damages either in a court or in an alternative administrative body. No prosecutors or other law enforcement personnel are involved, and there are no criminal penalties—only damages to plaintiffs who have proven the harms asserted.

The civil rights approach to pornography was built upon the experiences, perspectives, and interests of those most harmed. It originated in Minneapolis in an environment where neighborhood activists were exposed to the harms of pornography when the city zoned poor neighborhoods with relatively little political influence to permit pornography stores, strip clubs, and so-called adult movie theaters. The resulting conditions gave activists insight into the harms produced by the sex industry that is rare among those who are not themselves survivors of prostitution and gender-based violence. With the support of scholars and politicians, these activists took the challenge to the city council. From Minneapolis, the civil rights approach spread to other jurisdictions and succeeded in passing a similar ordinance in Indianapolis and in Bellingham, Washington (the latter by referendum). These cities were sued, and the law was invalidated in federal courts before anyone had the opportunity to use it, disposed of through lawsuits where no one with standing under the ordinance's own terms was represented, except among amici curiae.

In contrast to obscenity laws, criminal pornography laws, or other civil law approaches (e.g., sexual harassment laws that apply only in the workplace), the ordinances were drafted as a means of promoting substantive equality, recognizing disadvantaged groups, and representing the perspectives and interests of the groups demonstrably harmed by pornography according to the best empirical evidence available. The legislative findings that formed the basis of these legal challenges are consistent with the evidence assessed here. They correctly identified pornography as "central in creating and maintaining the civil inequality of the sexes," "a systematic practice of exploitation and subordination based on sex which differentially harms women."[37] This position clearly underscored substantive equality as what is at stake and recognized the indispensable role of disadvantaged groups comprised of those most harmed in the production of pornography and by its consumers.

Additionally, the ordinances specifically addressed such intersectional problems as poverty, racial discrimination, childhood abuse, and the lack of alternative sources of income, specifying defenses that may not be used to counter the claims of those who may use the ordinance to sue for coercion into pornography. Particular facts about the plaintiff that are readily subject to bias and misrepresentation were expressly barred, such as prior performance in pornography, purported consent to the conduct displayed, receipt of payment, or apparent cooperation.[38]

Compared with the other legal challenges studied here, the civil rights antipornography ordinances employ the most scientifically sound definition of pornography that is consistent with the evidence of its harms. Experiments with law students suggest that the ordinances can be applied to harmful materials without resulting in overbroad or vague misattributions to harmless materials, in contrast to U.S. obscenity law and other alternatives that are less amenable to uniform application.[39] The ordinance's definition of actionable materials as confined to the "graphic sexually explicit subordination of women" (or others similarly subordinated) is also more refined than the Canadian violence, degradation, and dehumanization test, in part because the ordinance includes at least one additional element, for example, women who are "presented as sexual objects who enjoy pain or humiliation . . . who experience sexual pleasure in being raped . . . [or] are presented as sexual objects for domination, conquest, violation, exploitation, possession, or use, or through postures or positions of servility or submission or display."[40] There is reciprocity between the definitional elements of pornography set forth in the civil rights ordinances and the categories of pornography demanded by consumers, the acts of abuse or subordination inflicted on women who must produce them, and the acts of abuse or subordination inflicted on women as a result of pornography consumption. In these senses, the ordinances represent the perspectives of those disadvantaged groups most harmed by the social practice of pornography. Corroborated by social science evidence and experiential accounts, the definition is also consistent with social reality. It was based on the latest research that existed at the time, the findings of which have since been strengthened through repeated corroboration.

Furthermore, by relying on civil rather than criminal law, the ordinances place the power in the hands of those who need it most, as opposed to public representatives with many other priorities, pressures, and interests besides benefiting those harmed by pornography. This shifting of legal power is consistent with promoting substantive equality at the level of procedure and makes pornographers directly accountable to those they harm rather than the state, as occurs under criminal obscenity laws. No criminal penalties, such as fines or imprisonment, would be applied—only damage awards to those plaintiffs who proved harm. The causes of action specified under the ordinances are only available to those who have been demonstrably harmed by pornography—not to prosecutors or others in law enforcement. Hence, (1) "trafficking in pornography" would be actionable because the dissemination of pornography contributes to discrimination against women; (2) "coercion into pornography performance" would be actionable because pornography production usually exploits those who are multiply disadvantaged and mired in circumstances that are tantamount to sexual coercion, rape, or sexual slavery; (3) "forcing pornography on a person" would be actionable much as it is in the sexual harassment context, but it would include non-work settings; and (4) "assault or physical attack due to pornography" would be actionable when it could be reasonably proven that an assault was inspired by pornography, such as when a john forces a prostituted person to imitate specific acts portrayed in pornographic materials or when a rapist repeatedly refers to them, as numerous studies have documented they do.

Several other laws contain some elements of the civil rights approach to pornography. These are exemplified in workplace sexual harassment law in the United States, constitutional litigation in Canada that incorporates processes that facilitate the intervention of disadvantaged groups, and sex crimes statutes in Sweden under which civil damages can be claimed by plaintiffs, a category that technically includes laws against the purchase of sex, procuring, and sex trafficking. Nevertheless, no jurisdiction has attempted to pursue the civil rights approach to pornography as it was envisioned in Minneapolis and Indianapolis in the mid-1980s. This study shows that there are no significant legal obstacles to undertaking such an effort either in the United States or Canada. Any jurisdiction that recognizes equality as a human right has the foundation necessary to pass an anti-pornography civil rights ordinance. It appears, however, that a constitutional amendment would be needed under current doctrine in Sweden to enact causes of actions that target dissemination, which would basically require two parliamentary decisions with a simple majority and an election in between.[41] That said, an amendment would not be needed to target pornography production using Sweden's trafficking laws or, more efficiently, to apply the procuring laws that criminalize anyone who promotes or exploits a person's paid temporary sex in order to make pornography.[42] Contrary to the government's inconsistent dismissal of the latter route in 2001,[43] these laws should already be applicable to pornography production in the same manner as a serious artist can be convicted for crimes like violent resistance or dishonest conduct, even when the conduct at issue is integral to the production of otherwise lawful expressive materials. Similarly, sexual offenders are not free from liability merely because they film their abuse.

Civil rights ordinances, more than any other kind of law, would promote the interests of those most affected by the harms of pornography. They would, for the first time, give those harmed a voice in the legal process and a tangible incentive to testify publicly to the injuries caused by pornography. No such incentives exist today. Quite the contrary, survivors continue to be disbelieved, ridiculed, trivialized, reviled, even persecuted for revealing their sexual abuse in public. Although the #MeToo movement seems to be changing the dynamic in at least some places, a noted effect on people who consume pornography is to make them more likely to trivialize violence against women. This effect, in turn, can make consumers even more defiant in denying harm. The pornography industry is also tirelessly trying to present itself as legitimate entertainment. The orchestrated P.R. campaign in 1986 to discredit the U.S. Attorney General's Commission on Pornography exemplifies its sway over public opinion,[44] including over women who, as recalled, may not be familiar with the actual content of pornography. By contrast, the civil rights approach to litigating the harms has the potential to make them much more visible to the public, thus not only providing remedies for those immediately affected but also properly educating the citizenry. Being founded on women's consciousness-raising and organizing against men's violence, it is no coincidence that the ordinances can have these extra-legal implications.

The Postmodern Critique of the Civil Rights Approach

The postmodern approach to legal challenges to practices of group subordination, which is opposed to hierarchy theory, has been held out as a viable theoretical alternative.[45] In the 1980s and 1990s, some postmodern theorists vocally opposed the American civil rights approach—not only as applied to pornography, but also in the case of hate speech. To cite one notable example, Judith Butler argued that the civil rights approach to pornography, or something similar applied to hate speech, might be "misappropriated" by the state.[46] Because the civil rights approach to adult pornography has never been systematically attempted, her argument relies on hypothetical scenarios and arguably analogous evidence. In order to evaluate her critique of the civil rights approach, it is, therefore, necessary to scrutinize the suitability and accuracy of Butler's hypotheticals and analogies, perforce given her stature within postmodern feminist thought.

Butler bases her argument mainly on two empirical examples: a 1990 obscenity prosecution that was ultimately unsuccessful, and a policy governing same-sex sexual conduct in the military from around the same time.[47] In her first example—the 1990 obscenity prosecution of the rap group 2 Live Crew—she provides no details about the events leading up to the case or the case itself, apparently presuming these facts are common knowledge, which they are not. However, others have also written about the indictment, including Crenshaw, who has commented on the intersection of racial and feminist politics in the public's response.[48] Informed observers thus know that members of 2 Live Crew were arrested for an allegedly obscene performance at an "adults-only club" in Florida in June 1990.[49] They were later acquitted of those charges.[50] Moreover, two days before their arrest, their album, *As Nasty As They Wanna Be*, had also been deemed obscene by a federal district court in Florida, although that determination was reversed on appeal.[51] Even though they were unsuccessful in the judicial outcomes, Butler interprets the indictments of 2 Live Crew as attempts to attack African American vernacular culture and governmental abuses of power. The rap genre "may not," she additionally contends, "be recognizable to the court."[52] Furthermore, she asserts, "the arbitrary and tactical use of obscenity law" invests "the courts with the power to regulate such expressions" and "produces new occasions for discrimination."[53] Yet Butler never mentions that 2 Live Crew's appearances were saturated with a discourse in which Black women were presented as " 'cunts,' 'bitches,' and all-purpose 'hos' "—a fact that Crenshaw highlights.[54] Although reluctant to quote their lyrics for fear of reinforcing racist stereotypes about Black men, Crenshaw explains that "listening to *Nasty*, we hear about 'cunts' being 'fucked' until backbones are cracked, asses being 'busted,' 'dicks' rammed down throats, and semen splattered across faces."[55]

Butler's analysis is not intersectional. It recognizes only the racist aspects of the government's pursuit of 2 Live Crew, ignoring the misogyny entirely. That said, the selective attempted enforcement of an obscenity law that is not employed to prosecute white misogynistic artists against a Black rap group—not to mention the nude dancing shows and "adult bookstores" that were selling pornography where the arrest took place—is suspicious.[56] Crenshaw notes that, while 2 Live Crew was arrested, the white comedy artist Andrew Dice Clay appeared on an HBO program singing lyrics like "'Eenie, meenie, minee, mo / Suck my [expletive] and swallow slow,' and 'Lose the bra, bitch.'"[57] A female cast member and the artist Sinead O'Connor canceled their scheduled appearances on the episode of *Saturday Night Live* that included Clay,[58] who is also known for his blatantly racist jokes.[59]

Using the unsuccessful prosecution of 2 Live Crew in an attempt to show how the civil rights anti-pornography ordinances could be misappropriated and thereby lead to discrimination against others relies on three misunderstandings. First, the type of expression produced by 2 Live Crew cannot be usefully reduced to "established African American genres of folk art," as Butler claims.[60] More precision is required. As Crenshaw observes, even though humor and irony can sometimes disarm an oppressor, as it sometimes does in popular culture, the identity of the performer matters:

> Although one could argue that Black comedians have broader license to market stereotypically racist images, that argument has no force here. 2 Live Crew cannot claim an in-group privilege to perpetuate misogynist humor against Black women: the members of 2 Live Crew are not Black women, and more importantly, they enjoy a power relationship over them.[61]

Because the indicted speech served not only a form of irony and humor among oppressed groups but also targeted Black women—making it a form of oppression—the example of 2 Live Crew cannot explain how a civil rights law against discrimination and oppression based on sex, both exacerbated by pornography, would not work as intended.

Butler's second misunderstanding is to ignore that the attempt to prosecute 2 Live Crew was made under an obscenity statute, not an anti-discrimination law. As a legal concept, obscenity has been roundly criticized for its conceptual problems, including within scholarship that contributed to the creation of the civil rights anti-pornography ordinance.[62] Butler's misappropriation claim is thus neither original nor integral to postmodernism. Furthermore, it appears she is simply barking up the wrong tree. The ordinance was proposed as an alternative to obscenity law, which would also reduce the potential for government misuse.[63] Obscenity is a vague and idiosyncratic concept that is not victim-centered. Thus, American obscenity law proscribes the appeal to prurient interests in the representation of sex, where it lacks cultural value and is patently offensive to prevailing community standards.[64] None of these strictures was incorporated into the civil rights anti-pornography ordinances. Indeed, one of the central reasons referred to for why the ordinance was struck down in *Hudnut* was that it did *not* track obscenity law.[65]

Butler's third error is to ignore that the attempted prosecution of 2 Live Crew is not equivalent to filing a civil complaint under an anti-discrimination or hate speech statute. The obscenity law applied was enforced by the state—not by an individual plaintiff able to prove harm. Under the civil rights ordinances, that power would not be accorded to the state. Only survivors of pornography-related injuries, or those provably impacted by sex discrimination, would be so empowered. In a sloppy legal analysis, Butler ignores these major distinctions. All in all, the use of 2 Live Crew to demonstrate the potential for governmental misuse of a civil rights ordinance aimed at either hate speech or pornography is tenuous at best, misleading at worst.

The second empirical example Butler proffers in support of her argument is the policy on same-sex sexual conduct in the military announced by President Clinton on July 19, 1993,[66] colloquially referred to as "don't ask, don't tell."[67] That policy was discontinued by President Obama approximately eighteen years later, when he proclaimed it ineffective as of September 20, 2011.[68] On its face, the intention of the policy was the opposite of a civil rights law meant to empower socially disadvantaged groups. Simply put, "don't ask, don't tell" discriminated against minorities. Members of the LGBTQ community could be discharged for conduct as benign as holding hands with or kissing a service member of the same sex, in or out of uniform. A serviceman or woman could be discharged for making "a statement" acknowledging that he or she was "homosexual or bisexual," or for entering into "a marriage or attempted marriage to someone of the same gender."[69] Needless to say, heterosexuals were not subject to separation for analogous conduct. One of the underlying objectives was to protect the perceived interest of heterosexual military personnel in avoiding exposure to non-conformist sexual identities and practices.[70] However, heterosexuals as a group have never been included among the protected "discrete and insular minorities" under the Fourteenth Amendment granted solicitude in the famous footnote 4 of the *Carolene Products* case.[71] Nor could they be. Heterosexuals are not, as a majority population, similar to vulnerable groups thought to be protected by hate speech statutes or anti-pornography ordinances. Obviously, then, "don't ask, don't tell" was not meant to counter discrimination; rather, the policy itself discriminated against sexual minorities.

A policy that on its face discriminates against a vulnerable minority is a singularly infelicitous means of demonstrating how another policy or law with the opposite intention might be misused by the state. Nonetheless, Butler queries: "As difficult and painful as it is to imagine, could the military have targeted this form of utterance as a codifiable offense without the precedent of sexual harassment law and its extension into the areas of pornography and hate speech?"[72] Yes, the military could. And did. Such "utterances," here, regarding coming out, were targeted long before the implementation of "don't ask, don't tell" and sexual harassment law. Gays had been officially banned from serving in the military fifty years before the prohibition was expressed in "don't ask, don't tell."[73] During that era, the U.S. military could discharge gay people solely for being gay, even when they had not stated, or "uttered," their sexual orientation. Investigations could be conducted to find out whether a service member was gay irrespective of any statement, much less conduct, to that effect.[74] That was perforce the outcome when a man or woman in the military verbally expressed their non-heterosexual status.

Besides Butler's misuse of legal terminology—a policy cannot create an "offense," and discharge is not a criminal sanction—her question as to whether "don't ask, don't tell" would have been possible without laws against sexual harassment and hate speech or the civil rights anti-pornography ordinances also presumes that such a discriminatory policy turned on an "utterance." However, whether official policies proscribed utterances or conduct, those that discriminate against socially vulnerable groups have existed for a very long time. Indeed, proscriptions on "utterances" predated those targeting sexual harassment, hate speech, and pornography, and existed before civil rights laws had been created. For instance, for ages, many countries criminalized utterances reflecting negatively on the head of state. Here, too, Butler is barking up the wrong tree. "Don't ask, don't tell" has an entirely different lineage and a theoretical basis that is antithetical to civil rights law. The association between a discriminatory policy against LGBTQ service members and laws against hate speech and forms of discrimination to which pornography contributes is therefore highly inapposite.

Just as the Seventh Circuit misrepresented the ordinance's definition of pornography as targeting "depictions" and "viewpoints" rather than a social "practice" of "subordination,"[75] Butler appears to have misapprehended the civil rights approach to pornography. For instance, she claims that the drafters of the anti-pornography ordinances were "[r]elying on recently proposed hate speech regulation"[76] but provides no support or citation to the regulation referenced.[77] Based on my extensive research, I am confident that no such regulation exists. Butler further contends that MacKinnon (one of the drafters) "never makes clear how being depicted within pornography is the same as being addressed by it. The equation, however, is central to her argument to extend [Mari] Matsuda's position to include the pornographic text."[78] Here, Butler fashions out of whole cloth an argument that has never been set forth in relation to the ordinances. Nowhere does the legislative history or MacKinnon herself refer to pornography as a "text," say that "being depicted" or "being addressed" by pornography is the target of the legislation, or make reference to "Matsuda's position." Butler should also know that the ordinances were proposed in 1983, antedating the relevant work of Matsuda.

Beyond the misinformation, misconceptions of the ordinances similar to Butler's mar the Seventh Circuit's opinion in *Hudnut*, which repeatedly equates pornography as defined by the ordinance with "speech" and "viewpoints."[79] In contrast to the professed analogy with pornography, Hitler did not need to exploit or abuse anyone to produce his orations, which may also be said to embody speech and viewpoints (e.g., claims that Jews and other minorities were *Untermenschen*). The court effectively casts the ordinance as if it provides a cause of action for publicly expressing, be it in a newspaper, on television, or at a conference, the viewpoint that women should be sexually subordinated—something it does not do. The ordinance does not reach expression that is neither graphic, explicit, nor sexually subordinating, as pornography demonstrably is.[80] In legal terms, like an ordinance prohibiting the destruction of public property, even if politically motivated, the interest of the anti-pornography ordinance is "unrelated to the suppression of free expression," and its "incidental restriction on alleged First Amendment freedoms is no greater than is essential to the furtherance of that interest."[81]

In contrast to Butler, though, the Seventh Circuit acknowledges that evidence substantiates the harmful effects of pornography.[82] Although the court erred in refusing to recognize these harms as a "compelling interest" that could sustain the ordinance,[83] at least their existence, and by implication their viability, was acknowledged. Butler never even considers pornography's harms. She devotes not a single sentence to what pogroms, rape, discrimination, and harassment mean concretely for those who are subjected to them.[84] Any extended analysis of the susceptibility of hate speech or pornography laws to governmental misuse that omits mention of the harmful effects that statutes and ordinances of this kind were intended to stop is inherently biased. It is possible that Butler ignores concrete harms based on the conviction that racists and their targets both have equal power over speech, including its impact on discourse and society, superstructure and base. At least, that is what she suggests: "[I]f utterances can be the bearers of equivocal meanings, then their power is, in principle, less unilateral and sure than it appears. Indeed . . . words that seek to injure might well miss their mark and produce an effect counter to the one that is intended."[85] But what if they "might well" not? If language was as ambivalent and airy as Butler claims it is, then Crenshaw must surely be wrong in asserting that because "the members of 2 Live Crew are not Black women, and more importantly, they enjoy a power relationship over them," it is inappropriate to equate their "misogynist humor against Black women" as "just jokes" not "meant to injure or to be taken literally."[86] At least the empirical social science data exposing the injuries of pornography is not as equivocal as Butler would have it.

When Butler questions whether language can produce meanings that are unambivalent, she is, in effect, questioning whether there is such a thing as social power over speech as Crenshaw and supporters of hate speech laws conceive it. In this respect, Butler goes even further than the Seventh Circuit in trivializing the harms accruing from hate speech and pornography. The Seventh Circuit at least acknowledges that different groups have unequal power over speech: "Racial bigotry, anti-Semitism . . . influence the culture and shape our socialization. None is directly answerable by more speech, unless that speech too finds its place in the popular culture. . . . At any time, some speech is ahead in the game; the more numerous speakers prevail."[87] Yet even this grudging acknowledgment misses the mark. It is not the case that more powerful speakers are necessarily more numerous; their voices are simply amplified by their power. In any event, following the liberal concept of negative rights, the court does not regard unequal access to speech as an issue calling for governmental intervention. For instance, the Seventh Circuit claims that the "Supreme Court has rejected the position that speech must be 'effectively answerable' to be protected by the Constitution."[88] However, it does not say that power over speech is equal, or that the speech of Nazis might produce pro-Jewish results. By contrast, Butler treats unequal access to speech as unproblematic.

Although this study has not taken as its task a thoroughgoing review of the postmodern approach to challenging gender-based violence and inequality, it is telling that one of its most celebrated exponents relies on misplaced analogies, even errors, in order to criticize the civil rights ordinances.

Butler's account minimizes the potential inherent in the civil rights antipornography ordinances. The ordinances are consistent with the social science evidence and aim to promote substantive equality. As such, they are narrowly tailored to reach only those materials that contribute to gender-based violence and other forms of discrimination. Unlike any legal approach conceived or attempted to date, laws of this kind would further the interests of those directly injured with minimal impact on other expressive interests.

Extended Implications

In light of the need for efficient and effective policy responses to the major problems of our times, it is also worthwhile to consider the broader insights that may be gained through the study of legal challenges to pornography. The findings set forth here suggest that the successful resolution of some of the most intractable problems relating to inequality and social dominance will require democracies to rethink their use of law. There is nothing inherently unique about this study's approach to the imperatives of substantive equality and its emphasis on the perspectives and interests of disadvantaged groups as a means of promoting it. Many contemporary political problems could be broached in a similar manner.

Reliance on criminal law, although useful where only the state can legitimately claim the initiative, is in many ways deficient. It is diminished both by a substantive equality deficit and a problem of legitimacy when it is used to represent democratic perspectives and interests under conditions of group oppression and social hierarchy. In such situations, police, prosecutors, and other public authorities, who might not have a vested interest in maintaining social dominance, may nevertheless lack the resolve necessary to counter oppression effectively. Accomplishing these ends calls for a shift in legal authority away from the state to make it more accessible to members of disadvantaged groups and their legitimate representatives whose commitment to achieving redress is bound to be stronger. There are undoubtedly other social maladies that would benefit from a similar change in focus toward the provision of civil rights to those in need of empowerment as well as to those who are already working within autonomous organizations to end their oppression.

Groups affected by hate crimes, systemic discrimination, or such forms of gender-based violence as rape and domestic abuse come to mind. The complaints routinely reported in media about law enforcement's failure to respond or act vigorously in response to these realities are instructive. Might an overall change in emphasis toward social groups, thereby facilitating a devolution of power that would redound to the benefit of civil rights, with support for autonomous organization and litigation, be a more appropriate approach for the twenty-first century? This study suggests as much. The state could provide its assistance, including a forum for civil society, rather than acting as a powerbroker and fountainhead of decision-making. Moreover, given the overburdened incarceration systems and finite resources that prevail in many democracies, a shift from criminal to civil sanctions and remedies merits further consideration. Prisons, jails, and other carceral institutions might be necessary in cases where perpetrators would otherwise cause serious harm or there are no viable alternative sanctions, remedies, and injunctions that can be reliably enforced. Examples include repeat offenders, members of organized crime syndicates, and terrorists. Apart from such examples, perhaps imprisonment should be restricted to those extreme circumstances in which no other sanction befits the crime (e.g., murder or manslaughter) or is proportional to the gravity of the offense (e.g., crimes against humanity or genocide).

Distinct conceptions of civil rights may also be more appropriate for developing countries. The forms of decision-making typically seen in international fora empower affluent countries with, for example, a veto against just compensation for their role in global warming. This power occurs, in Ian Shapiro's words, "by virtue of the decision-making procedure."[89] Recall that in March 2014, several affluent countries refused to accept the World Bank's $100 billion annual estimates of the cost of offsetting the adverse effects of climate change on poor countries that had contributed "virtually nothing" to global warming—countries that will be among the first to be victimized when "climatic disruptions intensify."[90] Climate politics is thus aggravated by an arguably unjust requirement that a consensus be reached among unequally situated parties—that is, between those who dominate and those who are subordinated. Democratic problems like these are similar to the politics of legal challenges to pornography and gender-based violence studied here. Both present complex and intractable challenges to strong "vested interests" that contribute to the "existing norms," which reproduce harmful practices at the expense of those harmed.[91] Such vested interests—wealthy countries, pornographers, and pornography consumers—are disinclined to change norms that demonstrably contribute to indefensible injustices, including gender-based violence and humanitarian catastrophes, despite overwhelming evidence of their culpability in causing the injuries from which they themselves may benefit.

During his career, James E. Hansen, a retired NASA climate scientist who participated in civil suits against the federal government and other entities, "repeatedly called for trying the most vociferous climate-change deniers for 'crimes against humanity.'"[92] Indeed, on account of the notoriety they have achieved for their reckless disregard for the ways in which the disinformation they promulgate may impact humanity, the idea of holding the most vociferous and influential climate-change deniers accountable is not entirely unprecedented. For instance, Julius Streicher, the infamous publisher of the well-circulated anti-Semitic publication *Der Stürmer* (1923–1945), in his "speeches and articles, week after week, month after month . . . infected the German mind with the virus of anti-Semitism and incited the German people to active persecution" by spreading lies, bigotry, and hatred.[93] He was subsequently convicted of crimes against humanity and sentenced to death by hanging.[94]

Certainly, many of us, if confronted with our undeserved privilege, might react by contesting the facts presented and disavowing any responsibility for the resulting injustice, just as deniers of the harms of pornography, global warming, and the Holocaust have done, at least initially. Yet, to have a substantial and sustainable impact on any major social problem, it is necessary for the public, political decision-makers, and the courts to face the facts as they are, illuminated by the knowledge gained through decades of rigorous scientific and social scientific study. Indeed, we take pride in distinguishing ourselves from earlier civilizations that believed the Earth was flat and the center of the universe. However, considering the harms of pornography and global warming, and the magnitude of the effort that will be required to overcome them, the distinction between contemporary enlightenment and past credulity may be more exaggerated than we would care to believe.

Like pornography, there are aspects of global warming that are related to social dominance and multiply disadvantaged groups that will necessitate concerted legal challenges in the future. Climate change will almost certainly affect populations around the globe asymmetrically and unequally. Developing nations have demanded compensation, most emphatically from the early industrializers, to offset the myriad adverse effects of global warming produced by the beneficiaries of cheap natural resources and laissez-faire regulation of the emission of greenhouse gases. The need for restitution is especially acute in the face of the tremendous sacrifices that may be required of people around the world if we are to reverse and protect ourselves from the profound effects of global warming that are now unavoidable. Indeed, even the Pentagon, not known as a leader in climate politics, has concluded that the effects of global warming include "increased risks from terrorism, infectious disease, global poverty and food shortages," as well as "rising demand for military disaster responses as extreme weather creates more global humanitarian crises."[95] Yet the political representatives of nations who are in a superior position economically, politically, and militarily have frequently exhibited greater interest in contesting the extent of their contribution to the vulnerability of developing countries to harms induced by climate change than committing to future change, far less compensation for the past.[96]

Presently, the problems attending global warming are, as with pornography, governed by a detached deliberative politics of "consensus" that is primarily controlled by dominant nations and interest groups far removed from those most adversely affected. To date, the politics of deliberation and consensus has yielded little of substance, as those contesting substantive legal challenges to pornography, be it pornographers, consumers, governments, or courts, rarely acknowledge the ideological basis of their resistance. As shown here, there are numerous legal routes available for challenging pornography more efficiently—none of which requires constitutional amendments or complex doctrinal changes. In Sweden, the existing procuring laws could be applied to pornography production. In the United States, a compelling governmental interest in eliminating sex discrimination can be found to sustain civil rights anti-pornography ordinances, which could be passed again at any time. Alternatively, the definition of pornography articulated in the model ordinance could be regarded as a new unprotected expressive category, as was done in the case of group libel in the mid-twentieth century. Then again, intermediate scrutiny could be applied, as the ordinances' incidental restrictions on expressive freedoms are proportional to the interest of countering sex discrimination and the target of regulation is the social practice of subordination, not any "viewpoints" expressed. Even in Canada, where it evidently has not been proposed, the community standard of tolerance test could be abandoned by the courts in favor of the more fact-sensitive dehumanization test.[97] And a civil law to remediate pornography's harms patterned on the civil rights ordinances would undoubtedly be regarded as a constitutional equality-promoting remedy.

As this study demonstrates, when the perspectives and interests of affected groups are not systemically taken into account, the result leads to useless obscenity laws, similarly ineffectual policies, or inefficient legislation that either does not pass or, when efficient, is shortly invalidated by courts that are variously misinformed and ideologically driven. What exists, then, is a limited and ineffective state-initiated regulatory regime that rests mainly on criminal laws that are hardly enforced, and when they are, it is typically the more extreme cases—cases that ought to be hard to lose—which are prosecuted, yet lose them prosecutors frequently do.[98] In this sense, and certainly in this instance, state-directed legal approaches that ignore multiply disadvantaged groups are bound to be incomplete and inefficient. Extending this insight to the context of global warming, organizations like the Pentagon and the World Bank—however laudable their concern about the impact of climate change—do not represent the most vulnerable and multiply disadvantaged populations. Not now, at least. In actuality, they represent an aggregation of national and global interests, channeled through deliberative procedures within governing bodies at both levels that, not unlike the underlying dynamics of criminal obscenity laws and contemporary community standards of tolerance, strive for consensus among those already empowered. These two organizations have neither the social consciousness nor the perspectives and interests of those most adversely affected in mind, as would be necessary to generate the knowledge most useful in designing appropriate policy. Here again, no meaningful steps toward remediation have thus far been taken. Yet, perhaps due to the dearth of available remedies, these organizations have articulated enlightened positions on global warming, underscoring the daunting challenges that lie ahead. Maybe it is because climate change affects them, too. Regardless, to actually address those compelling concerns, a more broadly empowering civil rights–focused legal challenge would surely be propitious.

It is certainly imperative that more power be granted to developing countries in climate change negotiations to offset and repair the damage caused by wealthier countries—preferably codified in international law rather than granted ad hoc on the basis of compromises grudgingly accepted in the interest of achieving a consensus that is often fleeting. Likewise, this study shows that we need to grant real, substantial, and effective legal power to members of those groups most affected if the harms of pornography are to be successfully addressed. This conclusion draws on empirical evidence of legal challenges undertaken in three diverse democracies. The evidence is further corroborated by research on social movements opposing gender-based violence and interpreted through the lenses of apposite political theories. The single most persistent, indeed salient, implication of this study is this: intractable problems of inequality, such as pornography and global warming, can only be successfully countered by placing the perspectives and interests of those most immediately affected at the law's center. In the case of pornography, these are the same groups that historically have been largely excluded from lawmaking, including in democracies.

With regard to the contemporary problems attending prostitution and pornography, survivor-led social movements in the form of numerous legitimate nongovernmental organizations already exist. In this instance, a public partnership may be most appropriate.[99] Concomitantly, the legal design of the civil rights anti-pornography approach is consistent with the empowerment of organizations like these, which could represent and assist individuals who would have greater difficulty attempting to enforce legal rights on their own. Under criminal laws, by contrast, the government has the power to initiate legal action, not those who are victimized. When governments do not act to apply their laws against pornography, there are no means for survivors to intervene. Civil rights laws would shift this distribution of power and put the legal initiative into the hands of those who are hurt, who have the most substantial incentives to act. The exploitation and abuse that pornography's production inflicts on members of the disadvantaged groups used to make it, with the sexual aggression and gender-based violence it inflicts on society at large, including in prostitution, through its consumers, pose urgent problems calling for democratic solutions. Nothing short of recognizing this reality for what it is, countering this powerful industry's propaganda and disinformation campaigns, while rethinking democratic mechanisms for representation and accountability to provide effective civil rights to the as yet forsaken people harmed, will change it.

Notes

Introduction

1. Helena Rohdén, Carin Nyman, and Maria Edström, "Påverkar omsorgsansvar våra åsikter?," in *I framtidens skugga*, ed. Lennart Weibull, Henrik Oscarsson, and Annika Bergström (Gothenburg: SOM Institute, 2012), 115.
2. Karin Johansson and Kenan Habul, "Varannan ung väljare vill förbjuda porr," *Sydsvenskan*, Aug. 13, 2006 [https://perma.cc/R59C-ZUFA].
3. Lucia C. Lykke and Philip N. Cohen, "The Widening Gender Gap in Opposition to Pornography, 1975–2012," *Soc. Curr.* 2, no. 4 (2015): 315.
4. Emma Green, "Most People Think Watching Porn Is Morally Wrong," *Atlantic*, Mar. 6, 2014 [https://perma.cc/3J2-QSB8] (citing the Public Religion Research Institute).
5. Jason S. Carroll et al., "Generation XXX: Pornography Acceptance and Use among Emerging Adults," *J. Adolescent Res.* 23, no. 1 (2008): 18 tbl. 1.
6. Mark Regnerus, David Gordon, and Joseph Price, "Documenting Pornography Use in America: A Comparative Analysis of Methodological Approaches," *J. Sex Res.* 53, no. 7 (2016): 878 tbl. 4.
7. Folkhälsomyndigheten [Swedish Public Health Agency], *Sexuell och reproduktiv hälsa och rättigheter i Sverige 2017: Resultat från befolkningsundersökningen SRHR2017* (Stockholm, 2019), 166–167 [https://www.folkhalsomyndigheten.se/].
8. Ibid.
9. For the population surveys on pornography consumption, see Chapter 1.
10. *See, e.g.*, Gert Martin Hald, "Gender Differences in Pornography Consumption among Young Heterosexual Danish Adults," *Arch. Sex. Behav.* 35 (2006): 582; Carl-Göran Svedin and Ingrid Åkerman, "Ungdom och pornografi: Hur pornografi i media används, upplevs och påverkar pojkar respektive flickor," in *Koll på porr: Skilda röster om sex, pornografi, medier och unga*, ed. Ann Katrin Agebäck (Stockholm: Medierådet, 2006), 92 (Sweden); E. Häggström-Nordin, U. Hanson, and T. Tydén, "Associations between Pornography Consumption and Sexual Practices among Adolescents in Sweden," *Int'l J. STD & AIDS* 16, no. 2 (Feb. 1, 2005): 102–103.
11. Hald, "Gender Differences in Pornography Consumption," 582.
12. Mike Allen et al., "The Connection between the Physiological and Psychological Reactions to Sexually Explicit Materials: A Literature Summary Using Meta-Analysis," *Commun. Monogr.* 74, no. 4 (2007): 551, 553.
13. Carroll et al., "Generation XXX," 17.
14. The idea of pornography as a "practice," as distinguished from "depictions" or "representations," was conceived by Andrea Dworkin and Catharine A. MacKinnon, who described it as "a systematic practice of exploitation and subordination based

on sex which differentially harms women" in a proposed statute drafted for the city of Minneapolis. Proposed Ordinance §1, to amend *Minneapolis, Minn. Code of Ordinances*, § 139.10(a)(1), 1st Reading, November 23, 1983, *reprinted in* Catharine A. MacKinnon and Andrea Dworkin, eds., *In Harm's Way: The Pornography Civil Rights Hearings* (Cambridge, MA: Harvard Univ. Press, 1997), 426–432.

15. This body of evidence is analyzed in Chapter 2.
16. The term "sexual aggression" refers to a "continuum of sexual activity involving increasing degrees of coercion up to and including rape." Mary P. Koss and Kenneth E. Leonard, "Sexually Aggressive Men: Empirical Findings and Theoretical Implications," in *Pornography and Sexual Aggression*, ed. Neil M. Malamuth and Edward Donnerstein (Orlando, FL: Academic Press, 1984), 213.
17. The studies that misleadingly control for interaction variables known to be impacted by pornography use constitute what the statistical methods literature terms "post-treatment bias." See Chapter 2 for further analysis of these studies.
18. *See* Dolf Zillmann and Jennings Bryant, "Pornography, Sexual Callousness, and the Trivialization of Rape," *J. Comm.* 32, no. 4 (1982): 17 tbl. 3.
19. *See infra* Chapter 2.
20. In this book, the terms "prostituted person" or "prostituted woman/man" are preferred, as they properly identify those in prostitution as being, to a large extent, placed and kept there by the acts of others, as the evidence proffered here shows. By contrast, "sex worker" implies a chosen occupation, and "prostitute" suggests a characteristic intrinsic to the person rather than an artifact of coercive social circumstances.
21. "John" is one word used to denote a purchaser of prostituted sex. Other commonly used words are "tricks," "punters," "buyers," and "clients."
22. This body of evidence is analyzed in Chapter 1.
23. The term "dehumanization" in this context describes the deprivation of women's unique humanity, for example, by presenting them as mere possessions, playthings, toys, and objects whose only purpose is to satisfy male sexual desires. Dehumanization thus disinhibits cruelty toward others in sexual relations. *See* James V. P. Check and Ted H. Guloien, "Reported Proclivity for Coercive Sex Following Repeated Exposure to Sexually Violent Pornography, Nonviolent Dehumanizing Pornography, and Erotica," in *Pornography: Research Advances and Policy Considerations*, ed. Dolf Zillmann and Jennings Bryant (Hillsdale, NJ: Lawrence Erlbaum, 1989), 160–161.
24. *See infra* Chapter 1.
25. Check and Guloien, "Reported Proclivity," 163.
26. Melissa Farley et al., "Prostitution and Trafficking in Nine Countries: An Update on Violence and Posttraumatic Stress Disorder," *J. Trauma Pract.* 2, nos. 3–4 (2004): 44–48, 56. Respondents were sampled from five continents (37–39).
27. Melissa Farley, "'Renting an Organ for Ten Minutes': What Tricks Tell Us about Prostitution, Pornography, and Trafficking," in *Pornography: Driving the Demand in International Sex Trafficking*, ed. David E. Guinn and Julie DiCaro (Los Angeles: Int'l Human Rights L. Inst., DePaul Univ., 2007), 145–146, 422 n.298.

28. U.N. Committee on the Elimination of Discrimination Against Women (CEDAW), 11th Sess., "General Recommendation No. 19," ¶ 6, U.N. Doc. A/47/38 (Feb. 1, 1992) [hereinafter: CEDAW, "General Recommendation No. 19"].
29. For applications and cases, see, e.g., CEDAW, Communication No. 18/2008 (Opt. Protocol), 46th Sess., July 12–30, 2010, U.N. Doc. CEDAW/C/46/D/18/2008 (Sept. 1, 2010) (on rape); M.C. v. Bulgaria, 15 Eur. Ct. H.R. 627 (2004) (on rape); Opuz v. Turkey, App. No. 33401/02, Eur. Ct. H.R. (2009) (on domestic violence). For regional and international instruments, see, e.g., Protocol to the African Charter on Human and Peoples' Rights on the Rights of Women in Africa, pmbl. para. 9 (following "further noting"), arts. 3(4), 4(2), July 11, 2003 (entry into force Nov. 26, 2005) [https://perma.cc/D3SB-L4Q3] (identifying gender-based violence and violence against women as practices incompatible with provisions guaranteeing human rights and the elimination of all forms of discrimination); Organization of American States, Inter-American Convention on the Prevention, Punishment and Eradication of Violence Against Women (Convention of Belém do Pará), art. 6, June 9, 1994, 33 I.L.M. 1534, 1536; Declaration on the Elimination of Violence Against Women, G.A. Res. 48/104, pmbl. para 6, U.N. doc. A/Res/48/104 (Dec. 20, 1993) [hereinafter U.N. Declaration on VAW]; Fourth World Conference on Women, Sept. 4–15, 1995, "Beijing Declaration and Platform for Action," ¶ 118, U.N. Doc. A/CONF.177/20/Rev.1 ("Violence against women is a manifestation of the historically unequal power relations between men and women, which have led to domination over and discrimination against women by men[.]"); CEDAW, "General Recommendation No. 19," *supra* note 28, ¶¶ 6–7. *See also* CEDAW, 8th Sess., "General Recommendation No. 12," U.N. Doc A/44/38 (Mar. 6, 1989).
30. World Health Organization, *Global and Regional Estimates of Violence against Women: Prevalence and Health Effects of Intimate Partner Violence and Non-Partner Sexual Violence* (Geneva: WHO, 2013), 20 tbl. 5 [https://perma.cc/C28W-WC7Y] (data from Western Pacific was incomplete); *see also* 19 tbl. 4 (noting missing data with respect to eastern Mediterranean).
31. Diana E. H. Russell, "The Prevalence and Incidence of Forcible Rape and Attempted Rape of Females," *Victimology: An Int'l J.* 7 (1982): 84, 91.
32. Dean G. Kilpatrick et al., *Drug-Facilitated, Incapacitated, and Forcible Rape: A National Study* (Charleston, SC: Nat'l Crime Victims Res. & Treatment Center, 2007), 56–58 [https://perma.cc/56W9-44Z3]; *also* 10 (definitions).
33. Ibid., 57, 59.
34. Michele C. Black et al., *The National Intimate Partner and Sexual Violence Survey (NISVS): 2010 Summary Report* (Atlanta, GA: Nat'l Ctr. for Injury Prevention & Control, 2011), 19 [https://perma.cc/PPP9-JTUM].
35. Tommy Andersson, Gun Heimer, and Steven Lucas, *Violence and Health in Sweden: A National Prevalence Study on Exposure to Violence among Women and Men and Its Association to Health* (Uppsala: Nat'l Centre for Knowledge on Men's Violence Against Women, Uppsala Univ., 2015), 39 [https://perma.cc/292S-NDFS] (definitions appear on 38, tbl. 3).
36. Ibid.

37. Mary P. Koss, Christine A. Gidycz, and Nadine Wisniewski, "The Scope of Rape: Incidence and Prevalence of Sexual Aggression and Victimization in a National Sample of Higher Education Students," *J. Consult. Clin. Psychol.* 55, no. 2 (1987): 166, 168 tbl. 4.
38. Ibid.
39. Catharine A. MacKinnon, *Toward a Feminist Theory of the State* (Cambridge, MA: Harvard Univ. Press, 1989), 150–151.
40. Margaret T. Gordon and Stephanie Riger, *The Female Fear: The Social Cost of Rape* (Urbana: Univ. of Illinois Press, 1991), 21.
41. MacKinnon, *Toward a Feminist Theory*, 3.
42. U.N. Declaration on VAW, *supra* note 29, pmbl., *para* 6; *cf. supra* note 29 (citing international law).
43. World Bank, *World Development Report: Gender Equality and Development* (Washington, DC: World Bank, 2011), xx [https://perma.cc/8GB2-VY5C].
44. International Labor Organization, *Global Wage Report 2008/09* (Geneva: Int'l Labor Office, 2008), 29 [https://perma.cc/D7BM-BPAD]; *cf.* International Trade Union Confederation, *The Global Gender Pay Gap* (Brussels: ITUC, 2008), 7, 13–14, 21–22 [https://perma.cc/7EMG-HLQS] (quoting country figures).
45. Sustainlabour, *Draft Report: Green Jobs and Women Workers* (Sustainlabour and U.N.'s Environmental Program, 2009), 5 (quotation), 7–16 (discussion and recommendations) [https://perma.cc/8GM3-MYN3].
46. Ibid., 8.
47. Ibid., 7 tbl. 1.
48. Ibid., 9.
49. U.S. Dep't of Labor, *Highlights of Women's Earnings in 2017*, Report 1075 (Washington, DC: Bureau of Labor Statistics, Aug. 2018), 1 [https://perma.cc/7Q7J-U4KA].
50. Paula England, "The Gender Revolution: Uneven and Stalled," *Gender & Soc'y* 24, no. 2 (2010): 153–154; *cf.* Asaf Levanon, Paula England, and Paul Allison, "Occupational Feminization and Pay: Assessing Causal Dynamics Using 1950–2000 U.S. Census Data," *Social Forces* 88, no. 2 (2009): 865–892.
51. "Balancing Paid Work, Unpaid Work and Leisure," *OECD: Better Policies for Better Lives*, Mar. 7, 2014 [https://perma.cc/J24R-X3U2] (scroll down).
52. Ibid.
53. Inter-Parliamentary Union, "Women in Parliaments: World and Regional Averages," accessed Dec. 12, 2018 [https://perma.cc/ME3N-QY9Q].
54. Inter-Parliamentary Union, "New Parline: The IPU's Open Data Platform (beta)," accessed Dec. 12, 2018 [https://data.ipu.org/]; *pinpoint archived* at https://perma.cc/8P9E-R66M.
55. Ibid., *pinpoint archived* at https://perma.cc/L9GP-YQ5J.
56. Inter-Parliamentary Union, "Women in National Parliaments: World Classification," accessed Dec. 12, 2018 [https://perma.cc/G9UY-MQG9] (ranking Canada fifty-ninth).
57. Ibid. (ranking Rwanda no. 1).

58. Statistics Sweden, "Elected Candidates in the Election to the Riksdag by Region, Party and Sex: Year of Election 1973–2014," accessed Dec. 12, 2018, [http://www.statistikdatabasen.scb.se/goto/en/ssd/Riksdagsledamoter] (select variables, create tables).
59. Women's Media Center, *The Status of Women in the U.S. Media in 2015* (WMC, 2015), 18 (tbl.) [https://perma.cc/X9TX-DPCV].
60. Women's Media Center, *The Status of Women in the U.S. Media in 2017* (WMC, 2017), 4 [https://perma.cc/QLA5-SFA4].
61. Ibid.
62. Ibid., 5.
63. Ian Shapiro, "Problems, Methods, and Theories in the Study of Politics, or What's Wrong with Political Science," *Polit. Theory* 30, no. 4 (2002): 598.
64. Ibid., 601–603.
65. *Cf.* ibid., 599–601.
66. Ibid., 598.
67. Quoted phrases are from Leigh Raymond et al., "Making Change: Norm-Based Strategies for Institutional Change to Address Intractable Problems," *Political Res. Q.* 67, no. 1 (2014): 197–211 (analyzing challenges to climate change and violence against women).
68. *Cf.* ibid.
69. *See, e.g.*, Justin Gillis, "Panel's Warning on Climate Risk: Worst Is to Come," *New York Times*, Mar. 31, 2014, A1 (Westlaw) (reporting that "several rich countries," including the United States, successfully requested the removal of a $100 billion annual estimate by the World Bank that was cited in the 48-page executive summary of a 2,500-page report from the U.N. Intergovernmental Panel on Climate Change of monies needed to offset the effects of climate change on poor countries that "had virtually nothing to do with causing global warming" but "will be high on the list of victims as climatic disruptions intensify," leaders of their countries believing they are paying for "decades of profligate Western consumption").
70. These theorists and their theories are introduced more fully in Chapter 3.
71. *See, e.g.*, Catharine A. MacKinnon, "Substantive Equality Revisited: A Reply to Sandra Fredman," *Int'l J. Const. Law* 14, no. 3 (2016): 739–746; *cf.* MacKinnon, *Toward a Feminist Theory*, 214–249 (using like terms throughout).
72. These critics are discussed further in Chapter 3.
73. The origins of the conceptual distinction between negative and positive freedom can be traced at least as far back as to Immanuel Kant. *See* Ian Carter, "Positive and Negative Liberty," in *Stanford Encyclopedia of Philosophy*, ed. Edward N. Zalta (Fall 2016) [https://plato.stanford.edu/entries/liberty-positive-negative/]. However, as Carter points out, the concepts were thoroughly "examined and defended by Isaiah Berlin in the 1950s and 1960s"; *cf.* Isaiah Berlin, "Two Concepts of Freedom," in *Liberty: Incorporating "Four Essays on Liberty,"* ed. Isaiah Berlin and Henry Hardy (Oxford: Oxford Univ. Press Scholarship Online, 2003), e-book, 169–181, doi:10.1093/019924989X.001.0001.

74. James Madison, "The Federalist No. 10," *in Alexander Hamilton, James Madison, and John Jay: The Federalist; With The Letters of Brutus*, ed. Terence Ball (Cambridge: Cambridge Univ. Press, 2003) (1787), PDF e-book, 40, 41.
75. See Chapter 3 for further discussion.
76. *See, e.g.*, Catharine A. MacKinnon, "Substantive Equality: A Perspective," 96 *Minn. L. Rev.* 1, 1–27 (2011); MacKinnon, "Substantive Equality Revisited."
77. For MacKinnon's substantive equality critique of the Aristotelian concept of equality, see, e.g., Catharine A. MacKinnon, *Sex Equality*, 3rd ed., Univ. Casebook Series (St. Paul, MN: Foundation Press, 2016), 5–13; Catharine A. MacKinnon, "Toward a New Theory of Equality," in *Women's Lives, Men's Laws* (Cambridge, MA: Belknap Press of Harvard Univ. Press, 2005), 44–54; MacKinnon, *Toward a Feminist Theory*, 215–234.
78. R. v. Kapp, 2008 SCC 41, [2008] 2 S.C.R. 483 ¶ 15 (Can.).
79. Withler v. Canada (A.G.), 2011 SCC 12, [2011] S.C.R. 396 ¶ 40 (Can.).
80. Andrews v. Law Soc'y of B.C., [1989] 1 S.C.R. 143 at 154, CarswellBC 16 ¶ 56 (Wilson, J.) (Can.); *accord* R. v. Turpin et al., [1989] 1 S.C.R. 1296 at 1333, CarswellOnt 76 ¶ 52 (Can.).
81. *See Andrews*, [1989] 1 S.C.R. 143 at 171, CarswellBC 16 ¶ 16 (McIntyre J.).
82. Ibid., 173–174.
83. These aspects of consciousness-raising and representation are elaborated in Chapter 3.
84. Wendy Brown, *States of Injury: Power and Freedom in Late Modernity* (Princeton, NJ: Princeton Univ. Press, 1995), 133.
85. Judith Butler, "Sovereign Performatives in the Contemporary Scene of Utterance," *Crit. Inq.* 23, no. 2 (1997): 376–377.
86. Brown, *States of Injury*, 134.
87. *See* Kimberle Crenshaw, "Mapping the Margins: Intersectionality, Identity Politics, and Violence against Women of Color," 43 *Stan. Law Rev.* 1241, 1296–1299 (1991) (criticizing "vulgar constructionism" within postmodern theory).
88. John Gerring, "What Is a Case Study and What Is It Good For?," *Am. Pol. Sci. Rev.* 98, no. 2 (2004): 342 (emphasis deleted).
89. *Cf.* John Gerring, *Case Study Research: Principles and Practices* (New York: Cambridge Univ. Press, 2007), 20.
90. *Cf.* Gerring, "What Is a Case Study?," 342.
91. Gerring, *Case Study Research*, 19–25.
92. Robert K. Yin, *Case Study Research: Design and Methods*, 5th ed. (Los Angeles: Sage, 2014), 40–44.
93. Matthew Lange, *Comparative-Historical Methods* (Los Angeles: Sage, 2013), 40–41, 110–112.
94. *Cf.* ibid., 110–114.
95. Ibid., 42.
96. *Cf.* ibid., 42–43.
97. Ibid., 43.
98. Yin, *Case Study Research*, 143 (citing Alexander L. George and Andrew Bennett, *Case Studies and Theory Development in the Social Science* (Cambridge, MA: MIT Press, 2004), chap. 9).

99. Lange, *Comparative-Historical Methods*, 53; Yin, *Case Study Research*, 143–147.
100. *See* Arend Lijphart, "The Comparable-Cases Strategy in Comparative Research," *Comp. Pol. Studies* 8, no. 2 (1975): 164; Adam Przeworski and Henry Teune, *The Logic of Comparative Social Inquiry* (New York: Wiley, 1970), 31–39.
101. Lange, *Comparative-Historical Methods*, 110–112.
102. *See, e.g.*, Samuel V. LaSelva, "'I Know It When I See It': Pornography and Constitutional Vision in Canada and the United States," in *Constitutional Politics in Canada and the United States*, ed. Steven L. Newman (Albany: State Univ. of New York Press, 2004), 133–151.
103. For the use of Weberian ideal types in comparative studies, see, e.g., Lange, *Comparative-Historical Methods*, 105–107; *cf.* Max Weber, *The Methodology of the Social Sciences*, trans. and ed. Edward A. Shils and Henry A. Finch (New York: Free Press, 1949), 90 (explaining the concept of ideal types).
104. For a thorough comparative constitutional analysis of US and Canadian law in these respects, see, e.g., MacKinnon, *Sex Equality*, esp. 13–41, 155–167, 1750–1822; MacKinnon, "Substantive Equality Revisited."
105. Virginia v. Black 538 U.S. 343, 362–63 (2003).
106. R.A.V. v. City of St. Paul, Minn., 505 U.S. 377, 380, 391 (1992) (citing a municipal bias-motivated crime ordinance at 380).
107. Criminal Code, R.S.C. 1985, c. C-46, ss. 319(2), 318(4) (Can.).
108. R. v. Keegstra, [1990] 3 S.C.R. 697 at 756, CarswellAlta 192 ¶ 80 (Can.).
109. *See* Beauharnais v. Illinois, 343 U.S. 250 (1952) (group libel); Robinson v. Jacksonville Shipyards, 760 F. Supp. 1486 (M.D. Fla. 1991) (settled before appeal) (sexual harassment including, inter alia, pornography displayed at work). For additional analysis of these cases, see Chapter 4.
110. Sweden's prostitution law is examined in Chapters 8 and 9, including the constitutional implications of its potential application to pornography production.
111. Yin, *Case Study Research*, 52.
112. *See Lov om straff (straffeloven) [Criminal Code]* Ch. 26, § 316 (Nor.) [https://lovdata.no/lov/2005-05-20-28/§316].
113. CEDAW, "Response to the Recommendations Contained in the Concluding Observations of the Committee Following the Examination of the Fifth and Sixth Periodic Reports of the State Party on 8 July 2008 (Iceland)," U.N. Doc. CEDAW/C/ICE/CO/6/Add.1 (May 27, 2011).
114. Bill C-36, *Protection of Communities and Exploited Persons Act*, 2nd Sess., 41st Parl., 2014 (Royal Assent, Nov. 6, 2014) (Can.). However, unlike Sweden, Canada's version of the Swedish law continues to criminalize prostituted people who solicit in a public place "that is or is next to a school ground, playground or daycare centre," or who obstruct public traffic when soliciting. *See* Criminal Code, R.S.C. 1985, c. C-46, s. 213 (Can.). Northern Ireland adopted a law similar to Sweden's at the end of 2014. *See* Chris Kilpatrick, "Stormont Bans Paying for Sex as Bulk of Our MLAs Support Clause," *Belfast Telegraph*, Oct. 21, 2014, p. 8 (Lexis).
115. For news reports of the enactment of France's law, see James McAuley, "France Declared War on Prostitution: Not on Prostitutes," *WashingtonPost.com*, Apr. 9, 2016

(Westlaw). For an English overview of the basics of the French law, which is delineated in different prostitution-related statutes, see Grégoire Théry and Claudine Legardinier, *The French Law of April 13, 2016, Aimed at Strengthening the Fight against the Prostitutional System and Providing Support for Prostituted Persons: Principles, Goals, Measures and Adoption*, trans. Caroline Degorce (Paris: Coalition for the Abolition of Prostitution, 2017) [https://perma.cc/3BUJ-NXXA].

116. Criminal Law (Sexual Offenses) Act, 2017 §§ 25–27 (Act No.2/2017) (Ireland). For news report on the enactment of Ireland's law, see Emma Batha, "Ireland Passes Law Making It a Crime to Buy Sex," *Thomson Reuters*, Feb. 23, 2017 (Westlaw).
117. *See* Vered Lee, "Israel's Law against Prostitution Heralds a New Era of Gender Equality," *Haaretz*, Jan. 1, 2019 [https://perma.cc/D5DJ-F6RN].
118. Proposition [Prop.] 1997/98:55 Kvinnofrid [government bill] 22 (Swed.).
119. Ibid., 104.
120. Ibid.
121. The impact of Sweden's law is addressed in Chapter 9.
122. *See Tryckfrihetsförordningen [TF] [Constitution]* 1:1(5) & 1:9 (Swed.); *Yttrandefrihetsgrundlagen [YGL] [Constitution]* 1:1(2) & 1:14 (Swed.).
123. *Regeringsformen [RF] [Constitution]* 8:14 (Swed.).
124. *TF* 1:1.
125. Statens Offentliga Utredningar [SOU] 1947:60 Förslag till tryckfrihetsförordning [government report series] 120 (Swed.); *cf.* Prop. 1948:230 Kungl. Maj:ts proposition till riksdagen med förslag till tryckfrihetsförordning m.m. [government bill] 172 (Swed.).
126. *See, e.g.*, SOU 2006:96 Ett nytt grundlagsskydd [government report series] 59–65 (Swed.); SOU 1947:60 at 250–251; *cf.* SOU 2016:58 Ändrade mediegrundlagar [government report series] 156–157 (Swed.); Prop. 1975/76:209 Om ändring i regeringsformen [government bill] 141–142 (Swed.).
127. Nils Alexanderson, *Föreläsningar öfver den svenska tryckfrihetsprocessen* (Uppsala: Almqvist & Wiksells Boktryckeri, 1907), 7–8; *cf.* SOU 1947:60 at 115–116, 120 (referring to Alexanderson); *see also* Gunnar Persson, *Exklusivitetsfrågan: Om förhållandet mellan tryckfrihet, yttrandefrihet och annan rätt* (Stockholm: Norstedts Juridik, 2002), 63–69 (discussing Alexanderson's work).
128. Persson, *Exklusivitetsfrågan*, 116–117.
129. Prop. 1997/98:43 Tryckfrihetsförordningens och yttrandefrihetsgrundlagens tillämpningsområden: Barnpornografifrågan m.m. [government bill] 67 (Swed.).
130. See Chapter 7 for further analysis of Canada.
131. *See* Prop. 1986/87:151 Om ändringar i tryckfrihetsförordningen m.m. [government bill] 102 (Swed.) (noting that efforts to promote equality between men and women are countered by the free dissemination of violent or sadistic pornography where women are "regularly" violated and degraded).
132. *See* R. v. Butler, [1992] 1 S.C.R. 452 at 509, CarswellMan 100 ¶¶ 126–127 (Can.).
133. These legislative attempts are analyzed in Chapter 8.
134. *See* Catharine A. MacKinnon, "Pornography's Empire," in *Are Women Human? And Other International Dialogues* (Cambridge, MA: Belknap Press of Harvard Univ.

Press, 2006), 113 (observing that the British legal approach to obscenity taken after 1868 "with minor local variations" has primarily grounded the "legal approach to pornography from India and Australia, to the United States and Canada, to Kenya and Zambia" (citations omitted)).

135. *See, e.g.*, Susan Cole, *Pornography and the Sex Crisis* (Toronto: Amanita Enterprises, 1989), 68–72; Donald Alexander Downs, *The New Politics of Pornography* (Chicago: Univ. of Chicago Press, 1989), 101–102; Kathleen E. Mahoney, "Obscenity, Morals and the Law: A Feminist Critique," 17 *Ottawa L. Rev.* 33, 37 (1985).
136. Catharine A. MacKinnon, "Pornography: Not a Moral Issue," *Women's Stud. Int'l F.* 9, no. 1 (1986): 70.
137. Miller v. California, 413 U.S. 15, 24 (1973) (citations omitted).
138. For discussion of recent U.S. obscenity cases, see Chapter 5.
139. These U.S. obstacles to pornography regulation are analyzed in Chapter 4.
140. Proposition [Prop.] 1970:125 Kungl. Maj:ts proposition nr 125 med förslag till ändring i tryckfrihetsförordningen m.m. [government bill] 79 (Swed.).
141. See Chapters 6–7 for Canada.
142. Criminal Code, R.S.C. 1985, c. C-46, s. 163(8) (Can.).
143. See Chapter 7 on Canada and Conclusions for further comparative analysis.
144. Some of my earlier publications provide analysis of documentation of this kind. *See, e.g.*, Max Waltman, "Sweden's Prohibition of Purchase of Sex: The Law's Reasons, Impact, and Potential," *Women's Stud. Int'l F.* 34, no. 5 (2011): 449–474. Among more recent evaluations are Länsstyrelsen Stockholm, *Prostitutionen i Sverige 2014: En omfattningskartläggning*, by Endrit Mujaj and Amanda Netscher (Stockholm: County Administrative Board, 2015) [https://perma.cc/2ML4-6LMR]; Carl Göran Svedin et al., *Prostitution i Sverige: Huvudrapport; Kartläggning och utvärdering av prostitutionsgruppernas insatser samt erfarenheter och attityder i befolkningen* (Linköping: Linköping Univ. Electronic Press, 2012) [https://perma.cc/P8DV-EGSF].
145. Michael Hill and Peter Hupe, *Implementing Public Policy: An Introduction to the Study of Operational Governance*, 2nd ed. (Los Angeles: Sage, 2009), 9.
146. Katharina Holzinger and Christoph Knill, "Theoretical Framework: Causal Factors and Convergence Expectations," in *Environmental Policy Convergence in Europe: The Impact of International Institutions and Trade*, ed. Katharina Holzinger, Cristoph Knill, and Bas Arts (Cambridge: Cambridge Univ. Press, 2008), 31.
147. This evidence is further analyzed in Chapter 9.
148. *See infra* Chapter 1.
149. Gerring, "What Is a Case Study?," 344.
150. Ibid.
151. The German proposal was published in a law review. *See* Susanne Baer and Vera Slupik, "Entwurf eines Gesetzes gegen Pornographie," *Kritische Justiz* 21 (1988): 171–181. *See also* Heather MacRae, "Morality, Censorship, and Discrimination: Reframing the Pornography Debate in Germany and Europe," *Soc. Politics* 10, no. 3 (2003): 314–345 (discussing the legal challenges to pornography attempted in Germany).

152. Tracy McVeigh, "Can Iceland Lead the Way towards a Ban on Violent Online Pornography?," *Observer*, Feb. 17, 2013, p. 31 (Lexis) (double quotation attributed to "Hildur Fjola Antonsdottir, a gender specialist at Iceland University"); *cf.* Alexandra Topping, "Battle to Block Online Porn in Iceland: Gender Equality Activists Press New Government to Be First in Europe to Ban Access," *Guardian*, May 27, 2013, p. 17 (Lexis).
153. *Cf.* Mark Jackson, "Excessive UK ISP Internet Filters Block Access to Vital Support Sites," *ISPReview*, Apr. 16, 2019 [https://perma.cc/2DPP-8UCZ] (describing the semi-official filter policy); Cara McGoogan, "Porn Blocking Legislation to Cement Internet Filtering in U.K. Law," *Telegraph* (online), Jan. 26, 2017 (Lexis) (describing a proposed law); Zachary Davies Boren, "Most Britons Don't Want David Cameron's Porn Filters; Less Than a Quarter Allow Their Internet Provider to Block Porn," *Independent* (online), Sept. 19, 2015 (Lexis).
154. *See, e.g.*, "Everything We Know about the U.K.'s Plan to Block Online Porn," *Wired*, Oct. 25, 2018 [https://perma.cc/WCC9-VGSE]; Graeme Burton, "David Cameron Forges Ahead with Adult Website Age-Verification Plans," *Computing*, Feb. 16, 2016 (Lexis). The British age verification plan was canceled in October 2019. *See* "U.K.'s Controversial 'Porn Blocker' Plan Dropped," *BBC News*, Oct. 16, 2019 [https://perma.cc/Q2FG-LK8D].

Chapter 1 Supply, Demand, and Production Harms

1. *See, e.g.*, Lori Watson, *Debating Pornography*, with Andrew Altman (Oxford: Oxford University Press, 2019); Walter S. DeKeseredy and Marilyn Corsianos, *Violence against Women in Pornography* (New York: Routledge, 2016); Christopher N. Kendall, *Gay Male Pornography: An Issue of Sex Discrimination* (Vancouver: Univ. of British Columbia Press, 2004); Catharine A. MacKinnon, *Only Words* (Cambridge, MA: Harvard Univ. Press, 1993); Andrea Dworkin, *Pornography: Men Possessing Women* (1981; London: Women's Press, 1984); Laura Lederer, ed., *Take Back the Night: Women on Pornography* (New York: Morrow, 1980).
2. Neil M. Malamuth, "Pornography," in *International Encyclopedia of Social and Behavioral Sciences*, ed. Neil J. Smelser and Paul B. Baltes (New York: Elsevier, 2001), 11817; *cf.* Drew A. Kingston et al., "The Importance of Individual Differences in Pornography Use: Theoretical Perspectives and Implications for Treating Sexual Offenders," *J. Sex Res.* 46, nos. 2–3 (2009): 216 (describing pornography as "primarily intended to sexually arouse the consumer and predominantly contains explicit sexual content").
3. Debby Herbenick et al., "Diverse Sexual Behaviors and Pornography Use: Findings from a Nationally Representative Probability Survey of Americans Aged 18 to 60 Years," *J. Sexual Medicine* 17, no. 4 (2020): 628 tbl. 3.
4. Gert Martin Hald, "Gender Differences in Pornography Consumption among Young Heterosexual Danish Adults," *Arch. Sex. Behav.* 35 (2006): 582 tbl. 3 ($p<.001$).

5. Magdalena Mattebo, *Use of Pornography and Its Associations with Sexual Experiences, Lifestyles and Health among Adolescents*, Digital Comprehensive Summaries of Uppsala Dissertations, Faculty of Medicine no. 974 (Uppsala: Acta Universitatis Upsaliensis, 2014), 34, 42, 45 ($p<.001$).
6. Mark Regnerus, David Gordon, and Joseph Price, "Documenting Pornography Use in America: A Comparative Analysis of Methodological Approaches," *J. Sex Res.* 53, no. 7 (2016): 875–876, 878 tbl. 4.
7. Ibid., 875.
8. David Gordon et al., *Relationships in America Survey* (Austin, TX: Austin Institute for the Study of Family and Culture, 2014), 27 (proportions), 53 (methodology) [https://perma.cc/X9NH-UQDB].
9. Regnerus, Gordon, and Price, "Documenting Pornography Use in America," 879.
10. Ibid.
11. Gordon et al., *Relationships in America Survey*, 27 fig. 10.1.
12. Ibid., 27.
13. Folkhälsomyndigheten [Public Health Agency of Sweden], *Sexuell och reproduktiv hälsa och rättigheter i Sverige 2017: Resultat från befolkningsundersökningen SRHR2017* (Stockholm: Folkhälsomyndigheten, 2019), 28, [https://www.folkhalsomyndigheten.se/].
14. Ibid.
15. Ibid., 164.
16. Ibid., 166–167.
17. Ibid.
18. Ibid. Among those aged 45–64 it was estimated that 4% of men and 0% of women watched pornography on a daily/almost daily basis, 6% of men and 0% of women watched pornography 3–5 times per week, and 13% of men and 1% of women watched pornography 1–2 times per week (ibid.). The same numbers for men aged 65–84 was 1%, 2%, 5%, respectively, and for women 0%, 0%, 0%, respectively (ibid.).
19. Ibid., 165.
20. *See, e.g.*, Jason S. Carroll et al., "Generation XXX: Pornography Acceptance and Use among Emerging Adults," *J. Adolescent Res.* 23, no. 1 (2008): 18 tbl. 1 (United States); Hald, "Gender Differences in Pornography Consumption," 582 tbl. 3 (Denmark); Carl-Göran Svedin and Ingrid Åkerman, "Ungdom och pornografi: Hur pornografi i media används, upplevs och påverkar pojkar respektive flickor" [Youth and Pornography], in *Koll på porr: Skilda röster om sex, pornografi, medier och unga*, ed. Ann Katrin Agebäck (Stockholm: Medierådet [Gov't Media Council], 2006), 89–92 & tbl. 2 (Sweden); E. Häggström-Nordin, U. Hanson, and T. Tydén, "Associations between Pornography Consumption and Sexual Practices among Adolescents in Sweden," *Int'l J. STD & AIDS* 16, no. 2 (Feb. 1, 2005): 102–103; Bente Træen, Kristin Spitznogle, and Alexandra Beverfjord, "Attitudes and Use of Pornography in the Norwegian Population 2002," *J. Sex Res.* 41, no. 2 (2004): 195; Mohsen Janghorbani, Tai Hing Lam, and The Youth Sexuality Study Task Force, "Sexual Media Use by Young Adults in Hong Kong: Prevalence and Associated Factors," *Arch. Sex. Behav.* 32, no. 6 (2003): 548 tbl. 3.

21. Hald, "Gender Differences in Pornography Consumption," 582 tbl. 3.
22. Carroll et al., "Generation XXX," 18 tbl. 1.
23. Ibid.
24. Svedin and Åkerman, "Ungdom och pornografi," 92 & tbl. 4.
25. Häggström-Nordin, Hanson, and Tydén, "Associations between Pornography Consumption and Sexual Practices," 102–103.
26. Hald, "Gender Differences in Pornography Consumption," 582 tbl. 3 ($p<.001$).
27. Elizabeth M. Morgan, "Associations between Young Adults' Use of Sexually Explicit Materials and Their Sexual Preferences, Behaviors, and Satisfaction," *J. Sex Res.* 48, no. 6 (2011): 523, 525–526 & tbl. 3.
28. Mike Allen et al., "The Connection between the Physiological and Psychological Reactions to Sexually Explicit Materials: A Literature Summary Using Meta-Analysis," *Comm. Monographs* 74, no. 4 (2007): 551, 553.
29. *See infra* Chapter 2.
30. For readers less familiar with anonymous surveys, several literature reviews in criminology have concluded that, when properly worded and administered, this methodology offers reliable estimates of even criminally sanctioned (as opposed to merely culturally disapproved) behaviors. *See, e.g.*, Terence P. Thornberry and Marvin D. Krohn, "The Self-Report Method for Measuring Delinquency and Crime," in *Measurement and Analysis of Crime and Justice*, vol. 4 of *Criminal Justice 2000*, ed. David Duffee (Washington, DC: Nat'l Inst. of Justice, 2000), 72; Josine Junger-Tas and Ineke Hean Marshall, "The Self-Report Methodology in Crime Research," 25 *Crime & Just.* 291, 354 (1999); David Huizinga and Delbert S. Elliot, "Reassessing the Reliability and Validity of Self-Report Delinquency Measures," *J. Quantitative Crim.* 2, no. 4 (1986): 294, 323–324.
31. Chyng Sun et al., "A Comparison of Male and Female Directors in Popular Pornography: What Happens When Women Are at the Helm?," *Psychol. Women Q.* 32, no. 3 (2008): 312 (citing figure mentioned by AVN).
32. Richard Corliss, "That Old Feeling: Porn Again," *Time*, May 7, 2005 [https://perma.cc/HW7F-MBAC].
33. Frank Rich, "Naked Capitalists," *New York Times Magazine*, May 20, 2001, p. 56 (Lexis) [http://www.nytimes.com/2001/05/20/magazine/naked-capitalists.html].
34. Dan Ackman, "How Big Is Porn," *Forbes.com*, May 25, 2001 [https://perma.cc/LMB6-J95B].
35. For instance, Ackman's lower estimations were based on a selling price of $20 per movie sold (ibid.), which does not seem to account for the fact that one video unit would likely have been rented out several times. *Cf.* Corliss, "That Old Feeling."
36. Somewhat confusingly, and without transparent sourcing, the business review website StatisticBrain.com estimated that the American "Adult Film Industry" had revenues of $13.3 billion in 2016—a figure comparable to Frank Rich's 2001 estimate of $10–14 billion. *See* Statistic Brain, "Adult Film Industry Statistics & Demographics," StatisticBrain.com, 2016 [https://perma.cc/7TFB-F28A].
37. Jerry Ropelato, "Pornography Statistics 2007," *Top Ten Reviews* (2007): 1 [https://perma.cc/Q9EQ-AK3T]. Among the sixteen countries included in this estimation,

nine countries—South Korea, Japan, the United States, Australia, the United Kingdom, Italy, Canada, the Philippines, and the Netherlands—were said to have provided more accessible data. In addition, seven countries with incomplete data were included: China, Taiwan, Germany, Finland, Czech Republic, Russia, and Brazil (1). Although sources are named, they are unaccompanied by such essential information as pinpointed publications, data sets, or websites. *See* 7.

38. Ibid., 1.
39. For the Commission's account on organized crime, see Att'y General's Comm., *Final Report of the Attorney General's Commission on Pornography*, ed. Michael J. McManus (Nashville, TN: Rutledge Hill Press, 1986), 29–30, 291–302. For a more detailed account, see the original edition of the report: Attorney General's Commission on Pornography, *Final Report*, 2 vols. (Washington, DC: U.S. Dept. of Justice, 1986), 291–297, 1037–1238.
40. *See infra* Chapter 5.
41. *See, e.g.*, Catharine A. MacKinnon, "Turning Rape into Pornography: Postmodern Genocide," *Ms.*, July/August 1993, *reprinted in Are Women Human? And Other International Dialogues* (Cambridge, MA: Belknap Press of Harvard Univ. Press, 2006), 160–168 (documenting pornography made of rapes during the Serbian-led genocide perpetrated in Bosnia-Herzegovina); Iris Chang, *The Rape of Nanking: The Forgotten Holocaust of World War II* (London: Penguin, 1998), 10, 162–163 (unnumbered photo section) (documenting pornography produced by Japanese soldiers of women they subjected to sexual violence in China).
42. *See, e.g.*, Robert K. Ressler, Ann Wolbert Burgess, and John E. Douglas, *Sexual Homicide: Patterns and Motives* (Lexington, MA: Lexington Books, 1988), 63 (documenting photographs taken as souvenirs before sexual murders of naked victims); *cf.* Eric W. Hickey, *Serial Murderers and Their Victims*, 3rd ed. (Belmont, CA: Wadsworth, 2002), 28. For legal cases where sexual murder was made into pornography, see, e.g., French Estate v. Ontario (Att'y Gen.) (1998), 38 O.R. (3d) 347, 350, 157 D.L.R. (4th) 144 (Ont. C.A.) (Can.) (Lexis); Schiro v. Clark, 963 F.2d 962, 965 (U.S. 7th Cir. 1992).
43. *See, e.g.*, Melissa Farley, "Legal Brothel Prostitution in Nevada," in *Prostitution and Trafficking in Nevada: Making the Connections*, ed. Melissa Farley (San Francisco: Prostitution Research & Education, 2007), 37 (describing a legal brothel in Nevada where prostituted women were pressured to allow their prostitution to be systematically filmed for use in pornography); Hilary Kinnell, *Violence and Sex Work in Britain* (Cullompton, Devon, UK: Willan, 2008), 42 (reporting "peeping toms" making covert photography). The association between prostitution and pornography production is further documented in this chapter, *infra*.
44. *See, e.g.*, Timothy Egan, "Erotica Inc.: A Special Report; Technology Sent Wall Street into Market for Pornography," *New York Times*, Oct. 23, 2000, A1; *cf.* Gail Dines, *Pornland: How Porn Has Hijacked Our Sexuality* (Boston: Beacon Press, 2010), 50 et seq.; Richard C. Morais, "Porn Goes Public: High Technology and High Finance Are Making the Smut Business Look Legitimate; How Did This Happen?," *Forbes*, June 14, 1999.

45. Benjamin Wallace, "The Geek-Kings of Smut," *New York Magazine*, Feb. 7, 2011 (Lexis).
46. Gail Dines and Dana Bialer, "Comment: The Porn Industry Isn't Dying; It's in Rude Health," *Guardian*, June 8, 2012, p. 36 (Lexis). But see Louis Theroux, "G2: Why Sex Isn't Selling," *Guardian*, June 6, 2012, p. 6 (Lexis), which focuses on those who have lost ground in the more competitive environment of the internet rather than those who reaped the benefits of those same conditions.
47. Dolf Zillmann and Jennings Bryant, "Shifting Preferences in Pornography Consumption," *Comm. Res.* 13, no. 4 (1986): 560–578.
48. Ibid., 565.
49. Ibid., 566.
50. Ibid., 567–569.
51. Ibid., 570–574.
52. Ibid., 575 tbl. 2.
53. Ibid., 573, 575.
54. Ibid., 576–577.
55. Aline Wery and J. Billieux, "Online Sexual Activities: An Exploratory Study of Problematic and Non-Problematic Usage Patterns in a Sample of Men," *Comp. Hum. Behav.* 56 (2016): 259–260. Most respondents, whose mean age was 29.5 (sd=9.5; range 18–72), had a BA or MA (81.8%) and were either employed (44.3%) or students (46.9%) (260).
56. Bryan Y. Park et al., "Is Internet Pornography Causing Sexual Dysfunctions? A Review with Clinical Reports," *Behav. Sciences* 6 (2016): 12–14.
57. Jodie L. Baer, Taylor Kohut, and William A. Fisher, "Is Pornography Use Associated with Anti-Woman Sexual Aggression? Re-examining the Confluence Model with Third Variable Considerations," *Can. J. Human Sexuality* 24, no. 2 (2015): 164 (r=.20, p<.01). Respondents were adult males whose mean age was 27.2 (sd=9.5; Median 24, Range 18–71) (163).
58. James V. P. Check and Ted H. Guloien, "Reported Proclivity for Coercive Sex Following Repeated Exposure to Sexually Violent Pornography, Nonviolent Dehumanizing Pornography, and Erotica," in *Pornography: Research Advances and Policy Considerations*, ed. Dolf Zillmann and Jennings Bryant (Hillsdale, NJ: Lawrence Erlbaum, 1989), 163.
59. Natalie Purcell, *Violence and the Pornographic Imaginary: The Politics of Sex, Gender, and Aggression in Hardcore Pornography* (New York: Routledge, 2012), 179 (quotes), 180.
60. Ibid., 181.
61. Ibid., 56.
62. Ibid., 107, 108 (quoting Mike Ramone et al., eds., *The AVN Guide to the 500 Greatest Adult Films of All Time* (New York: Thunder's Mouth, 2005), 142).
63. Purcell, *Violence and the Pornographic Imaginary*, 112–113; *cf.* Pamela Paul, *Pornified: How Pornography Is Damaging Our Lives, Our Relationships, and Our Families* (New York: Times Books, 2005), 123.
64. Purcell, *Violence and the Pornographic Imaginary*, 110.

65. Ibid., 115.
66. Ibid., 118.
67. Ana J. Bridges et al., "Aggression and Sexual Behavior in Best-Selling Pornography Videos: A Content Analysis Update," *Violence against Women* 16, no. 10 (2010): 1070–1071 (on sampling).
68. Ibid., 1074.
69. Ibid., 1075.
70. Ibid., 1072; for frequencies, see 1075 & tbl. 1.
71. Ibid., 1075–1077.
72. Ibid., 1074–1075.
73. Chyng Sun, Matthew B. Ezzell, and Olivia Kendall, "Naked Aggression: The Meaning and Practice of Ejaculation on a Woman's Face," *Violence against Women* 23, no. 14 (2017): 1725.
74. Ibid., 1716.
75. Ibid., 1725.
76. Ana J. Bridges et al., "Sexual Scripts and the Sexual Behavior of Men and Women Who Use Pornography," *Sexualization, Media, & Society* 2, no. 4 (2016): 4, 5 tbl. 2, doi: 10.1177/2374623816668275 (age m=22.55, sd=7.95).
77. Ibid., 8 tbl. 5.
78. Bridges et al., "Aggression and Sexual Behavior," 1079 tbl. 4.
79. Ibid., 1077–1078.
80. Purcell, *Violence and the Pornographic Imaginary*, 134.
81. Dines, *Pornland*, 68–69; *cf.* Rebecca Whisnant, "From Jekyll to Hyde: The Grooming of Male Pornography Consumers," in *Everyday Pornography*, ed. Karen Boyle (New York: Routledge, 2010), 118–119.
82. Bridges et al., "Sexual Scripts," 5 tbl. 2, 8 tbl. 5 (p<.001).
83. Purcell, *Violence and the Pornographic Imaginary*, 134.
84. Hearing on Proposed Ordinance § 1 to amend Minneapolis, Minn. Code of Ordinances, Ch. 7 Before the Government Operations Comm. Sess. I; Monday, December 12, 1983, 1:30 P.M. (testimony of Linda Marchiano), *transcribed in* Catharine A. MacKinnon and Andrea Dworkin, eds., *In Harm's Way: The Pornography Civil Rights Hearings* (Cambridge, MA: Harvard Univ. Press, 1997), 60–65; *see also* "Nat Laurendi, Polygraph Examination of Linda Lovelace, November 8, 1979," *submitted to* Minneapolis City Council, December 12–13, 1983, *reprinted in* MacKinnon and Dworkin, *In Harm's Way*, 205–213.
85. Purcell, *Violence and the Pornographic Imaginary*, 134.
86. Ibid., 135.
87. Ibid., 144 (citations omitted).
88. Ibid., 118.
89. Bridges et al., "Aggression and Sexual Behavior," 1074.
90. Purcell, *Violence and the Pornographic Imaginary*, 118–119.
91. Ibid., 118.
92. Ibid., 146, 213 n.103.
93. Bridges et al., "Sexual Scripts," 5 tbl. 2 (p=.988).

94. Ibid., 8 tbl. 5 ($p<.001$).
95. Cicely Marston and Ruth Lewis, "Anal Heterosex among Young People and Implications for Health Promotion: A Qualitative Study in the UK," *BMJ Open* 4, no. 8 (2014): 2, doi:10.1136/bmjopen-2014-004996. For details of the sample, see Ruth Lewis, Cicely Marston, and Kay Wellings, "Bases, Stages and 'Working Your Way Up': Young People's Talk about Non-Coital Practices and 'Normal' Sexual Trajectories," *Sociol. Res. Online* 18, no. 1 (2013) [http://www.socresonline.org.uk/18/1/1.html]. See Chapter 2 for further analysis of this study.
96. Marston and Lewis, "Anal Heterosex," 2.
97. Ibid., 4.
98. Breanne Fahs and Jax Gonzalez, "The Front Lines of the 'Back Door': Navigating (Dis)Engagement, Coercion, and Pleasure in Women's Anal Sex Experiences," *Feminism & Psychol.* 24, no. 4 (2014): 510 (quotes), 511.
99. Purcell, *Violence and the Pornographic Imaginary*, 130.
100. Ibid., 145.
101. Ibid., 145–146.
102. Martin J. Downing Jr. et al., "Sexually Explicit Media on the Internet: A Content Analysis of Sexual Behaviors, Risk, and Media Characteristics in Gay Male Adult Videos," *Arch. Sex. Behav.* 43 (2014): 813–815.
103. Ibid., 814–815.
104. Ibid., 819.
105. *See, e.g.*, S. T. Green, "HIV and AIDS, the Internet Pornography Industry and Safer Sex," *Int'l J. STD & AIDS* 15 (2004): 207; *cf.* Bridges et al., "Aggression and Sexual Behavior," 1074 (finding that among 304 scenes, only one (0.3%) presented characters discussing pregnancy or sexually transmitted diseases).
106. Sharif Mowlabocus, Justin Harbottle, and Charlie Witzel, "What We Can't See? Understanding the Representations and Meanings of UAI, Barebacking, and Semen Exchange in Gay Male Pornography," *J. Homosexuality* 61, no. 10 (2014): 1465–1466, 1478 n.7.
107. Shannon Gilreath, *The End of Straight Supremacy: Realizing Gay Liberation* (New York: Cambridge Univ. Press, 2011), 192.
108. Kimberly M. Nelson et al., "Sexually Explicit Online Media and Sexual Risk among Men Who Have Sex with Men in the United States," *Arch. Sex. Behav.* 43, no. 4 (2014): 839 & tbl. 3.
109. Ibid.
110. B. R. Simon Rosser et al., "The Effects of Gay Sexually Explicit Media on the HIV Risk Behavior of Men Who Have Sex with Men," *AIDS Behav.* 14, no. 4 (2013): 1493.
111. Ibid.
112. Bente Træen et al., "Examining the Relationship between Use of Sexually Explicit Media and Sexual Risk Behavior in a Sample of Men Who Have Sex with Men in Norway," *Scand. J. Psychol.* 56, no. 3 (2015): 292–293 & tbls. 1–2; *cf.* Yin Xu, Yong Zheng, and Qazi Rahman, "The Relationship between Self-Reported Sexually Explicit Media Consumption and Sexual Risk Behaviors among Men Who Have Sex with Men in China," *J. Sexual Medicine* 14, no. 3 (2017): 361 tbl. 2 (finding that

31.53% of participants in a survey with men who have sex with men in China reported that 50–100% of pornography they viewed the prior 3 months presented unprotected anal intercourse, 49.36% reported 1–49% presented it, and 19.11% claimed to have engaged in no viewing of it).

113. Downing et al., "Sexually Explicit Media," 815 & n.1.
114. See further discussion below.
115. Mowlabocus, Harbottle, and Witzel, "What We Can't See?," 1466.
116. Kendall, *Gay Male Pornography*, 56–68; *cf.* Gilreath, *The End of Straight Supremacy*, 169–203 (exemplifying and analyzing the cultural role of gay male pornography).
117. *See, e.g.*, Marty Rimm, "Marketing Pornography on the Information Superhighway: A Survey of 917,410 Images, Descriptions, Short Stories, and Animations Downloaded 8.5 Million Times by Consumers in Over 2000 Cities in Forty Countries, Provinces, and Territories," 83 *Geo. Law J.* 1849, 1891–1892 (1995) (finding that 48.4% of the files downloaded by internet users contained child pornography, sadomasochism, bestiality, "incest," or similarly extreme material, with more "common" pornography constituting 71.5% of the files sampled). For definitions, see 1855.
118. Alan McKee, "The Objectification of Women in Mainstream Pornographic Videos in Australia," *J. Sex Res.* 42, no. 4 (2005): 285.
119. Ibid., 282–283.
120. Bridges et al., "Aggression and Sexual Behavior," 1079–1080.
121. McKee, "Objectification of Women," 282.
122. *See, e.g.*, Edward Donnerstein and Leonard Berkowitz, "Victim Reactions in Aggressive Erotic Films as a Factor in Violence against Women," *J. Pers. & Soc. Psychol.* 41, no. 4 (1981): 720; Neil M. Malamuth and James V. P. Check, "Penile Tumescence and Perceptual Responses to Rape as a Function of Victim's Perceived Reactions," *J. Applied Soc. Psychol.* 10, no. 6 (1980): 538–540.
123. McKee, "Objectification of Women," 282.
124. *See infra* Chapter 2.
125. *See, e.g.*, Alan McKee, "Methodological Issues in Defining Aggression for Content Analyses of Sexually Explicit Material," *Arch. Sex. Behav.* 44, no. 1 (2015): 85. Quotations from respondents suggesting that pornography consumers "are very aware of consent" (85) are irrelevant in answering questions regarding the aggressive effects of consumption. Variables measuring aggressive consumption effects must include reliable measurements with construct validity that considers actual aggression or attitudes reflecting aggressive propensities. *See infra* Chapter 2. Moreover, if those made to perform, whom McKee explicitly refers to as "actors" throughout, are directed to *act as if* consenting, how can McKee be confident that what consumers are "aware" of is real or feigned?
126. Eran Shor and Kimberly Seida, "'Harder and Harder'? Is Mainstream Pornography Becoming Increasingly Violent and Do Viewers Prefer Violent Content?," *J. Sex Res.* 56, no. 1 (2019): 19–20, 23.
127. Ibid., 19.
128. Ibid.

129. Ibid., 26. "Bukkake" is slang for pornography where multiple men simultaneously ejaculate on a woman, usually on her face.
130. Ibid., 17.
131. Purcell, *Violence and the Pornographic Imaginary*, 179 (quote), 180.
132. Bridges et al., "Aggression and Sexual Behavior," 1070–1071.
133. Purcell, *Violence and the Pornographic Imaginary*, 183.
134. Ibid., 183–184.
135. Ibid., 183.
136. Melissa Farley et al., "Prostitution and Trafficking in Nine Countries: An Update on Violence and Posttraumatic Stress Disorder," *J. Trauma Practice* 2, nos. 3–4 (2004): 44, 46 tbl. 4. On sampling, see 37–39.
137. *See, e.g.*, Farley, "Legal Brothel Prostitution in Nevada," 31 (reporting that 21 of 45 persons prostituted in legal brothels in Nevada said they were used in order to make pornography in prostitution); Melissa Farley, "'Renting an Organ for Ten Minutes': What Tricks Tell Us about Prostitution, Pornography, and Trafficking," in *Pornography: Driving the Demand in International Sex Trafficking*, ed. David E. Guinn and Julie DiCaro (Los Angeles: Int'l Human Rights L. Inst., DePaul Univ., 2007), 145 (citing similar numbers from an oral history project undertaken in 1990).
138. Marjan Javanbakht et al., "Transmission Behaviors and Prevalence of Chlamydia and Gonorrhea among Adult Film Performers," *Sex. Transm. Dis.* 44, no. 3 (2017): 182–183.
139. Corita R. Grudzen et al., "Pathways to Health Risk Exposure in Adult Film Performers," *J. Urban Health: Bulletin of the New York Academy of Medicine* 86, no. 1 (2009): 69.
140. Melissa Farley, Julie Bindel, and Jacqueline M. Golding, *Men Who Buy Sex: Who They Buy and What They Know* (London: Eaves, 2009), 21 [https://perma.cc/QSU2-7AQV]; Rachel Durchslag and Samir Goswami, *Deconstructing the Demand for Prostitution: Preliminary Insights from Interviews with Chicago Men Who Purchase Sex* (Chicago: Chicago Alliance Against Sexual Exploitation, 2008), 14 [https://perma.cc/5V4Q-PH32].
141. Att'y General's Comm., *Final Report*, 224–245.
142. Ibid., 231 n.983.
143. Ibid., 242.
144. Corita R. Grudzen et al., "Comparison of the Mental Health of Female Adult Film Performers and Other Young Women in California," *Psychiatric Services* 62, no. 6 (2011): 639–645.
145. Ibid., 644.
146. Ibid., 641–642 ($p<.01$).
147. *See, e.g.*, Farley et al., "Prostitution and Trafficking in Nine Countries," 56–57, 66 n.4; Statens Offentliga Utredningar [SOU] 1995:15 Könshandeln: Betänkande av 1993 års Prostitutionsutredning [government report series] 144 (Swed.).
148. Grudzen et al., "Comparison of the Mental Health of Female Performers," 642.
149. Ibid., 641–642 & tbl. 1.
150. Att'y General's Comm., *Final Report*, 231.

151. *See, e.g.*, Alice Cepeda, "Prevalence and Levels of Severity of Childhood Trauma among Mexican Female Sex Workers," *J. Aggression, Maltreatment & Trauma* 20 (2011): 671–672 (citing research from both industrialized and developing regions highlighting poverty-related socioeconomic predictors of entry into prostitution); Cecilia Kjellgren, Gisela Priebe, and Carl Göran Svedin, *Utvärdering av samtalsbehandling med försäljare av sexuella tjänster (FAST): Delrapport 5 ur Prostitution i Sverige* (Linköping: Linköping Univ. Electronic Press, 2012), 21 [https://perma.cc/4RC8-36M5] (finding that, among 34 prostituted persons in Sweden, the most commonly stated reason for entry was the need for money to survive (*n*=14), sometimes specified as for paying the rent or bills, while earning money for drugs was second (*n*=10)); Chandré Gould, *Selling Sex in Cape Town: Sex Work and Human Trafficking in a South African City*, in collaboration with Nicole Fick (Pretoria: Inst. Security Studies, 2008), PDF e-book, 115 [https://perma.cc/D4TD-CDMX] (finding that the majority of respondents entered prostitution due to "financial need," i.e., the inability "to meet pressing financial obligations or to meet basic needs"); Special Committee on Pornography and Prostitution in Canada, *Pornography and Prostitution in Canada: Report of the Special Committee on Pornography and Prostitution in Canada*, vol. 2 (Ottawa: Supply & Services, 1985), 376 ("Overwhelmingly, prostitutes cite economic causes as the reason they are on the streets."); Mimi H. Silbert and Ayala M. Pines, "Entrance into Prostitution," *Youth & Soc'y* 13, no. 4 (1982): 486 (finding among 200 females prostituted in San Francisco that "[b]asic financial survival was mentioned by three-quarters of all subjects, by over 80% of the current prostitutes, and by close to 90% of the juveniles" as the reason for initial involvement).
152. *Cf.* Farley et al., "Prostitution and Trafficking in Nine Countries," 51 tbl. 8 & 65.
153. *See, e.g.*, ibid., 42–44, 57 (finding that 59% of 854 prostituted persons affirmed that they were hit or beaten by a caregiver during childhood until they were injured or bruised, and finding that 63% affirmed they were sexually abused during childhood while noting that the numbers are likely underestimations due to denial and minimization resulting from ongoing trauma); Chris Bagley and Loretta Young, "Juvenile Prostitution and Child Sexual Abuse: A Controlled Study," *Canadian J. Community Mental Health* 6 (1987): 12–14 tbl. 2 (reporting that 73.3% of 45 female prostitution survivors were subjected to child sexual abuse, compared to 28.9% of 45 women among a community control group); Silbert and Pines, "Entrance into Prostitution," 479 (finding that 60% of 200 current and former prostituted juvenile females and adult women reported childhood sexual abuse occurring between ages 3 and 16, of which 70% involved repeated abuse by the same persons, while 62% of those studied reported physical abuse); *cf.* Jennifer James and Jane Meyerding, "Early Sexual Experience as a Factor in Prostitution," *Arch. Sexual Behavior* 7 (1977): 33, 35. In-depth studies of survivors show higher frequencies of abuse. *See, e.g.*, Evelina Giobbe, "Confronting the Liberal Lies about Prostitution," in *Living with Contradictions*, ed. Alison M. Jaggar (Boulder, CO: Westview Press, 1994), 123 (referring to the organization WHISPER's survivor interviews conducted in Minneapolis, where 90% reported battery and 74% reported sexual abuse at some time between ages 3 and

14); Susan Kay Hunter, "Prostitution Is Cruelty and Abuse to Women and Children," *Mich. J. Gender & L.* 1 (1993): 92 n.2, 99 (finding that, among 123 prostitution survivors, 85% reported childhood incest, 90% physical abuse, and 98% emotional abuse). Likewise, in 1985, the Mary Magdalene Project in Reseda, California, reported that 80% of the prostituted women with whom it worked had been "sexually abused" during childhood, while Genesis House in Chicago reported "abuse" for 94%. Giobbe, "Confronting the Liberal Lies," 126 n.10. All these percentages, just as those of women in the general population, are likely significant underestimations. See Linda Meyer Williams, "Recall of Childhood Trauma: A Prospective Study of Women's Memories of Child Sexual Abuse," *J. Consulting & Clin. Psychol.* 62, no. 6 (1994):1167–1176 (interviewing 129 women subjected to *documented* childhood sexual abuse, finding 38% did not recall the abuse reported 17 years earlier, especially women who were younger during the abuse or those who were abused by someone they knew).

154. *See, e.g.*, John Briere and Diana M. Elliott, "Prevalence and Psychological Sequelae of Self-Reported Childhood Physical and Sexual Abuse in a General Population Sample of Men and Women," *Child Abuse & Neglect* 27 (2003): 1209–1210 (finding that 32.3% of 471 women in a geographically stratified, random sample of 935 men and women in the United States reported childhood sexual abuse); Nancy D. Vogeltanz et al., "Prevalence and Risk Factors for Childhood Sexual Abuse in Women: National Survey Findings," *Child Abuse & Neglect* 23 (1999): 583 (finding that the prevalence of child sexual abuse among 1,099 women (weighted n=733) ranged from 15.4% to 32.1%, depending upon the measurement criteria employed and the interpretation of incomplete data).
155. Grudzen et al., "Comparison of the Mental Health of Female Performers," 641 tbl. 1 & 642 (p<.01).
156. Bagley and Young, "Juvenile Prostitution," 14–16 & tbl. 3.
157. Mimi H. Silbert and Ayala M. Pines, "Sexual Child Abuse as an Antecedent to Prostitution," *Child Abuse & Neglect* 5 (1981): 409.
158. Ibid., 410.
159. Silbert and Pines, "Entrance into Prostitution," 474.
160. *See, e.g.*, SOU 1995:15 Könshandeln [government report series] 104 (Swed.); Ronald L. Simons and Les B. Whitbeck, "Sexual Abuse as Precursor to Prostitution and Victimization among Adolescent and Adult Homeless Women," *J. Fam. Issues* 12 (1991): 361; Bagley and Young, "Juvenile Prostitution," 17 tbl. 4. A Korean study found that women subjected to child sexual abuse by "a significant other" reported entering prostitution significantly earlier than did other prostituted women. Hyunjung Choi et al., "Posttraumatic Stress Disorder (PTSD) and Disorders of Extreme Stress (DESNOS) Symptoms Following Prostitution and Childhood Abuse," *Violence against Women* 15, no. 8 (2009): 942.
161. *See, e.g.*, Silbert and Pines, "Entrance into Prostitution," 485 (reporting that over half of 200 juvenile and adult, current and former prostituted females in San Francisco were runaways when entering prostitution; over two-thirds of those prostituted at the time were runaways, and 96% of the prostituted juveniles were runaways); Bagley and Young, "Juvenile Prostitution," 14 (reporting that three-quarters of 45

prostitution survivors left homes "riven by strife, drunkenness, and abuse" by age 16, compared to none of 45 women of in a community control group by that age, and that sexual abuse was the reason most frequently given for leaving home).

162. Farley et al., "Prostitution and Trafficking in Nine Countries," 40.
163. Jody Raphael and Deborah L. Shapiro, *Sisters Speak Out: The Lives and Needs of Prostituted Women in Chicago; A Research Study* (Chicago: Center for Impact Research, 2002), 13 [https://perma.cc/LH6K-N566].
164. Silbert and Pines, "Sexual Child Abuse as an Antecedent," 410.
165. Silbert and Pines, "Entrance into Prostitution," 486.
166. Ibid., 488–489.
167. Farley et al., "Prostitution and Trafficking in Nine Countries," 43–44.
168. *See* Jonna Abelsson and Anna Hulusjö, *I sexualitetens gränstrakter: En studie av ungdomar i Göteborg med omnejd som säljer och byter sexuella tjänster* (Gothenburg: Göteborgs Stad, Social resursförvaltning, 2008), 97–99 [https://perma.cc/TT7Z-8755].
169. Gisela Priebe and Carl-Göran Svedin, "Unga, sex och internet," in *Se mig: Unga om sex och internet*, ed. Ungdomsstyrelsen (Stockholm: Ungdomsstyrelsen, 2009), 74–75, 110, 112, 135 [https://perma.cc/Y37H-VFVJ]; Ungdomsstyrelsen, "Erfarenheter av sexuell exponering och sex mot ersättning," in Ungdomsstyrelsen, *Se mig*, 161–169.
170. A 2012 research report prepared by some of the same principal authors determined that people identified by the specialized Swedish health units treating prostituted people, of whom most are female, are "not likely reached" by larger population surveys. Carl Göran Svedin et al., *Prostitution i Sverige: Huvudrapport; Kartläggning och utvärdering av prostitutionsgruppernas insatser samt erfarenheter och attityder i befolkningen* (Linköping: Linköping Univ. Electronic Press, 2012), 17 [https://perma.cc/P8DV-EGSF].
171. SOU 2004:71 Sexuell exploatering av barn i Sverige, del 1 [government report series] 15–16 (Swed.).
172. Melissa Farley, Kenneth Franzblau, and M. Alexis Kennedy, "Online Prostitution and Trafficking," 77 *Alb. L. Rev.* 1039, 1041–1042 & n.14 (2014).
173. *See, e.g.*, Demand Abolition, *Who Buys Sex? Understanding and Disrupting Illicit Market Demand* (Washington, DC: Demand Abolition, 2018) (updated Mar. 2019), 7–8, 15 [https://perma.cc/SP9M-XKW3] (surveying 8,201 men across the U.S. of which 6.2% reported buying sex within the last year and 20.6% within their lifetime, their responses further suggesting that the people they buy for sex in the United States are "overwhelming young females, and disproportionally Black"); Jennifer James, *Entrance into Juvenile Prostitution: Final Report* (Washington, DC: Nat'l. Inst. of Mental Health, 1980), 17, 19 (finding that African American girls constituted 25% of sample (*n*=136) of prostituted girls interviewed in the Seattle area, where only 4.2% of the population was Black). Interviews conducted with over 3,000 "streetwalking prostitutes" for an outreach project in New York City found approximately half were African American, one-quarter Hispanic, and the remaining quarter white. Barbara Goldsmith, "Women on the Edge," *New Yorker*, Apr. 26, 1993, 65. *See also* Vednita Nelson, "Prostitution: Where Racism and Sexism Intersect," 1 *Mich. J. Gender & L.* 81, 83 (1993) (concluding, "Racism makes Black women and

girls especially vulnerable to sexual exploitation and keeps them trapped in the sex industry.").

174. *See, e.g.*, Andrea Krüsi et al., "Negotiating Safety and Sexual Risk Reduction with Clients in Unsanctioned Safer Indoor Sex Work Environments: A Qualitative Study," *Am. J. Pub. Health* 102, no. 6 (2012): 1155 (finding that 30 of 39 subjects in a sample of those living in a Vancouver public housing project for prostituted persons, which sanctioned indoor prostitution, "were of Aboriginal ancestry"); Cherry Kingsley and Melanie Mark, *Sacred Lives: National Aboriginal Consultation Project* (Vancouver: Save the Children Canada, 2010), 4, 8 [https://perma.cc/S97R-4PA2] (noting that Aboriginal children and youth comprise over 90% of "visible sex trade" in some areas of Canada where the Aboriginal population constitutes less than 10% of the whole); Melissa Farley, Jacqueline Lynne, and Ann J. Cotton, "Prostitution in Vancouver: Violence and the Colonization of First Nations Women," *Transcultural Psychiatry* 42 (2005): 242 (finding that 52% of 100 prostituted women were of First Nations Aboriginal descent, a group making up only 1.7–7% of Vancouver's total population); Julie Cool, *Prostitution in Canada: An Overview* (Ottawa: Parl. Info. & Res. Service, 2004), 3 & n.5 [https://perma.cc/AH29-G7FF] (citing Conseil du statut de la femme, *La prostitution: Profession ou exploitation? Une réflexion à poursuivre* (Québec: Gouvernement du Québec, 2002), 69) (observing an overrepresentation of First Nations Aboriginal and other ethnic minority women in Montréal prostitution); Cecilia Benoit et al., "In Search of a Healing Place: Aboriginal Women in Vancouver's Downtown Eastside," *Social Sci. & Med.* 56, no. 4 (2003): 824 (citing studies estimating that 70% of prostituted persons in Vancouver's Downtown Eastside are Aboriginal women).

175. Brottsförebyggande rådet [Swedish Nat'l Council for Crime Prevention], *The Organisation of Human Trafficking: A Study of Criminal Involvement in Sexual Exploitation in Sweden, Finland, and Estonia* (Stockholm: Brottsförebyggande rådet, 2008), 8, 36–43 [https://perma.cc/6TPL-RCFS].

176. Ungdomsstyrelsen, "Erfarenheter av sexuell exponering och sex mot ersättning," 158.

177. *See, e.g.*, Andrea Di Nicola and Paolo Ruspini, "Learning from Clients," in *Prostitution and Human Trafficking: Focus on Clients*, ed. A. Di Nicola et al. (New York: Springer, 2009), 231–232.

178. Melissa Farley et al., "Attitudes and Social Characteristics of Men Who Buy Sex in Scotland," *Psychol. Trauma: Theory, Res., Practice, & Pol'y* 3, no. 4 (2011): 372–373, 376 (quote). On sampling, see 371.

179. Melissa Farley et al., "Comparing Sex Buyers with Men Who Do Not Buy Sex: New Data on Prostitution and Trafficking," *J. Interpersonal Violence* 32, no. 23 (2017): 3614.

180. Farley, Bindel, and Golding, *Men Who Buy Sex [London]*, 16.

181. Durchslag and Goswami, *Deconstructing the Demand for Prostitution*, 20 (on child sexual abuse), 20–23 (other responses).

182. *See supra* note 140 and accompanying text.

183. *See supra* notes 59–117 and accompanying text.

184. Grudzen et al., "Pathways to Health Risk Exposure."

185. Ibid., 74.

186. Ibid., 73.

187. Ibid., 72–73, 75.
188. Att'y General's Comm., *Final Report*, 200 & n.765.
189. Ibid., 205–206.
190. Ibid., 206 & n.799.
191. Ms. P., "Statement," Minneapolis Press Conference, July 25, 1984, *transcribed in* MacKinnon and Dworkin, *In Harm's Way*, 265–266.
192. SOU 1995:15 Könshandeln [government report series] 96–97 (Swed.).
193. *See supra* note 84 and accompanying text.
194. The Minneapolis Hearings Dec. 12, 1983, 1:30 P.M., *supra* note 84, at 62 (testimony of Linda Marchiano).
195. Att'y General's Comm., *Final Report*, 204 & n.790 (quoting from Washington, DC, Hearing, Vol. I., 179–182).
196. Chapter 9 discusses the Swedish sex purchase law in detail.
197. SOU 1995:15 at 142.
198. Jody Raphael and Deborah L. Shapiro, "Violence in Indoor and Outdoor Prostitution Venues," *Violence against Women* 10, no. 2 (2004): 134–135.
199. Mimi H. Silbert and Ayala M. Pines, "Occupational Hazards of Street Prostitutes," *Crim. Just. Behav.* 8, no. 4 (1981): 397.
200. Hunter, "Prostitution Is Cruelty," 93–94.
201. *Cf.* Jody Raphael and Deborah L. Shapiro, "Reply to Weitzer," *Violence against Women* 11, no. 7 (2005): 967 (observing that prostitution survivors often describe how they fail to seek help due to fears of "being adversely judged by social services agencies"); SOU 1995:15 at 144 (acknowledging a need for a "long time and close contact with prostituted women in order to acquire knowledge of their real situation," and that a survival strategy "entails that the more gross the violence . . . the less becomes her propensity to report it"); Silbert and Pines, "Sexual Child Abuse as an Antecedent," 408 (noting that prostituted persons have little confidence in professionals, authorities, and others, which presents difficulties in interview situations).
202. Grudzen et al., "Pathways to Health Risk Exposure," 75.
203. Dawn Whittaker and Graham Hart, "Research Note: Managing Risks; The Social Organisation of Indoor Sex Work," *Soc. of Health & Illness* 18, no. 3 (1996): 404–405. For further discussion of research about the effects of legal prostitution, see Chapter 9.
204. Lenore Kuo, *Prostitution Policy: Revolutionizing Practice through a Gendered Perspective* (New York: NYU Press, 2002), PDF e-book, 84.
205. Farley, "Legal Brothel Prostitution in Nevada," 23–24.
206. R. v. Downey [1992] 2 S.C.R. 10, 36–39, 90 D.L.R. (4th) 449 (Can.).
207. Royal Canadian Mounted Police, *Human Trafficking in Canada* (Ottawa: RCMP, 2010), 38–39 [https://perma.cc/JJM7-XJN5].
208. American Psychiatric Association, *Diagnostic and Statistical Manual of Mental Disorders*, 5th ed. (Washington, DC: Am. Psychiatric Assoc., 2013), 271–280.
209. Ibid., 271–272.

210. Ingrid Melle, "The Breivik Case and What Psychiatrists Can Learn from It," *World Psychiatry* 12, no. 1 (2013): 16, 19.
211. Farley et al., "Prostitution and Trafficking in Nine Countries," 44, 47–48, 56. On sampling, see 37–39.
212. Ibid., 56.
213. Farley, "'Renting an Organ,'" 146.
214. Ibid. Put otherwise, except for the pornography variable, it was impossible to "differentiate how much each" of the other types of violence contributed to the respondents' "overall distress" (146).
215. Farley, "Legal Brothel Prostitution in Nevada," 37.
216. Choi et al., "Posttraumatic Stress Disorder," 942, 945–946.
217. Bagley and Young, "Juvenile Prostitution," 20–23, 21 tbl. 6, 23 tbl. 7. In analyzing the control group, the variable "practiced prostitution" was used instead of "months in prostitution."
218. Wulf Rössler et al., "The Mental Health of Female Sex Workers," *Acta Psychiatrica Scandinavica* 122 (2010): 144, 150 (quoted text).
219. Ibid., 145, 150.
220. Farley et al., "Prostitution and Trafficking in Nine Countries," 49 (reporting a special analysis of the Mexican subsample). Consistent with the similarity in PTSD severity, neither did the length of time in prostitution, exposure to child sexual abuse, childhood physical abuse, rape in prostitution, number of types of lifetime violence experienced, or the percentage who wanted to escape prostitution significantly differ among the three prostitution venues (49). However, significantly more women entered strip clubs when they were below age 18 than in brothel/massage or street prostitution (p=.03) (49).
221. Farley et al., "Attitudes and Social Characteristics," 376; Durchslag and Goswami, *Deconstructing the Demand for Prostitution*, 12.
222. Melissa Farley, "Prostitution, Trafficking, and Cultural Amnesia: What We Must Not Know in Order to Keep the Business of Sexual Exploitation Running Smoothly," 18 *Yale J.L. & Feminism* 109, 131 (2006) (quoting john saying, "If you look at it, it's paid rape"); *cf.* Farley, "Legal Brothel Prostitution in Nevada," 34 (reporting survivors use of similar terms); Giobbe, "Confronting the Liberal Lies," 121 (stating that survivors "described the act of prostitution as 'disgusting,' 'abusive,' and 'like rape'").
223. *See, e.g., supra* notes 213–215 and accompanying text.
224. John J. Potterat et al., "Mortality in a Long-Term Open Cohort of Prostitute Women," *Am. J. Epidemiol.* 159, no. 8 (2004): 780, 782–783. The homicide rate for prostituted women (204 per 100,000) was "many times higher than that for women and men in the standard occupations that had the highest workplace homicide rates in the United States during the 1980s (4 per 100,000 for female liquor store workers and 29 per 100,000 for male taxicab drivers)" (783).
225. Spec. Comm., *Pornography and Prostitution in Canada*, 350.
226. *See, e.g.*, Eric W. Hickey, *Serial Murderers and Their Victims*, 7th ed. (Boston: Cengage Learning, 2016), 363–365.

227. Bridges et al., "Aggression and Sexual Behavior in Pornography," 1076–1077; *cf.* Purcell, *Violence and the Pornographic Imaginary*, 118 (noting that pornographers, especially since 2000, have been "amping up overt expressions of hostility, anger, and contempt," which "are directed almost exclusively toward women").
228. Javanbakht et al., "Transmission Behaviors," 182–183.
229. *See, e.g.*, K. M. Coyne et al., "Sexual Health of Adults Working in Pornographic Films," *Int'l J. STD & AIDS* 20, no. 7 (2009): 508–509.
230. S. C. Hill, G. King, and A. Smith, "Condom Use and Prevalence of Sexually Transmitted Infection among Performers in the Adult Entertainment Industry;" *Int'l J. STD & AIDS* 20, no. 11 (2009): 809–810.
231. However, women used as pornography performers are more likely than men to have had plastic surgery, including breast augmentation or extreme breast implants. Grudzen et al., "Pathways to Health Risk Exposure," 73.
232. Ibid., 69–77.
233. Ibid., 69; *cf.* Javanbakht et al., "Transmission Behaviors," 182–183 (reporting median performer time 5 years for men (IQR 1–8), 2 years for women (IQR 1–5)).
234. SOU 1995:15 Könshandeln [government report series] 96–97 (Swed.).
235. Att'y General's Comm., *Final Report*, 235 (citing Bennet, "Breaking into X-Rated Films: A Guide for Prospective Porn Stars," *Hustler Erotic Video Guide*, May 1986, p. 72 (quoting an interview with William Margold)).
236. Ibid., 233 (citing Bennet, "Breaking into X-Rated Films," 71 (quoting interview with Margold)).
237. Att'y General's Comm., *Final Report*, 225.
238. Ibid., 232 n.987 (note continued from p. 231; brackets in original) (quoting *Adult Video News*, interviewing Harry Reems, Apr. 1985).
239. Att'y General's Comm., *Final Report*, 231–232 (also citing Charles Hix and Michael Taylor, *Male Model: The World behind the Camera* (New York: St. Martin's Press, 1979), 165–186).
240. Att'y General's Comm., *Final Report*, 233 & n.1004 (citing testimony presented at public hearings in Los Angeles and Washington, DC, in 1984); *cf.* 232 n.991 (citing Hix and Taylor, *Male Model*, 186) (quoting a male model who stressed the role of economic necessity, stating that it was the " 'same reason some people might end up in prostitution' " that propelled some men into nude modeling).
241. See, e.g., Kendall, *Gay Male Pornography*, 78–81.
242. Ibid.
243. Farley et al., "Prostitution and Trafficking in Nine Countries," 49.
244. Kendall, *Gay Male Pornography*, 85.
245. Rebecca Whisnant, "'But What about Feminist Porn?': Examining the Work of Tristan Taormino," *Sexualization, Media, & Society* 2, no. 2 (2016): 3 (internal citations omitted), doi: 10.1177/2374623816631727.
246. Ibid., 2–10.
247. Sun et al., "A Comparison of Male and Female Directors."
248. Ibid., 321–322.
249. Ibid., 321.

250. Ibid. ($p<.001$).
251. *See, e.g.*, Dines and Bialer, "Comment," 36.
252. Benjamin Wallace, "The Geek-Kings of Smut," *New York Magazine*, Feb. 7, 2011 (Lexis).
253. *See supra* notes 201–207 and accompanying text.
254. *Cf.* Margaret A. Baldwin, "Living in Longing: Prostitution, Trauma Recovery, and Public Assistance," *J. Trauma Practice* 2, nos. 3–4 (2004): 273.
255. Ibid (citation and footnote omitted).
256. *Cf.* SOU 1995:15 Könshandeln [government report series] 144 (Swed.).
257. James D. Griffith et al., "Pornography Actresses: An Assessment of the Damaged Goods Hypothesis," *J. Sex Res.* 50, no. 7 (2013): 621–632.
258. Ibid., 626.
259. Grudzen et al., "Comparison of the Mental Health of Female Performers," 643.
260. Griffith et al., "Pornography Actresses," 623–624.
261. *See, e.g.*, Molly Hennessy-Fiske, "Porn Health Clinic Closed," *Los Angeles Times*, Dec. 10, 2010, p. 3 (Westlaw); Molly Hennessy-Fiske, "Porn Clinic Denied State License," *Los Angeles Times*, Dec. 9, 2010, p. 3 (Westlaw); Molly Hennessy-Fiske and Rong-Gong Lin II, "Porn Industry Clinic Comes Under Fire for Its Handling of HIV Case," *Los Angeles Times*, Oct. 15, 2010 [https://perma.cc/DE5S-9VY4].
262. Griffith et al., "Pornography Actresses," 626–627.
263. *See* ibid., 623–625, on method and sampling.
264. Ibid., 630.
265. Ibid. (citation omitted).
266. Shira Tarrant, *The Pornography Industry: What Everyone Needs to Know* (New York: Oxford University Press, 2016), 64–66. *See also* Griffith et al., "Pornography Actresses," 625 (finding no statistically significant difference in child sexual abuse as it was reported by 36.2% of performers and 29.3% of the "matched sample").
267. Ronald Weitzer, "Interpreting the Data: Assessing Competing Claims in Pornography Research," in *New Views on Pornography: Sexuality, Politics, and Law*, ed. Lynn Comella and Shira Tarrant (Santa Barbara, CA: Praeger, 2015), 265–266.
268. Griffith et al., "Pornography Actresses," 629.
269. *Cf.* Dean G. Kilpatrick et al., *Drug-Facilitated, Incapacitated, and Forcible Rape: A National Study* (Charleston, SC: Nat'l Crime Victims Res. & Treatment Center, 2007), 24–25 [https://perma.cc/56W9-44Z3] (preferring "behaviorally specific terms" that will not "require women to label an event as 'rape'" in order to qualify as "rape").
270. I am indebted to Stella Marr, a sex trafficking survivor, activist, and organizer, for drawing attention to many of the organizations and individuals described below.
271. *See* Northern Ireland Assembly, Committee for Justice, "Human Trafficking and Exploitation (Further Provisions and Support for Victims) Bill: International Union of Sex Workers," *Official Report (Hansard)*, Session 2013/2014 (Jan. 9, 2014) at 4 [https://perma.cc/8XPJ-LQGH] (hearing with Ms. "Laura Lee," Int'l Union of Sex Workers).

272. "Douglas Fox: Profile," *Guardian*, Nov. 19, 2008 [https://perma.cc/L65X-Q9QH]; "UK Screen Association News: Evolutions and the Escort Agency," *UK Screen Association*, accessed Jan. 28, 2014 [https://perma.cc/35J7-KNWQ?type=image] (screenshot); *see also* N. Ire. Assembly, "Human Trafficking," *supra* note 271, at 4–5 (discussing Fox's activity); Julie Bindel, "An Unlikely Union: A World of Workers, Pimps and Punters," *Julie Bindel*, blog, Jan. 15, 2014 [https://perma.cc/BB3J-E3WX] (describing how the International Union of Sex Workers in the United Kingdom is dominated by third-party profiteers, not "workers"). Fox has also lobbied Amnesty International to consider a proposal calling for "legalized prostitution." *See* "Stormont Witnesses Deny Links to Pimps," *Belfast News Letter*, Jan. 31, 2014 [https://perma.cc/V3BB-QBM5]; Philip Bradfield, "Amnesty Sex Trade Row," *Belfast News Letter*, Feb. 1, 2014 [https://perma.cc/U3T5-LMMJ]. His efforts were successful. Amnesty International adopted a resolution in August 2015 favoring full decriminalization of prostitution, including not only prostituted persons but also the third parties and the buyers. *See* Editorial Board, "Solving Prostitution," *Washington Post*, Aug. 17, 2015, A12 (Westlaw) (criticizing Amnesty International's resolution for decriminalization while favoring the "so-called 'Nordic model' [law] . . . first passed in Sweden [that] decriminalizes the sale of sex but keeps the purchase illegal").
273. Turn Off the Blue Light, "About," accessed Jan. 28, 2014 [https://perma.cc/NW82-7A6G?type=image] (screenshot).
274. Eamond Dillon, "Sleaze to Meet You," *Sunday World.com*, Aug. 28, 2011 [https://perma.cc/TC82-ZZM6]. As of May 2010, the same man was said to be a businessman venturing into online advertising for prostitution and controlling a site where other convicted pimps and traffickers—among them, his 26-year-old son—had advertised their supply of women. *See, e.g.*, Tom Brady, "Family Ran Online Sex Advertisement Service in U.K.," *Irish Independent*, May 15, 2010 [https://perma.cc/84TK-7G59]; "Jail for Ulsterman Who Ran Brothel Network in Dublin," *Belfast Telegraph.co.uk*, May 15, 2010, p. 6 (Lexis). For an update, see Garreth MacNamee, "Convicted Pimp's Irish Escort Business Turned Over €6 Million in One Year," *TheJournal.ie*, Mar. 18, 2017 [https://perma.cc/5ALP-A5U3].
275. Valerie Jenness, "From Sex Work as Sin to Sex as Work: COYOTE and the Reorganization of Prostitution as a Social Problem," *Social Problems* 37, no. 3 (1990): 403–420.
276. Ibid., 403 (first quote), 404 (second quote).
277. International Sex Worker Foundation for Art, Culture and Education, "Norma Jean Almodovar: Biography," accessed July 1, 2018 [https://perma.cc/8C79-32J6].
278. Paul Feldman, "LAPD Traffic Officer-Turned-Call Girl Gets New Pandering Sentence—3 Years," *Los Angeles Times*, Aug. 1, 1987 (Westlaw); *cf.* Associated Press, "Ex-Policewoman Convicted by Jurors in Pandering Trial," *Register-Guard*, Sept. 27, 1984 [https://news.google.com/newspapers?id=Aa1jAAAAIBAJ&sjid=iuEDAAAAIBAJ&pg=6617%2C6534751].
279. Int'l Sex Worker Foundation, "Norma Jean Almodovar."
280. Jenness, "From Sex Work," 403.

281. *See* David McCumber, *X-Rated: The Mitchell Brothers; A True Story of Sex, Money and Death* (New York: Simon & Schuster, 1992), 45 (describing how attorneys "Kennedy and Rhine and Roberts" had referred to St. James and others as part of "an impressive stable of defense witnesses" in obscenity trials against two pornographers, the Mitchell brothers). My thanks to Professor Donna Hughes for tracking down this source.
282. Christine Beatty, "Margo St. James Runs for Supervisor," *Spectator Magazine*, Nov. 1, 1996, *transcript archived at* https://perma.cc/4GRK-FLQE; *cf.* Walli F. Leff and Marilyn G. Haft, *Time without Work: People Who Are Not Working Tell Their Stories* (Boston: South End Press, 1983), 184 (justifying the criminal charges, St. James says, "[I] always had people hanging out and smoking dope and partying. . . . I had people going in and out all the time. . . . [The cops] assumed that I must be charging").
283. Sex Workers Outreach Project Las Vegas, "People: Robyn Few," accessed Jan. 28, 2014 [https://perma.cc/WZ3F-6DAY].
284. Ken Garcia, "Keep Trafficking Out of City," *San Francisco Examiner*, Sept. 12, 2008 [https://perma.cc/KK8K-44WE].
285. Erotic Service Providers Union–CA, "About Erotic Service Providers Union," accessed Feb. 1, 2014, [https://perma.cc/5BJX-7JY7] (scroll down).
286. Rose Alliance: The National Organisation for Sex Workers, "About Rose Alliance," accessed Sept. 19, 2017 [https://perma.cc/7NA9-CK58].
287. Ibid.
288. Rose Alliance, "Resources and Links," accessed Sept. 19, 2017 [https://perma.cc/FU9Z-LA2S] (scroll down to "Our Sibling Organisations").
289. NSWP: Global Network of Sex Work Projects, "NSWP Elects New President, Pye Jakobsson," Jan. 31, 2014 [https://perma.cc/F8DH-2B6L].
290. *See* Kajsa Skarsgård, "Frontfigur också i styrelse för strippklubb," *Dagens Arena*, Jan. 14, 2013 [https://perma.cc/63XY-4HZF]; Gerda Christenson, "Swedish Rose Alliance—a Fraudulent Organization," *The Women's Front in Sweden*, Internal Newsletter no. 4, 2013, trans. Annina Claesson [https://perma.cc/7GZB-7TMB].
291. Coalition Against Trafficking in Women, "Survivors Connect Network: Sex Trafficking Survivors Worldwide Unite, Board to Meet in Washington DC," Oct. 17, 2012 [https://perma.cc/HW3N-MNU6].
292. Aphiwe Ngalo, "Reflections from a Parliamentary Summit: Sex Work vs Prostitution—Time to Get the Difference," *Daily Maverick*, Mar. 8, 2018 [https://perma.cc/FL4M-V7WF] (quoting Mickey Meji).
293. Mickey Meji, "ANC Resolution to Decriminalise Prostitution Fails Black Women," *News24*, Jan. 26, 2018 [https://perma.cc/E9ZG-H5SW].
294. *See, e.g.*, Prostituted Persons' Revenge in Society, "Goals," accessed June 20, 2017 [https://perma.cc/8XP9-DPVX].
295. *See* Survivor's of Prostitution Abuse Calling for Enlightenment, "Home," accessed July 1, 2018 [https://perma.cc/82FK-DHVK]; Coalition for the Abolition of Prostitution, "About," accessed July 1, 2018 [https://perma.cc/WFN8-6BLV]; Coalition Against Trafficking in Women, "Who We Are," accessed July 1, 2018 [https://perma.cc/C3WP-DZGZ].

296. *Cf.* Stella Marr, "Pimps Will Be Pimps Whether Male or Female or Posing as 'Sex Worker Activists' and Other Conflicts of Interest (Part 1 of 2)," *The Survivor's View* (blog), May 23, 2012 [https://perma.cc/KYV9-M5TJ] (suggesting that pimps use such organizations "to connect with Johns while they recruit vulnerable young women").
297. Farley et al., "Prostitution and Trafficking in Nine Countries," 44, 46 tbl. 4; Farley, "Legal Brothel Prostitution in Nevada," 31; Farley, "'Renting an Organ,'" 145 (citing similar numbers from an oral history project undertaken in 1990).
298. Javanbakht et al., "Transmission Behaviors," 182–183; Grudzen et al., "Pathways to Health Risk Exposure," 69.
299. Purcell, *Violence and the Pornographic Imaginary*, 146.
300. Ibid., 115.
301. Farley et al., "Prostitution and Trafficking in Nine Countries," 44, 47–48, 56.
302. Farley, "'Renting an Organ,'" 146.
303. *See infra* Chapter 2.

Chapter 2 Harm Caused by Consumers

1. Triangulation is understood here as a way to validate and strengthen scientific conclusions by using different methods and/or measurement instruments to study the same phenomenon. *See, e.g.*, Norman Blaikie, *Designing Social Research: The Logic of Anticipation* (Cambridge, UK: Polity Press, 2000), 262–270.
2. A *moderating* variable is usually posited when there are unexpected "weak or inconsistent" relations between independent and dependent variables, such as where the correlation between pornography and aggression is more applicable to one sub-population than for others. *Cf.* Reuben M. Baron and David A. Kenny, "The Moderator-Mediator Variable Distinction in Social Psychological Research: Conceptual, Strategic, and Statistical Considerations," *J. Pers. & Soc. Psychol.* 51, no. 6 (1986): 1178. The concept of a *mediating* variable refers to an intermediary variable that, in the most extreme cases, may entirely eliminate the measurable effect of an independent variable (1176). Statistical tests may control for the extent to which an independent effect can be attributed to the independent and the moderating or mediating variables, respectively. *See, e.g.*, 1174–1176 (describing tests and citing literature).
3. Several such studies claiming to investigate individual differences among pornography consumers are critically reviewed later in this chapter.
4. Many thanks to the political scientist Dr. Ana Catalano Weeks for reading a preliminary version of this chapter and suggesting that "post-treatment bias" was the most appropriate term for describing the criticism made here of several psychological studies.
5. *See* Gary King and Langche Zeng, "When Can History Be Our Guide? The Pitfalls of Counterfactual Inference," *Int'l Stud. Quart.* 51, no. 1 (2007): 201; *cf.* Jacob M.

Montgomery, Brendan Nyhan, and Michelle Torres, "How Conditioning on Posttreatment Variables Can Ruin Your Experiment and What to Do about It," *Amer. J. Political Sci.* 62, no. 3 (2018): 773 (recommending using only "pretreatment covariates as moderators, control variables, and attention checks"); Jason Seawright, *Multi-Method Social Science: Combining Qualitative and Quantitative Tools* (Cambridge: Cambridge University Press, 2016), 65–67 (explaining post-treatment bias and some ways to address it).

6. King and Zeng, "When Can History Be Our Guide?," 201; *cf.* Seawright, *Multi-Method Social Science*, 65–67.
7. King and Zeng, "When Can History Be Our Guide?," 201.
8. *See, e.g.*, Mike Allen et al., "Exposure to Pornography and Acceptance of Rape Myths," *J. Comm.* 45, no. 1 (1995): 5–26 (meta-analysis); Gert Martin Hald, Neil Malamuth, and Carlin Yuen, "Pornography and Attitudes Supporting Violence against Women: Revisiting the Relationship in Nonexperimental Studies," *Aggr. Behav.* 36, no. 1 (2010): 14–20 (meta-analysis).
9. Attorney General's Commission on Pornography, *Final Report of the Attorney General's Commission on Pornography*, ed. Michael J. McManus (Nashville, TN: Rutledge Hill Press, 1986), 281.
10. Between-method triangulation refers to the combination of "dissimilar methods to measure the same unit or concept" (e.g., experiments vs. naturalistic surveys), as distinguished from within-method triangulation, where, for example, a survey questionnaire uses different scales or different questions for measuring the same concept. Blaikie, *Designing Social Research*, 263. The term "between/within method triangulation" has been attributed to the sociologist Norman K. Denzin (263).
11. Paul J. Wright et al., "Pornography Consumption and Satisfaction: A Meta-Analysis," *Hum. Comm. Res.* 43, no. 3 (2017): 322.
12. Ibid.
13. Mike Allen, David D'Alessio, and Tara M. Emmers-Sommer, "Reactions of Criminal Sexual Offenders to Pornography: A Meta Analytic Summary," in *Comm. Yearbook 22*, ed. Michael E. Roloff (Thousand Oaks, CA: Sage, 1999), 146–147; Allen et al., "Exposure to Pornography," 12–13 (meta-analysis).
14. Thomas D. Cook and Laura C. Leviton, "Reviewing the Literature: A Comparison of Traditional Methods with Meta-Analysis," *J. Pers.* 48, no. 4 (1980): 453. For a useful critical appraisal of the method of meta-analysis, see Shinichi Nakagawa et al., "Meta-Evaluation of Meta-Analysis: Ten Appraisal Questions for Biologists," *BMC Biology* 15, Art. No. 18 (2017): doi:10.1186/s12915-017-0357-7.
15. Example modified from Allen et al., "Exposure to Pornography," 12 (meta-analysis).
16. Cook and Leviton, "Reviewing the Literature," 453–454.
17. Mike Allen, Keri Brezgel, and Dave D'Alessio, "A Meta-Analysis Summarizing the Effects of Pornography II: Aggression after Exposure," *Hum. Comm. Res.* 22, no. 2 (1995): 265.
18. Baron and Kenny, "Moderator-Mediator Variable Distinction," 1178.

19. *See, e.g.*, Hald, Malamuth, and Yuen, "Pornography and Attitudes Supporting Violence," 16 (meta-analysis); Allen et al., "Exposure to Pornography," 12 (meta-analysis).
20. Allen, D'Alessio, and Brezgel, "Meta-Analysis Summarizing the Effects," 268 (meta-analysis); *see also* Tania B. Huedo-Medina et al., "Assessing Heterogeneity in Meta-Analysis: Q Statistic or I^2 Index?," *Psychological Methods* 11, no. 2 (2006): 193; Allen et al., "Exposure to Pornography," 12 (meta-analysis).
21. *Cf.* Allen, D'Alessio, and Brezgel, "Meta-Analysis Summarizing the Effects," 268 (meta-analysis).
22. *See* Huedo-Medina et al., "Assessing Heterogeneity," 202–204.
23. Ibid.
24. *See, e.g.*, Nakagawa et al., "Meta-Evaluation of Meta-Analysis," 9–11.
25. Paul J. Wright, Robert S. Tokunaga, and Ashley Kraus, "A Meta-Analysis of Pornography Consumption and Actual Acts of Sexual Aggression in General Population Studies," *J. Comm.* 66, no. 1 (2016): 188, 195, 199; Wright et al., "Pornography Consumption and Satisfaction," 322, 333, 334.
26. *See, e.g.*, Allen, Brezgel, and D'Alessio, "Meta-Analysis Summarizing the Effects," 276 (meta-analysis).
27. Martha R. Burt, "Cultural Myths and Supports for Rape," *J. Pers. & Soc. Psychol.* 38, no. 2 (1980): 217.
28. *See, e.g.*, Hald, Malamuth, and Yuen, "Pornography and Attitudes Supporting Violence," 15.
29. Burt, "Cultural Myths and Supports for Rape," 217–218, 222–223.
30. Ibid.; *cf.* Neil M. Malamuth, "Aggression against Women: Cultural and Individual Causes," in *Pornography and Sexual Aggression*, ed. Neil M. Malamuth and Edward Donnerstein (Orlando, FL: Academic Press, 1984), 24 (exemplifying rape myths).
31. *See, e.g.*, Mary P. Koss et al., "Nonstranger Sexual Aggression: A Discriminant Analysis of the Psychological Characteristics of Undetected Offenders," *Sex Roles* 12 (1985): 989; Neil M. Malamuth, "Predictors of Naturalistic Sexual Aggression," *J. Pers. & Soc. Psychol.* 50, no. 5 (1986): 955–957, 959; Neil M. Malamuth et al., "The Characteristics of Aggressors against Women: Testing a Model Using a National Sample of College Students," *J. Consult. Clin. Psychol.* 59, no. 5 (1991): 673, 676–677.
32. John Briere and Neil M. Malamuth, "Self-Reported Likelihood of Sexually Aggressive Behavior: Attitudinal versus Sexual Explanations," *J. Res. Pers.* 17, no. 3 (1983): 318 (quote), 318–322; *see also* Neil M. Malamuth, "Rape Proclivity among Males," *J. Social Issues* 37, no. 4 (1981): 144; Todd Tieger, "Self-Rated Likelihood of Raping and the Social Perception of Rape," *J. Res. Pers.* 15, no. 2 (1981): 154–156; Neil M. Malamuth, Scott Haber, and Seymour Feshbach, "Testing Hypotheses regarding Rape: Exposure to Sexual Violence, Sex Differences, and the 'Normality' of Rapists," *J. Res. Pers.* 14, no. 1 (1980): 130–131 & tbl. 4, 134–135; Neil M. Malamuth and James V. P. Check, "Penile Tumescence and Perceptual Responses to Rape as a Function of Victim's Perceived Reactions," *J. Applied Soc. Psychol.* 10, no. 6 (1980): 540–541 & tbl. 3, 544–545.

33. Neil M. Malamuth, "Predicting Laboratory Aggression against Female and Male Targets: Implications for Sexual Aggression," *J. Res. Pers.* 22, no. 4 (1988): 487–489; *see also* Neil M. Malamuth, "Factors Associated with Rape as Predictors of Laboratory Aggression against Women," *J. Pers. & Soc. Psychol.* 45, no. 2 (1983): 439–440; Malamuth, "Aggression against Women," 36–39 (summarizing studies).
34. Malamuth, "Predicting Laboratory Aggression," 489–491.
35. *See* Malamuth, "Aggression against Women," 25–26 & fig. 1.1 (summarizing studies); Malamuth, "Rape Proclivity," 145–147 & 148 fig. 1 (summarizing studies).
36. *See, e.g.*, Diana Scully and Joseph Marolla, "Convicted Rapists' Vocabulary of Motive: Excuses and Justifications," *Social Problems* 31, no. 5 (1984): 534–537; Allen, D'Alessio, and Emmers-Sommer, "Reactions of Offenders," 154–156 (meta-analysis); *see also* Malamuth, "Rape Proclivity," 142–143 (citing and summarizing studies).
37. Min-Sun Kim and John E. Hunter, "Attitude-Behavior Relations: A Meta-Analysis of Attitudinal Relevance and Topic," *J. Comm.* 43, no. 1 (1993): 101–142; Min-Sun Kim and John E. Hunter, "Relationships among Attitudes, Behavioral Intentions, and Behavior: A Meta-Analysis of Past Research, Part 2," *Comm. Res.* 20, no. 3 (1993): 331–364.
38. *See, e.g.*, Dolf Zillmann and Jennings Bryant, "Pornography, Sexual Callousness, and the Trivialization of Rape," *J. Comm.* 32, no. 4 (1982): 13–14 (using exposure over six weeks followed by a two-week break before measuring effects); James V. P. Check and Ted H. Guloien, "Reported Proclivity for Coercive Sex Following Repeated Exposure to Sexually Violent Pornography, Nonviolent Dehumanizing Pornography, and Erotica," in *Pornography: Research Advances and Policy Considerations*, ed. Dolf Zillmann and Jennings Bryant (Hillsdale, NJ: Lawrence Erlbaum, 1989), 166 (using 3 exposures during 6 days and a 4–5-day break before measuring effects).
39. *See, e.g.*, Edward Donnerstein and Leonard Berkowitz, "Victim Reactions in Aggressive Erotic Films as a Factor in Violence against Women," *J. Pers. & Soc. Psychol.* 41, no. 4 (1981): 713–714 (describing methodology); Edward Donnerstein and John Hallam, "Facilitating Effects of Erotica on Aggression against Women," *J. Pers. & Soc. Psychol.* 36, no. 11 (1978): 1272 (describing methodology).
40. *See, e.g.*, Gert Martin Hald and Neil N. Malamuth, "Experimental Effects of Exposure to Pornography: The Moderating Effect of Personality and Mediating Effect of Sexual Arousal," *Arch. Sex. Behav.* 44, no. 1 (2015): 99–109 (reporting no age differences in exposure effects when using a random stratified sample of 350 adults aged 18–30 living in Aarhus, Denmark, stratified by sex/gender, age, place of birth, and citizenship, determined by sociodemographic analysis to be nationally representative); Dolf Zillmann and Jennings Bryant, "Shifting Preferences in Pornography Consumption," *Comm. Res.* 13, no. 4 (1986): 560–578 (sampling 80 nonstudents, mean age approx. 35, and 80 students, mean age approx. 22, and finding similar patterns with minor differences in exposure effects between the groups); Dolf Zillmann and Jennings Bryant, "Effects of Prolonged Consumption of Pornography on Family Values," *J. Fam. Issues.* 9, no. 4 (1988): 533, 538–539 (sampling 80 nonstudents and 80 students, mean ages approx. 35/22, where exposure to common nonviolent pornography, among other things, produced (1) more perceptions of women as sexually

promiscuous; (2) more acceptance of male dominance; and (3) more acceptance of female servitude, with no interaction effects between exposure and student/nonstudent status except for female servitude (4), where effects on nonstudents were weaker and nonsignificant compared to students).

41. Wright, Tokunaga, and Kraus, "Meta-Analysis of Pornography Consumption," 193.
42. *See supra* notes 33–34 and accompanying text.
43. *E.g.*, Donnerstein and Hallam, "Facilitating Effects Erotica," 1270–1277; Edward Donnerstein, "Pornography: Its Effect on Violence against Women," in Malamuth and Donnerstein, *Pornography and Sexual Aggression*, 56 (citing studies).
44. Donnerstein and Hallam, "Facilitating Effects Erotica," 1270–1277.
45. Ibid., 1275–1276.
46. Dolf Zillmann, James L. Hoyt, and Kenneth D. Day, "Strength and Duration of the Effect of Aggressive, Violent, and Erotic Communications on Subsequent Aggressive Behavior," *Comm. Res.* 1, no. 3 (1974): 286–306.
47. Ibid., 294.
48. Donnerstein and Berkowitz, "Victim Reactions," 713–714.
49. Ibid., 717 & n.2.
50. Ibid., 720.
51. Ibid., 718–719.
52. Allen, D'Alessio, and Brezgel, "Meta-Analysis Summarizing the Effects," 266. The researchers scanned 1,300 studies on pornography before determining which to include (265).
53. Ibid., 266, 269.
54. Ibid., 269–274.
55. *See* Huedo-Medina et al., "Assessing Heterogeneity," 202–203.
56. The heterogeneity test for nonviolent pornography was relatively more powerful, if not quite within the recommended range ($k=24$, $\bar{N}=51$), while both the violent test ($k=7$, $\bar{N}=50$) and the nudity test ($k=9$, $\bar{N}=45$) were considerably less powerful. See Allen, D'Alessio, and Brezgel, "Meta-Analysis Summarizing the Effects," 271 (average sample sizes rounded).
57. *Cf.* Montgomery, Nyhan, and Torres, "How Conditioning on Posttreatment Variables," 767, 770–771; King and Zeng, "When Can History Be Our Guide?," 201; Seawright, *Multi-Method Social Science*, 65–67.
58. Allen, D'Alessio, and Brezgel, "Meta-Analysis Summarizing the Effects," 271.
59. Ibid., 269.
60. This category was defined by the researchers as "nudity (a single person depicted with minimal or a complete lack of clothing but not engaged in a sexual activity)" (ibid., 267). Some experiments in this category used pictures from publications such as *Playboy* or *Penthouse*. *See, e.g.*, John Ramirez, Jennings Bryant, and Dolf Zillmann, "Effects of Erotica on Retaliatory Behavior as a Function of Level of Prior Provocation," *J. Pers. & Soc. Psychol.* 43, no. 5 (1982): 974; Edward Donnerstein, Marcia Donnerstein, and Ronald Evans, "Erotic Stimuli and Aggression: Facilitation or Inhibition," *J. Pers. & Soc. Psychol.* 32, no. 2 (1975): 239. For the other studies included in the meta-analysis, see Allen, D'Alessio, and Brezgel, "Meta-Analysis Summarizing the Effects," 270.

61. Allen, D'Alessio, and Brezgel, "Meta-Analysis Summarizing the Effects," 271.
62. Donnerstein, Donnerstein, and Evans, "Erotic Stimuli and Aggression," 242.
63. Ibid (citing other studies).
64. Kyra Lanis and Katherine Covell, "Images of Women in Advertisements: Effects on Attitudes Related to Sexual Aggression," *Sex Roles* 32, nos. 9–10 (1995): 639–649; Nathalie J. MacKay and Katherine Covell, "The Impact of Women in Advertisements on Attitudes toward Women," *Sex Roles* 36, nos. 9–10 (1997): 573–583; Michael A. Milburn, Roxanne Mather, and Sheree D. Conrad, "The Effects of Viewing R-Rated Movie Scenes That Objectify Women on Perceptions of Date Rape," *Sex Roles* 43, nos. 9–10 (2000): 645–664.
65. See Mónica Romero-Sanchez et al., "More Than a Magazine: Exploring the Links between Lads' Mags, Rape Myth Acceptance, and Rape Proclivity," *J. Interpers. Violence* 32, no. 4 (2015): 525–527. Although these statistical findings only held for those men who also perceived a higher legitimacy in magazines like these and exhibited higher rape myth acceptance than other men, these moderating variables may lead to post-treatment bias in the model insofar as such moderators can be caused by consumption of objectifying magazines over time. Thus, while not wholly eliminating experimental exposure effects, if these moderators are caused by exposure to the same type of magazine covers in social reality it would be wrong to assume based on this experiment that only men sharing those characteristics are at risk of being affected by such exposure.
66. Paul J. Wright and Robert S. Tokunaga, "Men's Objectifying Media Consumption, Objectification of Women, and Attitudes Supportive of Violence against Women," *Arch. Sex. Behav.* 45, no. 3 (2016): 957, 960 (quote).
67. *See* Chapter 1 for studies of consumer desensitization.
68. *See supra* notes 31–37 and accompanying text.
69. *See, e.g.*, Briere and Malamuth, "Self-Reported Likelihood of Sexually Aggressive Behavior," 318-322; Tieger, "Self-Rated Likelihood of Raping," 154–156; Malamuth, Haber, and Feshbach, "Testing Hypotheses regarding Rape," 130–131 & tbl. 4, 134–135; Malamuth and Check, "Penile Tumescence," 540–541 & tbl. 3, 544–545; Malamuth, "Rape Proclivity," 144.
70. *E.g.*, Dolf Zillmann and James B. Weaver, "Pornography and Men's Callousness toward Women," in Zillmann and Bryant, *Pornography*, 118–119 & tbl. 4.3; Zillmann and Bryant, "Pornography, Sexual Callousness," 17 tbl. 3.
71. Allen et al., "Exposure to Pornography," 17–18 (meta-analysis). Note that the same article also reports a meta-analysis of *nonexperimental* studies that is not discussed here. That part was found to contain errors by Hald, Malamuth, and Yuen, "Pornography and Attitudes Supporting Violence," 15–16 (meta-analysis). The errors were acknowledged by Allen in personal communications with Hald, Malamuth, and Yuen in 2005. *See* 16.
72. Allen et al., "Exposure to Pornography," 14–15 tbl. 2.
73. Ibid., 18–19.
74. Ibid.; *see also* Huedo-Medina et al., "Assessing Heterogeneity," 202–203.

75. Allen et al., "Exposure to Pornography," 19.
76. Ibid. Parameters for violent pornography–control were $k=5$; $\bar{N}=144$; for nonviolent pornography–control groups $k=7$; $\bar{N}=150$; and for violent pornography–nonviolent pornography, $k=8$; $\bar{N}=95$ (19) (average sample sizes rounded).
77. *See, e.g.*, William A. Fisher et al., "Pornography, Sex Crime, and Paraphilia," *Curr. Psychiatry Rep.* 15, no. 6, (2013): art. no. 362, which purports to provide an analytical literature review, but already in its abstract claims that only experiments with violent pornography have shown aggressive effects, even though meta-analyses performed in 1995 plainly show the contrary. Later in their article, Fisher et al. admit that a few nonexperimental naturalistic survey studies they selectively looked at actually suggested a sexually aggressive association with nonviolent pornography, but then incorrectly claimed that there exists "no compelling explanation offered to conceptualize a linkage between nonviolent sexual imagery and attitudes and behavior involving sexual violence" (4). As the paragraphs to follow demonstrate, such a "linkage" had already been conceptualized in the 1980s.
78. *See* Zillmann and Weaver, "Pornography and Men's Callousness," 109–115 (summarizing studies).
79. Kenneth E. Leonard and Stuart P. Taylor, "Exposure to Pornography, Permissive and Nonpermissive Cues, and Male Aggression toward Females," *Motivation & Emotion* 7, no. 3 (1983): 293–294.
80. Ibid., 295.
81. Ibid., 294.
82. Ibid., 296.
83. Ibid., 296–297.
84. Zillmann and Weaver, "Pornography and Men's Callousness," 114.
85. Ibid.
86. *See* ibid., 115–121, for a report of the whole experiment.
87. Ibid., 116.
88. Ibid., 118 tbl. 4.3.
89. Ibid., 115, 118 tbl. 4.3
90. When separating male and female subjects exposed to rape pornography, only the sentence recommended by women was significantly lower than controls at $p<.05$. Ibid., 118 tbl. 4.3 (two-tailed *t* test).
91. When separating male from female subjects exposed to erotized violence, only the sentence recommended by men was significantly lower than controls at $p<.05$. Ibid., 118 tbl. 4.3 (two-tailed *t* test).
92. Ibid., 118 tbl. 4.3; $p>.05$ (two-tailed *t* test).
93. Ibid., 116.
94. Ibid., 116–117 & tbl. 4.1.
95. Ibid., 117 tbl. 4.1; $p>.05$ (two-tailed *t* test).
96. Ibid., 119.
97. *See* Zillmann and Bryant, "Effects of Prolonged Consumption," 529–530 tbl. 1, 532–533 & tbl. 2, 538–539.

98. Zillmann and Bryant, "Pornography, Sexual Callousness," 15 & tbl. 1.
99. Ibid., 17 tbl. 3.
100. Ibid., 17–18 & tbl. 4. The Sexual Callousness scale developed by Mosher was used (14), which contains items similar to, inter alia, Burt's rape myth acceptance and acceptance of interpersonal violence scales. *Cf.* Burt, "Cultural Myths and Supports for Rape," 222–223.
101. R. v. Wagner, 1985 CarswellAlta 35 ¶¶ 58–60, 36 Alta. L.R. (2d) 301 (Can. Alta. Q.B.) (Westlaw), *aff'd* 1986 CarswellAlta 26, 69 A.R. 78 (Can. Alta. C.A.).
102. Ibid. ¶¶ 63–64.
103. Ibid. ¶ 62.
104. This experiment is reported in Check and Guloien, "Reported Proclivity for Coercive Sex."
105. Ibid., 163.
106. Ibid., 168.
107. Ibid., 168–169.
108. Ibid., 166.
109. Ibid., 165.
110. Ibid., 171 & tbl. 6.1; $p<.05$.
111. Zillmann and Weaver, "Pornography and Men's Callousness," 120.
112. *Indianapolis, Ind. Code* ch. 16 § 16-3(q) (1984) (emphasis added), *invalidated by* American Booksellers Ass'n v. Hudnut, 771 F.2d 323 (7th Cir. 1985), *reprinted in* Catharine A. MacKinnon and Andrea Dworkin, eds., *In Harm's Way: The Pornography Civil Rights Hearings* (Cambridge, MA: Harvard Univ. Press, 1997), 438–457.
113. King and Zeng, "When Can History Be Our Guide?," 201.
114. *See* Montgomery, Nyhan, and Torres, "How Conditioning on Posttreatment Variables," 761–762 (noting that "the dangers of posttreatment conditioning are either not understood or are being ignored" (761), and finding that 35 of 75 experimental studies published from 2012 to 2014 in three leading political science journals (*APSR*, *AJPS*, *JOP*) "engaged in posttreatment conditioning," 762).
115. Check and Guloien, "Reported Proclivity for Coercive Sex," 175.
116. Ibid., 175–176.
117. Ibid., 176–177.
118. *See, e.g.*, Michele L. Ybarra and Richard E. Thompson, "Predicting the Emergence of Sexual Violence in Adolescence," *Prevention Science* 19, no. 4 (2018): 403–415 (finding violent pornography exposure significantly increased the likelihood of first sexual violence perpetration, rejecting reverse causation since no sexual aggression predated pornography exposure); Jane D. Brown and Kelly L. L'Engle, "X-Rated: Sexual Attitudes and Behaviors Associated with U.S. Early Adolescents' Exposure to Sexually Explicit Media," *Comm. Res.* 46, no. 1 (2009): 137, 139, 142 tbl. 3, & 143 (finding that, when controlling for other baseline predictors, pornography still predicted significantly more sexual harassment perpetration after two years among 12- to 14-year-old males).
119. Check and Guloien, "Reported Proclivity for Coercive Sex," 168.

120. S. B. G. Eysenck and H. J. Eysenck, "The Measurement of Psychoticism: A Study of Factor Stability and Reliability," *Br. J. Soc. Clin. Psychol.* 7, no. 4 (1968): 286 (quoting H. J. Eysenck and S. B. G. Eysenck, "A Factorial Study of Psychoticism as a Dimension of Personality," *Multivariate Behav. Res.* All-Clin. Spec. Issue (1968): 15–31).
121. Gary R. VandenBos, ed., *APA Dictionary of Psychology* (Washington, DC: American Psychological Association, 2015), PDF e-book, 864.
122. Check and Guloien, "Reported Proclivity for Coercive Sex," 164 (citing Hans J. Eysenck, *Sex and Personality* (London: Sphere, 1978)).
123. Ibid., 168.
124. Ibid., 172–173 & tbl. 6.2.
125. Ibid., 174 (p<.05).
126. Wright, Tokunaga, and Kraus, "Meta-Analysis of Pornography Consumption," 193.
127. Allen et al., "Exposure to Pornography," 18–19 (meta-analysis).
128. Ibid. (k=16; n=141). No information about between-studies correlation is provided. For statistical power in heterogeneity tests, see Huedo-Medina et al., "Assessing Heterogeneity," 202–203.
129. Allen et al., refer to a prior publication ("Check 1985, Experiment I") where the same data that Check and Guloien reported in 1989 was found. *See* Allen et al., "Exposure to Pornography," 14 tbl. 2, 17 tbl. 3.
130. Neil M. Malamuth, Tamara Addison, and Mary Koss, "Pornography and Sexual Aggression: Are There Reliable Effects and Can We Understand Them?," *Ann. Rev. Sex Res.* 11 (2000): 61–63, 77–78. *See also* Mary P. Koss, Christine A. Gidycz, and Nadine Wisniewski, "The Scope of Rape: Incidence and Prevalence of Sexual Aggression and Victimization in a National Sample of Higher Education Students," *J. Consult. Clin. Psychol.* 55, no. 2 (1987): 165 tbl. 2 (describing the "present sample" as having been surveyed in 1984–1985). The study by Malamuth, Addison, and Koss, "Pornography and Sexual Aggression," 61, makes clear it is based on the same survey.
131. Malamuth, Addison and Koss, "Pornography and Sexual Aggression," 63.
132. Koss, Gidycz, and Wisniewski, "Scope of Rape," 165 & 167 tbl. 3.
133. Malamuth, Addison, and Koss, "Pornography and Sexual Aggression," 77–78.
134. Ibid., 78.
135. Ibid., 64–65.
136. Vanessa Vega and Neil M. Malamuth, "Predicting Sexual Aggression: The Role of Pornography in the Context of General and Specific Risk Factors," *Aggr. Behav.* 33, no. 2 (2007): 105.
137. *See, e.g.*, ibid., 107 (using the scales Acceptance of Interpersonal Violence (AIV), Rape Myth Acceptance (RMA), Adversarial Sexual Beliefs (ASB), Hostility toward Women (HTW), and Sexual Dominance (DOM) to measure the HM moderator); Malamuth et al., "Characteristics of Aggressors," 673 (using HTW, ASB, and Negative Masculinity (NM) to measure HM). For meta-analysis on pornography exposure effects using scales of this type, see, e.g., Allen et al., "Exposure to Pornography" (experiments); Hald, Malamuth, and Yuen, "Pornography and Attitudes Supporting Violence" (naturalistic studies). Other individual studies are discussed above.

138. Malamuth, Addison, and Koss, "Pornography and Sexual Aggression," 64–65.
139. *See* Laura Vandenbosch and Steven Eggermont, "Sexually Explicit Websites and Sexual Initiation: Reciprocal Relationships and the Moderating Role of Pubertal Status," *J. Res. on Adolescence* 23, no. 4 (2013): 628–629, 631–632; *cf.* Brown and L'Engle, "X-Rated," 143 (finding that males with higher levels of exposure to pornography, but no experience of oral sex or sexual intercourse during baseline, were significantly more likely to have engaged in these forms of sexual conduct two years later).
140. Emily L. Harkness, Barbara M. Mullan, and Alex Blaszczynski, "Association between Pornography Use and Sexual Risk Behaviors in Adult Consumers: A Systematic Review," *Cyberpsychology, Behavior, and Social Networking* 18, no. 2 (2015): 68–69 (reviewing ten cross-sectional studies with adults and finding a "robust" and "strong association" between more pornography consumption and more sexual partners); Meghan Donevan and Magdalena Mattebo, "The Relationship between Frequent Pornography Consumption, Behaviors, and Sexual Preoccupancy among Male Adolescents in Sweden," *Sexual & Reproductive Healthcare* 12 (2017): 86(finding "frequent" pornography consumers "more often report behaviors associated with sexual risk taking including earlier age at sexual debut, anal sex, and having tried acts seen in pornography").
141. Malamuth, Addison, and Koss, "Pornography and Sexual Aggression," 75.
142. Jodie L. Baer, Taylor Kohut, and William A. Fisher, "Is Pornography Use Associated with Anti-Woman Sexual Aggression? Re-examining the Confluence Model with Third Variable Considerations," *Can. J. Human Sexuality* 24, no. 2 (2015): 165 tbl. 1. The respondents had a mean age of 27.2 (Range 18–71) (163).
143. Ibid., 164.
144. *See* Chapter 1.
145. *Cf.* King and Zeng, "When Can History Be Our Guide?," 201; Seawright, *Multi-Method Social Science*, 65–67.
146. Christopher J. Ferguson and Richard D. Hartley, "Pornography and Sexual Aggression: Can Meta-Analysis Find a Link?," Trauma, Violence, & Abuse, published ahead of print, July 21, 2020, at 9–10, doi:10.1177/1524838020942754. The references list, inter alia, Malamuth, Addison, and Koss, "Pornography and Sexual Aggression" and Vega and Malamuth, "Predicting Sexual Aggression," as being included in the meta-analysis.
147. Ferguson and Hartley, "Pornography and Sexual Aggression," 3.
148. Wright, Tokunaga, and Kraus, "Meta-Analysis of Pornography Consumption," 192; Hald, Malamuth, and Yuen, "Pornography and Attitudes Supporting Violence," 18; Allen, Brezgel, and D'Alessio, "Meta-Analysis Summarizing the Effects," 269; Allen et al., "Exposure to Pornography," 18–19.
149. Ferguson and Hartley, "Pornography and Sexual Aggression," 5.
150. Malamuth, Addison, and Koss, "Pornography and Sexual Aggression," 63 (capitalization and italics omitted).

151. Allen, D'Alessio, and Brezgel, "Meta-Analysis Summarizing the Effects," 269 (meta-analysis).
152. Malamuth, Addison, and Koss, "Pornography and Sexual Aggression," 62.
153. Koss, Gidycz, and Wisniewski, "Scope of Rape," 169.
154. Malamuth, Addison, and Koss, "Pornography and Sexual Aggression," 77–78.
155. Seawright, *Multi-Method Social Science*, 66.
156. VandenBos, *APA Dictionary of Psychology*, 864.
157. Check and Guloien, "Reported Proclivity for Coercive Sex," 175–176.
158. *Cf.* King and Zeng, "When Can History Be Our Guide?," 201.
159. *See* Chapter 1.
160. Check and Guloien, "Reported Proclivity for Coercive Sex," 168.
161. Gert Martin Hald and Neil N. Malamuth, "Experimental Effects of Exposure to Pornography: The Moderating Effect of Personality and Mediating Effect of Sexual Arousal," *Arch. Sex. Behav.* 44, no. 1 (2015): 99–109.
162. Ibid., 103–104 & tbl. 1.
163. Ibid., 100 (citations omitted).
164. Ibid., 106.
165. Ibid., 104 & tbl. 2.
166. Ibid., 104–105. Quote at 100.
167. Ibid., 102.
168. *Cf.* Montgomery, Nyhan, and Torres, "How Conditioning on Posttreatment Variables," 8, 11–12; Seawright, *Multi-Method Social Science*, 65–67; King and Zeng, "When Can History Be Our Guide?," 201.
169. For an analysis of the influence of pornography on mainstream culture, see, e.g., Catharine A. MacKinnon, "X-Underrated," in *Butterfly Politics* (Cambridge, MA: Belknap Press of Harvard Univ. Press, 2017), 199–206. On the sexualization of youth culture, see, e.g., Patrice A. Oppliger, *Girls Gone Skank: The Sexualization of Girls in American Culture* (Jefferson, NC: McFarland, 2008); American Psychological Ass'n, *Report of the APA Task Force on the Sexualization of Girls*, ed. Eileen L. Zurbriggen et al. (Washington, DC: APA, 2007) [https://perma.cc/7TE5-2YFC].
170. Wright, Tokunaga, and Kraus, "Meta-Analysis of Pornography Consumption," 183–205.
171. Ibid., 201.
172. Ibid., 193–195.
173. Ibid., 199.
174. Ibid., 194–195.
175. *See supra* notes 27–37 and accompanying text.
176. Hald, Malamuth, and Yuen, "Pornography and Attitudes Supporting Violence," 15–16 (meta-analysis).
177. Studies were included when (1) defining pornography according to the norm within this body of research, (2) having a valid indicator of ASV, (3) offering sufficient statistical information to measure the association between naturalistic consumption and ASV, and (4) providing data from samples of non-convicts since "the veridicality

and validity of self-reports" from convicted offenders had been questioned by "various researchers." Ibid., 16 (citing studies).

178. The meta-analysis excluded data from female participants except for a fraction of 10 women involved in one study. Ibid., 16.

179. Ibid., 18.

180. Neil M. Malamuth, Gert Martin Hald, and Mary Koss, "Pornography, Individual Differences in Risk and Men's Acceptance of Violence against Women in a Representative Sample," *Sex Roles* 66, nos. 7–8 (2012): 427–439.

181. Malamuth, Addison, and Koss, "Pornography and Sexual Aggression."

182. Ibid., 433.

183. Hald, Malamuth, and Yuen, "Pornography and Attitudes Supporting Violence," 18.

184. Malamuth, Hald, and Koss, "Pornography, Individual Differences," 435–436.

185. For the 2012 study's methods in these regards, see ibid., 431. Moreover, since the 2012 study divided respondents into six risk groups based on their Hostile Masculinity and Interpersonal Sex scores (434–436), Type II errors became more likely when comparing group differences in ASV, contrasting with the 2000 study on sexual aggression, where three risk groups were deemed "more appropriate" due to statistical power problems that more subgroups would cause. Malamuth, Addison, and Koss, "Pornography and Sexual Aggression," 77.

186. Malamuth, Hald, and Koss, "Pornography, Individual Differences," 432. Negative Masculinity measures traits like arrogance, boastfulness, egoism, greed, cynicism, self-interestedness, hostility, and dictatorial attitudes. *See* Janet T. Spence, Robert L. Helmreich, and Carole K. Holahan, "Negative and Positive Components of Psychological Masculinity and Femininity and Their Relationships to Self-Reports of Neurotic and Acting Out Behaviors," *J. Pers. & Soc. Psychol.* 37, no. 10 (1979): 1675–1676. It can be measured by the degree of adherence to statements such as "Most people are out for themselves and I don't trust them very much." Malamuth, Hald, and Koss, "Pornography, Individual Differences," 432. Notably, all three scales indicating ASV in the 2012 study (432) also measure similar manifestations of hostility, for instance, adherence to statements like "In a dating relationship a woman is largely out to take advantage of a man" (Adversarial Sexual Beliefs (ASB)). Burt, "Cultural Myths and Supports for Rape," 222–223. Likewise, Hostility toward Women can be measured by undesirable hostility and, inversely, adherence to statements such as "I rarely become suspicious with women who are more friendly than I anticipate." Malamuth, Hald, and Koss, "Pornography, Individual Differences," 432. Not coincidentally, very similar characteristics are included in ASV, for instance, "Women are usually sweet until they've caught a man, but then they let their true self show" (ASB). Burt, "Cultural Myths and Supports for Rape," 222–223.

187. *See, e.g.*, Vega and Malamuth, "Predicting Sexual Aggression," 107 (using the scales Acceptance of Interpersonal Violence (AIV), Rape Myth Acceptance (RMA), Adversarial Sexual Beliefs (ASB), Hostility toward Women (HTW), and Sexual Dominance (DOM) to measure the Hostile Masculinity moderator); Malamuth et al., "Characteristics of Aggressors," 673 (using HTW, ASB, and Negative Masculinity (NM) to measure HM); Malamuth, Hald, and Koss, "Pornography,

Individual Differences," 432 (using AIV, RMA, and ASB to measure the dependent variable ASV).

188. Malamuth, Hald, and Koss, "Pornography, Individual Differences," 432.
189. For an explanation of this problem in post-treatment bias, see King and Zeng, "When Can History Be Our Guide?," 201; Seawright, *Multi-Method Social Science*, 65–67.
190. Malamuth, Addison, and Koss, "Pornography and Sexual Aggression," 75; Baer, Kohut, and Fisher, "Is Pornography Use," 165 tbl. 1.
191. Malamuth, Hald, and Koss, "Pornography, Individual Differences," 435 tbl. 2.
192. Both the study from 2012 and the study from 2000 used subjectively worded survey questions about consumption frequency and replaced missing data with sample averages. Typically, these procedures would underestimate group differences. *See supra* notes 150–152, 185 and accompanying text.
193. Ybarra and Thompson, "Predicting the Emergence of Sexual Violence."
194. Ibid., 406, 409, & 410 tbl. 2.
195. Ibid., 409, & 410–411 tbls. 2–3.
196. *See* Brown and L'Engle, "X-Rated," 137, 139, 142 tbl. 3, & 143.
197. *See* Jochen Peter and Patti M. Valkenburg, "Adolescents' Exposure to Sexually Explicit Internet Material and Notions of Women as Sex Objects: Assessing Causality and Underlying Processes," *J. Communication* 59, no. 3 (2009): 422. The mediation analysis seems superfluous, though, since consumers who did not "like" pornography would probably not consume it on their own initiative. Adding such a mediating variable may cause a statistical "post-treatment bias" that underestimates the effects of pornography.
198. Brown and L'Engle, "X-Rated," 146–147.
199. Ybarra and Thompson, "Predicting the Emergence of Sexual Violence," 406.
200. *Compare* Allen, D'Alessio, and Brezgel, "Meta-Analysis Summarizing the Effects," 267 (defining nonviolent pornography in a meta-analysis as "nonviolent sexual behavior (including petting, autoerotica, and fondling of genitals, as well as oral, vaginal, or anal intercourse))," *with* Ybarra and Thompson, "Predicting the Emergence of Sexual Violence," 406 (defining nonviolent pornography as "sexualized media," e.g., "kissing, fondling, having sex").
201. Ybarra and Thompson, "Predicting the Emergence of Sexual Violence," 406.
202. *See* Chapter 1.
203. When comparing Ybarra and Thompson's finding that the adjusted odds for a first sexually violent behavior were not significantly predicted by nonviolent pornography consumption with the much stronger significant finding regarding violent pornography exposure ("Predicting the Emergence of Sexual Violence," 410–411 tbls. 2–3), that comparison is likely confounded by the unmeasured frequency of consumption in both instances. Had the study measured frequency of consumption with greater precision, those who increased their consumption over time—whether or not the pornography was violent—might also have evinced significantly elevated adjusted odds of being sexually aggressive.
204. Ibid., 409.

205. *Cf.* ibid., 411–412. For instance, table 2 reports an astonishing number: among the sample of 361 male youths, prior violent pornography exposure predicted significantly increased adjusted odds of 46.10 ($p<.01$; 95% CI 3.05, 697.84) compared to those unexposed to any pornography of committing a first "sexual assault" (the umbrella measure during 2006–2012) (410 tbl. 2). Ybarra and Thompson do not mention this number in the main text likely because its 95% confidence interval ranged from about 3 to almost 700. They caution that the odds of "sexual assault" as well as "sexual harassment"—the latter 10.96 among 327 males ($p<.01$; 95% CI 2.78, 43.18)—"preclude any strong conclusions" due to "small sample sizes and wide confidence intervals" (411).
206. Catherine Moreau et al., "Capturing Sexual Violence Experiences among Battered Women Using the Revised Sexual Experiences Survey and the Revised Conflict Tactics Scales," *Arch. Sex. Behav.* 40, no. 1 (2015): 225, 227.
207. Ibid., 227–228 & tbl. 3.
208. Catherine A. Simmons, Peter Lehmann, and Shannon Collier-Tenison, "Linking Male Use of the Sex Industry to Controlling Behaviors in Violent Relationships: An Exploratory Analysis," *Violence against Women* 14, no. 4 (2008): 409–410.
209. Ibid., 411.
210. Ibid., 412 tbl. 1.
211. Ibid., 412 tbl. 2.
212. *See* ibid., 411, 414.
213. Janet Hinson Shope, "When Words Are Not Enough: The Search for the Effect of Pornography on Abused Women," *Violence against Women* 10, no. 1 (2004): 61.
214. Ibid., 63.
215. Ibid., 63–64 & tbl. 2 ($p<.05$).
216. Ibid., 65 & tbl. 3 ($p<.01$).
217. Raquel Kennedy Bergen and Kathleen A. Bogle, "Exploring the Connection between Pornography and Sexual Violence," *Violence and Victims* 15, no. 3 (2000): 230.
218. Ibid., 230–231.
219. Elizabeth Cramer et al., "Violent Pornography and Abuse of Women: Theory to Practice," *Violence & Victims* 13, no. 4 (1998): 319–332.
220. Ibid., 326.
221. Ibid. ($\chi^2=13.93$, $p<.001$). No post-hoc analysis of differences among these three groups was reported.
222. Ibid., 327. These results remained consistent after controlling for age. There were no significant differences in the severity of violence experienced by women who reported that their partners only used violent pornography (20.2%)—i.e., without forcing imitation, posing, or viewing—compared to those whose partners reportedly did not use violent pornography (54%) (327).
223. Elizabeth Cramer and Judith McFarlane, "Pornography and Abuse of Women," *Pub. Health Nursing* 11, no. 4 (1994): 268–272.
224. Ibid., 270.

225. The authors report 74%, which appears to be a typographical error considering that 75% is an exact number (27) while 74% is not (26.64).
226. Walter S. DeKeseredy and Amanda Hall-Sanchez, "Adult Pornography and Violence against Women in the Heartland: Results from a Rural Southeast Ohio Study," *Violence against Women* 23, no. 7 (2017): 834–838.
227. Ibid., 838–843.
228. Ibid., 842.
229. Letter from Flora Colao to the Minneapolis City Council, November 10, 1983, *reprinted in* MacKinnon and Dworkin, *In Harm's Way*, 214–215.
230. "Hearing on Proposed H. Bill 5194, An Act to Protect the Civil Rights of Women and Children," Boston, MA, March 16, 1992 (submission of Gail Kielson) [hereinafter Massachusetts Hearing], *reprinted in* MacKinnon and Dworkin, *In Harm's Way*, 423–424.
231. "Hearing on Proposed Ordinance § 1 to amend *Minneapolis, Minn. Code of Ordinances*, Ch. 7, Before the Government Operations Comm.," December 13, 1983 [hereinafter Minneapolis Hearing] (testimonies of Gary Kaplan and Richelle Lee, sex offender treatment specialists; Charlotte Kasl and Sue Schafer, survivors' therapists), *transcribed in* MacKinnon and Dworkin, *In Harm's Way*, 165–168, 171–172, 172–175, 179; "Hearing to Consider an Amendment to Ch. XVI of the Indianapolis, Ind. City Code Before the Indianapolis City-Council Administration Committee," April 16, 1984 (testimony of Detective Terry Hall, Ind. Police Dept.), *reprinted in* MacKinnon and Dworkin, *In Harm's Way*, 279–280; Massachusetts Hearing, *supra* note 230, at 411–412 (testimony of Betsy Warrior, founder of the Battered Women's Directory in Boston, MA); Att'y General's Comm., *Final Report*, 208–209 & n.817 (quoting a letter from the Harriet Tubman Women's Shelter to the Commission (1986)).
232. *See, e.g.*, Diana E. H. Russell, *Sexual Exploitation: Rape, Child Sexual Abuse, and Workplace Harassment* (Beverly Hills, CA: Sage, 1984), 124–126; Att'y General's Comm., *Final Report*, 197–223 passim; Minneapolis Hearing, *supra* note 231, at 108–114, 145–147; Massachusetts Hearing, *supra* note 231, at 370–425 passim; Minneapolis Press Conference, July 25, 1984, *reprinted in* MacKinnon and Dworkin, *In Harm's Way*, 260–265.
233. Walter S. DeKeseredy and Martin D. Schwartz, *Woman Abuse on Campus: Results from the Canadian National Survey* (Thousand Oaks, CA: Sage, 1998), 25 (on sample), 110 (on pornography).
234. Russell, *Sexual Exploitation*, 124.
235. DeKeseredy and Schwartz, *Woman Abuse on Campus (Canada)*, 110.
236. Ibid., 110–111.
237. Mimi H. Silbert and Ayala M. Pines, "Entrance into Prostitution," *Youth & Soc'y* 13, no. 4 (1982): 474.
238. Mimi H. Silbert and Ayala M. Pines, "Pornography and Sexual Abuse of Women," *Sex Roles* 10, nos. 11–12 (1984): 863–865.

239. Melissa Farley et al., "Prostitution and Trafficking in Nine Countries: An Update on Violence and Posttraumatic Stress Disorder," *J. Trauma Practice* 2, nos. 3–4 (2004): 44 & 46.
240. SOU 1995:15 Könshandeln: Betänkande av 1993 års Prostitutionsutredning [government report series] 135 (Swed.).
241. Silbert and Pines, "Pornography and Sexual Abuse," 865–866.
242. *See, e.g.*, Minneapolis Hearing, *supra* note 231, at 162–164, 166–169, & 171–179 (testimonies of Cheryl Champion, Gary Kaplan, Nancy Steele, Richelle Lee, Charlotte Kasl, Sue Santa, Sherry Arndt, and Sue Schafer).
243. *E.g.*, Margaret A. Baldwin, "Pornography and the Traffic in Women: Brief on Behalf of Trudee Able-Peterson et al., Amici Curiae in Support of Defendant and Intervenor-Defendants, *Village Books v. City of Bellingham*," 1 *Yale J. L. & Feminism* 111, 141–142 (1989) (quoting Minneapolis Public Hearings); *cf.* Att'y General's Comm., *Final Report*, 204 (quoting a public hearing in Washington, DC, where a prostitution survivor testified to being exploited in connection with New York City conventions on weekends when pornographic films were first shown to male audiences, which "'most often set the tone for the kinds of acts we were expected to perform'").
244. Minneapolis Hearing, *supra* note 231, at 116 (testimony by T.S.).
245. Silbert and Pines, "Pornography and Sexual Abuse," 863.
246. Ibid.
247. Ibid., 864.
248. Ibid., 864–865.
249. Ibid., 864.
250. Ibid., 865.
251. *Indianapolis, Ind. Code* ch. 16 § 16-3(q) (1984), *invalidated by* American Booksellers Ass'n v. Hudnut, 771 F.2d 323 (7th Cir. 1985).
252. See Chapter 4 further on the civil rights challenges.
253. *See* Andrea Dworkin and Catharine A. MacKinnon, *Pornography and Civil Rights: A New Day for Women's Equality* (Minneapolis, MN: Organizing against Pornography, 1988) [http://www.nostatusquo.com/ACLU/dworkin/other/ordinance/newday/TOC.htm].
254. Melissa Farley et al., "A Thorn in the Heart: Cambodian Men Who Buy Sex," paper presented at the Focus on Men Who Buy Sex: Discourage Men's Demand for Prostitution, Stop Sex Trafficking conference, Phnom Penh, Cambodia, July 17, 2012, p. 26 [https://perma.cc/KU76-5FT5].
255. Melissa Farley et al., "Comparing Sex Buyers with Men Who Don't Buy Sex: 'You Can Have a Good Time with the Servitude' vs. 'You're Supporting a System of Degradation,'" paper presented at the Annual Conference of Psychologists for Social Responsibility, Boston, July 15, 2011, pp. 30–31 [https://perma.cc/LX9L-2VK2].
256. Rachel Durchslag and Samir Goswami, *Deconstructing the Demand for Prostitution: Preliminary Insights from Interviews with Chicago Men Who Purchase*

Sex (Chicago: Chicago Alliance against Sexual Exploitation, 2008), 13 [https://perma.cc/5V4Q-PH32].

257. Farley et al., "Comparing Sex Buyers [Boston]," 30 (as reported 2011).
258. Melissa Farley et al., "Comparing Sex Buyers with Men Who Do Not Buy Sex: New Data on Prostitution and Trafficking." *J. Interpersonal Violence* 32, no. 23 (2017): 3613.
259. Melissa Farley et al., "Attitudes and Social Characteristics of Men Who Buy Sex in Scotland," *Psychological Trauma: Theory, Research, Practice, and Policy* 3, no. 4 (2011): 374.
260. Melissa Farley, Julie Bindel, and Jacqueline M. Golding, *Men Who Buy Sex: Who They Buy and What They Know* (London: Eaves, 2009), 21–22, 26 [https://perma.cc/QSU2-7AQV].
261. Farley et al., "Cambodian Men," 13.
262. Ibid.
263. Ibid., 26; *see also* 13 (referring to the more elaborate questionnaire with regard to pornography as compared to previous similar studies).
264. Ibid., 27.
265. Janet Bradley et al., "Pornography, Sexual Enhancement Products, and Sexual Risk of Female Sex Workers and Their Clients in Southern India," *Arch. Sex. Behav.* 45, no. 4 (2016): 950 tbl. 3 (95% CI: 1.66–12.1; p=.003).
266. Farley et al., "Attitudes and Social Characteristics . . . Scotland," 376. On sampling, see 371.
267. Durchslag and Goswami, *Deconstructing the Demand*, 12.
268. Ibid. One john expressed this idea in more general terms: "I want to pay someone to do something a normal person wouldn't do. To piss on someone or pay someone to do something degrading who is not my girlfriend" (12).
269. According to the reports of the 110 johns in Scotland, the more frequent pornography consumers (more than once monthly) were significantly more likely to buy sex more often than less frequent consumers (once or twice per year). Farley et al., "Attitudes and Social Characteristics . . . Scotland," 374.
270. Farley et al., "Cambodian Men," 26.
271. Ibid., 26 n.6 (reporting a result from the Boston study).
272. *See* Martin A. Monto and Nick McRee, "A Comparison of the Male Customers of Female Street Prostitutes with National Samples of Men," *Int'l J. Offender Therapy & Comp. Criminol.* 49, no. 5 (2005): 515 tbl. 1, 520–521 & tbl. 2, 523.
273. Ibid., 520 tbl. 2. First-time offenders and national men reporting buying sex at some previous point in their lives both reported lower pornography consumption than repeat offenders, but higher consumption than non-buyers. All statistical comparisons among these four groups were strongly significant (p<.001) (520 tbl. 2).
274. *See* Bidhubhusan Mahapatra and Niranjan Saggurti, "Exposure to Pornographic Videos and Its Effect on HIV-Related Sexual Risk Behaviours among Male Migrant Workers in Southern India," *PLOS One* 9, no. 11 (2014): 5 & 8 tbl. 3 (95% CI: 3.7–4.8).
275. Farley et al., "Comparing Sex Buyers [Boston]," 31 (as reported 2011).
276. Farley et al., "Cambodian Men," 14.

277. Ibid., 30.
278. Ibid., 32.
279. Ibid., 26.
280. Ibid., 30–31.
281. Ibid., 31.
282. Ibid.
283. Ibid., 30.
284. Ibid., 30; $r = -.20$, $p = .018$. This correlation was retrieved with age transformed into a continuous log variable (30 n.7).
285. Ibid., 32 ($p = .010$).
286. Ibid. ($p = .0124$)
287. SOU 1995:15 Könshandeln [government report series] 96–97 (Swed.).
288. Att'y General's Comm., *Final Report*, 204.
289. Durchslag and Goswami, *Deconstructing the Demand*, 13.
290. Ibid., 11.
291. Farley et al., "Attitudes and Social Characteristics . . . Scotland," 375 (quote).
292. Farley et al., "Cambodian Men," 31.
293. Ibid.
294. Farley et al., "Attitudes and Social Characteristics . . . Scotland," 374.
295. *See supra* note 244 and accompanying text.
296. *Cf.* Natalie Purcell, *Violence and the Pornographic Imaginary: The Politics of Sex, Gender, and Aggression in Hardcore Pornography* (New York: Routledge, 2012) (analyzing content changes over time).
297. Paul J. Wright et al., "Pornography, Alcohol, and Male Sexual Dominance," *Comm. Monographs* 82, no. 2 (2015): 252–270.
298. Ibid., 258.
299. Ibid., 259.
300. Ibid., 260 tbl. 1. The questionnaire does not reveal whether those who had tried a specific act had a desire to try it further; rather, it seems to assume that once a person has engaged in a behavior, they will continue "desiring" it. However, a similar survey conducted in the United States that also included women (*see infra* notes 303–311 and accompanying text) showed that is not always a reasonable assumption, especially with respect to women, and possibly not with all men.
301. Ibid., 260–61 & tbl. 2; *cf.* 262 tbl. 3.
302. Chapter 1 discusses evidence showing that "gonzo" predominates among male consumers.
303. Ana J. Bridges et al., "Sexual Scripts and the Sexual Behavior of Men and Women Who Use Pornography," *Sexualization, Media, & Society* 2, no. 4 (2016): doi:10.1177/2374623816668275.
304. Ibid., 4.
305. Ibid., 6 tbl. 3.
306. Ibid., 5 tbl. 2, 8 tbl. 5. In contrast to the study from Germany, this U.S. study seems to have had separate questions regarding imitation and interest in trying behaviors.

307. Chyng Sun, Matthew B. Ezzell, and Olivia Kendall, "Naked Aggression: The Meaning and Practice of Ejaculation on a Woman's Face," *Violence against Women* 23, no. 14 (2017): 1716, 1725.
308. Bridges et al., "Sexual Scripts," 5 tbl. 2, 8 tbl. 5.
309. Ibid., 7 & tbl. 4.
310. Ibid., 8–9 & tbl. 6.
311. Ibid., 10–11.
312. Cicely Marston and Ruth Lewis, "Anal Heterosex among Young People and Implications for Health Promotion: A Qualitative Study in the UK," *BMJ Open* 4, no. 8 (2014): 2, doi:10.1136/bmjopen-2014-004996.
313. For details of the sample, see Ruth Lewis, Cicely Marston, and Kay Wellings, "Bases, Stages and 'Working Your Way Up': Young People's Talk about Non-Coital Practices and 'Normal' Sexual Trajectories," *Sociol. Res. Online* 18, no. 1 (2013) [http://www.socresonline.org.uk/18/1/1.html].
314. Marston and Lewis, "Anal Heterosex," 2.
315. Ibid., 4.
316. Ibid., 3.
317. Breanne Fahs and Jax Gonzalez, "The Front Lines of the 'Back Door': Navigating (Dis)Engagement, Coercion, and Pleasure in Women's Anal Sex Experiences," *Feminism & Psychol.* 24, no. 4 (2014): 507, 510 (quotes).
318. Ibid., 510 (quote), 512.
319. Ibid., 512.
320. Marston and Lewis, "Anal Heterosex," 3.
321. Chapter 1 reviews studies of pornography consumption frequencies among men and women.
322. Marston and Lewis, "Anal Heterosex," 3.
323. Debby Herbenick et al., "Diverse Sexual Behaviors and Pornography Use: Findings from a Nationally Representative Probability Survey of Americans Aged 18 to 60 Years," *J. Sexual Medicine* 17 (2020): 623–633.
324. Ibid., 628.
325. Ibid., 627 tbl. 2.
326. Neil M. Malamuth and Eileen V. Pitpitan, "The Effects of Pornography Are Moderated by Men's Sexual Aggression Risk," in *Pornography: Driving the Demand in International Sex Trafficking*, ed. David E. Guinn and Julie DiCaro (Los Angeles: Int'l Human Rights L. Inst., DePaul Univ., 2007), 140–141.
327. Ibid., 138–140.
328. Drew A. Kingston and Neil M. Malamuth, "Problems with Aggregate Data and the Importance of Individual Differences in the Study of Pornography and Sexual Aggression: Comment on Diamond, Jozifkova, and Weiss (2010)," *Arch. Sex. Behav.* 40, no. 5 (2011): 1045–1046.
329. Dean G. Kilpatrick et al., *Drug-Facilitated, Incapacitated, and Forcible Rape: A National Study* (Charleston, SC: Nat'l Crime Victims Res. & Treatment Center, 2007), 47–48 & Exhibit 41 [https://perma.cc/56W9-44Z3]. These percentages are for "forcible rape."

330. Ibid., 44. The study's operative definition of rape included "forcible rape," "drug and alcohol facilitated rape," or "incapacitated rape" (10).
331. Ferguson and Hartley, "Pornography and Sexual Aggression," 7–10 (listing, inter alia, works by Diamond et al., Kimmel and Linders, Scott and Schwalm, as well as Winnick and Evans that are based on data on reported sex crimes and arrests).
332. Larry Baron and Murray A. Straus, "Four Theories of Rape: A Macrosociological Analysis," *Soc. Problems* 34, no. 5 (1987): 467–489.
333. Joseph E. Scott and Loretta A. Schwalm, "Rape Rates and the Circulation Rates of Adult Magazines," *J. Sex Res.* 24, no. 1 (1988): 241–250.
334. Baron and Straus, "Four Theories of Rape," 480; Scott and Schwalm, "Rape Rates," 245–246.
335. Baron and Straus, "Four Theories of Rape," 478 fig. 2, 480.
336. The fact that the proportion of African Americans in the population correlates with more reports of rape crimes does not mean that the actual prevalence is greater; it simply means that it is more common that crimes supposed to be committed by African Americans than, most often, white Americans, are *reported* rather than *suppressed*—an outcome that may be influenced by several factors, among them racism and poverty.
337. Baron and Straus, "Four Theories of Rape," 477; Scott and Schwalm, "Rape Rates," 244–245.
338. Baron and Straus, "Four Theories of Rape," 472–477; *cf.* Scott and Schwalm, "Rape Rates," 244–245.
339. Baron and Straus, "Four Theories of Rape," 473.
340. *See, e.g.*, Patricia Tjaden and Nancy Thoennes, *Full Report of the Prevalence, Incidence, and Consequences of Violence against Women* (Washington, DC: Nat'l Inst. of Justice, 2000), 15 & passim [https://perma.cc/9WFU-8E9D]; Wesley G. Skogan, "A Review: The National Crime Survey Redesign," *Publ. Opinion Quart.* 54, no. 2 (1990): 258; Kilpatrick et al., *Drug-Facilitated, Incapacitated*, 24–25.
341. Baron and Straus, "Four Theories of Rape," 474–475 tbl. 1; Scott and Schwalm, "Rape Rates," 247 tbl. 1.
342. *Cf.* Malamuth and Pitpitan, "Effects of Pornography," 140–142 (discussing similar methodological problems).
343. Scott and Schwalm, "Rape Rates," 243.
344. Ibid., 245.
345. Ibid., 246.
346. Ibid., 246–247.
347. Ibid., 245–246; $p > .05$.
348. Milton Diamond, Eva Jozifkova, and Peter Weiss, "Pornography and Sex Crimes in the Czech Republic," *Arch. Sex. Behav.* 40, no. 5 (2011): 1039–1040.
349. When the Cold War officially ended in 1989, epitomized by the dismantling of the Berlin Wall, a considerable liberalization of the former Soviet bloc took place. The introduction of market economies and more freedom of movement for goods and people reduced many previous obstacles to obtain pornography, thus Diamond, Jozifkova, and Weiss' assumption that its consumption increased.

350. Diamond, Jozifkova, and Weiss, "Pornography and Sex Crimes," 1038–1040.
351. Given space constraints, only the determinants of rapes will be discussed here, but the Czech study's analysis of other sexual crimes is equally problematic and has been closely scrutinized elsewhere. *See* Max Waltman, *The Politics of Legal Challenges to Pornography: Canada, Sweden, and the United States*, Stockholm Studies in Politics 160, PhD diss. (Stockholm: Stockholm University, 2014), 134–138.
352. Diamond, Jozifkova, and Weiss, "Pornography and Sex Crimes," 1039 & fig. 1.
353. Ibid., 1040.
354. Malamuth and Pitpitan, "Effects of Pornography," 140–141 (emphasis omitted).
355. Kilpatrick et al., *Drug-Facilitated, Incapacitated*, 44, 47–48 & Exhibit 41.
356. Diamond, Jozifkova, and Weiss, "Pornography and Sex Crimes," 1040.
357. Ibid., 1039.
358. A study published in 2007 estimated that 18% of *all* U.S. women had been raped, of whom only 18% reported a crime, while finding that the reporting frequency did *not* increase between 1991 and 2005. Kilpatrick et al., *Drug-Facilitated, Incapacitated*, 56–59. Notably, the *prevalence* of "forcible rape" was estimated to have increased by 27.3% per capita since 1991 (57). In terms of reporting trends, FBI statistics counted 84,767 reports of forcible rape in 2010 in all states, yet only 20,088 of these reports led to arrest of a suspect. *See* Federal Bureau of Investigation, U.S. Dep't of Justice, *Crime in the United States, 2010 Uniform Crime Reports* (2011) [https://perma.cc/Z3WT-HEL5] (tbl. 1, reports); [https://perma.cc/NGS9-SMMH] (tbl. 29, arrests). Moreover, alcohol- and drug-facilitated/incapacitated rapes (accomplished without physical force) have been reported at about half the frequency as forcible rapes. Kilpatrick et al., *Drug-Facilitated, Incapacitated*, 59. Only a minority of arrests have resulted in conviction in the United States. *See, e.g.*, Kathleen Daly and Brigitte Bouhours, "Rape and Attrition in the Legal Process: A Comparative Analysis of Five Countries," *Crime & Just.* 39, no. 1 (2010): 605–607. The U.S. Senate Committee on the Judiciary's 1993 majority report concluded that 98% of those subjected to forcible rape never receive justice. Majority Staff of Senate Comm. on the Judiciary, 103d Cong., *The Response to Rape: Detours on the Road to Equal Justice* (1993), 2, 11, 34–37 (with an introduction by Chairman Senator Joseph R. Biden Jr.). Similar figures appear in the academic literature. *See, e.g.*, Jane Kim, "Taking Rape Seriously: Rape as Slavery," 35 *Harvard J. Gender & Law* 263, 264–265 (2012); Joan McGregor, "Introduction to Philosophical Issues in Rape Law," 11 *Law & Phil.* 1, 2 (1992); *see also* Mary P. Koss et al., *No Safe Haven: Male Violence against Women at Home, at Work, and in the Community* (Washington, DC: APA, 1994), 167–171 tbl. 1 (reviewing prevalence rates set forth in the literature).
359. *See, e.g.*, Baron and Straus, "Four Theories of Rape," 472; *cf.* John H. Court, "Sex and Violence: A Ripple Effect," in Malamuth and Donnerstein, *Pornography and Sexual Aggression*, 154–155 (discussing demographic rape predictors); Malamuth and Pitpitan, "Effects of Pornography," 141.
360. *Indianapolis, Ind. Code* ch. 16 § 16-3(q) (1984), *invalidated in* American Booksellers Ass'n v. Hudnut, 771 F.2d 323 (7th Cir. 1985).

Chapter 3 Democracy and Hierarchy

1. *See, e.g.*, Catharine A. MacKinnon, "Substantive Equality Revisited: A Reply to Sandra Fredman," *Int'l J. Const. Law* 14, no. 3 (2016): 739–746; *cf.* Catharine A. MacKinnon, *Toward a Feminist Theory of the State* (Cambridge, MA: Harvard Univ. Press, 1989), 214–249 (using like terms throughout).
2. David Held, *Models of Democracy*, 3rd ed. (Cambridge, UK: Polity Press, 2006), 19.
3. David Held, "Democracy: From City-States to a Cosmopolitan Order?," *Political Studies* 40, no. s1 (1992): 13.
4. *See, e.g.*, Held, *Models of Democracy*, 22–23.
5. *See, e.g.*, Niccolò Machiavelli, *Machiavel's Discourses upon the First Decade of T. Livius*, trans. Edward Dacres, 2nd ed. (London: Charles Harper, 1674) (ca. 1513–1519), digital image archive, 1st book, chaps. 3–6, 55–58, [http://eebo.chadwyck.com/home].
6. *See* John Stuart Mill, *On Liberty*, ed. Gertrude Himmelfarb (London: Penguin, 1974), 123–138. "Genius" at 130.
7. Ibid., 139–140.
8. *See* Held, *Models of Democracy*, 86–87 (citing Mill).
9. Another assumption often invoked in Mill's defense is that economic equality would counter incentives for productivity—a metaphysical claim not susceptible to empirical testing except in a minimal sense, for example, in a specific competitive workplace or society. Community recognition, intellectual stimulation, or social solidarity may provide incentives for growth and progress that are just as strong as direct economic benefits, the aptness of which is manifest not least by the many unpaid activists who work tirelessly for essentially altruistic objectives, such as human rights, justice, or the environment.
10. John Locke, *Two Treatises of Government and a Letter concerning Toleration*, ed. Ian Shapiro (New Haven, CT: Yale Univ. Press: 2003) (1690), 160–161 ¶ 137 (Second Treatise).
11. Ibid., 140 ¶ 93.
12. *See, e.g.*, ibid., 156–62 ¶¶ 131 & 138.
13. *See* Held, *Models of Democracy*, 68 (discussing Montesquieu's work).
14. Whitney v. California, 274 U.S. 357, 375 (1927) (Brandeis, J., concurring).
15. Mill, *On Liberty*, 68.
16. Ibid., 119.
17. Ibid.
18. Ibid., 158.
19. Ibid.
20. For a critical review of this concept, see Frederick Schauer, "Slippery Slopes," 99 *Harv. L. Rev.* 361, 361–383 (1985); *cf.* Catharine A. MacKinnon, *Only Words* (Cambridge MA: Harvard Univ. Press), 75–78.
21. James Madison, "The Federalist No. 10," in *Alexander Hamilton, James Madison, and John Jay: The Federalist; with The Letters of Brutus*, ed. Terence Ball (Cambridge: Cambridge Univ. Press, 2003) (1787), PDF e-book, 40–41; *cf.* Held, *Models of Democracy*, 72 (discussing Madison).

22. *See* Robert A. Dahl, *A Preface to Democratic Theory* (Chicago: Univ. of Chicago Press, 1956), 83.
23. Ibid., 58–59.
24. *See, e.g.*, Carole Pateman, *The Sexual Contract* (Cambridge, UK: Polity Press, 1988).
25. *See* Catharine A. MacKinnon, "On Torture," in *Are Women Human? And Other International Dialogues* (Cambridge, MA: Belknap Press of Harvard Univ. Press, 2006), 17–27, for a critical analysis of gender-based violence compared to state-sanctioned terror.
26. *See* Ian Carter, "Positive and Negative Liberty," in *Stanford Encyclopedia of Philosophy* (Fall 2016 Edition), ed. Edward N. Zalta (2003–2012), [https://plato.stanford.edu/archives/spr2016/entries/liberty-positive-negative/].
27. Ibid; *cf.* Isaiah Berlin, "Two Concepts of Freedom," in *Liberty: Incorporating "Four Essays on Liberty,"* ed. Isaiah Berlin and Henry Hardy (Oxford: Oxford Univ. Press Scholarship Online, 2003), e-book (paginated), 169–181, doi:10.1093/019924989X.001.0001.
28. *Cf.* Hilary Charlesworth and Christine Chinkin, *The Boundaries of International Law: A Feminist Analysis* (Manchester: Manchester Univ. Press, 2000), 231–244 (discussing the three "generations" of rights, the first directed against state (or public) action aligned with the concept of negative rights, the second and third directed toward private or group rights aligned with the concept of positive rights).
29. DeShaney v. Winnebago County Dept. of Social Services, 489 U.S. 189, 196 (1989) (6-3) (citations omitted). For facts acknowledged regarding the child's injuries, see 193.
30. *See, e.g.*, Town of Castle Rock, Colo. v. Gonzales, 545 U.S. 748, 755, 768–769 (2005) (7-2) (citing *DeShaney*, 489 U.S. 189, while finding that a mother could not sue a town and its police department for failing to enforce a restraining order against her estranged husband, who ultimately murdered all three of their children). *But see* Jessica Lenahan (Gonzales) et al. v. United States, Case 12.626, Inter-Am. Comm'n H.R., Report No. 80/11 (July 21, 2011) [http://www.oas.org/en/iachr/decisions/2011/USPU12626EN.doc] (finding the United States responsible for human rights violations against the plaintiff and her three deceased children and issuing recommendations for changing U.S. laws and policies related to domestic violence).
31. Carmichele v. Minister of Safety and Security, 2001 (4) SA 938 (CC) (S. Afr.).
32. *Carmichele*, ¶ 23.
33. *Carmichele*, ¶ 45 (quoting Osman v. United Kingdom, 29 E.H.R.R. 245 at 305, ¶ 115 (Eur. Ct. H.R. 1998)).
34. Opuz v. Turkey, App. No. 33401/02, Eur. Ct. H.R. (2009).
35. Declaration on the Elimination of Violence Against Women, G.A. Res. 48/104, pmbl. *para* 6, U.N. doc. A/Res/48/104 (Dec. 20, 1993).
36. See, e.g., Charlesworth and Chinkin, *Boundaries of International Law*, 231–44.
37. For details, see introduction.
38. U.N. Comm. on the Elimination of Discrimination Against Women, 11th Sess., "General Recommendation No. 19," ¶ 12, U.N. Doc. A/47/38 (Feb. 1, 1992).
39. Ibid., ¶ 24(t), t(i).

40. Human Rights Comm., 68th Sess., 1834th Mtg., "General Comment No. 28," ¶ 22, U.N. Doc. CCPR/C/21/Rev.1/Add.10 (Mar. 29, 2000).
41. *See* Fourth World Conference on Women, Sept. 4–15, 1995, "Beijing Declaration and Platform for Action," ¶ 118, U.N. Doc. A/CONF.177/20/Rev.1.
42. Protocol to the African Charter on Human and Peoples' Rights on the Rights of Women in Africa, art. 13(m), July 11, 2003 (entry into force Nov. 26, 2005) [http://perma.cc/D3SB-L4Q3].
43. "Resolution on Pornography," *Eur. Parl.* 1994 O.J. (C 20) 546, 548 (¶K) (Dec. 17, 1993).
44. "Resolution on Discrimination Against Women in Advertising," *Eur. Parl.* 1997 O.J. (C 304) 60, 61–62 (¶5) (Oct. 6, 1997).
45. *See* Vishaka v. State of Rajasthan, [1997] 3 L.R.C. 361, A.I.R. [1997] S.C. 3011 (Aug. 13, 1997) (India Sup. Ct.); Apparel Export Promotion Council v. A. K. Chopra, (1999) 1 S.C.C. 759, A.I.R. [1999] S.C. 625 (India Sup. Ct.).
46. *See, e.g.*, Carolyn Bronstein, *Battling Pornography: The American Feminist Anti-Pornography Movement, 1976–1986* (Cambridge: Cambridge Univ. Press, 2011), 83–92, 139–157; Susan Brownmiller, *In Our Time: Memoir of a Revolution* (New York: Random House, 1999), 295–325. Notable early U.S. organizations against pornography were Women Against Violence Against Women, formed in 1976 in Los Angeles; Women Against Violence in Pornography and Media, formed in early 1977 in Berkeley; and Women Against Pornography, formed in 1979 and based in New York City—the largest thereto organized attempt against pornography by the women's movement. Some more well-known activists during the early days were Kathleen Barry, Susan Brownmiller, Lynn Campbell, Andrea Dworkin, Laura Lederer, Dorchen Leidholdt, Julia London, Robin Morgan, Amina Abdur Rahman, Diana Russell, and Gloria Steinem.
47. Brownmiller, *In Our Time*, 297–98; Susan Cole, *Pornography and the Sex Crisis* (Toronto: Amanita Enterprises, 1989), 72; Laura Lederer, ed., *Take Back the Night: Women on Pornography* (New York: William Morrow, 1980), 15.
48. *See* Cole, *Pornography and the Sex Crisis*, 72.
49. *See* Dany Lacombe, *Blue Politics: Pornography and the Law in the Age of Feminism* (Toronto: Univ. of Toronto Press, 1994), 78–79.
50. *See infra* Chapter 7.
51. *See* MacKinnon, *Toward a Feminist Theory*, 97.
52. *See* ibid., 89–90.
53. Ibid., 83.
54. However, women as a group also have conflicting social interests on racial, economic, ethnic, age, and other grounds. As MacKinnon observes, "[a]ll women possess ethnic (and other definitive) particularities that mark their femaleness; at the same time their femaleness marks their particularities and constitutes one." Ibid., xii.
55. For instance, in Chapter 1 studies suggested that most johns understand that women are harmed in prostitution—i.e., the same men who themselves exploit and abuse these women irrespective of the harms.
56. For a discussion of this tension, see MacKinnon, *Toward a Feminist Theory*, 195–214. For a critical analysis of obscenity law from a feminist anti-pornography perspective,

see Catharine A. MacKinnon, *Feminism Unmodified: Discourses on Life and Law* (Cambridge, MA: Harvard Univ. Press, 1987), 146–162.

57. *See* MacKinnon, *Toward a Feminist Theory*, 184–185 ("The more intimate one is with one's accused rapist, the less likely a court is to find that what happened was rape. . . . Under these conditions, women often do not use birth control because of its social meaning, a meaning women did not create. Using contraception means acknowledging and planning the possibility of intercourse, accepting one's sexual availability, and appearing nonspontaneous.").
58. Ibid., 180.
59. *Cf.* ibid., 180–183.
60. Ibid., 114.
61. Ibid., chaps. 6, 9, & 11.
62. S. Laurel Weldon and Mala Htun, "The Civic Origins of Progressive Policy Change: Combating Violence against Women in Global Perspective, 1975–2005," *Am. Pol. Sci. Rev.* 106, no. 3 (2012): 548–569.
63. Ibid., 550–551.
64. Ibid., 548, 564. Other significant predictors of lesser magnitude were withdrawal of reservations to international and regional human rights instruments on gender-based violence, or ratification of such instruments (but only when accompanied by a stronger domestic feminist movement); similarly, regional diffusion of efficient policies was a significant, though weaker, predictor (561–563).
65. Ibid., 563–564.
66. Ibid., 560.
67. Ibid., 553 (citations omitted).
68. Ibid., 553.
69. Ibid., 555.
70. Iris Marion Young, "Polity and Group Difference: A Critique of the Ideal of Universal Citizenship," in *Throwing Like a Girl and Other Essays in Feminist Philosophy and Social Theory* (Bloomington: Indiana Univ. Press, 1990), 121 (citing Jane Mansbridge, *Beyond Adversary Democracy* (New York: Basic Books, 1989)).
71. Young, "Polity and Group Difference," 121.
72. Ibid. (citing Amy Gutmann, *Liberal Equality* (Cambridge, MA: Cambridge Univ. Press, 1980), 191–202).
73. *Cf.* Iris Marion Young, *Justice and the Politics of Difference* (Princeton, NJ: Princeton Univ. Press, 1990), 183–191, esp. 183–186.
74. *Cf.* Iris Marion Young, "Activist Challenges to Deliberative Democracy," *Political Theory* 29, no. 5 (Oct. 2001): 673–684 (discussing how the constraints imposed by deliberative institutions affect social justice activism).
75. Weldon and Htun, "Civic Origins," 553.
76. *See* Iris Marion Young, *Inclusion and Democracy* (Oxford: Oxford Univ. Press, 2000), 134–141 (conceptualizing the distinction between "perspective" and "interest").
77. Weldon and Htun, "Civic Origins," 553 (citations omitted).
78. Young, "Polity and Group Difference," 124.

79. Ibid. *Cf.* Young, *Justice and the Politics of Difference*, 184.
80. See Chapter 1 for a discussion of credible representation.
81. *Cf.* Young, *Inclusion and Democracy*, 149.
82. Young, "Polity and Group Difference," 124; Young, *Justice and the Politics of Difference*, 184.
83. Young, *Justice and the Politics of Difference*, 185–186.
84. Young, *Inclusion and Democracy*, 40–44.
85. Young, *Justice and the Politics of Difference*, 185.
86. For an analysis of how, while ostensibly being protected as "speech," pornography silences women in society, see Catharine A. MacKinnon, "Francis Biddle's Sister," in *Feminism Unmodified: Discourses on Life and Law* (Cambridge, MA: Harvard Univ. Press, 1987), 192–197.
87. *Cf.* Young, *Justice and the Politics of Difference*, 186.
88. Ibid., 185.
89. Ian Shapiro, *The State of Democratic Theory* (Princeton, NJ: Princeton Univ. Press, 2003), 4.
90. Ibid., 3.
91. Ibid.
92. Ibid., 48.
93. Ibid., 49.
94. Young, *Justice and the Politics of Difference*, 184.
95. Shapiro, *State of Democratic Theory*, 5.
96. Ibid., 48 (citations omitted).
97. Jane Mansbridge, "Should Blacks Represent Blacks and Women Represent Women? A Contingent 'Yes,'" *J. Politics* 61, no. 3 (1999): 641.
98. Ibid.
99. Ibid., 639.
100. As expressed in a brief filed on behalf of the plaintiff-respondent in the first U.S. Supreme Court case to recognize sexual harassment at work as sex discrimination: "All too often, it is Black women like Ms. Vinson who have been specifically victimized by the invidious stereotype of being scandalous and lewd women, perhaps targeting them to would-be perpetrators. This is not to say that this is a case of race discrimination, but rather that minority race aggravates one's vulnerability as a woman by reducing one's options and undermining one's credibility and social worth." Brief of Respondent Mechelle Vinson at 67–68, Meritor Savings Bank v. Vinson, 477 U.S. 57 (1986) (9-0) (No. 84-1979) (Lexis). Brief authored by Catharine MacKinnon, joint representation with co-counsel Patricia Barry. *See* Catharine A. MacKinnon, "Intersectionality as Method: A Note," *Signs: Journal of Women in Culture and Society* 38, no. 4 (2013): 1025 n.23.
101. On pornography's effect on sexual harassment specifically, see, e.g., Jane D. Brown and Kelly L. L'Engle, "X-Rated: Sexual Attitudes and Behaviors Associated with U.S. Early Adolescents' Exposure to Sexually Explicit Media," *Comm. Res.* 46, no. 1 (2009): 137, 142 tbl. 3, & 143; Michele L. Ybarra and Richard E. Thompson,

"Predicting the Emergence of Sexual Violence in Adolescence," *Prevention Science* 19, no. 4 (2018): 409, 410 tbl. 2.

102. *Cf.* Kimberle Crenshaw, "Mapping the Margins: Intersectionality, Identity Politics, and Violence against Women of Color," 43 *Stanford Law Rev.* 1241, 1268 (1991) (comparing the "special attention given to the rape of the Central Park [white] jogger during a week in which twenty-eight other cases of first-degree rape or attempted rape were reported in New York," most involving women of color, some being gang rapes and many "as horrific as the rape in Central Park, yet all were virtually ignored by the media") (citations omitted).
103. Mansbridge, "Should Blacks Represent Blacks," 640–641.
104. *Cf.* ibid.
105. *See* Kimberle Crenshaw, "Demarginalizing the Intersection of Race and Sex: A Black Feminist Critique of Antidiscrimination Doctrine, Feminist Theory and Antiracist Politics," 1989 *U. Chi. Legal F.* 139, 139–167 (1989). For an application to gender-based violence, see Crenshaw, "Mapping the Margins," 1241–1299 passim.
106. Crenshaw, "Demarginalizing the Intersection," 151.
107. Ibid., 151–152.
108. *See, e.g.*, Melissa Farley, *Prostitution and Trafficking in Nevada: Making the Connections* (San Francisco: Prostitution Research & Education, 2007), 34; Evelina Giobbe, "Confronting the Liberal Lies about Prostitution," in *Living with Contradictions*, ed. Alison M. Jaggar (Boulder, CO: Westview Press, 1994), 121; *cf.* Melissa Farley, "'Bad for the Body, Bad for the Heart': Prostitution Harms Women Even If Legalized or Decriminalized," *Violence against Women* 10, no. 10 (2004): 1100.
109. *See, e.g.*, Melissa Farley, "Prostitution, Trafficking, and Cultural Amnesia: What We Must *Not Know* in Order to Keep the Business of Sexual Exploitation Running Smoothly," 18 *Yale J.L. & Feminism* 109, 131 (2006) (quoting johns).
110. *See, e.g.*, Catharine A. MacKinnon, *Sex Equality*, 3rd ed., Univ. Casebook Series (St. Paul, MN: Foundation Press, 2016), 915–1002 (discussing, inter alia, different requirements for a showing of violence, threats of violence, and similar forced conditions under various U.S. rape laws); Catharine A. MacKinnon, "Rape Redefined," 10 *Harv. L. & Pol'y Rev.* 431, 474 (2016) (analyzing the shortcomings of rape law and introducing a domestic alternative defining rape as "a physical invasion of a sexual nature under circumstances of threat or use of force, fraud, coercion, abduction, or of the abuse of power, trust, or a position of dependency or vulnerability").
111. *See, e.g.*, Max Waltman and Catharine A. MacKinnon, "Suggestions to the Government's Review of the Sex Purchase Act" (Sweden) (13 signatories) (submission received by government on Mar. 17, 2010), 22–29 [https://ssrn.com/abstract=2416479] (providing examples of rape committed through force and duress against prostituted women in Sweden, but not recognized as such by the courts).
112. Crenshaw, "Demarginalizing the Intersection," 152.
113. Ibid., 149.

114. *See, e.g.*, Melissa Farley et al., "Prostitution and Trafficking in Nine Countries: An Update on Violence and Posttraumatic Stress Disorder," in *Prostitution, Trafficking, and Traumatic Stress*, ed. Melissa Farley (Binghamton, NY: Haworth Maltreatment & Trauma Press, 2003), 48, 51, 56 [http://perma.cc/V7FM-YXKQ] (finding that 89% of 785 prostituted persons in nine countries said they wanted to escape prostitution); MacKinnon, *Sex Equality*, 1571–1572 (citing *Elizabeth Fry Society of Toronto, Streetwork Outreach with Adult Female Prostitutes: Final Report* (1987) (finding that approximately 90% of a sample of 243 women in street prostitution indicated that they wanted to escape); *cf.* Farley, *Prostitution and Trafficking in Nevada*, 23–24, 29 (finding that 81% of 45 respondents in legal brothels said they wished to leave prostitution during interviews, with many speaking in whispers because their conversations were subject to surveillance by listening devices and they were under intense pressure not to disclose information to outsiders that "reflected badly" on the brothels).
115. Crenshaw, "Demarginalizing the Intersection," 167.
116. Ibid. (paraphrasing the title of Paula Giddings, *When and Where I Enter: The Impact of Black Women on Race and Sex in America* (New York: William Morrow, 1984)).
117. *Cf.* Weldon and Htun, "Civic Origins," 553; Young, *Justice and the Politics of Difference*, 185–86.
118. As described in Chapter 1, among other sources of confusion are third-party profiteers that falsely pretend to represent those who are exploited in prostitution.
119. See Chapter 1 for background information and discussion of organizations representing persons used for commercial sex.
120. Judith Butler, "Sovereign Performatives in the Contemporary Scene of Utterance," *Critical Inquiry* 23, no. 2 (1997): 376; *cf.* Judith Butler, *Excitable Speech: A Politics of the Performative* (New York: Routledge, 1997), 101.
121. Butler, "Sovereign Performatives," 352 (footnote omitted). In *Excitable Speech*, Butler changed this sentence. While beginning with the uncited claim that MacKinnon is "[r]elying on recently proposed hate speech regulation," Butler then proceeds differently: "pornography ought to be construed as a kind of 'wound,' according to MacKinnon, because it proclaims and effects the subordinated status of women." Butler, *Excitable Speech*, 73 (note omitted).
122. The grounds for Butler's misunderstanding can be seen in her attached footnote, where she quotes text in which MacKinnon never mentions pornography: "Whatever damage is done through such words is done not only through their context but through their content, in the sense that if they did not contain what they contain, and convey the meanings and feelings and thoughts they convey, they would not evidence or actualize the discrimination that they do." Butler, "Sovereign Performatives," 352 n.4 (quoting MacKinnon, *Only Words*, 14); *cf.* Butler, *Excitable Speech*, 174 n.4. Further omitted from the quotation is the explanation MacKinnon offers for why the "words" she refers to are legally regarded as sex discriminatory in case law (words like "help wanted—male," "sleep with me and I'll give you an A," or "it was essential that the understudy to my Administrative Assistant be a man"). *See* MacKinnon, *Only Words*, 13–14. Butler

also omits the passage immediately following her selected passage, which plainly shows why MacKinnon could not have conceived an argument equating such speech with pornography: "Pornography, by contrast [to discriminatory speech], has been legally framed as a vehicle for the expression of ideas. The Supreme Court of Minnesota recently observed of some pornography before it that 'even the most liberal construction would be strained to find an "idea" in it,' limited as it was to 'who wants what, where, when, how, how much, and how often.' Even this criticism dignifies the pornography. The *idea of* who wants what, where, and when sexually can be expressed without violating anyone and without getting anyone raped. There are many ways to say what pornography says, in the sense of its content. But nothing else does what pornography does." MacKinnon, *Only Words*, 14–15 (footnote omitted). Butler further claims, based on her misreading and without further citation, that "pornography is considered by MacKinnon, through a legal catachresis, to be a form of *speech* and a harmful *utterance* at that." Butler, "Sovereign Performatives," 353 (emphasis added).

123. Butler, "Sovereign Performatives," 376–377; *cf.* Butler, *Excitable Speech*, 102.
124. In *Excitable Speech*, but not in *Critical Inquiry*, Butler states: "I am not opposed to any and all regulations, but I am skeptical. . . . I do think that the ritual chain of hateful speech cannot be effectively countered by means of censorship." Butler, *Excitable Speech*, 102.
125. *Cf.* Martha C. Nussbaum, "The Hip Defeatism of Judith Butler: The Professor of Parody," *New Republic*, Feb. 22, 1999, p. 38 (noting that "a large proportion of the sentences in any book by Butler—especially sentences near the end of chapters—are questions" and non-interrogative sentences in which "Butler never quite tells the reader whether she approves of the view described").
126. Wendy Brown, *States of Injury: Power and Freedom in Late Modernity* (Princeton, NJ: Princeton Univ. Press, 1995), 99.
127. Ibid., 114.
128. As stated previously, negative rights have traditionally created an illusory distinction between public and private that is incapable of apprehending abuses of power or forms of dominance that are not public, for instance, the social subordination of women by men, dominance through entrenched inequality, or private non-state discrimination against minority populations.
129. Brown, *States of Injury*, 99.
130. Ibid., 114.
131. Ibid.
132. Ibid., 140.
133. Ibid., 141.
134. Wendy Brown, "Revaluing Critique: A Response to Kenneth Baynes," *Political Theory* 28, no. 4 (2000): 475 (quoting Kenneth Baynes, "Rights as Critique and the Critique of Rights: Karl Marx, Wendy Brown, and the Social Function of Rights," *Political Theory* 28, no. 4 (2000): 467 [correct is 464]).
135. Brown, "Revaluing Critique," 476.
136. Brown, *States of Injury*, 141; *cf.* Brown, "Revaluing Critique," 476.

137. Note that roughly the same proportion of all live births ended in an abortion while it was illegal in the United States as when it became legal. *See* Brief for the National Coalition Against Domestic Violence as Amicus Curiae Supporting Appellees at 17–18, Webster v. Reproductive Health Servs., 492 U.S. 490 (1989) (No. 88-605) (citing sources suggesting 20–30% of live births ended in abortions in the 1960s, while 27–30% did so in the late 1970s through the 1980s). Moreover, abortion-related maternal deaths were estimated to be roughly eight times higher for illegal abortions right before *Roe v. Wade*, 410 U.S. 113 (1973), than for legal abortions. *See* Willard Cates Jr. and Roger W. Rochat, "Illegal Abortions in the United States: 1972–1974," *Fam. Plan. Persp.* 8, no. 2 (1976): 92. Considering that illegal abortion jeopardized the lives of women, those undertaking such a risk likely do so because of external constraints. For further discussion of reproductive politics, see Catharine A. MacKinnon, "Reflections on Sex Equality under Law," in *Women's Lives, Men's Laws* (Cambridge, MA: Belknap Press of Harvard Univ. Press, 2005), 136–150.
138. Young, *Justice and the Politics of Difference*, 184.
139. *See, e.g.*, Catharine A. MacKinnon, *Sexual Harassment of Working Women: A Case of Sex Discrimination* (New Haven, CT: Yale Univ. Press, 1979); Catharine A. MacKinnon, "Pornography, Civil Rights, and Speech," 20 *Harvard C.R.-C.L. Law Rev.* 1 (1985).
140. Brown, *States of Injury*, 133.
141. Ibid., 141.
142. Butler, "Sovereign Performatives," 376–377; Butler, *Excitable Speech*, 101–102.
143. Butler, "Sovereign Performatives," 376–377; *cf.* Butler, *Excitable Speech*, 101–102.
144. Brown, *States of Injury*, 134.
145. As recalled, Brown criticized universal abstract rights in the context of abortion as "a liberal discourse of generic personhood." Ibid., 141.
146. Ibid., 134.
147. Judith Butler, "Against Proper Objects," *Differences: A Journal of Feminist Cultural Studies* 6, nos. 2–3 (1994): 16.
148. Ibid., 18.
149. Brown, *States of Injury*, 134.
150. Ibid., 95 (emphasis added).
151. Considering that Brown often criticizes other theories as "totalizing," this danger is notable. *See* ibid. (alleging that "the very structure and categories of her [MacKinnon's] theory—its tautological and totalizing dimensions"—are related to a "potentially fascistic interplay of manipulated despair and libidinal arousal"); *cf.* 133 (implying that representing the experiences of subordinated groups in law may lead to "inevitably totalized formulations of identity" that "produce levels of regulation . . . not imagined even by Foucault").
152. Crenshaw, "Mapping the Margins," 1297.
153. Ibid.
154. Ibid., 1296.
155. Brown, *States of Injury*, 133–134.
156. *Cf.* Crenshaw, "Mapping the Margins," 1296.

157. Ibid., 1296 n.180.
158. Brown, *States of Injury*, 134.
159. Gary King, Robert O. Keohane, and Sidney Verba, *Designing Social Inquiry: Scientific Inference in Qualitative Research* (Princeton, NJ: Princeton Univ. Press, 1994), 104.
160. Butler's critique will be revisited in the concluding chapter's discussion, where it will be assessed for it veracity and persuasiveness, particularly in light of the legal challenges to pornography in the United States that Butler has specifically addressed.
161. Discussion of the research design may be found in the introduction.
162. Butler, "Sovereign Performatives," 376–377; Butler, *Excitable Speech*, 101–102.
163. Brown, *States of Injury*, 134.
164. Crenshaw, "Mapping the Margins," 1296–1298.

Chapter 4 The Anti-pornography Civil Rights Ordinances, 1983–1991

1. *See, e.g.*, Brief of the Neighborhood Pornography Task Force [at 321–324] as *Amicus Curiae*, Supporting Appellant Hudnut v. American Booksellers Ass'n, 771 F.2d 323 (7th Cir. 1985), *reprinted in* Catharine A. MacKinnon and Andrea Dworkin, eds., *In Harm's Way: The Pornography Civil Rights Hearings* (Cambridge, MA: Harvard Univ. Press, 1997), 321–331; Paul Brest and Ann Vandenberg, "Politics, Feminism, and the Constitution: The Anti-Pornography Movement in Minneapolis," 39 *Stan. Law Rev.* 607, 608–609 (1987).
2. *See* Brief of Minneapolis Neighborhood Task Force, *supra* note 1, at 322–323; Brest and Vandenberg, "Politics, Feminism," 609; *cf.* Alicia M. Turner, "Feminist Resistance: An Oral History of the Dworkin-MacKinnon Anti-Pornography Civil Rights Ordinance," B.A. thesis, Kalamazoo College, Winter 1997, 26 (on file with Kalamazoo College [https://cache.kzoo.edu/handle/10920/29011]).
3. Brief of the Minneapolis Neighborhood Task Force, *supra* note 1, at 324 & 327; *cf.* Donald Alexander Downs, *The New Politics of Pornography* (Chicago: Univ. of Chicago Press, 1989), 25 (noting that a contemporaneous study suggested "community leaders" and especially "legal elites" were more supportive of protecting pornography than was the "mass public").
4. Brief of Minneapolis Neighborhood Task Force, *supra* note 1, at 327.
5. Catharine A. MacKinnon, "Testimony on Pornography, Minneapolis," in *Butterfly Politics* (Cambridge, MA: Belknap Press of Harvard Univ. Press, 2017), 96 (preface to and dated transcript of MacKinnon's speech at Zoning and Planning Commission hearing); *cf.* Brest and Vandenberg, "Politics, Feminism," 613–615; Downs, *New Politics*, 56–59; Turner, "Feminist Resistance," 26–28.
6. Brest and Vandenberg, "Politics, Feminism," 615 (quoting Dworkin's speech).
7. MacKinnon, "Testimony . . . Minneapolis," 97.
8. Ibid.
9. Brest and Vandenberg, "Politics, Feminism," 616–617.

10. *See* Downs, *New Politics*, 87 (estimating numbers); *cf.* Brest and Vandenberg, "Politics, Feminism," 620, 641–42. Turner, "Feminist Resistance," 23–24, 34–39.
11. Brest and Vandenberg, "Politics, Feminism," 620.
12. Ibid. For complete documentation and transcripts of the Minneapolis hearings, see MacKinnon and Dworkin, *In Harm's Way*, 39–268.
13. For hearing transcripts, see MacKinnon and Dworkin, *In Harm's Way*, 39–202.
14. Brest and Vandenberg, "Politics, Feminism," 644.
15. Ibid., 653.
16. *Indianapolis, Ind. Code* ch. 16 § 16-3(q) (1984), *invalidated by* American Booksellers Ass'n v. Hudnut, 771 F.2d 323 (7th Cir. 1985), *reprinted in* MacKinnon and Dworkin, *In Harm's Way*, 438–457.
17. Susan Brownmiller, *In Our Time: Memoir of a Revolution* (New York: Random House, 1999), 323–325.
18. Andrea Dworkin, "Beaver Talks," in *Life and Death: Unapologetic Writings on the Continuing War against Women* (New York: Free Press, 1997), 92.
19. Turner, "Feminist Resistance," 118; *cf.* Dworkin, "Beaver Talks," 92 (mentioning the court intervention).
20. Dworkin, "Beaver Talks," 92; Turner, "Feminist Resistance," 121.
21. Margaret A. Baldwin, "Pornography and the Traffic in Women: Brief on Behalf of Trudee Able-Peterson et al., Amici Curiae in Support of Defendant and Intervenor-Defendants, *Village Books v. City of Bellingham*," 1 *Yale J. L. & Feminism* 111, 112 (1989); Dworkin, "Beaver Talks," 92; Turner, "Feminist Resistance," 136.
22. Village Books v. City of Bellingham, No. C88-1470D (W.D. Wash. Feb. 9, 1989) (unreported) [https://perma.cc/K7S5-VJPU]. The district court also cited the Supreme Court's summary affirmance of the Seventh Circuit opinion. Ibid. *See* Hudnut v. American Booksellers Ass'n, 475 U.S. 1001 (1986) (6-3) (summary affirmance without opinion). For a discussion of the limited precedential value of that summary affirmance, see *infra* notes 124–127 and accompanying text.
23. *See* Turner, "Feminist Resistance," 144 (interviewing activists involved in the Bellingham challenges).
24. Catharine A. MacKinnon, "The Roar on the Other Side of Silence," in MacKinnon and Dworkin, *In Harm's Way*, 18.
25. Proposed Ordinance § 1, to amend *Minneapolis, Minn. Code of Ordinances* § 139.10(a)(1), 1st Reading, Nov. 23, 1983 (all caps neutralized), *reprinted in* MacKinnon and Dworkin, *In Harm's Way*, 426–432 [hereinafter *Minneapolis Proposed Ordinance*].
26. *Minneapolis Proposed Ordinance*, *supra* note 25, § 139.10(a)(1).
27. Ibid.
28. *See, e.g.*, Margaret T. Gordon and Stephanie Riger, *The Female Fear: The Social Cost of Rape* (Urbana: Univ. of Illinois Press, 1991), 21.
29. *Minneapolis Proposed Ordinance*, *supra* note 25, § 139.10(a)(1).
30. See Chapter 3.
31. *Minneapolis Proposed Ordinance*, *supra* note 25, §§ 139.20(gg)(1)–(2).
32. See Chapter 2 for research definitions of harmful pornography categories.
33. Miller v. California, 413 U.S. 15, 24 (1973) (citations omitted).

34. U.N. Econ. & Soc. Council [ECOSOC], "Preliminary Report of the Special Rapporteur on Violence Against Women," ¶ 240, U.N. Doc. E/CN.4/1995/42 (Nov. 22, 1994) (*submitted by* Radhika Coomaraswamy). *Cf.* ¶¶ 240–242.
35. James Lindgren, "Defining Pornography," 141 *U. Penn. Law. Rev.* 1153 (1993).
36. Ibid., 1161–1167, 1188 tbl. 4.
37. *See* ibid., 1189; *see also* 1187–1191 (providing further details concerning these comparisons).
38. Ibid., 1210.
39. For documentation of the hearings in Minneapolis, Indianapolis, Los Angeles, and Massachusetts, see MacKinnon and Dworkin, *In Harm's Way*, 39–425. Lindgren seemingly did not summarize or otherwise present the ordinances' legislative history to his survey respondents. *See* Lindgren, "Defining Pornography," 1174–1180 (describing the administration of questionnaires), 1223–1275 (appending the questionnaires).
40. *Minneapolis Proposed Ordinance*, *supra* note 25, §§ 139.20(gg)(1)(i)(v).
41. *See* Kyra Lanis and Katherine Covell, "Images of Women in Advertisements: Effects on Attitudes Related to Sexual Aggression," *Sex Roles* 32, nos. 9–10 (1995): 639–649; Nathalie J. MacKay and Katherine Covell, "The Impact of Women in Advertisements on Attitudes toward Women," *Sex Roles* 36, nos. 9–10 (1997): 573–583; Michael A. Milburn, Roxanne Mather, and Sheree D. Conrad, "The Effects of Viewing R-Rated Movie Scenes That Objectify Women on Perceptions of Date Rape," *Sex Roles* 43, nos. 9–10 (2000): 645–664.
42. *Minneapolis Proposed Ordinance*, *supra* note 25, §§ 139.20(gg)(1)(v–vii).
43. Ibid., § 139.20(gg)(1)(i) & (viii).
44. Ibid., § 139.20(gg)(1)(ii–iv) & (ix).
45. Turner, "Feminist Resistance," 30 (interviewing MacKinnon).
46. Dworkin, "Beaver Talks," 87–90.
47. For accounts of hearings, see MacKinnon and Dworkin, *In Harm's Way* and Attorney General's Commission on Pornography, *Final Report of the Attorney General's Commission on Pornography*, ed. Michael J. McManus (Nashville, TN: Rutledge Hill Press, 1986), 197–245.
48. *See, e.g.*, Catharine A. MacKinnon, "Consciousness Raising," in *Toward a Feminist Theory of the State* (Cambridge, MA: Harvard Univ. Press, 1989), 83–105.
49. *Cf.* S. Laurel Weldon and Mala Htun, "The Civic Origins of Progressive Policy Change: Combating Violence against Women in Global Perspective, 1975–2005," *Am. Pol. Sci. Rev.* 106, no. 3 (2012): 553 (discussing ways that historically oppressed groups have self-organized). For further information, see Chapter 3.
50. For a conceptualization distinguishing between "perspective" and "interest," see Iris M. Young, *Inclusion and Democracy* (Oxford: Oxford Univ. Press, 2000), 134–141.
51. For an explanation of the civil rights ordinance that, while written for a popular audience, is nonetheless thorough, see Andrea Dworkin and Catharine A. MacKinnon, *Pornography and Civil Rights: A New Day for Women's Equality* (Minneapolis, MN: Organizing against Pornography, 1988) [http://www.nostatusquo.com/ACLU/dworkin/other/ordinance/newday/TOC.htm].

52. *Minneapolis Proposed Ordinance*, *supra* note 25, §§ 139.40(l)(m)(n)(o).
53. Ibid., § 139.40(l).
54. Ibid., § 139.40(l)(3).
55. Ibid.
56. Ibid., § 139.40(l)(1).
57. Ibid., § 139.40(m).
58. Ibid., § 139.40(m)(2)(i–xiii).
59. Ibid., § 139.40(n).
60. *See supra* note 28.
61. Robinson v. Jacksonville Shipyards, 760 F. Supp. 1486, 1494, 1523 (M.D. Fla. 1991) (settled before appeal).
62. For a description of the pornographic materials found in Robinson's workplace, see, e.g., ibid., 1493–98.
63. Ibid., 1523.
64. Ibid., 1534.
65. *See, e.g.*, Williams v. CSX Transp. Co., 533 Fed. App'x 637, 642–643 (6th Cir. 2013); Greene v. A. Duie Pyle, Inc., 371 F. Supp. 2d 759, 763 (D. Md. 2005); Lyle v. Warner Bros. Television Prods., 132 P.3d 211, 229–230 (Cal. 2006).
66. *Robinson*, 760 F. Supp. at 1535 (citing Roberts v. United States Jaycees, 468 U.S. 609, 626 (1984); Rotary Int'l v. Rotary Club of Duarte, 481 U.S. 537, 549 (1987)).
67. *Roberts*, 468 U.S. at 623.
68. Ibid., 628.
69. *Minneapolis Proposed Ordinance*, *supra* note 25, § 139.40(o).
70. Att'y Gen. Comm., *Final Report*, 201 (citing a presentation from the National Women Judge Conference delivered in October 1986).
71. Letter from Flora Colao to the Minneapolis City Council, Nov. 10, 1983, *reprinted in* MacKinnon and Dworkin, *In Harm's Way*, 214–215.
72. "Hearing on Proposed Ordinance § 1 to amend *Minneapolis, Minn. Code of Ordinances*, Ch. 7, Before the Government Operations Comm.," Sess. II; Dec. 12, 1983, 5:00 P.M. [hereinafter "Minneapolis Hearing"] (testimony of R.M.M.), *transcribed in* MacKinnon and Dworkin, *In Harm's Way*, 113–114.
73. Jane Mansbridge, "Should Blacks Represent Blacks and Women Represent Women? A Contingent 'Yes,'" *J. Politics* 61, no. 3. (1999): 641.
74. *Cf.* Kimberle Crenshaw, "Demarginalizing the Intersection of Race and Sex: A Black Feminist Critique of Antidiscrimination Doctrine, Feminist Theory and Antiracist Politics," 1989 *U. Chi. Legal F.* 139, 151–152, 166–167 (1989).
75. See *Minneapolis Proposed Ordinance*, *supra* note 25, §§ 139.40(m)(2)(i–xiii).
76. For a transcription of the Minneapolis hearings, see MacKinnon and Dworkin, *In Harm's Way*, 39–202.
77. MacKinnon notes that Downs' account does not cite transcripts, but rather what seem to be incomplete notes from the hearings ("Administration Committee Notes"). MacKinnon, "The Roar," 9 n.24. When asked to provide the source documents he cited seven years after publication of his book, he reportedly said that he did not have them (9 n.24).

78. Downs, *New Politics*, 81–88.
79. "Minneapolis Hearing," *supra* note 72, at 76–81, Session I: Dec. 12, 1983, 1:30 P.M. (testimony of Strauss and Alberta); "Minneapolis Hearing," *supra* note 72, at 82–95, Session II: Dec. 12, 1983, 5:00 P.M. (testimony of Beaver, Warwick, Osborne, Laurence, Greene, Campbell, and Halfhill).
80. "Minneapolis Hearing," *supra* note 72, at 201, Session III: Dec. 13, 1983, 5:00 P.M. (statements by Chairman White and MacKinnon).
81. Downs, *New Politics*, 66.
82. Ibid.
83. Brest and Vandenberg, "Politics, Feminism," 644, 653.
84. Diane Kuschel, "A Tale of Two Cities: Civil Rights Antipornography Legislation in Minneapolis and Indianapolis," M.A. thesis: University of Missouri, Columbia, 1995, 90 (quoting "New Tack Sought in Porn Fight," *Indianapolis Star*, Mar. 27, 1984, p. 6).
85. Ibid.
86. Downs, *New Politics*, 66.
87. Giovanni Sartori, "Concept Misformation in Comparative Politics," *Am. Pol. Sci. Rev.* 65, no. 4 (1970): 1034.
88. Downs, *New Politics*, 65.
89. Ian Shapiro, *The State of Democratic Theory* (Princeton, NJ: Princeton Univ. Press, 2003), 44.
90. Ibid.
91. Ibid.
92. Ibid.
93. See the testimonies offered during the public hearings in MacKinnon and Dworkin, *In Harm's Way*, passim.
94. Downs, *New Politics*, 68.
95. Ibid., 91 (citations omitted).
96. Ibid., 142.
97. Iris Marion Young, *Justice and the Politics of Difference* (Princeton, NJ: Princeton Univ. Press, 1990), 183–184.
98. Brest and Vandenberg, "Politics, Feminism," 641–643.
99. Turner, "Feminist Resistance," 94 (citing Martha Allen, "Antiporn Group Rallied at City Hall," *Minneapolis Star & Tribune*, June 22, 1984); *cf.* Kuschel, "A Tale of Two Cities," 63. This event is noted in the index files of the Minnesota Historical Society. *See* "City Hall Pornography Dump 1984 (box 2), Organizing against Pornography" (Organizational Rec., Minn. Hist. Soc'y, 1984) [http://www2.mnhs.org/library/findaids/00183.xml] (index).
100. Brest and Vandenberg, "Politics, Feminism," 653; *cf.* Downs, *New Politics*, 64–65, 87; Kuschel, "A Tale of Two Cities," 64–66; *see also* Michael Atkinson, "An Antiwar Flame That Flickered Glows Brightly Again," *New York Times*, Aug. 28, 2013, C5 (Westlaw) (mentioning Norman Morrison's 1965 Vietnam War protest).
101. Downs, *New Politics*, xviii, 91, 129.
102. *Cf.* Young, *Inclusion and Democracy*, 47–51 (arguing that a strong deliberative norm of "orderliness" silences disadvantaged subordinated groups).

103. Brest and Vandenberg, "Politics, Feminism," 653–654; MacKinnon, "The Roar," 12–13.
104. Downs, *New Politics*, 77–81.
105. Brest and Vandenberg, "Politics, Feminism," 644–645.
106. Downs, *New Politics*, 63.
107. Turner, "Feminist Resistance," 87–88.
108. Downs, *New Politics*, 63–65.
109. Ibid.; *cf.* Brest and Vandenberg, "Politics, Feminism," 646–653 (describing events that occurred after new elections were held).
110. Downs, *New Politics*, 63–65; Brest and Vandenberg, "Politics, Feminism," 653.
111. *Cf.* Shapiro, *State of Democratic Theory*, 44.
112. Dany Lacombe, *Blue Politics: Pornography and the Law in the Age of Feminism* (Toronto: Univ. of Toronto Press, 1994), 152–153.
113. Kimberle Crenshaw, "Mapping the Margins: Intersectionality, Identity Politics, and Violence against Women of Color," 43 *Stanford L. Rev.* 1241, 1296 (1991).
114. *Indianapolis, Ind. Code* ch. 16 § 16-3(q) (1984) [hereinafter *Indianapolis Code* (1984)], *invalidated by* American Booksellers Ass'n v. Hudnut, 771 F.2d 323 (7th Cir. 1985), *reprinted in* MacKinnon and Dworkin, *In Harm's Way*, 438–457.
115. American Booksellers Ass'n v. Hudnut, 598 F. Supp. 1316, 1318–1320 (S.D. Ind. 1984).
116. Downs, *New Politics*, 131.
117. Turner, "Feminist Resistance," 70; *cf.* Downs, *New Politics*, 131 (noting that the preliminary injunction against enforcement was "uncontested").
118. Baldwin, "Pornography and the Traffic in Women," 137.
119. American Booksellers Ass'n v. Hudnut, 771 F.2d 323, 327 (7th Cir. 1985).
120. Baldwin, "Pornography and the Traffic in Women," 137.
121. Catharine A. MacKinnon and Andrea Dworkin, "Appendix: American Booksellers Ass'n Inc. v. Hudnut; Editors' Note," in MacKinnon and Dworkin, *In Harm's Way*, 462 (quoting Motion to Intervene as Plaintiffs, Cause No. IP 84-791C, U.S. Dist. Ct. S.D. Ind. (May 1984), §3).
122. American Booksellers Ass'n v. Hudnut, 650 F. Supp. 324, 331 (S.D. Ind. 1986).
123. MacKinnon and Dworkin, "Appendix," 463.
124. American Booksellers Ass'n v. Hudnut, 598 F. Supp. 1316, 1318–1320 (S.D. Ind. 1984), *aff'd* 771 F.2d 323 (7th Cir. 1985), *aff'd mem.* 475 U.S. 1001 (1986) (6-3) (summary affirmance without opinion), *reh'g denied* 475 U.S. 1132 (1986).
125. *See* Catharine A. MacKinnon, *Sex Equality*, 3rd ed. (St. Paul, MN: Foundation Press, 2016), 1757 (citing Robert L. Stern et al., *Supreme Court Practice*, 7th ed. (Washington, DC: Bureau of Nat'l Affairs, 1993), 215–221).
126. MacKinnon, *Sex Equality*, 1757 (citing cases).
127. *Hudnut*, 475 U.S. at 1001 (6-3).
128. American Booksellers Ass'n v. Hudnut, 771 F.2d 323, 327 (7th Cir. 1985) (citations omitted).

129. The appellate case was decided by a three-judge panel that produced Judge Easterbrook's opinion (ibid., 323–334) and a brief concurring opinion (334) authored by the Senior Circuit Judge.
130. *Cf.* Shapiro, *State of Democratic Theory*, 44.
131. Ibid.
132. *Hudnut*, 771 F.2d at 327 (describing that "plaintiffs . . . *read* . . . material that could be affected by the ordinance") (emphasis added).
133. *Cf.* Justin Gillis, "Panel's Warning on Climate Risk: Worst Is to Come," *New York Times*, Mar. 31, 2014, A1 (Westlaw).
134. Christine Sypnowich, "Law and Ideology," in *Stanford Encyclopedia of Philosophy*, ed. Edward N. Zalta (2014) [https://plato.stanford.edu/archives/spr2017/entries/law-ideology/].
135. *Indianapolis Code* (1984), *supra* note 114, ch. 16 §§ 16-1(2) (1984), *invalidated by Hudnut*, 771 F.2d at 323.
136. *Hudnut*, 771 F.2d at 328.
137. Ibid., 329.
138. Ibid.
139. Ibid.
140. Ibid. (quoting *Indianapolis Code* (1984), *supra* note 114, ch. 16 § 16-1(a)(2)) (brackets in opinion).
141. Ibid., 329–330.
142. New York v. Ferber, 458 U.S. 747, 763–764 (1982).
143. *See, e.g.*, United States v. Norris, 159 F.3d 926, 930 (5th Cir. 1998).
144. *Indianapolis Code* (1984), *supra* note 114, ch. 16 §§ 16-3(g)(4–7).
145. *Hudnut*, 771 F.2d at 328 (citing Brandenburg v. Ohio, 395 U.S. 444 (1969); DeJonge v. Oregon, 299 U.S. 353 (1937); Collin v. Smith, 578 F.2d 1197 (7th Cir. 1978), *cert. denied*, 439 U.S. 916 (1978)).
146. Brandenburg v. Ohio, 395 U.S. 444, 449 (1969).
147. Ibid., 446 n.1.
148. Schenck v. United States, 249 U.S. 47, 52 (1919).
149. Charles L. Lumpkins, *American Pogrom: The East St. Louis Race Riot and Black Politics* (Athens: Ohio Univ. Press, 2008), 1.
150. *E.g.*, Chaplinsky v. New Hampshire, 315 U.S. 568, 571–572 (1942); Beauharnais v. Illinois, 343 U.S. 250 (1952).
151. New York v. Ferber, 458 U.S. 747, 757, 763–764 (1982).
152. *See, e.g.*, Citizens United v. FEC, 558 U.S. 310, 340 (2010); Pacific Gas & Electric Co. v. Public Utilities Comm'n, 475 U.S. 1, 19 (1986); Globe Newspaper Co. v. Superior Court, 457 U.S. 596, 606–607 (1982).
153. *Indianapolis Code* (1984), *supra* note 114, ch. 16 § 16-3(q).
154. *See supra* notes 35–39 and accompanying text.
155. *E.g.*, Lanis and Covell, "Images of Women in Advertisements"; MacKay and Covell, "Impact of Women in Advertisements"; Milburn, Mather, and Conrad, "Effects of Viewing."
156. See Chapter 2.

157. American Booksellers Ass'n v. Hudnut, 771 F.2d 323, 325 (7th Cir. 1985) (quoting Indianapolis ordinance).
158. Ibid., 326.
159. Ibid., 324, 326.
160. *Cf.* Downs, *New Politics*, 132–133.
161. *Hudnut*, 771 F.2d at 329.
162. New York v. Ferber, 458 U.S. 747, 761 (1982).
163. *Hudnut*, 771 F.2d at 325 (citation omitted).
164. *See* ibid., 327, 332; 334 (Swygert, J., concurring).
165. *Cf.* Crenshaw, "Demarginalizing the Intersection," 167.
166. *Compare* 18 U.S.C. § 2259(b)(1) (2014) (directing the defendant "to pay . . . the full amount of the victim's losses" due to child pornography), *with* Paroline v. United States, 572 U.S. 434, 458–459 (2014) (5-4) ("The amount [of damages] would not be severe. . . . It would not, however, be a token or nominal amount"). For cases illustrating the levels of awards, see, e.g., United States v. Funke, 846 F.3d 998, 1002 (8th Cir. 2017) (ordering a consumer of twenty child pornography videos made with a victim then aged 10–11 to pay $3,500 in restitution under the law); United States v. Darbasie, 164 F. Supp. 3d 400, 408 (E.D.N.Y. 2016) (ordering a consumer to pay $2,000 in restitution to the same victim); United States v. DiLeo, 58 F. Supp. 3d 239, 245, 247, 249 (E.D.N.Y. 2014) (ordering a consumer to pay $2,000 in restitution to the same victim while noting that as of May 7, 2014, the victim had estimated her total loss at roughly $1.1 million and had received about $600,000 from 475 child pornography restitution orders, the defendant excluded); *see also* United States v. Hite, 113 F. Supp.3d 91, 99 (D.D.C. 2015) (ordering restitution awards to be paid by a consumer of five different series of photographed child pornography, with two victims receiving $5,000 each, two receiving $2,500 each, and one receiving $1,750).
167. Emily Bazelon, "Money Is No Cure," *New York Times Magazine*, Jan. 27, 2013, M22 (Lexis).
168. Attorney General's Comm., *Final Report*, 214.
169. Melissa Farley, *Prostitution and Trafficking in Nevada: Making the Connections*, ed. M. Farley (San Francisco: Prostitution Research & Education, 2007), 37.
170. Robinson v. Jacksonville Shipyards, 760 F. Supp. 1486, 1535–1536 (M.D. Fla. 1991) (settled before appeal); *see also supra* note 65 and accompanying text at p. 178.
171. *Hudnut* was decided on August 27, 1985; *see* American Booksellers Ass'n v. Hudnut, 771 F.2d 323 (7th Cir. 1985). *Roberts* had been decided July 3, 1984; *see* Roberts v. United States Jaycees, 468 U.S. 609, 626 (1984).
172. *Robinson*, 760 F. Supp. at 1535 (citing *Roberts*, 468 U.S. at 626; Rotary Int'l v. Rotary Club of Duarte, 481 U.S. 537, 549 (1987)).
173. *Roberts*, 468 U.S. at 623.
174. Ibid., 628.
175. Catharine A. MacKinnon, *Toward a Feminist Theory of the State* (Cambridge, MA: Harvard Univ. Press, 1989), 225.

176. Ibid.
177. Ibid., 233–234.
178. Catharine A. MacKinnon, "On Torture," in *Are Women Human? And Other International Dialogues* (Cambridge, MA: Belknap Press of Harvard Univ. Press, 2006), 26.
179. Crenshaw, "Demarginalizing the Intersection," 145.
180. Ibid.
181. Ibid., 167.
182. Attorney General's Comm., *Final Report*, 244 (citing Hensen v. City of Dundee, 682 F.2d 897, 908 (11th Cir. 1982); Bundy v. Jackson, 641 F.2d 934 (D.C. Cir. 1981); Miller v. Bank of America, 600 F.2d 211 (9th Cir. 1979); Tomkins v. Public: Service Electric & Gas, 568 F.2d 1044 (D.C. Cir. 1979) [corrected]; 29 C.F.R. § 1064.11a [corrected]).
183. Ibid., 244 (internal citations omitted).
184. Attorney General's Comm., *Final Report*, 245 (footnote omitted).
185. American Booksellers Ass'n v. Hudnut, 771 F.2d 323, 325 (7th Cir. 1985).
186. Brief for Feminist Anti-Censorship Taskforce et al. as Amici Curiae Supporting Plaintiffs at xiii–xxii, in American Booksellers Ass'n v. Hudnut, 771 F.2d 323 (7th Cir. 1984) (presenting information about the co-signers), *reprinted in* Nan D. Hunter and Sylvia A. Law, "Brief Amici Curiae of Feminist Anti-Censorship Taskforce et al.," 21 *U. Mich. J.L. Reform* 69 (1987) [hereinafter FACT brief]. Pagination to original brief in reprint.
187. FACT brief, *supra* note 186, at 22.
188. Ibid. (quoting Ellen Willis, "Feminism, Moralism and Pornography," in *Powers of Desire: The Politics of Sexuality*, ed. Ann Barr Snitow, Christine Stansell, and Sharon Thompson (New York: Monthly Review Press, 1983), 464).
189. *See, e.g.*, Farley, *Prostitution and Trafficking in Nevada*, 34; *cf.* Evelina Giobbe, "Confronting the Liberal Lies about Prostitution," in *Living with Contradictions*, ed. Alison M. Jaggar (Boulder, CO: Westview Press, 1994), 121.
190. FACT brief, *supra* note 186, at 33 (quoting Orr v. Orr, 440 U.S. 268, 283 (1979)).
191. Crenshaw, "Mapping the Margins," 1297.
192. FACT brief, *supra* note 186, at 34–35.
193. Lacombe, *Blue Politics*, 152–153; *cf. supra* note 112 and accompanying text at p. 186.
194. *See* FACT brief, *supra* note 186, at 34–35 (advocating public education and support for female survivors of male violence).
195. R. v. Butler, [1992] 1 S.C.R. 452 at 508, 89 D.L.R. (4th) 449 (Can.).
196. Ibid.
197. *Cf.* MacKinnon, "On Torture," 26; MacKinnon, *Toward a Feminist Theory*, 225, 233–234.
198. FACT brief, *supra* note 187, at 22 (quoting Willis, "Feminism, Moralism and Pornography," 464).
199. Crenshaw, "Demarginalizing the Intersection," 167.
200. *See* FACT brief, *supra* note 186, at 21.
201. *Indianapolis Code* (1984), *supra* note 114, ch. 16 § 16-3 (g)(4)(c).
202. Ibid., § 16-3(q)(2).

203. United States v. O'Brien, 391 U.S. 367, 377 (1968).
204. Snyder v. Phelps, 562 U.S. 443, 460 (2011) (8-1) (admitting that funeral picketing was "certainly hurtful").
205. Ibid., 457.
206. Simon & Schuster, Inc. v. Members of the N.Y. State Crime Victims Bd., 502 U.S. 105, 116 (1991).
207. *Cf.* Daniel A. Farber, *The First Amendment*, 4th ed. (St. Paul, MN: Foundation Press, 2014), 65; Catharine A. MacKinnon, *Only Words* (Cambridge MA: Harvard Univ. Press, 1993), 38.
208. American Booksellers Ass'n v. Hudnut, 771 F.2d 323, 328–329 (7th Cir. 1985) (internal quotation quoting *Indianapolis Code* (1984), *supra* note 114, ch. 16 § 16-1(a)(2)).
209. Ibid., 328.
210. *See, e.g.*, ibid., 324–325 ("The Indianapolis ordinance .... demands attention to particular depictions."); 325 ("The ordinance discriminates on the ground of the content of the speech. ... The state may not ordain preferred viewpoints in this way."); 334 ("Indianapolis might choose to have no ordinance if it cannot be limited to viewpoint-specific harms, or it might choose to extend the scope to all speech, just as the law of libel applies to all speech.").
211. Ibid., 329.
212. United States v. O'Brien, 391 U.S. 367 (1968).
213. Ibid., 377.
214. Perry Educ. Ass'n v. Perry Local Educators' Ass'n, 460 U.S. 37, 53 (1983).
215. *O'Brien*, 391 U.S. at 377.
216. *Indianapolis Code* (1984), *supra* note 114, ch. 16 § 16-3(g)(5).
217. United States v. Roeder, 526 F.2d. 736, 739 (10th Cir. 1975) (citations omitted).
218. People v. Kovner, 409 N.Y.S.2d 349, 352 (Sup. Ct. 1978).
219. *See* MacKinnon, *Sex Equality*, 1704–1711 (describing a number of factually similar cases with different legal outcomes).
220. People v. Freeman, 758 P.2d 1128, 1131 (Cal. Sup. Ct., 1988) (holding there was no "purpose of sexual arousal or gratification" behind the paying of "acting fees," a purpose required according to relevant state statutes on prostitution).
221. California v. Freeman, 488 U.S. 1311, 1314–1315 (1989) (O'Connor, Circuit Justice, 9th Cir., 1989).
222. Ibid., 1313.
223. United States v. Stevens, 559 U.S. 460 (2010) (animal cruelty); New York v. Ferber, 458 U.S. 747 (1982) (child pornography); Giboney v. Empire Storage & Ice Co., 336 U.S. 490 (1949) (labor picketing).
224. *Stevens*, 559 U.S. at 471 (quoting *Ferber*, 458 U.S. at 761–762 (quoting Giboney, 336 U.S. at 498)) (internal quotation marks omitted).
225. American Booksellers Ass'n v. Hudnut, 771 F.2d 323, 332 (7th Cir. 1985).
226. Ibid., 330.
227. Protocol to Prevent, Suppress and Punish Trafficking in Persons, Especially Women and Children, Supplementing the United Nations Convention Against

Transnational Organized Crime, art. 3(a), *opened for signature* Dec. 12, 2000, T.I.A.S. No. 13127, 2237 U.N.T.S. 319 (entered into force Dec. 25, 2003) (a.k.a. the Palermo Protocol).

228. Rep. of the Ad Hoc Comm. on the Elaboration of a Convention Against Transnational Organized Crime on the Work of Its First to Eleventh Sessions, Addendum, Interpretative Notes for the Official Records (*Travaux Préparatoires*) of the Negotiation of the United Nations Convention Against Transnational Organized Crime and the Protocols Thereto, ¶ 63, U.N. Doc. A/55/383/Add.1 (Nov. 3, 2000).
229. *Hudnut*, 771 F.2d at 330.
230. *Indianapolis Code* (1984), *supra* note 114, ch. 16 § 16-3(g)(5)(a).
231. *Hudnut*, 771 F.2d at 330.
232. United States v. O'Brien, 391 U.S. 367, 370 (1968).
233. People v. Kovner, 409 N.Y.S.2d 349, 352 (Sup. Ct. 1978); United States v. Roeder, 526 F.2d 736, 739 (10th Cir. 1975).
234. *O'Brien*, 391 U.S. at 377.
235. *Cf.* Farber, *The First Amendment*, 65; MacKinnon, *Only Words*, 38.
236. Whitney v. California, 274 U.S. 357, 375 (1927) (Brandeis, J., concurring).
237. Karl Marx and Friedrich Engels, *The German Ideology*, ed. C. J. Arthur, 2nd ed. (London: Electric Book Co., 2001), 68–69.
238. Chaplinsky v. New Hampshire, 315 U.S. 568 (1942).
239. United States v. Orito, 413 U.S. 139 (1973).
240. Beauharnais v. Illinois, 343 U.S. 250 (1952).
241. American Booksellers Ass'n v. Hudnut, 771 F.2d 323, 331–332 & n.3 (7th Cir. 1985).
242. *Accord Hudnut*, 771 F.2d at 331 ("Some cases hold that speech far removed from politics and other subjects at the core of the Framers' concerns may be subjected to special regulation.") (citations omitted).
243. Williamson v. Lee Optical of Oklahoma, Inc., 348 U.S. 483, 487–488 (1955). For a case that did not sustain this standard, see, e.g., Romer v. Evans 517 U.S. 620, 635 (1996).
244. *Orito*, 413 U.S. at 143–144. For the Third Circuit decision, see United States v. Extreme Assocs., 431 F.3d 150, 154 (3rd Cir. 2005), *cert. denied* 547 U.S. 1143 (2006).
245. *See Hudnut*, 771 F.2d at 331–332 n.3 (7th Cir. 1985) (reporting that "Indianapolis briefly argues that Beauharnais v. Illinois, 343 U.S. 250 (1952) . . . supports the ordinance").
246. Beauharnais v. Illinois, 343 U.S. 250, 251 (1952) (quoting § 224a of the Illinois Criminal Code, Ill. Rev. Stat., 1949, c. 38, Div. 1, § 471).
247. Ibid., 263.
248. Ibid., 259 (citations omitted).
249. Ibid., 261 (quoting Cantwell v. Connecticut 310 U.S. 296, 310 (1940)) (emphasis added).
250. *See supra* notes 35–39 and accompanying text at p. 172.

251. American Booksellers Ass'n v. Hudnut, 771 F.2d 323, 331 n.3 (7th Cir. 1985) (citing Collin v. Smith, 578 F.2d 1197, 1205 (7th Cir. 1978), *cert. denied* 439 U.S. 916 (1978) (7-2); and New York Times v. Sullivan, 376 U.S. 254 (1964)).
252. *Collin*, 578 F.2d at 1199 n.3, 1204–1205.
253. *Collin*, 439 U.S. at 916 (7-2) (Blackmun, J., dissenting; joined by White, J.).
254. United States v. Stevens, 559 U.S. 460, 468 (2010) (8-1) (citing *Beauharnais*).
255. *See* New York v. Ferber, 458 U.S. 747, 763 (1982) ("Leaving aside the special considerations when public officials are the target, New York Times Co. v. Sullivan, 376 U.S. 254 (1964), a libelous publication is not protected by the Constitution. Beauharnais v. Illinois, 343 U.S. 250 (1952). . . . When a definable class of material, such as that [child pornography] covered by § 263.15, bears so heavily and pervasively on the welfare of children . . . it is . . . without the protection of the First Amendment").
256. Gertz v. Robert Welch, Inc., 418 U.S. 323, 344 (1974).
257. American Booksellers Ass'n v. Hudnut, 771 F.2d 323, 331–332 & n.3 (7th Cir. 1985).
258. Beauharnais v. Illinois, 343 U.S. 250, 251 (1952) (quoting § 224a of the Illinois Criminal Code, Ill. Rev. Stat., 1949, c. 38, Div. 1, § 471).
259. *Hudnut*, 771 F.2d at 331–332 (citations to law reviews omitted).
260. *Beauharnais*, 343 U.S. at 251 (quoting legislation).
261. *Hudnut*, 771 F.2d at 331–332.
262. *Beauharnais*, 343 U.S. at 257–258.
263. Ibid., 258.
264. Ibid.
265. Ibid., 263.
266. Miller v. California, 413 U.S. 15, 24 (1973).
267. For historical accounts of the law of obscenity, see, e.g., Leonard W. Levy, *Blasphemy: Verbal Offense against the Sacred, from Moses to Salman Rushdie* (New York: Knopf, 1993); Albert B. Gerber, *Sex, Pornography, and Justice* (New York: Lyle Stuart, 1965).
268. Downs, *New Politics*, 63–65.
269. United States v. Carolene Products Co., 304 U.S. 144, 152 n.4 (1938).
270. American Booksellers Ass'n v. Hudnut, 771 F.2d 323, 332 (7th Cir. 1985).
271. Christine Sypnowich, "Law and Ideology," in *Stanford Encyclopedia of Philosophy*, ed. Edward N. Zalta (2014) [https://plato.stanford.edu/archives/spr2017/entries/law-ideology/].
272. United States v. O'Brien, 391 U.S. 367, 377 (1968).

Chapter 5 Federal Responses, 1984–2014

1. Richard D. Lyons, "William French Smith Dies at 73; Reagan's First Attorney General," *New York Times*, Oct. 30, 1990, B6 (Lexis).
2. "Charter of the Attorney General's Commission on Pornography," *reprinted in* Attorney General's Commission on Pornography, *Final Report of the Attorney*

General's Commission on Pornography, ed. Michael J. McManus (Nashville, TN: Rutledge Hill Press, 1986), li.

3. Ibid., li–lii.
4. Michael J. McManus, Introduction to ibid., ix.
5. *See, e.g.*, ibid., xvii–xviii, xxiii.
6. Att'y Gen. Comm., *Final Report*, 224–245.
7. Ibid., 197–223.
8. Ibid., 189.
9. See Chapter 3 for an intersectional analysis of the politics of pornography.
10. Att'y Gen. Comm., *Final Report*, 186–189.
11. Brown v. Bd. of Educ., 347 U.S. 483 (1954).
12. Muller v. Oregon, 208 U.S. 412 (1908).
13. Att'y Gen. Comm., *Final Report*, 187–188.
14. Ibid., 187.
15. Beauharnais v. Illinois, 343 U.S. 250, 258 (1952).
16. *Cf.* Att'y Gen. Comm., *Final Report*, 187–188.
17. American Booksellers Ass'n v. Hudnut, 771 F.2d 323, 331 (7th Cir. 1985).
18. Plessy v. Ferguson, 163 U.S. 537, 544 (1896).
19. Brown v. Board of Education, 347 U.S. 483, 489 (1954).
20. Ibid., 494.
21. Ibid. (quoting the Kansas court without citation) (first and last bracket in original).
22. *Hudnut*, 771 F.2d at 329.
23. *Brown*, 347 U.S. at 494.
24. Ibid., 494 n.11
25. Ibid., 495.
26. Ibid., 494 (describing the ruling by the Kansas lower court).
27. For this analysis, see Chapter 4.
28. Att'y Gen. Comm., *Final Report*, 187. For the chapters on performers and victim testimony, see 197–246.
29. Ibid., 188.
30. *See* Proposed Ordinance § 1, to amend *Minneapolis, Minn. Code of Ordinances* § 139.40(m)(2)(i–xiii), 1st Reading, Nov. 23, 1983, *reprinted in* Catharine A. MacKinnon and Andrea Dworkin, eds., *In Harm's Way: The Pornography Civil Rights Hearings* (Cambridge, MA: Harvard Univ. Press, 1997), 426–432.
31. Ibid., 189.
32. *See, e.g.*, Ronald J. Ostrow, "Meese Panel Asks Porn Crackdown: Sexually Violent Materials and Actions Connected, Commission Concludes," *Los Angeles Times*, July 10, 1986, p. 1 (Lexis); *cf.* "Defeated by Pornography," *New York Times*, June 2, 1986, A16 (Lexis) ("[C]ommissioners [were] chosen by Attorney General Edwin Meese"); "Balancing Liberty and Libertinism," *Chicago Tribune*, July 13, 1986, C2 (Lexis) ("The Meese Commission on Pornography"); Jonathan Yardley, "The Porn Commission's Hidden Agenda," *Washington Post*, July 14, 1986, C2 (Lexis) ("Though Meese . . . had not read the report, the fact remains that the commission . . . is commonly known, whether fairly or not, as 'the Meese Commission.'"); Robert Fulford, "Beware of

Supposition: We're Making a Lot of Judgments—and in Danger of Making Laws before We Have Needed Information," *Toronto Star*, Sept. 27, 1986, M5 (Lexis) ("[T]he Meese commission, responding, stepped forward[.]").

33. "Charter of the Attorney General's Commission on Pornography," li–lii.
34. Catharine A. MacKinnon, "The Roar on the Other Side of Silence," in MacKinnon and Dworkin, *In Harm's Way*, 14.
35. This account and analysis of the P.R. campaign and the media response build on contemporaneous news reporting and investigative work by journalists, such as Susan B. Trento and Michael J. MacManus. Individual sources are footnoted throughout.
36. "Extracts from the Letter to the Council for Periodical Distributors Associations from Gray and Co., June 5, 1986," in *Pornography: Women, Violence and Civil Liberties*, ed. Catherine Itzin (Oxford: Oxford Univ. Press, 1992), 599 (quoting a letter from Steve M. Johnson, Senior Vice President of Gray & Company, to John M. Harrington, Executive Vice President of the Council for Periodical Distributors Associations., June 5, 1986); *cf.* McManus, Introduction to *Final Report*, xlvi (describing Gray & Company's strategy); Lois Sweet, "A Deluge of Porn Predicted by Study as Free Trade Result," *Toronto Star*, Nov. 24, 1986, C2 (Lexis) (quoting the letter from Johnson, Gray & Co).
37. *See supra* note 36.
38. See Susan B. Trento, *The Power House: Robert Keith Gray and the Selling of Access and Influence in Washington* (New York: St. Martin's Press, 1992), 196, 407 n.7 (chap. 10). Trento does not specify whether *Playboy* and *Penthouse* contributed funding to the Media Coalition directly or indirectly.
39. "Charter of the Attorney General's Commission on Pornography," lii.
40. Trento, *Power House*, 197.
41. "Extracts," in Itzin, *Pornography*, 600; *cf.* McManus, Introduction to *Final Report*, xlvi; Sweet, "Deluge of Porn," C2; Trento, *Power House*, 197.
42. McManus, Introduction to *Final Report*, xlviii; *cf.* MacKinnon, "The Roar," 21–23.
43. "Extracts," in Itzin, *Pornography*, 600–601.
44. McManus, Introduction to *Final Report*, xviii (mentioning that Edward Donnerstein and Neil Malamuth had criticized the Commission).
45. Edward P. Mulvey and Jeffrey L. Haugaard, *Report of the Surgeon General's Workshop on Pornography and Public Health: June 22–24, 1986, Arlington, Virginia* (Washington, DC: U.S. Dept. Health & Hum. Services, Aug. 4, 1986), 1.
46. Ibid., 13, 17, 19, 23, & 28.
47. "Balancing Liberty," C2.
48. Fulford, "Beware of Supposition," M5.
49. Yardley, "Porn Commission's Hidden Agenda," C2.
50. "Defeated by Pornography," A16.
51. "Extracts," in Itzin, *Pornography*, 601 (quoting Gray's letter, which outlines the strategy to circulate these claims); *cf.* McManus, Introduction to *Final Report*, xlviii (concluding that the claims dominated media reporting and analysis, and stating that people behind Gray's P.R. campaign confirmed the strategy's implementation).

52. Richard Stengel, "Sex Busters," *Time*, July 21, 1986 [http://perma.cc/S8ZU-4XMG (wrong date in byline)]; Ostrow, "Meese Panel," 1.
53. *See* Chapter 4.
54. McManus, Introduction to *Final Report*, xxxvi.
55. "Statement of Park Elliot Dietz, M.D., M.P.H., Ph.D.," in Att'y General's Comm., *Final Report*, 490 (Commissioner Cusack, concurring).
56. Ibid., 492 (Personal statement by Commissioner Elliot Dietz, Chairman Hudson and Commissioners Dobson, Lazar, Garcia and Cusack, concurring).
57. Pornography Victims Protection Act, S. 3063, 98th Cong. (1984); H.R. 5509, 99th Cong. (1986). When introducing his bill in Congress, Senator Specter made numerous comparative references to the Minneapolis and Indianapolis anti-pornography civil rights ordinances, including ordering them to be reprinted as part of the record. *See* 130 *Cong. Rec.* 29169–29175 (Oct. 3, 1984) (statement of Sen. Specter).
58. S. 3063, § 2(3); H.R. 5509, § 2(3).
59. S. 3063, § 4; H.R. 5509, § 4.
60. S. 3063, § 2(3); H.R. 5509, § 2(3).
61. *See* Minneapolis Proposed Ordinance, *supra* note 30, § 139.40(m)(2)(i–xiii).
62. *See, e.g.*, United States v. Roeder, 526 F.2d. 736, 739 (10th Cir. 1975); People v. Kovner, 409 N.Y.S.2d 349, 352 (Sup. Ct. 1978). For additional discussion of these cases, see Chapter 4.
63. United States v. O'Brien, 391 U.S. 367, 377 (1968).
64. S. 3063, § 2(3); H.R. 5509, § 2(3).
65. Am. Booksellers Ass'n v. Hudnut, 771 F.2d 323, 332 (7th Cir. 1985).
66. S. 3063, 98th Cong. (1984); S. 1187, 99th Cong. (1985); H.R. 5509, 99th Cong. (1986); S. 703, 100th Cong. (1987); H.R. 1213, 100th Cong. (1987).
67. Pornography Victims' Compensation Act, S. 1226, 101st Cong. (1989).
68. S. 1226, 101st Cong. § 3(b) (1989); *cf.* S. 983, 102d Cong. § 3(b) (1991).
69. Kitty Dumas, "Future Unclear for Pornography Bill," *C.Q. Weekly Report* 50, no. 26 (June 27, 1992): 1887.
70. *See* Minneapolis Proposed Ordinance, *supra* note 30, § 139.40(o); and Chapter 4.
71. *Compare* S. 1521, 102d Cong. § 3(c) (as reported by S. Comm. on the Judiciary, July 22, 1991) (stating that "[i]n determining whether the material was a substantial cause of the offense," any evidence would be "admissible under the Federal Rules of Evidence, except the testimony of the offender"), *with* S. 983, 102d Cong. § 3(c), (2) (as introduced in the Senate, Apr. 25, 1991) (stating that "the finder of fact may reasonably infer that the sexually explicit material was a proximate cause of the offense" if, e.g., there is a "testimony of the offender to the effect that such material influenced or incited the commission of the offense").
72. *See, e.g.*, Anna-Liza Kozma, "Porn Ruling: Canadian Court Ties Obscenity, Violence," *Chicago Tribune*, June 14, 1992 (Lexis); Lewis Beale, "Porn Bill in Senate Fueling Debate," *Philadelphia Inquirer*, Apr. 12, 1992 [http://perma.cc/B2A4-LZKQ].
73. Kozma, "Porn Ruling"; *cf.* Beale, "Porn Bill in Senate."
74. *See* S. 1521, 102d Cong. § 4(d)(2) (as reported with a substitute amendment to the S. Comm. on the Judiciary, Aug. 12, 1992) ("On motion of the plaintiff or the

defendant . . . the court may order a physical or mental examination . . . of a sex offender."); *cf. S. Rep. No.* 102-372, at 16 (1992) (clarifying that "[o]ffender testimony may also be introduced" as evidence).

75. For contemporaneous reporting of the legislative deliberations, see Kitty Dumas, "Backers of Porn-Victims Bill Fight for Panel Approval," *C.Q. Weekly Report* 50, no. 24 (June 13, 1992): 1711; Dumas, "Future Unclear for Pornography Bill," 1887; "Pornography Victims' Compensation Act," *C.Q. Almanac* 48 (1992): 331. *See also* S. Rep. No. 102-372, at 5–6 (1992) (describing bill S. 1521's legislative history).
76. S. 1521, § 4(c)(1) (Aug. 12, 1992); *cf.* Transcript of Proceedings at 14, S. Comm. on the Judiciary, Committee Business, 102d Cong. (June 25, 1992 at 2.25 pm) (pdf via Lexis) (Statement by Sen. Grassley) ("Senator Heflin's amendment requires the plaintiff [to] be barred from bringing a civil action under the bill until the sex offender is convicted of the sex offense").
77. Transcript of Proceedings at 14 (Statement by Sen. Grassley) (describing Sen. Specter's amendment); *see also* S. 1521, § 4(c)(4) (Aug. 12, 1992).
78. *See* S. 983, 102d Cong. § 4(1)(F), (2)(A)(C) (as introduced in the Senate, Apr. 25, 1991) (subparts defining "(1) sexually explicit" as "graphically" depicting or describing "(F) sadistic or masochistic abuse, including but not limited to torture, dismemberment, confinement, bondage, beatings, or bruises or other evidence of physical abuse, which are presented in a sexual context or which appear to stimulate sexual pleasure in the abuser or the recipient of such abuse; however . . . not . . . an isolated passage . . . (2) 'violent' describes any acts or behavior . . . in which women, children, or men are (A) victims of sexual crimes such as rape, sexual homicide, or child sexual abuse; (B) . . . or (C) tortured, dismembered, confined, bound, beaten, or injured, in a context that makes these experiences sexual or indicates that the victims derive sexual pleasure from such experiences."); *cf.* S. 1226, 101st Cong. § 5(1)(F), (2)(A)(C) (as introduced in the Senate, June 22, 1989) (see under "Definitions"). For comparison, see Minneapolis Proposed Ordinance, *supra* note 30, § 139.20 (gg).
79. *See* S. Rep. No. 102-372, at 6 (1992) (describing Sen. Biden's attempt to amend bill S. 1521 on June 25); *cf.* Dumas, "Backers of Porn-Victims Bill," 1711; "Pornography Victims' Compensation Act," 331.
80. *See* Transcript of Proceedings at 19–20 & attachment (Statement by Sen. Biden) (explaining and quoting proposed amendment to S. 1521, 102d Cong. § 4(c)(4) (Aug. 12, 1992)); *cf.* S. Rep. No. 102-372, at 6.
81. Transcript of Proceedings at 31 (Statement by Sen. Thurmond); *cf.* Dumas, "Future Unclear for Pornography Bill," 1887; "Pornography Victims' Compensation Act," 332.
82. *Cf.* MacKinnon, "The Roar," 18 n.58.
83. S. Rep. No. 102-372, at 5–6 (1992).
84. *See, e.g.*, S. Rep. No. 103-30, at 52 (1993) (reporting that "[n]o action was taken by the full Senate on S. 1521 during the 102d Congress.").
85. Dumas, "Future Unclear for Pornography Bill," 1887
86. Att'y Gen. Comm., *Final Report*, 186–189.

87. Paula Reed Ward, "Federal Obscenity Case, Filed 5 Years Ago, Has Stalled," *Pittsburgh Post-Gazette*, Aug. 26, 2008, A1 (Lexis) (quoting the political science professor Todd Lochner).
88. Ibid. (citing Lochner).
89. *See infra* notes 116–131 and accompanying text.
90. Miller v. California, 413 U.S. 15, 24–25 (1973).
91. "Pornography on the Internet: Hearing, Oct. 15, Before the S. Comm. On the Judiciary," 108th Cong. 266–267 (2003) (submission by Mary Beth Buchanan, U.S. Attorney for the Western District of Pennsylvania).
92. Ibid., 267.
93. Ibid., 266.
94. Ibid.
95. *Miller*, 413 U.S. at 24.
96. Unites States v. Extreme Assocs, Inc., 352 F. Supp. 2d 578 (W.D. Pa., 2005), *rev'd and remanded*, 431 F.3d 150, 161 (3rd Cir. 2005).
97. Brief of Petitioner-Appellant at 7 n.2, United States v. Extreme Assocs, Inc., 431 F.3d 150 (3rd Cir. 2005) (No. 05-1555), 2005 WL 6104849.
98. *Extreme Assocs*, 431 F.3d at 151 (emphasis added).
99. *Extreme Assocs.*, 352 F. Supp. 2d at 591–92, *rev'd and remanded*, 431 F.3d at 161, *cert. denied* 547 U.S. 1143 (2006).
100. Lawrence v. Texas, 539 U.S. 558 (2003).
101. *Extreme Assocs.*, 352 F. Supp. 2d at 587, 591, *rev'd*, 431 F.3d at 150.
102. *See, e.g.*, Leif Silbersky and Carlösten Nordmark, *Såra Tukt och Sedlighet: En debattbok om pornografin* (Stockholm: Bokförlaget Prisma/RFSU, 1969), 22–27 (describing one of lawyer Silbersky's more significant cases).
103. Ibid., 184.
104. Prop. 1970:125 Kungl. Maj:ts proposition nr 125 med förslag till ändring i tryckfrihetsförordningen m.m. [government bill] 79 (Swed.).
105. Prop. 1986/87:151 Om ändringar i tryckfrihetsförordningen m.m. [government bill] 2, 8, 12–14 (Swed.); *Lag om ändring i brottsbalken* (Svensk författningssamling [SFS] 1988:835) (Swed.) (amending the Criminal Code on Jan. 1, 1989); *Lag om ändring i tryckfrihetsförordningen* (SFS 1988:1448) (amending the constitution on Jan. 1, 1989).
106. United States v. Extreme Assocs, Inc., 431 F.3d 150 (3rd Cir. 2005).
107. *See, e.g.*, ibid., 155 (citing Rodriguez de Quijas v. Shearson/American Express Inc., 490 U.S. 477, 484 (1989); and Agostini v. Felton, 521 U.S. 203, 236–238 (1997)).
108. The Third Circuit emphasized that there was no indication that the Supreme Court's prior decision holding that "'commerce in obscene material is unprotected by any constitutional doctrine of privacy'" would not be applicable to internet commerce. *Extreme Assocs*, 431 F.3d at 161 (quoting Paris Adult Theatre I v. Slaton, 413 U.S. 49, 69 (1973)). Although the Supreme Court has carved out a right to enjoy obscenity in the privacy of one's home, Stanley v. Georgia, 394 U.S. 557, 564–565 (1969), this zone of privacy no longer exists "once material leaves [the home], regardless of a transporter's professed intent." United States v. Orito, 413 U.S. 139, 143 (1973).

109. Lawrence v. Texas, 539 U.S. 558, 590 (2003) (Scalia, J., dissenting, joined by Rehnquist C.J., and Thomas, J.) (emphasis added).
110. *See, e.g.*, Clay Calvert and Robert D. Richards, "Vulgarians at the Gate: Privacy, Pornography and the End of Obscenity Law as We Know It," 34 *Southwestern U. L. Rev.* 427 (2005); Jennie G. Arnold, Comment, "*United States v. Extreme Associates Inc.*: The Substantive Due Process Death of Obscenity Law," 74 *U. Cincinnati L. Rev.* 607 (Winter 2005).
111. Paula Reed Ward, "Porn Producer, Wife Get 1-year Jail Terms: Acrimonious Obscenity Case Took 7 Years," *Pittsburgh Post-Gazette*, July 2, 2009, A1 (Lexis).
112. Ibid. (quoting and citing H. Louis Sirkin, a well-known defense attorney regularly employed by pornographers).
113. U.S. Dept. of Justice, "Producer Paul Little Indicted on Obscenity Charges," news release, May 31, 2007 [http://perma.cc/R6ZG-8YWD].
114. *See* United States v. Little, 365 Fed. App'x 159 (11th Cir. 2010) (affirming convictions for obscenity charges in the Middle District of Florida, but vacating a sentence enhancement for pecuniary gain); U.S. Dept. of Justice, "Adult Entertainment Producer Sentenced to 46 Months in Prison on Obscenity Charges," news release, Oct. 3, 2008 [https://perma.cc/96K2-JGV4].
115. *See* "Inmate Locator: Find an Inmate," Federal Bureau of Prisons [http://www.bop.gov/Locate/] (choose "Find by Number," choose "BOP Register Number," add "44902-112").
116. Victoria Kim, "Mistrial in L.A. Obscenity Case: Jurors Deadlock 10 to 2 in Favor of Convicting Ira Isaacs, a Fetish Film Producer, Distributor," *Los Angeles Times*, Mar. 7, 2012, AA3 (Lexis).
117. Federal Bureau of Investigation, L.A. Div., "Ira Isaacs Sentenced in Adult Obscenity Case," FBI/Los Angeles, Jan. 16, 2013 [https://perma.cc/HSV9-L4DW].
118. Ibid. The official counts convicted for were mailing, transporting, transporting for sale or distribution, and producing and selling "obscene matter." *See* United States v. Isaacs, 565 F. App'x 637, 639 (9th Cir. 2014). (citing 18 U.S.C. §§ 1461, 1462(a), 1465, 1466(a)).
119. *Isaacs*, 565 F. App'x at 639–640.
120. Kim, "Mistrial in L.A.," AA3.
121. Greg Piper, "Indicted Porn Producer Plans Challenge to Obscenity Law," *Washington Internet Daily*, Apr. 22, 2008 (Westlaw; 2008 WLNR 7662080); *cf.* Natalie Purcell, *Violence and the Pornographic Imaginary: The Politics of Sex, Gender, and Aggression in Hardcore Pornography* (New York: Routledge, 2012), 87 (describing Stagliano as the originator of "gonzo" pornography).
122. Spencer S. Hsu, "Judge Drops Porn Case for Insufficient Evidence, Rebukes Government, Urges Better Guidance on Obscenity Statutes," *Washington Post*, July 17, 2010, A2 (Lexis).
123. Ibid.
124. *See* Amanda Hess, "Opening Arguments in the U.S. vs. John 'Buttman' Stagliano," *Washington City Paper*, July 13, 2010 [https://perma.cc/V6KJ-2PDD] (referencing ass-to-mouth); Juliana Brint, "Buttman Trial: Courthouse Porn Shows Milk Enemas,

Racial Epithets to D.C. Jurors," *Washington City Paper*, July 14, 2010 [https://perma.cc/6BTN-B6PK].

125. Carmen M. Cusack, *Pornography and the Criminal Justice System* (Boca Raton, FL: CRC Press, Taylor & Francis, 2015), 48.
126. Hsu, "Judge Drops Porn Case," A2 (interviewing Robert D. Richards, a professor at Penn State University and expert on the First Amendment). *Cf.* Jennifer M. Kinsley, "The Myth of Obsolete Obscenity," 33 *Cardozo Arts & Ent. Law J.* 607, 640 (2015) (suggesting that the government intentionally waited to charge the relatively more "mainstream" Stagliano after first having "secured pleas and convictions in the *Extreme Associates* and *Paul Little* cases"). Note that Kinsley acknowledges having been counsel for the defense in *Stagliano* and other obscenity cases (7 n.*).
127. Hsu, "Judge Drops Porn Case," A2.
128. *Cf.* Amanda Hess, "Buttman v. the Man," *Washington City Paper*, July 23, 2010 (Westlaw; 2010 WLNR 28492168) (reporting that "in the end . . . [t]he government failed to prove that Stagliano actually sent anything to anyone"); Cusack, *Pornography*, 48 (noting that the case was dismissed for lack of evidence).
129. United States v. Stagliano, 693 F.Supp. 2d 25, 37 (D.C. 2010) (footnote text omitted).
130. Ibid., 38 (citations omitted).
131. Ibid.
132. Ward, "Porn Producer, Wife," A1 (quoting Bill [William] Margold).
133. Ibid.
134. Ibid.
135. Purcell, *Violence and the Pornographic Imaginary*, 179–181 (discussing sampling and methodology).
136. Ibid., 118.
137. *See* Cicely Marston and Ruth Lewis, "Anal Heterosex among Young People and Implications for Health Promotion: A Qualitative Study in the UK," *BMJ Open* 4, no. 8 (2014): doi:10.1136/bmjopen-2014-004996; Breanne Fahs and Jax Gonzalez, "The Front Lines of the 'Back Door': Navigating (Dis)Engagement, Coercion, and Pleasure in Women's Anal Sex Experiences," *Fem. Psychol.* 24, no. 4 (2014): 500–520.
138. Purcell, *Violence and the Pornographic Imaginary*, 118.
139. Ibid., 119.
140. Ana J. Bridges et al., "Sexual Scripts and the Sexual Behavior of Men and Women Who Use Pornography," *Sex. Media Soc.* 2, no. 4 (2016): 5 tbl. 2 (p=.988), doi: 10.1177/2374623816668275.
141. Ibid., 8 tbl. 5; p<.001.
142. *See* Chapter 4.
143. Minneapolis Proposed Ordinance, *supra* note 30, § 139.40(l)(3).
144. For an overview of these state-level prosecutions, see Kinsley, "Myth of Obsolete Obscenity."
145. Ibid., 641.
146. Ibid.
147. *See supra* notes 67–85 and accompanying text.
148. Miller v. California, 413 U.S. 15, 24 (1973).

149. Robinson v. Jacksonville Shipyards, 760 F. Supp. 1486, 1535 (M.D. Fla. 1991) (settled before appeal).
150. *Miller*, 413 U.S. at 24–25.

Chapter 6 Legislative Attempts, 1983–1988

1. R. v. Hicklin, (1868) L.R. 3 Q.B. 360, 371 (Lord Cockburn, C.J.).
2. R. v. Martin Secker Warburg Ltd., [1954] 1 W.L.R. 1138, [1954] 2 All E.R. 683, (Cent. Crim. Ct.) (requiring that obscenity determinations of books be based also on the authors' purposes and the literary contexts of the publications, rather than on isolated passages).
3. Kathleen E. Mahoney, "Obscenity, Morals and the Law: A Feminist Critique," 17 *Ottawa L. Rev.* 33, 58 (1985).
4. Criminal Code, R.S.C. 1985, c. C-46, s. 163(8) (Can.).
5. Brodie v. The Queen, [1962] S.C.R. 681, 706 (Can.).
6. Mahoney, "Obscenity, Morals," 58.
7. Ibid.
8. R. v. Hicklin, (1868) L.R. 3 Q.B. 360, 371 (Lord Cockburn, C.J.).
9. Susan Cole, *Pornography and the Sex Crisis* (Toronto: Amanita Enterprises, 1989), 72.
10. Dany Lacombe, *Blue Politics: Pornography and the Law in the Age of Feminism* (Toronto: Univ. of Toronto Press, 1994), 78–79.
11. Ibid., 79 (footnote citations omitted).
12. Kathleen E. Mahoney, "Defining Pornography: An Analysis of Bill C-54," 33 *McGill L. J.* 575, 576 (1988); *cf.* Lacombe, *Blue Politics*, 81.
13. Special Committee on Pornography and Prostitution in Canada, *Pornography and Prostitution in Canada: Report of the Special Committee on Pornography and Prostitution in Canada* (Ottawa: Supply & Services, 1985), 2:vii, 7.
14. Mahoney, "Defining Pornography," 578.
15. Ibid., 579.
16. *Cf.* R. v. Ramsingh (1984), 29 Man. R. (2d) 110 at 112, 14 C.C.C. (3d) 230 (Can. Man. Q.B.) (stating that "we deal not with 'exploitation' of sex, but with 'undue' exploitation of sex"); R. v. Doug Rankine Co. (1983), 9 C.C.C. (3d) 53 at 60, 36 C.R. (3d) 154 (Can. Ont. Cty. Ct.) (stating that "it is not sufficient that a dominant characteristic" of a publication "has been the exploitation of sex. There must have been an 'undue' exploitation of sex").
17. Mahoney, "Defining Pornography," 579; *cf.* Spec. Comm., *Pornography and Prostitution in Canada*, 114.
18. Attorney General's Commission on Pornography, *Final Report of the Attorney General's Commission on Pornography*, ed. Michael J. McManus (Nashville, TN: Rutledge Hill Press, 1986), 226.
19. Spec. Comm., *Pornography and Prostitution in Canada*, 265.
20. Ibid., 87, 153–154.

21. For this paragraph, see ibid., 9–10, 63–64.
22. For this paragraph, see ibid., 352–354; quote at 354.
23. There were only a few exceptions to criminalization, such as outcall/escort prostitution without the involvement of third parties, which would not be conducted inside a "bawdy house" or being solicited publicly (e.g., street prostitution). *Cf.* ibid., 404 et seq.
24. Spec. Comm., *Pornography and Prostitution in Canada*, 351.
25. Ibid., 25.
26. *Cf.* Kimberle Crenshaw, "Demarginalizing the Intersection of Race and Sex: A Black Feminist Critique of Antidiscrimination Doctrine, Feminist Theory and Antiracist Politics," 1989 *U. Chi. Legal F.* 139, 167 (1989).
27. Att'y Gen. Comm., *Final Report*, 224–245.
28. Ibid., 189.
29. Ibid., 187–189.
30. Spec. Comm., *Pornography and Prostitution in Canada*, 309.
31. Ibid., 308.
32. Ibid.
33. Ibid., 64–67.
34. Ibid.
35. Ibid., 67.
36. Ibid.
37. Ibid., 64.
38. *See, e.g.*, Edward P. Mulvey and Jeffrey L. Haugaard, *Report of the Surgeon General's Workshop on Pornography and Public Health: June 22–24, 1986, Arlington, Virginia* (Washington, DC: U.S. Dept. Health & Hum. Services, Aug. 4, 1986); Mimi H. Silbert and Ayala M. Pines, "Pornography and Sexual Abuse of Women," *Sex Roles* 10, nos. 11–12 (1984): 857–868.
39. Spec. Comm., *Pornography and Prostitution in Canada*, 268.
40. *Canadian Charter of Rights and Freedoms*, s. 15, Part 1 of the *Constitution Act, 1982*, being Schedule B to the *Canada Act 1982* (U.K.), 1982, c. 11 [hereinafter: *Canadian Charter*].
41. Spec. Comm., *Pornography and Prostitution in Canada*, 266–268.
42. To reiterate, section 1 "guarantees the rights and freedoms set out in it subject only to such reasonable limits prescribed by law as can be demonstrably justified in a free and democratic society." *Canadian Charter*, *supra* note 40, s. 1.
43. Spec. Comm., *Pornography and Prostitution in Canada*, 266–268.
44. R. v. Keegstra, [1984] 87 A.R. 200, CarswellAlta 428 (Can. Alta. Q.B.) [*Keegstra* 1984 cited to CarswellAlta].
45. Spec. Comm., *Pornography and Prostitution in Canada*, 266–268.
46. *See* R. v. Keegstra, [1990] 3 S.C.R. 697, 114 A.R. 81 (Can.), *rev'g* [1988] 87 A.R. 177, 5 W.W.R. 211, CarswellAlta 280 (C.A.) (invalidating the hate propaganda provision on the ground of expressive freedom).
47. See *Keegstra*, [1984] CarswellAlta 428 ¶¶ 55–62.
48. Spec. Comm., *Pornography and Prostitution in Canada*, 276–279.

49. *See, e.g.*, Mahoney, "Obscenity, Morals."
50. Spec. Comm., *Pornography and Prostitution in Canada*, 271.
51. Ibid.; *cf.* 276.
52. *Cf.* Att'y Gen. Comm., *Final Report*, 226.
53. Spec. Comm., *Pornography and Prostitution in Canada*, 271, 276–277.
54. Ibid., 271, 278.
55. *Indianapolis, Ind. Code* ch. 16 § 16-3 (g)(4)(c) (1984), *invalidated in* American Booksellers Ass'n v. Hudnut, 771 F.2d 323 (7th Cir. 1985), *reprinted in* Catharine A. MacKinnon and Andrea Dworkin, eds., *In Harm's Way: The Pornography Civil Rights Hearings* (Cambridge, MA: Harvard Univ. Press, 1997), 438–457.
56. Spec. Comm., *Pornography and Prostitution in Canada*, 271–272, 278.
57. *Ind. Code* ch. 16 § 16-3(q) (6) (1984).
58. Spec. Comm., *Pornography and Prostitution in Canada*, 265.
59. Att'y Gen. Comm., *Final Report*, 226.
60. *See, e.g.*, Proposed Ordinance § 1, to amend *Minneapolis, Minn. Code of Ordinances* § 139.40(m)(2)(i–xiii), 1st Reading, Nov. 23, 1983 [hereinafter Proposed Minneapolis Ordinance], *reprinted in* MacKinnon and Dworkin, *In Harm's Way*, 426–432.
61. *See, e.g.*, Little Sisters v. Canada, 2000 SCC 69, [2000] 2 S.C.R. 1120 ¶ 33 (Can.) (remarking that in criminal trials, obscenity must be proven "beyond a reasonable doubt").
62. *E.g.*, ibid., ¶ 104 (remarking that the seizure of obscene materials by customs is "a civil proceeding which generally requires proof only on a balance of probabilities").
63. Spec. Comm., *Pornography and Prostitution in Canada*, 311.
64. Ibid.
65. Ibid., 309.
66. Ibid., 313.
67. Ibid., 195–201.
68. U.N. Comm. on the Elimination of Discrimination Against Women, 11th Sess., "General Recommendation No. 19," ¶¶ 11–12, 24(t), U.N. Doc. A/47/38 (Feb. 2, 1992).
69. Human Rights Comm., 68th Sess., 1834th Mtg., "General Comment No. 28," ¶ 22, U.N. Doc. CCPR/C/21/Rev.1/Add.10 (Mar. 29, 2000).
70. Fourth World Conference on Women, Sept. 4–15, 1995, "Beijing Declaration and Platform for Action," ¶ 118, U.N. Doc. A/CONF.177/20/Rev.1.
71. Protocol to the African Charter on Human and Peoples' Rights on the Rights of Women in Africa, art. 13(m), July 11, 2003 (entered into force Nov. 26, 2005) [http://perma.cc/D3SB-L4Q3].
72. On postmodernism, see Chapter 3.
73. Spec. Comm., *Pornography and Prostitution in Canada*, 260. For an alternative critique of the notion of rational compromise, see Lacombe, *Blue Politics*, 81–92.
74. Spec. Comm., *Pornography and Prostitution in Canada*, 260.
75. Ibid., 277.
76. Criminal Code, R.S.C. 1985, c. C-46, s. 163(8) (Can.) (emphasis added).
77. Spec. Comm., *Pornography and Prostitution in Canada*, 201.

78. *See* Bill C-36, *Protection of Communities and Exploited Persons Act*, 2nd Sess., 41st Parl., 2014 (Royal Assent, Nov. 6, 2014) (Can.); Proposition [Prop.] 1997/98:55 Kvinnofrid [Women's Sanctuary] [government bill] (Swed.).
79. Bill C-114, *An Act to amend the Criminal Code and the Customs Tariff*, 1st Sess., 33d Parl., 1986 (1st reading, June 10) [hereinafter bill C-114]; Lacombe, *Blue Politics*, 81, 99 (mentioning the two different governments).
80. Bill C-114, *supra* note 79, ss. 138 (definition of "other pornography"), 159.3 (penalties). All bill C-114 citations are to section numbers as they would have appeared in an amended *Criminal Code* had the bill been passed in the proposed form.
81. Ibid., s. 138.
82. Ibid.
83. Proposed Minneapolis Ordinance, *supra* note 60, §§ 139.10(a)(1), 139.20(gg)(1).
84. *Cf.* Mahoney, "Defining Pornography," 596 (discussing artistic defenses set forth in the bill proposed one year after bill C-114).
85. See Chapter 2 for an analysis of studies of johns who imitate pornography.
86. Lacombe, *Blue Politics*, 114–116.
87. Ibid., 115 (double quotation marks quoting Louise Dulude, President of the National Action Committee on the Status of Women, as portrayed by the *Toronto Star*, June 11, 1986). Further citations in text.
88. Ibid.
89. Ibid., 112 (quote), 111.
90. Ibid., 116.
91. Bill C-54, *An Act to Amend the Criminal Code and Other Acts in Consequence Thereof*, 2nd sess., 33d Parl., 1987 (1st reading, May 4) [hereinafter bill C-54]. All citations are to section numbers as they would have appeared in an amended *Criminal Code* had the bill been passed in the proposed form.
92. Bill C-54 s. 138.
93. Ibid., ss. 159.4, 159.5, 159.7.
94. Ibid., s. 138 (*a*)(i)–(iv).
95. Ibid., s. 138 (*b*).
96. *Cf.* R. v. Doug Rankine Co. (1983), 9 C.C.C. (3d) 53 at 66, 36 C.R. (3d) 154 (Can. Ont. Cty. Ct.) ("The familiar saying that one picture is worth a thousand words applies with special force in the field of obscenity.")
97. For studies using audiotaped and written representations of rape, see, e.g., Neil M. Malamuth and James V. P. Check, "Penile Tumescence and Perceptual Responses to Rape as a Function of Victim's Perceived Reactions," *J. Applied Soc. Psychol.* 10, no. 6 (1980): 528–547; Neil M. Malamuth, Scott Haber, and Seymour Feshbach, "Testing Hypotheses regarding Rape: Exposure to Sexual Violence, Sex Differences, and the 'Normality' of Rapists," *J. Res. Pers.* 14, no. 1 (1980): 121–137; *see also* Martin L. Lalumière and Vernon L. Quinsey, "The Discriminability of Rapists from Non-Sex Offenders Using Phallometric Measures: A Meta-Analysis," *Crim. Just. Behav.* 21, no. 1 (1994): 150–175; Gordon C. Nagayama Hall, Denise D. Shondrick, and Richard Hirschman, "The Role of Sexual Arousal

in Sexually Aggressive Behavior: A Meta-Analysis," *J. Consult. Clin. Psychol.* 61 (1993): 1091–1095.

98. Etymologically, "obscenity" traces back to the Latin, meaning "ill-omened," "adverse," or "not for stage." Donald Alexander Downs, *The New Politics of Pornography* (Chicago: Univ. of Chicago Press, 1989), 9.
99. Kirsten Johnson, *Undressing the Canadian State: The Politics of Pornography from Hicklin to Butler* (Halifax: Fernwood, 1995), 50 (quoting Canadian Advisory Council on the Status of Women, *Pornography: An Analysis of Proposed Legislation (Bill C-54): A Brief Presented to the Hon. Ray Hnatyshyn, Minister of Justice* (Ottawa: The Council, 1988)).
100. Cole, *Pornography and the Sex Crisis*, 78; *cf.* Mahoney, "Defining Pornography," 583–584.
101. Bill C-54, *supra* note 91, s. 138.
102. Mahoney, "Defining Pornography," 584.
103. Bill C-54, *supra* note 91, s. 138 (*a*)(vi).
104. Cole, *Pornography and the Sex Crisis*, 78 (quote), 176 n.31 (citing Steinem).
105. Gloria Steinem, "Erotica and Pornography: A Clear and Present Difference," in *Take Back the Night: Women on Pornography*, ed. Laura Lederer (New York: Morrow, 1980), 37.
106. *Indianapolis, Ind. Code* ch. 16 § 16-3(q) (6) (1984), *invalidated in* American Booksellers Ass'n v. Hudnut, 771 F.2d 323 (7th Cir. 1985).
107. Bill C-54, *supra* note 91, ss. 138 (*a*)(iv)–(vi).
108. Ibid., s. 159.1(1).
109. *Cf.* Mahoney, "Defining Pornography," 588 (footnote citations omitted).
110. Ibid., 588–589.
111. Ibid., 589
112. Johnson, *Undressing the Canadian State*, 52–53 (citing/quoting Nat'l Action Comm. Status of Women, *Brief to the House of Commons Justice Comm. on Bill-C54*, prepared by Kate Andrew and Debra J. Lewis (Toronto: NAC, Feb. 1988)).
113. Lacombe, *Blue Politics*, 118 (quoting *Toronto Star*, May 23, 1987).
114. Lacombe, *Blue Politics*, 124.
115. *See, e.g.*, R. v. Doug Rankine Co. (1983), 9 C.C.C. (3d) 53, 36 C.R. (3d) 154 (Can. Ont. Cty. Ct.).
116. Lacombe, *Blue Politics*, 126 (citing Edward L. Greenspan, "Correspondence to the Canadian Civil Liberties Ass'n Re the Potential Vulnerability of Library Personnel to Bill C-54," (1987), at 4).
117. Lacombe, *Blue Politics*, 123; *see also* Kirk Makin, "Join Battle against Anti-Porn Bill, Librarians Urged," *Globe and Mail*, Nov. 21, 1987.
118. Makin, "Join Battle."
119. Ibid.
120. Lacombe, *Blue Politics*, 127.
121. Ibid., 128 (quoting MP Richard Grisé, parliamentary secretary to the deputy prime minister and president of the Privy Council).
122. Lacombe, *Blue Politics*, 128.

123. Ibid.
124. Ibid., 118–120.
125. Ibid., 128–129.
126. *Cf.* ibid., 120–123, 129–133.
127. Ibid., 130.
128. *Cf.* Mahoney, "Defining Pornography," 584, 596.
129. Johnson, *Undressing the Canadian State*, 53.
130. Ibid., 97 n.43 (quoting Jane Rhodes, "Silencing Ourselves? Pornography, Censorship and Feminism in Canada," *Resources for Feminist Research / Documentation sur la Recherche Feministe* 17, no. 3 (1988): 134).
131. *E.g.*, Mahoney, "Obscenity, Morals"; Mahoney, "Defining Pornography."
132. *Cf.* Johnson, *Undressing the Canadian State*, 48; Cole, *Pornography and the Sex Crisis*, 72.

Chapter 7 Judicial Challenges, 1982–2019

1. Criminal Code, R.S.C. 1985, c. C-46, s. 163(8) (Can.) (*italics* added).
2. In my own analysis of this case law, I have benefited from the scholarship of Kathleen Mahoney, Christopher Kendall, Catharine MacKinnon, Susan Cole, Kirsten Johnson, and Janine Benedet, among others.
3. *Canadian Charter of Rights and Freedoms*, s. 32(2), Part 1 of the *Constitution Act, 1982,* being Schedule B to the *Canada Act 1982* (U.K.), 1982, c. 11 [hereinafter: *Canadian Charter*] (barring section 15 from taking effect until 1985).
4. Alberta (Aboriginal Affairs & N. Dev.) v. Cunningham, 2011 SCC 37, [2011] 2 S.C.R. 670 ¶¶ 39–40 (Can.).
5. For a similar argument, see, e.g., Andrea Dworkin, "Against the Male Flood: Censorship, Pornography, and Equality," *in Letters from a War Zone* (Brooklyn, NY: Lawrence Hill Books, 1993) (1988), 268–270 (discussing the silencing effects of pornography on women while presenting masochism as women's true "speech"); Catharine A. MacKinnon, "Francis Biddle's Sister," in *Feminism Unmodified: Discourses on Life and Law* (Cambridge, MA: Harvard Univ. Press, 1987), 192–197 (discussing pornography as a practice that silences women).
6. For instance, the First Amendment is worded in more absolute terms: "Congress shall make no law . . . abridging the freedom of speech, or of the press." *U.S. Const.* amend. I [1791].
7. R. v. Doug Rankine Co. (1983), 9 C.C.C. (3d) 53 at 68, 36 C.R. (3d) 154 (Ont. Cty. Ct.).
8. Ibid., 70.
9. Kathleen E. Mahoney, "Obscenity, Morals and the Law: A Feminist Critique," 17 *Ottawa L. Rev.* 33, 62 (1985).
10. *E.g.*, *Rankine*, 9 C.C.C. (3d) at 68, 70.
11. Mahoney, "Obscenity, Morals," 58–61.
12. Ibid., 60–61.

13. Ibid., 61.
14. R. v. Ramsingh (1984), 29 Man. R. (2d) 110 at 116, 1984 CarswellMan 230 (Q.B.) (Lexis/WL).
15. Ibid., 116.
16. See ibid., 112, 118–119, 121.
17. *Canadian Charter, supra* note 3, s. 32(2) (barring s. 15 from taking effect until 1985).
18. *Ramsingh*, 29 Man. R. (2d) at 115, 117.
19. *See, e.g.*, "Hearing on Proposed Ordinance § 1 to amend *Minneapolis, Minn. Code of Ordinances*, Ch. 7 Before the Government Operations Comm.," Sess. I; Monday, Dec. 12, 1983, 1:30 P.M. (testimony of Linda Marchiano), *transcribed in* Catharine A. MacKinnon and Andrea Dworkin, eds., *In Harm's Way: The Pornography Civil Rights Hearings* (Cambridge, MA: Harvard Univ. Press, 1997), 60–65; *see also* "Nat Laurendi, Polygraph Examination of Linda Lovelace, November 8, 1979" (lie detector test and analysis), *submitted to* the Minneapolis City Council, Dec. 12–13, 1983 ("exhibit 3 [10]"), *reprinted in* MacKinnon and Dworkin, *In Harm's Way*, 205–213; *see also* Linda Lovelace, *Ordeal: An Autobiography*, with Mike McGrady (Secaucus, NJ: Citadel Press, 1980).
20. *Ramsingh*, 29 Man. R. (2d) at 115, 116.
21. Kathleen E. Mahoney, "Defining Pornography: An Analysis of Bill C-54," 33 *McGill L. J.* 575, 596 (1988).
22. Letter from Flora Colao to the Minneapolis City Council, Nov. 10, 1983, *reprinted in* MacKinnon and Dworkin, *In Harm's Way*, 214–215.
23. See Chapter 2 for analysis of these studies on imitation of pornography.
24. R. v. Wagner, 1985 CarswellAlta 35 ¶ 64, 36 Alta. L.R. (2d) 301 (Q.B.) (WL), *aff'd* (1986) 69 A.R. 78, 43 Alta. L.R. (2d) 204 (C.A.), *leave to appeal refused* 1986 CarswellAlta 1148, 50 C.R. (3d) 175n (S.C.C.).
25. Ibid., ¶¶ 58–60, 64, 87.
26. See Chapter 2 for additional discussion.
27. Miller v. California, 413 U.S. 15, 24 (1973). That said, recent applications have tended to focus on extreme violence and degradation. *See* Chapter 5.
28. *Wagner*, 1985 CarswellAlta 35 ¶¶ 86, 87.
29. Ibid., ¶ 65.
30. Ibid., ¶ 31.
31. Towne Cinema Theatres, Ltd. v. R., [1985] 1 S.C.R. 494 at 497, 61 A.R. 35 (Dickson, C.J., plurality opinion). The trial court found that a cinema had presented an "obscene entertainment" by showing *Dracula Sucks* to an audience in Edmonton, Alberta (497–501).
32. Ibid., 505.
33. Ibid.
34. *Cf.* ibid., 523 (Wilson, J., concurring) (quoting and referring approvingly to the dehumanization approach taken in R. v. Doug Rankine Co. (1983), 9 C.C.C. (3d) 53 at 70 (Ont. Cty. Ct.)); *see also Towne Cinema*, [1985] 1 S.C.R. at 518 (Beetz, Estey, JJ., concurring); 518–519 (McIntyre, J., concurring).
35. *Towne Cinema*, [1985] 1 S.C.R. at 505 (citing *Rankine* and *Wagner*).

36. Ibid.
37. Ibid., 501, 502 (citing Brodie v. The Queen, [1962] S.C.R. 681).
38. Ibid., 505.
39. Ibid., 502–505.
40. *See Canadian Charter*, *supra* note 3, s. 32(2).
41. R. v. Red Hot Video Ltd., [1985] B.C.J. No. 2279 ¶¶ 3, 37, 41, 53, 18 C.C.C. (3d) 1 (B.C.C.A.) (Anderson, J.) (Lexis).
42. For this paragraph, see ibid., ¶¶ 27–30, 31 (quoting the Charter), 32.
43. See Chapter 6.
44. R. v. Butler, [1992] 1 S.C.R. 452, 78 Man. R. (2d) 1 [*Butler* cited to S.C.R.].
45. Ibid., 461–469.
46. Ibid., 460; *see also* Women's Legal Education and Action Fund, *Equality and the Charter: Ten Years of Feminist Advocacy before the Supreme Court of Canada* (Montgomery: Emond Montgomery, 1996), 204 (describing the intervener's positions).
47. *See, e.g.*, Factum of the Intervener Women's Legal Education and Action Fund ¶¶ 7, 22, in R. v. Butler, [1992] 1 S.C.R. 452, *reprinted in* LEAF, *Equality and the Charter*, 201–217 [hereinafter: Factum of LEAF in *Butler*].
48. *Butler*, [1992] 1 S.C.R. at 509–511.
49. Catharine A. MacKinnon, *Sex Equality*, 3rd ed., Univ. Casebook Series (St. Paul, MN: Foundation Press, 2016), 1795.
50. For hierarchy theory, see Chapter 3.
51. Jeff Sallot, "Legal Victory Bittersweet GOOD; BAD NEWS: The Supreme Court's Pornography Ruling Is Hailed as a Stunning Advance. But a Program That Helped Make It Possible Has Been Cut," *Globe and Mail*, Feb. 29, 1992, A6 (Westlaw). For the background of the program, see Government of Canada, "Summary Report on The Court Challenges Program Consultations," last modified Aug. 10, 2017 [https://perma.cc/88YH-557C]; *see also* Shelagh Day, "History of the Court Challenges Program" (2006) [https://perma.cc/P3DN-RQVD].
52. Sallot, "Legal Victory Bittersweet."
53. Ibid.
54. *See* Government of Canada, "Summary Report"; Day, "History of the Court Challenges Program."
55. *See* Government of Canada, "Court Challenges Program," last modified Sept. 13, 2019 [https://perma.cc/TJ9A-VNNM].
56. *Cf.* Iris Marion Young, *Justice and the Politics of Difference* (Princeton, NJ: Princeton Univ. Press, 1990), 185–186.
57. *Cf.* ibid.
58. Factum of LEAF in *Butler*, *supra* note 47, ¶ 4.
59. Ibid., ¶¶ 4–5.
60. Chapter 1 reviews studies on aggression and subordination in popular pornography.
61. *Indianapolis, Ind. Code* ch. 16 §§ 16-3(q) (1–6) (1984), *invalidated in* American Booksellers Ass'n v. Hudnut, 771 F.2d 323 (7th Cir. 1985), *reprinted in* MacKinnon and Dworkin, *In Harm's Way*, 438–457.

62. For the civil rights ordinances, see Chapter 4.
63. Factum of LEAF in *Butler*, *supra* note 47, ¶¶ 7, 22.
64. R. v. Keegstra, [1990] 3 S.C.R. 697 (Can.).
65. *See* R. v. Jones, [1986] 2 S.C.R. 284 at 308, 1986 CarswellAlta 181 ¶ 1 (WL) (Can.) (McIntyre, J.); Operation Dismantle Inc. et al. v. R. et al., [1985] 1 S.C.R. 441 at 489, 491, 1985 CarswellNat 151 ¶¶ 102 & 106 (WL) (Can.) (Wilson, J., concurring).
66. Factum of LEAF in *Butler*, *supra* note 47, ¶ 55.
67. Ibid., ¶¶ 28–29. *See* Irwin Toy Ltd. v. Quebec (A.G.), [1989] 1 S.C.R. 927 at 978, 1989 CarswellQue 115 ¶ 56; *cf.* Rocket v. Royal College of Dental Surgeons of Ontario, [1990] 2 S.C.R. 232 at 245, 1990 CarswellOnt 1014 ¶ 24 (WL) ("a law prohibiting violence or threats of violence might be held not to be protected by s. 2(b) because of the expression's offensive form") (citation omitted); R.W.D.S.U. v. Dolphin Delivery Ltd., [1986] 2 S.C.R. 573 at 588, 1986 CarswellBC 411 ¶ 27 (WL) ("Charter protection for freedom of expression . . . of course, would not extend to protect threats of violence or acts of violence"); *see also* Reference re ss. 193 & 195.1(1)(c) of Criminal Code (Man.), [1990] 1 S.C.R. 1123 at 1182, 1990 CarswellMan 206 ¶ 78 (WL) (Lamer, J.) (stating that "threats of violence," inter alia, "have not received protection under s. 2(b)").
68. Factum of LEAF in *Butler*, *supra* note 47, ¶¶ 27–34.
69. Ibid., ¶¶ 33–34 (citing research).
70. Ibid., ¶¶ 30–31, 32 (citing U.S. cases).
71. *Irwin Toy*, [1989] S.C.R. at 971–976, 1989 CarswellQue 115 ¶¶ 48–52.
72. United States v. O'Brien, 391 U.S. 367, 376 (1968).
73. City of Renton v. Playtime Theatres, Inc., 475 U.S. 41, 47 (1986).
74. Factum of LEAF in *Butler*, *supra* note 47, ¶ 51.
75. *Irwin Toy*, [1989] S.C.R. at 976, 1989 CarswellQue 115 ¶ 54.
76. Factum of LEAF in *Butler*, *supra* note 47, ¶ 55.
77. *Canadian Charter*, *supra* note 3, s. 28.
78. R. v. Red Hot Video Ltd., [1985] B.C.J. No. 2279 ¶ 31 (B.C.C.A.) (Anderson, J.).
79. Factum of LEAF in *Butler*, *supra* note 47, ¶ 43.
80. *Cf.* Janine Benedet, "Pornography at Work: Sexual Harassment, Sex Equality and Freedom of Expression," SJD diss., Univ. of Mich. Law School, Ann Arbor, UMI Microform/ProQuest, 2003, viii.
81. Factum of LEAF in *Butler*, *supra* note 47, ¶ 45.
82. *See, e.g.*, R. v. Kapp, 2008 SCC 41, [2008] 2 S.C.R. 483 ¶ 15.
83. Factum of LEAF in *Butler*, *supra* note 47, ¶ 40.
84. *See Canadian Charter*, *supra* note 3, s. 15(1).
85. R. v. Turpin, [1989] 1 S.C.R. 1296 at 1333, 1989 CanLII 98.
86. *Cf.* Factum of LEAF in *Butler*, *supra* note 47, ¶ 55.
87. Ibid., ¶ 56.
88. *Canadian Charter*, *supra* note 3, s. 1.
89. R. v. Oakes, [1986] 1 S.C.R. 103 at 138–139, 1986 CarswellOnt 95 ¶ 73 (quoting R. v. Big M Drug Mart Ltd., [1985] 1 S.C.R. 295 at 352, 1985 CarswellAlta 316 ¶ 140).
90. *Oakes*, 1 S.C.R. at 139, CarswellOnt 95 ¶ 74 (paraphrasing the *Canadian Charter*).

91. *Oakes*, 1 S.C.R. at 139, CarswellOnt 95 ¶ 74 (internal quotation to *Big M Drug Mart*, [1985] 1 S.C.R. at 352, 1985 CarswellAlta 316 ¶ 140).
92. *E.g.*, Factum of LEAF in *Butler*, *supra* note 47, ¶¶ 30–34, 44–48.
93. Ibid., ¶ 59.
94. Ibid., ¶¶ 57–63.
95. Ibid., ¶ 60; *cf.* ¶¶ 16–26.
96. Ibid., ¶¶ 65, 67 (quoting R. v. Edwards Book and Art Ltd., [1986] 2 S.C.R. 713 at 779, 35 D.L.R. (4th) 1).
97. R. v. Butler, [1992] 1 S.C.R. 452 at 489.
98. Ibid., 509–511.
99. Ibid., 479.
100. R. v. Wagner, 1985 CarswellAlta 35 ¶ 65 (Q.B.).
101. *Butler*, [1992] 1 S.C.R. at 479.
102. Ibid., 479–480.
103. Ibid., 493.
104. Ibid., 509.
105. See Chapter 4 for a critique of how the strict scrutiny standard was applied to the Indianapolis ordinance.
106. *Compare* Virginia v. Black, 538 U.S. 343, 362–363 (2003), *with* R.A.V. v. City of St. Paul, Minn., 505 U.S. 377, 380, 391 (1992).
107. United States v. O'Brien, 391 U.S. 367, 377 (1968).
108. City of Renton v. Playtime Theatres, Inc., 475 U.S. 41, 47 (1986).
109. R. v. Butler, [1992] 1 S.C.R. 452 at 483 (Can.).
110. *See* R. v. Wagner, 1985 CarswellAlta 35 ¶¶ 58–60, 64 (Q.B.).
111. *Butler*, [1992] 1 S.C.R. at 484–485.
112. Ibid., 479 (citations omitted).
113. Ibid. Though it referenced another page range, this citation was located in the same paragraph.
114. Attorney General's Commission on Pornography, *Final Report of the Attorney General's Commission on Pornography*, ed. Michael J. McManus (Nashville, TN: Rutledge Hill Press, 1986), 33.
115. *See, e.g.*, Factum of LEAF in *Butler*, *supra* note 47, ¶¶ 34, 44–46 (citing studies on harms caused by consumers); Att'y Gen. Comm., *Final Report*, 31–48, 197–290 (analyzing research on production harms and harms caused by consumers); Dolf Zillmann and Jennings Bryant, eds., *Pornography: Research Advances and Policy Considerations* (Hillsdale, NJ: Lawrence Erlbaum, 1989); Neil M. Malamuth and Edward Donnerstein, eds., *Pornography and Sexual Aggression* (Orlando, FL: Academic Press, 1984).
116. *Butler*, [1992] 1 S.C.R. at 504, 509.
117. Ibid., 504.
118. Ibid., 484.
119. Ibid.

120. Special Committee on Pornography and Prostitution in Canada, *Pornography and Prostitution in Canada: Report of the Special Committee on Pornography and Prostitution in Canada* (Ottawa: Supply & Services, 1985), 2:51.
121. *See, e.g.*, James V. P. Check and Ted H. Guloien, "Reported Proclivity for Coercive Sex Following Repeated Exposure to Sexually Violent Pornography, Nonviolent Dehumanizing Pornography, and Erotica," in Zillmann and Bryant, *Pornography*, 159–184.
122. Ibid., 168.
123. *Butler*, [1992] 1 S.C.R. at 485 (emphasis added).
124. R. v. Wagner, 1985 CarswellAlta ¶ 64 (Q.B.), *aff'd* (1986) 69 A.R. 78 (C.A.), *leave to appeal refused* (1986), 50 C.R. (3d) 175n (S.C.C.).
125. As section 15 was not yet in force, Judge Anderson had only section 28 on which to rely. *See* R. v. Red Hot Video Ltd., [1985] B.C.J. No. 2279 ¶ 31 (B.C.C.A.) (Anderson, J.) (judgment filed Mar. 18, 1985, invoking s. 28 to sustain the obscenity law against expressive challenges under the Charter); *Canadian Charter*, *supra* note 3, s. 32(2) (barring section 15 from taking effect until Apr. 17, 1985).
126. R. v. Keegstra, [1990] 3 S.C.R. 697 at 755–757.
127. *Butler*, [1992] 1 S.C.R. at 486–490.
128. R. v. Butler, 1990 CarswellMan 228 ¶ 30, 73 Man. R. (2d) 197 (C.A.) (Huband, J.) (3–2), *modified* [1992] 1 S.C.R. 452.
129. Factum of LEAF in *Butler*, *supra* note 47, ¶ 52.
130. *Butler*, 1990 CarswellMan 228 ¶ 37.
131. Mahoney, "Obscenity, Morals," 60–61.
132. Ibid., 61.
133. *Butler*, [1992] 1 S.C.R. 452 at 460.
134. LEAF, *Equality and the Charter*, 204.
135. Lise Gotell, "Shaping *Butler*: The New Politics of Anti-Pornography," in *Bad Attitude/s on Trial: Pornography, Feminism, and the* Butler *Decision*, ed. Brenda Cossman et al. (Toronto: Univ. of Toronto Press, 1997), 102 n.2.
136. R. v. Hawkins (1993), 15 O.R. (3d) 549, 1993 CarswellOnt 133 (C.A.).
137. R. v. Ronish, 1993 CarswellOnt 75 ¶¶ 5, 7, 11(4), 18 C.R. (4th) 165 (Ont. Ct. J. (Prov. Div.)).
138. R. v. Hawkins, 1992 CarswellOnt 1940 ¶¶ 7–13 (Ont. Ct. J. (Gen. Div.)).
139. *See* Factum of LEAF in *Butler*, *supra* note 47, ¶ 4. *See supra* notes 58–61 and accompanying text (synopsizing LEAF's descriptions of the *Butler* materials).
140. *Hawkins*, 15 O.R. (3d) at 562–563.
141. Ibid., 563.
142. Ibid.
143. Ibid., 564 (quoting R. v. Butler, [1992] 1 S.C.R. 452 at 485 (emphasis omitted)).
144. Ibid., 565–568, 573.
145. Ibid., 564.
146. Ibid., 565.
147. Ibid., 566.
148. Ibid.

149. R. v. Butler, [1992] 1 S.C.R. 452 at 485 (emphasis added).
150. *Hawkins*, 15 O.R. (3d) at 566 (quotes), 568, 573.
151. Ibid., 562.
152. *Cf.* Check and Guloien, "Reported Proclivity," 171 & tbl. 6.1 (finding that the dehumanizing nonviolent, rather than the violent, pornography produced the strongest effect on the likelihood of forcing a female to have sex scale); Dolf Zillmann and James B. Weaver, "Pornography and Men's Callousness toward Women," in Zillmann and Bryant, *Pornography*, 120 (finding that exposure to unambiguous presentations of "nymphomania" with a "total absence of coercive or violent action" nonetheless led to "the strongest trivialization of rape" among research subjects compared to other pornography).
153. R. v. Hawkins, 1992 CarswellOnt 1940 ¶¶ 14–15 (Ont. Ct. J. (Gen. Div.)) (Misener, J.).
154. Zillmann and Weaver, "Pornography and Men's Callousness," 120.
155. See the introduction for a discussion of systemic indices of male dominance.
156. *See* R. v. Ronish, 1993 CarswellOnt 75 ¶¶ 5, 7, 11(4), 18 C.R. (4th) 165 (Ont. Ct. J., Prov. Div.) (describing nonviolent materials presented in the case); R. v. Hawkins, 1992 CarswellOnt 1940 ¶¶ 7–13 (Ont. Ct. J. (Gen. Div.)) (describing nonviolent materials presented in the case).
157. *Hawkins*, 15 O.R. (3d) at 564.
158. Ana J. Bridges et al., "Sexual Scripts and the Sexual Behavior of Men and Women Who Use Pornography," *Sexualization, Media, & Society* 2, no. 4 (2016): doi:10.1177/2374623816668275.
159. Ibid., 4, 5 tbl. 2, 8 tbl. 5.
160. James Lindgren, "Defining Pornography," 141 *U. Penn. Law. Rev.* 1153, 1210 (1993) (emphasis added).
161. Check and Guloien, "Reported Proclivity," 163.
162. Ibid., 168–169.
163. Ibid., 179.
164. Factum of LEAF in *Butler*, *supra* note 47, ¶¶ 45–46.
165. *See* R. v. Erotica Video Exchange Ltd. (1994), 163 A.R. 181 at 184, 1994 CarswellAlta 820 (Alta. Prov. Ct.) ("[T]he defense concedes that each of the three videos contains degrading and dehumanizing pornography."). *See* 197, for convictions and acquittals.
166. Ibid., 192.
167. Ibid., 187 (quoting Berl Kutchinsky, "Pornography and Rape: Theory and Practice? Evidence from Crime Data in Four Countries Where Pornography Is Easily Available," *Int'l J. Law & Psychiatry* 14, nos. 1–2 (1991): 62).
168. Kutchinsky, "Pornography and Rape," 57 fig. 7.
169. See Chapter 2 for a more thorough critique of aggregated longitudinal studies.
170. *Cf.* Neil M. Malamuth and Eileen V. Pitpitan, "The Effects of Pornography Are Moderated by Men's Sexual Aggression Risk," in *Pornography: Driving the Demand in International Sex Trafficking*, ed. David E. Guinn and Julie DiCaro (Los Angeles: Int'l Human Rights L. Inst., DePaul Univ., 2007), 140–141 (discussing problems of causal overdetermination in aggregated studies).

171. *See, e.g.*, Att'y Gen. Comm., *Final Report*, 259–261 (discussing and citing scholarly criticism voiced since the 1970s against longitudinal research on pornography and sex crime reports).
172. Drew A. Kingston and Neil M. Malamuth, "Problems with Aggregate Data and the Importance of Individual Differences in the Study of Pornography and Sexual Aggression: Comment on Diamond, Jozifkova, and Weiss (2010)," *Arch. Sex. Behav.* 40, no. 5 (2011): 1045. *Cf.* Malamuth and Pitpitan, "Effects of Pornography," 138–141.
173. R. v. Erotica Video Exchange Ltd. (1994), 163 A.R. 181 at 192 (Alta. Prov. Ct.).
174. *See, e.g.*, Check and Guloien, "Reported Proclivity," 159–184; Neil M. Malamuth and James V. P. Check, "The Effects of Aggressive Pornography on Beliefs in Rape Myths: Individual Differences," *J. Res. Pers.* 19 (1985): 299–320; Neil M. Malamuth and James V. P. Check, "The Effects of Mass Media Exposure on Acceptance of Violence against Women: A Field Experiment," *J. Res. Pers.* 15 (1981): 436–446.
175. Christopher Nowlin, *Judging Obscenity: A Critical History of Expert Evidence* (Montreal: McGill-Queen's Univ. Press, 2003), 131.
176. This observation was made in November 2019.
177. R. v. Butler, [1992] 1 S.C.R. 452 at 485 (emphasis added).
178. R. v. Hawkins (1993), 15 O.R. (3d) 549 at 559–561, 568–570, 573 (C.A.).
179. R. v. Jorgensen, [1995] 4 S.C.R. 55, 129 D.L.R. (4th) 510 [*Jorgensen* cited to S.C.R.]. The defendant's appeal had previously been dismissed by the Court of Appeal for Ontario, which affirmed the Ontario Court Provincial Division's conviction for "selling obscene material without lawful justification or excuse." *See Hawkins* (1993), 15 O.R. (3d) at 559 (quote), 573 (dismissing appeal).
180. *Jorgensen*, [1995] 4 S.C.R. at 84–122 (a partial concurrence was delivered by Lamer, J., 61–84). For Sophinka's opinion in *Butler*, see [1992] 1 S.C.R. at 460–511 (Sophinka, J.).
181. *See Jorgensen*, [1995] 4 S.C.R. at 61.
182. Criminal Code, R.S.C. 1985, c. C-46, s. 163(1)(2) (Can.).
183. Ibid., s. 163(2) (emphasis added).
184. *See* ibid., s. 163(1).
185. *Jorgensen*, [1995] 4 S.C.R. at 95–96.
186. Ibid., 96–97.
187. Ibid., 92. The fact that provincial film review boards classified pornography at the time was also taken into account as evidence of contemporary community standards, but a provincial body could not be given the constitutional power to "preclude the prosecution" (116) since the Criminal Code is a federal law.
188. Ibid., 107–108. If prosecutors, as reported, used the word "morally" blameworthy rather than simply saying "blameworthy," that was indicative of a concern with "morals" rather than with law.
189. Ibid., 108–111.
190. Ibid., 110.
191. Ibid., 111.

192. S. Laurel Weldon and Mala Htun, "The Civic Origins of Progressive Policy Change: Combating Violence against Women in Global Perspective, 1975–2005," *Am. Pol. Sci. Rev.* 106, no. 3 (2012): 548–569.
193. *See* Day, "History of the Court Challenges Program."
194. *Jorgensen* appealed a decision from Ontario on Oct. 19, 1993, and the Supreme Court heard the case on Feb. 21, 1995. *See Jorgensen*, [1995] 4 S.C.R. at 55, 61.
195. This observation was made in November 2019.
196. R. v. Price, 2004 BCPC 103, [2004] B.C.J. No. 814, 2004 CarswellBC 895 (Prov. Ct. Crim. Div.).
197. Ibid., ¶ 18.
198. For this paragraph, see ibid., ¶¶ 59–65.
199. For this paragraph, see ibid., ¶¶ 29, 30, 35–36. It is conceivable that the defense believed a mother involved in BDSM activities would be seen as a favorable female witness, presuming mothers are more cautious not to expose themselves to harm due to their parental responsibilities compared to other women.
200. For this paragraph, see ibid., ¶¶ 34–43, 58, 68–69.
201. See Chapter 1 for further discussion.
202. For this paragraph, see R. v. Price, 2004 BCPC 103, [2004] B.C.J. No. 814 ¶¶ 46–51, 53, 55 (Prov. Ct. Crim. Div.).
203. Malamuth and Pitpitan, "Effects of Pornography," 138–141; *cf.* Kingston and Malamuth, "Problems with Aggregate Data," 1045–1046.
204. *See especially* Larry Baron and Murray A. Straus, "Four Theories of Rape: A Macrosociological Analysis," *Social Problems* 34, no. 5 (1987): 478 fig. 2, 480; Joseph E. Scott and Loretta A. Schwalm, "Rape Rates and the Circulation Rates of Adult Magazines," *J. Sex Res.* 24, no. 1 (1988): 245–246.
205. See Chapter 2 for these studies.
206. Dean G. Kilpatrick et al., *Drug-Facilitated, Incapacitated, and Forcible Rape: A National Study* (Charleston, SC: Nat'l Crime Victims Res. & Treatment Center, 2007), 43, 57, 59 [http://perma.cc/56W9-44Z3].
207. Factum of LEAF in *Butler*, *supra* note 47, ¶¶ 15, 23, 31, 34, 44–46.
208. Weldon and Htun, "Civic Origins," 561–564.
209. *See supra* notes 51–56 and accompanying text paragraphs.
210. For this paragraph, see R. v. Price, 2004 BCPC 103, [2004] B.C.J. No. 814 ¶¶ 51, 86, 88 (Prov. Ct. Crim. Div.)
211. For this paragraph, see ibid., ¶¶ 21, 22, 25, 27, 89, 95.
212. Ibid., ¶¶ 99–100.
213. Ibid., ¶¶ 76–79 (quote at ¶ 79).
214. R. v. Butler, [1992] 1 S.C.R. 452 at 485.
215. Miller v. California, 413 U.S. 15, 24–25 (1973).
216. R. v. Smith, 2012 ONCA 892, 2012 CarswellOnt 15792 (C.A.) [*Smith* 2012 cited to Carswell], *leave to appeal refused* [2013] CarswellOnt 9111 (Fish, Moldaver, Rothstein JJ.) (S.C.C.).
217. R. v. Smith (2005), 76 O.R. (3d) 435, CanLII 23805 (C.A.).
218. *Smith*, [2012] CarswellOnt 15792 ¶¶ 38–44.

219. *See* retrial-judgment on application to exclude evidence in R. v. Smith, [2007] O.J. No. 3075 ¶ 12, 2007 CarswellOnt 6286 (Super. Ct.) (Lexis).
220. R. v. Smith, 2002 CarswellOnt 6125 ¶¶ 4–9, O.J. No. 5018 (Super. Ct. J.) ("brutal rape" quotation at ¶ 9); *Smith* (2005), 76 O.R. (3d) at 438, ¶ 4 (C.A.) ("intercourse or fellatio" quote).
221. *Smith*, 2002 CarswellOnt 6125 ¶ 4.
222. Ibid., ¶¶ 5–7.
223. *Smith*, 2012 CarswellOnt 15792 ¶¶ 27–32; *Smith* (2005), 76 O.R. (3d) at 440–41, ¶¶ 11–14.
224. *Smith* (2005), 76 O.R. (3d) at 441, ¶¶ 15–16.
225. For this paragraph, see ibid., 441, ¶¶ 13–15.
226. *See Smith*, 2002 CarswellOnt 6125 (Super. Ct. J.) (judgment delivered Dec. 3, 2002); R. v. Price, 2004 BCPC 103, 2004 CarswellBC 895 (Prov. Ct. Crim. Div.) (judgment delivered Apr. 23, 2004).
227. *See, e.g.*, Neil M. Malamuth, Tamara Addison, and Mary Koss, "Pornography and Sexual Aggression: Are There Reliable Effects and Can We Understand Them?," *Ann. Rev. Sex Res.* 11 (2000): 26–91; Neil M. Malamuth, James V. P. Check, and John Briere, "Sexual Arousal in Response to Aggression: Ideological, Aggressive, and Sexual Correlates," *J. Pers. & Soc. Psychol.* 50, no. 2 (1986): 330–340.
228. *Price*, 2004 BCPC 103 ¶¶ 91–93, 99–100.
229. *Smith*, 2002 CarswellOnt 6125 ¶ 30.
230. Ibid., ¶¶ 31–32 (Pierce, J.).
231. R. v. Smith (2005), 76 O.R. (3d) 435 at 441, ¶ 14, CanLII 23805 (C.A.).
232. R. v. Smith, 2012 ONCA 892 ¶ 29, 2012 CarswellOnt 15792 (C.A.).
233. R. v. Labaye, 2005 SCC 80, [2005] 3 S.C.R. 728.
234. Ibid., ¶¶ 1, 13, 72 (quoting in ¶ 1 Criminal Code, R.S.C. 1985, c. C-46, s. 210(1) (Can.), *invalidated in* Canada (A.G.) v. Bedford, 2013 SCC 72, [2013] 3 S.C.R. 1101 ¶ 164).
235. *Labaye*, 2005 SCC 80 ¶¶ 9–10, 18, 24, 33.
236. Ibid., ¶ 20.
237. Ibid., ¶ 21.
238. Richard Jochelson and Kirsten Kramar, *Sex and the Supreme Court: Obscenity and Indecency Law in Canada* (Halifax: Fernwood, 2011), 59–60; *cf.* 64–65.
239. *Labaye*, 2005 SCC 80 ¶ 21 (quoting R. v. Butler, [1992] 1 S.C.R. 452 at 485).
240. R. v. Smith (2005), 76 O.R. (3d) 435 at 440–442 (quotation at 441), 2005 CarswellOnt 2872 ¶¶ 11–17 (quotation at ¶ 15) (C.A.).
241. *Labaye*, 2005 SCC 80 ¶ 21.
242. R. v. Katigbak, 2011 SCC 48, [2011] 3 S.C.R. 326 ¶ 67.
243. Ibid., ¶ 78 (quoting R. v. Katigbak, 2010 ONCA 411 ¶ 76 (C.A.); emphasis added by Supreme Court).
244. Ibid. ¶ 78.
245. Little Sisters Book & Art Emporium v. Canada, 2000 SCC 69, [2000] 2 S.C.R. 1120 ¶ 1 (Binnie, J.).
246. Ibid., ¶¶ 1, 6–7, 8–10, 11.

247. *Cf.* Susan Cole, *Pornography and the Sex Crisis* (Toronto: Amanita Enterprises, 1989), 70 (noting that obscenity law was historically used to repress women's reproductive and sexual autonomy); MacKinnon, *Sex Equality*, 1696 (mentioning "years of litigation resisting attempted censorship of literary works that offended the establishment" following the obscenity rule in *Roth v. United States*, 354 U.S. 476 (1957) (citation omitted)).
248. *Little Sisters*, 2000 SCC 69 ¶ 63.
249. Ibid.
250. Ibid., ¶ 66.
251. Ibid., ¶¶ 60 (second quote), 68 (first quote).
252. Janine Benedet, "The Paper Tigress: Canadian Obscenity Law 20 Years after *R. v. Butler*," 93 *Canadian Bar Review* 1, 13 (2015).
253. For Benedet's article, see ibid., 12–13, 13 n.48, 18–20,
254. My search included cases involving charges for obscenity offenses under s. 163 of the Canadian Criminal Code. In one case, the obscenity law was used to charge a man for having published "a video depicting the murder and dismemberment of a human victim," seemingly without pornographic or other sexual elements. R. v. Marek, 2016 ABQB 18, 2016 CarswellAlta 28 ¶ 2 (Q.B.) (on the admissibility of evidence). Occasionally, s. 163 appears as a subsidiary charge to child pornography offenses because of a plea; *see* R. v. C. (J.), 2013 BCPC 237, 2013 CarswellBC 2780 (Prov. Ct.); R. v. Rogers, 2012 BCPC 518, 2012 CarswellBC 4284 (Prov. Ct.); or as a subsidiary charge to other sexual offenses against children; *see* R. v. Danylak, 2012 ABCA 179, 2012 CarswellAlta 1026 ¶ 2, 10 (C.A.) (reporting that defendant was found not guilty of distributing obscene matter at trial while ordering retrial for other offenses); or as an ancillary charge to other offenses; *e.g.*, R. v. Magnotta, 2014 QCCS 4247 (CanLII) (Quebec Super. Ct., Dist. Montreal) (adding obscenity charges to first-degree murder, criminal harassment of the prime minister and members of Parliament, and offenses involving dead bodies).
255. *See* "Summary Report," Government of Canada (under subheading 2.1.a.ii).
256. *See supra* notes 54–55 and accompanying text.

Chapter 8 Challenging Production, 1993–2005

1. *See* introduction for a brief comparative discussion of Sweden's sex purchase law.
2. *See* Meghan Donevan, *Out of Sight, Out of Mind—Insights into the Swedish Pornography Industry* (Stockholm: Talita, 2019), 3 (summary) [https://perma.cc/HAL4-YUY8].
3. Protocol to Prevent, Suppress and Punish Trafficking in Persons, Especially Women and Children, Supplementing the United Nations Convention Against Transnational Organized Crime, *opened for signature* Dec. 12, 2000, T.I.A.S. No. 13127, 2237 U.N.T.S. 319 (entered into force Dec. 25, 2003) [hereinafter Palermo Protocol].
4. Ibid., art. 3(a) (emphasis added).
5. Rep. of the Ad Hoc Comm. on the Elaboration of a Convention Against Transnational Organized Crime on the Work of Its First to Eleventh Sessions,

Addendum, Interpretative Notes for the Official Records (*Travaux Préparatoires*) of the Negotiation of the United Nations Convention Against Transnational Organized Crime and the Protocols Thereto, ¶ 63, U.N. Doc. A/55/383/Add.1 (Nov. 3, 2000) (emphasis added).

6. Palermo Protocol, *supra* note 3, art. 3(b).
7. *Brottsbalken [BrB] 4:1a [Criminal Code]* (Swed.).
8. *BrB* 6:12(1).
9. *Lag om ändring i brottsbalken* (Svensk författningssamling [SFS] 2018:601) (Swed.) (entering into force July 1, 2018), *amending BrB* 6:12.
10. *Cf.* Royal Canadian Mounted Police, *Human Trafficking in Canada* (Ottawa: RCMP, 2010), 37 [https://perma.cc/JJM7-XJN5] (noting that trafficking charges are "sometimes omitted as other associated charges are believed to have greater odds of a successful prosecution," even in cases with "strong elements of human trafficking" due for instance to difficulties "in 'measuring' exploitation"); 11 (noting that massage parlors make prostitution payments private, separated from ostensibly legitimate payments); 38–39 (discussing witness intimidation and difficulties getting prostituted persons to testify against traffickers); *see also* Max Waltman, "Assessing Evidence, Arguments, and Inequality in *Bedford v. Canada*," 37 *Harvard J. Law & Gender* 459, 511–528 (2014) (demonstrating how other Canadian prostitution laws cover a broader range of third-party conduct otherwise not effectively covered under anti-trafficking laws).
11. Brottsförebyggande rådet, "Personer lagförda för brott," accessed Feb. 12, 2019 [https://www.bra.se/brott-och-statistik/kriminalstatistik/personer-lagforda-for-brott.html] (scroll down and select "Tabeller"; select "Lagföringsbeslut efter huvudbrott och huvudpåföljd"; select "period," "population," and "område" from the respective drop-down menus; press "Visa"; select "Ladda ner ditt urval som excelfil"; then repeat that procedure for every year from 2002 through 2019).
12. Statens Offentliga Utredningar [SOU] 1995:15 Könshandeln: Betänkande av 1993 års Prostitutionsutredning [government report series] (Swed.).
13. Proposition [Prop.] 1997/98:55 Kvinnofrid [government bill] (Swed.). The current version of the sex purchase law is in the criminal code. *See BrB 6:11* (Swed.).
14. SOU 1995:15 p. 136.
15. Ibid., 230; *cf.* 33.
16. Ibid., 230.
17. Ibid., 231.
18. Ibid., 55. The statutory language has changed only slightly in the years since. *See BrB* 6:12(3).
19. See SOU 1995:15 p. 231, for all quotes and references in this paragraph.
20. *BrB* 6:12(1).
21. SOU 1995:15 p. 231.
22. *BrB* 6:12(1).
23. Nytt Juridiskt Arkiv [NJA] [Weekly Law Reports] [Supreme Court] 1979-09-28 p. 602 (reporting from all judicial instances).
24. Ibid., 605–606 (HovR) [Ct. App.].
25. SOU 1995:15 pp. 231.

26. Ibid., 231–232. A similar law covering adults performing in a pornographic movie was also said to exist in the Danish criminal code at the time (232).
27. Prop. 1997/98:55 Kvinnofrid [government bill] 106 (Swed.).
28. Kommittédirektiv [dir.] 1998:48 Översyn av lagstiftningen om sexualbrott [government committee directive] 12 (Swed.), *available as appendix in* SOU 2001:14 Sexualbrotten: Ett ökat skydd för den sexuella integriteten och angränsande frågor [government report series] 609 (Swed.).
29. Ibid.
30. Ibid.
31. S. Laurel Weldon and Mala Htun, "The Civic Origins of Progressive Policy Change: Combating Violence against Women in Global Perspective, 1975–2005," *Am. Pol. Sci. Rev.* 106, no. 3 (2012): 548, 564.
32. Motion till Riksdagen [Mot.] 1999/2000:Ju710 Pornografi [parliamentary motion] (Sept. 28, 1999) (Swed.) (Ulla Hoffmann et al.; Left Party) (rejected). Swedish public parliamentary documents are generally available at https://www.riksdagen.se.
33. Ibid.
34. Riksdagens snabbprotokoll 1999/2000:67 JuU7 Straffrättsliga frågor: Mom. 3; pornografi ur könspolitisk synvinkel [parliamentary minutes] (Feb. 16, 2000) (Swed.) [https://perma.cc/4XM8-9FK2].
35. Mot. 2001/02:K348 Pornografins utveckling [parliamentary motion] (Oct. 3) (Swed.) (Ewa Larsson and Kia Andreasson; Greens).
36. Ibid.
37. Ibid.
38. Mot. 2000/01:K351 Pornografi i kabelTV-kanaler (Oct. 4) (Birgitta Sellén and Rigmor Stenmark; Center Party).
39. Mot. 2000/01:K375 TV-kanaler med pornografiska sändningar (Oct. 2) (Carina Hägg, Birgitta Ahlqvist, and Agneta Brendt; Social Democrats); Mot. 1999/2000:K304 Pornografiska sändningar (Sept. 30) (containing the same authors and content as the preceding citation).
40. Mot. 2000/01:N310 Export av pornografiskt material (Sept. 26) (Carina Hägg: Social Democrats).
41. Mot. 1998/99:K224 Videovåld och pornografi (Oct. 21) (Margareta Viklund; Christian Democrats).
42. Ibid.
43. Ibid.
44. Mot. 1998/99:K285 Pornografi (Oct. 27) (Gudrun Schyman et al.; Left Party, 10 MPs); *cf.* Mot. 1997/98:K342 Pornografi m.m. (Oct. 7) (Swed.) (Johan Lönnroth et al.; Left Party, 8 MPs) (containing similar content as above).
45. Mot. 1998/99:K285; *cf.* Mot. 1997/98:K342.
46. Mot. 1998/99:K285 ("completely toothless"); *cf.* Mot. 1997/98:K342 (denouncing the law as "insufficient" even for addressing "the most gross forms of violent pornography").
47. Mot. 1998/99:K285; *cf.* Mot. 1997/98:K342.

48. SOU 2001:14 Sexualbrotten: Ett ökat skydd för den sexuella integriteten och angränsande frågor [government report series] 415 (Swed.).
49. Ibid.
50. Prop. 2004/05:45 En ny sexualbrottslagstiftning [government bill] (Swed.) (passed).
51. *See* Christine Sypnowich, "Law and Ideology," in *Stanford Encyclopedia of Philosophy*, ed. Edward N. Zalta (2014) [https://plato.stanford.edu/archives/spr2017/entries/law-ideology/] (distinguishing between law and ideology).
52. SOU 2001:14 Sexualbrotten, 411.
53. Ibid., 411–412.
54. Ibid., 412.
55. Ibid.
56. Ibid. (citing SOU 1999:30 Yttrandefrihet och konkurrensen: Förslag till mediekoncentrationslag m.m. [government report series] 150–151, 208–209 (Swed.); SOU 1980:28 Massmediekoncentration: Lagförslag och motiv [government report series] 64–65, 92–93 (Swed.)).
57. SOU 2001:14 p. 412 n.13.
58. Ibid., 412.
59. SOU 1999:30 Yttrandefrihet och konkurrensen, 219.
60. Ibid.
61. SOU 1999:30 pp. 206–222; *also* SOU 1980:28 Massmediekoncentration, 92–94.
62. SOU 1999:30 pp. 206–222; SOU 1980:28 p. 93.
63. Catharine MacKinnon makes a similar point, arguing that at the same time pornography is being protected as "speech," in actuality it is silencing the speech of women. Catharine A. MacKinnon, "Francis Biddle's Sister," in *Feminism Unmodified: Discourses on Life and Law* (Cambridge, MA: Harvard Univ. Press, 1987), 192–197.
64. SOU 1980:28 Massmediekoncentration, 92–94.
65. SOU 1999:30 Yttrandefrihet och konkurrensen, 218.
66. Ibid.
67. Ibid.
68. SOU 2001:14 Sexualbrotten [government report series] 412 & n.14 (Swed.) (citing Prop. 1979/80:83 Om ändring i konkurslagen [On Amendments to the Bankruptcy Act] [government bill] 184–185 (Swed.) (submitted Feb. 7, 1980)).
69. Prop. 1979/80:83 at 184–186 (reprinting a statement by the Council on Legislation).
70. *Konkurslagen [KonkL] [Bankruptcy Code]* 6:1 (Swed.).
71. *Compare* Prop. 1979/80:83 pp. 183–192 (discussing the Council on Legislation's response and the waiver), *with* SOU 2001:14 Sexualbrotten, 412 & n.14 (only citing Prop. 1979/80:83 pp. 184–185).
72. Prop. 1979/80:83 at 191.
73. Ibid.
74. Ibid.
75. SOU 2001:14 p. 412.
76. Ibid., 413.
77. Ibid.
78. The introduction briefly described the "Alexanderson doctrine" and Sweden's constitutional framework within which child pornography is regulated.

79. *See, e.g.*, SOU 1947:60 Förslag till tryckfrihetsförordning [government report series] 120 (Swed.); *cf.* Prop. 1975/76:209 Om ändring i regeringsformen [government bill] 141 (Swed.); Prop. 1948:230 Kungl. Maj:ts proposition till riksdagen med förslag till tryckfrihetsförordning m.m. [government bill] 172 (Swed.).
80. *See BrB [Criminal Code]* 16:10a (Swed.).
81. Prop. 1997/98:43 Tryckfrihetsförordningens och yttrandefrihetsgrundlagens tillämpningsområden: Barnpornografifrågan m.m. [government bill] 67 (Swed.).
82. SOU 2001:14 Sexualbrotten [government report series] 413–414 (Swed.) (citing NJA II [Weekly Law Reports II] 1984 pp. 156–157 (Swed.)); *cf.* Prop. 1983/84:105 Om ändring I brottsbalken m.m. (sexualbrotten) [government bill] 55–56 (Swed.).
83. SOU 2001:14 p. 414 (citing NJA II 1984 pp. 156–157); *cf.* Prop. 1983/84:105 p. 56.
84. Prop. 1983/84:105 p. 56; *cf.* NJA II 1984 pp. 156–157.
85. *BrB* 16:10c.
86. *Tryckfrihetsförordningen [TF] [Constitution]* 7:7 (Swed.), *passed by Lag om ändring i tryckfrihetsförordningen* (SFS 1988:1448) (Swed.); *cf. Yttrandefrihetsgrundlagen [YGL] [Constitution]* 5:1 (Swed.); *BrB* 16:10c.
87. SOU 2001:14 p. 414.
88. Prop. 1983/84:105 p. 56; *cf.* NJA II 1984 pp. 156–157.
89. *See, e.g.*, Prop. 1997/98:43 Tryckfrihetsförordningens och yttrandefrihetsgrundlagens tillämpningsområden: Barnpornografifrågan m.m. [government bill] 13 (Swed.) (listing the prior location of child pornography as a Crime Against Freedom of Expression in the Freedom of the Press Act, *TF* 7:4(12) (as per 1997)).
90. SOU 2001:14 p. 414.
91. Ibid. At the end of the same paragraph (415), the Committee cited Hans Gunnar Axberger, *Tryckfrihetens gränser* (Stockholm: Liber Förlag, 1984), 68–69.
92. Gunnar Persson, *Exklusivitetsfrågan: Om förhållandet mellan tryckfrihet, yttrandefrihet och annan rätt* (Stockholm: Norstedts Juridik, 2002), 359.
93. Axberger, *Tryckfrihetens gränser*, 69.
94. Ibid.
95. Persson, *Exklusivitetsfrågan*, 359. For relevant legislative history, see, e.g., SOU 1947:60 Förslag till tryckfrihetsförordning [government report series] 115–120 (Swed.); *cf.* Prop. 1975/76:209 Om ändring i regeringsformen [government bill] 141 (Swed.); Prop. 1948:230 Kungl. Maj:ts proposition till riksdagen med förslag till tryckfrihetsförordning m.m. [government bill] 172 (Swed.).
96. Persson, *Exklusivitetsfrågan*, 360.
97. Ibid., 361.
98. SOU 2001:14 Sexualbrotten [government report series] 414–415 (Swed.).
99. *Tryckfrihetsordningen [TF] [Constitution]* 1:1 (Swed.).
100. SOU 2001:14 p. 415.
101. Ibid.
102. Ibid., 412.
103. *See* NJA [Supreme Court Reports] 1979 pp. 602, 608 (Swed.); *cf.* Prop. 1986/87:151 Om ändringar i tryckfrihetsförordningen m.m. [government bill] 21 (Swed.).
104. *TF* 1:1.

105. *BrB [Criminal Code]* 6:12(1) (Swed.).
106. *See* Sypnowich, "Law and Ideology," (distinguishing between *law* and *ideology*); *see also* introduction to Part II.
107. Stockholms tingsrätt [Stockholm Dist. Ct.], 2009-08-31, B 3870-09 (Swed.).
108. These two crimes are only found in the criminal code. *See BrB* 17:4 (violent resistance), 9:8 (dishonest conduct).
109. See Stockholms tingsrätt, B 3870-09, at 1, 3, 5, 7–9 (quote at 5).
110. SOU 2001:14 Sexualbrotten [government report series] 412 (Swed.).
111. Stockholms tingsrätt, B 3870-09, at 1, 9.
112. SOU 2010:49 Förbud mot köp av sexuell tjänst: En utvärdering 1999–2008 [government report series] 23 (Swed.) (summary).
113. NJA [Weekly Law Reports] [Supreme Court] 1999 pp. 275, 275–281 (Swed.) (containing all instances of judicial opinions).
114. Ibid., 275 (reporting the Stockholm District Court's opinion).
115. Ibid., 281 (Supreme Court).
116. Ibid., 279.
117. Ibid., 277 (reporting the District Court's opinion).
118. Ibid., 278 (reporting Svea Court of Appeal's opinion) (convicting defendant), *rev'd* 281 [Sup. Ct.].
119. Ibid., 281 (Supreme Court).
120. *BrB [Criminal Code]* 6:12(1) (Swed.).
121. Gross violation of a woman's integrity is an umbrella crime covering offenses that form a pattern of repeated violations. *See BrB* 4:4a, para. 2.
122. Hovrätten över Skåne och Blekinge [Ct. App.] 2009-05-18, B 452-09 (Swed.), *modifying* Malmö tingsrätt [Dist.Ct.] 2009-02-03, B 6656-08 (Swed.).
123. HovR Skåne & Blekinge, B 452-09 pp. 26–27, 34–35.
124. See Chapter 1 for examples of abusive conditions often associated with pornography production.
125. Malmö tingsrätt, B 6656-08 pp. 18, 41.
126. Ibid., 17–18, 41.
127. Ibid., 17–18, 41.
128. NJA [Supreme Court] 1979 pp. 602, 608 (Swed.); *cf.* Prop. 1986/87:151 Om ändringar i tryckfrihetsförordningen m.m. [government bill] p. 21 (Swed.) (stating that the purpose of freedom of the press is also to protect presentations that may fairly be "characterized as pure entertainment").
129. Hovrätten över Skåne och Blekinge [Ct. App.] 2009-05-18, B 452-09 p. 14 (Swed.); *cf.* 15; *also* Malmö tingsrätt, B 6656-08 pp. 13, 65.
130. HovR Skåne & Blek., B 452-09 pp. 14–15; Malmö tingsrätt, B 6656-08 pp. 13, 64–65.
131. Hovrätten för Västra Sverige [Ct. App.] 2009-05-15, B 3766-08 pp. 2, 5–6 (Swed.), *rev'g* Varbergs tingsrätt [Dist Ct.] 2008-07-22, B 2771-07 (Swed.).
132. HovR Västra Sverige, B 3766-08, at 6.
133. For pinpoint citations, see *infra* note 134.
134. *See, e.g.*, Hovrätten för Västra Sverige [Ct. App.] 2011-04-15, B 1607-11 p. 8 (Swed.) (concluding that since a film could not be permanently deleted from a cell phone with certainty, forfeiture of a seized cell phone containing a film of a sexual crime

was appropriate); Svea hovrätt [Ct. App.] 2010-04-23, B 5077-09 (Swed.), *aff'g* Södertälje tingsrätt [Dist. Ct.] 2009-05-19, B 366-06 pp. 11, 15 & appendix file no. 140 p. 3 (Swed.); Svea hovrätt [Ct. App.] 2009-08-11, B 5284-09 p. 2 (Swed.) (affirming the forfeiture of the cell phone, but dismissing the rape charge), *partially dismissing* Södertörns tingsrätt [Dist. Ct.] 2009-06-05, B 6371-09 pp. 6, 18 (Swed.) (noting that the rape defendant, relying on no particular legal grounds, protested unsuccessfully against the cell phone's forfeiture). See also Svea hovrätt [Ct. App.] 2009-09-07, B 6354-09 pp. 4–5 (Swed.), where the court forfeits a seized cell phone containing a copy of a movie thought to have been deleted through forfeiture of another cell phone in a prior rape case against the same defendant, B 5284-09, *supra* at 2, over the defendant's objections that, because the prior rape case was dismissed, the movie should be considered to be "of a noncriminal and private nature and that there is thus no legal grounds for forfeiture." B 6354-09, *supra* at 4.

135. NJA [Weekly Law Reports] [Supreme Court] 2015 pp. 45, 45–61 (Swed.).
136. Ibid., 51 (reporting the Malmö District Court's opinion). The conviction was affirmed on appeal. *See* 57 (Scania & Blekinge Ct. App.), *aff'd but reducing penalty*, 61 (Sup. Ct.).
137. *See* NJA [Weekly Law Reports] [Supreme Court] 2015 p. 59, ¶ 13 (Supreme Court).
138. *TF [Constitution]* 1:12 (6) (Swed.); *cf. YGL [Constitution]* 1:18 (Swed.).
139. NJA 2015 pp. 45, 59, ¶ 13 (Supreme Court).
140. NJA [Supreme Court Reports] 1979 pp. 602, 608 (Swed.).
141. NJA 2015 pp. 45, 60, ¶ 17 (Supreme Court).
142. Ibid.
143. This distinction of ideology in relation to law builds on Sypnowich, "Law and Ideology."
144. *See supra* notes 32–47 and accompanying text.
145. Inter-Parliamentary Union, "Women in Parliaments: World Classification," IPU PARLINE, accessed May 26, 2014 [https://perma.cc/N5AG-DDHW] (Sweden's election Sept. 1998).
146. Inter-Parliamentary Union, "Women in Parliaments," [https://perma.cc/N73A-X888] (Sweden's election Sept. 2002).
147. See Chapters 1 & 2 for the evidence of pornography's harm to sex equality.
148. *Cf.* Iris Marion Young, *Inclusion and Democracy* (Oxford: Oxford Univ. Press, 2000), 149.

Chapter 9 Substantive Equality Prostitution Law, 1999–2019

1. *Brottsbalken [BrB] [Criminal Code]* 6:11 (Swed.).
2. The increase to a maximum penalty of one year's imprisonment was accomplished through an Act of Parliament. *See Lag om ändring i brottsbalken* (Svensk författningssamling [SFS] 2011:517) (passed 282 to 1, 66 absent); *see also* Proposition [Prop.] 2010/11:77 Skärpt straff för köp av sexuell tjänst [government bill] (Swed.).

3. Prop. 1997/98:55 Kvinnofrid [government bill] 104 (Swed.).
4. *Nev. Rev. Stat.* § 244.345 (2019). Under this law, unlicensed prostitution is still regarded as a misdemeanor.
5. *See, e.g.*, Canada (Att'y Gen.) v. Bedford, 2013 SCC 72, [2013] 3 S.C.R. 1101 ¶¶ 63–67 (Can.); *but see* Max Waltman, "Assessing Evidence, Arguments, and Inequality in *Bedford v. Canada*," 37 *Harvard J. Law & Gender* 459, esp. at 479–511 (2014) (finding that the *Bedford* decision relied on inaccurate evidence).
6. Chapter 1 includes a description of more recent research on international prostitution finding that johns tend to know critical facts about prostitution.
7. *See* Mary Sullivan, *What Happens When Prostitution Becomes Work? An Update on Legalisation of Prostitution in Australia* (North Amherst, MA: Coalition Against Trafficking in Women, 2005), 7, 20–21 [https://perma.cc/0vmQYRcckgR].
8. Ibid., 20.
9. Ibid.; *cf.* Priscilla Pyett and Deborah Warr, "Women at Risk in Sex Work: Strategies for Survival," *J. Sociology* 35, no. 2 (1999): 186, 190 (noting that prostituted women in some licensed brothels report that unsafe sex is either encouraged or tacitly condoned).
10. Sullivan, *What Happens*, 21.
11. Pyett and Warr, "Women at Risk," 190.
12. Report of the Prostitution Law Review Committee on the *Operation of the Prostitution Reform Act 2003* (Wellington, NZ: Ministry of Justice, 2008), 14, 57 [https://perma.cc/0dW66NBn2Ti].
13. Fed. Ministry for Family Affairs, Senior Citizens, Women and Youth, Ger. Fed. Gov't, *Report by the Federal Government on the Impact of the Act Regulating the Legal Situation of Prostitutes* (Rostock: Publikationsversand der Bundesregierung, 2007), 79 [https://perma.cc/0sd3L6pB1CE].
14. Ibid.
15. *See* Cordula Meyer et al., "Unprotected: How Legalizing Prostitution Has Failed," *Der Spiegel Online Int'l*, May 30, 2013 (Christopher Sultan trans.) (Westlaw).
16. Melissa Farley, *Prostitution and Trafficking in Nevada: Making the Connections*, ed. Melissa Farley (San Francisco: Prostitution Research & Education, 2007), 44.
17. Lenore Kuo, *Prostitution Policy: Revolutionizing Practice through a Gendered Perspective* (New York: New York Univ. Press, 2002), PDF e-book, 84.
18. Ibid.
19. Jayme Ryan, "Legalized Prostitution: For Whose Benefit?," *Sojourner: The Women's Forum*, July, 1989, p. 23; Farley, *Prostitution and Trafficking in Nevada*, 44 (interviewing a woman prostituted in a legal brothel saying that in her brothel, if the women "insist" on condoms with johns, the johns would complain via bedroom-phones to the management, who would then instruct the women to "'comply'")
20. *See* Anastasia Volkonsky, "Legalizing the 'Profession' Would Sanction the Abuse," *Insight on the News*, Feb. 27, 1995, p. 22 (referring to interviews with about a dozen women prostituted in legal brothels in Nevada, which revealed that "contrary to the common claim that the brothel will protect women from the dangerous, crazy clients on the streets, rapes and assaults by customers are covered up by the management.");

Ryan, "Legalized Prostitution," 22 (discussing her many years of experience from being prostituted in legal brothels in Nevada while stating that "[o]nce you were alone in your room with a customer you had no protection from him. There were many different occasions where a woman was brutally beaten or raped by a john, but as long as he paid the house, it was kept quiet"); *cf.* Farley, *Prostitution and Trafficking in Nevada*, 29–30 (interviewing a former brothel manager who admitted that "only a small percentage of brothel violence is reported"); Kuo, *Prostitution Policy*, 84 (noting, when pressed, that all her interviewees in Nevada's legal brothels "acknowledged" that third parties and johns who patronized these establishments were "occasionally" abusive); *see also* Dan Kulin, "Prostitute Sues Musician Neil, Brothel over Alleged Assault," *Las Vegas Sun*, Apr. 16, 2004 [https://perma.cc/03Lm5Jxxs83].

21. Farley, *Prostitution and Trafficking in Nevada*, 23, 31.
22. See Chapter 2.
23. *Cf.* Dawn Whittaker and Graham Hart, "Research Note: Managing Risks; the Social Organisation of Indoor Sex Work," *Sociol. Health & Illness* 18, no. 3 (1996): 409 (reporting on legal apartment prostitution in London, where prostituted "women are subject to violence and . . . the presence of the [assistant] maid has only a limited protective value"); Melissa Farley, "'Bad for the Body, Bad for the Heart': Prostitution Harms Women Even If Legalized or Decriminalized," *Violence against Women* 10, no. 10 (2004): 1103 (noting that "[p]anic buttons in brothels make as little sense as panic buttons in the homes of battered women," as they will not "be answered quickly enough to prevent violence"); Suzanne Daley, "New Rights for Dutch Prostitutes, but No Gain," *New York Times*, Aug. 12, 2001 (quoting a Dutch owner of a legal brothel who was critical of a government regulation requiring a pillow in the room: "'You don't want a pillow in your room. It's a murder weapon.'").
24. *See, e.g.*, Mary Sullivan, *Making Sex Work: A Failed Experiment with Legalized Prostitution* (North Melbourne: Spinifex Press, 2007), 186, 201–203, 205–206, 225–226, 242–243; Janice G. Raymond, "Ten Reasons for Not Legalizing Prostitution and a Legal Response to the Demand for Prostitution," in *Prostitution, Trafficking, and Traumatic Stress*, ed. Melissa Farley (Binghamton, NY: Haworth Maltreatment & Trauma Press, 2003), 320–321.
25. Farley, *Prostitution and Trafficking in Nevada*, 103–105, 118–122. In 1989, a prostitution survivor with experience in legal brothels in Nevada remarked that the age of young recruits was deliberately not verified. Ryan, "Legalized Prostitution," 22. *See also* Brian Bahouth, "Nevada's Illegal Sex Industry is the Nation's Largest and a Hub for Sex Trafficking," *Sierra Nevada Ally*, Jan. 21, 2021 [https://perma.cc/HJF7-BDJEs] (interviewing former trafficking victim who said her pimp send her to legal brothels "'as a form of punishment': 'If you weren't making enough money, if you were getting arrested too often, he would send you to the brothels. Because then he had other pimps watching over you, and he knew that you'd be forced to get off your butt and make money because the brothels aren't going to let you sit around and say no all the time.'"); Kathleen Barry, *Female Sexual Slavery*, with a new introduction (New York: New York Univ. Press, 1984 [1979]), 132 (noting that when the police in Oakland, San Francisco, or Los Angeles were going after or had arrested the pimps, the women were

sent to the Mustang Ranch brothel in Nevada until it was possible to prostitute them on the streets again).

26. *Report of the Prostitution Law Review Committee (NZ)*, at 154.
27. Daley, "New Rights for Dutch Prostitutes." *Cf.* Michelle L. Price, "Pandemic Makes Prostitution Taboo in Nevada's Legal Brothels," *Associated Press*, Feb. 20, 2021 (Westlaw, 2/20/21 AP Bus. News) (interviewing a prostituted woman at the Moonlite Bunny Ranch brothel in Carson city: "Finding a job outside the stigmatized sex industry also can be tough, [she] said, because background checks can reveal the work authorization cards prostitutes must have in brothels.").
28. Ger. Fed. Gov't, *Report by the Federal Government*, 79.
29. Canada (Att'y Gen.) v. Bedford, 2013 SCC 72, [2013] 3 S.C.R. 1101 (Can.), *rev'g in part*, 2012 ONCA 186, 346 D.L.R. (4th) 385 (Ont. C.A.), *rev'g in part* 2010 ONSC 4264, 102 O.R. (3d) 321 (Ont. Super. Ct.).
30. *Bedford*, 2010 ONSC 4264 ¶ 325.
31. Waltman, "Assessing Evidence," part II.
32. *See Bedford*, 2010 ONSC 4264 ¶ 325(e) (citing Barbara G. Brents and Kathryn Hausbeck, "Violence and Legalized Brothel Prostitution in Nevada: Examining Safety, Risk, and Prostitution Policy," *J. Interpersonal Violence* 20, no. 3 (2005): 270–295).
33. Brents and Hausbeck, "Violence and Legalized Brothel Prostitution in Nevada," 294 n.1.
34. *See, e.g.*, Farley, *Prostitution and Trafficking in Nevada*, 23 (reporting being denied entry by 6 out of 14 Nevada brothels); Kuo, *Prostitution Policy*, 79–80 (noting that, when attempting to access brothels in Nevada for research purposes, the author was "consistently informed that women were permitted entrance only under the auspices of George Flint, president of the Nevada Brothel Association."); Barry, *Female Sexual Slavery*, 131 (describing how Joe Conforte, then owner of the legal brothel Mustang Ranch in Nevada, told Barry on the phone to "'come on up,'" but when she arrived with a friend, they were refused to talk with any prostituted women there, denied "a tour of the premises as had been promised," and finally "mysteriously turned away"); *cf.* Tooru Nemoto et al., "HIV Risk among Asian Women Working at Massage Parlors in San Francisco," *AIDS Education and Prevention* 15, no. 3 (2003): 247 (reporting the denial of entry to 13 out of 25 parlors where men could buy sex in San Francisco).
35. Brents and Hausbeck, "Violence and Legalized Brothel Prostitution in Nevada," 271.
36. *See supra* notes 16–25 and accompanying text.
37. *Bedford,* 2010 ONSC 4264¶ 325(d) (citing Whittaker and Hart, "Research Note," 399–414).
38. *Bedford*, 2010 ONSC 4264 ¶ 325(d).
39. Whittaker and Hart, "Research Note," 399, 406.
40. Ibid., 404–405.
41. Ibid.
42. Ibid., 405.
43. Ibid.; *see also* 402 (describing Dawn Whittaker's "dual role" as a health practitioner who both interviewed research subjects and performed drop-in visits at the apartments).

44. Ibid., 408 (first quotation), 409 (second quotation).
45. *See* Bedford v. Canada (Att'y Gen.), 2010 ONSC 4264, 102 O.R. (3d) 321 ¶ 325(a)–(b) (citing Stephanie Church et al., "Violence by Clients towards Female Prostitutes in Different Work Settings: Questionnaire Survey," *Brit. Med. J.* 322 (2001): 524–525; Libby Plumridge and Gillian Abel, "A 'Segmented' Sex Industry in New Zealand: Sexual and Personal Safety of Female Sex Workers," *Austl. & N.Z. J. Pub. Health* 25, no. 1 (2001): 78–83). For critical analysis, see Waltman, "Assessing Evidence," part II.D.
46. Plumridge and Abel, " 'Segmented' Sex Industry," 82 tbl. 6.
47. Church et al., "Violence by Clients," 524, 525 tbl. 1.
48. Plumridge and Abel, " 'Segmented' Sex Industry," 80–81; Church et al., "Violence by Clients," 524–525.
49. *Cf.* Whittaker and Hart, "Research Note," 406 (noting that their study of indoor prostitution in London flats found that older women were more "experienced and skilled at managing interactions with clients," while younger women seemed to work longer hours, saw more johns, and knew "considerably less" about condom safety).
50. Plumridge and Abel, " 'Segmented' Sex Industry," 80–81; Church et al., "Violence by Clients," 525. For more detailed analysis, see Waltman, "Assessing Evidence," part II.D.
51. *Bedford*, 2010 ONSC 4264 ¶¶ 325 & (a) & (b).
52. Jody Raphael and Deborah L. Shapiro, "Violence in Indoor and Outdoor Prostitution Venues," *Violence against Women* 10, no. 2 (2004): 135.
53. Melissa Farley et al., "Prostitution and Trafficking in Nine Countries: An Update on Violence and Posttraumatic Stress Disorder," *J. Trauma Practice* 2, nos. 3–4 (2004): 48, 56.
54. Ibid., 49.
55. Ibid.
56. Wulf Rössler et al., "The Mental Health of Female Sex Workers," *Acta Psychiatrica Scandinavica* 122 (2010): 150.
57. Statens Offentliga Utredningar [SOU] 1995:15 Könshandeln: Betänkande av 1993 års Prostitutionsutredning [government report series] 10, 98–99 (Swed.).
58. Socialstyrelsen [Nat'l Bd. Health & Welfare], Swed. Gov't, *Prostitution in Sweden 2003* (Stockholm: Socialstyrelsen, 2004), 23 [https://perma.cc/0vWJVmQN1Ea].
59. Charlotta Holmström, "Prostitution och människohandel för sexuella ändamål i Sverige: Omfattning, förekomst och kunskapsproduktion," in *Prostitution i Norden: Forskningsrapport*, ed. Charlotta Holmström and May-Len Skilbrei (Copenhagen: Nordic Council of Ministers, 2008), 314 [https://perma.cc/U4WP-PTJA]. For an abbreviated English version, see Charlotta Holmström and May-Len Skilbrei, *Prostitution in the Nordic Countries: Conference Report, Stockholm, October 16–17, 2008* (Copenhagen: Nordic Council of Ministers, 2008), 15 [https://perma.cc/H499-T54S]; *cf.* Socialstyrelsen, *Prostitution in Sweden 2007* (Stockholm: Socialstyrelsen, 2008), 52 [https://perma.cc/DS2K-36HS] (estimating online prostitution).
60. Länsstyrelsen Stockholm [a], *Prostitutionen i Sverige 2014: En omfattningskartläggning*, by Endrit Mujaj and Amanda Netscher (Stockholm: County Administrative Board, 2015), 9–10, 18–19 [https://perma.cc/2ML4-6LMR].

61. Jeanett Bjønness, "Holdninger til prostitution i Danmark," in Holmström and Skilbrei, *Prostitution i Norden*, 108; Charlotta Holmström and May-Len Skilbrei, "Nordiska prostitutionsmarknader i förändring: En inledning," in Holmström and Skilbrei, *Prostitution i Norden*, 14; *cf.* Holmström and Skilbrei, *Prostitution in Nordic Countries*, 15–16. The Danish numbers appear not to have included prostituted males. *See* Bjønness, "Holdninger," 108.
62. Holmström and Skilbrei, "Nordiska prostitutionsmarknader," 14; *cf.* Holmström and Skilbrei, *Prostitution in Nordic Countries*, 16.
63. For population estimates for 2007, see Statistics Denmark, "StatBank Denmark," accessed Jan. 10, 2019 [https://www.statbank.dk/]; *see also* Statistics Sweden, "Population and Population Changes 1749–2013," accessed Oct. 13, 2019 [https://perma.cc/G8L5-DTQF].
64. *See* Sexarbejdernes Interesseorganisation, "Svensk rapport bygger på forkerte tal for Danmark: Nu må Reden sige sandheden," news release, July 4, 2010, accessed May 31, 2014 [https://perma.cc/Q6W2-FYW4].
65. Holmström and Skilbrei, "Nordiska prostitutionsmarknader," 14.
66. *See* Bjønness, "Holdninger," 107 (noting that indoor and escort prostitution was estimated based on advertisements and number of parlors).
67. Statistics Norway, "Population per 1 April 2007 and Population Changes During 1st Quarter of 2007," accessed June 21, 2014 [https://perma.cc/D9YT-L43T].
68. Norway enacted a law criminalizing the purchase of sex in 2009. *See* Lov om straff (straffeloven) [Criminal Code] Ch. 26, § 316 (Nor.) [https://lovdata.no/lov/2005-05-20-28/], §316.
69. Marianne Tveit and May-Len Skilbrei, "Kunnskap om prostitusjon og menneskehandel i Norge," in Holmström and Skilbrei, *Prostitution i Norden*, 220–221.
70. Ibid. Among those not observed on the street in Norway, the extent of prostitution was determined on the basis of encounters with social workers through outreach and service activities, as well as advertisements in newspapers and on the internet (221); *cf.* Holmström and Skilbrei, "Nordiska prostitutionsmarknader," 13.
71. SOU 2010:49 Förbud mot köp av sexuell tjänst: En utvärdering 1999–2008 [government report series] 118 (Swed.).
72. Ibid.
73. Holmström, "Prostitution och människohandel," 314.
74. Ibid.
75. SOU 2010:49 at 152.
76. *Cf.* ibid., 120.
77. Socialstyrelsen, *Prostitution in Sweden 2007*, 34; *cf.* 61.
78. *Cf.* Rikspolisstyrelsen, [Nat'l Criminal Investigation Dep't], Swed. Gov't, *Trafficking in Women: Situation Report no. 5* (Stockholm: Rikspolisstyrelsen, 2003), 35 [https://perma.cc/QXD7-DVMN] ("The fact that the prostitution and the trafficking are not visible does not mean that the police do not receive information of what is going on. Daily the police receive such information through Internet surveillance, physical surveillance, tip-offs from the public at large and other sources.")
79. Noting that its estimate that 200–250 people were involved in street prostitution in 2014 was based on the number encountered by organizations doing outreach and

support work on the streets, the County Administrative Boards' report allows that some may have been missed. Länsstyrelsen [a], *Prostitutionen i Sverige 2014*, at 19. However, given that the same method of relying on specialized social workers to estimate street prostitution has been used over time, any underestimations that may result will be relatively similar from 1993 to 2014. *See* SOU 1995:15 Könshandeln [government report series] 81–82, 85–87, 98–99, 153–158 (Swed.); Socialstyrelsen, *Prostitution in Sweden 2003*, 23–25 (reporting numbers for 1998–2003); Socialstyrelsen, *Prostitution in Sweden 2007*, 11, 33–34.

80. Rikspolisstyrelsen, *Trafficking in Women*, 34.
81. Ibid.; *see also* Rikspolisstyrelsen, *Lägesrapport 10: Människohandel för sexuella och andra ändamål 2007–2008* (Stockholm: Rikspolisstyrelsen, 2009), 10 [https://perma.cc/9ZAV-N8CQ] (referencing information derived from social workers and police about other Nordic countries).
82. Rikspolisstyrelsen, *Trafficking in Women*, 34.
83. Ibid.
84. Ibid.
85. Ibid.
86. SOU 2010:49 Förbud mot köp av sexuell tjänst: En utvärdering 1999–2008 [government report series] 122 (Swed.); *cf.* Rikspolisstyrelsen, *Lägesrapport 10*, 10; *see also* Polismyndigheten, *Människohandel för sexuella och andra ändamål: Lägesrapport 19* (Stockholm: Nationella operativa avdelningen, 2018), 119–123 [https://perma.cc/3CUX-YR7G] (reporting convictions during 2017 for procuring and trafficking for sex where 4 cases involved 1 prostituted woman as a plaintiff/injured party, 2 cases involved 2 women each, 1 case involved 4 women, and 1 involved 5 women).
87. See Chapter 2.
88. *See, e.g.*, SOU 1995:15 at 140–143.
89. *See* "Prostitution in Germany: Homicides and Attempted Homicides since 2002," *Ressources Féministes*, accessed Jan. 21, 2021 [https://perma.cc/XMS9-J8PD] (providing a list of links to information about known prostitution homicides and attempts in Germany, as reported in the media or as verified through other sources).
90. Penny White, "Remembering the Murdered Women Erased by the Pro-Sex Work Agenda." *feministcurrent.com*, Nov. 13, 2015 [https://perma.cc/CS8A-JMPU].
91. Suzann Larsdotter, Jonas Jonsson, and Mina Gäredal, *Osynliga synliga aktörer: Hbt-personer med erfarenhet av att sälja och/eller köpa sexuella tjänster* (Stockholm: RFSL Förbundet, 2011) [https://perma.cc/X5PY-TSB3]; Niklas Eriksson and Hans Knutagård, *Sexmänsäljer.se/x: Nöje blir funktion* (Malmö: RFSL Rådgivningen Skåne, 2005) [https://perma.cc/YEV7-M4KF].
92. Larsdotter, Jonsson, and Gäredal, *Osynliga synliga aktörer*, 98–99, 245, 260; Eriksson and Knutagård, *Sexmänsäljer.se/x*, 54, 76.
93. Socialstyrelsen, *Prostitution in Sweden 2003*, 34.
94. SOU 2010:49 Förbud mot köp av sexuell tjänst: En utvärdering 1999–2008 [government report series] 130 (Swed.).
95. See Anna Helmerson/TT (News Agency Sweden), "Anmälda sexköp har fördubblats," *Dagens Nyheter*, July 27, 2010 [https://perma.cc/5X5N-FN72].

96. Brottsförebyggande rådet [Nat'l Council for Crime Prevention], Nat'l Criminal Statistics Database, Sweden (2018) [https://www.bra.se].
97. Ibid.
98. Undecided responses were not reported in the 1996 survey. Sven-Axel Månsson, "Commercial Sexuality," in *Sex in Sweden: On the Swedish Sexual Life 1996*, ed. Bo Lewin, Kerstin Fugl-Meyer, and Folkhälsoinstitutet (Stockholm: Nat'l Institute of Public Health, 2000), 249.
99. Charlotta Holmström and May-Len Skilbrei, "The Swedish Sex Purchase Act: Where Does It Stand?," *Oslo Law Rev.* 4, no. 2 (2017): 92.
100. *See* Gisela Priebe and Carl Göran Svedin, *Sälja och köpa sex i Sverige 2011: Förekomst, hälsa och attityder. Delrapport 1 ur Prostitution i Sverige* (Linköping: Linköping Univ. Electronic Press, 2012), 27 tbl. 1.6 [https://perma.cc/YBQ3-EHDV]; Jari Kuosmanen, "Attitudes and Perceptions about Legislation Prohibiting the Purchase of Sexual Services in Sweden," *Eur. J. Soc. Work* 14, no. 2 (2011): 253–254; Niklas Jakobsson and Andreas Kotsadam, "Gender Equity and Prostitution: An Investigation of Attitudes in Norway and Sweden," *Feminist Economics* 17, no. 1 (2011): 38, 39 tbl. 1 (not reporting separate gender data).
101. Holmström and Skilbrei, "Swedish Sex Purchase Act," 92.
102. Priebe and Svedin, *Sälja & köpa sex i Sverige 2011*, 25 tbl. 1.4.
103. Ibid.
104. *See, e.g.*, Proposition [Prop.] 1997/98:55 Kvinnofrid [government bill] 22 (Swed.).
105. Brottsförebyggande rådet, *Prostitution och människohandel för sexuella ändamål: En första uppföljning av regeringens handlingsplan; Rapport 2010:5*, by Anna Eklund and Stina Holmberg (Stockholm: BRÅ, 2010), 71 [https://perma.cc/LH86-ES5U].
106. Ibid., 70 (quoting Månsson, "Commercial Sexuality," 249 (original emphasis)).
107. Månsson, "Commercial Sexuality," 250 tbl. 13:16.
108. Kuosmanen, "Attitudes and Perceptions," 254 tbl. 2; Svedin & Priebe, *Sälja & köpa sex i Sverige 2011*, 27 tbl. 1.6.
109. Holmström and Skilbrei, "Swedish Sex Purchase Act," 92 (citing David Garland, *The Culture of Control* (Chicago: Univ. of Chicago Press, 2001)).
110. Sofia Jonsson and Niklas Jakobsson, "Is Buying Sex Morally Wrong? Comparing Attitudes toward Prostitution Using Individual-Level Data across Eight Western European Countries," *Women's Stud. Int'l F.* 61 (2017): 62 & tbl. 2.
111. Ibid., 62–63 & tbl. 3.
112. For this paragraph, see ibid., 62 tbl. 2.
113. In all surveys cited in this paragraph, the percentage of women reporting sex purchasing is minuscule compared to men.
114. Månsson, "Commercial Sexuality," 238. The total number of paper surveys is reported in Kuosmanen, "Attitudes and Perceptions," 250.
115. This survey is cited in Kuosmanen, "Attitudes and Perceptions," 250, 257.
116. Ibid., 251, 256 & tbl. 5. Kuosmanen reports that seven additional respondents among the 448 men indirectly admitted having bought sex in their responses to a follow-up question, thus raising the corresponding percentage.
117. Priebe and Svedin, *Sälja & köpa sex i Sverige 2011*, 33 tbl. 10.

118. Länsstyrelsen [a], *Prostitutionen* 2014, 25 tbl. 3; Länsstyrelsen Stockholm [b], *Prostitutionen i Sverige 2014: Bilaga 2; Fördjupad metodbeskrivning, tillvägagångssätt och resultat*, by Endrit Mujaj and Amanda Netscher (Stockholm: County Administrative Board, 2015), 9 tbl. 1 [https://perma.cc/V5UX-YV8V] (describing sample size and demographics).
119. Folkhälsomyndigheten, *Sexuell och reproduktiv hälsa och rättigheter i Sverige 2017: Resultat från befolkningsundersökningen SRHR2017* (Stockholm, 2019), 191–192 [https://www.folkhalsomyndigheten.se/].
120. Ibid., 194.
121. *E.g.*, Max Waltman, "Sweden's Prohibition of Purchase of Sex: The Law's Reasons, Impact, and Potential," *Women's Stud. Int'l F.* 34, no. 5 (2011): 460; Holmström and Skilbrei, "Sex Purchase Act," 88–89.
122. Holmström and Skilbrei, "Sex Purchase Act," 88 (citing Waltman, "Sweden's Prohibition," 460). A number of literature reviews conclude that anonymous surveys of criminal behavior are not generically unreliable and do not typically underreport. *See, e.g.*, Terence P. Thornberry and Marvin D. Krohn, "The Self-Report Method for Measuring Delinquency and Crime," in *Measurement and Analysis of Crime and Justice*, Criminal Justice 2000, ed. David Duffee (Washington, DC: Nat'l Inst. of Justice, 2000), 4:72; Josine Junger-Tas and Ineke Hean Marshall, "The Self-Report Methodology in Crime Research," 25 *Crime & Just.* 291, 354 (1999); David Huizinga and Delbert S. Elliot, "Reassessing the Reliability and Validity of Self-Report Delinquency Measures," *J. Quantitative Crim.* 2, no. 4 (1986): 294, 323–324. By first quoting my later conclusion that the sex purchasing law had a deterrent effect—a conclusion based on a number of other sources of information about the prostitution market, including those previously presented here—Holmström and Skilbrei's later discussion of reliability gives readers the erroneous impression that my conclusions were based solely on the 1996 and 2008 surveys. Holmström and Skilbrei, "Sex Purchase Act," 88 (quoting and citing Waltman, "Sweden's Prohibition," 460).
123. Länsstyrelsen [a], *Prostitutionen 2014*, 26. The report also argues that although the incidence of sex purchasing during the prior 12 months has been reported in some Swedish surveys undertaken since 1996, it is still a blunt measure that needs to be complemented by findings from other studies in order to reliably describe the characteristics of johns (26).
124. Andreas Kotsadam and Niklas Jakobsson, "Shame on You, John! Laws, Stigmatization, and the Demand for Sex," *Eur. J. Law & Econ.* 37 (2014): 393–404.
125. Ibid., 395.
126. Ibid., 395–396 (reporting Fisher's exact test); *cf.* 396 tbl. 1. In total, there were 51 men (and 3 women) reporting sex purchasing during the preceding 6 months, 26 of the men in Denmark, 20 in Norway, and 5 in Sweden.
127. May-Len Skilbrei and Charlotta Holmström, *Prostitution Policy in the Nordic Region: Ambiguous Sympathies* (London: Routledge, 2016), 69.
128. Ibid., 68.
129. SOU 1995:15 Könshandeln [government report series] 94 (Swed.).
130. Ibid., 77.
131. Ibid.

132. Skilbrei and Holmström, *Prostitution Policy*, 68.
133. Ibid., 68–69. Skilbrei and Holmström are citing SOU 2010:49 Förbud mot köp av sexuell tjänst: En utvärdering 1999–2008 [government report series] 285–287 (Swed.).
134. *See supra* notes 81–86 and accompanying text.
135. Skilbrei and Holmström, *Prostitution Policy*, 68.
136. Ibid. (citing SOU 2010:49 p. 287).
137. *See* SOU 2010:49 p. 287.
138. Skilbrei and Holmström, *Prostitution Policy*, 68.
139. Ibid.
140. Ibid.
141. Socialstyrelsen, *Prostitution in Sweden 2007*, 15.
142. Skilbrei and Holmström, *Prostitution Policy*, 67.
143. Ibid., 67–68 n.16.
144. Rikspolisstyrelsen, *Trafficking in Women*, at 34; *see also supra* notes 80–86 and accompanying text.
145. Jay Levy, *Criminalising the Purchase of Sex: Lessons from Sweden* (Abingdon: Routledge, 2015), 110–111.
146. *See supra* notes 95–97 and accompanying text.
147. See Levy, *Criminalising the Purchase of Sex*, chap. 3.
148. Ibid., 126.
149. *See supra* notes 57–126 and accompanying text.
150. Giovanni Sartori, "Concept Misformation in Comparative Politics," *Am. Pol. Sci. Rev.* 65, no. 4 (1970): 1033.
151. SOU 1995:15 Könshandeln: Betänkande av 1993 års Prostitutionsutredning [government report series] 153–158 (Swed.) (describing the origins of these public organizations).
152. Carl Göran Svedin et al., *Prostitution i Sverige: Huvudrapport; Kartläggning och utvärdering av prostitutionsgruppernas insatser samt erfarenheter och attityder i befolkningen [Primary Report]* (Linköping: Linköping Univ. Electronic Press, 2012), 2 [https://perma.cc/P8DV-EGSF] (citing the national action plan).
153. Ibid., 2, 4.
154. Cecilia Kjellgren, Gisela Priebe, and Carl Göran Svedin, *Utvärdering av samtalsbehandling med försäljare av sexuella tjänster (FAST): Delrapport 5 ur Prostitution i Sverige* (Linköping: Linköping Univ. Electronic Press, 2012), 27 & tbl. 10.5 [https://perma.cc/4RC8-36M5].
155. Ibid. (citing Gunilla Lundqvist et al., "Group Therapy for Women Sexually Abused as Children: Mental Health before and after Therapy," *J. Interpersonal Violence* 21, no. 12 (2006): 1665–1677).
156. *See* Farley et al., "Prostitution and Trafficking in Nine Countries," 56.
157. Kjellgren, Priebe, and Svedin, *Utvärdering av samtalsbehandling*, 24–25.
158. Ibid., 26 tbl. 5.9. The estimates of childhood sexual abuse are likely significant underestimations. See Linda Meyer Williams, "Recall of Childhood Trauma: A Prospective Study of Women's Memories of Child Sexual Abuse," *J. Consulting & Clin. Psychol.* 62, no. 6 (1994):1167– (interviewing 129 women subjected to

documented childhood sexual abuse, finding 38% did not recall the abuse reported 17 years earlier, especially women who were younger during the abuse or those who were abused by someone they knew).

159. See Chapter 1 for citations to and discussion of these studies.
160. Kjellgren, Priebe, and Svedin, *Utvärdering av samtalsbehandling*, 5.
161. Svedin et al., *Prostitution i Sverige: Huvudrapport*, 9.
162. Ibid.
163. Ibid.
164. Ibid.
165. Kjellgren, Priebe, and Svedin, *Utvärdering av samtalsbehandling*, 36.
166. Ibid., 35–36 & tbl. 5.19.
167. Svedin et al., *Prostitution i Sverige: Huvudrapport*, 10.
168. Ibid.
169. Cecilia Kjellgren, Jonna Abelsson, and Carl Göran Svedin, *Intervjuer med personer som tidigare fått samtalsbehandling vid FAST: Delrapport 7 ur Prostitution i Sverige* (Linköping; Linköping Univ. Electronic Press, 2012), 6 [https://perma.cc/ZB8U-XJ7U].
170. SOU 2010:49 Förbud mot köp av sexuell tjänst: En utvärdering 1999–2008 [government report series] 232 (Swed.).
171. Svedin et al., *Prostitution i Sverige: Huvudrapport*, 13; *see also* Linda Jonsson and Carl Göran Svedin, *"Online är jag någon annan. . . ." Unga kvinnor med erfarenhet av att sälja sexuella tjänster online: Delrapport 8 ur Prostitution i Sverige* (Linköping; Linköping Univ. Electronic Press, 2012), 12–13 [https://perma.cc/KAQ2-3ZKH] (describing the recruitment procedure of the 11 informants).
172. Svedin et al., *Prostitution i Sverige: Huvudrapport*, 14.
173. Ibid.
174. Ibid., 17.
175. Ibid.
176. *See* Grégoire Théry and Claudine Legardinier, *The French Law of April 13, 2016, Aimed at Strengthening the Fight against the Prostitutional System and Providing Support for Prostituted Persons: Principles, Goals, Measures and Adoption*, trans. Caroline Degorce (Paris: Coalition for the Abolition of Prostitution, 2017), 39 [https://perma.cc/3BUJ-NXXA] (summarizing various laws pertaining to prostitution contained in different French legal codes).
177. Ibid., 38–39. *Cf.* James McAuley, "France Declared War on Prostitution: Not on Prostitutes," *WashingtonPost.com*, Apr. 9, 2016 (Westlaw) (explaining that the French law allocates funding for prostituted persons "to receive training in other industries" and eases "immigration restrictions on foreign sex workers").
178. Théry and Legardinier, *French Law*, 10.
179. *See, e.g.*, Kajsa Ekis Ekman et al., "Stockholm har raserat en världsledande behandling," Debatt, *Svenska Dagbladet*, Jan. 13, 2018 [https://www.svd.se/stockholm-har-raserat-en-varldsledande-behandling]; Malin Jenstav et al., "Förstör inte stödet att lämna prostitution," Opinion, *SVT Nyheter*, Dec. 8, 2016 [https://perma.cc/ZP7B-87YP].
180. See Chapter 5.

181. Petra Östergren, "Sexworkers Critique of Swedish Prostitution Policy," petraostergren.com, accessed Feb. 17, 2014 [https://perma.cc/MZS9-ZDCD?type=image].
182. *See, e.g.*, Emily van der Meulen, "Sex Work and Canadian Policy: Recommendations for Labor Legitimacy and Social Change," *Sexuality Res. & Soc. Pol'y* 8, no. 4 (2011): 352; Jane Scoular, "What's Law Got to Do with It? How and Why Law Matters in the Regulation of Sex Work," *J.L. & Soc'y* 37, no. 1 (2010): 20; Janet Halley et al., "From the International to the Local in Feminist Legal Responses to Rape, Prostitution/Sex Work, and Sex Trafficking: Four Studies in Contemporary Governance Feminism," 29 *Harv. J. L. & Gender* 335, 396 n. 206 (2006); John Lowman, "Dealing with Prostitution in Canada," letter, *CMAJ* 172, no. 1 (2005): 14; Jane Scoular, "Criminalizing 'Punters': Evaluating the Swedish Position on Prostitution," *J. Soc. Welfare & Fam. Law* 26, no. 2 (2004): 200, 202.
183. Eric Harper, Dianne Massawe, and Vivienne Mentor-Lalu, Sex Worker Education and Advocacy Taskforce, "Submission to the South African Law Reform Commission: Project 107 Sexual Offences Adult Prostitution; Discussion Paper 0001/2009" (2009), 41–42 [https://perma.cc/5DFN-TKKS]; *cf.* Nicole Frick, SWEAT, "Well Intentioned but Misguided? Criminalizing Sex Workers' Clients," *S. African Crime Q.*, no. 22 (2007): 35 (citing only Östergren's unpublished piece and a Norwegian government report to support claims about Sweden's prostitution law that are contradicted by the Swedish research and other evidence cited here).
184. Östergren, "Sexworkers Critique."
185. Ibid.
186. Levy, *Criminalising the Purchase of Sex*, 184.
187. Ibid., 185–190. Regarding prices, a woman in internet escort prostitution told Levy she could charge two or three times more in Sweden than in "the rest of Europe"; another said she migrated to Sweden because the prices were the highest in the EU; and a third believed her hourly rate of 3,000 SEK (ca. $400) was relatively "good pay" in 2009 (188).
188. Socialstyrelsen, *Kännedom om prostitution 1998–1999* (Stockholm: Socialstyrelsen, 2000) ("inaktuellt") [https://perma.cc/8RXR-ZEP5].
189. Socialstyrelsen, *Prostitution in Sweden 2003*, 34 (emphasis added).
190. Socialstyrelsen, *Prostitution in Sweden 2007*, 28.
191. Ibid.
192. Ibid.
193. Östergren, "Sexworkers Critique."
194. Ibid., 48.
195. Östergren, "Sexworkers Critique."
196. Jay Levy and Pye Jakobsson, "Sweden's Abolitionist Discourse and Law: Effects on the Dynamics of Swedish Sex Work and on the Lives of Sweden's Sex Workers," *Criminology & Crim. Just.* 14, no. 5 (2014): 603.
197. In his book, Levy quotes a "founder of Rose Alliance," likely Jakobsson, who maintains that "sometimes" the police "call the landlord" and threaten him or her with procuring charges for having a prostituted person as a tenant; however, no further information is provided to indicate whether any such evictions ensued, whether the calls concerned residential or business premises, or when and where these alleged incidents took place. Levy, *Criminalising the Purchase of Sex*, 196.

198. *See* Niina Vuolajärvi, "Governing in the Name of Caring—The Nordic Model of Prostitution and Its Punitive Consequences for Migrants Who Sell Sex," *Sexuality Res. & Soc. Pol'y* 16, no. 2 (2019): 160–162.
199. Levy and Jakobsson, "Sweden's Abolitionist Discourse," 600–601; *cf.* Levy, *Criminalising the Purchase of Sex*, 139, 142–153, 190–192.
200. If "the vast majority" of the prostituted people who participated in the Swedish survey cited by Levy and Jakobsson already acknowledged that oral sex was less safe without a condom, yet about half admitted providing unprotected oral sex, it is because the johns demand it—not, as disingenuously implied, because of "a dearth in harm reduction initiatives designed to translate knowledge to practice." Levy and Jakobsson, "Sweden's Abolitionist Discourse," 600. *Cf.* Levy, *Criminalising the Purchase of Sex*, 191 ("'[O]n the street it's very common, clients, they [are] asking to do it without a condom[.] And they are very much allergic to condoms *laughs*.'" (quoting female "sex worker")); 191 ("'[C]ustomers who do not wish to use a condom seem to be frequent'" (citing Larsdotter, Jonsson, and Gäredal, *Osynliga synliga aktörer*, 130) (Levy's translation)).
201. Petra Östergren, *Porr, horor och feminister* (Stockholm: Natur och kultur, 2006), 168.
202. Ibid., 169.
203. Petra Östergren, "Synden Ideologiserad: Modern svensk prostitutionspolicy som identitets- och trygghetsskapare," master's thesis, Stockholm University, spring 2003, 17 [https://perma.cc/3CAS-ZSDU].
204. Östergren, "Sexworkers Critique."
205. Ibid.
206. Scoular, "What's Law?," 20; *see also* Scoular, "Criminalizing 'Punters,'" 200 (citing Östergren's interviews to support a critique of the Swedish law).
207. Scoular, "What's Law?," 18.
208. Ibid.
209. Ibid., 19 n.27.
210. Ibid.
211. *See supra* notes 188–194 and accompanying text.
212. Scoular, "What's Law?," 38.
213. Ronald Weitzer, "Legalizing Prostitution: Morality Politics in Western Australia," *Brit. J. Criminology* 49, no. 1 (2009): 100 (referring, with no pinpoint citation, to Scoular, "Criminalizing 'Punters'")
214. Halley et al., "From the International to the Local," 396 & nn.206 & 207.
215. Ibid., 397 (emphasis added).
216. *See* ibid., 397 n.209.
217. Socialstyrelsen, *Prostitution in Sweden 2003*, 34.
218. van der Meulen, "Sex Work and Canadian Policy," 352.
219. Lowman, "Dealing with Prostitution," 14.
220. SOU 2010:49 Förbud mot köp av sexuell tjänst: En utvärdering 1999–2008 [government report series] 127–30 (Swed.).
221. Proposed Ordinance § 1, to amend *Minneapolis, Minn. Code of Ordinances* § 139.40(m), 1st Reading, Nov. 23, 1983, *reprinted in* Catharine A. MacKinnon and Andrea Dworkin, eds., *In Harm's Way: The Pornography Civil Rights Hearings* (Cambridge, MA: Harvard Univ. Press, 1997), 426–432.
222. *Rättegångsbalken* [RB] *[Code of Judicial Procedure]* 22:1, 22:3, 22:5–7 (Swed.), *semi-official translation archived at* https://perma.cc/9GND-TEDP (as amended Jan. 1, 1999).

223. RB 20:8(4).
224. Ibid.
225. *See* RB chap. 22; *see also* 1 § *Lag om målsägandebiträde [Act on Victim's Legal Counsel]* (Svensk författningssamling [SFS] 1988:609) (Swed.). If they are not available for all crimes, victims' legal counsel are at least available for provisions falling under chapter 6 of the Criminal Code dealing with Sexual Crimes.
226. NJA [Weekly Law Reports] [Supreme Court] 2001 pp. 527, 533 (Swed.).
227. Ibid., 529 (reporting the district court's opinion), 532 (reporting the court of appeal's opinion).
228. For legislative history prior to the 2001 Supreme Court decision, see Prop. 1997/98:55 Kvinnofrid [government bill] (Swed.); SOU 1995:15 Könshandeln [government report series] (Swed.).
229. See Chapters 1–2 for an analysis of contemporary research on the associations among prostitution, pornography, and gender-based violence.
230. NJA 2001 p. 529 (reporting the district court's opinion).
231. Rättsfall från hovrätterna [RH] [cases from the Courts of Appeal] 2008:59 (Swed.) (Zeteo online).
232. Ibid. (no pagination).
233. NJA 2001 p. 529 (reporting the district court's opinion).
234. Ibid., 532–533 (reporting the court of appeal and the Supreme Court's opinions).
235. SOU 2010:49 Förbud mot köp av sexuell tjänst: En utvärdering 1999–2008 [government report series] 217 (Swed.).
236. Ann Johansson and Per Nygren, "Polisen tar tuffare tag mot sexköparna runt Rosenlund," *Göteborgs-Posten*, Apr. 11, 2010, p. 9.
237. "Fakta: Expert vill se hårdare straff," *Expressen*, May 23, 2010, p. 9.
238. SOU 2016:42 Ett starkt straffrättsligt skydd mot köp av sexuell tjänst och utnyttjande av barn genom köp av sexuell handling, m.m. [government report series] 22 (Swed.).
239. *BrB [Criminal Code]* 25:7 (Swed.).
240. *See, e.g.*, Théry and Legardinier, *French Law*, 39.
241. Socialstyrelsen, "Socialstyrelsens yttrande över betänkandet Förbud mot köp av sexuell tjänst—en utvärdering 1999–2008 (SOU 2010:49)" [remissvar] [submission as considerate party in legislative process] (Stockholm: Socialstyrelsen, 2010), 7 [https://perma.cc/CP6M-DQHQ].
242. Socialtjänstlagen [SoL] [Social Welfare Service Act] 5:11 (Swed.).
243. For example, the Social Welfare Service Act does not specify to what standard of support crime victims are entitled.
244. SOU 2010:49 Förbud mot köp av sexuell tjänst: En utvärdering 1999–2008 [government report series] 249 (Swed.).
245. *See* Annelie Siring, "Sexhandel, sexköpslagstiftning och myndighetsförståelse: Ett svenskt exempel," in Holmström and Skilbrei, *Prostitution i Norden*, 341–343 (quoting and citing interviews with police officers); *cf.* Sanna Jansson, "Få sexköpare åker fast i regionen," *Göteborgs Fria tidning*, Jan. 21, 2010 [https://perma.cc/4TDY-HKTJ] (interviewing a police officer and a prosecutor).
246. Kammarrätten i Stockholm [KR] [Admin. Ct. App.] 2007-03-19, Mål nr 2231-06 (Swed.).

247. Ibid., 1.
248. Brendan Riley, "Prostitution Tax Dies," *Casper Star-Tribune (Wyoming)*, Apr. 9, 2009 [https://perma.cc/TCK5-JXPX].
249. Prop. 1997/98:55 Kvinnofrid [government bill] 22 (Swed.).
250. Ibid., 104.
251. *RB [Code of Judicial Procedure]* 20:8(4) (Swed.).
252. *BrB [Criminal Code]* 6:11 (Swed.).
253. This phrase was originally introduced by Catharine MacKinnon. *See* Catharine A. MacKinnon and Max Waltman, "A Response to *Prohibition against Purchase of Sexual Service: An Evaluation 1999–2008 (SOU 2010:49)*" (12 signatories) (submission officially received by Swedish government on Feb. 2, 2011), 2 n.3 [https://ssrn.com/abstract=2450513].
254. Prop. 2010/11:77 Skärpt straff för köp av sexuell tjänst [government bill] 15 (Swed.); *cf.* SOU 2010:49 Förbud mot köp av sexuell tjänst: En utvärdering 1999–2008 [government report series] 247–251 (Swed.).
255. *See, e.g.*, Fanny Holm and Brottsoffermyndigheten [The Swedish Crime Victim Compensation and Support Authority], *Utbetalning av brottsskadeersättning till offer för människohandel* (Umeå: Brottsoffermyndigheten, 2010), 14–20 [https://perma.cc/HKC2-ZS7M]; Christina Halling, Charlotta Holmström, and Sven-Axel Månsson, *Svårigheter och möjligheter i organiseringen av stöd till offer för människohandel för sexuella ändamål i Sverige* (Malmö: Malmö högskola [Malmö University], 2012), 13–16, 29–30, 40–41 [https://perma.cc/6GV8-DZCB]; *cf.* Christian Diesen, "Målsägande?" [Injured Party?], in *Festskrift till Lars Heuman*, ed. J. Kleineman, P. Westberg, and S. Carlsson (Stockholm: Jure Förlag, 2008), 140.
256. *E.g.*, Halling, Holmström, and Månsson, *Svårigheter och möjligheter*, 10–16; *cf.* Svedin et al., *Prostitution i Sverige: Huvudrapport*, 21 (noting that some women declined further contacts with the specialized social services if they had to testify in procuring or trafficking cases, which in practice entailed them being expelled).
257. Polismyndigheten, *Människohandel*, 68–70.
258. Ibid., 70.
259. *See, e.g.*, Vuolajärvi, "Governing in the Name of Caring."
260. *See* Kommittédirektiv [dir.] 2008:44 Utvärdering av förbudet mot köp av sexuell tjänst [government committee directives] 4, 6 (Swed.).
261. *See* SOU 2010:49 Förbud mot köp av sexuell tjänst: En utvärdering 1999–2008 [government report series] (Swed.).
262. Ibid., 96, 116–117, 121.
263. Ibid., 247–251.
264. Brown v. Board of Education, 347 U.S. 483, 489 (1954).
265. *See* ibid., 494 ("Whatever may have been the extent of psychological knowledge at the time of *Plessy v. Ferguson*, this finding [that segregation is harmful and inherently unequal] is amply supported by modern authority [n.11]."); *cf.* 494 n.11 (citing a number of scientific sources).
266. Beauharnais v. Illinois, 343 U.S. 250, 258 (1952).
267. SOU 2010:49 p. 250.
268. *Rättegångsbalken [RB] [Code of Judicial Procedure]* 45:4(2) (Swed.).

269. *RB* 22:2.
270. For these statutes, see *RB* 22:2, 23:3.
271. SOU 2010:49 at 245 (emphasis added); *cf.* Prop. 2010/11:77 Skärpt straff för köp av sexuell tjänst [government bill] 11 (Swed.).
272. Ibid., 81 (first quote), 245 (second quote).
273. *Cf.* Prop. 1997/98:55 Kvinnofrid [government bill] 102–103 (Swed.) (emphasizing the deprivation, neglect, and childhood sexual abuse commonly seen in the histories of prostituted women and the negative self-image that tends to result).
274. *Cf.* MacKinnon and Waltman, "A Response to *Prohibition against Purchase*," 3.
275. Rikspolisstyrelsen, *Trafficking in Women*, at 35.
276. *See* Chapter 1 (discussing harms inflicted on persons used as performers during production).
277. *See* Jonsson and Jakobsson, "Is Buying Sex Morally Wrong?," 62 tbl. 2.
278. For an explanation of this aspect of the data, see Brottsförebyggande rådet, *Kvalitetsdeklaration: Personer lagförda för brott* (Stockholm: Brottsförebyggande rådet, 2018), 4–5 [https://perma.cc/JMA4-KMNU]. In Sweden, a waiver of prosecution (*åtalsunderlåtelse*), *Rättegångsbalken [RB] [Code of Judicial Procedure]* 20:7 (Swed.), still produces a criminal record for the defendant. *See* § 3(4) *Lag om belastningsregister* (Svensk författningssamling [SFS] 1998:620). Note as well that the sex purchase law was not inserted into the criminal code until April 1, 2005, but was instead cited as a special law: *Lag om förbud mot köp av sexuella tjänster* (SFS 1998:408), *superseded by statute*, *BrB [Criminal Code]* 6:11 (Swed.).

Conclusions

1. For a general distinction between law and ideology, see Christine Sypnowich, "Law and Ideology," in *Stanford Encyclopedia of Philosophy*, ed. Edward N. Zalta (2014) [https://plato.stanford.edu/archives/spr2017/entries/law-ideology/].
2. The concepts of "negative" and "positive" rights are explained more fully in Chapter 3.
3. *See* Kimberle Crenshaw, "Demarginalizing the Intersection of Race and Sex: A Black Feminist Critique of Antidiscrimination Doctrine, Feminist Theory and Antiracist Politics," 1989 *U. Chi. Legal F.* 139 (1989).
4. R. v. Butler, [1992] 1 S.C.R. 452 at 509, 89 D.L.R. (4th) 449 (Can.).
5. *See* Miller v. California, 413 U.S. 15 (1973).
6. American Booksellers Ass'n v. Hudnut, 771 F.2d 323 (7th Cir. 1985).
7. Kirsten Johnson, *Undressing the Canadian State: The Politics of Pornography from Hicklin to Butler* (Halifax: Fernwood, 1995), 53.
8. Ibid., 97 n.43 (quoting Jane Rhodes, "Silencing Ourselves? Pornography, Censorship and Feminism in Canada," *Resources for Feminist Research / Documentation sur la Recherché Féministe* 17, no. 3 (1988): 134).
9. Beauharnais v. Illinois, 343 U.S. 250 (1952).
10. New York v. Ferber, 458 U.S. 747 (1982).
11. Nytt Juridiskt Arkiv [NJA] [Weekly Law Reports] 2015-03-04 pp. 45, 45–61 (Swed.). This case, along with others mentioned here, is also discussed in Chapter 8.

12. Karl Marx and Friedrich Engels, *The German Ideology*, ed. C. J. Arthur, 2nd ed. (London: Electric Book Co., 2001), 68.
13. *Cf.* Beauharnais v. Illinois, 343 U.S. 250, 258 (1952) (recognizing that neither "history" nor "practice" answers the question of whether or not group libel is unprotected expression).
14. Brown v. Bd. of Educ., 347 U.S. 483 (1954).
15. American Booksellers Ass'n v. Hudnut, 771 F.2d 323, 329 n.2 (7th Cir. 1985).
16. *Brown*, 347 U.S. at 489 ("[A]lthough these sources [of law] cast some light . . . they are inconclusive.").
17. Ibid., 494–495.
18. Plessy v. Ferguson, 163 U.S. 537, 544 (1896) (holding that although the "object of the [Fourteenth A]mendment was undoubtedly to enforce the absolute equality of the two races before the law . . . it could not have been intended to abolish distinctions based upon color, or to enforce social, as distinguished from political, equality, or a commingling of the two races upon terms unsatisfactory to either"), *invalidated in Brown*, 347 U.S. 483.
19. R. v. Labaye, 2005 SCC 80, [2005] 3 S.C.R. 728 (Can.).
20. R. v. Katigbak, 2011 SCC 48, [2011] 3 S.C.R. 326 ¶¶ 67, 78 (Can.).
21. See Chapter 7 for further discussion of *Labaye* and *Katigbak*.
22. *See* James Lindgren, "Defining Pornography," 141 *U. Penn. L. Rev.* 1153, 1187–1191 (1993) (surveying law students' application of the anti-pornography civil rights ordinance); *see also* 1210 (discussing the "Lindgren Variation"); James V. P. Check and Ted H. Guloien, "Reported Proclivity for Coercive Sex Following Repeated Exposure to Sexually Violent Pornography, Nonviolent Dehumanizing Pornography, and Erotica," in *Pornography: Research Advances and Policy Considerations*, ed. Dolf Zillmann and Jennings Bryant (Hillsdale, NJ: Lawrence Erlbaum, 1989), 168–169 (surveying lay persons' rating of pornography as violent, degrading/dehumanizing, or "erotic").
23. See Chapter 1.
24. Melissa Farley et al., "Prostitution and Trafficking in Nine Countries: An Update on Violence and Posttraumatic Stress Disorder," *J. Trauma Practice* 2, nos. 3–4 (2004): 44, 47–48, 56.
25. Theoretically speaking, there may be unreported cases; however, that is unlikely considering their precedential value.
26. *See, e.g.*, Catharine A. MacKinnon, *Toward a Feminist Theory of the State* (Cambridge, MA: Harvard Univ. Press, 1989), 225, 233–234.
27. *Cf.* Kimberle Crenshaw, "Demarginalizing the Intersection of Race and Sex: A Black Feminist Critique of Antidiscrimination Doctrine, Feminist Theory and Antiracist Politics," 1989 *U. Chi. Legal F.* 139, 149 (1989).
28. See Chapters 1 and 2.
29. See Chapter 5.
30. *See* Spencer S. Hsu, "Judge Drops Porn Case for Insufficient Evidence; Rebukes Government, Urges Better Guidance on Obscenity Statutes," *Washington Post*, July 17, 2010, A2 (Lexis).
31. For information about the content of the indicted movies as reported by the press, see Chapter 5's discussion of the *Stagliano* case.

32. R. v. Price, 2004 BCPC 103, [2004] CarswellBC 895 ¶¶ 99–100 (Can. B.C. Prov. Ct. Crim. Div.).
33. This case is analyzed in depth in Chapter 7.
34. R. v. Smith, [2002] CarswellOnt 6125 ¶¶ 4–9 (Can. Ont. Super. Ct. J.), *aff'd with sentence modification* 2012 ONCA 892, [2012] CarswellOnt 15792 (C.A.).
35. S. Laurel Weldon and Mala Htun, "The Civic Origins of Progressive Policy Change: Combating Violence against Women in Global Perspective, 1975–2005," *Am. Pol. Sci. Rev.* 106, no. 3 (2012): 548–569.
36. Ibid., 560–564.
37. Proposed Ordinance § 1, to amend *Minneapolis, Minn. Code of Ordinances* § 139.10(a)(1), 1st Reading, Nov. 23, 1983 (all-caps neutralized), *reprinted in* Catharine A. MacKinnon and Andrea Dworkin, eds., *In Harm's Way: The Pornography Civil Rights Hearings* (Cambridge, MA: Harvard Univ. Press, 1997), 426–432.
38. *See* ibid., § 139.40(m)(2)(i–xiii)) (listing all impermissible defenses).
39. Lindgren, "Defining Pornography," 1187–1191. Lindgren also found that the ordinances' definition of pornography was easier to apply when qualified to cover materials "whose dissemination in context would tend to subordinate women" (1210). He evidently did not summarize the legislative history of the ordinances for his respondents. *See* 1174–1180 (describing questionnaire administration), 1223–1275 (appending questionnaires). The legislative history alone, including in the testimonies and written submissions of survivors, researchers, and other authorities attesting to the harms that the dissemination of pornography causes within the context of male dominance, gender-based violence, including prostitution, supports a finding of subordination. *See* MacKinnon and Dworkin, *In Harm's Way*, 39–425 (documenting the ordinances' legislative hearings).
40. *Indianapolis, Ind. Code* ch. 16 § 16-3(q) (1984), *invalidated by* American Booksellers Ass'n v. Hudnut, 771 F.2d 323 (7th Cir. 1985), *reprinted in* MacKinnon and Dworkin, *In Harm's Way*, 438–457 (original brackets).
41. *Regeringsformen [RF] [Constitution]* 8:14 (Swed.).
42. For legislation specifically targeting production, see Chapter 8.
43. For an analysis and critique of the government's arguments, see Chapter 8.
44. See Chapter 5.
45. This postmodern theory is discussed in Chapter 3.
46. Judith Butler, "Sovereign Performatives in the Contemporary Scene of Utterance," *Critical Inquiry* 23, no. 2 (1997): 376. *Cf.* Judith Butler, *Excitable Speech: A Politics of the Performative* (New York: Routledge, 1997), 101.
47. Butler, "Sovereign Performatives," 354–356.
48. Kimberle Crenshaw, "Mapping the Margins: Intersectionality, Identity Politics, and Violence against Women of Color," 43 *Stanford Law Rev.* 1241, 1283–1295 (1991).
49. Ibid., 1283.
50. Ibid.
51. Skywalker Records, Inc. v. Navarro, 739 F. Supp. 578 (S.D. Fla. 1990), *rev'd sub nom.* Luke Records, Inc. v. Navarro, 960 F.2d. 134 (11th Cir. 1992).
52. Butler, "Sovereign Performatives," 354 (italics omitted).
53. Ibid. (citation omitted).

54. Crenshaw, "Mapping the Margins," 1285.
55. Ibid., 1284–1285 & n.147 (citing "*see generally*" 2 Live Crew, *As Nasty as They Wanna Be* (Luke Records, 1989); N.W.A., *Straight Outta Compton* (Priority Records, Inc., 1988); N.W.A., *N. W.A. & The Posse* (Priority Records, Inc., 1989)).
56. Crenshaw, "Mapping the Margins," 1285–1286.
57. Ibid., 1286 & n.150 (quoting Derrick Z. Jackson, "Why Must Only Rappers Take the Rap?," *Boston Globe*, June 17, 1990, A17).
58. Jean Seligmann, "Dicey Problem," *Newsweek*, May 21, 1990, p. 95 (Lexis).
59. Crenshaw, "Mapping the Margins," 1286 & n.150.
60. Butler, "Sovereign Performatives," 354.
61. Crenshaw, "Mapping the Margins," 1293.
62. *See, e.g.*, Catharine A. MacKinnon, "Pornography: Not a Moral Issue," *Women's Stud. Int'l F.* 9, no. 1 (1986): 63–78.
63. See Chapter 4 for further discussion.
64. Miller v. California, 413 U.S. 15, 24–25 (1973).
65. *See* American Booksellers Ass'n v. Hudnut, 771 F.2d 323, 324–325, 327, 331 (7th Cir. 1985).
66. Butler, "Sovereign Performatives," 355.
67. *See* "Gay Rights in the Military: The Pentagon's New Policy Guidelines on Homosexuals in the Military," *New York Times*, July 20, 1993, A16 (Westlaw); Thomas L. Friedman, "Chiefs Back Clinton on Gay-Troop Plan: President Admits Revised Policy Isn't Perfect," *New York Times*, July 20, 1993, A1 (Westlaw); William B. Rubenstein, "'Don't Ask, Don't Tell.' Don't Believe It," *New York Times*, July 20, 1993, A19 (Westlaw).
68. Elisabeth Bumiller, "A Final Phase for Ending 'Don't Ask, Don't Tell,'" *New York Times*, July 23, 2011, A13 (Westlaw); Charley Keyes, "End of 'Don't Ask, Don't Tell' Brings Relief, Celebration," *CNN.com*, Sept. 20, 2011 [https://perma.cc/9TFE-4ZCL].
69. "Gay Rights in the Military," A16.
70. *Cf.* Rubenstein, " 'Don't Ask, Don't Tell.' Don't Believe It," A19 ("The 'don't ask, don't tell' solution also concedes that gay people are not disruptive unless others know we are among them.").
71. United States v. Carolene Products Co., 304 U.S. 144, 152 n.4 (1938).
72. Butler, "Sovereign Performatives," 355.
73. Friedman, "Chiefs Back Clinton," A1.
74. *Cf.* ibid. (noting that Clinton's plan made "it difficult for commanders to initiate investigations without clear evidence of homosexual behavior").
75. *See* Chapter 4.
76. Butler, "Sovereign Performatives," 352.
77. See also Chapter 3, pages 155 and 156 and accompanying notes 121–122, for a discussion of Butler's misplaced equation of pornography with hate speech and her misattribution of this theory to MacKinnon.
78. Butler, "Sovereign Performatives," 353.
79. *See, e.g.*, American Booksellers Ass'n v. Hudnut, 771 F.2d 323, 325, 330 (7th Cir. 1985).
80. Moreover, at a minimum one of the six sub-definitions has to be included in order to state a viable cause of action. *Indianapolis, Ind. Code* ch. 16 § 16-3(q) (1984), *invalidated in Hudnut*, 771 F.2d 323.
81. United States v. O'Brien, 391 U.S. 367, 377 (1968).

82. *Hudnut*, 771 F.2d 323, 328–329 & n.2.
83. See Chapter 4, which criticizes the Seventh Circuit's application of the strict scrutiny standard.
84. Butler, "Sovereign Performatives," 350–377.
85. Ibid., 365.
86. Crenshaw, "Mapping the Margins," 1293.
87. *Hudnut*, 771 F.2d at 330–331.
88. Ibid., 331.
89. Ian Shapiro, *The State of Democratic Theory* (Princeton, NJ: Princeton Univ. Press, 2003), 44.
90. Justin Gillis, "Panel's Warning on Climate Risk: Worst Is to Come," *New York Times*, Mar. 31, 2014, A1 (Westlaw).
91. The quoted phrases are taken from Leigh Raymond et al., "Making Change: Norm-Based Strategies for Institutional Change to Address Intractable Problems," *Political Res. Quart.* 67, no. 1 (2014): 197–211 (analyzing challenges to climate change and violence against women).
92. Justin Gillis, "Climate Maverick to Quit NASA," *New York Times*, Apr. 2, 2013, D1 (Westlaw).
93. *Trial of the Major War Criminals before the International Military Tribunal, vol. 22: 14 Nov. 1945–1 Oct. 1946* (Nuremberg, Germany, 1948), 547 [https://perma.cc/VDQ8-JAQ5].
94. *See* ibid., 549 (finding Streicher guilty of crimes against humanity), 588 (reporting conviction).
95. Coral Davenport, "Pentagon Signals Security Risks of Climate Change," *New York Times*, Oct. 14, 2014, A14 (Westlaw); *see also* CNA Military Advisory Bd., *National Security and the Accelerating Risks of Climate Change* (Alexandria, VA: CNA Corp., 2014) [https://perma.cc/GU8A-DETF].
96. *See, e.g.*, Mike Ives, "Promised Billions for Climate Change, Poor Countries Are Still Waiting," *New York Times*, Sept. 10, 2018, A10 (Lexis).
97. The related decisions on indecency and child pornography, which criticized community standards, appear to move in this direction. R. v. Labaye, 2005 SCC 80, [2005] 3 S.C.R. 728 (Can.); R. v. Katigbak, 2011 SCC 48, [2011] 3 S.C.R. 326 ¶¶ 67, 78 (Can.).
98. *See, e.g.*, R. v. Price, 2004 BCPC 103, [2004] B.C.J. No. 814 (Can. B.C. Prov. Ct., Crim. Div.) (acquitting producer and distributor of violent dehumanizing pornography); R. v. Erotica Video Exchange Ltd. (1994), 163 A.R. 181 at 184, [1994] CarswellAlta 820 (Can. Alta. Prov. Ct.) (acquitting sellers of videos where the defense conceded that "each" of the videos contained "degrading and dehumanizing pornography"); Hsu, "Judge Drops Porn Case" (reporting unsuccessful prosecution of pornographer John Stagliano); Amanda Hess, "Buttman v. The Man," *Washington City Paper*, July 23, 2010 (Westlaw; 2010 WLNR 28492168) ("The government failed to prove that Stagliano actually sent anything to anyone."). These cases are analyzed in depth in Chapter 5 and 7.
99. See also Chapter 1 for a discussion of organizations recognized as legitimate by prostitution survivors.

Index

For the benefit of digital users, indexed terms that span two pages (e.g., 52–53) may, on occasion, appear on only one of those pages.

Tables are indicated by *t* following the page number

abortion, 145, 157, 460n.137
abuse of power, 138–39
  expressive rights and, 137
  negative rights and, 14, 15–16, 19, 141–42, 156–57, 158, 332–33, 459n.128
abusive materials, 39, 41
abusive pornography, 64–66, 148, 272, 344
  economic incentives for production, 5, 34, 41–42, 337, 369
  prevalence, 35–36, 64
  prostitution and, 72–73
  types of, 35–36, 64, 373 (*see also* anal sex)
abusive production conditions, 39–40, 49–51
abusive sex, demand for, 337–38
actionable content, defined, 181
actionable materials, defined, 171–72, 193–94, 213–14, 223–24, 388
activists. *See* anti-pornography activists; sex worker activists and organizations
Adult Industry Medical Healthcare Foundation (AIM), 58
African Americans, 48, 192–93, 218–19. *See also* racism
  Kimberle Crenshaw on oppression of, 152–54, 391–92, 395–96
African Union's Protocol on Women's Human Rights in Africa, 142–43, 248–49
aggression. *See also* cruelty; psychoticism; sexual aggression; violence; *specific topics*
  contending perceptions of, 37–44
  imitation of pornography and, 3–4, 70, 104–5, 113–14, 119, 120–22, 131, 179–80, 252
agreeableness, 94–96
Alexanderson, Nils, 21–22
Alexanderson doctrine, 21–22, 326, 329
  challenges to, 21–22
  child pornography law and, 322–23
  Gunnar Persson on, 21–22, 324–26
  Hans-Gunnar Axberger and, 324–26
  Sexual Crimes Committee and, 322–23, 325–26
Alexanderson model of constitutional interpretation, 324–26
Almodovar, Norma Jean, 60–61
alternative production. *See also* female-directed pornography
  myth of, 56–57
American Booksellers Ass'n v. Hudnut. See *Hudnut, American Booksellers Ass'n v.*
anal sex, 38–39, 41, 49, 83–84, 119–20, 233–34. *See also* "ass-to-mouth"
  aggression, abuse, and, 5, 120, 121, 233–34
  in gay pornography, 39–40, 64
  imitation of pornography and, 83–84, 110–11, 116, 119, 120–21, 131–32, 232–33
  painful, 39, 49, 119–21, 131–32, 232–33
  prevalence, 38–41, 111, 119–20, 233
  as "primary event," 38
  with prostituted persons, 53, 110–11, 116
  reasons for having, 120–21 (*see also* imitation of pornography)

anal sex (*cont.*)
  unprotected, 39–41, 64
  women pressured into, 4, 39, 49, 119–21, 131–32, 232–33
Anderson, Judge, 268, 273–74, 281–82
anti-pornography activists, 259
  in Minneapolis, 167–68, 182, 184–86, 387
antitrust law, 319–21
Aristotelian approach. *See* formal equality
"artist's case" (Sweden), 327–33, 376–77
assault, 315. *See also* sexual assault
  of prostituted persons, 50, 109–10, 339–40
"assault or physical attack due to pornography" ("assault" provision), 179–80, 193, 388–89
"ass-to-mouth," 36–38, 118, 119, 231, 233–34
attitudes, measuring, 72–74
attitudes about criminalization of "sale of sex," 347. *See also under* substantive equality prostitution law
attitudes about pornography, 1–2
  gender differences in, 1, 2
attitudes supporting violence, 96–101
attitudes supporting violence against women (ASV), 73, 95. *See also* legitimate targets of sexual aggression; methods assessing effects from exposure
  aggression and, 73, 93–94, 112
    sexual, 73, 79–80, 87, 93–94, 97–98, 112
  agreeableness and, 94–96
  Hostile Masculinity and, 90–91, 98–99
  objectifying materials and, 78–79
  pornography consumption and, 2–3, 79–81, 89–91, 92–95, 97–99, 100–1, 129–30, 132–33, 298–99
Australia. *See* Victoria
autonomy, bodily, 145
Axberger, Hans-Gunnar, 324–26

bankruptcy law, 319, 321–22
barebacking, 39–41, 64
Baron, Larry, 124–26
battered women, 131–32. *See also* violence against women
  forced to imitate pornography, 103, 104–7, 170, 179–80
  impact of pornography in the lives of, 103–7
BDSM, 41, 292–94. *See also* pain; violent pornography
Beauharnais v. Illinois, 208, 209, 210–12, 217–18, 365–66, 375–76, 378
  Brown v. Board of Education and, 217–18, 365–66, 378
  Seventh Circuit Court of Appeals and, 209–12, 217–18, 378
Bedford, Canada v., 338–40
Beijing Declaration, 142–43, 248–49
Berlin, Isaiah, 140
between-method triangulation, defined, 432n.10
Biden, Joseph R. ("Joe"), 225
bill C-54. *See* parliamentary bill C-54
bill C-114. *See* parliamentary bill C-114
binary stereotypes. *See under* stereotypes: of women
Blacks. *See* African Americans
blame, 291. *See also* victim blaming
body-parts approach to definitions, 245, 251, 254–55
bondage and sadomasochism. *See* BDSM
Boreman, Linda ("Linda Lovelace"), 38, 50, 263–64
Borins, Stephen, 262
bourgeois rights, 156–58
Brandenburg v. Ohio, 192–93
Bridges, Ana J., 36–38, 41–42
Britain. *See* London studies; United Kingdom
British Columbia court cases and legal decisions, 268, 292, 299, 384–85
Brodie v. The Queen, 239, 267
brothels, 60–61
  abuse, assault, and trauma in, 51, 52–53, 337–38, 339–40, 502–3n.20
  finances, 336–37
  law enforcement and, 60–61, 336
  legal, 50–51, 52, 336–37, 338, 348, 502–3n.20
  management, 51, 336–38

in Nevada, 51, 52, 196–97, 336–38
pornography production and, 52, 196–97
unsafe sex in, 50–51, 335–37
Brown, Wendy, 156–61
on abortion, 157
bourgeois rights and, 156–58
dominance, subordination, and, 156–58, 159–61
group rights and, 157–58, 160–61
Judith Butler and, 156, 158, 159–61
Marxism and, 156–57
negative rights and, 156–58, 159
neutrality and, 156–57, 159
postmodernism of, 160, 161, 162
Brown v. Board of Education of Topeka, 219, 365–66, 379
Beauharnais v. Illinois and, 217–18, 365–66, 378
Hudnut and, 218, 219, 378, 379
Plessy v. Ferguson and, 218–19, 379
Seventh Circuit Court of Appeals and, 217–19, 378
Bryant, Jennings, 34–35
Buchanan, Mary Beth, 226–27
bukkake, 43. *See also* ejaculation sites
Bundy, Theodore R. ("Ted"), 224
Butler, Judith, 158, 159–60
and the ambivalence of language, 395–96
Catharine MacKinnon and, 155–56nn.121–22, 156, 159–60, 394–95
civil rights approach to pornography and, 390–91, 394–95, 396–97
"don't ask, don't tell" and, 393–94
gender and, 159–60
harms and, 395–96
hate speech and, 155–56, 158, 390–91, 393–95, 396
hierarchy theory and, 160–61
inequality and, 159–60
Kimberle Crenshaw and, 161, 392, 395–96
on language, 159–60, 395–96
misuse of legal terminology, 393–94
obscenity law and, 391, 392–93
postmodernism and, 155, 161, 162, 390–97
racism and, 155–56, 391–92, 395–96
Seventh Circuit Court of Appeals and, 277–78, 394–96
subordination and, 155, 156
on 2 Live Crew, 391–93, 395–96
unequal access to speech and, 395–96
Wendy Brown and, 156, 158, 159–61
Butler, R. v., 366–67, 374, 379–80, 383, 384–87
consolidation and progression in balancing substantive equality under Section 1, 276–78
Butler's remaining problems, 278–84
representation of perspectives and interests, 269–75
and definitions of pornography, 271, 277–78, 280–81
gay pornography after, 303–5
LEAF and, 271–72, 282–84, 288, 295–96, 304, 305, 385–86
post-*Butler* Law (1993–2019), 284, 375, 379, 385–86
the future of community standards: *R. v. Labaye*, *R. v. Katigbak*, 300–3
gay pornography after *Butler*: *Little Sisters v. Canada*, 303–5
R. v. Erotica Video, nonviolent dehumanizing materials non-obscene, 288–90
R. v. Hawkins, nonviolent dehumanizing materials non-obscene, 284–88
R. v. Jorgensen, "un-knowingly" selling violent obscenity, 290–92
R. v. Price, violent pornography not obscene, 292–97
R. v. Smith, violent pornography obscene, 297–300
R. v. Doug Rankine Co. and, 276, 283–84
Seventh Circuit Court of Appeals and, 277–78, 394–96
tripartite test of obscenity, 285–86, 296, 299
buyers (prostitution). *See* johns

Call Off Your Old Tired Ethics (COYOTE), 60–61
Cambodia, 110–11, 113, 114–16

Cambridge, Massachusetts, 168–69
camera obscura analogy, 207, 377–78
Canada. *See also* British Columbia court cases and legal decisions
  negative rights and, 20, 22–23, 305, 379
  viewpoint neutrality and, 274, 277–78, 289, 305, 375–76
Canadian Charter of Rights and Freedoms (the "Charter")
  Canadian Supreme Court and, 244–45, 260–61, 269, 271–72, 274–75, 276
  expressive freedoms and, 244–45, 261, 263, 268, 277, 281–82, 374
  LEAF and, 269, 271, 273–75, 277
Canadian Civil Liberties Association, 256–57, 269
Canadian Criminal Code, 239, 240, 244–45, 249–50, 266, 290–91
Canadian Supreme Court. *See* Supreme Court of Canada
Carolene Products Co., United States v., 212, 393
case study(ies), 14–15
  comparative qualitative, 16–18
  defined, 16
categorization. *See* name-calling; stereotypes
causal overdetermination
  in aggregated longitudinal studies, 126–29, 132
  defined, 122–23
CEDAW (Committee on the Convention on the Elimination of All Forms of Discrimination Against Women), 142–43, 248–49
Check, James V. P., 278–79, 287–88
  expert testimony, 264–65, 288–89
  research, 35, 84–85, 86–89, 93–96
  three-pronged definition of pornography, 84–85, 264–65, 267, 278–79, 281, 288–89
Chicago, 47, 48, 50, 53, 111, 115, 211–12, 340
child pornography, 50
child pornography law, 21–22, 192, 193, 196–97, 213–14, 323–24, 377. See also *Ferber, New York v.*; *Katigbak, R. v.*; *Labaye, R. v.*
  Alexanderson doctrine and, 322–23
  Arlen Specter and, 224–25
  bill C-54 and, 253–54, 255–57
  Canadian Supreme Court and, 272, 300–1, 302–3, 385
  constitutional regulations and, 322, 323–24
  enforcement, 226, 306
  Fraser Committee and, 246
  obscenity law and, 224–25, 302–3, 306, 379–80, 385
  procuring law and, 322–23
  Sexual Crimes Committee and, 322–24, 325–26
  U.S. Supreme Court and, 192, 195, 204–5, 209, 272
child sexual abuse, 46, 196, 241–42, 246, 317
  child molestation vs. child pornography analogy, 322–24
  defining, 46, 59
  portrayed in pornography, 227
  prevalence, 46–47, 48, 52–53, 107, 108, 353, 421–22n.153
  prostituted persons and, 46–47, 48, 52–53, 108, 196, 242–43, 353, 421–22n.153
choking, 118, 119. *See also* gagging
civil liability, 196–97, 360. *See also* "injured party"; U.S. anti-pornography civil rights ordinances
"civil obscenity law," 234–35
Civil Rights Act of 1964. *See* Title VII of Civil Rights Act
civil rights approach (to pornography), 174, 184, 187–88, 196–97, 219–20, 386–87. *See also under* civil rights approach; Fraser Committee; U.S. anti-pornography civil rights ordinances
  Andrea Dworkin, Catharine MacKinnon, and, 110, 167–68
  anti-pornography civil rights movement, 24–25, 86, 110
  Fraser Committee and, 247–48, 249–50
  Judith Butler and, 390–91, 394–95, 396–97
  postmodern critique of, 390–97

potential of a Swedish (*see* Sex Purchase Law of 1999)
and the potential of civil rights laws, 386–90
Clay, Andrew Dice, 391–92
climate change, 11–12, 189–90, 398–402
Code of Judicial Procedure (Sweden), 360, 363–64, 366
coercion, 247, 273, 332–33. *See also* "consent"; forced sex acts; forcing pornography on someone
acceptance of, 221
continuum of, 331
epidemiology of sexual, 289
filming coercive sexual acts, 330
financial, 50
normalization of, 120–21
obscenity law and, 264, 272
into performing particular acts or practices, 49–50, 119–20, 121–22
pornography made through, 205, 223–24, 243, 271–72 (see also *Deep Throat*)
procuring and unlawful, 326, 331
of prostituted persons, 131, 242, 250–51
viewpoint neutrality and, 205–6
"coercion into pornography performance," 175, 203–4, 212, 388–89
"coercion" provision. *See under* Indianapolis ordinance; Minneapolis ordinance
coercive circumstances, 155, 157, 367–68, 371
underlying prostitution, 155, 335, 361, 363
coercive encounters in pornography, 35–36, 323. *See also* rape pornography
Cold War, ending of the, 450n.349
Cole, Susan, 254–55
Collins, Peter, 298–99
Commission on Pornography. *See under* Smith, William French
"community standard of tolerance" test (community standards test), 276–77, 300–2
vs. dehumanization test, 305–6, 379–80, 401
nature of, 211–12
obscenity law and, 211–12, 239, 249–50, 262, 281–82, 384–85, 388
R. v. Butler and, 278–79, 281–82, 296, 301–2
R. v. Labaye and, 300–2
Towne Cinema Theatres, Ltd. v. R. and, 266–68
community standards
Canadian Supreme Court and, 239, 266–67, 297, 300–1, 302–3, 385
R. v. Labaye, *R. v. Katigbak*, and the future of, 300–3, 385
role in obscenity law, 379–80, 385
community standards as arbiter of obscenity, 279–80
competition law, 319–21
condoms, 49. *See also* unsafe sex
for anal sex, 39–41 (*see also* anal sex: unprotected)
distribution of free, 357–58
in pornography, 39–41, 49, 54
prostitution and, 335–37
consciousness raising. *See under* hierarchy theory
consensus approach, 234
consensus decision-making, 185–86, 187, 189–90. *See also* consensus politics
consensus politics, 183–84, 398–99, 400. *See also* consensus decision-making
consensus statements about the effects of pornography, 220–22
consensus test, viewpoint neutrality as a, 212
"consent." *See also* coercion
BDSM and, 293–94
obscenity law and, 276
Palermo Protocol and, 311–12
pornography and, 205–6, 219–20, 223, 247, 250, 265–66, 276, 286, 293–94, 329–30, 419n.125
prostitution and, 153, 360–61, 382, 383
Constitutional Court of South Africa, 141–42
Convention on the Elimination of All Forms of Discrimination Against Women, 142–43, 248–49

Court Challenges Program of Canada, 269–70, 292, 295–96, 306–7, 366–67
Court of Appeal for Ontario, 284–85, 297–98, 302
COYOTE (Call Off Your Old Tired Ethics), 60–61
Crenshaw, Kimberle Williams
basement metaphor, 152–53, 154–55
Feminist Anti-Censorship Taskforce (FACT) and, 200, 201
on humor, 391–92
intersectionality and, 152–55, 198–99, 201, 372–73, 382
Judith Butler and, 161, 392, 395–96
on oppression of black women, 152–54, 391–92, 395–96
pornography and, 152, 153, 154–55, 198–99, 372–73
prostitution and, 153–55, 198
speech and, 396
2 Live Crew and, 391–392, 395
on vulgar constructionism, 161, 187
Criminal Code of Canada. *See* Canadian Criminal Code
Criminal Code of Sweden. *See* Swedish Criminal Code
criminal laws. *See also under* Fraser Committee; *specific topics*
limits of, 380–86
criminal liability. *See* criminal laws; liability
criminal mind. See *mens rea*
cross-sectional studies, 69–70, 107, 131–32. *See also* longitudinal and cross-sectional surveys
aggregated comparative, 124–26
cruelty, 39, 204–5, 262. *See also* dehumanization; torture
cultural value, pornography as lacking, 330, 331–32, 392–93
Czech Republic, longitudinal study in, 126–28

Dahl, Robert A., 138–39
Day, Shelagh, 269–70
decision making. *See* consensus decision-making
Declaration on the Elimination of Violence Against Women, 7, 141–42
Deep Throat (film), 38, 46, 106–7, 179–80, 263–64
"deep throating," 179–80
degradation test. *See* dehumanization test
degrading pornography. *See* dehumanizing/degrading pornography
dehumanization, 82. *See also* name-calling; sexual objectification
defined, 404n.23
and the definition of pornography, 170
pornography and, 109–10, 119
of racial groups, 192–93
subordination and, 171
dehumanization test, 267–68, 281, 287–89, 302–3. *See also* Check, James: three-pronged definition of pornography
vs. community standards test, 305–6, 379–80, 401
dehumanizing/degrading pornography, 78, 84–85, 267, 270–71, 285–86, 287–88, 373. *See also* "ass-to-mouth"; forced sex acts
alternative production and, 56–57
anal sex and, 39
bill C-54 and, 253–54, 255–57
bill C-114 and, 251–52
defined, 251–52
exposure to, 87
effects of, 85, 86–87, 88, 89, 93–94, 129–30, 246, 265, 305
Fraser Committee and, 240, 244, 246, 251, 258–59, 280–81
gay pornography and, 304–5
John Sophinka and, 276–77, 278–81
legislation and, 317
a new approach to degrading materials, 226–27
obscenity law and, 262, 264–66, 267, 276–77, 279–80, 281, 290–91, 384 (*see also under Butler*; dehumanization test; *Hawkins*
prostitution and, 131, 344
R. v. Towne Cinema Theatres and, 267–68

taboo violation and, 38
William Margold on, 232–33
democracies, western, 9, 18, 22, 23
democracy
implications for, 9–10
challenging subordination: a problem-driven theory, 10–13
hierarchy theory and its critics, 13–16
John Stuart Mill on, 135–37
democratic theory, 10–11, 13, 154–55, 157, 163, 183
substantive inequality in, 135–39
democratic values and ideals, 9–10, 86, 110
Denmark
pornography consumption in, 29–30, 31–32
prostitution in, 341–42, 351
compared with Sweden, 341, 342, 348, 349, 368–69, 380
DeShaney v. Winnebago, 140–41
Dietz, Park Elliot, 222–23
dishonest conduct, artist convicted of, 327–28, 331–33, 376–77
domestic violence. *See* battered women
dominance/domination, 150–51, 270, 397. *See also* BDSM; hierarchy theory; women
climate change politics and, 398–400
democracy and, 149–50
language and, 160–61
male, 7, 115–16, 118
Judith Butler on, 155, 158
pornography and, 83–84, 121, 150–52, 160–61, 164, 252–53, 268, 298–99
usefulness of legal rights for challenging, 155, 158 (*see also* postmodern theory)
Wendy Brown and, 156–58, 159–61
"don't ask, don't tell," 393–94
Doug Rankine Co., R. v., 262–63, 283–84
Downs, Donald Alexander, 182–84, 185–86, 187
Due Process Clause, 140
Dworkin, Andrea, 86, 110, 168, 172, 188
anti-pornography ordinances and, 168, 173, 186, 217, 403–4n.14
definitions of pornography and, 86, 110, 188
Woman Hating, 173
on zoning laws, 167–68

Easterbrook, Frank H., 189
ecological fallacy, 122–23, 295
economic incentives for producing abusive pornography, 5, 34, 41–42, 337, 369
economics. *See also* poverty
of brothels, 336–37
economic sex inequality, 8–9
ejaculation sites, 37, 118, 119, 270–71, 287
Eleven Videos/Eleven Movies, 292–94, 296–97
Elman, R. Amy, 168–69
Engels, Friedrich. *See camera obscura* analogy
England. *See* United Kingdom
entertainment, pornography as pure, 326–27, 330, 331–32, 390
equality. *See also* sex inequality; substantive equality
implications for, 5–6
in context of indices of sex inequality, 8–9 (*see also under* gender-based violence)
LEAF and, 269, 273–74, 385–86
substantive vs. formal, 15
Equality Now, 245
equality rights. *See also* equality
expressive freedoms and, 11, 142, 178–79, 197–98, 208, 261, 303, 320, 374
equal opportunity employment. *See* Title VII of Civil Rights Act
Equal Protection Clause, 200, 212, 217–18
"erotica"
bill C-54 and, 253–55, 257–58
as category of pornography, 84–85, 86–87, 88, 264–66, 276, 278–79, 280–81
definitions, 253–55, 257–58
vs. pornography, 253–55
Erotica Video, R. v., 295
nonviolent dehumanizing materials non-obscene, 288–90
ethnic minorities. *See* racial minorities

European Court of Human Rights, 141–42
European Parliament, 142–43
European Union (EU), 142–43, 316–17, 364–65
exclusivity, principle of, 21
experimental research, 68–70, 72–75. *See also* methods and research design
attitudes supporting violence against women, 79–81
early findings on aggression, 75–77
individual differences and post-treatment bias, 86–96
understanding meta-analysis on general aggression, 77–79
why nonviolent pornography feeds violence against women, 81–86
expressive content and underlying crimes, 324–26
expressive rights, 137–38. *See also* freedom of expression; *specific topics*
Extreme Associates, Inc., United States v., 227–32, 233–34, 235
Eyesenck, Hans, 88

fantasies, rape, 199, 201
"fantasy-based" pornography, 35–36
fellatio, 38, 118. *See also* "ass-to-mouth"; ejaculation sites; oral sex
female-directed pornography, 56–57, 64–65
female-instigated sex, films showing, 82–83, 284–85, 286–88
feminism, xiii
Canadian legislation and, 252–53, 257–59, 374–75
Catharine MacKinnon and, 7, 13, 134, 144, 146
hierarchy and, 13, 134
postmodernism and, xiii, 157–58, 390–91
Feminist Anti-Censorship Taskforce (FACT), 199–201
feminist anti-pornography movement, 143–44, 146, 258–59
feminist critique of pornography, 167
feminist movements, 146, 386
feminist opposition to pornography, 143–44, 186–87, 240
feminist organizations, 252–53, 316
feminist politics and political theory, xiii, 139, 391
"feminist" pornography, 56, 64–65
feminist scholars, questions asked by, 145
Ferber, New York v., 192, 195, 196–97, 375–76
Ferg, Patrick, 262, 263–64
finances. *See* economics; poverty
financial coercion, 50
First Amendment, 178–79, 192, 193, 203–5, 231–32. *See also* freedom of expression; viewpoint neutrality
anti-pornography ordinances and restrictions on, 214–15, 255–56, 378, 395
Fraser Committee and, 247
Miller v. California and, 22–23
obscenity and, 22–23, 208–9
Pornography Victims Protection Act and, 223–24
Seventh Circuit Court of Appeals and, 206, 207–9, 210–11
sex discrimination and, 193–201, 277–78
unprotected expressive categories under, 211–12
viewpoint neutrality and, 204–5, 206–7
Five Factor Model, 94–95. *See also* agreeableness
Forced Entry (video), 227
forced prostitution, 153, 382
forced sex acts. *See also* anal sex: women pressured into; coercion; forcing pornography on someone; rape
forcing/pressuring women to imitate pornography, 3–4, 103, 105–7, 120, 131–32, 133, 170, 179–80, 232–33, 287 (*see also* imitation of pornography: aggressive behavior and)
forcing prostituted persons to imitate pornography, 108–9, 113–17, 264, 371, 383–84
likelihood of forcing a woman to have sex (*see* rape proclivity)
in pornography, 49
portrayed in pornography, 227, 293 (*see also* rape pornography)

forcing pornography on someone
  forced viewing of pornography, 103, 105, 177, 181, 197, 219–20
    sexual harassment law and, 177–79, 181, 193, 197, 213–14, 382–83
    at work, 177–78, 179, 193, 197, 213–14, 235
  "forcing pornography on a person," 177–78, 388–89
  women forced to participate in the making of pornography, 104–6, 114–15 (*see also under* forced sex acts)
formal equality, 15
Fourteenth Amendment, 393
  Due Process Clause, 140
  Equal Protection Clause, 200, 212, 217–18
  object of, 217–18, 517n.18
Fox, Douglas, 60
France, prostitution law in, 355, 362–63
Fraser, Donald, 168–69
Fraser Committee (1983–1985), 240–41, 251, 258–59
  civil rights vs. criminal law, 247–49
  concluding analysis, 249–51
  constitutional substantive equality and, 243–45
  degrading pornography and, 240, 244, 246, 251, 258–59, 280–81
  hearings, 241, 242, 244
  recommended legal definitions, 245–47
  Special Report, 251, 273–74, 280–81
  vulnerability, legal distinctions, intersectionality, 241–43
freedom of expression, 21–22, 137–38, 208, 261, 315–16, 327, 371–72. *See also* "artist's case"; First Amendment; hate speech
  antitrust law and, 319–21
  Canadian Charter and, 244–45, 261, 263, 268, 277, 281–82, 374
  equality rights and, 11, 142, 178–79, 197–98, 208, 261, 303, 320, 374
  limits on, 213–14, 244–45, 261, 263, 277, 303, 319–20, 327, 330, 377, 400
    obscenity law and, 265, 268–69, 276, 277, 281–82, 283–84, 374
Freedom of Expression Act, 328
freedom of speech, 178, 212, 244–45, 320. *See also* hate speech; *specific topics*
  Seventh Circuit Court of Appeals and, 210–12, 214–15, 217–18, 375–76, 396
freedom of the press, 315–16, 317–18, 323–25
Freeman, People v., 204–5
Fundamental Law on Freedom of Expression, 21–22, 318–19, 327–29. *See also* Freedom of Expression Act

gagging, 36–37, 38, 64, 116–18, 270–71. *See also* choking; throat rape
gang rape, 113–16, 179–80
gay male performers, 55–56
gay pornography
  after *Butler*, 303–5
  anal sex in, 39–40, 64
  subordination in, 41, 64
gays in the military, 393–94
gender-based violence, 9–11, 24–25, 141–45, 146, 155. *See also specific topics*
  defined, 5–6
  as linchpin of sex inequality, 5–7
gender differences
  in attitudes about pornography, 1, 2
  in pornography consumption, 1–2, 29–32
gender discrimination, 304
gender inequality. *See* sex inequality
gender neutrality, 156
  pornography and, 245, 287
gender renaturalization. *See* renaturalization: gender
gender roles. *See* stereotypes: of women
gender theory, 159–60
Germany, 117–18, 336, 338, 344, 399
global warming. *See* climate change
gonzo pornography, 36, 39, 57, 117–18, 231
  anal sex in, 233
  Natalie Purcell on, 35–36, 39, 233
  violence and cruelty in, 39, 50
"gonzo" standard, 35–36
government abuse of power. *See* abuse of power

governmental interest, 197, 202, 203, 206, 214, 235
Grant, Barry, 298–99
Gray & Company, 220–23
Green, Sedgwick "Bill," 223
Greenhorn (film), 265–66
Greenspan, Edward L., 256–58
Griffith, James D., 58–59
Group Against Pornography, 269, 283–84
group rights, 157–58, 160–61
  Wendy Brown and, 157–58, 160–61
Grudzen, Corita R., 58

Hald, Gert Martin, 94–96
Halley, Janet, 359
Hansen, James E., 399
harms. *See also* Butler, Judith; injury(ies); Mill, John Stuart; production harms; *specific topics*
  assessing the, 2–5
  Canadian Supreme Court and, 266, 300–1, 302, 304–5
  evaluating the evidence, 57–59 (*see also* methods assessing effects from exposure)
    credibility of representation, 60–63
  indirect, 137–38, 192–93
  LEAF and, 269, 270–74, 305, 385–86
harms-based test, 301–2
hate speech, 191, 192–93, 328–29
  Catharine MacKinnon and, 156
  Judith Butler and, 155–56, 158, 390–91, 393–95, 396
  postmodernism and, 155–56, 158, 163–64, 390–91, 393–96
hate speech laws, 158, 163–64, 393–96
Hawkins, R. v., 290, 297
  nonviolent dehumanizing materials non-obscene, 284–89
Heflin, Howell, 224–25
Hicklin, R. v., 239, 301
hierarchy theorists, 13, 163–64, 292, 333
hierarchy theory, 14, 189–90, 225, 269
  consciousness raising and, 144–47
  criticisms of and other theories contrasted with, 13–16, 163–64, 183, 187, 234, 252, 390–91
  group representation and, 147–52
  intersectionality and, 152–55
  negative rights and, 14, 163–64, 179
  obscenity law and, 373
  overview and nature of, 13
  positive rights and, 14
  predictive capacity, 374–75
  prostitution and, 213–14, 250–51, 335, 340–41
  substantive equality and, 14, 169, 170, 173–74, 179, 180, 184, 187, 213–14, 234, 340–41
Hnatyshyn, Ramon, 253, 256–57
Holder, Eric, 231
Holmström, Charlotta, 342, 347, 348–51
Hostile Masculinity, 90–92, 98–99
hostility, gestures associated with, 38
Hoyt, Charlee, 185–86
Htun, Mala, 146–47
Hudnut, American Booksellers Ass'n v., 187–88, 192, 197, 202–3, 374–76, 378–79
  Brown v. Board of Education of Topeka and, 218, 219, 378, 379
  Seventh Circuit Court of Appeals and, 188–89, 218, 376, 378, 395
  U.S. Supreme Court and, 188–89, 210–11, 219
human rights law, 142–43, 248–49
human rights organizations, 146–47, 245

Iceland, 24–25
identity politics, 161, 163–64
Illinois, 208–11, 214–15. See also *Beauharnais v. Illinois*
imitation of pornography, 3–4, 131–32
  aggressive behavior and, 3–4, 70, 104–5, 113–14, 119, 120–22, 131, 179–80, 252 (*see also under* battered women; forced sex acts)
  anal sex and, 83–84, 110–11, 116, 119, 120–21, 131–32, 232–33
  in popular surveys, 116–22
  targeted groups, perpetrators, and, 103–7
Impersonal Sex, 99
incest. *See* child sexual abuse
India, 111, 112

Indianapolis ordinance
"coercion" provision, 193, 199, 205–6, 214, 223–24 (*see also* "coercion into pornography performance")
definition of pornography, 172–73, 188, 190–91, 193–94, 203–4, 211–12, 213–15, 223–24, 246, 287–88
viewpoint neutrality and, 202–4, 205–6, 207, 214, 223–24
indirect harm, 137–38, 192–93
indirect restrictions, 318–20, 328, 330
inequality, ideology, and the law. *See also* sex inequality; substantive equality
challenging, 371–80
information, item of, 331–32
"injured party" (status), 360, 361, 366–67, 369–70, 381–82, 383
injury(ies), 158, 190–91, 205–6, 393. *See also* Butler, Judith; harms
intermediate scrutiny, 193–94, 214, 277–78, 400. *See also* viewpoint neutrality
"internal necessities" test and "internal necessities" defense, 284–85, 302–3
International Covenant on Civil and Political Rights (ICCPR), 142–43, 248–49
internet, 25, 39–40
impact, 33–34, 227, 229, 294–95
regulation of obscenity on the, 207–8
intersectional approach/intersectional perspective, 196, 201, 216–17, 243, 304, 372–73
intersectional disadvantages, 154–55, 169
intersectional discrimination, 152–53, 163, 177, 198, 213–14, 383. *See also* intersectional theory of discrimination
intersectionality, 15–16, 152–55, 163–64
civil rights approach and, 386–87
concept of, 153–55, 198–99
Kimberle Crenshaw and, 152–55, 198–99, 201, 372–73, 382
legal reform and, 243
of prostitution and pornography, 372–73, 382–83, 386–87
vulnerability, legal distinctions, and, 241–43
intersectional theory of discrimination, 177, 198, 372–73. *See also* intersectional discrimination
Ireland, 60
Irwin Toy Ltd. v. Quebec, 271–72, 273, 282–83
Isaacs, Ira, 231
I.S.S.I. Theater, Inc., 188
"item of information," 331–32

Jakobsson, Pye, 61–62, 357–58
johns (clients of prostituted persons)
awareness of prostituted persons' social circumstances, 48
convictions in Sweden (1999–2019), 344–45
criminalization of, 348 (*see also* Sex Purchase Law of 1999)
definition of and synonyms for, 404n.21
seeking to imitate pornography, 70, 108, 110–14, 115–17, 131, 252
Jorgensen, R. v., and "un-knowingly" selling violent obscenity, 290–92
Judicial Procedure, Code of, 360, 363–64, 366
judicial review, 182, 189–90
standards of, 193–94 (*see also* rational basis review; scrutiny)

Katigbak, R. v., 302–3, 379–80, 385
Keegstra, R. v., 19, 244–45, 271, 282
Kendall, Christopher, 41, 55, 56
King, Gary, 93–94
Kinsley, Jennifer M., 234
Kovner, People v., 204–5, 206
Ku Klux Klan (KKK), 192–93
Kuo, Lenore, 51, 336–37
Kutchinsky, Berl, 288–89
Kvinnofrid. *See* Sex Purchase Law of 1999

Labaye, R. v., 379–80
community standards and, 300–3, 379–80, 385
R. v. Katigbak and, 302–3, 379–80, 385

Lacombe, Dany, 186–87, 200, 252–53, 256–57
language, 160–61
  ambivalence of, 395–96
  Judith Butler on, 159–60, 395–96
  male, 199, 201
Lawrence v. Texas, 228–29, 231–32
LEAF. *See* Women's Legal Education and Action Fund
legal frameworks, comparative predominance of, 18–23, 19*t*
legitimate targets of sexual aggression, women as, 75–76, 82, 83, 84, 86, 109–10, 116–17
lesbian, gay, bisexual, transgender, and queer (LGBTQ). *See* gay pornography; gays in the military
"lesbian scenes," 284–85
Levy, Jay, 351–52, 356, 357–58, 512n.197
"lewd" acts, 245. *See also* obscenity
LGBTQ. *See* gay pornography; gays in the military
liability, 312–14. *See also* civil liability; *Jorgensen, R. v.*; parliamentary bill C-54
liberalism, classical, 13–16, 18–20, 135, 136–37, 139, 371–72. *See also* negative rights
libraries and librarians, 256–58
linguistics. *See* language
Little, Paul F. ("Max Hardcore"), 230–31
Little Sisters Book & Art Emporium v. Canada, 303–5
Locke, John, 136–37
London studies, 50–51, 54, 110–11, 338–39
longitudinal and cross-sectional surveys, population-based naturalistic, 96–101
longitudinal research design, advantages of, 69–70, 101–3
longitudinal studies, 116–17, 130, 131, 132
  causal overdetermination in aggregated, 126–29, 132
  nature of, 69–70
Los Angeles, 44, 60–61, 168–69
  studies in, 49, 50–51, 54, 58, 65
  well-known producers in L.A. imprisoned, 230–32
Lovelace, Linda, 38, 50. See also *Deep Throat*

Machiavelli, Niccolò, 135, 149–50
MacKinnon, Catharine A., xiii, 167–68, 173
  anti-pornography ordinances and, 168, 217, 403–4n.14
  civil rights approach to pornography as sex discrimination, 86, 110, 386–87
  comparative constitutional analysis, 409n.104
  criticism of pornography, 403–4n.14, 458–53nn.121–22
  definitions of pornography and, 86, 110, 188
  equality law and, 110, 197–99
  on femaleness, 454n.54
  feminism and, 7, 13, 134, 144, 146
  free speech and, 498n.63
  on gender-based violence and sexuality, 7
  hierarchy and, 7, 13
  Judith Butler and, 394–95, 155–56nn.121–22
  neutrality and, 144, 145–46
  obscenity law and, 22, 269, 495n.247
  on pornography as speech, 458–59n.122
  on rape, 145, 455n.57, 457n.110, 458–59n.122
  on subordination, 7, 86, 110
  substantive equality and, 14
Madison, James, 14, 138–39
madonna–whore dichotomy, 86
Mahoney, Kathleen E., 239, 254–55, 256, 262
"mainstreaming" of pornography, 96
Malamuth, Neil M., 94–96, 298–99, 304–5
male performers, 54–56
male privilege, 103–4, 157–58. *See also* dominance/domination: male
Manitoba, 262, 263, 264, 269, 270–71, 282–83
Mansbridge, Jane, 147, 150–51, 180–81
Maputo Protocol. *See* African Union's Protocol on Women's Human Rights in Africa

Marciano, Linda. *See* Boreman, Linda
Margold, William ("Bill"), 232–33
marital rape, 330
Marxism, 156–57. *See also camera obscura* analogy
masochism, 262, 388. *See also* BDSM; pain
masturbation
  with pornography, 31–32, 65–66, 94, 112–13, 117–18, 119, 120–21
  portrayed in pornography, 255–56
Matsuda, Mari, 394–95
McConnell, Mitch, 224
McKee, Alan, 41–42, 419n.125
"meaning"
  (restrictions on) expression and attempts to convey, 272, 282–83
  vs. "form" of expression, 271–72
Media Coalition, 220
media companies, application of competition law to, 319–21
Media Concentration Committee of 1999, 319
Media Concentration Inquiry report (1980), 320
mediating variable, defined, 431n.2
mediators (statistics), 68
Meese Commission. *See* Smith, William French: Commission on Pornography
Meji, Mickey, 62–63
mens rea, 145, 290, 291–92
mental health
  mental sequelae of pornography production, 51–54
  of pornography performers, 45, 58 (*see also under* posttraumatic stress disorder)
  of prostituted persons, 52–53, 340, 353, 381
methods and research design
  alternative selection, 24–25
  case selection framework, 18–23
  comparative qualitative case studies, 16–17
  policy output and policy outcome, 23–24
  primary vs. secondary methods, 17
  unreliable methods, 122–23
    aggregated comparative cross-sectional studies, 124–26
    causal overdetermination in aggregated longitudinal studies, 126–29, 132
methods assessing effects from exposure, 67–68. *See also* experimental research
  experiments and naturalistic studies, 68–70
  measuring sexual aggression, experimental predictors, and attitudes, 72–74
  meta-analysis, 70–72
  population-based naturalistic longitudinal and cross-sectional surveys, 96–101
#MeToo movement, 144, 174, 266, 390
Mill, John Stuart
  on democracy, 135–37
  on direct vs. indirect harm, 137–38, 192–93
  on diversity, 135–36
  on liberty and harm, 137–38
  methods of agreement or difference, 17–18
  on power and equality, 135–37
Miller v. California, 22–23, 171–72
Minneapolis, anti-pornography activists in, 167–68, 182, 184–85
Minneapolis City Council, 182, 184–86. *See also* Minneapolis ordinance
  Andrea Dworkin, Catharine MacKinnon, and, 167–68, 186
  civil rights approach and, 387
  criticism of, 185–86
  hearings, 168–69, 173, 179–80, 182, 184–85, 186–87
  on pornography, 169–70, 251–52
  Zoning and Planning Committee, 167–68
Minneapolis ordinance
  "assault" provision (*see* "assault or physical attack due to pornography")
  "coercion" provision, 175–77, 193, 212 (*see also* "coercion into pornography performance")
  definition of pornography, 170–72, 179–80, 185–86, 193–94, 213–14, 251–52, 403–4n.14

moderators (statistics), 68, 431n.2
Montesquieu, Charles de, 136–37
Mosher, Dr., 293–94
most similar systems design (MSSD) and most different systems design (MDSD), 18
Muller v. Oregon, 217

name-calling, 36–37, 64, 118, 270–71
National Board of Health and Welfare (Sweden), 342–43, 344, 352–53, 356–57, 358–59, 362–63
negative rights, 140, 150, 201, 320, 371–72, 376, 378
  abuse of power and, 14, 15–16, 19, 141–42, 156–57, 158, 332–33, 459n.128
  Canada and, 20, 22–23, 305, 379
  child abuse and, 140
  disadvantaged groups and, 15–16, 19
  hierarchy theory and, 163–64, 179
  obscenity law and, 22–23, 212
  vs. positive rights, 140–42, 150, 159, 184, 320, 371–72, 378
  Sexual Crimes Committee and, 320–21, 332–33
  Sweden and, 305, 376, 379
  United States and, 14, 19, 20, 22–23, 140, 305, 379
  Wendy Brown and, 156–58, 159
neo-Nazis, 328–29
neutrality, 144, 145, 159. *See also* gender neutrality; viewpoint neutrality
  Catharine MacKinnon and, 144, 145–46
  Wendy Brown and, 156–57, 159
Nevada, prostitution in, 334–35, 336–38, 363
  brothels, 51, 52, 196–97, 336–38
New Zealand, 336
"nice, virtuous girls," 83
nonviolent pornography. *See also specific topics*
  defined, 102, 172–73, 443n.200
  why it feeds violence against women, 81–86
Norway, prostitution in, 342, 349, 368–69

Oakes, R. v., 274–75
objectification. *See* sexual objectification
objectivity, 144–46
O'Brien, United States v., 203–4, 206, 223–24
obscenity, 245. *See also under* community standards
  defined, 22–23, 211–12, 265, 301, 374
    "undue exploitation of sex," 23, 239, 240, 249–50, 260, 266, 305–6 (*see also* "undue exploitation of sex")
  as a legal concept, 392–93
  tests for assessing, 301–3 (*see also* "community standard of tolerance" test; dehumanization test)
obscenity law, 22–23. *See also under* dehumanizing/degrading pornography; obscenity; "undue exploitation of sex"
  Canada's 1959 law, 260, 267
  Canadian Supreme Court and, 266–67, 269, 277–78, 290, 302–3
  Catharine MacKinnon and, 22, 269, 495n.247
  enforcement, 393
  expressive freedoms and, 265, 268–69, 276, 277, 281–82, 283–84, 374
  LEAF and, 271, 272, 277, 385–86
  in 21st century (2002–2014), 226
    the first trials, 227–30
    new approach to violent, aggressive, and degrading materials, 226–27
    results, potential, and limitations, 232–35
    well-known producers in L.A. imprisoned, 230–32
  substantive equality in, 262–68
  viewpoint neutrality and, 203, 211–12
O'Connor, Sandra Day, 204–5
Ontario Court of Appeal, 284–85, 297–98, 302
oppositional consciousness, 15, 148, 152, 161, 173
oral sex, 38, 39–40, 111, 118. *See also* fellatio
Orito, United States v., 207–8
Östergren, Petra, 355–59

"paid rape"
  pornography as, 153, 199
  prostitution as, 53, 382

pain, 42, 265–66. *See also* cruelty; torture
women portrayed as enjoying/desiring, 109, 262 (*see also* violent pornography: with positive outcomes)
painful anal sex, 39, 49, 119–21, 131–32, 232–33
Palermo Protocol, 311–12
parliamentary bill C-54, 253–56, 258–59
bill C-114 and, 254, 255, 256, 258–59
child pornography law and, 253–54, 255–57
dehumanizing/degrading pornography and, 253–54, 255–57
responses (1987–1988), 256–58
parliamentary bill C-114 (1986–1987), 251–53
bill C-54 and, 254, 255, 256, 258–59
definitions of pornography, 251–52, 253–57
Penthouse magazine, 78–79, 220
Perry Educ. Ass'n v. Perry Local Educators Ass'n, 203–4
Persson, Gunnar, 21–22
on Alexanderson doctrine, 21–22, 324–26
Axberger's model and, 324–26
photographs
nude/pornographic, 49, 77–79, 176, 178
women photographed by their partners, 103, 105–6
threatening, 328–29
physical abuse, 329–30. *See also* "assault or physical attack due to pornography"; violence
in gay pornography, 41
pimps and pimping, 50–51, 60, 336–38, 357
Linda Boreman and, 38, 263–64
pornography production as (*see under* procuring)
Playboy magazine, 78–79, 220
Plessy v. Ferguson, 218–20, 379
policy outputs and policy outcomes, 23–24
distinction between, 23–24
Pornhub, 42–44
pornography. *See also specific topics*
definitions of, 84–85, 102, 172, 223, 224–25, 228–29, 245, 280–81, 287–88, 374–75, 388, 394–95
Attorney General's Commission definition, 219–20
in bill-C114, 251–52, 253–57
definition in Indianapolis ordinance, 172–73, 188, 190–91, 193–94, 203–4, 211–12, 213–15, 223–24, 246, 287–88
definition in Minneapolis ordinance, 170–72, 179–80, 185–86, 193–94, 213–14, 251–52, 403–4n.14
Fraser Committee's definition, 245, 249–50, 251
"graphic sexually explicit subordination of women" (Dworkin-MacKinnon), 86, 110, 129–30, 172–73, 194, 214–15, 245, 246, 271, 300, 374–75, 388, 394–95, 400
James Check's three-pronged definition, 84–85, 264–65, 267, 278–79, 281, 288–89
Pornography Victims Protection Act definition, 223–25
R. v. Butler and, 271, 277–78, 280–81
recommended legal (Fraser Committee), 245–47
speech and, 191
subordination and, 86, 110, 170, 171–73, 190–91, 194, 203–4, 223–25, 249–50
as a "practice" (vs. depictions/representations), 403–4n.14
pornography consumption. *See also* methods assessing effects from exposure; supply and demand; *specific topics*
in Denmark, 29–30, 31–32
effects of
on attitudes supporting violence against women, 2–3, 79–96, 97–101, 129–31, 132–33, 298–99
on general aggression, 75–79
on sexual aggression, 96–103, 100*t*
gender differences in, 1–2, 29–32
as a "symptom," 133
pornography genres, most popular, 35–39
pornography performers. *See* male performers; mental health; *specific topics*

Pornography Victims' Compensation Act in 1989, 224–25
Biden, Joe, amendment requiring repeated dissemination of obscenity to, 225
"Bundy Bill" provision on offender testimony in, 224–25
Heflin, Howell, amendment requiring offender conviction to, 224–25
McConnell, Mitch, introducing, 224
Specter, Arlen, amendment requiring obscenity conviction to, 224–25
Thurmond, Strom, "foolish enough" comment, 225
Pornography Victims Protection Act in 1984, 223–24
Specter, Arlen, introducing the, 223
Green, Sedgwick "Bill," introducing House companion to, 223
position of vulnerability, 205, 311–12
defined, 311–12
prostitution and, 62–63, 311–12
positive outcomes, violent pornography with, 42, 76–77, 270–71
positive rights, 140–43, 159, 261, 320
vs. negative rights, 140–42, 150, 159, 184, 320, 371–72, 378
postmodern critique of the civil rights approach, 390–97
postmodernism
feminism and, xiii, 157–58, 390–91
hate speech and, 155–56, 158, 163–64, 390–91, 393–96
postmodern theory, 155–64, 199–201, 249
Judith Butler and, 155–56, 158, 159–62, 390–97
Wendy Brown and, 156–62
postmodern vulgar constructionism, 161, 163–64, 187
posttraumatic stress disorder (PTSD), 51–52
in pornography performers, 4–5, 52, 55, 57–58, 64–65
in prostituted persons, 4–5, 52–53, 55, 57–58, 64–65, 340, 353, 381
post-treatment bias, 69, 78, 80–81, 86–96, 98–101, 130–31, 436n.65, 443n.197
defined, 69
sexual aggression, attitudes supporting violence, and, 98–101
poverty, 45–46, 48, 49, 50. *See also* economic sex inequality
power. *See also* abuse of power
John Stuart Mill on equality and, 135–37
prey. *See also* legitimate targets of sexual aggression
easy, 55
Price, R. v., 299, 300, 301–2, 305–6
violent pornography not obscene, 292–97
private sphere, 15–16, 139. *See also* public/private dichotomy
privilege, 147–48, 149, 150, 184, 270, 275. *See also* intersectionality
male, 103–4, 157–58
proceduralism, 186
procuring, 312–13
gross, 312, 313
laws, 312
law, ideology, and representation of, 332–33
pornography production as, 312–16, 317–18
1979 Supreme Court (Sweden) prostitution advertisement decision and, 314–15
1993 Prostitution Inquiry's proposal of, 312–15
Alexanderson doctrine (e.g., fraud and misleading ads) applied to but contrasted with, 324–26
analogous case law supports treating, 327–32
artist's case analogy supports treating, 327–29
Axberger's interpretive model and, 324–26
balancing harm with "publication interest" analogy and, 331–32
child molestation analogy with, 322–24
child pornography dissemination contrasted with, 322–24
committee dismissal of, 318–27
committee distortion of legal landscape of, 319–22

committee "mixes apples and oranges" of, 322–24
dishonest conduct case law analogy with, 327–29
filmed artistic rape analogy with, 330
filmed gross violation of a woman's integrity and gross artistic rape analogy with, 329–30
filmed sexual crimes case law analogy with, 329–31
filmed sexual crimes on cell phones analogy with, 331
government circumscribes investigation of, 315–18
"illusory rights" argument attempted on, 326–27
Persson's considerations applied to, 324–26
potential policy impact of, 368–70
tabloid press illegal weapons purchase case analogy with, 331–32
threatening photos of neo-Nazis contrasted with, 328–29
violent resistance case law analogy with, 327–29
producers. *See under* Los Angeles
as pimps and procurers (*see* procuring: pornography production as)
production. *See also* supply and demand
as pimping and procuring (*see* procuring: pornography production as)
challenging, 311–33 (*see also* procuring: pornography production as; Prostitution Inquiry of 1993; Sexual Crimes Committee)
law, ideology, and representation of, 332–33
production harms. *See also* mental health
conflicts of interest in representing, 60–63
evaluating misleading studies of, 57–59
to male performers, 54–56
mental sequelae as indicator of abusive, 51–54
myth of alternative pornography without, 56–57
physical abuse, coercion, and sexual exploitation as systemic indicators of, 49–51
preconditions of abuse and vulnerability, 44–48
survivors' lack of conflict of interest in representing, 62–63
promiscuity, 90–91, 99, 109–10
pornography and, 81–84, 86, 90–91, 129–30
as target of sexual aggression, 73, 81–84, 86, 109–10
as moderator of sexual aggression, 90–91, 99
prostituted persons. *See also* "sex workers"
evidence from, 108–10
imitation in popular surveys, 117–22
PTSD in, 4–5, 52–53, 55, 64–65, 340, 353, 381
use of the term, 404n.20
violence against, 50 (*see also* rape: of prostituted persons)
Prostituted Persons' Revenge in Society, 62–63
prostitution, 311. *See also* brothels; johns; pimps and pimping; substantive equality prostitution law
ages of entry into, 47
"consent" and, 153, 360–61, 382, 383
definitions, 363–64 (*see also* "sexual services")
hierarchy theory and, 213–14, 250–51, 335, 340–41
Kimberle Crenshaw and, 153–55, 198
legal, 50–51, 335–41 (*see also* brothels: legal)
pornography production as, 311, 311–33 *et passim* (*see also* procuring: pornography production as)
in San Francisco, 46–47, 50, 108–10
as a social practice, 311, 334–35
terminology, 363–64, 404n.20 (*see also* "paid rape"; "sexual services")
as a "victimless" crime, 300, 361, 381

prostitution disclosure, perpetrators' reactions to, 108–9
Prostitution Inquiry of 1993 (Sweden), 50, 319, 324–25, 327, 341, 349–50
final report (1995), 108, 114–15, 322
and 1998 government demands for further inquiry, 315–18
overview of pornography production as procuring, 312–15
Prostitution Reform Act 2003 (New Zealand), 336
protest tactics, 184–85. *See also* anti-pornography activists
psychoticism, 88–89, 93–94
defined, 88
nature of, 93–94
public/private dichotomy, 142. *See also* private sphere
public virtues, 184
Purcell, Natalie
on anal sex, 38, 233
on "ass-to-mouth," 36, 37–38
content analysis of pornographic movies, 35–38, 43–44, 232–33
on gonzo pornography, 35–36, 39, 233
on taboo acts, 38, 233
"pure entertainment," pornography as, 326–27, 330, 331–32, 390

racial minorities, 105
overrepresented in prostitution, 48
racial segregation, 147, 217–19, 379. See also *Brown v. Board of Education of Topeka*
racism, 19, 192–93, 231, 391–92
Judith Butler and, 155–56, 391–92, 395–96
Ramsingh, R. v.
Deep Throat and, 263–64
obscenity law and, 262, 263–65
R. v. Doug Rankine and, 262, 263
R. v. Wagner and, 264–66
Rankine, Doug. See *Doug Rankine Co., R. v.*
rape, 84–85, 329–30. *See also* coercion; forced sex acts; "paid rape"; sexual aggression; throat rape
Catharine MacKinnon on, 145, 455n.57, 457n.110, 458–59n.122
in Czech Republic, 126–28
defined, 457n.110
epidemiology, 6–7, 45, 46, 78–79, 90, 101, 103, 127–28, 289, 294–95
gang, 113–16, 179–80
pornography and, 78–79, 127, 133, 262, 316–17 (*see also* rape pornography)
dehumanizing, 85, 86–87, 88, 93–94, 129–30
of prostituted persons, 50, 108–9, 113–14, 153, 344 (*see also* forced prostitution)
statutory, 46 (*see also* child sexual abuse)
rape fantasies, 199, 201
rape laws, 145, 153, 457n.110
rape myths, 3, 69, 73, 145, 196
rape pornography, 42, 82–83, 106, 270–71, 298, 330. *See also under* coercion; forced sex acts
positive-outcome, 42, 270–71
rape proclivity (likelihood of raping/forcing sex), 78–79, 85, 86–87, 88, 89, 93–94
rape shield laws, 176, 247
rape trials, simulated, 79–80, 83–84
rapists
law privileges the state of mind of, 145
pornography provided a "manual for abuse" for, 317
references to pornography, 108–10, 388–89
use of pornography, 105–6
rational basis review, 193–94, 207–8, 214–15, 228, 235, 378
alternative balancing, 207–12
Reden, 341–42
Red Hot Video Ltd., R. v., 268, 281–82
renaturalization
gender, 162
of subordination and oppression, 15–16, 158, 159, 161–62, 249

research design. *See* methods and research design
reverse causation hypothesis, 69–70, 94, 96–97, 101
rights approach. *See also* negative rights; positive rights
  new, 140–44
Roberts v. United States Jaycees, 178–79, 197
Robinson v. Jacksonville Shipyards, 178–79, 193, 197
Roeder, United States v., 204–5, 206
role-playing, 41, 330. *See also specific topics*
romance, 82–83
Romano, Janet, 230–31, 232. See also *Extreme Associates, Inc., United States v.*
Rose Alliance, 61–62

sadism, 104–5. *See also* aggression; BDSM; cruelty
safe sex. *See* condoms; unsafe sex
"sale of sex." *See also* prostitution
  attitudes regarding criminalization of the, 347
San Francisco, 109–10
  prostitution in, 46–47, 50, 108–10
Sartori, Giovanni, 182–83, 352
Schwalm, Loretta A., 124–26
scientific method
  vs. aggregated methodology, 128–29
  objectification as a, 145
Scotland, prostitution in, 48, 53, 110–12, 115–16
Scott, Joseph E., 124–26
Scoular, Jane, 358–59
scrutiny, tiers of, 192, 193–94. *See also* intermediate scrutiny; judicial review: standards of; strict scrutiny
Seawright, Jason, 93
secondary effects
  of prostitution, 381
  of speech, 272, 277–78, 375–76
selection techniques, 18
Seventh Circuit Court of Appeals. *See* U.S. Court of Appeals for the Seventh Circuit
sex crimes
  crime reports and the prevalence of, 122–23
  pornography and crime reports of, 123–29
sex inequality, 8–9
  economic, 8–9
  gender-based violence as linchpin of, 5–7
Sex Purchase Law of 1999 (Sweden), 20–21, 334–35, 341–70
  civil liability under, 360
  civil remedies as support for exit, 362–64
  enforcement, 328, 360–62
  impact, 341–52, 380
  interpretive problems under, 360–62
  2011 legislative clarifications, 364–67
  legislative history, 20–21, 50, 364, 365–66
  and political obstacles to substantive equality, 367–68
  1993 Prostitution Inquiry and, 312–13, 315–16
  support for (and opposition to), 346*t*, 346, 369
sex purchasers. *See* johns
sex purchasing, criminalizing, 348, 369. *See also* Sex Purchase Law of 1999
sex trafficking. *See* trafficking
sexual abuse, 196, 222–23. *See also* child sexual abuse; sexual aggression
  association between pornography and, 104, 105–7, 317
  legislation and, 153, 205, 262, 272, 275
  minimalization, trivialization, and normalization of, 132–33, 174, 203, 205–6, 246, 287, 304, 305–6, 317 (*see also* violence against women: trivialization of)
  in pornography, 35–36, 194, 300, 317
  prevalence, 5–7, 107
sexual aggression, 87, 89–93. *See also* aggression; coercion; dehumanizing/degrading pornography; legitimate targets of sexual aggression; rape

sexual aggression (*cont.*)
attitudes supporting violence against women and, 73, 79–80, 87, 93–94, 97–98, 112
defined, 404n.16
measuring, 72–74
pornography consumption and, 96–101, 100*t*
promiscuity and, 73, 81–84, 86, 90–91, 99, 109–10
psychoticism and, 88, 93–94
sexual assault, 329–30. *See also* assault; rape; throat rape
Deep Throat and, 38, 106–7, 179–80, 264
epidemiology, 102, 106, 109, 294–95
pornography and, 102, 106
Sexual Crimes Committee (1998–2001), 315–18, 320–22, 325–26, 329–30, 332–33
Alexanderson doctrine and, 322–23, 325–26
bankruptcy law and, 319, 321–22
case law rebuts Committee's theory, 327–32 (*see also* "artist's case")
Charter, 316–17
children and, 317–18, 322–24, 325–26
1998–2001 Committee's dismissal, 318–19
the indirect standard, 319–22
competition law and, 319–21
constitutional regulations and, 315–16, 317–27, 328
expressive content and underlying crimes, 324–26
and freedom of press and expression, 315–33
negative rights and, 326–27
the seriousness of expressive infringement, 326–27
sexual harassment, 93–94, 185, 222–23
obscenity law and, 226, 235
as sex discrimination, 197
sexual harassment law
"don't ask, don't tell" and, 394
and forcing pornography on employees, 177–79, 181, 193, 197, 213–14, 382–83
sexualization
of society, 96
of women, 7
of women's subordination, 7
sexually transmitted infections (STIs), 54. *See also* unsafe sex
sexual objectification. *See also* dehumanization; women
obscenity and, 227
pornography and, 86, 170, 172–73, 186–87, 194, 241–42
Sexual Promiscuity. *See* promiscuity
"sexual services," purchase of, 61–62, 334, 354, 363–64. *See also* prostitution
sexual terminology, slang, 36–37, 64, 118, 270–71
sex worker activists and organizations, 60–63, 65, 341–42, 355–56
"sex workers." *See also* prostituted persons
terminology and use of the term, 63, 404n.20
third parties calling themselves, 60–63
Sex Workers Outreach Project (SWOP), 61
Shannon, Melvin Earl, 264–66, 276
Shapiro, Ian, 149–50, 183, 398–99
shelters, women's, 103–4, 106–7
SIO (Danish sex workers organization), 341–42
Skilbrei, May-Len, 347, 348–51, 509n.122
slavery. *See also* trafficking
conditions tantamount to, 65–66, 340–41, 388–89
pornography as, 206, 214, 317
slippery slope, 138
Smith, William French, 216
Commission on Pornography (1985–1986), 216–20
Final Report, 44–45, 216–17, 220, 222–23
P.R. campaign against, 220–23
Snuff (film), 143–44, 240
social contract, 136–37, 139, 140–41
social dominance. *See* dominance/domination
social practices, 160–61, 272, 282–83

Sophinka, John, 276–77
  dehumanizing/degrading pornography and, 276–77, 278–81
  R. v. Butler and, 278–81, 282
  R. v. Wagner and, 278–79, 281
South African Constitutional Court, 141–42
South Korea, 52–53
Specter, Arlen, 223, 224–25, 475n.57
speech. *See* freedom of speech
Stagliano, John, 231–32
statistical analysis, 68. *See also* methods assessing effects from exposure
statistical hypothesis tests, 71–72, 431n.2
statutory rape, 46. *See also* child sexual abuse
Steinem, Gloria, 255
stereotypes, 200
  racist, 391, 392 (*see also* racism)
  of women, 161, 200 (*see also* name-calling)
    binary/dichotomous, 81, 83, 109–10, 176
    pornography and, 81, 82, 83, 84, 109–10, 186–87, 200, 246, 255
Stevens, United States v., 204–5
Stockholm Administrative Court of Appeal, 363
Straus, Murray A., 124–26
Streicher, Julius, 399
strict scrutiny, 195, 196–97, 208–9, 213–14, 228, 277–78
  child pornography and, 193
  equality as a compelling interest, 193–201
subject positions, 186–87
submission, female. *See* dominance/domination: male
subordination, 86. *See also* renaturalization
  Catharine MacKinnon on, 7, 86, 110
  challenging, 10–13
  and the definition of pornography, 86, 110
  dehumanization and, 171 (*see also* dehumanization)
  in gay pornography, 41, 64
  hierarchy theory and, 15–16
  johns and, 112–13, 115–16
  in popular pornography, 35–39
  of the prostituted woman, 109–10
  violence and, 7–8, 10, 13, 41, 64, 86, 109–10, 121–22, 129–30
  Wendy Brown and, 156, 157–58, 161
substantive equality, 14. *See also* hierarchy theory
  Canadian equality law and, 15
  hierarchy theory and, 14, 169, 170, 173–74, 179, 180, 184, 187, 213–14, 234, 340–41
substantive equality prostitution law, 1999–2019, 334–35. *See also* Sex Purchase Law of 1999
  evidence from legal prostitution, 335–41
  impact of Swedish prostitution law
    comparing prostitution prevalence in Scandinavia over time, 341–43
    consistent patterns of attitudes and sex purchasing, 346–49
    corroborating evidence of a prostitution decrease and increased safety, 343–45
    unwarranted skepticism, 349–52
  importance of specialized exit programs, 352–55
  lessons for legal challenges to pornography, 368–70
  symptomatic misinformation about Sweden's law, 355–59
suffocation, 38
Sunstein, Cass R., 172
supply and demand. *See also* gay pornography; pornography consumption
  aggression and subordination in popular pornography, 35–39
  consumer desensitization, 34–35
  contending perceptions of aggression, 37–44
  men and women's consumption, 29–32
  size and economics of the pornography industry, 33–34

Supreme Court of Canada, 51, 244–45, 262, 277–78, 290–91, 385. *See also* *specific cases*
  Canadian Charter and, 244–45, 260–61, 269, 271–72, 274–75, 276
  child pornography and, 272, 300–1, 302–3, 385
  community standards and, 239, 266–67, 297, 300–1, 302–3, 385
  discrimination and, 260–61
  equality and, 15, 277–78
  harms and, 266, 300–1, 302, 304–5
  law vs. non-mandatory measures and, 200
  LEAF and, 269, 271–72, 274–75, 276, 283–84, 304
  obscenity law and, 266–67, 269, 277–78, 290, 302–3
Supreme Court of Sweden, 314–15, 328–29, 331–32, 360–62
Sweden. *See also* substantive equality prostitution law
  1984 bill amending the crime of child molestation, 323–24
  Cabinet, 315–16, 317–18, 334
  Council on Legislation, 321
  Ministry of Justice, 315–16, 317–18, 365–66
  negative rights and, 305, 376, 379
Swedish Code of Judicial Procedure, 360, 363–64, 366
Swedish Code of Statutes. *See* Swedish Criminal Code
Swedish Criminal Code, 312, 313, 315–16, 327–28, 362–63
Swedish National Board of Health and Welfare, 342–43, 344, 352–53, 356–57, 358–59, 362–63
Swedish National Council for Crime Prevention, 347
Swedish Sex Purchase Law. *See* Sex Purchase Law of 1999
Swedish Supreme Court, 314–15, 328–29, 331–32, 360–62
swingers clubs. See *Labaye, R. v.*
"symbolic speech," 203–4

taboo acts, 38, 233, 270–71
target devaluation and target depersonalization, 82
Tarrant, Shira, 59
taxation, 363
Taylor-Munro, Sheryl, 257
Third Circuit Court of Appeals. *See* U.S. Court of Appeals for the Third Circuit
threats, 38, 51, 271–72, 328–29
throat rape, 38, 106–7, 179–80, 264. *See also* gagging
throat sex, 36
Thurmond, Strom, 225
Title VII of Civil Rights Act (equal opportunity employment), 199
Törnell, Inga-Britt, 312–16
Toronto Public Library Board, 257
tort liability. *See* civil liability; "injured party"
torture, 50, 317
trafficking, 48
  Fraser Committee and, 243–44, 248
  scope of the term, 311–12
  in Sweden, 343–44, 345, 350–51, 352–53, 357, 361–62, 364–65, 368–69, 380
"trafficking in pornography" ("trafficking" provision Minneapolis ordinance), 175, 185–86, 195
  lawsuits under, 175, 201, 234
trafficking laws and provisions, 205, 206, 226, 311–12, 377, 388–89. *See also* "trafficking in pornography"
trauma. *See* posttraumatic stress disorder
triangulation (of research methods), 67–68, 74, 96, 97–98, 116–17, 121–22, 171–72, 289, 432n.10
  between-method, 69–70, 112, 131–32, 432n.10
Turpin, R. v., 274
  2 Live Crew, 391–393, 395
  Kimberle Crenshaw and, 391–92, 395–96

"undue exploitation of sex," 266–67, 279, 281, 290–91, 297, 300, 301–2, 305–6
  and the definition of obscenity, 23, 239, 240, 249–50, 260, 266, 305–6
  meanings of the term until the early 1980s, 239

tests for determining/interpreting, 267–68, 296
Towne Cinema Theatres, Ltd. v. R. and, 266–68
United Kingdom (U.K.), 25. *See also* London studies
research in, 39–40, 41, 119–21, 232–33
United Nations (UN). *See also* CEDAW
Human Rights Committee, 142, 248–49
unlawful portrayal of violence, 322–24
unsafe sex. *See also* condoms
pornography and, 54, 64, 369
prostitution and, 39–42, 44, 49, 50–51, 335–39, 344–45, 356
unprotected anal sex, 39–41, 64
U.S. anti-pornography civil rights ordinances, 1983–1991, 167–69
evidence, equality, and representation, 169, 180–81
causes of action, 175–80
representing interests, 173–74
substantive equality and perspective, 169–73
judicial responses and ideological clashes
constitutional review, 190–92
John Stuart Mill's distinctions, 192–93
representation and ripeness, 187–90
strict scrutiny: equality as a compelling interest, 193–201
public responses and ideological clashes, 182–87
U.S. congressional hearings, 225, 226, 231
U.S. Constitution. *See* First Amendment; Fourteenth Amendment
U.S. Court of Appeals for the Seventh Circuit
Attorney General's Commission and, 217–18, 219–20
Beauharnais v. Illinois and, 217–18, 378
Brown v. Board of Education and, 217–19, 378
free speech and, 210–12, 214–15, 217–18, 375–76, 396
Hudnut and, 188–89, 218, 376, 378, 395
Indianapolis and, 209–10, 211–12, 213, 214–15, 217, 218, 223–24, 277–78
Plessy and, 218, 219
R. v. Butler and, 277–78, 394–96
U.S. Supreme Court and, 210, 214–15, 217–18, 396
viewpoint neutrality doctrine applied by, 214
U.S. Court of Appeals for the Third Circuit, 207–8, 228, 229
U.S. Department of Justice, 226, 227, 230–31, 253–54
U.S. Supreme Court. *See also specific cases*
child pornography law and, 192, 195, 204–5, 209, 272
Hudnut and, 188–89, 210–11, 219
Seventh Circuit Court of Appeals and, 210, 214–15, 217–18, 396

victim blaming, 242–43
"victimless" crimes, 300, 361, 381
Victoria, Australia
prostitution in, 335–38
viewpoint neutrality, 202–7, 371–73. *See also* neutrality
Canada and, 274, 277–78, 289, 305, 375–76
as a consensus test, 212
Indianapolis ordinance and, 202–4, 205–6, 207, 214, 223–24
obscenity law and, 203, 211–12
Seventh Circuit Court of Appeals and, 202–4, 205–7, 211–12, 214, 223–24, 375–76
violence. *See also* aggression; assault; attitudes supporting violence; gender-based violence
definitions, 6–7, 41–42
eroticized, 82–83
male perceptions of, 262, 283
threats of (*see* threats)
unlawful portrayal of, 322–24
violence against women, 5–6, 143–44. *See also* attitudes supporting violence against women; battered women; methods assessing effects from exposure; *Price, R. v.*; rape; *specific topics*
legislation, 315–16 (*see also* Sex Purchase Law of 1999)
prostitution and, 20–21
subordination and, 7–8

violence against women (*cont.*)
  trivialization of, 32, 42, 73, 79–80, 82–84, 86, 92–93, 109–10, 123, 127–28, 133, 390 (*see also under* pain; sexual abuse)
  why nonviolent pornography feeds, 81–86
Violence Against Women Act (Sweden). *See* Sex Purchase Law of 1999
violence/dehumanization test. *See* dehumanization test
violent pornography, 49. *See also* BDSM
  defined, 41–42
  with negative outcomes, 76–77
  with positive outcomes, 42, 76–77, 270–71
  prevalence, 41–42
violent resistance, artist convicted of, 327–28, 331–33, 376–77. *See also* "artist's case"
virtues, 184. *See also* "nice, virtuous girls"
  public, 184
vulgar constructionism, 161, 163–64, 187
vulnerability. *See* position of vulnerability

Wagner, R. v., 268, 275, 276, 281
  Check's three-pronged definition of pornography and, 84–85, 264–65, 278–79, 281, 288–89
  civil rights and, 266
  and definitions of and standards for obscenity, 264–65, 266
  John Sophinka and, 278–79, 281
  Judge Shannon and, 264–66, 276
  R. v. Ramsingh and, 264–66
Weaver, James B., 82–84
Weitzer, Ronald, 59, 359
Weldon, S. Laurel, 146–47
white supremacy, 192–93, 328–29
Woman Hating (Dworkin), 173. *See also* Dworkin, Andrea
women. *See also* feminism; gender differences; *specific topics*
  as sexual objects for domination, conquest, violation, exploitation, possession, or use, 194, 195, 246, 255, 388
Women Against Violence Against Women, 143–44
Women's Legal Education and Action Fund (LEAF), 269–74, 283, 304
  Canadian Charter and, 269, 271, 273–75, 277
  Canadian Supreme Court and, 269, 271–72, 274–75, 276, 283–84, 304
  equality and, 269, 273–74, 385–86
  harms and, 269, 270–74, 305, 385–86
  obscenity law and, 271, 272, 277, 385–86
  R. v. Butler and, 271–72, 282–84, 288, 295–96, 304, 305, 385–86
women's organizations, 143–44
women's shelters, 103–4, 106–7
workplace, pornography forced on employees in, 177–78, 179, 197, 213–14, 235

Young, Iris Marion, 147–50, 184, 270, 333

Zicari, Rob, 230–31, 232. See also *Extreme Associates, Inc., United States v.*
Zillmann, Dolf, 82–84
zoning laws, 167–68, 185–86